1998-99

EVANGELICAL
SUNDAY SCHOOL
LESSON
COMMENTARY

FORTY-SEVENTH ANNUAL VOLUME

Based on the

Evangelical Bible Lesson Series

Editorial Staff

James E. Humbertson—*EDITORIAL DIRECTOR*

Homer G. Rhea—*EDITOR IN CHIEF*

H. Bernard Dixon—*GENERAL DIRECTOR OF PUBLICATIONS*

Lesson Exposition Writers

Eugene C. Christenbury   James E. Humbertson

Rodney Hodge   Jerald Daffe

Betty Spence   Oliver McMahan

Published by
PATHWAY PRESS
Cleveland, Tennessee

Lesson treatments in the *Evangelical Sunday School Lesson Commentary* for 1998-99 are based upon the outlines of the Evangelical Bible Lesson Series prepared by the Evangelical Curriculum Commission (formerly the Curriculum Commission of the National Sunday School Association).

Copyright 1998

PATHWAY PRESS, Cleveland, Tennessee
ISBN: 0-87148-981-3

Printed in the United States of America

TABLE OF CONTENTS

INTRODUCING THE 1998-99 COMMENTARY

The *Evangelical Sunday School Lesson Commentary* contains in a single volume a full study of the Sunday school lessons for the months beginning with September 1998 and running through August 1999. The 12 months of lessons draw from both the Old Testament and the New Testament in an effort to provide balance and establish relationship between these distinct but inspired writings. The lessons in this 1998-99 volume are drawn from the seventh year of a seven-year cycle, which will be completed in August 1999. (The cycle is printed in full on page 16 of this volume.)

The lessons for the *Evangelical Commentary* are based on the Evangelical Bible Lesson Series Outlines, prepared by the Evangelical Curriculum Commission. (The Evangelical Curriculum Commission is a member of the National Association of Evangelicals.) The lessons in this volume are drawn from the Old and New Testaments; and taken together with the other annual volumes of lessons in the cycle, they provide a valuable commentary on a wide range of Biblical subjects. Each quarter is divided into two or more units of study.

The 1998-99 commentary is the work of a team of Christian scholars and writers who have developed the volume under the supervision of Pathway Press. All the major writers, introduced on the following pages, represent a team of ministers committed to a strictly Evangelical interpretation of the Scriptures. The guiding theological principles of this commentary are expressed in the following statement of faith:

1. WE BELIEVE the Bible to be the inspired, the only infallible, authoritative Word of God.

2. WE BELIEVE that there is one God, eternally existing in three persons: Father, Son, and Holy Spirit.

3. WE BELIEVE in the deity of our Lord Jesus Christ, in His virgin birth, in His sinless life, in His miracles, in His vicarious and atoning death through His shed blood, in His bodily resurrection, in His ascension to the right hand of the Father, and in His personal return in power and glory.

4. WE BELIEVE that for the salvation of lost and sinful men, personal reception of the Lord Jesus Christ and regeneration by the Holy Spirit are absolutely essential.

5. WE BELIEVE in the present ministry of the Holy Spirit by whose cleansing and indwelling the Christian is enabled to live a godly life.

6. WE BELIEVE in the personal return of the Lord Jesus Christ.

7. WE BELIEVE in the resurrection of both the saved and the lost—they that are saved, unto the resurrection of life; and they that are lost, unto the resurrection of damnation.

8. WE BELIEVE in the spiritual unity of believers in our Lord Jesus Christ.

USING THE 1998-99 COMMENTARY

The *Evangelical Sunday School Lesson Commentary* for 1998-99 is presented to the reader with the hope that it will become his weekly companion through the months ahead.

The fall quarter 1998 continues a seven-year cycle of lessons which will be completed with the summer quarter 1999. The 28 quarters of studies, divided into two or more units each, draw from both the Old and New Testaments. Also a number of studies will be topical in nature as attention is focused on contemporary issues. A complete listing of the themes that will be included in the seven-year cycle is printed on page 16 of this volume.

Quarterly unit themes for the 1998-99 volume are as follows:

Fall Quarter—Unit One: "Life and Teachings of Paul"; Unit Two: "Help for Life's Journey"

Winter Quarter—Unit One: "God's Plan of Redemption"; Unit Two: "Truths From the Tabernacle"

Spring Quarter—Unit One: "People Who Met Jesus"; Unit Two: "Personal Evangelism"

Summer Quarter—Unit One: "Revelation"; Unit Two: "Mission of the Church"

The lesson sequence used in this volume is prepared by the Evangelical Curriculum Commission. (The Evangelical Curriculum Commission is a member of the National Association of Evangelicals.)

The specific material used in developing each lesson is written and edited under the guidance of the editorial staff of Pathway Press.

STUDY TEXT: At the opening of each week's lesson, you will see printed the study text. These references point out passages of Scripture that are directly related to the lesson, and it is advisable for you to read each one carefully before beginning the lesson study.

TIME and PLACE: A time and place is given for each lesson. Where there is a wide range of opinions regarding the exact time or place, the printed New Testament works of Merrill C. Tenney and Old Testament works of Samuel J. Schultz are used to provide the information.

PRINTED TEXT and CENTRAL TRUTH: The printed text is the body of Scripture designated each week for verse-by-verse study in the classroom. Drawing on the study text the teacher delves into this printed text, expounding its content to the students. Although the printed text contains different insights for each teacher, the central truth states the single unifying principle that the expositors attempted to clarify in each lesson.

DICTIONARY: A dictionary, which attempts to bring pronunciation and clarification to difficult words or phrases, is included with most lessons. Pronunciations are based on the phonetic system used by Field Enterprises Educational Corporation of Chicago and New York in *The World Book Encyclopedia*. Definitions are generally based on *The Pictorial Bible Dictionary*, published by Zondervan Publishing Company, Grand Rapids, Michigan.

EXPOSITION and LESSON OUTLINE: The heart of this commentary—and probably the heart of the teacher's instruction each week—is the exposition of the printed text. This exposition material is preceded by a lesson outline, which indicates how the material is to be divided for study. These lesson outlines are not exhaustive but, rather, provide a skeleton for the teacher to amplify upon and to build around.

REVIEW and DISCUSSION QUESTIONS: Immediately following the expository material in each lesson are five review questions. These questions are designed as discussion starters, along with the discussion questions appearing throughout the expository material. The review questions also serve to restate the major bits of information in the text and may be supplemented by questions of your own drawn from the expository material.

GOLDEN TEXT HOMILY: The golden text homily for each week is a brief reflection on that single verse. As the word *homily* implies, it is a discourse or sermon on a particular point. The homily may often be used effectively to give the lesson a life-related slant.

SENTENCE SERMONS: Two or more sentence sermons—popular and pithy single-line thoughts on the central truth of the lesson—are included each week.

EVANGELISM APPLICATION: The evangelism application relates the general theme of the week's lesson to the ongoing task of evangelism. The theme of the lesson (but not necessarily of the lesson text) is used to make this application. At times the emphasis of the section bears on direct evangelism of class members who may not be Christians; at other times the emphasis bears upon exhorting the class members to become more involved in evangelizing others.

ILLUMINATING THE LESSON: In this section, illustrative material is provided for the teacher to use to support the lesson at whatever point seems most appropriate.

DAILY BIBLE READINGS: The daily Bible readings are included for the teacher to use in his own devotions throughout the week, as well as to share with members of his class.

EXPOSITION WRITERS

Writers for the expository materials for the 1998-99 volume are as follows:

The lesson expositions for the fall quarter (September, October, November) were prepared by a team of Bible scholars including the Reverend Dr. James E. Humbertson (B.A., M.R.E., D.Min.), the Reverend Dr. Oliver McMahan (B.A., M.Div., D.Min.), and the Reverend Dr. Jerald Daffe (B.A., M.A., D.Min.).

The Reverend James E. Humbertson, who wrote lessons 1, 2, 4-8, is editorial director of the *Evangelical Sunday School Lesson Commentary* at the Church of God Publishing House, Cleveland, Tennessee.

The Reverend Dr. Humbertson holds an undergraduate degree in Biblical education and two graduate degrees, including a master of religious education and a doctor of ministry in the field of Christian education.

Dr. Humbertson's experience includes years of service as a seminary and college professor, college administrator, a chairman of boards of Christian education, and a lecturer at writers' and educational seminars.

The Reverend Dr. Humbertson has written many articles and book chapters published in Pathway Press magazines and workers training courses. He has also written three courses including "The History and Philosophy of Christian Education" for Lee University.

The Reverend Dr. Oliver McMahan, who wrote lesson 3, is former dean of students and associate professor at Northwest Bible College, Minot, North Dakota. Presently, he is associate professor of pastoral studies and director of external studies at the Church of God Theological Seminary, Cleveland, Tennessee. He is a graduate of West Coast Bible College and of Brite Divinity School at Texas Christian University.

An ordained minister in the Church of God, Dr. McMahan has served his denomination as pastor, educator, and personal counselor. From 1976-1981 he served as minister of youth and outreach at the Oak Cliff Church of God in Dallas, Texas.

Dr. McMahan has written a number of articles for the *Church of God Evangel* and is a contributor of definitions and articles for the *Complete Biblical Library*.

Dr. McMahan is a member of the Evangelical Theological Society and the Association for Clinical Pastoral Education.

The Reverend Dr. Jerald Daffe, who wrote lessons 9-13, is associate professor of pastoral studies and serves as chairman of the Department of Bible and Christian Ministries, Lee University, Cleveland, Tennessee.

Dr. Daffe earned his bachelor of arts degree at Northwest Bible College, a master of arts degree at Wheaton College Graduate School, and his doctorate of ministry degree at Western Conservative Baptist Seminary. An ordained minister in the Church of God, Dr. Daffe has served in the pastoral ministry for 10 years and has been a faculty member on two college campuses—Northwest Bible College and Lee University—for over 20 years.

Dr. Daffe has been recognized and listed in *Outstanding Educators of America 1974-75* and *Outstanding Young Men of America 1984.* He also received the Excellence in Teaching Award at Lee College in 1990. Recognized for his professional knowledge and communicative skills, Dr. Daffe is a popular speaker at camp meetings, retreats, seminars, and churches in many denominations. In addition to many magazine articles and Sunday school lessons, he has written several books, including *Handbook for Special Services; Instructor's Guide for Sunday School in the '90s; In the Face of Evil;* and *Revival: God's Plan for His People.*

Lesson expositions for the winter quarter (December, January, February) were written by the Reverend Dr. Eugene C. Christenbury (B.A., M.A., M.S., Ed.D.) and Mrs. Betty Spence (B.A.) of Mobile, Alabama.

The Reverend Dr. Eugene C. Christenbury wrote lessons 1-8. (See spring quarter information for academic, professional, and practical experiences of this writer.)

Mrs. Betty Spence, who wrote lessons 9-13, is a professional writer, with a long list of credits to her Kingdom service. She has written Sunday school Adult Teacher's Guides for the International Pentecostal Holiness Church through the years and has a unique ability to relate Scripture with applications.

Mrs. Betty Spence is a member of the Alabama Writers' Conclave; Alabama State Poetry Society; and the National League of American Pen Women, Incorporated. She is a past president of the Pensters and the Mobile Branch of NLAPW and is currently president (1996-98) of the State Association, NLAPW.

Mrs. Spence has taught creative writing courses at the Eastern Shore Institute of Lifelong Learning and currently teaches creative writing for the City of Mobile Community Programs.

In 1988 she was a recipient of the Gayfer's Career Club, Outstanding Career Woman Award, and in 1990 she received a resolution of commendation for outstanding professional achievement and community service by the State of Alabama House of Representatives.

Mrs. Spence lives with Pete, her husband of 45 years, and their grown son, Chuck, in west Mobile, where she is a member of the Forest Hill Church of God.

Lesson expositions for the spring quarter (March, April, May) were written by the Reverend Dr. Eugene C. Christenbury.

Dr. Christenbury earned his bachelor of arts and master of arts degrees at George Peabody College for Teachers and his doctorate of education from the University of Tennessee. He also earned the M.S. degree in religion from the Church of God School of Theology, Cleveland, Tennessee. An ordained minister in the Church of God, Dr. Christenbury has served as state youth and Christian education director, pastor, and assistant superintendent at the Home for Children in Sevierville, Tennessee. He is retired after serving as senior adjunct professor of education at Lee College, Cleveland, Tennessee.

Dr. Christenbury is a member of Phi Delta Kappa and the Council on Public Education of Religious Studies. Recognized for his academic and religious knowledge, he is a popular speaker on the Lee University campus and in the broader church community.

Lesson expositions for the summer quarter (June, July, August) were written by the Reverend Rodney Hodge, an ordained minister who has served as minister of music for 24 years at Northwood Temple Pentecostal Holiness Church in Fayetteville, North Carolina. He holds degrees from Emmanuel College and the University of Georgia and did graduate studies in history at the University of Georgia.

The Reverend Hodge has written numerous Bible study programs, as well as dramas and music productions, and has produced an entire series of theater productions for church use.

The Reverend Hodge presently writes adult Sunday school literature for the International Pentecostal Holiness Church.

GOLDEN TEXT HOMILY WRITERS
1998-99

French L. Arrington, Ph.D.
Professor of New Testament Greek
and Exegesis
Church of God Theological Seminary
Cleveland, Tennessee

Richard Y. Bershon, Ph.D.
Chaplain, State Veterans Home
Hot Springs, South Dakota

Noel Brooks, D.D. (Retired)
Writer, *Adult Sunday School Teacher
Quarterly*
International Pentecostal Holiness
Church
Oklahoma City, Oklahoma

Eugene C. Christenbury, Ed.D. (Retired)
Former Faculty Member at Lee
University
Cleveland, Tennessee

James L. Durel, Captain
The Salvation Army
Vacaville, California

Joel Harris
Pastor, Church of God
Mobile, Alabama

Willie F. Lawrence, D.D.
Pastor, Church of God
Danville, Illinois

William R. McCall
Missionary, Church of God
Cleveland, Tennessee

Aaron D. Mize, Chaplain I
Alcohol and Drug Treatment Center
Parchman, Mississippi

Levy E. Moore, Mayor
City of Franklin Springs
Franklin Springs, Georgia

Ronald M. Padgett, Chaplain
Director of Religious Programs
Mississippi Department of Corrections
Parchman, Mississippi

O.W. Polen, D.D. (Retired)
Former Editor in Chief
Pathway Press
Cleveland, Tennessee

Wayne S. Proctor, Coordinator
Autumn Ministries of Illinois
Harrisburg, Illinois

Jerry Puckett
Customer Service Representative
Pathway Press
Cleveland, Tennessee

Homer G. Rhea, Editor in Chief
Pathway Press
Cleveland, Tennessee

Marion H. Starr, Pastor
Church of God
Marion, South Carolina

Michael S. Stewart, Senior Pastor
First Assembly of God
Raleigh, North Carolina

Robert B. Thomas, Vice President for
Administration
Church of God Theological Seminary
Cleveland, Tennessee

Dennis W. Watkins
Director of Legal Services
Church of God International Offices
Cleveland, Tennessee

Fred H. Whisman (Lt. Col.)
Group II Chaplain
Civil Air Patrol
Chattanooga, Tennessee

Charles G. Wiley, Pastor
Church of God
Graham, Texas

Florie Brown Wigelsworth, M.Div.
Elizabeth City, North Carolina

Sabord Woods, Ph.D.
Professor of English
Lee University
Cleveland, Tennessee

SCRIPTURE TEXTS USED IN LESSON EXPOSITION

Genesis		Exodus (Cont.)	
3:1, 4-7, 9-15, 22-24	December 6	25:21, 22	February 21
18:19	November 15	25:23, 30	February 14
		26:33	February 21
Exodus		27:1, 2	February 7
12:2, 6, 7, 12, 13,	December 27	30:1, 7	February 14
48-50		30:18-20	February 7
25:8, 9	January 31	40:34, 35	January 31

Leviticus

1:2, 3	February 28
2:1, 2	February 28
3:1, 2	February 28
9:7	February 7
16:30, 33, 34	February 21
24:2, 3	February 14

Numbers

28:2-4	February 7

Deuteronomy

12:10, 11	January 31

Psalm

51:1-4	November 22
71:1-9, 15-24	November 29

Ecclesiastes

2:15-17	November 22
11:1-10	November 1
12:1	November 1

Isaiah

53:1-12	January 3

Matthew

5:14-16	November 15
7:13, 14	November 8
19:16-21, 29	November 8
27:50, 51	February 21
27:57-60	April 4
28:1-10, 18-20	April 4

Mark

5:1-9, 14-20	March 28
14:6-9	April 11
16:14-20	August 15

Luke

2:1-14, 20	December 20
2:25-32	December 13
4:16-19	August 8
5:27-32	August 15
7:19-23	December 13
17:11-18	April 11
19:1-10	March 21
22:19	February 28
22:31, 32	November 22
22:33, 34, 56-62	April 18

John

1:4	February 14
1:29-32	December 13
1:35-49	May 9
3:1-16	March 7
3:36	November 8
4:3, 4, 7-15, 27-30	April 25
4:23, 24	January 31
6:48-51	February 14
8:1-11	March 14
10:9	February 7
15:3	February 7
21:15-17	April 18

Acts

1:4-8	August 29
1:5-8	May 23
2:1-4, 13-16, 21, 40, 41	May 23

Acts (Cont.)

4:31-35	August 29
8:26-40	May 16
9:1-9, 15-20	September 6
13:1-4	August 22
16:16-31	May 30
23:1-7, 9	October 4
25:9-12	October 4
28:30, 31	October 4

Romans

3:21-26	May 2
3:22-24	December 27
5:6-8	May 2
5:18-21	March 14
6:23	May 2
8:18, 22, 23	January 24
10:9, 10	May 2
12:4-8	August 22
12:17, 18	November 15

1 Corinthians

1:4-9, 18-25	September 13
2:7, 8, 10, 13	September 13
5:7	December 27
11:23-26	February 14
13:1-13	September 27

2 Corinthians

5:16-19	March 21

Galatians

1:6-16	September 20
2:1-5	September 20
3:1-5, 10, 11, 13, 14, 22-27	January 10
4:4-7	January 10
6:7-9	November 22

Ephesians

1:3-8	August 29
1:7	February 28
2:4-7	August 15
2:8, 9	May 2
2:13	February 28
2:13-19	January 17
4:11-16	August 22
5:2	February 28
5:25, 26	February 7
6:4	November 15

Philippians

2:5-11	August 8
4:4-19	October 11

Colossians

1:13, 14, 19-23	January 17
3:17	April 11
3:18, 19	November 15

1 Thessalonians

4:3, 4, 7	November 22
4:11, 12	November 15
4:16-18	January 24
5:18	April 11

2 Thessalonians

3:10-12	November 15

1 Timothy
5:8	November 15

2 Timothy
1:5	May 9
1:8, 9, 13, 14	October 25
3:11-15	October 25
4:6-8, 16-18	October 25

Titus
2:11-14	January 17

Philemon
3-21	October 18

Hebrews
1:5, 6	August 8
3:12-14	November 22
8:1, 2	January 31
9:6, 11, 12	January 31
9:24, 28	February 21
10:9, 10	February 7
10:19, 22	February 21
11:24-27	November 8
13:15, 16	August 8

1 Peter
1:18, 19	December 27
2:11, 12, 15	November 15
3:10-12	November 1

2 Peter (cont.)
1:10, 11	November 8
3:13, 14	January 24

1 John
2:1, 2	February 21

Revelation
1:5	February 28
1:9-20	June 6
2:1-3, 19	June 13
3:2, 3, 15-22	June 13
4:2, 3, 5, 6, 8	June 20
5:1-5, 9-12	June 20
6:1-5, 7, 8, 11-14	June 27
7:9, 10	June 27
8:1-6, 13	July 4
8:3	February 14
9:20, 21	July 4
11:14, 15, 18	July 4
12:9-11	July 11
13:4-9, 11, 12, 16-18	July 11
14:6, 7, 12, 13	July 18
15:4-8	July 18
16:1, 4-7	July 18
19:5-7, 9, 11, 13, 15, 19, 20	July 25
20:1, 2, 7, 10	July 25
21:1-5	August 1
22:1-5	August 1
22:1-7	January 24

SCRIPTURE TEXTS USED IN GOLDEN TEXT HOMILIES

Genesis
3:15	December 6

Deuteronomy
30:19	November 8

Psalm
71:18	November 29
107:6	March 28

Proverbs
4:14	November 22

Isaiah
53:6	January 3

Matthew
28:6	April 4

Luke
2:11	December 20
12:48	November 15
21:28	June 27
24:49	August 29

John
1:29	December 13
3:3	March 7
4:23	January 31
4:35	April 25
8:12	February 14

Acts
1:8	May 23
16:31	May 30
22:10	September 6

Romans
5:8	May 2
5:21	March 14

1 Corinthians
1:18	September 13
5:7	December 27
13:13	September 27

2 Corinthians
5:17	March 21
5:19	October 18

Galatians
1:11, 12	September 20
3:24	January 10

Ephesians
5:2	February 28
5:15, 16	November 1

Philippians
2:9	August 8
4:11	October 11

Colossians
3:17	April 11

1 Timothy
1:15	August 15

2 Timothy
1:12	October 4
3:15	May 9
4:7	October 25

Titus
2:14	January 17
3:5	February 7

Hebrews		**1 John**	
10:22	February 21	2:1	April 18
1 Peter		**Revelation**	
3:15	May 16	1:8	June 6
4:10	August 22	3:5	June 13
5:8	July 11	5:9	June 20
		11:15	July 4
2 Peter		15:4	July 18
3:13	January 24	19:6	July 25
		21:7	August 1

ACKNOWLEDGMENTS

Many books, magazines, and newspapers have been used in the research that has gone into this 1998-99 *Evangelical Commentary*. A few of the major books that have been used are listed below.

Bibles

King James Version, Oxford University Press, Oxford, England
New American Standard Bible (NASB), A.J. Holman Co., Publishers, New York, New York
New English Bible (NEB), Oxford University Press, Oxford, England
New International Version (NIV), Zondervan Publishing House, Grand Rapids, Michigan
New King James Version (NKJV), Thomas Nelson Publishers, Nashville, Tennessee
The Berkeley Version, Zondervan Publishing House, Grand Rapids, Michigan

Commentaries

Clarke's Commentary, Abingdon-Cokesbury, Nashville, Tennessee
Commentaries on the Old Testament (Keil & Delitzsch), Eerdmans Publishing Co.,
  Grand Rapids, Michigan
Ellicott's Bible Commentary, Zondervan Publishing House, Grand Rapids, Michigan
Expositions of Holy Scriptures (Alexander MacLaren), Eerdmans Publishing Co.,
  Grand Rapids, Michigan
The Broadman Bible Commentary, Volumes 10 and 11, Broadman Press, Nashville, Tennessee
The Expositor's Greek Testament, Eerdmans Publishing Co., Grand Rapids, Michigan
The Interpreter's Bible, Abingdon Press, New York, New York
The Letters to the Corinthians, William Barclay, Westminster Press, Philadelphia, Pennsylvania
The Pulpit Commentary, Eerdmans Publishing Co., Grand Rapids, Michigan
The Wesleyan Commentary, Eerdmans Publishing Co., Grand Rapids, Michigan

Illustrations

Dictionary of Illustrations for Pulpit and Platform, Moody Press, Chicago, Illinois
I Quote, George W. Stewart Publishers, Inc., New York, New York
Knight's Master Book of New Illustrations, Eerdmans Publishing Co., Grand Rapids,
  Michigan
Notes and Quotes, The Warner Press, Anderson, Indiana
1,000 New Illustrations, Al Bryant, Zondervan Publishing Co., Grand Rapids,
  Michigan
Quotable Quotations, Scripture Press Publications, Wheaton, Illinois
The Encyclopedia of Religious Quotations, Fleming H. Revell Co., Old Tappan, New
  Jersey
The Pointed Pen, Pathway Press, Cleveland, Tennessee
The Speaker's Sourcebook, Zondervan Publishing House, Grand Rapids, Michigan
3,000 Illustrations for Christian Service, Eerdmans Publishing Co., Grand Rapids, Michigan

General Reference Books

Harper's Bible Dictionary, Harper and Brothers Publishers, New York, New York
Pictorial Dictionary of the Bible, Zondervan Publishing House, Grand Rapids,
  Michigan
The International Standard Bible Encyclopedia, Eerdmans Publishing Co., Grand
  Rapids, Michigan
The Interpreter's Dictionary of the Bible, Abingdon Press, Nashville, Tennessee
The World Book Encyclopedia, Field Enterprises Education Corp., Chicago, Illinois
Word Pictures in the New Testament (Robertson), Broadman Press, Nashville, Tennessee

Evangelical Bible Lesson Series (1992-1999)

Fall Quarter September, October, November	Winter Quarter December, January, February	Spring Quarter March, April, May	Summer Quarter June, July, August
1992 Unit One—Personalities in Genesis Unit Two—Psalms, Proverbs and Ecclesiastes	**1992-93** Unit One—Following Jesus Unit Two—Evangelism	**1993** Unit One—Building Positive Relationships Unit Two—Life and Teachings of Moses	**1993** Unit One—The Church Is Launched Unit Two—Ministry in the Church
1993 Unit One—Learning From Israel's Experiences Unit Two—Living in Today's World	**1993-94** Unit One—The Gospel According to John Unit Two—Christian Growth	**1994** Unit One—Covenants in the Bible Unit Two—Joshua and Ruth	**1994** Unit One—Understanding Cultism Unit Two—Spiritual Revival and Renewal Unit Three—Ezra, Nehemiah, Ruth
1994 Unit One—Truths From Romans Unit Two—Spiritual Warfare	**1994-95** Unit One—Mosaic Law and New Testament Counterparts Unit Two—Worship in the OT and NT	**1995** Unit One—1 & 2 Corinthians Unit Two—Strengthening Marriage and Family Ties	**1995** Unit One—Principles of Godly Leadership Unit Two—Christian Values
1995 Unit One—Galatians and Ephesians Unit Two—Christian Fellowship	**1995-96** Unit One—Wisdom Literature Unit Two—Building a Consistent Devotional Life	**1996** Unit One—Triumphing Over Life's Crises Unit Two—Philippians and Colossians	**1996** Unit One—Isaiah Unit Two—God's Providential Care
1996 Unit One—Insights from 1 & 2 Timothy, Titus Unit Two—Ministering to One Another	**1996-97** Unit One—Christ in Prophecy Unit Two—Teachings from Ezekiel and Daniel	**1997** Unit One—Teachings of Jesus Unit Two—Basic Christian Truths	**1997** Unit One—God's Word for Difficult Times Unit Two—Servanthood
1997 Unit One—James, 1 & 2 Peter Unit Two—Work of the Spirit	**1997-98** Unit One—Celebrating Advent Unit Two—God's Word in Psalm 119	**1998** Unit One—The Book of Hebrews Unit Two—Lessons From the Patriarchs	**1998** Unit One—Messages of Minor Prophets Unit Two—Bible Answers to Current Issues
1998 Unit One—Life and Teachings of Paul Unit Two—Help for Life's Journey	**1998-99** Unit One—God's Plan of Redemption Unit Two—Truths From the Tabernacle	**1999** Unit One—People Who Met Jesus Unit Two—Personal Evangelism	**1999** Unit One—Understanding Revelation Unit Two—The Mission of the Church

INTRODUCTION
TO FALL
QUARTER

September marks the fall quarter and the beginning of a series of lessons divided into two distinct units of study. Unit One (lessons 1-8) is presented under the theme "Life and Teachings of Paul." Appearing perhaps providentially, the apostle Paul was used mightily for the Lord during this momentous time in the formation of the early church. The eight lessons included in the unit of study are but a small part of the work and ministry of this gifted leader, but they are sufficient to alert us to the potential service resident in one who was consecrated to the Lord.

The lessons of Unit Two (9-13) are presented under the theme "Help for Life's Journey." As the theme implies, the lessons are of a practical nature and are certain to be a challenge to the avid student of God's Word.

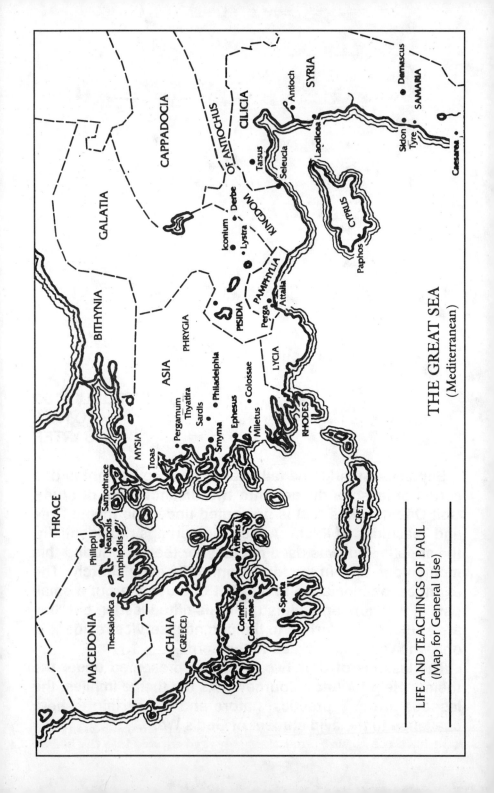

THE GREAT SEA
(Mediterranean)

LIFE AND TEACHINGS OF PAUL
(Map for General Use)

Conversion Means an About-Face

Study Text: Acts 9:1-31

Objective: To understand that conversion means a changed life and turn our lives completely to Christ.

Time: The Book of Acts was written between A.D. 61 and 63. Paul's conversion probably took place in A.D. 37.

Place: The Book of Acts was probably written at Caesarea or Rome.

Golden Text: "What shall I do, Lord?" (Acts 22:10).

Central Truth: God's grace saves penitent sinners and transforms them for His service.

Evangelism Emphasis: God saves us from sin so that we can serve in His kingdom.

PRINTED TEXT

Acts 9:1. And Saul, yet breathing out threatenings and slaughter against the disciples of the Lord, went unto the high priest,

2. And desired of him letters to Damascus to the synagogues, that if he found any of this way, whether they were men or women, he might bring them bound unto Jerusalem.

3. And as he journeyed, he came near Damascus: and suddenly there shined round about him a light from heaven:

4. And he fell to the earth, and heard a voice saying unto him, Saul, Saul, why persecutest thou me?

5. And he said, Who art thou, Lord? And the Lord said, I am Jesus whom thou persecutest: it is hard for thee to kick against the pricks.

6. And he trembling and astonished said, Lord, what wilt thou have me to do? And the Lord said unto him, Arise, and go into the city, and it shall be told thee what thou must do.

7. And the men which journeyed with him stood speechless, hearing a voice, but seeing no man.

8. And Saul arose from the earth; and when his eyes were opened, he saw no man: but they led him by the hand, and brought him into Damascus.

9. And he was three days without sight, and neither did eat nor drink.

15. But the Lord said unto him, Go thy way: for he is a chosen vessel unto me, to bear my name before the Gentiles, and kings, and the children of Israel:

16. For I will shew him how great things he must suffer for my name's sake.

17. And Ananias went his way, and entered into the house;

and putting his hands on him said, Brother Saul, the Lord, even Jesus, that appeared unto thee in the way as thou camest, hath sent me, that thou mightest receive thy sight, and be filled with the Holy Ghost.

18. And immediately there fell from his eyes as it had been scales: and he received sight forthwith,

and arose, and was baptized.

19.   And when he had received meat, he was strengthened.   Then was Saul certain days with the disciples which were at Damascus.

20.   And straightway he preached Christ in the synagogues, that he is the Son of God.

DICTIONARY

Damascus (duh-MAS-kus)—Acts 9:2—A city 40 miles east of Lake Galilee.

Ananias (an-uh-NY-us)—Acts 9:17—A Christian of Damascus who helped Paul.

LESSON OUTLINE

I.   CONFRONTED BY CHRIST

   A.   A Zealous Persecutor

   B.   A Persecutor Learns Truth About Christ

II.   SUBMISSION TO CHRIST

   A.   Instructions Sought

   B.   Instructions Obeyed

III.   COMMISSIONED BY CHRIST

   A.   Vision-Directed Service

   B.   A Chosen Vessel

   C.   A Mighty Healing

   D.   A Powerful Preacher

LESSON EXPOSITION

INTRODUCTION

Today begins a series of eight lessons from the life and teachings of the great apostle Paul. The lessons cover, in a much less than exhaustive manner, his conversion, some of his teachings, and his last days as he awaited death. Paul had a dramatic but genuine conversion that resulted in his service to the Christian church, fulfilling what the Lord Jesus had told Ananias: "He is a chosen vessel unto me, to bear my name before Gentiles, and kings, and the children of Israel" (Acts 9:15).

Recent surveys by pollsters point up the broad range of opinions that exist concerning conversion. Those opinions range from the belief that conversion is the signing of a church membership roster to the idea that a total about-face results from conversion, as was well evidenced in the case of the apostle Paul. Few conversions are as dramatic as that of the apostle Paul, but true conversion means a changed life and lifestyle as that life is turned completely to Christ.

As we look at today's lesson, it becomes easy to understand why Paul became such an important link in the spread of the gospel. He made a complete about-face, submitted to Christ, and took seriously Christ's commission to him.

Although the emphasis of this

lesson is on Paul's conversion, it is good to keep in mind the unfolding of God's plan for redemption of the human family. One of the great objectives of the appearance of Christ was to break down the wall of separation between Jew and Gentile and make the blessings of salvation the property of all men, without distinction of race or language. But Christ was not Himself permitted to carry the change into practical realization, for He was cut off in the midst of His days and had to leave the task to His followers. The apostle Paul became a most important person in continuing the work of Christ.

I. CONFRONTED BY CHRIST
(Acts 9:1-5)

Saul, or Paul as he was later to be called, was born into a strict Hebrew family near the beginning of the first century. His native city was Tarsus, a busy metropolis in Cilicia, situated on the northern corner of the Mediterranean Sea. In this city was the University of Tarsus, which was noted for its courses in philosophy and medicine. Whether Paul ever attended the university is doubtful, but he could scarcely have escaped the influence of the Hellenistic thinking and life of the city. He was educated strictly in good Jewish fashion, learning the Hebrew language and the Scriptures, and also the trade of tentmaking. He was acquainted with the Aramaic language, which he probably spoke at home, and the Greek language, which was the prevalent language of Tarsus.

At the age of 12 he was sent to Jerusalem to study with Gamaliel (Acts 22:3). By conviction he was a Pharisee, and his zeal was measured by the intensity with which he persecuted the church (26:9-11).

The death of Stephen seems to have been the signal for an immediate campaign of repression against the Jerusalem church, although some persecution is mentioned in Acts 4. If we read Acts 8:1-3, in its wider context, one may conclude that it was the Hellenists in the church (the group in which Stephen had been a leader) who were the main target of attack, and that they, for the most part, made up the group of believers who were compelled to leave Jerusalem. From that time onward the Jerusalem church appears to have consisted almost entirely of Hebrew Christians. The 12 apostles remained in Jerusalem, partly no doubt because they were convinced that it was their duty to stay at their posts, and partly because the popular resentment was directed not so much toward them as at the leaders of the Hellenists in the church. It is of special importance to note that the persecution and dispersion brought about a beginning of the fulfillment of our Lord's commission to His disciples: "Ye shall be witnesses unto me both in Jerusalem, and in all Judaea, and in Samaria, and unto the uttermost part of the earth" (Acts 1:8).

A. A Zealous Persecutor (vv. 1, 2)

1. And Saul, yet breathing out threatenings and slaughter against the disciples of the Lord, went unto the high priest,
2. And desired of him letters to Damascus to the synagogues, that if he found any of this way, whether they were men or women, he might bring them

bound unto Jerusalem.

The prime mover in the repressive effort to stamp out "this way" was Saul of Tarsus. He now carried into more effective action the attitude toward the new movement which he had displayed at the stoning of Stephen. Armed with the necessary authority from the Sanhedrin's chief priest and other leaders, he harried or ravaged ("made havock") the body of Christ, arresting men and women in their own homes and sending them off to prison. The Greek word used for "harried" or "ravaged" is *elumaineto* (Acts 8:3) and suggests "the ruin and devastation as caused by an army." "In the Septuagint (Greek version of the Hebrew Old Testament), the word is used in reference to that of a wild boar ravaging a vineyard" (*The Expositor's Greek Testament*).

The relentless efforts to stamp out the Christian way did not stop with Jerusalem. Paul sought to eliminate the Christians in Damascus. Consequently, he requested and received the necessary authority from the high priest as head of the Sanhedrin, and then set out for Damascus with a group of men. In reality, the Sanhedrin had direct authority only within the boundaries of Judea, but its orders were regarded as binding over every Jewish community. The extent to which the outlying communities cooperated with the directives of the Sanhedrin depended on the attitude that Jewish community had toward the Sanhedrin.

As the facts of the persecution unfold, it is well to keep in mind the effectiveness of God's plan. James Stalker says: "It was the persecutor's hope to exterminate

Christianity, but little did he understand its genius. It thrives on persecution. . . . Heretofore, the church had been confined within the walls of Jerusalem, but now all over Judea and Samaria and in distant Phoenicia and Syria, the beacon of the gospel began in many a town and village to twinkle through the darkness, and twos and threes met together in upper rooms to impart to each other their joy in the Holy Ghost" (*The Life of Saint Paul*).

B. A Persecutor Learns Truth
   About Christ (vv. 3-5)

3. And as he journeyed, he came near Damascus: and suddenly there shined round about him a light from heaven:

4. And he fell to the earth, and heard a voice saying unto him, Saul, Saul, why persecutest thou me?

5. And he said, Who art thou, Lord? And the Lord said, I am Jesus whom thou persecutest: it is hard for thee to kick against the pricks.

Saul had nearly reached Damascus when a miraculous light flashed out of heaven and surrounded him. It was noonday (22:6), and the light was brighter than the sun (26:13). Paul's mentioning of both the time of day when an Eastern sun was at its brightest and the brightness of the light indicates it was not a natural phenomenon.

Instantly, Saul fell prostrate to the ground from the animal he was riding. Then he heard the voice that said, "Saul, Saul, why persecutest thou me?" And Saul asked in response to the voice and the strange experience, "Who art thou, Lord?"

When the voice replied, "I am Jesus whom thou persecuteth"

PERSECUTION BACKFIRED

Saul's conscience must have convulsed when he heard the name Jesus. Saul had been serving his Jewish belief that Christ was dead and the group of followers were fanatical and out of touch with reality. But the words that fell upon his ears awakened Saul to the fact that Jesus and the church were indeed one in purpose (a solemn truth that Saul wrote about later in his letters).

G. Campbell Morgan says: "It is as though Christ had said to him, those men and women whom you have haled to prison have suffered; but it is I Who have suffered in their suffering, Saul. The brutal stones that you saw hurled upon Stephen, cutting into his flesh, and giving him physical pain, reached Me, hurt Me. I felt every throb of Stephen's pain.

"But there was another meaning in the words 'Why persecutest thou Me?' I am above thee in the heavens; thou canst not undo My work; that against which thou art fighting is not the fanaticism of a mistaken fanatic; it is the march of God through human history" (*The Acts of the Apostles*). We do not wonder that Saul never looked back. His gaze was now heavenward, and he was trying to make up for lost time.

What does the term conversion mean to you?

II. SUBMISSION TO CHRIST (Acts 9:6-9)

A. Instructions Sought (vv. 6, 7)

6. And he trembling and astonished said, Lord, what wilt thou have me to do? And the Lord said unto him, Arise, and go into the city, and it shall be told thee what thou must do.

7. And the men which journeyed with him stood speechless, hearing a voice, but seeing no man.

The Lord who had answered Saul's question "Who art thou, Lord?" continued His encounter with the determined persecutor. But by now Saul was submissive and ready to listen. The Jesus whom he thought a fanatic was at the center of heavenly glory. That same Jesus whom he hated spoke to him in a language of divine love. No wonder he was ready to change his direction as he asked, "What wilt thou have me to do?"

The immediate instructions were simple: "Arise, and go into the city, and it shall be told thee what thou must do." Although the instructions were simple, the severity of the visit to Damascus must have created mixed emotions in the mind of Saul. Indeed, those who were opposed to Christ were expecting Saul to be their leader, while the Christians in Damascus were braced for persecution similar to the experiences of other followers of Christ.

In verse 7 it is evident that the revelation was directly to Saul, but the men who journeyed with him did not understand, though they were aware that some strange, frightening phenomenon had occurred. Adam Clarke says, "It has been a question among scholars whether Jesus really did appear to Saul on this occasion. Luke tells us that those who were with him heard the voice but saw no man; which is a strong indication that Saul saw what they did not see. Ananias, it seems, was informed that there had been a real appearance, for in addressing Saul, verse 17, he says, 'The Lord . . . Jesus that appeared unto thee in the way.'

. . .' Also in Paul's own words (1 Corinthians 15:8), 'and last of all he was seen of me also, as of one born out of due time'" (*Clarke's Commentary*, Vol. 5).

B. Instructions Obeyed (vv. 8, 9)

8. And Saul arose from the earth; and when his eyes were opened, he saw no man: but they led him by the hand, and brought him into Damascus.

9. And he was three days without sight, and neither did eat nor drink.

Saul came into Damascus blind, defeated, captured, and led by others. He who had come armed with official authority to end the Nazarene heresy was led in as the blind slave of Christ. Those perhaps were wonderful days, the three days and nights that the blindness continued, especially as he reflected on that experience later in his life. It is not surprising to read that during those days he neither ate nor drank anything. One little word in the Book of Philippians gives us a clue as to his thinking during that experience: "What things were gain to me, those I counted loss for Christ" (3:7). He was finding a true balance of things. His Hebrew birthright, his role in positions of authority, even his attachment to Pharisaism now seemed as nothing compared to his new life he was finding in Christ. It is certain that during those three days and nights when he was stricken with blindness he was gaining new insights and a consciousness, not of loss, but of gain.

G. Campbell Morgan comments: "Mark the fitness in the choice of the instrument. To see the Hebraism and Hellenism merging in Paul, read in Galatians 2:20 these

words: 'I am crucified with Christ,' that is Hebraism, restraint; 'and it is no longer I that live,' that is Hellenism, culture. Then he merged the two, 'but Christ liveth in me,' and that is Christianity. In that final sentence Hebraism and Hellenism have joined hands; culture is seen resulting from restraint, and restraint merging into culture. In this story then, we see Heaven's arrest of the apostle who passed through the Asian cities to carry the evangel [gospel] to these regions beyond" (*The Acts of the Apostles*).

Discuss God's manifestation of mercy through acts of severe discipline.

III. COMMISSIONED BY CHRIST (Acts 9:10-22)

A. Vision-Directed Service (vv. 10-14)

(Acts 9:10-14 is not included in the printed text.)

Verses 10-14 tell the story of how a godly disciple in Damascus, named Ananias, was directed through a vision to render a valuable service to Saul and ultimately to the Christian church worldwide. While the emphasis is on Saul's conversion, it is important to note that the role of lesser-known individuals was a common occurrence in the body of Christ following the Day of Pentecost and the outpouring of the Holy Spirit. That has not changed, as evidenced by the tremendous service that is rendered through lay ministries.

The use of visions has been one of the most common methods God implements to gain the attention of a servant He desires to use. He often depends on those who are loyal to

Him for their assistance. Ananias was directed to go to Damascus "and enquire in the house of Judas for one called Saul, of Tarsus: for, behold, he prayeth, and hath seen in a vision a man named Ananias coming in, and putting his hand on him, that he might receive his sight" (vv. 11, 12). It is interesting to notice how God worked on both ends of the line. Ananias was instructed, but so was Saul. Once the men met, there was confirmation.

Ananias was obviously reluctant to walk into the situation since the reputation of Saul as a persecutor was well known. He did not question the Lord's directive, but he did make the comment that he knew something about the action of Saul and his backing by the chief priests to bind all who called on the name of Jesus.

Human nature doesn't change much since it is rather natural to reason things out in our own way and follow that rationale. But many have learned and been blessed by following the admonition of Proverbs 3:5, 6, which says, "Trust in the Lord with all thine heart; and lean not unto thine own understanding. In all thy ways acknowledge him, and he shall direct thy paths."

B. A Chosen Vessel (vv. 15, 16)

15. But the Lord said unto him, Go thy way: for he is a chosen vessel unto me, to bear my name before the Gentiles, and kings, and the children of Israel:

16. For I will shew him how great things he must suffer for my name's sake.

Beginning with verse 15, Ananias was instructed to carry out the directive from the Lord inasmuch as Saul was a chosen vessel

to Christ. The message called attention to three things that would mark Saul's ministry. First, he was a chosen vessel unto the Lord. Paul, as he was later called, had a deep sense of being chosen and was never ashamed of the gospel, even in the face of death. Second, he would take the gospel to the Gentiles, Jews, and even kings. The details of that mission are vividly recounted in Acts 26. The third revelation concerning the future of Saul was that he would suffer great things for the name of the Lord. Paul's whole life after his conversion was a fulfillment of that prediction. Philippians 3:7-11 gives evidence of Paul's willingness to suffer for Christ.

C. A Mighty Healing (vv. 17-19)

17. And Ananias went his way, and entered into the house; and putting his hands on him said, Brother Saul, the Lord, even Jesus, that appeared unto thee in the way as thou camest, hath sent me, that thou mightest receive thy sight, and be filled with the Holy Ghost.

18. And immediately there fell from his eyes as it had been scales: and he received sight forthwith, and arose, and was baptized.

19. And when he had received meat, he was strengthened. Then was Saul certain days with the disciples which were at Damascus.

Ananias obeyed the directive of the Lord and went straight to Paul. When he was convinced that Christ had adopted Saul into the heavenly family, he had no hesitation to fellowship with him and indeed used the term "Brother Saul." Ananias gave Saul the information he had been given by the Lord regarding the healing of his blindness and of his being filled with the Holy Ghost. Certainly Christ could have brought healing and the Holy Spirit baptism without human means, just as he had enlightened Saul's mind and heart without human help, but He honors human beings by making them agents even in the working of miracles.

After Ananias delivered his message to Saul and put his hands on him, something like scales fell from Saul's eyes and he could see. Ananias played an important part in ministry to Paul.

It is noteworthy to remember that these were not the hands of an apostle or a deacon, but the hands of a disciple—a disciplined one who apparently was a leader but not of the standing of an apostle. Christ sent a disciple to lay hands on His chosen vessel who was to bear His name before kings, Jews, and Gentiles.

Saul ended his three-day fast and received strength physically. He then spent a number of days with the disciples at Damascus.

D. A Powerful Preacher (vv. 20-22)

(Acts 9:21, 22 is not included in the printed text.)

20. And straightway he preached Christ in the synagogues, that he is the Son of God. Immediately Paul began to proclaim Jesus in the synagogues. His message was "Jesus is the Son of God." The great question to be determined for the conviction of the Jews was whether Jesus was indeed the Son of God. Saul was now convinced that Jesus, whom the Jews crucified and who had appeared to him on the road to Damascus, was the Son of God and the Messiah.

Paul's first preaching was not to the heathens of Damascus but to the Jews in their synagogues.

Paul's preaching generated some amazement because these people knew him as the leader who, while in Jerusalem, had destroyed those who called on the name of Jesus and had made his way to Damascus to inflict the same persecution there. So powerful and convincing, however, was the preaching of this Spirit-led messenger that the people were confounded and became uncertain about their own position.

Great Spirit-led preaching has the power to cause hearers to be affected and disturbed. Such was the response Paul saw and heard as he moved across the vast expanse of land from Damascus to Corinth, Ephesus, and beyond.

REVIEW QUESTIONS

1. Why was Saul so strongly opposed to the early Christian worshipers of Christ?

2. Who was Ananias? What part did he play in the follow-up of Saul's conversion?

3. What does the lesson teach us about being chosen vessels for the Lord?

4. For what reason, according to Acts 9:15, had the Lord chosen Saul?

5. How soon after receiving his sight did Saul begin to preach Christ?

GOLDEN TEXT HOMILY

"WHAT SHALL I DO, LORD?" (Acts 22:10).

This brief text is a part of Paul's retelling of his conversion as recorded in Acts 9, where he used the expression "Lord, what wilt thou have me to do?"

Conversion means a changed heart, changed thoughts, changed feeling, a changed air and light. But it means nothing if it does not mean also a genuinely, practically changed career. No sublime enjoyment, no rich experience, no flight of sanctified imagination, no foretaste in saintly, heavenly communings with unseen realities, of "the joys" that are to come, shall satisfy Jesus, nor can satisfy Scripture's conception and representation of the convert of Christ. His life must be "Christ"; and he must await death to know his full "gain." His life must be a witness to Christ, albeit it be first strong witness against his old past self, and ever a quiet rebuke of those who live not after the same rule. The amazement and the solemn dread of those minutes of blindness and strongest excitement, when Saul lay on the earth, and was already summoned as it were to the bar of his Maker, did not prevent him, as a true convert and as type of a true convert, asking for his practical work. "Lord, what wilt thou have me to do?" In our ignorance, perhaps we should have thought a more reasonable question, a more modest question, might have been, "Lord, where wilt thou have me to go"—go hide myself? "Where wilt thou have me go, that I may shed bitter tears and do penance for the past?" But no, the question cannot be mistaken, misreported, or altered. It is, "What wilt thou have me to do?" And Jesus tells him, and does not say now, "This is the work of God, that you believe on me." He tells him, and it proves very shortly, how really he had "to do," to "spend and be spent," "to labour more abundantly than they

all," and to prove his conversion by his changed life and its fruits. For vain, unspeakably vain, the profession of a changed heart and the hopes of Christ and of heaven, without the proof that lies in the changed life.—**Excerpts from** *The Pulpit Commentary*, **Vol. 18**

SENTENCE SERMONS

GOD'S GRACE saves penitent sinners and transforms them for His service.

—Selected

CONVERSION IS a deep work—a heart work. It goes throughout the man, throughout the mind, throughout the members, throughout the entire life.

—Joseph Alleine

NO MAN ever really comes to himself without meeting Christ somewhere along the way.

—Roy L. Smith

CONVERSION IS moving from living death to deathless life.

—Quotable Quotations

DAILY BIBLE READINGS

M. Transformation Sought.
    Psalm 51:1-10
T. Invitation to Transformation.
    Isaiah 1:16-18
W. Yield to God.
    Isaiah 6:1-8
T. Follow Christ.
    Luke 5:27-29
F. New Birth Needed.
    John 3:1-7
S. Transformed by the Spirit.
    Romans 8:1-6

True Wisdom and Power

Study Text: 1 Corinthians 1:1 through 2:16

Objective: To comprehend that spiritual wisdom and power are found in Christ and seek these qualities for daily living.

Time: The Book of 1 Corinthians was probably written in the spring of A.D. 57.

Place: The Book of 1 Corinthians was written at Ephesus.

Golden Text: "The preaching of the cross is to them that perish foolishness; but unto us which are saved it is the power of God" (1 Corinthians 1:18).

Central Truth: The wisdom and power of God are found in Jesus Christ.

Evangelism Emphasis: The Cross seems foolish to the world, but it is the only means God uses to save sinners.

PRINTED TEXT

1 Corinthians 1:4. I thank my God always on your behalf, for the grace of God which is given you by Jesus Christ;

5. That in every thing ye are enriched by him, in all utterance, and in all knowledge;

6. Even as the testimony of Christ was confirmed in you:

7. So that ye come behind in no gift; waiting for the coming of our Lord Jesus Christ:

8. Who shall also confirm you unto the end, that ye may be blameless in the day of our Lord Jesus Christ.

9. God is faithful, by whom ye were called unto the fellowship of his Son Jesus Christ our Lord.

18. For the preaching of the cross is to them that perish foolishness; but unto us which are saved it is the power of God.

19. For it is written, I will destroy the wisdom of the wise, and will bring to nothing the understanding of the prudent.

20. Where is the wise? where is the scribe? where is the disputer of this world? hath not God made foolish the wisdom of this world?

21. For after that in the wisdom of God the world by wisdom knew not God, it pleased God by the foolishness of preaching to save them that believe.

22. For the Jews require a sign, and the Greeks seek after wisdom:

23. But we preach Christ crucified, unto the Jews a stumblingblock, and unto the Greeks foolishness;

24. But unto them which are called, both Jews and Greeks, Christ the power of God, and the wisdom of God.

25. Because the foolishness

of God is wiser than men; and the weakness of God is stronger than men.

2:7. But we speak the wisdom of God in a mystery, even the hidden wisdom, which God ordained before the world unto our glory:

8. Which none of the princes of this world knew: for had they known it, they would not have crucified the Lord of glory.

10. But God hath revealed them unto us by his Spirit: for the Spirit searcheth all things, yea, the deep things of God.

13. Which things also we speak, not in the words which man's wisdom teacheth, but which the Holy Ghost teacheth; comparing spiritual things with spiritual.

LESSON OUTLINE

I. ENRICHED BY CHRIST
   A. True Thanksgiving
   B. The Purpose of His Gifts

II. POWER, WISDOM, AND THE CROSS
   A. The Power of God
   B. The Wisdom of God
   C. The Foolishness of God

III. TRUTH SPIRITUALLY DISCERNED
   A. Demonstration of the Spirit
   B. Revelation Through the Spirit
   C. Discernment by the Spirit

LESSON EXPOSITION

INTRODUCTION

Lesson 1, which introduced this unit theme, "Life and Teachings of Paul," gave some insights into Paul's conversion and serious commitment to Christ and the call that was placed upon his life. Today's lesson, however, jumps ahead nearly 20 years to a time when he communicated with the Corinthian church, which he had founded on his second missionary journey and where he had remained for about 18 months around A.D. 51-53. Now in early A.D. 57, the apostle Paul found it necessary to instruct the Corinthians concerning some problems that had arisen. After Paul left Corinth, some other ministers came to the city and preached. It is likely that Christians who had been converted under yet other ministers had also moved to Corinth, all with various interpretations of what Christianity really meant. It also appears that the influences of the Corinthian environment began to find their way into the church. In Paul's absence, these influences created divisions within the church. Most troubling were the factions which divided the church and resulted in individual ministers being glorified, in corruption of personal living, and in corruption of worship and doctrine.

I. ENRICHED BY CHRIST
(1 Corinthians 1:4-9)

A. True Thanksgiving (vv. 4-6)

4. I thank my God always on your behalf, for the grace of God

which is given you by Jesus Christ;

5. That in every thing ye are enriched by him, in all utterance, and in all knowledge;

6. Even as the testimony of Christ was confirmed in you.

The church at Corinth was a shining testimony of how the marvelous grace of God saves individuals from the grip of sin and darkness. But on the other hand, this church's history was also a record of how easily people slip back into lives of sin, forgetting what it really means to be a Christian. In verses 1-3, the apostle Paul reminded the Corinthians that they had been called by God into a spiritual fellowship. This set the stage for his later appeal for unity.

Paul's compassion and shepherding concern for the people at Corinth was evidenced by his expression of thanksgiving for them. The fact that later in the letter he would have to deal with some difficult problems did not blind him to the fact that this group of people had been enriched by the experience of grace through Christ. The enrichment which began at conversion had increased as they remained submissive to Christ.

The term *every thing* in verse 5 refers to the many charismatic gifts which he planned to discuss later in his letter (chapters 12-14). The gifts of utterance and knowledge enriched the church and confirmed the witness of Christ in their lives. The Greek word *logos* is translated "utterance" here. Paul was saying the Corinthians were enriched with a "word, or deposit" to be declared. They had a message, an utterance, but it was not merely a word of wisdom for their own possession. It

was a word of wisdom which they were to utter or declare to others. Paul talked about what grace had done for them, and he reminded them that whatever had come to them had come as a deposit for which they were responsible for sharing with other people.

The word *knowledge* conveys the idea of intellectual understanding. The Corinthians were enriched experientially by God's grace, and that constituted a message, an "utterance," which should be shared.

How emphatic is the Bible about the responsibility of Christians to share the message of Christ?

The expression "even as the testimony of Christ was confirmed in you" (v. 6) means that the gospel message (Christ's testimony) was planted solidly in the hearts of the Corinthians by faith. Through them, Christ was to be revealed and manifested; the message was to be not only proclaimed but also intelligently demonstrated in them. The verb *confirmed* (Greek, *bebaioo*) means that when the Corinthians accepted the gospel as preached to them by Paul, they received a down payment of spiritual wealth which was delivered as promised. When God guarantees delivery, the goods are already in transit.

B. The Purpose of His Gifts
(vv. 7-9)

7. So that ye come behind in no gift; waiting for the coming of our Lord Jesus Christ:

8. Who shall also confirm you unto the end, that ye may be

blameless in the day of our Lord Jesus Christ.

9. God is faithful, by whom ye were called unto the fellowship of his Son Jesus Christ our Lord.

In the expression "so that ye come behind in no gift," the verb phrase *come behind* means "to be deficient in, to fall short, to be lacking." Stated positively, the Corinthians had an abundance of gifts. The gifts were given by the Holy Spirit through Christ. The Corinthians had everything they needed for the fulfilling of their function as a church; and they were to use their gifts in view of the Lord's return, when He will "confirm," or make them to stand that they might be "blameless in the day of our Lord Jesus Christ." The apostle was fully persuaded that the grace of God produces lives that will be irreproachable, or unimpeachable, when they stand before Christ. This blameless life is the life of holiness.

Paul, with the Corinthians, was waiting for the return of the Lord Jesus Christ, and he therefore combined present spiritual engagement with future spiritual anticipation. The apostle looked at life realistically, knowing the sins of the human family and proclaiming the redemptive grace of God. He also looked up expectantly, knowing that the return of Christ was the Christian's hope. Paul always made the gospel relevant to the current needs of the human family. He, along with other New Testament writers, always made the expectation of the return of Christ an incentive to spiritual pursuits and a means of spiritual enrichment and power (see 2 Peter 3:11, 12; 1 John 3:2, 3).

In verse 9 the original Greek text states, "Faithful is God." This differs from the way the King James translators rendered the verse when they said, "God is faithful." By placing the adjective (Greek, *pistos*) forward in the sentence construction, the Greeks gave special emphasis to the word *faithful*, thus rendering it "trustworthy and reliable." The earlier verses show in what respect this is true; namely, to all that God does for our final salvation. Left to depend on himself, man would surely be lost, but he can fully trust in God. The work He has begun in us, He will most certainly complete. God is faithful, trustworthy, and reliable not only in regard to what He will do for our salvation from now on but also because His faithfulness reaches back to the very moment of our saving contact with Him. God, who began the blessed work in the Corinthians, will not at any time become indifferent or show neglect for their well-being.

The phrase "unto the fellowship of his Son Jesus Christ our Lord" embraces the entirety of communion with Christ, including the consummation at the Last Day. Our part of this fellowship and communion with Christ is mediated by faith. Love, devotion, worship, and all works by which we serve Him are never independent but spring forth as the fruit of faith. Consequently, our fellowship and communion with Christ are pure and intense in the same measure as our faith.

G. Campbell Morgan comments about verse 9 as follows: "So in this one verse there is at once a revelation of the Church's power and the Church's responsibility. What is the Church's power? Her fellowship with her Lord . . . What is the Church's responsibility? 'Be ye steadfast, unmoveable, always abounding in the work of the Lord.' Not by our trying to find something to do for Him, but to get into His business. What is His business in the world? Whatever it is, we are committed to it in fellowship with Him. That is our responsibility" (The Corinthian Letters of Paul).

II. POWER, WISDOM, AND THE CROSS (1 Corinthians 1:18-25).

In verses 10-17, the apostle Paul condemned the divisions in the church which had given occasion for false concepts of loyalty to human leaders to arise. He stressed the cardinal fact that the cross of Christ effected unity as the normal result of true Christian fellowship. So Paul followed up that emphasis with a rather casual reference to the nature of preaching and focused on the contrast of human wisdom with that of godly wisdom.

A. The Power of God (vv. 18-20)

18. For the preaching of the cross is to them that perish foolishness; but unto us which are saved it is the power of God.

19. For it is written, I will destroy the wisdom of the wise, and will bring to nothing the understanding of the prudent.

20. Where is the wise? where is the scribe? where is the disputer of this world? hath not God made foolish the wisdom of this world?

In verse 18, the apostle Paul takes up the subtle problem of the rhetorical utterances of Greek philosophic wisdom in contrast to

Christian preaching. The contrast is between "wisdom of words" (v. 17) and "the preaching [words] of the cross" (v. 18).

G. Campbell Morgan states: "The word of the Cross, or to give the phrase its full value, the logos of the Cross, is the whole totality of truth contained in and revealed through the Cross. Logos is truth, and not truth merely, but truth revealed, truth manifested. So the Greeks used the word. So it is used in our Scriptures. 'The word of the Cross,' the truth embodied, embedded in the Cross, and that truth declared and revealed. Paul tells us the effect. 'To them that are perishing' it is 'foolishness.' That is a true and accurate word. Really, the Greek word [moria] has more acid in it. We could translate it by our word 'silliness,' quite accurately, or by the word 'absurdity.' 'To them that are perishing, silliness, absurdity.'

"What does that mean? Is it absurd to them? Is it foolishness to them because they are perishing? No, they are perishing because they are treating the Cross as silliness and foolishness, as absurd. The reason for the perishing is in their attitude. These people were refusing to examine something outside of, or contrary to, their own thinking, contrary to their own philosophies" (The Corinthian Letters of Paul).

It is important to keep in mind that the word philosopher does not mean a wise man, but only one who loves wisdom. But there is within the mind-set of the non-Christian philosopher the exclusion of wisdom gained through faith or revelation as set forth in the Bible. Consequently, his wisdom has an obvious weakness, even though he loves wisdom that cannot be holistic or that encompasses a proper view of life. It has often been said, "A Christian philosopher can see more while on his knees than the secular philosopher, who excludes faith and revelation as a basis for wisdom and knowledge, can see while standing on his tiptoes."

"But unto us which are saved it is the power of God." This last phrase from verse 18 verifies Paul's conviction that the gospel is much more than theory or speculation; it is the "power of God." So men and women, boys and girls down through the ages have testified to the transforming effect of the message of the Cross. They have been set free from the bondage of sin, and through their relationship with Christ they see the "wisdom of preaching that focuses on the Cross." But only those who have experienced the "saved" relationship with Christ know anything of this mighty power. Indeed the power of Christianity is reserved for those who submit to God's redemptive plan.

In verses 19 and 20, the apostle points out the futility of earthly wisdom by citing the words of Isaiah the prophet (29:14). The people of whom Isaiah spoke had departed from God. They took His name, professing that they were true to God, while in fact they gathered around their own views and concepts. But of this condition God said He would destroy the wisdom of the wise. Paul quoted Isaiah's words, applying them to the people in Corinth of whom they were also true. The Corinthians turned their attention to the thinking of men, to the philosophers, and created divisions in matters of opinions within the church,

even gathering around individuals such as Paul or Apollos or Cephas, while some insisted on the fact that they alone were true because they named the name of Christ.

In verse 20, the apostle asked: "Where is the wise? [What has he done?] Where is the scribe? [a reference to the Jewish attitude] Where is the disputer of this world? [a reference to the Greek attitude]." In essence, Paul was asking, "What does it all amount to?" The overruling God made the whole business foolish and made all such wisdom silly and absurd. Paul's message to the Corinthians was that although they looked on the Cross as "silly or absurd," God had proved by what He had done—by the very message of the Cross—the silliness and absurdity of all their own thinking. In writing to the Romans, Paul said, "Professing themselves to be wise, they became fools" (Romans 1:22).

Why was it necessary for God to give man a special revelation? Why must a valid philosophy give place for revelation (both natural and special) in the pursuit of truth?

B. The Wisdom of God (vv. 21-24)

21. For after that in the wisdom of God the world by wisdom knew not God, it pleased God by the foolishness of preaching to save them that believe.

22. For the Jews require a sign, and the Greeks seek after wisdom:

23. But we preach Christ crucified, unto the Jews a stumblingblock, and unto the Greeks foolishness;

24. But unto them which are

called, both Jews and Greeks, Christ the power of God, and the wisdom of God.

When the world's wisdom failed to reveal God (see Acts 17:27), God in His own wisdom used the very thing which they called *foolishness.* The "foolishness of preaching" does not mean the act of preaching but the thing preached that centered in the Cross. The mystery religions so common in Paul's day centered on rites and ceremonies, but God's plan reached the heart of man through faith in the crucified and risen Christ.

The apostle Paul distinguished between Jews and Greeks and their concepts. The Jews were skeptical about anything that was added to their already accepted revelation without some kind of earth-shattering sign of verification. The Greeks represented themselves as the ultimate in human wisdom that was based on human reasoning.

In verse 23, the apostle alluded to the fact that the Jews considered the crucified Christ "a stumbling-block," for they looked for a conquering military Messiah. The Greeks considered the preaching of the Cross foolish or moronic (see also Acts 17:32). They were caught up in the philosophies of men such as Plato, Socrates, and Aristotle. They felt they were too intelligent to accept such an absurd story.

Verse 24 in the Corinthians passage testifies to the fact that there were both Jews and Greeks on the side of Christ. These converts had been made aware of a higher revelation and a more profound wisdom. They had accepted the gospel and found that real truth comes through God's revelation. The message of the cross of Christ still changes lives of people today who are hungry for life-giving truth.

C. The Foolishness of God (v. 25)

25. Because the foolishness of God is wiser than men; and the weakness of God is stronger than men.

The initial word of verse 25, *because*, resolves the whole argument of the source of wisdom. What unregenerate men regard as God's foolish and weak act is indeed wiser and stronger than the acts of men. William Barclay states: "The Greeks were intoxicated with fine words; and to them the Christian preacher with his blunt message seemed a crude and uncultured figure, to be laughed at and ridiculed rather than to be listened to and respected.

"It looked as if the Christian message had little chance of success against the background of Jewish or Greek life; but, as Paul said, 'What looks like God's foolishness is wiser than men's wisdom; and what looks like God's weakness is stronger than men's strength'" (*The Letters to the Corinthians*).

III. TRUTH SPIRITUALLY DIS-CERNED (1 Corinthians 2:1-16)

A. Demonstration of the Spirit (vv. 1-5)

(1 Corinthians 2:1-5 is not included in the printed text.)

After discussing the matter of human wisdom and the wisdom of God, the apostle Paul focused on his manner of preaching with simplicity to the Corinthians. At some time in his service to Christ, either by direct instruction from the Lord or by personal choice based on his understanding of the weakness of high Grecian rhetoric and heavy theological jargon, Paul made a deliberate choice in his method of preaching to frame the gospel message according to divine revelation. His preaching was simple and Christ-centered, and it conveyed concern, purpose, and power.

The simplicity with which Paul preached the gospel does not mean shallowness, nor that it lacked arduous study and careful preparation. Rather, his approach was that of stating truth in clear, direct, and understandable language. His preaching was not characterized by subtle philosophical or psychological suggestions, nor did it contain theological double-talk or mysterious and hidden concepts.

Paul's message was Christ-centered. Consequently, he excluded from his message everything except the revelation of the redemptive work of Christ. Unmoved by what the Grecian mind might have considered weak oratory, Paul was concerned that through his message, the message of the Cross would show forth. It is commendable that many of our seminaries and Bible scholars have stressed the necessity of simplicity in preaching. Leon Morris, in his volume *The First Epistle of Paul to the Corinthians,* states: "Preaching the gospel is not delivering edifying discourses, beautifully put together [to gain applause for great rhetoric]. It is bearing witness to what God has done in Christ for man's salvation." When Paul preached "Jesus Christ, and him crucified," he selected the one point that was the most criticized by both Jews and Greeks.

Discuss the matter of simplicity in the presentation of the gospel message, both in preaching and in teaching in a classroom setting.

In verse 3, Paul refers to his earlier visit to Corinth and acknowledges his personal fears and struggles at that time. Adam Clarke comments on that experience in Acts 18:9, 10 as follows: "It is likely that Paul was at this time much discouraged by the violent opposition of the Jews, and probably was in danger of his life (v. 10); and might have been entertaining serious thoughts of ceasing to preach, or leaving Corinth. To prevent this, and comfort him, God was pleased to give him this vision" (*Clarke's Commentary*, Vol. V).

The message from the Lord was, "Be not afraid, but speak, and hold not thy peace: for I am with thee, and no man shall set on thee to hurt thee: for I have much people in this city" (Acts 18:9, 10). Paul was totally dependent on the Lord for his strength.

In verse 4 of our study text, the apostle Paul indicates that he did not speak with persuasive doctrines of human wisdom, but with the grand, but simple, truths of the gospel. The doctrine that he preached was revealed by the Spirit; and the potency and power of the doctrine was evidenced by the souls who were converted by the overthrow of idolatrous practices.

Verse 5 indicates that Paul was committed to building the faith of the Corinthians on the power of God and not on the eloquence of man's enticing words. Faith built on God's power can stand against the onslaughts of evil and has the courage to be bold in the midst of personal fear. This reality Paul could verify by his early experience at Corinth.

B. Revelation Through the Spirit (vv. 6-13)

(1 Corinthians 2:6, 9, 11, 12 is not included in the printed text.)

7. But we speak the wisdom of God in a mystery, even the hidden wisdom, which God ordained before the world unto our glory:

8. Which none of the princes of this world knew: for had they known it, they would not have crucified the Lord of glory.

10. But God hath revealed them unto us by his Spirit: for the Spirit searcheth all things, yea, the deep things of God.

13. Which things also we speak, not in the words which man's wisdom teacheth, but which the Holy Ghost teacheth; comparing spiritual things with spiritual.

The apostle Paul had no faith in man's wisdom concerning redemption, for the gospel message was from God himself who revealed His own purpose and plan of redemption. Man's knowledge cannot bring about redemption, peace, or permanent security for the searching soul.

In verse 7, Paul refers to the "wisdom of God in a mystery." To him God's wisdom was a mystery in the sense that human wisdom was not able to penetrate or discover it. Also the term indicates the sense of something hidden from the person not willing to submit to the demands of the Christian way of life. By contrast, when those demands are met, that which was a mystery becomes clear.

Despite the eminence of the "princes of this world" (v. 8) as leaders of society, they did not discern the true nature of redemption. In fact, Paul indicates that if the leaders had known who Christ really was, "they would not have crucified the Lord of glory."

In verse 9 the apostle alludes to Isaiah 64:4 in a rather free rendering of that verse. He indicates that man cannot grasp the wisdom of God by his perceptive abilities or his human reasoning. Such knowledge is gained only through God's special revelation. Believers gain true wisdom and spiritual power through Christ. But even beyond such a great benefit, there are additional benefits awaiting the child of God—"the things which God hath prepared for them that love him" (v. 9).

No person is able to know the things of God except through the ministry of the Holy Spirit. The Spirit possesses complete and accurate knowledge of truth resident in God. "[Even] the deep things of God" (v. 10) probably refers to His essence, attributes, volition, and plans; but the Holy Spirit knows and gives understanding of these deep things to those who love Him.

Paul indicates there are two kinds of truth and two kinds of people. First, there is spiritual truth which comes through the Holy Spirit and is understood by spiritual people. There is also a natural wisdom which is opposed to spiritual truth. Spiritual people accept and understand spiritual truth which the natural man does not. The "spirit of the world" (v. 12) is manifested through man in his sinful state; it is the principle which pervades human society in its alienation from God. In contrast to the spirit of the world is the Spirit of

God, that is, the Holy Spirit who is given by God to believers.

In verse 13, Paul indicates that as God has revealed Himself to man, He enables man to present the revealed truth to other persons. Consequently, divine truth does not depend upon human contrivances in its presentation. Also the spiritual man makes a practice of "comparing spiritual things with spiritual." This seems to indicate that interpreting, adapting, and applying spiritual teachings to spiritual persons should be done with discernment. Paul certainly makes clear the fact that human learning and human salvation are not sufficient to present the gospel. Salvation truth is a revealed message which is taught under the direction of the Spirit.

C. Discernment by the Spirit
(vv. 14-16)

(1 Corinthians 2:14-16 is not included in the printed text.)

The natural man is one who possesses simply the ability of human cognition, but has not the ability of spiritual understanding and knowledge. He has only the common powers of a man separated from God, and as such he cannot receive the "things . . . of God . . . neither can he know them, because they are spiritually discerned" (v. 14). Since the natural abilities of man are altogether corrupt because of sin, every activity of his soul and mind will be darkened accordingly. Spiritual things are foolish to such a person because he sees life in relationship only to this present world. Since the natural man does not open his life to the Holy Spirit, he counts all spiritual life and values as foolishness.

Verse 15 bears out the fact that because of the presence of the Holy Spirit, "he that is spiritual judgeth all things, yet he himself is judged of no man." This passage by no means grants a license for a Christian to sit in judgment of the activities of others, nor does it mean the spiritual man is immune to criticism or evaluation by the world. The spiritual man, however, does have a spiritual capacity to sift, investigate, examine, and discern all things within the scope of divine revelation of redemption.

In verse 16, Paul quotes from Isaiah 40:13. God's ways and methods are beyond the understanding of man. Consequently, it is a waste of time for the natural man to attempt to understand the operation of divine redemption. In fact, it is the height of egotism for a man to attempt to instruct the Lord. But the indwelling Spirit reveals Christ and the power of God to the redeemed person. The spiritual man does not evaluate things from the point of view of the world, but sees things in the light of the revelation of God in Christ.

REVIEW QUESTIONS

1. What were the conditions of the Corinthian church that caused the apostle Paul to write the letter to them?

2. What is lacking in the wisdom of natural man so far as a basis for understanding redemption is concerned?

3. In 1 Corinthians 2:3, Paul refers to his visit when he was weak and fearful. What were the conditions that created the fear, and how was it controlled?

4. Why, according to 1

Corinthians 2:7, 8, is the wisdom of God connected with mystery?

5. Do Christians sometimes fall prey to the wisdom of this world? In what ways?

GOLDEN TEXT HOMILY

"THE PREACHING OF THE CROSS IS TO THEM THAT PERISH FOOLISHNESS; BUT UNTO US WHICH ARE SAVED IT IS THE POWER OF GOD" (1 Corinthians 1:18).

At the heart of our faith stands the cross of Christ. Death by means of crucifixion was reserved for criminals. Our Savior suffered this death—the most shameful death known to humankind. But Christ's death cannot be seen in the same light as the death of other men by crucifixion. His death was unique, for it has a twofold effect: To those who are on their way to destruction, it makes no sense, and it is foolish, cruel, and crude. But to believers it is the greatest power, transforming their lives and setting them free from the power of sin and death.

Christ's death is not something nice to think about or to talk about. The Cross was so radical that it was a stumbling block to the Jews and foolishness to the Greeks. When we really hear the message of the Cross, it also makes us uncomfortable. The One crucified in weakness condemns human pride, self-righteousness, and looking out for number one, especially when such a person is clothed in the garb of piety and religion.

Can we join Paul and declare, "God forbid that I should glory, save in the cross of our Lord Jesus Christ" (Galatians 6:14)? The Cross shaped Paul's life. But so often we do not want the Cross to determine the kind of people we are. Should the Cross be allowed to do that, it could very well get in our way and hinder what we want to do and accomplish. However, that is precisely what we need—to allow the Cross to shape our lives. It is the only remedy for what is spiritually and morally wrong with us. So nothing else can offer us the help, comfort, and assurance that the message of the Cross offers. The Cross provided the power of God for our salvation, and it is our only hope of everlasting life.—**French L. Arrington, Ph.D., Professor of New Testament Greek and Exegesis, Church of God School of Theology, Cleveland, Tennessee**

SENTENCE SERMONS

THE WISDOM AND POWER of God are found in Jesus Christ.

—Selected

HE WHO PROVIDES for this life, but takes no care for eternity, is wise for a moment, but a fool forever.

—John Tillotson

DAILY BIBLE READINGS

M. Wisdom of Unity.
    Psalm 133:1-3
T. Source and Benefits of
    Wisdom. Proverbs 9:6-12
W. Divine Power Promised.
    Acts 1:1-9
T. Human Wisdom Is Weak.
    1 Corinthians 1:26-31
F. Triumphant Power Through
    Christ. 2 Corinthians 4:8-18
S. God Gives Wisdom.
    James 1:2-5

Defending the Gospel

Study Text: Galatians 1:1 through 2:10

Objective: To recognize and accept our responsibility to defend the gospel.

Time: The Book of Galatians was written around A.D. 55-56.

Place: The Book of Galatians was probably written at Antioch or Ephesus.

Golden Text: "The gospel which was preached of me is not after man . . . but by the revelation of Jesus Christ" (Galatians 1:11, 12).

Central Truth: Our doctrine must be in accordance with God's revealed Word.

Evangelism Emphasis: The power of the gospel can deliver sinners.

PRINTED TEXT

Galatians 1:6. I marvel that ye are so soon removed from him that called you into the grace of Christ unto another gospel:

7. Which is not another; but there be some that trouble you, and would pervert the gospel of Christ.

8. But though we, or an angel from heaven, preach any other gospel unto you than that which we have preached unto you, let him be accursed.

9. As we said before, so say I now again, If any man preach any other gospel unto you than that ye have received, let him be accursed.

10. For do I now persuade men, or God? or do I seek to please men? for if I yet pleased men, I should not be the servant of Christ.

11. But I certify you, brethren, that the gospel which was preached of me is not after man.

12. For I neither received it of man, neither was I taught it, but by the revelation of Jesus Christ.

13. For ye have heard of my conversation in time past in the Jews' religion, how that beyond measure I persecuted the church of God, and wasted it:

14. And profited in the Jews' religion above many my equals in mine own nation, being more exceedingly zealous of the traditions of my fathers.

15. But when it pleased God, who separated me from my mother's womb, and called me by his grace,

16. To reveal his Son in me, that I might preach him among the heathen; immediately I conferred not with flesh and blood.

2:1. Then fourteen years after I went up again to Jerusalem with Barnabas, and took Titus with me also.

2. And I went up by revelation, and communicated unto them that gospel which I preach among the Gentiles, but privately to them which were of reputation, lest by any means I should run, or had run, in vain.

3. But neither Titus, who was with me, being a Greek, was compelled to be circumcised:

4. And that because of false brethren unawares brought in, who came in privily to spy out our liberty which we have in Christ Jesus, that they might bring us into bondage:

5. To whom we gave place by subjection, no, not for an hour; that the truth of the gospel might continue with you.

LESSON OUTLINE

I. OPPOSE FALSE TEACHING
   A. Perversion of the Gospel
   B. Reject Any Other Gospel

II. REVELATION OF THE GOSPEL
   A. Not Received From Man
   B. Not by Religion
   C. Not Originated by the Apostles

III. CONTINUE IN THE TRUE GOSPEL
   A. Gospel Preached by Paul
   B. Defense Against False Brethren
   C. Commission to Proclaim the Gospel

LESSON EXPOSITION

INTRODUCTION

The lesson for today is taken from the Book of Galatians as the study continues under the theme of "Life and Teachings of Paul." Galatia was located in what is today the modern country of Turkey. The churches there had been initially established and visited by Paul during his first missionary journey.

The apostle Paul was now writing the churches because he had received startling news that false teachers had come into their midst. They were preaching a gospel different from the one Paul preached. They were evidently from Jerusalem and perhaps claiming the authority of the Jerusalem church fathers.

They were claiming that Christians had to come under certain aspects of Jewish law in order to obtain salvation. These included the observance of certain festival days, dietary restrictions, and circumcision. Paul was concerned because these teachers had reduced Christ and elevated these practices until both were on an equal level.

Paul defended the gospel of Christ which he preached. He called the Galatians to a firm faith in Christ. Christ's work purchased the redemption of the Galatian believers, not certain religious practices. Paul exposed the false teachers and vindicated his own authority to preach. God had commissioned him with the true gospel. The Galatian believers needed to retain the gospel that Paul had originally preached to them.

I. OPPOSE FALSE TEACHING
(Galatians 1:6-9)

A. Perversion of the Gospel
(vv. 6, 7)

6. I marvel that ye are so soon removed from him that called you into the grace of Christ unto another gospel:

7. Which is not another; but there be some that trouble you, and would pervert the gospel of Christ.

Paul immediately identified the central problem troubling the Galatian Christians; they had allowed themselves to be moved away from Christ. Christ is the only Lord and Savior of the believer. No other person can take His place, and everything the believer does *NOT* must be in Christ. *EYES ON CHRIST*

The issue was more than doctrinal; they had left the worship and service of Christ himself. This implied the seriousness of the condition. The problem was not merely in the ideas they were embracing. They had allowed these erroneous teachings to move them away from Christ.

This is the great peril of false doctrine; it leads people away from Christ. Error is not neutral. It is not like an alternative way of solving a problem. Christ is the only way of salvation. No other doctrine is an option. Heresy is wrong and a threat to the very life of the believer's faith.

The phrase "grace of Christ" signifies that the gospel depends only on Christ and what He has provided. *Grace* comes from a concept representing the favor Christ bestowed on lost mankind. It is favor undeserved. This grace does not come to man as the result of anything he has done. It comes from Christ and Christ alone.

The perversion of the false teachers in Galatia was precisely on this point of grace. They had perverted this gospel of grace in Christ. *Pervert* (v. 7) is translated from a Greek term which literally means "to completely turn around and change." They had taken the meaning of grace in Christ and made it into something completely different, a gospel of works. They no longer were living in the favor freely given by Christ. They were seeking to earn His favor through works and observances.

What is the meaning of the phrase "grace of Christ"?

B. Reject Any Other Gospel
(vv. 8, 9)

8. But though we, or an angel *DEEP* **from heaven, preach any other gospel unto you than that which we have preached unto you, let him be accursed.**

9. As we said before, so say I now again, If any man preach any other gospel unto you than that ye have received, let him be accursed.

In these verses Paul conveyed the seriousness of the need to reject false teachings. He said that anyone who comes preaching an erroneous gospel should be *accursed*. The Greek word is *anathema,* and it is comprised of two words: *ana,* "back again," and *tithemi,* "to place." The words combined mean "to place back."

As the word is used here and elsewhere by Paul (Romans 9:3; 1 Corinthians 16:22), it means the giving of a person over into the hands of God for judgment and for destruction. It was a terrible thing to be placed into the hands of God's judgment, but this is the seriousness with which Paul confronted the Galatians. The false teachers were not to be tolerated. Paul called for God's judgment to be placed on them.

Paul was so serious about this matter that he repeated the command. The first time (v. 8) he said that if anyone should possibly do this, he would be accursed. The second time (v. 9) the command is reinforced by a different form of the Greek verb translated "preach." Paul said that if anyone was currently preaching a false gospel, he too would be accursed. In other words, if the possibility existed or if at any time a false teacher should come into their midst, they should place him in the hands of God's judgment.

The critical point here is that believers must be on guard against false teaching and not expect to merely handle it themselves. The solution is not in dialogue or mutual understanding. The command is to place these false teachers before God and allow Him to deal with them. This is best done through the Word and work of the Holy Spirit.

II. REVELATION OF THE GOSPEL
(Galatians 1:10-24)

A. Not Received From Man
(vv. 10-12)

10. For do I now persuade men, or God? or do I seek to please men? for if I yet pleased men, I should not be the servant of Christ.

11. But I certify you, brethren, that the gospel which was preached of me is not after man.

12. For I neither received it of man, neither was I taught it, but by the revelation of Jesus Christ.

In these verses Paul identified the source and nature of the gospel he had delivered to the Galatians. This was the gospel they were to remain faithful to.

Paul prefaced his remarks by testifying that he preached this gospel holding himself answerable to God and not man. His task was not to persuade or please men but to be a servant of Christ. He delivered the gospel with only one commitment and motivation—to serve Christ.

To be a servant of Christ is usually not the motivation of false teachers. The commitment of a false teacher is usually to a selfish and godless cause, though they may profess to be rendering the gospel of Christ. A close examination of the gain they seek through their teaching will reveal their true motives. Having a servant's spirit is one of the marks of a teacher of the true gospel of Christ.

Certify (v. 11) is translated from a Greek word meaning "to bring to one's knowledge." It indicates that Paul was informing, as well as announcing to his brethren, something they may not have currently understood about the gospel. This point was to be very important in Paul's defense of the gospel.

Paul told the Galatians that the gospel he preached did not come from man. It was not handed to him by anyone, neither was he taught this message by sitting under someone's instruction or training.

False doctrine can often be identified by its claim to have come through a special revelation or teaching. Many false teachers claim they received a special insight, or boast about receiving some mystical revelation or instruction. Paul fully clarified that these were not the sources of the gospel he preached. He emphatically declared that it came "by the revelation of Jesus Christ"—He was the source and guide of his gospel!

A revelation was something which could not be known except by one revealing a matter.

Revelation (Greek, _apokalupsis_, from which we get our English word _apocalypse_) literally means "to unveil." It is as though the knowledge of the gospel was hidden from man and thus impossible for him to receive. The only manner in which the gospel could come was by God's lifting the veil which kept it hidden.

This revelation was not the result of any human effort. It came only by the grace and power of God. The false teachers were claiming that certain religious observances were required before access to Christ could be attained. To the contrary, the true gospel of Christ is the message that has been revealed by God's grace.

B. Not by Religion (vv. 13, 14)

13. For ye have heard of my conversation in time past in the Jews' religion, how that beyond measure I persecuted the church of God, and wasted it:

14. And profited in the Jews' religion above many my equals in mine own nation, being more exceedingly zealous of the traditions of my fathers.

In these two verses Paul declared that the gospel did not come to him through religion, even though he had excelled in religion. He had already established the source of the gospel as the revelation of Jesus Christ. Now he reviewed his past history in the religion of the Jews, rejecting it as the source of the gospel he preached.

By reviewing his experience in the religion of the Jews, Paul demonstrated that he had as much opportunity as anyone to receive special insight from that religion. He excelled in that religion, yet it did not reveal the gospel of Christ to him.

The Greek term for _conversation_ essentially means "manner of living

or practice." In verses 13 and 14 Paul reviewed the way his manner of living excelled that of many of his fellow Jews. In five different references Paul told how he excelled in the practice of the religion of the Jews:

1. He had acquired such a reputation for the practice of his religion that the Galatians had already heard of it.

2. He had not only persecuted the church but had done so "beyond measure."

3. He had _profited_, or "cut forward" (Greek meaning), in Judaism. In other words, he was a teacher ambitiously cutting down those who opposed the religion.

4. In comparison to theirs he was above them.

5. He was extremely zealous in his religious pursuits.

In effect, Paul was saying to the Judaizers (who had infiltrated the Galatian church and were teaching false doctrine) that if religion was the way to serve Christ, he would be a great success. However, as he proceeded to write to the Galatians, Paul rejected religious practice as the source of man's salvation.

It must be clarified that Paul was not rejecting religion or tradition in and of themselves. Religion and tradition based on the revelation of God's Word and the gospel of Christ are necessary. Religion is an expression of faith. Tradition is the preservation of godly practices. However, Paul was attacking religion and tradition only when they are used to replace Christ. Only Christ is the author and finisher of the faith of the Christian (Hebrews 12:2).

C. Not Originated by the Apostles (vv. 15-24)

(Galatians 1:17-24 is not included in the printed text.)

15. But when it pleased God,

who separated me from my mother's womb, and called me by his grace,

16. To reveal his Son in me, that I might preach him among the heathen; immediately I conferred not with flesh and blood.

In verses 16-19, Paul said that once the gospel was revealed to him by Christ, he did not confer with the other apostles. This demonstrated that the gospel did not come from consultation with or by the instruction of the apostles. This is another part of Paul's emphatic message. The validity of the gospel rests on the revelation of Christ and not by man, not even the apostles.

In verses 15 and 16 Paul especially referred back to the fact that the gospel came from God alone. He said the imparting of the gospel pleased God. Further, God "separated" him to preach the gospel even from his mother's womb. Finally, God was the One who called him to the gospel. God himself had revealed the gospel of Christ to him.

Separated (v. 15) may have been a special twist used by Paul to address the false teachers in Galatia. The Judaizers were preaching a message similar to that of the Pharisees, whose name derived from the Hebrew word meaning "separated ones." The Judaizers' message was that observance of laws and traditions would lead to godliness. The Pharisees felt they were set apart because of their observance of laws and traditions. But God is the One who separates, not man nor man-made traditions. Neither was Paul special or set apart because of his own good works. He was called of God.

Verses 17-24 review the steps Paul took immediately after he received the revelation of Christ. This brief report assured the

Galatians that not even the apostles contributed to the origin of the gospel which Paul received. He went immediately into Arabia before going to Jerusalem where he met with Peter. Beyond that experience, Paul mentioned his going into Syria and Cilicia, but he was unknown by face to the churches in Judea. When the Judean Christians heard that he was the one who previously ravished the churches, hauling away the Christians, they glorified God inasmuch as that persecutor had been saved and now preached Christ.

Perhaps the false teachers were from Jerusalem and claimed superiority over Paul because of their proximity to the apostles there. It is not unusual for false teachers to base their credibility on the significance of geography or associations. On the basis of having been someplace special or with well-known individuals, they may have tried to justify their erroneous doctrines.

The Christian must firmly hold to Christ the source of the gospel. Religion, tradition, special locations, or important individuals should never be elevated above the grace of God through Christ.

What was the basis of Paul's being separated?

III.   CONTINUE IN THE TRUE GOSPEL (Galatians 2:1-10)

A.   Gospel Preached by Paul (vv. 1-3)

1. Then fourteen years after I went up again to Jerusalem with Barnabas, and took Titus with me also.

2. And I went up by revelation, and communicated unto them that gospel which I preach among the Gentiles, but privately to

them which were of reputation, lest by any means I should run, or had run, in vain.

3. But neither Titus, who was with me, being a Greek, was compelled to be circumcised.

A very important point was made by Paul about the gospel he had preached. It was in agreement with the doctrine of the apostles in Jerusalem. This is important because God is not the author of any interpretation that comes exclusively from one man. The true gospel is open to investigation. It is a credible gospel even under the scrutiny of God's people.

False teachers often avoid scrutiny from others, making special claims about their doctrine and refusing to come under the authority of anyone.

By contrast Paul was seen here as putting himself under the gaze and authority of the church at Jerusalem. In humility he sought them out to make sure the gospel he had been preaching was not in error.

He was wise in the process of selecting those who could be qualified by reputation—that is, a position of authority—to give him counsel. Paul would have been foolish to have asked the opinion of those who had not ministered the gospel themselves nor ministered with authority in the church. He sought the advice which could legitimately offer him guidance and wisdom.

Paul needed to know if the gospel he preached was correct lest his preaching had been in vain. If a person preaches an erroneous "gospel" his work is in vain. This points out the necessity of a humble spirit that is willing to come under correction and guidance. If a person persists in false doctrine, unwilling to be corrected, his efforts will be fruitless.

The defense of the gospel requires a proper attitude. A haughty spirit unwilling to come under correction does not help the defense of the gospel; rather it causes distortion and falsehood.

Verse 3 identifies a particular point that was no doubt under question by the false teachers in Galatia. Evidently, they were claiming that circumcision was a requirement for believers. Paul said that while he was in Jerusalem making sure that his preaching was correct, no one required circumcision of Titus the Greek, who had not been circumcised.

Verse 3 also demonstrates a vital part of the defense of the gospel— proper clarification of the issues. One tactic of false teachers is to confuse the facts of Christianity. Then based on this confusion, erroneous doctrine is taught. The defender of the gospel must be willing to tackle these erroneous assumptions. Quite often, it is a matter of looking at what a false teacher is claiming about Christianity and pointing out how his interpretation is in error. The Judaizers had evidently been claiming that the Jerusalem apostles had required circumcision. Paul proved them wrong.

B. Defense Against False Brethren (vv. 4-6)

(Galatians 2:6 is not included in the printed text.)

4. And that because of false brethren unawares brought in, who came in privily to spy out our liberty which we have in Christ Jesus, that they might bring us into bondage:

5. To whom we gave place by subjection, no, not for an hour; that the truth of the gospel might continue with you.

In verses 4 and 5 Paul gave a description of the nature in which false doctrine had infiltrated the Galatian churches. This description fits the manner in which the church today is assaulted by false doctrine.

First, the character of the teachers of heresy is revealed by the very name "false brethren." This term was aptly defined by the Greek scholar Hermann Cremer. He said it referred to "those who had become members of the Christian church, shared in the fellowship of life and love, but were not so really, that is inwardly, and therefore had no right to be called [brethren]. They had companionship of the [brethren], but real kinship of spiritual life was wanting (see 2 Corinthians 11:26). By claiming the name 'brethren,' they began the weakening of the brethren" (*Biblico-Theological Lexicon of New Testament Greek*).

Second, the manner of false teachers is identified. They come into the church unsuspected ("unawares"). Unawares is translated from a Greek word which literally means "to sneak in alongside." The emphasis of the word is upon the way someone who is totally alien to the church is able to sneak in and be accepted by other believers as a believer. They come in even though they are the very thing that threatens the church.

Third, the method by which these false teachers come into a church and teach their doctrine is expanded by use of the words "came in privily," that is, secretly or by stealth.

Fourth, the purpose of these individuals is revealed in the phrase "spy out." This phrase comes from a single Greek word which means "to examine very carefully." It was used most often where treacherous intent was involved. The purpose of

these false brothers is to pick apart and scrutinize the precious faith of the saints in order to propagate their own heresy.

Fifth, the result of the work of false teachers is seen. They turn the liberty of the Christian into bondage. These concepts are exact opposites. This is the nature of the work of heretics. They distort the truths of the gospel until the people of God actually believe something that is directly opposed to sound doctrine.

How important is clarification of issues in defending the gospel?

This fivefold description of the work of false teachers is very insightful. Once they are let in and become a part of the fellowship of a group of believers, they twist the teachings of Christ so convincingly that believers accept as truth what is in reality a lie. Sadly, many people unwittingly allow false teachers to come into a fellowship and teach them distortions.

Paul set the example in verse 5 for all believers by citing his reaction to false teachers: he did not tolerate them. This is the meaning of the statement "We gave place by subjection, no, not for an hour." He did not put up with them at any time. This was the best way to make sure "that the truth of the gospel might continue with" the Galatian saints.

False doctrine and false teachers must not be tolerated by the church. This does not mean that believers should become militant or go on "witch-hunts." Neither does it mean that love should not be shown toward those who do not hold beliefs exactly like ours. However, when a doctrine is clearly in error, the Body should be on guard and determine not to tolerate heresy. Christians should be wary about the fact that false teachers can easily slip in beside them and convince them to believe a lie.

C. Commission to Proclaim the Gospel (vv. 7-10)

(Galatians 2:7-10 is not included in the printed text.)

In verses 7-10 Paul told how his ministry was further vindicated by the men of the Jerusalem church. He had already discussed the acceptance of the message he preached after he first returned from the Arabian wilderness (1:15-24). Now, he explained that his ministry to the Gentiles and the gospel he preached to them were also accepted by the brethren of Jerusalem at a later time. This defense was to further respond to claims by false teachers in Galatia.

In this lesson Paul certainly demonstrates the need to effectively make a stand against false teachers. He did not become proud or brash in his response to their heresy. Rather he consistently clarified the facts and then exposed the error of their teaching.

The decisiveness of Paul's attitude should instruct the church today. False teachers are very dangerous and must not be tolerated. With a spirit of love the church today can clarify the nature of the true gospel and then expose the error of those who would slip into the church in an attempt to distort the gospel.

REVIEW QUESTIONS

1. What is the purpose of Paul's letter to the Galatians?
2. What is the meaning of the term *revelation*?
3. What may have been some of the claims of the false teachers who got into the Galatian churches?
4. How does Paul describe the methods of false teachers?
5. What should be the response of the church today to false teachers? Are there false teachers?

GOLDEN TEXT HOMILY

"THE GOSPEL WHICH WAS PREACHED OF ME IS NOT AFTER MAN . . . BUT BY THE REVELATION OF JESUS CHRIST" (Galatians 1:11, 12).

Paul wanted the people to understand that the gospel is a revelation of Jesus Christ. Its importance lies in the fact that man-made religion is so common. Man's attempt to fashion Christianity into his desires and his standards is the highest form of idolatry. In so doing, God is pulled down to the level of man, Christianity is empty, and man is left to struggle without hope.

Paul pointed out that human reasoning cannot understand the deep needs of the soul and the spirit. That which is carnal and temporal cannot comprehend that which is spiritual and eternal. Only the Word of God has the key to open the hearts of mankind to see their spiritual need. Therefore, the gospel could not have come from man, because man is not spiritual in nature. He only becomes a spiritual being after he has had an encounter with Jesus Christ.

In the verses following, Paul gave his personal testimony to declare the divine origin of Scripture. In times past he had persecuted the church of God. He had been zealous in the Jews' religion, which was so opposed to the teachings of Christianity. All that changed when he gave his life to Christ. Paul, who had once been a destroyer, was now a disciple; he who had been a doubter was now a teacher and a writer of the gospel.

This gospel that Paul preached enables us to be forgiven of our sins and brings us into a relationship with God. Our lives are changed; our goals, our desires, and our purposes have new meaning. All this can only be accomplished by the revelation of the Word of God and through the indwelling of the Holy Spirit. Only a message of divine origin can accomplish such spiritual realities in our lives.—**Jerry Puckett, Customer Service Representative, Pathway Press, Cleveland, Tennessee**

SENTENCE SERMONS

OUR DOCTRINE must be in accordance with God's revealed Word.

—Selected

THE GLORY of the gospel is its freedom.

—A.W. Tozer

THE GOSPEL IS neither a discussion nor a debate. It is an announcement.

—Paul Stromberg Rees

THE WORLD has many religions; it has but one true gospel.

—George Owen

EVANGELISM EMPHASIS

THE POWER OF THE GOSPEL CAN DELIVER SINNERS.

The world today is filled with cures and remedies. Entertainment, popularity, drugs, passionate lifestyles, and other temptations send the message that life's problems can easily be removed by these means. They offer quick relief for a nagging chronic problem—sin.

As great as the claims of the world may be, there is still only one remedy which is strong enough to remove sin from a life. This cure, faith in the Lord Jesus Christ, is eternal and everlasting. This is the message available to whoever will call on the name of the Lord, confess his sins, and accept Christ as Lord and Savior. Once this is done, newness of life and freedom from the guilt of sin is given to the repentant sinner. Only the power of the gospel can deliver from sin.

ILLUMINATING THE LESSON

During the Civil War in America, those throughout the country who were loyal displayed the banner of the United States. Such was the case in the town of Fredericksburg. But when the inhabitants found that Stonewall Jackson and a regiment of Confederate soldiers were approaching, they were all with one exception frightened and concealed their signs of loyalty. An elderly woman named Barbara Frike had the courage to display the banner outside the window. When the general saw it, he ordered the soldiers to fire at it. In the midst of the fire and the smoke, the old dame put her head out and shouted with an electric voice, "Strike my grey head if you like, but spare the banner of my country." Her courage overpowered the general and he ordered his men to leave her alone.

The gospel of Christ, unadulterated in its Scriptural simplicity, has been the banner of our country for ages. It merits our most courageous defense.

—D. Rees

DAILY BIBLE READINGS

M. God's Power Revealed.
   1 Kings 18:30-39
T. Trusting God. Psalm 27:1-6
W. Truth Confessed.
   Daniel 6:24-27
T. Contending for the Truth.
   Acts 15:1-5, 13-20
F. Manifestation of the Gospel.
   1 Timothy 3:14-16
S. Beware of Deception.
   2 Peter 2:1-9

Love—the Supreme Virtue

Study Text: 1 Corinthians 13:1-13

Objective: To recognize that love is the most important virtue and make it the rule of daily living.

Time: The Book of 1 Corinthians was probably written in the spring of A.D. 57.

Place: The Book of 1 Corinthians was written at Ephesus.

Golden Text: "Now abideth faith, hope, charity, these three; but the greatest of these is charity" (1 Corinthians 13:13).

Central Truth: Love is the greatest Christian virtue.

Evangelism Emphasis: God's greatest manifestation of love was sending Jesus Christ to die for sinners.

PRINTED TEXT

1 Corinthians 13:1. Though I speak with the tongues of men and of angels, and have not charity, I am become as sounding brass, or a tinkling cymbal.

2. And though I have the gift of prophecy, and understand all mysteries, and all knowledge; and though I have all faith, so that I could remove mountains, and have not charity, I am nothing.

3. And though I bestow all my goods to feed the poor, and though I give my body to be burned, and have not charity, it profiteth me nothing.

4. Charity suffereth long, and is kind; charity envieth not; charity vaunteth not itself, is not puffed up,

5. Doth not behave itself unseemly, seeketh not her own, is not easily provoked, thinketh no evil;

6. Rejoiceth not in iniquity, but rejoiceth in the truth;

7. Beareth all things, believeth all things, hopeth all things, endureth all things.

8. Charity never faileth: but whether there be prophecies, they shall fail; whether there be tongues, they shall cease; whether there be knowledge, it shall vanish away.

9. For we know in part, and we prophesy in part.

10. But when that which is perfect is come, then that which is in part shall be done away.

11. When I was a child, I spake as a child, I understood as a child, I thought as a child: but when I became a man, I put away childish things.

12. For now we see through a glass, darkly; but then face to face: now I know in part; but then shall I know even as also I am known.

13. And now abideth faith, hope, charity, these three; but the greatest of these is charity.

LESSON OUTLINE

LESSON EXPOSITION

INTRODUCTION

The lesson for today is about the apostle Paul's teaching about love. His emphasis on love, however, comes as a parenthetical statement as he teaches on a broader context about the gifts of the Spirit, the body of Christ, and worship.

Perhaps no topic is more important and essential than that of love. Yet secular-minded individuals, as well as many who desire to follow Christ, practice and reflect little of the real characteristics of love. In our human frailty we will doubtlessly ever reach a plateau of love that our inner man at its most dedicated state cries out for. But help for such a worthy objective can come to us from the Lord.

"Love is not a possession but a growth," said Henry Ward Beecher. "The heart is a lamp with just oil enough to burn for an hour, and if there be no oil put in again, its light will go out. God's grace is the oil that fills the lamp of love." (*The Encyclopedia of Religious Quotations*).

Much of the world, especially the English-speaking cultures, use the single word *love* to express a lot of relationships. The Greeks, however, had different words for *love* to describe relationships. William Barclay notes four words used by Greek-speaking people:

"*Eros* is the word that characterized the love of a man and a woman. It always had a predominately physical side and it always involved sex. The New Testament writers did not use this word as it had come to be related to more lust than a normal marital love.

"*Philia* is the highest word in secular Greek for love. It describes a warm, intimate, tender relationship of body, mind, and spirit. It describes close friendship and brotherhood. Note the word *Philadelphia*—city of brotherly love.

"*Storge* is a word not found in the New Testament. It describes the love between family members.

"*Agape* is the word used in the New Testament to describe godly love. It is the word of Christian fellowship and God's love for the human family in Jesus Christ. Agape is the spirit in the heart which will never seek anything but the highest good of its fellowman. It does not matter how its fellowman treats it. It does not matter what and who its fellowmen are. It does not matter what the attitude is to be, it will never seek anything but the highest and their best good" (*Flesh and Spirit: an Examination of Galatians*).

Agape is the word translated "charity" in 1 Corinthians and used in the lesson today.

Our Lord himself was emphatic about the need for *agape* love: "Love your enemies" (Luke 6:27); "Love one another" (John 15:17). And in John 3:16 He shared with Nicodemus the ultimate expression of love: "For God so loved the world, that he gave his only begotten Son, that whosoever believeth in him should not perish, but have everlasting life."

Samuel M. Shoemaker said, "In the triangle of love between ourselves, God, and other people, is found the secret of existence, and the best foretaste, I suspect, that we can have on earth of what heaven will probably be like" (*The Encyclopedia of Religious Quotations*).

Perhaps it is not too bold to think that as the merits of godly love are studied and applied, preparations are being made not only for this life but also for eternal life with the Lord.

I. LOVE IS ESSENTIAL
(1 Corinthians 13:1-3)

The church at Corinth was established during Paul's second missionary journey. According to Acts 18:11, the apostle had been in Corinth for 18 months, but the young congregation was a vexing problem to Paul because of its instability. Since it was composed largely of Gentiles who had no training in Old Testament Scriptures and whose religious and moral antecedents were the exact opposites of Christian principles, much training was required to bring them up to the place of spiritual maturity.

The problems at Corinth ranged from schisms to finances and from church doctrine to the Resurrection. In essence, the problems at Corinth reflected the conflicts which take place when Christian experience and Christian ideals of conduct come into conflict with the concepts and practices of the pagan world.

Beginning with chapter 12, the apostle Paul discussed the abuses in spiritual matters such as the gifts of the Spirit and the body of Christ. He concluded the exhortation with chapter 14, where he discussed the proper use of spiritual gifts particularly as they relate to prophecy and worship.

Consequently, chapter 13—the chapter on love—comes in the middle of the broad context, not so much as an essay or a poetic "ode to love," but as a well-placed climax of studied argument or reasoning. It was the logical conclusion to bring a godly solution to conditions that were disrupting the church.

Discuss the essential part that love plays in bringing harmony to otherwise divisive situations.

A. The Language of Love (v. 1)

1. Though I speak with the tongues of men and of angels, and have not charity, I am become as sounding brass, or a tinkling cymbal.

At the conclusion of chapter 12 (v. 31), the apostle Paul promised to show the Corinthians "a more excellent way" than that in which they were now proceeding. They were so distracted with contentions, divided by parties, and envious of each other's gifts that unity was nearly destroyed. This was full proof that love to God and man was wanting, and that without this their numerous gifts and other graces were nothing in the eyes of God; for it was evident that they did not love one another, which is a proof that they did not love God and, consequently, did not have true religion. Having corrected many abuses by his advice and directions, and having shown them how in outward things they should walk so as to please God, Paul now showed them the spirit, temper, and disposition in which this should be done, and without which all the rest would be ineffectual.

Paul, much aware of the priority the Grecian culture placed on oratory, assured the Corinthians that all human languages, with all the eloquence of the most accomplished orators, are as sounding brass and tinkling cymbals unless they are accompanied by love. The reference to "tongues . . . of angels" probably means only "the most splendid eloquence," as is sometimes applied to the word *angelic* to indicate something is sublime, grand, and beautiful.

Dr. A.D. Beacham says: "Paul recognized that speaking in tongues could actually be a manifestation of pagan worship if the believer did not have Christian love in his heart. The 'sounding brass' was a gong used in pagan worship. In Greek it is the *chalkos echon*. The 'cymbal' was the instrument known as a *kumbalon*. It was also used in pagan cults. Conzeilmann quotes from an ancient text describing the pagan worship of Attis: 'I have eaten from the tambourine, I have drunk from the cymbal, I have become an initiate of Attis.'

"The cymbal was used extensively in the cult of Cybele. This was the 'Great Mother goddess' of the Anatolian cults from Persia that merged with the Greeks in the centuries before the Christian era. Attis was her son and consort. The great temple of Artemis at Ephesus was one site of her worship (Acts 19:23-41). This was the dominant cult of Asia Minor. The preaching of the gospel challenged the supremacy of this pagan cult. The Corinthians,

like nearly everyone in the ancient world, understood the point Paul was making in comparing worship without love to pagan worship" (*Evangelical Sunday School Lesson Commentary, Vol. 40*).

B. Spiritual Gifts and Love (v. 2)

2. And though I have the gift of prophecy, and understand all mysteries, and all knowledge; and though I have all faith, so that I could remove mountains, and have not charity, I am nothing.

The apostle Paul continues his emphasis on the necessity of love by pointing up that the absence of it in connection with ministry gifts leads to nothingness. Though one could receive from God the knowledge of future events, so that he could correctly foretell future events "and understand all mysteries," such as the types and figures in the Old Testament and all the unexplored secrets of nature, and have enough faith to move mountains, but have not godly love, that person is nothing—nothing in the sight of God, the church, and mankind.

Adam Clarke says of this "nothingness": "We daily see many men who are profound scholars, and well skilled in arts and sciences, and yet not only careless about religion but downright infidels! It does not require the tongue of the inspired to say that these men, in the sight of God are nothing; nor can their literary or scientific acquisitions give them a passport to glory" (*Clarke's Commentary*, Vol. VI).

C. Sacrifice and Love (v. 3)

3. And though I bestow all my goods to feed the poor, and though I give my body to be burned, and have not charity, it

profiteth me nothing.

This verse is proof that the word *charity* in modern usage is not what the apostle Paul meant; for surely giving can go no further than to give up all that one possesses in order to relieve the wants of others, and this is recognized as "charity." Yet Paul is saying that it must be done with *agape love*.

To give out of a grim duty or with contempt or rebuke is not charity, but a manifestation of pride; and pride is always cruel, for it knows no love.

Paul goes further by saying, "Though I give my body to be burned, but have not love, it is of no profit to me" (paraphrased). The apostle might have been thinking of some Christians whose lives were given in martyrdom; or he might have been thinking of Shadrach, Meshach, and Abed-nego and the burning fiery furnace (Daniel 3). But if the motive that makes a person give his life for Christ is merely pride and self-display, then even martyrdom is without value. It is difficult to accept the fact that many deeds which look sacrificial are the products of pride rather than true devotion. FASTING/PRAYING

Discuss the matter of giving for flood relief, tornado relief, or relief for famine-ravished areas, as has been the case in the last few years. Do you feel giving was done, even on the part of non-Christians, on the basis of anything but love and concern? Explain.

II. CHARACTERISTICS OF LOVE
(1 Corinthians 13:4-7)

4. Charity suffereth long, and is kind; charity envieth not; charity vaunteth not itself, is not puffed up,

5. Doth not behave itself unseemly, seeketh not her own, is not easily provoked, thinketh no evil;

6. Rejoiceth not in iniquity, but rejoiceth in the truth;

7. Beareth all things, believeth all things, hopeth all things, endureth all things.

In verses 4-7 the apostle Paul lists 15 characteristics of *agape* love. He uses both positive and negative statements to focus on the many dimensions of this greatest of all virtues. In essence, Paul is saying that Christian love can be depended on both for what it does and what it does not do.

Love is long-suffering. The Greek word *makrothumeo*, as used in the New Testament, always describes long-suffering or patience with people and not patience with circumstances. Chrysotom said that it is the word used of a person who has been wronged and who has it easily within his power to avenge himself and yet will not do it. God is like that in His relationship to the human family. Certainly Paul was pointing out that in dealing with people regardless of however unkind and hurting they are, care should be taken to exercise the same long-suffering or patience that God exercises with us. Such patience is not a sign of weakness but of strength; it is the way to victory rather than defeat.

Love is kind. The kindness of love performs good deeds for others. It desires to be useful, obliging, and helpful, and it remains kind after much suffering and ill use. Love shows mercy and is gracious in the face of unkindness from others.

Love knows no envy. There are two kinds of envy. The one covets the possessions of other people; such envy is very difficult to avoid because it is very human. The other is worse—it resents the very fact that others have what it has not; it does not so much want things for itself as wish that others did not have them. Meanness of soul can sink no further than that.

Love does not boast ("*vaunteth not itself*"). The word *vaunteth* is translated by many authors as "bragging" or engaging in "vain glory." The whole emphasis in this characteristic of love is on the word *itself*. In some individuals more than in others, there is an observable disposition toward bragging or display. There may be real ability, and yet there may be the vanity which counterfeits the proofs of that ability; on the other hand, there may be an absence of ability, and yet the fool may not be able to conceal his folly but must make himself the laughingstock of all sound-thinking individuals. Christian love does not delight in the display of real or imaginary power that does not exist.

Love is not puffed up. The Greek word for *puffed up* means just that—"inflated." Godly love keeps one's estimate of his own importance in perspective and has no desire to appear greater or more important than others or to attempt to make them appear insignificant.

Love does not behave unseemly. The word *unseemly* means that love is not rude. It has good manners and realizes that crude and ridiculous manners are offensive to others. Christian love has proper respect for those in authority as well as proper regard for those over whom authority is exercised. The apostle Paul is not merely referring to an illusive ideal. He points rather to an exercise in love which is an immediate, present possibility.

Love seeks not her own. Love is not selfish. Perhaps this characteristic of love describes best the self-emptying capacity of love. Those filled with such love are genuinely concerned with the comfort and well-being of others rather than with an egotistical focus on themselves.

Love is not easily provoked. The Greek word for *provoked* means "to sharpen, rouse to anger." Christian love is not soon angered nor is it given to outbursts of temper. It is restrained and is in control of expressions made that are later apologized for.

Discuss the matter of being "easily provoked." What can the church do to help people keep their tempers under control and not to be "easily provoked"?

Love thinks no evil. Love does not keep a record of wrongs with intentions of settling the score sometime later. Many people nurse their wrath to keep it warm. They brood over the wrongs until they are impossible to forget. Christian love has learned the secret of forgetting.

Love does not rejoice in iniquity, but rejoices in the truth. Dr. A.D. Beacham writes: "The heart that keeps score also has a tendency to rejoice when bad things happen to others." Martin Luther translated this verse, 'Love does not laugh in her sleeve when the pious suffer violence and wrong.'

"The English translation of this verse cannot capture the subtle dynamic of the Greek text. In 'rejoiceth not in iniquity,' *rejoice* denotes a 'standing off' and looking at a situation with a sense of happiness that iniquity has occurred. In 'rejoiceth in the truth,' *rejoice* means to 'rejoice with' and denotes a 'standing with' the triumph of truth. The first position is the position of unrighteous judgment; the second position is the position of siding with God's view of the situation" (*Evangelical Sunday School Lesson Commentary*, Vol. 40).

With verse 7, the apostle Paul gives four concluding characteristics of love. These four are expressed in a positive mode after a series of "love-does-nots." The four include *beareth, believeth, hopeth,* and *endureth.*

Love bears all things. The Greek word for *beareth* means to "endure patiently." Its connotation suggests the idea of putting up with something at a personal sacrifice. Love enables the Christian to bear, or suffer, the loss of things which he had a legitimate claim on. The bearing of all things also applies to controlling one's feelings under pressure.

Love believes all things. To believe all things does not imply that the person is gullible. Rather this characteristic of love implies the absence of suspicion. "The flesh," says Lenski, "is ready to believe all things about a brother and fellow man in an evil sense. Christian love does the opposite, it is confident till the last" (*Interpretation of I and II Corinthians*).

Love hopes all things. "Love never gives up," states Donald S. Metz, "it follows a man to the edge of the grave always expecting the best. Love does not produce a kind of sentimental optimism which blindly refuses to face reality, but it refuses to take failure as final. Rather than accept failure of another, love will hold on to this hope until all possibility of such a result has vanished and it is compelled to believe that the conduct is not susceptible to fair explanation" (*Beacon Bible Commentary*, Vol. 5).

Love endures all things. The phrase "endureth all things" conveys the thought of brave perseverance. It is the person who, under a great array of trials, bears up and does not lose heart and courage. Love undergirds the Christian with strength and faith during trials and difficult circumstances, because he can see the working of God in his behalf.

In these statements of the characteristics of love, the inner power of that love is revealed. It can hold its head up high, and its heart is strong with strength from heaven. It is such love that has rightly been called "the greatest thing in this world." Paul does not enumerate the sacrifices, triumphs, and mighty works of love. Rather he focuses on the ordinary circumstances of life where love is so sorely needed, even in the church. It is easy to find excuses when great things are made the goal of life and failure ensues. But with genuine Christian love, excuses are cut off. Being a true Christian every day in the exercise of love readies that person for the performance of extraordinary opportunities.

III.　LOVE IS ETERNAL
　　　(1 Corinthians 13:8-13)

A.　Love Is Permanent (vv. 8-10)

8. Charity never faileth: but whether there be prophecies, they shall fail; whether there be

tongues, they shall cease; whether there be knowledge, it shall vanish away.

9. For we know in part, and we prophesy in part.

10. But when that which is perfect is come, then that which is in part shall be done away.

In verses 8-13, the apostle Paul comes to the conclusion of his exhortation about love—the supreme virtue. In verses 8-10 he calls attention to the temporary existence of three of the most highly regarded gifts—the gift of prophecy, the gift of tongues, and the gift of knowledge. But over against the temporary existence of all other virtues stands love which is permanent.

In verse 8, Paul assures us that love never fails. In the previous section (vv. 4-7, "Characteristics of Love") a reminder was given that only Christian love can truly love. Natural man cannot generate such love. It is given as man accepts the redemptive work of Christ and is led by the Spirit to new relationships with God and with his fellow human beings.

Consequently, love becomes a part of the redeemed person's life and serves as the guiding principle of his relationships—as Paul says, "Love never fails [ends]" (*NKJV*). It is eternal and will never come to an end because it is grounded in God who is eternal. Unending love is always the same love. It is the love by which we accepted the work of Christ in redemption to bring us into fellowship with God. The love we know today is the love we will have as we stand before God.

"Our future has begun [as Christians] because love already possesses us. Love is the promise fulfilled already in the present. It is the connecting link between now and then, and between here and the hereafter" (Karl Barth, *Church Dogmatics*).

In contrast to the permanence of *agape* love, when the redeemed stand before God, prophecies will no longer be needed. The gift of tongues so highly esteemed by the Corinthians will cease when the era of redemptive work is finished, and believers will be delivered from all that separates them from God and others. Also, the gift of knowledge, both the learning acquired by the human family and the mysteries revealed by God, will cease to be needed in the light of the perfect knowledge of God.

In commenting on the time when prophecies, tongues, and the gift of knowledge will cease, Dr. A.D. Beacham states: "The important thing to note is that these verbs [the verbs relating to prophecy, tongues, and knowledge] are all in the future tense. There are those who argue that these three things came to an end at the close of the first century. This view imposes a theological/ historical slant upon Scripture that cannot be supported in any way other than the interpreter's bias. Prophecy, tongues, and knowledge will continue to exist as ministries of the Holy Spirit for the church throughout the church age. When the Lord returns in power and glory, these gifts will cease because they will have fully accomplished their purpose.

"The point is further clarified by the impact of verse 10. It is not until 'that which is perfect is come' that those things which are 'in part' shall be done away with. We surely cannot claim that the 'perfect' has already come! We are still awaiting His glorious return, and then the perfect will have come" (*Evangelical Sunday School Lesson Commentary*, Vol. 40).

In verse 9, we are reminded that we know only "in part." Our knowing is partial and inadequate. We never know with full comprehension, full penetration, and complete mastery. In all our knowing, there is something left that we do not know, a beyond to which our feeble brain has not allowed us to go.

Such limitations seem humiliating and irritating to many, but there are limits. We cannot fully comprehend many of the truths of Scripture—the Trinity, the Incarnation, the working of Providence, and others. Even in regard to the lower domain of nature we know only in part. Who fully understands life, light, electricity, and many other things? Even Martin Luther said, "I do not pretend to understand fully the Incarnation or the Trinity along with many other mysteries. I don't even know how it is that I lie down and fall asleep and when rested I wake up."

We are also reminded that "we prophesy in part." This is further proof of our limitations of powers, and it should be observed that Paul includes himself along with all other Christians. Even the most dedicated prophetic ministers have been able to say but little of some heavenly things. It pleases God that only glimpses and whisperings of divine revelations are afforded to us. It should be remembered, however, that we have much to learn from God; and for this, one must diligently wait on Him by reading His Word and by incessant prayer.

The limitations of knowledge and prophecy should not destroy the value of what we do know and what has been revealed to us; for in reality, to know God, Christ, and the Holy Spirit in faith is "life eternal" (John 17:3).

What is the general opinion about individuals who feel they fully understand all things both in the spiritual and natural world?

Verse 10 provides for the Christian the assurance that there will come a change in the final consummation of redemptive history. "That which is in part" will be replaced with "that which is perfect." The imperfections will vanish, and all that appears dim and obscure will be made plain.

B. Love Is Unlimited (vv. 11-13)

11. When I was a child, I spake as a child, I understood as a child, I thought as a child: but when I became a man, I put away childish things.

12. For now we see through a glass, darkly; but then face to face: now I know in part; but then shall I know even as also I am known.

13. And now abideth faith, hope, charity, these three; but the greatest of these is charity.

In verse 11 Paul used the typical singular "I" when he was speaking about that which is true of all people. He might have continued to use "I" in the next verse, but he inserted one clause which has the plural "we" in the verb and thereby shows that every "I" refers to all of us.

Present knowledge compared to that which we will have in heaven is like knowledge of the infant compared with the knowledge of the mature person. The word *child* (Greek, *nepios*) denotes a baby, an infant, although without any age limit. It does, however, refer to the early stages of life.

By the word *understood*, Paul refers to the earlier undeveloped experiences of the childish mind, a time of thinking which is not yet to the stage of developed reasoning. The word *thought*, however, is from the Greek word *logizomai* and conveys the idea of a progression over *understood* by inferring that reasoning is a capability. But as Paul grew, he matured in Christian love. He put away childish things with finality.

In verse 12, the apostle Paul continues his contrasts regarding knowledge. "Now we see through a glass, darkly" conveys the fact that our present knowledge, as dear as it is to us, is an indirect and partial knowledge. The word *glass* (Greek, *esoptron*) means a mirror. The mirrors of Paul's days were thin disks of metal polished on one side. At best they gave only a dim reflection. Paul also used the word *darkly*, suggesting that what was reflected in the mirror was limited and incomplete. The Greek word for *darkly* is *en ainigmati* and literally means "a riddle." Consequently, Paul says the reflection is obscure, dark, and leaves one guessing as is the case of a riddle.

The expression "but then face to face" suggests a bright future. The limited vision of the present will give way to a clear vision of the future. Our understanding will no longer be obscure, dim, and limited, but complete, direct, and unlimited. This reality is based on the promise that the believer will "know even as [he is] known."

In verse 13, Paul reaches the highest point in the 13th chapter. The time will come when all the gifts of God in the church on earth will have fulfilled God's purpose and the faithful will dwell in their Father's house, where faith, hope, and love will mark the lives of the saints forever. Faith will remain, for it is trust in God's saving work revealed in Christ. Those who trust will know the eternal presence of God. Hope will abide because it is faith that perseveres and is serene in confidence in God. Love, "the greatest of these," abides because it is God's nature and is therefore as everlasting as the Father.

"God's love, which cares," says Raymond Bryan Brown, "is answered by man's love, which cares. And love which cares is everlasting.

"Love is the reality by which God the Father unveils his heart to man and, by God's grace, the reality by which man unveils his heart to God and neighbor. It does not cease. And in the life to come it will abide in understanding the Father, who calls forth the love of men by his love for them (cf. 1 John 4:19).

"Love is the greatest of all because it expresses God's being, as faith and hope do not. God's love gives man a basis for faith and hope, which are marks of man's life, not God's" (*The Broadman Bible Commentary*, Vol. 10).

REVIEW QUESTIONS

1. What conditions were existing in the Corinthian church that made it essential for Paul to write to them concerning *love*, the highest virtue?

2. What four words did the Greeks use to define *love* in different relationships?

3. Why are the characteristics of love given in both positive and negative statements?

4. When will prophecies, tongues, and the gift of knowledge cease to be needed?

5. What did Paul mean by the statement "Now we see through a glass, darkly"?

GOLDEN TEXT HOMILY

"NOW ABIDETH FAITH, HOPE, CHARITY, THESE THREE; BUT THE GREATEST OF THESE IS CHARITY" (1 Corinthians 13:13).

Larry couldn't understand love. He'd been brought up on a ranch in California and had known only hard work. His father, a hard man, drove himself and his family and never gave a word of praise. Larry desperately needed his father's approval, but his father never seemed to approve. Larry was an unhappy person, struggling to do his best. He had no joy. Every day was tinged with the misery of trying to prove himself.

Many of us have been in that same place—our personalities are scarred; we doubt our own worth. We act out of fear, constantly trying to win the approval of others. We demand perfection and can never believe that others accept and appreciate us. How desperately we need God's kind of love—the love that is kind, caring, unfailing, and enduring. This unconditional, worth-asserting love is a different kind of love from the one Larry knew. This is a freeing love. We do not have to fear, because we know our acceptance is not based on our efforts. We don't have to prove ourselves. We have worth as individuals. Duty and struggle are replaced with joy when we return the love of

Him who loves us. With our motivation changed, with the focus shifted from us, and with our efforts toward God and His love, we grow and change.

Larry's idea of love was shaped by what he experienced in his relationship with his father. His personality was a reflection of the kind of love he was given. Each of us has been so shaped. And each of us can be freed to grow and change by experiencing God's kind of love.—**James L. Durel, Pastor, Salvation Army, Vacaville, California.**

SENTENCE SERMONS

LOVE IS the greatest Christian virtue.

—Selected

HUMAN THINGS must be known to be loved; but divine things must be loved to be known.

—Blaise Pascal

I NEVER KNEW how to worship until I knew how to love.

—Henry Ward Beecher

LOVE CAN HOPE where reason would despair.

—Lord George Lyttleton

DAILY BIBLE READINGS

M. Love Intercedes for Others. Exodus 32:30-34

T. Love Never Fails. Ruth 1:11-18

W. Love Is Forgiving. John 8:1-11

T. Love Is Not Selfish. John 15:9-14

F. Love Is Patient. James 5:7-10

S. Love Is Compassionate. 1 John 3:14-23

Face Adversity With Confidence

Study Text: Acts 23:1-11; 25:7-12; 28:16-31

Objective: To know that Christians often face adversity and determine to place our confidence in God.

Time: The Book of Acts was written between A.D. 61 and 63. The events of this lesson happened between the summer of A.D. 58 and the spring of A.D. 61.

Place: The Book of Acts was probably written at Caesarea or Rome.

Golden Text: "I know whom I have believed, and am persuaded that he is able to keep that which I have committed unto him against that day" (2 Timothy 1:12).

Central Truth: The Lord is aware of the adverse circumstances His people face and keeps them in His care.

Evangelism Emphasis: Adverse circumstances may provide opportunities to witness for Christ.

PRINTED TEXT

Acts 23:1. And Paul, earnestly beholding the council, said, Men and brethren, I have lived in all good conscience before God until this day.

2. And the high priest Ananias commanded them that stood by him to smite him on the mouth.

3. Then said Paul unto him, God shall smite thee, thou whited wall: for sittest thou to judge me after the law, and commandest me to be smitten contrary to the law?

4. And they that stood by said, Revilest thou God's high priest?

5. Then said Paul, I wist not, brethren, that he was the high priest: for it is written, Thou shalt not speak evil of the ruler of thy people.

6. But when Paul perceived that the one part were Sadducees, and the other Pharisees, he cried out in the council, Men and brethren, I am a Pharisee, the son of a Pharisee: of the hope and resurrection of the dead I am called in question.

7. And when he had so said, there arose a dissension between the Pharisees and the Sadducees: and the multitude was divided.

9. And there arose a great cry: and the scribes that were of the Pharisees' part arose, and strove, saying, We find no evil in this man: but if a spirit or an angel hath spoken to him, let us not fight against God.

25:9. But Festus, willing to do the Jews a pleasure, answered Paul, and said, Wilt thou go up to

Jerusalem, and there be judged of these things before me?

10. Then said Paul, I stand at Caesar's judgment seat, where I ought to be judged: to the Jews have I done no wrong, as thou very well knowest.

11. For if I be an offender, or have committed any thing worthy of death, I refuse not to die: but if there be none of these things whereof these accuse me, no man may deliver me unto them. I appeal unto Caesar.

12. Then Festus, when he had conferred with the council, answered, Hast thou appealed unto Caesar? unto Caesar shalt thou go.

28:30. And Paul dwelt two whole years in his own hired house, and received all that came in unto him,

31. Preaching the kingdom of God, and teaching those things which concern the Lord Jesus Christ, with all confidence, no man forbidding him.

DICTIONARY

Ananias (an-uh-NY-us)—Acts 23:2—A high priest at Paul's trial.

Sadducees (SAD-you-seez)—Acts 23:6—A Jewish religious group that did not believe in angels or resurrection.

Pharisees (FARE-ih-seez)—Acts 23:6—A Jewish religious group who followed Jewish laws strictly.

Festus (FES-tus)—Acts 25:9—The governor of Judea after Felix.

LESSON OUTLINE

I. STAND FIRM
   A. Paul Before the Sanhedrin
   B. Paul Appeals to the Pharisees

II. PROTECTION ASSURED
   A. Divine Visitation
   B. Paul Before Festus
   C. Paul Appeals to Caesar

III. CONSISTENT MINISTRY
   A. Paul Arrives in Rome
   B. Paul Ministers to the Jews
   C. Paul Ministers to the Gentiles

LESSON EXPOSITION

INTRODUCTION

Adversity can either destroy or build up confidence. It all depends on one's chosen response. Certainly adversity has left the biographies of many with indelible markings and frustrated lives. But there are countless others who through perseverance, prayer, and confidence in God have weathered the storms of life and have had their relationships with God strengthened.

The lesson for today touches on some periods of adversity in the life of the apostle Paul. At times his life was in danger of being destroyed, but nearly always he lived with harassment and opposition from

Jewish leaders who contended that some tenets of Jewish belief were being ignored by those who had accepted Christ. Through the adversity he faced, he learned to stand firm in his Christian convictions; he consoled himself with the protection assured to him by God; and he persevered with a consistent ministry.

Certainly the experiences of the great apostle Paul can serve as reminders that adversities come to all of God's dear children. But the adversities, rather than destroying us, can serve as building blocks for a closer relationship with our heavenly Father.

I. STAND FIRM (Acts 23:1-9)

A. Paul Before the Sanhedrin (vv. 1-5)

1. And Paul, earnestly beholding the council, said, Men and brethren, I have lived in all good conscience before God until this day.

2. And the high priest Ananias commanded them that stood by him to smite him on the mouth.

3. Then said Paul unto him, God shall smite thee, thou whited wall: for sittest thou to judge me after the law, and commandest me to be smitten contrary to the law?

4. And they that stood by said, Revilest thou God's high priest?

5. Then said Paul, I wist not, brethren, that he was the high priest: for it is written, Thou shalt not speak evil of the ruler of thy people.

The apostle Paul completed his third missionary journey and was determined to go to Jerusalem, although he had been warned not to go by prophetic communication (Acts 21:10-12) and by the advice of dear friends. So it was not a surprise to the apostle that he was confronted by the Sanhedrin Council when he arrived in Jerusalem. However, the account of the hearing in this section of the lesson is only the beginning of a series of hearings in which he firmly stood for and witnessed about his Christian convictions.

Paul began his defense by addressing his hearers as "men and brethren." Then he made a bold claim of having "lived in all good conscience before God until this day." Paul's righteousness, which gave him the benefit of a good conscience, was that which he was assured would also provide his justification in the heavenly court. However, the purest conscience was an uncertain refuge under the scrutiny of God, as Paul reflected and wrote in 1 Corinthians 4:4: "For I know nothing [against] myself; yet am I not hereby justified: but he that judgeth me is the Lord."

Whether Paul's claim to a good conscience or the high priest's envy of it caused his actions, Ananias was wrong and acted illegally when he commanded those near Paul to strike him on the mouth. Paul's response revealed some of the characteristics of Ananias. The metaphor of the "whited wall" suggests a tottering wall whose precarious condition has been disguised by a generous coat of whitewash. Ananias was one of the most disgraceful profaners of the sacred office. Josephus tells how Ananias seized for himself the tithes that ought to have gone to the common priests, causing them to die for "want of food." (*Antiquities* XX. 9.2)

The pro-Roman policy of Ananias made him an object of intense hostility to the national party in Judea, and when the war against Rome broke out in A.D. 66, he was dragged by the insurgents from an aqueduct in which he had tried to hide. He was put to death along with his brother Hezekiah.

The bystanders did not appear to have been surprised by Ananias' outburst, even though it was not a proper way for a high priest to speak. But they were shocked at Paul's response. When it was pointed out that the man to whom he spoke was the high priest, Paul apologized to the official, if not to Ananias himself. Paul was well acquainted with the passage in Exodus 22:28 that states, "Thou shalt not . . . curse the ruler of thy people."

F.F. Bruce questions the statement "I did not know he was the high priest." "What did he [Paul] mean that he did not know that the speaker was the high priest? At a regular meeting of the Sanhedrin the high priest presided, and would surely have been identifiable for that reason. Or was Paul not looking in the direction from which the words came, so that he could not be sure who actually uttered them? Or was he speaking ironically, as if to say, I did not think a man who spoke like that could possibly be the high priest. The context leaves the matter uncertain. We may bear in mind, however, that it was not a regular session of the Sanhedrin, but a meeting convened by the tribune, and in that case the high priest may not have occupied his usual place or worn his robes of office" (*Commentary on the Book of Acts*).

B. Paul Appeals to the Pharisees
   (vv. 6-9)

(Acts 23:8 is not included in the printed text.)

6. But when Paul perceived that the one part were Sadducees, and the other Pharisees, he cried out in the council, Men and brethren, I am a Pharisee, the son of a Pharisee: of the hope and resurrection of the dead I am called in question.

7. And when he had so said, there arose a dissension between the Pharisees and the Sadducees: and the multitude was divided.

9. And there arose a great cry: and the scribes that were of the Pharisees' part arose, and strove, saying, We find no evil in this man: but if a spirit or an angel hath spoken to him, let us not fight against God.

The high priest's interruption of the council by his outburst to have Paul slapped in the mouth had the effect of changing the tactics the apostle used. It must have become apparent that he was not going to get a fair trial. The actions so far revealed that the pattern had been set. Paul took note that the Sanhedrin was made up of Sadducees and Pharisees, with the Sadducees having the majority of members. So Paul announced that he was indeed a Pharisee and was now being examined concerning the national hope of the Jewish people. This hope was based on the resurrection; however, the Sanhedrin majority did not believe in the resurrection of the dead. Paul was a believer in the resurrection and hope beyond the grave, but only in Christ. The apostle knew that he would have defenders of the resurrection in the Pharisees. Since he was himself a Pharisee, he knew well their position, but he also knew the persuasion of the Sadducees, who were materialistic and politically minded and held no hope of a resurrection or life beyond the grave.

The Pharisees were immediately inclined to concede that a man who was sound on central Pharisaic doctrine could not be so wrong. But the Sadducees were more enraged than ever over what appeared to them to be a new-fangled heresy.

The dispute which broke out between the two parties at the Council made it impossible to arrive at a conclusion. Some of the Pharisaic scholars contended that Paul had done no wrong. If he spoke of receiving divine instructions in visions, it might well be that some spirit or angel had communicated with him. The Sadducees repudiated the very possibility that such a communication could be made. And so the Sanhedrin was at an impasse, but the Lord's hand was upon Paul, and he was protected.

II. PROTECTION ASSURED
(Acts 23:10, 11; 25:7-12)

A. Divine Visitation (23:10, 11)

10. And when there arose a great dissension, the chief captain, fearing lest Paul should have been pulled in pieces of them, commanded the soldiers to go down, and to take him by force from among them, and to bring him into the castle.

11. And the night following the Lord stood by him, and said, Be of good cheer, Paul: for as thou hast testified of me in Jerusalem, so must thou bear witness also at Rome.

Verse 10 gives additional insight into the wrangling that developed between the Pharisees and Sadducees as mentioned in verses 7-9 and discussed above. The dispute which broke out between the two parties in the council chambers blotted out any possibility of having a serious examination of Paul or a clarification of the charges against him. Consequently, the officer ordered the guard to snatch Paul out of the midst of them and take him to the castle. Except for the quick action of the Romans, the apostle might have suffered injury, and this would not have set well with the Roman authorities who took seriously their responsibility to treat their citizens with proper respect.

Commenting on the interpretation of this encounter experienced by Paul, *The Layman's Bible Commentary* states, "There are two possible interpretations of this episode. One is that the tribune actually wanted to dispose of Paul's case by having him tried by the Sanhedrin. The other is that it merely presented him before the Sanhedrin to gather more information about the case, intending to turn Paul over to the Roman procurator when next he visited Jerusalem. In either case, he failed. Nothing was to be learned or decided by the riotous outcome of Paul's visit to the Sanhedrin."

In verse 11, the picture begins to change for Paul. His worst apprehensions of what might happen to him at Jerusalem now appear that they will be fulfilled. His plans for carrying the gospel to the Far West and for visiting Rome on the way begin to seem questionable. Paul might have felt somewhat dejected and despondent after the events of these two days. However, the following night the Lord stood by him, as He had done at critical moments before, and encouraged him: "As thou hast testified of me in Jerusalem, so must thou bear witness also at Rome." The reference to bearing witness in Jerusalem probably refers to Paul's speech at the top of the steps to the crowd in the temple court. It could also refer to the many other times Paul's influence and stand for Christianity were shared in Jerusalem. But the message from the Lord also assured Paul that he would live to bear witness in Rome. Certainly this assurance must have meant much to Paul during the delays and anxieties that confronted him in the next two years.

We gather from the broader context that the assurance from the Lord enabled Paul to remain calm and act with dignity as he gained a reputation for being a master rather than a victim of events.

B. Paul Before Festus (vv. 25:7-9)

(Acts 25:7, 8 is not included in the printed text.)

In the sequence of events between Acts 23:10, 11 and Acts 25:7, where the exposition picks up again, a number of things happened to Paul. Consequently, the following brief summary will give continuity to the broader context.

As a result of the conflict between the Pharisees and Sadducees, a number of Zealots who felt they had missed their chance to kill Paul banned together under an oath not to eat or drink until they had killed the apostle. They reported their plans to the chief priests and elders and requested that Paul be brought before the council. However, the plan was to slay Paul before he came near the council chambers.

The son of Paul's sister heard of the scheme and told Paul. The young man then reported the plan to the chief captain, who readied a protective army to move Paul that night to Caesarea, where he would be under the protection of Felix, the governor of the Roman province. In conjunction with the move of Paul to Caesarea, Claudius Lysias, who was in charge of the Roman garrison at Jerusalem and was stationed in the Castle of Antonia, adjoining the temple, wrote to Felix giving the details of the Jewish charges against Paul and the plot to kill him. He informed Felix of the fruitless interviews with the Sanhedrin. From these Lysias had gathered only that the dispute was not one of which Roman law took cognizance, but one of Jewish theological interpretation. He felt it necessary, therefore, to send Paul to Caesarea so the case might be dealt with in the procurator's court. Felix assured Paul that he would hear his case when his accusers came down from Jerusalem.

Five days after Paul's first interview with Felix, Ananias and some elders arrived at Caesarea. Ananias also brought a lawyer by the name of Tertullus to plead their cause. The charges were presented against Paul after which Paul was permitted to defend himself against the accusations. After the presentation by both sides the procurator was to render a decision.

Felix immediately realized that there was no case against Paul. However, Paul continued to be held in protective custody with the privilege of having friends visit him—generally under house arrest. Luke indicates that Felix and his wife Drusilla had frequent conferences with Paul during the two-year period he was held for. And Luke also indicates that Felix hoped that Paul would give him money. This was tantamount expecting a bribe, which was against Roman law. But the law was broken more times than obeyed.

After Paul had been held as a prisoner for two years, Felix was recalled to Rome because of an incident that occurred in Caesarea. Violence broke out between the Jews and Gentiles of the city, and Felix turned his troops on the rioting. Many Jews were killed, and Felix permitted the troops to ransack and loot the houses of the wealthy Jews; but the Jews reported the action to Rome. Since Felix was leaving Caesarea under serious conditions, he attempted to curry the favor of the Jews by retaining Paul in prison. Felix was replaced by Porcius Festus.

In the first 6 verses of Acts 25, the new procurator of Judea became acquainted with the Jewish case against Paul. Three days after he arrived in Caesarea he went to Jerusalem to pay his respects to the religious leaders and to cultivate their friendship. Immediately the Jewish leaders asked that Festus grant them a favor. They told him about Paul and asked that he send the prisoner to Jerusalem.

Luke informs us that the Jews planned a second ambush to kill Paul; he does not mention how the plot was disclosed. Although Festus wanted the goodwill of the Jewish leaders, he was wise enough to detect a sinister dimension to their request. So Festus told the Jews to come to Caesarea and present their case there. The Jews agreed and sent a delegation to accompany the procurator on his return trip to the capital of the province.

7. And when he was come, the Jews which came down from Jerusalem stood round about, and laid many and grievous complaints against Paul, which they could not prove.

8. While he answered for himself, Neither against the law of the Jews, neither against the temple, nor yet against Caesar, have I offended any thing at all.

9. But Festus, willing to do the Jews a pleasure, answered Paul, and said, Wilt thou go up to Jerusalem, and there be judged of these things before me?

The Jews issued the same charges against Paul with the additional charge of treason against Caesar. This charge seems to have come from Tertullus' accusation that Paul had agitated the "Jews throughout the world" (24:5).

Paul denied all charges, but the Jews still charged him with heresy because he did not require his Gentile converts to observe Jewish law.

Festus was caught in a difficult position. He wanted to retain favor with the Jews, but he was obliged to respect Roman justice. As a compromise, he asked Paul if he would be willing to go to Jerusalem and there be judged on the charges before Festus himself.

C. Paul Appeals to Caesar (25:10-12)

10. Then said Paul, I stand at Caesar's judgment seat, where I ought to be judged: to the Jews have I done no wrong, as thou very well knowest.

11. For if I be an offender, or have committed any thing worthy of death, I refuse not to die: but if there be none of these things whereof these accuse me, no man may deliver me unto them. I appeal unto Caesar.

12. Then Festus, when he had conferred with the council, answered, Hast thou appealed

unto Caesar? unto Caesar shalt thou go.

Paul's response to the request of the Roman procurator was couched in a restatement of his innocence and with an affirmation that if he were an offender he was willing to die. He also reminded Festus that he had done no wrong to the Jews "as thou very well knowest." Paul knew that Festus was not well-acquainted with the subtle tactics of the Jews and that there was a chance the Jews could outwit the procurator. Consequently, Paul felt that he stood a better chance of getting justice from the Romans than from the Jews, so he made his appeal to go to Caesar.

Do you feel that Paul was consciously cooperating with God's arrangement to get him to witness "of Christ also at Rome"?

Commenting on the Roman's right of appeal, T.C. Smith writes, "The privilege of a Roman to make his appeal to Caesar grew out of an old law prevalent in the sixth century B.C., called 'an appeal to the people.' In Paul's day no citizen could ask for a trial before Caesar's court if he had already been sentenced by a lower tribunal. Since no judgment had been passed upon the apostle, he was well within his rights to make the appeal. He took advantage of his inherited prerogative, not simply for his own safety, but for use as a wedge to gain legal recognition of the Christians in the Empire" (*The Broadman Bible Commentary*, Vol. 10).

Festus was apparently fearful of having to refer his first case to the imperial government. So he conferred with the council (v. 12) to be advised if Paul was within his right to make such an appeal. From his response Festus seemed to have been assured that Paul was within his rights and privileges to appeal to Caesar, and he consented for Paul to go to Rome.

III. CONSISTENT MINISTRY (Acts 28:16-31)

A. Paul Arrives in Rome (v. 16)

(Acts 28:16 is not included in the printed text.)

The apostle Paul's dream of visiting the imperial city of Rome had finally become a reality. He apparently did not think that he would make that visit as a prisoner, but since that was the means by which his visit developed, he would make his appeal to Ceasar just as he had defended himself in Jerusalem and Caesarea. His defense gave opportunity to witness to the reality of the risen Lord and the truths of Jewish theology which supported belief in the Resurrection and life beyond the present world.

In Rome, Paul was permitted to live in a private residence with a soldier guarding him. This allowed a good deal of freedom to have visitors and to visit Christians in the area, especially those of the church in Rome to which he had written some 10 years earlier.

B. Paul Ministers to the Jews (vv. 17-24)

(Acts 28:17-24 is not included in the printed text.)

The apostle Paul had been in Rome only three days before he called a meeting of the local leaders of the Jews. His desire to stay in touch with and minister to the Jews is a manifestation of the deep love and hope he had for the Jewish nation, despite the fact that there was hostility against Paul from the time he first became a follower of Christ.

Paul briefly introduced himself and summarized the events that brought him to Rome. He was careful not to say too much about the authorities in Jerusalem, but emphasized his innocence of any breach of the ancestral law or tradition of his people. He emphasized his defense and innocence, and explained that the appeal to Ceasar was simply the continuation of his efforts to establish his innocence. In Rome as in Jerusalem, he told of the Christian message, and he proclaimed that it, far from undermining the religion of Israel, was its divinely appointed fulfillment.

The Jews informed the apostle Paul that they had received no report from Jerusalem concerning these matters. If any attempt by the authorities in Jerusalem had been made, it is likely that the stormy seas and delays in transportation had delayed the letter and that Paul had arrived before the information. Adam Clarke says of this lack of communication, "This is very strange and shows us that the Jews knew their cause to be hopeless and therefore did not send it forward to Rome. They wished for an opportunity to kill Paul; and when they were frustrated by his appeal to the emperor, they permitted the business to drop" (*Clarke's Commentary*, Vol. V).

The Jewish leaders of Rome seem mostly to have been concerned with the apostle's views of the new sect. They knew of its existence and had heard much about opposition to the new sect. They were probably thinking about the edict of Claudius which expelled the Jews from Rome because of a riot which occurred concerning the preaching of Christ.

The apostle was willing to give the information the leaders requested, and a day was set for a large number of Jews to come to Paul's lodging. Consequently, for a whole day Paul preached about the Kingdom of God and used proof from the Bible that Jesus was the Messiah that the Law and Prophets talked about. Some of the Jews believed Paul's message, and some did not. Despite the apostle Paul's love for his people and his desire to see them accept Christ, they did not accept his message with full accord. Consequently, he would turn to the Gentiles.

What important lessons on witnessing can be drawn from the example of Paul's efforts to work with the Jewish people?

C. Paul Ministers to the Gentiles (vv. 25-31)

(Acts 28:25-29 are not included in the printed text.)

Paul used a quotation from Isaiah 6:9,10 that indicated that the Jews would not respond favorably to Christianity. The prophet had also called the Jewish people hard of understanding, dull of hearing, and unwilling to see. Paul experienced a repeat of the type of reaction he had found among the Jewish people in Pisidian Antioch, Corinth, and elsewhere, so he announced that henceforth the Gentiles would have the priority in receiving the message of salvation.

With the negative response to Paul's message, it appears that he was ready to move on. In his letter to the Romans he had said, "I could wish that myself were accursed from Christ for my brethren, my kinsmen according to the flesh"

(9:3). It may have proven a discouragement to Paul when he realized the Jews were not going to respond positively to God's revelation in Christ. However, along with the sorrow that must have come to him as a result of the Jews' attitude toward the Lord Jesus, Paul was joyful that the Gentiles had believed and would continue to respond positively to the message of Christ.

30. And Paul dwelt two whole years in his own hired house, and received all that came in unto him,

31. Preaching the kingdom of God, and teaching those things which concern the Lord Jesus Christ, with all confidence, no man forbidding him.

As a Roman prisoner, Paul probably had a small single room in the prison, and he was granted a favor in that he was permitted to dwell alone with the soldier who guarded him. But his liberty also included the privilege of preaching the gospel to those who would come to him. Many reliable expositors indicate that his ability to preach to many persons caused him to need "his own hired house." Chrysostom observes that Paul paid for the hired house by the fruits of his own labor.

The matter of the two years seems to be explained by the existence of a statutory period within which the prosecution might state its case against a defendant. For capital cases which were brought to Rome from Roman provinces across the seas, the time limit appears to have been 18 months. If the time period was exceeded the case defaulted.

The Sanhedrin's case against Paul probably was allowed to default, the prosecutor's judging it neither practical nor wise to pursue it any further. Roman law was not likely to deal with unsuccessful prosecutors, especially if their charges appeared under examination to be mere vexations.

During those two years, the gospel was proclaimed freely in Rome through the lips of its chief messenger. He was a serious contender for the faith and a champion for the cause of Christ.

The teaching of "those things which concern the Lord Jesus Christ" certainly would have included the subjects of Christ as Lord who upholds all things by the word of His power; Christ as He who governs the world and the church; and Christ who has all things under his control and all His enemies under His feet. In essence, Paul proclaimed Christ as the Maker and Upholder of all things and the Judge of all persons.

As Savior, Christ was proclaimed as the One who saves, delivers, and preserves those who believe on Him. As the Messiah, He was the Anointed One who is the Appointed One, who has the Spirit without measure, and who anoints and communicates the gifts and graces of the Spirit to true believers. As the Messiah, Christ was foretold by the prophets and expected by the Jews.

While these are the essentials of the gospel, the apostle Paul would also have included the whole account of the incarnation, of Christ's preaching in Judea, and of His miracles, persecutions, passion, death, burial, resurrection, ascension, and work as Intercessor. Certainly the apostle Paul was capable of covering every essential detail of the gospel message, and he carried out the work for two full years.

Verse 31 also indicates that Paul carried out his ministry "with all confidence, no man forbidding him." It seems as though Paul had complete liberty and freedom to say all he pleased when he pleased. He had full tolerance from the Roman government, and the unbelieving Jews had no power to prevent him from preaching.

It is supposed that it was during his two years in Rome that Onesimus was converted and sent back to Philemon with the epistle that bears the receiver's name. In verses 23 and 24 of that letter of chapter one, we learn that Paul then had the companionship of Epaphras, Marcus, Aristarchus, Demas, and Luke. Although a prisoner by providential appointment, the great apostle Paul did much to spread the message of the Lord Jesus to the Romans.

REVIEW QUESTIONS

1. What conditions required Paul's appearance before the Sanhedrin Council?

2. Who were the opposing religious groups that made up the Council Paul addressed?

3. What were the main theological differences between the Pharisees and the Sadducees?

4. How did the conspirators plot to kill Paul?

5. What was the theme and manner of Paul's witness in Rome?

GOLDEN TEXT HOMILY

"I KNOW WHOM I HAVE BELIEVED, AND AM PERSUADED THAT HE IS ABLE TO KEEP THAT WHICH I HAVE COMMITTED UNTO HIM AGAINST THAT DAY" (2 Timothy 1:12).

The sentence on a blackboard in a high school classroom read, "The intensity of one's convictions is a measure of the depth of his ignorance." Think of the implications of that statement! Those students were being taught that to have definite convictions on anything meant they were intellectually deficient. In his *An Essay on Morals*, Philip Wylie utters the same nonsense when he says that "the really mature mind is one which readily surrenders its inner convictions."

If this is true, Socrates, Galileo, Newton, Kepler, Edison, Steinmetz, Pasteur, and Einstein must have been very immature mentally because they had some very intense convictions in the scientific field.

A study of history indicates that the men and women who have made a worthwhile contribution to life have been those who had such definite convictions—so blazing and intense—that they were willing to die rather than sacrifice their integrity or compromise their convictions.

The apostle Paul was a man of deep convictions and undaunted courage. Second Timothy 1:12 is one of the finest Christian testimonies in the Bible. Timothy's life shows that faith grows into knowledge. Steadfastness in belief produces the vast evidence of experience. Continuing in faith unafraid brings that which approaches certainty.

Paul committed his person and everything he had to his Lord for safekeeping. Why? Because he knew that Christ had died for him and was his personal Guardian and would hold his deposit safe until the time when he would be welcomed home.

So may we follow Paul's example and commit to our Lord our life, energy, reputation, marriage, business, profession, integrity—and what we will against the day of vindication, fulfillment, honor, satisfaction, and judgment.—**Eugene C. Christenbury, Professor of Education, Lee University, Cleveland, Tennessee**

SENTENCE SERMONS

THE LORD IS aware of the adverse circumstances His people face and keeps them in His care.
—**Selected**

ADVERSITY IS the diamond dust heaven polishes its jewels with.
—**Robert Leighton**

WE OUGHT as much to pray for a blessing on our daily rod as upon our daily bread.
—**John Owen**

IF GOD sends us on stony paths, He will provide us with strong shoes.
—**Alexander MacLaren**

EVANGELISM APPLICATION

ADVERSE CIRCUMSTANCES MAY PROVIDE OPPORTUNITIES TO WITNESS FOR CHRIST

Our Father, who seeks to perfect His saints in holiness, knows the value of the refiner's fire. An earnest Christian worker had been treated most unkindly, and was crying brokenheartedly when a neighbor came in and, laying a hand on his shoulder, said quietly, "Why Mrs. ___, you're wriggling." Lifting her head, the other replied, "I don't think this is a time to be funny." "Oh, I am not that. But don't you know that God has permitted this trouble to touch you because He sees something in your life that grieves Him, and He has put you in the furnace. When a goldsmith puts gold into the crucible and the fire begins to work on the dross, it begins to wriggle and wriggle, and as the dross is burned out it gets quieter, until at last the surface is so calm that the refiner sees his own face reflected and puts out the fire."
—*Knight's Masterbook of New Illustrations*

ILLUMINATING THE LESSON

When Martin Luther was in the throes of the Reformation and the pope was trying to bring him to the Catholic Church, he sent a cardinal to deal with Luther and buy him with gold. The cardinal wrote to the pope, "The fool does not love gold." The cardinal, when he could not convince Luther, said to him, "What do you think the pope cares for the opinion of a German boor? The pope's little finger is stronger than all Germany. Do you expect your princes to take up arms to defend you—you a wretched worm like you? I tell you No! And where will you be then?" Luther's reply was simply, "Where I am now, In the hands of Almighty God.
—*Christian Digest*

DAILY BIBLE READINGS

M. God's Servant Pursued.
    1 Samuel 23:1-8
T. God's Servant Delivered.
    1 Samuel 23:9-14
W. Divine Help Given.
    Daniel 3:16-25
T. Blessed in Persecution.
    Matthew 5:10-12
F. Evil Action Thwarted.
    Acts 23:12-24
S. Delivered From Peril.
    Acts 27:13-25

Joy and Contentment Through Christ

Study Text: Philippians 4:1-23

Objective: To appreciate the contentment gained in serving Christ and rejoice in His blessings.

Time: The Book of Philippians was probably written around A.D. 62-63.

Place: The Book of Philippians was written from Rome.

Golden Text: "I have learned, in whatsoever state I am, therewith to be content" (Philippians 4:11).

Central Truth: In every circumstance, Christians can count on God's faithfulness.

Evangelism Emphasis: Despite personal inconvenience and deprivation, Christians must witness for Christ.

PRINTED TEXT

Philippians 4:4. Rejoice in the Lord alway: and again I say, Rejoice.

5. Let your moderation be known unto all men. The Lord is at hand.

6. Be careful for nothing; but in every thing by prayer and supplication with thanksgiving let your requests be made known unto God.

7. And the peace of God, which passeth all understanding, shall keep your hearts and minds through Christ Jesus.

8. Finally, brethren, whatsoever things are true, whatsoever things are honest, whatsoever things are just, whatsoever things are pure, whatsoever things are lovely, whatsoever things are of good report; if there be any virtue, and if there be any praise, think on these things.

9. Those things, which ye have both learned, and received, and heard, and seen in me, do: and the God of peace shall be with you.

10. But I rejoiced in the Lord greatly, that now at the last your care of me hath flourished again; wherein ye were also careful, but ye lacked opportunity.

11. Not that I speak in respect of want: for I have learned, in whatsoever state I am, therewith to be content.

12. I know both how to be abased, and I know how to abound: every where and in all things I am instructed both to be full and to be hungry, both to abound and to suffer need.

13. I can do all things through Christ which strengtheneth me.

14. Notwithstanding ye have well done, that ye did communicate with my affliction.

15. Now ye Philippians know also, that in the beginning of

the gospel, when I departed from Macedonia, no church communicated with me as concerning giving and receiving, but ye only.

16. For even in Thessalonica ye sent once and again unto my necessity.

17. Not because I desire a gift: but I desire fruit that may abound to your account.

18. But I have all, and abound: I am full, having received of Epaphroditus the things which were sent from you, an odour of a sweet smell, a sacrifice acceptable, wellpleasing to God.

19. But my God shall supply all your need according to his riches in glory by Christ Jesus.

DICTIONARY

Macedonia (mas-eh-DOH-nee-uh)—Philippians 4:15—The northern part of present-day Greece.

Thessalonica (THES-ah-lah-NY-kah)—Philippians 4:16—The capital of the country of Macedonia, which is now northern Greece.

Epaphroditus (ee-PAF-ro-DYE-tus)—Philippians 4:18—A Christian in the church at Philippi.

LESSON OUTLINE

I. REJOICE IN THE LORD

    A. Stand Fast in the Lord

    B. Strive for Unity

    C. Be Courteous

II. THINK GOOD THOUGHTS

    A. Expect the Peace of God

    B. Meditate on Wholesome Things

III. BE CONTENT

    A. Content in All Circumstances

    B. Content by Faith

    C. Content Through Christ

LESSON EXPOSITION

INTRODUCTION

The church at Philippi in ancient Macedonia was the first European church founded by the apostle Paul and thereby represents the first major penetration of the gospel into Gentile territory. The events leading to the founding of that congregation are recorded in Acts 16:9-40. The apostle Paul, along with his helpers Silas, Timothy, and Luke, was on his second missionary journey through Asia Minor. When Paul was forbidden by the Holy Spirit to preach in Asia and Bithynia to the north, he and his fellow workers made their way to Troas on the Agean Sea. At Troas, Paul received a vision from the Lord to take the gospel to Europe: "There stood a man of Macedonia, and prayed him, saying, Come over into Macedonia, and help us" (Acts 16:9). Paul and his companions immediately answered the divine call and set sail for the nearest port—Neapolis near Philippi, where the gospel message was heartily received and a loyal congregation emerged.

Now nearly a decade later, the Philippian church learned of the disaster in Jerusalem and of Paul's subsequent imprisonment in Rome. The news evoked a renewed sympathetic interest, and they reactivated their charitable giving to Paul's needs much as the church had done from the very founding of that congregation. Epaphroditus, the messenger from the church at Philippi, had brought to Paul their gifts, and he in turn had been taken seriously ill. Paul considered his recovery an answer to prayer (Philippians 2:25-27) and sent him back to Philippi with the letter which he wrote.

Although the entire Book of Philippians has an emphasis on "joy and rejoicing," chapter 4 is more on the practical side of arriving at complete joy and contentment. This chapter may be divided into three sections: An appeal is made for (1) unity, (2) a challenge is set forth to think good thoughts, and (3) an exhortation is given emphasizing the need to be content. All three points are attainable when one's life is Christ-centered as was that of the apostle Paul. "To gain Him," "to know Him," "to be found in Him," and "to attain the goal" set in Christ were the pressing desires that engaged all of Paul's attention (see 1:21; 3:9-14).

I. REJOICE IN THE LORD
(Philippians 4:1-5)

A Stand Fast in the Lord (v. 1)

1. Therefore, my brethren dearly beloved and longed for, my joy and crown, so stand fast in the Lord, my dearly beloved.

The first four verses of this chapter may seem somewhat disjointed since they appear to be a part of a larger context, beginning with verse 17 of chapter 3. The initial word of verse 1 is *therefore*, which signals that it is tied to something earlier. While there is a general tie to all

three preceding chapters, the link to the preceding five verses is rather pointed.

In the passage of 3:17-21, Paul called attention to the fact that in the church at Philippi there were men whose conduct was an open scandal and who by their lifestyles showed themselves to be enemies of the cross of Christ (v. 18). These men lived gluttonous and immoral lives and used their so-called Christianity to justify themselves. It is likely they were of one or more branches of the Gnostics or Epicureans, who existed in large numbers throughout the Roman Empire. These ungodly men were persons "whose glory is in their shame, who mind earthly things" (v. 19).

In contrast to such persons, the people who choose to follow Christ recognize a standard upon something far more important than earthly pursuits. The Christian is a citizen of heaven and he longs for the kingdom of heaven to become a present reality (Matthew 6:10; Ephesians 2:19). In a sense the church is a "colony of heaven" as much as Philippi was a Roman colony. And the realization that the Savior will one day return for those citizens of heaven is a powerful incentive for godly living.

In verse 21, Paul reminded the Philippians that when Christ returns for His church, the bodies of the believers will be changed like His own (1 John 3:2). Redeemed souls will occupy redeemed bodies such as Christ's after the Resurrection. So it follows that since doctrine determines conduct and destiny, Christians must avoid doctrines or philosophies that allow for such actions as the ungodly lives mentioned in Philippians 3:18, 19.

As the apostle reflected on the "day of Christ," when He will fashion anew "our vile body, that it may be fashioned like unto his glorious body" (v. 21), he appealed to the Philippians to stand firm in the Lord. Only with Jesus Christ can a person resist the seductions of temptation and the weakness of cowardice. The Greek word Paul used for "stand fast" (4:1) is *steko*, which means "to be stationary"; it is the word used for a soldier standing fast in the shock of battle, with the enemy advancing down upon him. Neither the church nor the individual can stand fast except when they stand with the help of Christ.

Why is it so essential to "stand fast" in Christ regardless of the circumstances? Name some persons who paid with their lives when they stood fast in the Lord.

B. Strive for Unity (vv. 2, 3)

(Philippians 4:2, 3 is not included in the printed text.)

In verse 2 the apostle Paul made a direct reference to a difference of opinions between two women of prominence in the Philippian church. The unity that Paul exhorted these ladies to seek is unity in the Lord. They had need of the mind that is in Christ Jesus (see 2:5).

While the problem of differences of opinions are common in churches of this age, a recognition of the common lordship of Christ would do much to make Christians like-minded. Those that have the mind of Christ must of necessity be "of one mind, of one accord" (see 2:2).

According to 4:3, the two women, Euodias and Syntyche, had assisted Paul in his ministry at Philippi, and he apparently had great appreciation for their work. In any event Paul was not willing for a little difference of opinion to rob the ladies

of the joy that could be theirs when true unity prevailed. The apostle asked a third party to assist in settling the dispute.

Commentators disagree as to whether "true yokefellow" merely describes the person addressed or whether his actual name was *Suzugos*, the literal Greek noun from which the word *yokefellow* comes. It probably refers to a prominent individual in the church so well known that Paul did not need to name him. Such a view seems to coincide with many Bible translations of the verse. The *New Century Bible* renders verse 3: "And I ask you, my faithful friend, to help these women. They served with me in telling the Good News, together with Clement and others who worked with me, whose names are written in the book of life."

C. Be Courteous (vv. 4, 5)

4. Rejoice in the Lord alway: and again I say, Rejoice.

5. Let your moderation be known unto all men. The Lord is at hand.

The apostle continued his general exhortation on the need to have a right spirit and right conduct of life. "Rejoice in the Lord" expresses the predominant mood of the entire Epistle to the Philippians, which was a mood characteristic of Paul's closing years. He doubled the exhortation with "and again I say, Rejoice" to take away any loophole of those who might say, "What, shall we rejoice in afflictions?" He asked that they come out openly, avow their faith, take their stand, and rejoice as they do it.

The word *moderation* (v. 5) is from the Greek word *epieikes* and is the same term as used in 2 Corinthians 10:1, where it refers to Christ and means "gentleness, courteousness, or meekness." It is what we often associate with Christlikeness. It means an attitude that will pardon human feelings and look to the intention and not to the act, to the whole and not to the part, and to remember the good rather than the evil.

The apostle was urging the Philippians to be characterized by a spirit of meekness, courtesy, and reasonableness such as marked the character of Jesus. The appeal for such a triad is noted throughout the New Testament. With our lives patterned after Him, we are certain to "rejoice in the Lord."

"Why," asks William Barclay, "should [man] have this joy and gracious gentleness in his life? Because, says Paul, the Lord is at hand. If we remember the coming triumph of Christ, we can never lose our hope and our joy. If we remember that life is short, we will not wish to enforce the stern justice which so often divides men but will wish to deal with men in love, as we hope that God will deal with us" ("The Letters to the Philippians, Colossians, and Thessalonians," *The Daily Study Bible Series*).

II. THINK GOOD THOUGHTS
(Philippians 4:6-9)

A. Expect the Peace of God
(vv. 6, 7)

6. Be careful for nothing; but in every thing by prayer and supplication with thanksgiving let your requests be made known unto God.

7. And the peace of God, which passeth all understanding, shall keep your hearts and minds through Christ Jesus.

In his scholarly work on Christian apologetics, Edward J. Carnell reminds us: "Man is a creature in time and space who is primarily interested in [peace] and happiness. Yet before this desired state of well-being can become real, three definite conditions must be met. First, the hope for immortality must be secured, because without this hope man is harassed and vexed by the fear of death. Secondly, a rational view of the universe must be plotted, for the fear of death cannot be dissipated simply by rubbing some wonderful lamp of Aladdin. It can be disposed of only when man succeeds in learning that death is not his final judge. Thirdly, man must know what truth is that he may have a norm by which a true solution to the problem of the one [truth] within the many [claimed truths] may be recognized when it comes along" (*An Introduction to Christian Apologetics*).

For the Philippians to have arrived at truth in an environment filled with many false philosophies was indeed a tribute to Paul's labors and the guidance of the Holy Spirit. The believers of Philippi had gained the assurance of life after death and the essential steps to take to avoid vexation regarding death. They had learned what truth is in spite of the many warped philosophies and "claimed truths" which sought for their allegiance. But for the Philippians, as it is for all people, life can be troublesome because humanity is vulnerable to all the chances and changes of this mortal life. To the normal troubling aspects of human existence in the early church, there was the reality of added worry that your life was marked if you professed to be a Christian. The Philippians were much aware of the problems Paul and countless other Christians faced in their stand for Christ. Consequently, they needed encouragement and guidance.

The apostle Paul's admonition to the Philippians was to "be careful for nothing." This phrase is perhaps best translated "Be anxious about nothing." Jesus laid great emphasis on anxiety, indicating such an emotion is the result of fear. The meaning is "In no case should you permit yourself to be full of fear."

Paul further exhorted the Philippians to rid themselves of worry and anxiety by engaging in faith-centered prayer. Instead of worrying, which all people deplore but few escape, Paul urged his readers to find peace of heart by turning to God and seeking fellowship with Him: "In every thing by prayer and supplication with thanksgiving let your requests be made known unto God" (v. 6).

In everything we are to find relief in prayer. Nothing is too big, nothing is too small to be beyond God's care. Prayer, as Paul here urges, expresses the act of devotion and love to God; supplication expresses the cry of conscious need; and the admonition regarding requests focuses on the actual favors which are asked of God.

All is to be done with gratitude—"with thanksgiving." Every prayer must surely include thanks for the privilege of prayer itself. Paul insists that we must give thanks in everything—in sorrows and in joys alike. When prayer is offered with such a mind-set, it implies true gratitude and perfect submission to the will of God. "When we pray," says William Barclay, "we must always remember three things. We must remember *the love of God*, which ever desires only what is best for us. We must remember *the wisdom of God*, which alone knows what is best for us. We must remember *the power of God*, which alone can bring to pass that which is best for us. . . . The result of believing prayer is that the peace of

God will stand like a sentinel on guard upon our hearts" ("The Letters to the Philippians, Colossians, and Thessalonians," *The Daily Study Bible Series*).

How is true, lasting personal peace obtained?

B. Meditate on Wholesome Things (vv. 8, 9)

8. Finally, brethren, whatsoever things are true, whatsoever things are honest, whatsoever things are just, whatsoever things are pure, whatsoever things are lovely, whatsoever things are of good report; if there be any virtue, and if there be any praise, think on these things.

9. Those things, which ye have both learned, and received, and heard, and seen in me, do: and the God of peace shall be with you.

In verses 8 and 9, the apostle Paul continued his appeal to the Philippians on how they could arrive at the state of joy and contentment through the work of Christ. Not only must they let God know their desires through prayer and thanksgiving, as admonished in verses 6 and 7, but they must meditate on wholesome things.

An individual will always set his mind on something, and the apostle wanted to be sure the Philippians would set their minds on right things. The main verb used in verse 8, as Paul listed the wholesome things he wanted them to meditate on, is *think*, or consider. In other words, he was asking his readers to be logical, be thoughtful, meditate, reflect upon, and give consideration to wholesome and good things.

The term *true* implies integrity and sincerity with no falsehood or hypocrisy (see Genesis 42:11, "we are true men"). The virtue of truthfulness was greatly praised among the best of Greeks and Persians as well as the Jewish people. Jesus called himself "the way, the truth, and the life" (John 14:6), and He declared God's Word to be truth (17:17).

Honest relates to things worthy of honor, or things worthy of reverence. When used to describe a person, the term *honest* describes one who moves throughout the world as if it were the temple of God. There are things in this world which are flippant and cheap and attractive to the light-minded, but it is on the things which are serious and dignified that the Christian will set his mind.

The term *just* has to do with what is right according to God's standards which are spelled out in Scripture. In other words, *just* is the term used to describe duty faced and duty done. There are those who set their minds on pleasure, comfort, and easy ways. The Christian's thoughts are on "just" things with a feel for proper duty to God and man.

Pure describes that which is morally undefiled. When the term is used ceremonially, it describes that which has been so cleansed that it is fit to be brought into the presence of God and used in His service. Consequently, the apostle Paul's appeal to his readers is that their minds will be set on things that are pure, and their thoughts so clean that they can stand the scrutiny of a holy God.

The term *lovely* means "winsome, attractive, affectionate, or beloved." The Greek term for *lovely* (*prosphiles*) occurs nowhere else in the New Testament. It might be paraphrased as "that which calls forth love." The mind of the Christian is set on lovely things—kindness, sympathy, forbearance—so he is a "winsome" or "attractive" person whom to see is to love.

Good report refers to things attractive in character. William Barclay says, "It is not easy to get the meaning of this Greek word *euphema*—good report. It literally means 'air speaking,' but it was specially connected with the holy silence at the beginning of a sacrifice in the presence of gods. It might not be going too far to say that it describes 'the things which are fit for God to hear.'" ("The Letters to the Philippians, Colossians, and Thessalonians," *The Daily Study Bible Series*).

It follows from these exhortations that we should not occupy our minds, or at least feed our minds, on anything to which any of these wholesome qualities could not be applied. Not only do unedifying subjects bring moral pollution, but they usurp the place of something better. Indeed there are so many worthy things to occupy one's mind that there should be given no place for the frivolous or immoral matters.

In verse 9, Paul admonished that the good things which they had learned from him be practiced and remembered. He was confident that as they do so, the "God of peace" would be with them. The assurance of God's presence is the greatest possible source of joy, contentment, as well as security.

III.   BE CONTENT
       (Philippians 4:10-19)

A.   Content in all Circumstances
     (vv. 10-12)

10.   But I rejoiced in the Lord

greatly, that now at the last your care of me hath flourished again; wherein ye were also careful, but ye lacked opportunity.

11. Not that I speak in respect of want: for I have learned, in whatsoever state I am, therewith to be content.

12. I know both how to be abased, and I know how to abound: every where and in all things I am instructed both to be full and to be hungry, both to abound and to suffer need.

In Paul's closing words to the Philippians, he took the opportunity to thank them for their financial support and to impart to them his secret of real contentment even in dire circumstances. The phrase "your care of me hath flourished again" (v. 10) may indicate a temporary suspension of their financial support for a time, perhaps due to the lack of a way to get the support to him, or even because of the influence of some false teachers. The fact that their giving had been reactivated was cause for Paul to rejoice.

In verse 11, Paul shared one of his three secrets of life—a life of contentment. The apostle declared his independence of creature comforts. The Greek word autarkes, which Paul used for content, means "self-sufficient." It was the highest aim of Stoic ethics, and by it the Stoics meant a state of mind in which a man was absolutely independent of all things and all people. They proposed to reach that state by a certain pathway of the mind. Paul's contentment, however, was in Christ and the faith he had in Him (v. 13).

At some point in his life Paul made a commitment to serve the Lord regardless of circumstances. The results of that decision was still evi-

dent in his life when he wrote to the Philippians. Acts 9 reminds us that shortly after Paul's conversion he faced persecution, and certain enemies of the gospel attempted to kill him; but God protected him in that confrontation and many more after that (see 2 Corinthians 11:24-27).

In Acts 4:12, the apostle Paul reminded his readers that he had experienced both sorrow and joy, both distress and comfort, and he knew how to bear himself in any circumstance because his joy and contentment were in Christ. Such an abiding joy and contentment raised him above the hard blows of mortal life and gave him a Christian viewpoint which enabled him to act becomingly both in adversity and in prosperity. One has only to hear the stories of missionaries and pioneer pastors to realize that they, like Paul, found joy and contentment in Christ even when they were persecuted and deprived of ample funds to care for their families.

Discuss the merits of contentment in Christ as compared with temporary contentment through financial strength or status in life. Can both avenues be merged? Explain.

B. Content by Faith (v. 13)

13. I can do all things through Christ which strengtheneth me.

Paul ascribed the source of his strength to Christ. Unlike the Stoic, it was not something he could be proud of as a personal achievement, but something for which he was grateful because of the indwelling Christ.

The soul, by faith and in communication with God, learns many mysteries of spiritual experiences: mysteries of grace, mysteries of self-renunciation, and mysteries of self-consecration. Paul had been initiated into all of them. Long training under the guidance of the Holy Spirit had led him through the deep and holy mysteries of life that is hid with Christ in God. We can, and must, ask the same Holy Spirit to guide us into all truth, for it is only in spiritual union with Christ that the Christian possesses strength to cope with the realities of life. The Christian must not be discouraged; he must not shrink from the battle against evil in himself and in the world. He is indeed weak and helpless in himself, but he has the presence of Christ, and in the strength of His presence the Christian can do all things.

C. Content Through Christ
   (vv. 14-19)

14. Notwithstanding ye have well done, that ye did communicate with my affliction.

15. Now ye Philippians know also, that in the beginning of the gospel, when I departed from Macedonia, no church communicated with me as concerning giving and receiving, but ye only.

16. For even in Thessalonica ye sent once and again unto my necessity.

17. Not because I desire a gift: but I desire fruit that may abound to your account.

18. But I have all, and abound: I am full, having received of Epaphroditus the things which were sent from you, an odour of a sweet smell, a sacrifice acceptable, wellpleasing to God.

19. But my God shall supply all your need according to his riches in glory by Christ Jesus.

In verse 14, the apostle Paul commended the Philippians for the gifts they had sent. The Greek text uses the word for *fellowship* instead of *communicate* and the word for *tribulation* instead of *affliction.* Consequently, the verse would then read, "Ye had fellowship with my tribulation." This fellowship was in the area of stewardship.

It is readily apparent that Paul valued the sympathy, this fellow feeling, perhaps even more than the gift itself. It certainly was not an easy period of time for the apostle, and he wanted the Philippians to know they had done well to share with him. In fact, the Philippian church seems to have been the only one that faithfully supported him over an extended period of time.

In verses 15-19, Paul reflected on the continuous support, excluding a brief period of inactivity, of the Philippians. He prized this expression not only because of the intrinsic merit of the gift, but even more because it symbolized their affection, love, and loyalty. The apostle was saying, in so many words, "It is not that I desire a present from you for my own sake, although your gift touches my heart and makes me very glad. I don't need anything; for I have more than enough, and I have learned to be content in Christ regardless of circumstances." Their generosity made him glad not for his sake but for theirs, because their gift was, in reality, a sacrifice to God—"an odour of a sweet smell" (v. 18). For such love and generosity, "God shall supply all your need according to his riches in glory by Christ Jesus" (v. 19).

REVIEW QUESTIONS

1. What were the conditions under which Paul wrote to the Philippians?

2. Name the two ladies that Paul mentioned in verse 2. What admonition did he have for them?

3. What admonition did Paul give regarding *moderation* (v. 5)? What does the term mean?

4. What is meant by the phrase "Be careful for nothing" (v. 6)?

5. What was the basis of Paul's great joy in the Philippian Christians?

GOLDEN TEXT HOMILY

"I HAVE LEARNED, IN WHATSOEVER STATE I AM, THEREWITH TO BE CONTENT" (Philippians 4:11).

The definition of the word *learned* is "having or showing much learning; being well informed."

Paul was a well-informed person. He had studied at the feet of Camalliel, a great Jewish teacher.

He had gained understanding of what the will of God was for his life. He knew he was to suffer many things and endure hardships for the sake of Christ.

The word *state* implies a "position" or a "standing." Paul's position or standing after his conversion was in Christ. He was to obey the commands of Christ and go minister to the Gentile nations and train workers to carry on the ministry of the church. Paul knew that this was his ministry and calling, and he carried it out with great dedication till the end of his life.

The word *content* suggests a satisfaction or happiness with what one has or is—not desiring something more or different, but truly being satisfied. The Holy Spirit enabled Paul to be happy in life with what Jesus Christ had called him to do. He could write and carry out his ministry even while a prisoner. Paul's happiness was to win people to the Lord Jesus Christ regardless of nationality. He wrote to Timothy, "But godliness with contentment is great gain" (1 Timothy 6:6).

As children of God we need to be content in whatever position and service God has called us into. It is a high calling to be able to serve the Lord Jesus even if the task is minor.—**Charles G. Wiley, Pastor, Church of God, New Boston, Texas**

SENTENCE SERMONS

IN EVERY CIRCUMSTANCE, Christians can count on God's faithfulness.

—Selected

IF YOU HAVE no joy in your religion, there is a leak in your Christianity somewhere.

—W.A. (Billy) Sunday

JOY IS more divine than sorrow, for joy is bread and sorrow is medicine.

—Henry Ward Beecher

SUBMISSION IS the only reasoning between man and his Maker, and contentment in His will is the best remedy one can apply to misfortune.

—Sir William Temple

DAILY BIBLE READINGS

M. Joyful Confidence.
   Psalm 31:19-24
T. Security. Psalm 91:5-15
W. Peace. John 20:19-22
T. Contentment.
   Hebrews 13:1-5
F. Christ Gives Hope.
   1 Peter 1:1-5
S. Christ Gives Joy.
   1 Peter 1:6-11

Striving for Reconciliation

Study Text: Philemon 1-25

Objective: To recognize and accept opportunities to work for reconciliation between people.

Time: The Book of Philemon was probably written in late A.D. 62 or early A.D. 63.

Place: The Book of Philemon was written from Rome, where Paul was under house arrest.

Golden Text: "God was in Christ, reconciling the world unto himself . . . and hath committed unto us the word of reconciliation" (2 Corinthians 5:19).

Central Truth: Our reconciliation to God enables us to treat others as we have been treated.

Evangelism Emphasis: Christians should share God's message of reconciliation through Christ.

PRINTED TEXT

Philemon 3. Grace to you, and peace, from God our Father and the Lord Jesus Christ.

4. I thank my God, making mention of thee always in my prayers,

5. Hearing of thy love and faith, which thou hast toward the Lord Jesus, and toward all saints;

6. That the communication of thy faith may become effectual by the acknowledging of every good thing which is in you in Christ Jesus.

7. For we have great joy and consolation in thy love, because the bowels of the saints are refreshed by thee, brother.

8. Wherefore, though I might be much bold in Christ to enjoin thee that which is convenient,

9. Yet for love's sake I rather beseech thee, being such an one as Paul the aged, and now also a prisoner of Jesus Christ.

10. I beseech thee for my son Onesimus, whom I have begotten in my bonds:

11. Which in time past was to thee unprofitable, but now profitable to thee and to me:

12. Whom I have sent again: thou therefore receive him, that is, mine own bowels;

13. Whom I would have retained with me, that in thy stead he might have ministered unto me in the bonds of the gospel:

14. But without thy mind would I do nothing; that thy benefit should not be as it were of necessity, but willingly.

15. For perhaps he therefore departed for a season, that thou shouldest receive him for ever;

16. Not now as a servant, but

above a servant, a brother beloved, specially to me, but how much more unto thee, both in the flesh, and in the Lord?

17. If thou count me therefore a partner, receive him as myself.

18. If he hath wronged thee, or oweth thee ought, put that on mine account;

19. I Paul have written it with mine own hand, I will repay it: albeit, I do not say to thee how thou owest unto me even thine own self besides.

20. Yea, brother, let me have joy of thee in the Lord: refresh my bowels in the Lord.

21. Having confidence in thy obedience I wrote unto thee, knowing that thou wilt also do more than I say.

DICTIONARY

Onesimus (oh-NES-ih-mus)—Philemon 10—The slave of a Christian named Philemon.

LESSON OUTLINE

I. BASIS FOR RECONCILIA-
    TION

    A. Love

    B. Communication of Faith

II. INTERCEDING FOR
    ANOTHER

    A. Boldness and Love

    B. Reception Requested

    C. Service as a Brother

III. RESTORATION SOUGHT

    A. Plea for Acceptance

    B. Obedience Anticipated

LESSON EXPOSITION

INTRODUCTION

The letter of Paul to Philemon is the only surviving example of private letters written by the apostle; furthermore, it is one that sheds abundant light on his character and Christian viewpoint. The dispatch of the letter to Philemon was combined with a letter to the church at Colosse and possibly a letter to the church at Ephesus.

Paul, however, was a prisoner in Rome when he received word from Epaphras (probably the founder of the predominantly Gentile church at Colosse) of subversive teachings which were plaguing the Colossian congregation. Paul became convinced that a letter must be dispatched to the brethren who were in danger of being led astray. At the same time, the recently converted fugitive slave Onesimus had to be returned to his master Philemon, one of the pillars of the church at Colosse. Philemon loved the Lord and the brethren and had given evidence of that in many ways (v. 7). He was Paul's spiritual son, for the Lord had used the preaching of Paul to change his heart (v. 19).

Onesimus, whose name means "useful" or "beneficial," was one of the slaves of Philemon's household. The slave had run away, journeying all the way to Rome where he came into contact with Paul. Just as the Lord had formerly blessed the sermons of Paul to the heart of

Philemon, the master, so He now blessed them to the heart of the slave. Onesimus became so dear to Paul that Paul referred to him as "my son . . . whom I have begotten in my bonds" (v. 10).

Paul did not feel it was right to keep Onesimus with him in Rome, although he was useful to the apostle. Consequently, Paul decided to send him back to his master with a very carefully and politely worded request that Philemon welcome back this runaway slave as a brother in the Lord.

Of special importance in this lesson is the impact of the message of reconciliation as taught by the apostle Paul years earlier when he wrote 2 Corinthians: "And all things are of God, who hath reconciled us to himself by Jesus Christ, and hath given to us the ministry of reconciliation" (5:18). In the ministry of reconciliation covered in this lesson, we first have the picture of a servant who was reconciled to God through the ministry of Paul. Then, the effort to reconcile two individuals who are Christians is considered.

I. BASIS FOR RECONCILIATION
(Philemon 3-7)

A. Love (vv. 3-5)

3. Grace to you, and peace, from God our Father and the Lord Jesus Christ.

4. I thank my God, making mention of thee always in my prayers,

5. Hearing of thy love and faith, which thou hast toward the Lord Jesus, and toward all saints.

The apostle Paul opens his letter with a typical salutation: "Unto Philemon our dearly beloved, and fellowlabourer, and to our beloved

Apphia, and Archippus . . . and to the church in thy house" (vv. 1, 2). The church in the house of Philemon undoubtedly refers to the group of Christians who were accustomed to assembling in that home for worship. This group would be interested in the return of Onesimus, but all would need the commendation of the apostle in order to be willing to receive a fugitive slave as a Christian brother. The appeal he would make later would be based on the Christian love that Paul knew existed in those he addressed.

There is little if any doubt that love is an essential factor in the reconciliation of godly individuals. Indeed, reconciliation with God is based on the love God manifested through the sacrifice of Christ. And reconciliation of Christians with other Christians is based on godly love flowing through them that provides an understanding of the responsibility, opportunity, and joy of being reconciled to a person or individuals who were previously estranged because of antagonism.

The letter to Philemon is a treasured document on the manifestation of love. It is evident that the source of Paul's courtesy was the kindness of his heart which motivated him to act with unselfish consideration for the feelings and happiness of others. He declared his love not only for the generous and wealthy householder Philemon but also for the fugitive slave.

"Grace to you, and peace, from God our Father and the Lord Jesus Christ" may be regarded as a wish, prayer, or promise. But it expresses the greatest good that one may desire for another. It requests that such good may be granted by a loving God.

Beginning with verse 4, the apostle follows his salutation with a thanksgiving and prayer. In fact, the thanksgiving is expressed in his prayer and is the occasion of his prayer. It both precedes and follows his petition and establishes gratitude and praise as the spirit of intercession.

The apostle expressed gratitude for the reports which he had received of the love that Philemon had shown toward his fellow believers and for the faith he had in Christ, the source of his love. He expressed his gratitude every time he remembered Philemon in prayer. The love which possessed Philemon was no mere sentiment, weak emotion, or empty profession. It was expressed in deeds that resulted in generous gifts to his fellow Christians.

B. Communication of Faith
   (vv. 6, 7)

6. That the communication of thy faith may become effectual by the acknowledging of every good thing which is in you in Christ Jesus.

7. For we have great joy and consolation in thy love, because the bowels of the saints are refreshed by thee, brother.

Philemon was a man whose faith in Christ and love to the brethren was well known, and the story of them had even reached Rome, where Paul was a prisoner. His house must have been like an oasis in a desert, for he had "refreshed" the hearts of God's people. Indeed, it is a real testimony to be thought of as a person in whose house God's people are rested and refreshed.

The word *communication* (Greek,

koinonia) in verse 6, is rendered "fellowship" in many other translations. Of this verse William Barclay states: *"Koinonia* [among other translations] can mean 'the act of sharing;' in that case the verse will mean: 'It is my prayer that your way of generously sharing all that you have will lead you more and more deeply into the knowledge of the good things which lead to Christ.' . . . Obviously Christian generosity was a characteristic of Philemon; he had love to God's people and in his home they were rested and refreshed. And now Paul is going to ask the generous man to be more generous yet. There is a great thought here, if this interpretation is correct. It means that we learn about Christ by giving to others. It means that by emptying ourselves we are filled with Christ. It means that to be open-handed and generous-hearted is the surest way to learn more and more of the wealth of Christ. The man who knows most of Christ is not the intellectual scholar . . . but the man who moves in loving generosity amongst his fellow-men" ("The Letters to Timothy, Titus, and Philemon," *The Daily Bible Study Series*).

Is the sharing (communicating) of one's faith a means of strengthening and deepening that faith? Explain.

II. INTERCEDING FOR ANOTHER
    (Philemon 8-16)

A. Boldness and Love (vv. 8-10)

8. Wherefore, though I might be much bold in Christ to enjoin thee that which is convenient,

9. Yet for love's sake I rather beseech thee, being such an one

as Paul the aged, and now also a prisoner of Jesus Christ.

10. I beseech thee for my son Onesimus, whom I have begotten in my bonds.

There was no lower status in the Roman Empire than that of a runaway slave. Runaway slaves were not protected by any law and were subject to all kinds of punishment. Generally when a runaway slave was captured, he was seriously beaten and sold to work as a miner or put to work in some occupation with a short life expectancy. Consequently, by sending Onesimus back to Philemon, the apostle was putting the slave in a most dangerous position.

In view of the serious condition under which the slave returned to Philemon, Paul felt constrained to make the most emphatic, urgent appeal he could for his son in the faith. The apostle opened the matter of his relationship to Onesimus and of the return of the runaway to Philemon by suggesting he could have appealed to Philemon's sense of duty as a Christian. In making such an appeal, he confessed to much boldness. So Paul's implication was that he could have appealed to an ethical obligation inherent in Christian living, but he made his appeal on the basis of love, a compliment to the kind and generous nature of his friend Philemon.

In his appeal to the Christian grace of love, Paul appealed to the specific love Philemon had for Paul himself. This love would be even more emphasized because of the circumstances under which Paul was writing the letter. It is apparent that the language he used in describing his circumstances was

deliberate and personal, referring to himself both as "the aged" and as "a prisoner." The term *aged* could refer to his age, but it is more likely a reference to his office. He emphasized also the fact that he was a "prisoner of Jesus Christ," or a prisoner for Christ's sake.

B. Reception Requested (vv. 11-14)

11. Which in time past was to thee unprofitable, but now profitable to thee and to me:

12. Whom I have sent again: thou therefore receive him, that is, mine own bowels;

13. Whom I would have retained with me, that in thy stead he might have ministered unto me in the bonds of the gospel:

14. But without thy mind would I do nothing; that thy benefit should not be as it were of necessity, but willingly.

Before Onesimus became a runaway, his relationship with Philemon was that of an "unprofitable" servant. However, the apostle now indicated that the slave he was sending back would fit the role of a "profitable" servant. But he emphasized the fact that Onesimus would be profitable not only to Philemon but also to Paul himself. It was with the changed status of the slave clearly indicated that the apostle sent the letter to Philemon, by all indications by the hand of Onesimus himself. In his letter, Paul asked that Philemon give this runaway a warm reception. The Greek word for "bowels" that he used means "inward affection," or "my very own heart," and it expresses the emotional bond between Paul and Onesimus.

Discuss the matter of work ethics. Does a Christian feel a greater responsibility than a non-Christian to give an employer a proper day's work for the money he is paid? Explain.

Paul was not reluctant to let Philemon know that he would have liked to have kept Onesimus with him because Onesimus could have rendered valuable service to the apostle, who was a prisoner and had restricted freedom. Paul had every right to request Onesimus' assistance in the gospel ministry, but he respected his friend Philemon too much to take advantage of the situation. The apostle used a very descriptive phrase, "the bonds of the gospel," to indicate his state as a prisoner enduring hardship for the sake of the gospel. Onesimus had been a great blessing to him, but now Paul would no longer have the comfort and assistance of this one he had led to the Lord.

Paul did not take the liberty to assume that Philemon would concur with Paul's desire to keep Onesimus with him. He did not want to act without Philemon's consent. Paul further indicated that he did not want to manipulate or pressure someone into doing something out of necessity, but rather he wanted Philemon to act by his own volition.

C. Service as a Brother (vv. 15, 16)

15. For perhaps he therefore departed for a season, that thou shouldest receive him for ever;

16. Not now as a servant, but above a servant, a brother beloved, specially to me, but how

much more unto thee, both in the flesh, and in the Lord?

In verse 15, Paul suggested that Philemon look for a hidden meaning behind Onesimus' departure and return. Perhaps God worked things out that the slave might return home as a brother. He caused an evil circumstance to "work together for good." Onesimus heard the message of salvation, gave his life to the Lord Jesus Christ through the ministry of Paul, and became a new creation in the Lord. Commenting on this verse, William Barclay states: "[Onesimus] went away as a heathen slave; he comes back as a brother in Christ. It is going to be hard for Philemon to regard a runaway slave as a brother; but that is exactly what Paul demands. 'If you agree,' says Paul, 'that I am your partner in the work of Christ and that Onesimus is my son in the faith, you must receive him as you would receive myself' (v. 17).

"Here . . . is something very significant. The Christian must always welcome back the man who has made a mistake. Too often we regard the man who has taken the wrong turning with suspicion and show that we are never prepared to trust him again. We believe that God can forgive him but we, ourselves, find it too difficult. It has been said that the most uplifting thing about Jesus Christ is that He trusts us on the very field of our defeat. When a man has made a mistake, the way back can be very hard, and God cannot readily forgive the man who, in his self-righteousness or lack of sympathy, makes it harder" ("The Letters to Timothy, Titus, and Philemon," *The Daily Study Bible Series*).

Paul used the word *season*

(Greek, *hora*), which means "an hour or a short period of time," to emphasize the short duration of time Onesimus had been away when compared with the restoration, which would be "forever." Though Paul had a special love for Onesimus because he was a father to him in the Lord, he also believed that Philemon would come to have a deeper affection for him "both in the flesh, and in the Lord."

Discuss the matter of providential care as it relates to verse 15.

III. RESTORATION SOUGHT
      (Philemon 17-21)

A.   Plea for Acceptance
      (vv. 17, 18)

17. If thou count me therefore a partner, receive him as myself.

18. If he hath wronged thee, or oweth thee ought, put that on mine account.

In verse 17, Paul makes a final and definite request that Onesimus be given a kind reception. It is significant that all the preceding sentences of the letter have been written in preparation for this emphatic appeal for acceptance of his son in the faith. Charles R. Erdman, in his volume *The Epistles of Paul to the Colossians and to Philemon*, makes this observation: "Among the grounds for such a plea for acceptance, the following have been advanced: The proposed action is just, or 'befitting'; but 'for love's sake' the request takes the place of what might have been a command. The petitioner is an aged Christian prisoner. He is under obligation to seek the welfare of one of his own converts. The changed character of

the man justifies the request. Paul is sacrificing his own desire to his sense of duty to Philemon. He is leaving Philemon absolutely free to make his decision. He has implied that Philemon would willingly have allowed Onesimus to remain with Paul. He has intimated that the hand of God may be seen in the flight and return of the slave. Onesimus is returning not merely as a fugitive but actually as a beloved brother in Christ.

Enforced by such facts Paul makes his request: 'If thou count me therefore a partner, receive him as myself.' Even in voicing this petition, so long delayed by graceful preliminary pleas, Paul appeals to a tender motive, namely that of friendship."

The word *partner* denotes more than just a friendship or comrade relationship. It denotes a relationship so close in its experiences as to involve mutual responsibilities. Because of their close relationship, Paul requested Philemon to give Onesimus the same Christian welcome he would have extended to Paul himself.

There could have remained one reason Philemon might have been hesitant to grant the runaway slave full pardon. Repentance should include restitution, and Onesimus might show his willingness to surrender and face any penalty. Onesimus would have needed money to get all the way to Rome. Paul perhaps entertained the idea that Onesimus may have helped himself to some of Philemon's resources. At least Paul had anticipated such and indicated, "If he hath wronged thee, or oweth thee ought, put that on mine account" (v. 18).

B. Obedience Anticipated (vv. 19-21)

19. I Paul have written it with mine own hand, I will repay it: albeit, I do not say to thee how thou owest unto me even thine own self besides.

20. Yea, brother, let me have joy of thee in the Lord: refresh my bowels in the Lord.

21. Having confidence in thy obedience I wrote unto thee, knowing that thou wilt also do more than I say.

Paul's customary method of writing letters was by the use of a secretary-helper. However, since this letter was so short and perhaps because he did not have his helper on hand, the apostle himself wrote the letter to Philemon (v. 19). In making that statement Paul was saying more than declaring that he himself had written the letter or simply signed his name. The statement also signified that Paul was taking responsibility for debts Onesimus might owe to Philemon.

In a very gentle way Paul reminded Philemon of his own debt to Paul—a debt that involved much more than money. Under Paul's ministry, Philemon had come to know the Lord. So in some respects, Philemon was more deeply in debt to Paul than Onesimus was to Philemon.

Many Bible scholars differ on the thought conveyed in verse 20. It contains a unique structure in the Greek language. *The Expositor's Greek Testament* points out that the optative "let me have joy" is the only proper optative in the New Testament which is not in the third person. Much more significantly, the verb in the Greek represents a play on the word *Onesimus,* as if Paul were saying, "You can now bring profit to me, Philemon, as the return of Onesimus will bring profit to you." Then comes the final simple challenge, "Refresh my bowels in the Lord." Again with a unique way of expressing it, Paul was asking Philemon to refresh his heart (inner man) just as Philemon had often refreshed the hearts and souls of the saints.

In verse 21, the apostle expressed his confidence that Philemon would comply with his request and even go beyond that. Indeed, one wonders how anyone could have turned down a request set in such emphatic phrases and thoughts as the one delivered to Philemon. We are not told what Philemon's response was. However, it would not be too difficult for a spiritually minded individual to conclude that Philemon responded positively to the request without hesitation.

There are times when all of us have the need to make serious requests. Perhaps Paul's pattern and approach to making a request could be a great help to us.

REVIEW QUESTIONS

1. What were the circumstances under which Onesimus met Paul?

2. What was Philemon's reputation?

3. How did Paul want Philemon to receive Onesimus?

4. Discuss Paul's understanding of God's providence in this situation.

5. What did Paul say regarding the debt Onesimus probably owed to Philemon?

GOLDEN TEXT HOMILY

"GOD WAS IN CHRIST, RECONCILING THE WORLD UNTO HIMSELF . . .

AND HATH COMMITTED UNTO US THE WORD OF RECONCILIATION" (2 Corinthians 5:19).

Reconciliation—oh, the preciousness of that word and thought!

Reconciliation denotes that an estrangement has taken place and that the one involved because of the estrangement is willing to do whatever is necessary to bring about a restoration of fellowship.

God, in His infinite knowledge, knew man would stray from Him. He permitted him, of his own free will, to choose life or death. God loved him in spite of his unbelieving rebelliousness in accepting Satan's lies.

The enormity of reconciling his relationship with God was more than any could pay. Man had sinned grossly. He needed a Savior. Jesus was the only Lamb without blemish. He was of the nature of God yet knew the frailty of the flesh.

When asked to pay the ultimate price for this needed peace, Jesus requested He be relieved of it. Later He yielded to His Father's will.

John 3:16 reveals to whom this restoration was intended—all mankind who would seek Him. "For all have sinned" (Romans 3:23).

As Christians, it is our blessed privilege and responsibility to assist in bringing reconciliation. We are "ambassadors" and "reconcilers." It is for us to reunite prodigals with their heavenly Father. At times it may even mean "pulling them out of the fire" (Jude 23).

We are to be keenly aware of Jesus' rhetorical question "What shall it profit a man, if he shall gain the whole world and lose his own soul?" (Mark 8:36). The Bible says, "He that winneth souls is wise" (Proverbs 11:30). "And they that be wise shall shine as the brightness of the firmament; and they that turn many to righteousness as the stars for ever and ever" (Daniel 12:3).— **Fred H. Whisman, Cost Analyst, Pathway Press, Cleveland, Tennessee**

SENTENCE SERMONS

OUR RECONCILIATION to God enables us to treat others as we have been treated.

—Selected

HE WHO CANNOT forgive and reconcile with others breaks the bridge over which he himself must pass.

—George Herbert

WE WIN by tenderness; we conquer by forgiveness and reconciliation.

—Fredrick W. Robertson

A MAN CANNOT touch his neighbor's heart with anything less than his own.

—Anonymous

DAILY BIBLE READINGS

M. Reconciled and United.
   Genesis 33:1-16
T. Forgiveness and Reconciliation.
   Genesis 45:1-15
W. Showing Kindness.
   2 Samuel 9:1-13
T. Reconciliation, Condition for Worship. Matthew 5:21-24
F. Reconciliation, Ministry to Fulfill. 2 Corinthians 5:11-19
S. Reconciliation, Service of Love. Colossians 4:1-9

Facing Death Triumphantly

Study Text: 2 Timothy 1:6-14; 3:10-17; 4:6-18

Objective: To know that Christians can face death victoriously and determine to be faithful to Christ.

Time: The Book of 2 Timothy was written around A.D. 66-67.

Place: The Book of 2 Timothy was written from a prison in Rome where Paul awaited his death sentence.

Golden Text: "I have fought a good fight, I have finished my course, I have kept the faith" (2 Timothy 4:7).

Central Truth: Those who believe in Christ face death with the assurance of eternal life.

Evangelism Emphasis: A life lived without faith in Christ results in eternal loss.

PRINTED TEXT

2 Timothy 1:8. Be not thou therefore ashamed of the testimony of our Lord, nor of me his prisoner: but be thou partaker of the afflictions of the gospel according to the power of God;

9. Who hath saved us, and called us with an holy calling, not according to our works, but according to his own purpose and grace, which was given us in Christ Jesus before the world began.

13. Hold fast the form of sound words, which thou hast heard of me, in faith and love which is in Christ Jesus.

14. That good thing which was committed unto thee keep by the Holy Ghost which dwelleth in us.

3:11. Persecutions, afflictions, which came unto me at Antioch, at Iconium, at Lystra; what persecutions I endured: but out of them all the Lord delivered me.

12. Yea, and all that will live godly in Christ Jesus shall suffer persecution.

13. But evil men and seducers shall wax worse and worse, deceiving, and being deceived.

14. But continue thou in the things which thou hast learned and hast been assured of, knowing of whom thou hast learned them;

15. And that from a child thou hast known the holy scriptures, which are able to make thee wise unto salvation through faith which is in Christ Jesus.

4:6. For I am now ready to be offered, and the time of my departure is at hand.

7. I have fought a good fight, I have finished my course, I have kept the faith:

8. Henceforth there is laid up for me a crown of righteousness,

which the Lord, the righteous judge, shall give me at that day: and not to me only, but unto all them also that love his appearing.

16. At my first answer no man stood with me, but all men forsook me: I pray God that it may not be laid to their charge.

17. Notwithstanding the Lord stood with me, and strengthened me; that by me the preaching might be fully known, and that all the Gentiles might hear: and I was delivered out of the mouth of the lion.

18. And the Lord shall deliver me from every evil work, and will preserve me unto his heavenly kingdom: to whom be glory for ever and ever. Amen.

DICTIONARY

Antioch (AN-tee-ahk), Iconium (eye-KOH-nee-um), Lystra (LIS-tra)— 2 Timothy 3:11—Cities in which Paul preached and met persecutions.

LESSON OUTLINE

I. VICTORIOUS FAITH
   A. Perseverance Needed
   B. Suffering Endured

II. VICTORIOUS MINISTRY
   A. Teaching by Word and Example
   B. Encouraging Steadfastness
   C. Acknowledging the Source and Function of Scripture

III. VICTORIOUS LIFE
   A. Triumphant Testimony
   B. Appeal for Human Presence and Service
   C. Warning About Opposition
   D. Strengthened by the Lord's Presence

LESSON EXPOSITION

INTRODUCTION

The Second Epistle to Timothy was probably the last correspondence the apostle Paul ever wrote. At least there is no record of any later letters. By a study of this epistle we get a feeling of the burdens, the faith, the optimism, and the confidence the great apostle Paul manifested in the face of impending martyrdom. While we get from this study the facts about one who faced death triumphantly, we learn also of the important responsibilities of leaders who must encourage and instruct those who will carry the work of the Lord into the future. By example, the apostle Paul showed great faith that the work which Christ had begun would not be extinguished by the persecution of Nero or by any future tyrant who worked against the Christ of Calvary. The work needed only faithful men like Paul, Timothy, and others to serve in responsible leadership roles.

The Roman historian Tacitus, as well as other reliable sources, recorded the persecution of the Christians following the great fire of

Rome in A.D. 64. The fire is commonly regarded by historians to have been set by Emperor Nero in order to allow him to rebuild the city—a high priority with him. In order to divert suspicion of arson from himself, he accused the Christians of burning the city and ordered their punishment.

In the wake of this persecution, Paul was rearrested, possibly at Troas (see 2 Timothy 4:13) and taken back to Rome. This time the arrest was by the henchmen of Nero, not by the Jews. And he was arrested as a criminal (2:9), not on some point of Jewish law as he was at first. Death was almost certain for him, and he wrote his final message to his helper in Kingdom service.

In his last hours, the apostle talked about himself, giving a picture of a lonely man abandoned by his friends, cold and longing for warmer clothes, wishing he had his books, and wanting some human hand to touch him in friendship and fellowship in the hour of his trial. Yet he triumphed and looked forward to his crown. He could boldly say, "I have fought a good fight, I have finished my course, I have kept the faith" (4:7). May we accept Paul's words as a challenge for us to do likewise.

I. VICTORIOUS FAITH
(2 Timothy 1:6-14)

A. Perseverance Needed (vv. 6-11)

(2 Timothy 1:6, 7, 10, 11 is not included in the printed text.)

8. Be not thou therefore ashamed of the testimony of our Lord, nor of me his prisoner: but be thou partaker of the afflictions of the gospel according to the power of God;

9. Who hath saved us, and called us with an holy calling, not according to our works, but according to his own purpose and grace, which was given us in Christ Jesus before the world began.

In verses 1-4, the apostle addressed Timothy and declared his deep affection for him as "my dearly beloved son" (v. 2), one who was brought to salvation through Christ by Paul's ministry. Probably the apostle spoke here according to a Jewish maxim which states, "He who teaches the law to his neighbor's son is considered by Scripture as if he had begotten him."

Paul had great love for the young man Timothy and desired to see him, "being mindful of thy tears" (v. 4). Perhaps the apostle was referring to the parting with the Ephesian church, mentioned in Acts 20:37, or to the deep impressions made on Timothy when he instructed him in the doctrine of the crucified Christ. The mention of the affection is certainly proof of the apostle's love and concern for his son in the Lord and explains that seeing Timothy would fill his heart with joy.

Beginning with verse 5, the apostle reflected on the piety of Timothy's mother and grandmother and the religious education they had given him. The "unfeigned faith" that Paul alluded to indicates Timothy had given the fullest proof of the sincerity of his conversion and of the purity of his faith.

Verse 6 begins Paul's appeal to Timothy regarding the need to persevere in the faith and ministry of the Lord. He reminded his son in the faith that it is necessary to "stir up the gift of God, which is in thee."

The gift which Timothy had received was the Holy Spirit, and through the Holy Spirit he had a particular power to preach and defend the truth. The Greek word *anazopureo* which is used here signifies "to stir up the fire; to add fresh fuel to it." If this is not done, the fire will go out.

Whether Timothy had withdrawn to an extent from an aggressive role in ministry is uncertain, although the fact that Paul made such a special appeal to Timothy raises that probability. The persecutions going on in Rome and in other parts of the Christian world, along with the reality of Paul's imprisonment and impending death, certainly made many fearful and less vocal than in earlier years. The apostle reminded Timothy that "God hath not given us the spirit of fear [timidity]" (v. 7). Instead of fear, God has given us power to work miracles, confound enemies, support each other in trials, and do that which is right and lawful in His sight. Instead of fear, God has also given the spirit of *love*, which enables the committed Christian to hear, believe, hope, and endure all things. And instead of fear, God has given a *sound mind*, which means that one has the ability to understand clearly and to have sound judgment, holy passions, and controlled tempers. In essence, it means to think, speak, and act right in all things—to be self-disciplined.

The apostle Paul pointed out two things in verse 8 that Timothy was not to be ashamed of: (1) the testimony of Jesus Christ and (2) Paul as a prisoner for Christ. Perhaps the admonition here is not in terms of being disgraced or embarrassed by the testimony of Christ and of

Paul's imprisonment. Rather the emphasis has consistently been on being without fear. The thought of timidity and inhibition is familiar to many modern-day Christians, although the reaction to sharing the message of Christ is not as hostile as it would have been for Timothy.

What can be done to offset timidity on the part of those who should be witnessing for Christ?

In verses 9 and 10 the apostle Paul reminded Timothy of the essentials of redemption through Christ and of the purpose for which Christ died. Indeed, the gospel of Christ—which was made possible by His coming, death, and resurrection—abolished death and brought new life. Many Jews, especially the Pharisees, believed in life after death, but other groups of Jews did not hold to this theology. When Jesus died and rose again, He verified the doctrine of the Resurrection. In the sight of His disciples, He took the same body up into heaven and now He ever appears in the presence of God for us. Through this act He also illustrated the doctrine of incorruption. For all these benefits, boldness in testimony should be the pattern of those who claim the name *Christian.*

Paul said he was appointed a preacher, an apostle, and a teacher to the Gentiles (v. 11). He never shirked his duty to fulfill the appointment. With persistence he held high the gospel of Jesus Christ regardless of hardship, threats, or confinements. His appointment as a preacher, apostle, and teacher brought him face-to-face with those of morbid, idolatrous practices and lifestyles. Yet he kept a victorious faith that enabled him to set a good example for Timothy and to encourage the young man to a bold ministry for Christ.

B. Suffering Endured (vv. 12-14)

(2 Timothy 1:12 is not included in the printed text.)

13. Hold fast the form of sound words, which thou hast heard of me, in faith and love which is in Christ Jesus.

14. That good thing which was committed unto thee keep by the Holy Ghost which dwelleth in us.

Verse 12 includes a very familiar portion of Scripture which has become a standard position for Christians: "I am not ashamed: for I know whom I have believed, and am persuaded that he is able to keep that which I have committed unto him against that day."

Reflecting back on his suffering, Paul could say that though he suffered for the gospel, he was not ashamed of the gospel neither was he confounded in his expectations, since he knew the grace of God was sufficient for him.   *LIFE, Soul, Gospel*

The phrase "that which I have committed unto him" has been understood in various ways by Bible scholars. Some think Paul was talking about his life. Others think he meant his soul; while others hold the position that Paul was speaking of the gospel. One thing is certain, whether Paul was referring to any one of the three or indeed to all three—they were in safekeeping since Paul knew experientially the One to whom he had committed his life and all things.

"Hold fast the form of sound words" (v. 13) refers to the plan of salvation which the apostle Paul

had taught Timothy. The Greek word *hupotuposis* ("form") signifies the "sketch, plan, or outline" of a building or picture and fittingly is applied to salvation's plan.

Although some men have tried, no person is free to invent or advance a religion for his own use and after his own mind. God alone knows that with which He can be pleased. If God had not given a revelation of Himself, the religious inventions of men would be endless error involved in contortions of unlimited confusion. God through His mercy gave "the form of sound words" (doctrine)—a perfect plan and sketch with well-defined outlines of everything concerning the present and eternal welfare of the human family and man's future glory.

"In faith and love" indicates the conditions under which Paul shared the "form of sound words" with Timothy. Faith credits the sound doctrine to God, the originator of the sound words, and love reduces them to practice. Faith lays hold on Jesus Christ and obtains that outflowing love by which every sound word is cheerfully obeyed.

In verse 14, Paul appealed to Timothy to keep "that good thing"— the everlasting gospel—by the power of the Holy Ghost which was resident in Timothy. The apostle Paul was confident that the indwelling Holy Spirit would continue to make the gospel effective in Timothy's own life and enable him to preach these sound words to others who would accept God's plan of salvation.

Discuss the turmoil and end results of man-made, philosophical religions that are out of harmony with God's divine plan of redemption.

II. VICTORIOUS MINISTRY
(2 Timothy 3:10-17)

A. Teaching by Word and Example (vv. 10-12)

(2 Timothy 3:10 is not included in the printed text.)

11. Persecutions, afflictions, which came unto me at Antioch, at Iconium, at Lystra; what persecutions I endured: but out of them all the Lord delivered me.

12. Yea, and all that will live godly in Christ Jesus shall suffer persecution.

Verse 10 begins a new section which is in reality Paul's final advice to Timothy and considers the example of the apostle's own experiences. The "but thou" is emphatic and shows the contrast between Timothy and the kind of people Paul wrote about in the first nine verses of chapter 3. A bit of reflection on those earlier verses will help to make the present exposition more meaningful.

Paul reminded Timothy that "in the last days perilous times shall come" (3:1). The grossly immoral character of life of those who had an outward "form of godliness, but denying the power thereof" (v. 5) convinced Paul that what he had observed as being already present was ample proof that moral conditions would continue to deteriorate. But what was more alarming was that the features of life he just described, although in the personal family and social relations of those within the church, were "more closely akin to paganism than to Christianity" (J.P. Lilley, *The*

Pastoral Epistles).

Unlike the people Paul described, Timothy was commended for being a different person who had given ear to the apostle's doctrines. The phrase "thou hast fully known" (v. 10) is translated from the Greek word *parakoloutheo,* which means literally "to follow alongside." However, it is used with a magnificent width of meaning. "It means to follow a person *physically,*" says William Barclay, "to stick by him through thick and thin. It means to follow a person *mentally,* to attend diligently to his teaching and fully to understand the meaning of what he says. It means to follow a person *spiritually,* not only to understand what he says, but also to carry out his ideas and be the kind of person he wishes us to be. *Parakolouthein* is indeed the word for the disciple, for it includes the unwavering loyalty of the true comrade, the full understanding of the true scholar and the complete obedience of the dedicated servant" ("The Letters to Timothy, Titus, and Philemon," *The Daily Study Bible Series*).

Paul went on to list nine things that Timothy had observed as his disciple (vv. 10, 11). The interest of that list is that it consists of the strands out of which the life and work of an apostle were woven. In it were the duties, qualities, and experiences of an apostle.

Doctrine is a major theme of both letters to Timothy. *Manner of life* denotes Paul's general behavior and Christlike attitude under trying circumstances. The word *purpose* refers to the apostle's main aim in life. *Faith* is the body of truth that constitutes the gospel. The term *longsuffering* denotes Paul's patience with people. Charity reflects a love (agape) that seeks the best for others. Patience is a term that denotes the apostle's endurance or steadfastness.

The list continues in verse 11 with the words persecutions and afflictions, which Paul had suffered on his missionary journeys in Antioch (Acts 13:50), Iconium (14:5, 6), and Lystra (14:19, 20). Lystra was Timothy's hometown (16:1), and the young man may have been an eyewitness to many of the abuses and persecutions of Paul at Lystra and elsewhere.

Paul mentioned these persecutions to magnify the fact that "out of them all the Lord delivered me" (2 Timothy 3:11). But he was convinced that the deliverance which now awaited him was the best of all (see 4:8). The apostle's example and steadfastness certainly must have been an incentive to Timothy to fully trust Paul's example and to be assured that God could deliver under any conditions.

Every true Christian must be prepared to accept the fact that "all that will live godly in Christ Jesus shall suffer persecution" (v. 11). R.F. Horton writes: "He who gives himself entirely up to God, making the Holy Scriptures the rule of his words and actions, will be more or less reviled and persecuted.

"The life in Christ is a life of spiritual mystical identification with him, and consequently it involves a partaking of his sufferings as surely as a partaking of his victory. The persecution in the Christian life is intrinsic. . . . [It] arises from the fact that the life in Christ is alien to this present world, and involves an inward and outward crucifixion of lusts and tendencies, which the world admits, but which Christ destroys. . . . The life of Christ in which the believer shares is a life which, if not against, is always athwart the world. Its motives and springs, its standards and precepts, its modes and development, its goals and its ends are as different from the world's as light is from darkness" (The Pastoral Epistles).

Discuss present-day persecutions that Christians face in many parts of the world.

B. Encouraging Steadfastness (vv. 13-15)

13. But evil men and seducers shall wax worse and worse, deceiving, and being deceived.

14. But continue thou in the things which thou hast learned and hast been assured of, knowing of whom thou hast learned them;

15. And that from a child thou hast known the holy scriptures, which are able to make thee wise unto salvation through faith which is in Christ Jesus.

Those who advance in the Christian life will suffer some degree of persecution, but there is another side of the picture—"evil men and seducers shall wax worse and worse." Their deterioration will continue on a descending scale. But the church will flourish even in the midst of persecution; those who try to thwart her work will sink deeper into sin and misery.

"Deceiving, and being deceived" states an inexorable law of our moral being. Self-delusion costs men their ability to distinguish between truth and error and thereby weakens their power of resistance to self-deceit and to imposition by others.

Timothy was encouraged to continue on in the things which he had learned, probably many of those things through hard knocks, but always with the impact of godly advice and instruction of the Old Testament Scriptures—taught to him by earnest, faithful leaders such as Paul, his mother, grandmother, and others. Also, Timothy had heard of the Old Testament prophecies and how many of them were related to the truths of the coming of Christ and the spread of the gospel. Indeed Timothy's moral strength and ministerial effectiveness lay in the fact that he had been grasped and held by the certainty of those great fundamental truths of the gospel: God, Christ, sin, salvation, repentance, faith, life in the Spirit, and the blessed hope of the Lord's return.

C. Acknowledging the Source and Function of Scripture (vv. 16, 17)

(2 Timothy 3:16, 17 is not included in the printed text.)

Timothy was encouraged to be fearless concerning the authority of his Bible-based message, which was indeed built on the Holy Scriptures—the inspired, God-given words communicated through divinely designed channels to serve a divine purpose. The usefulness of these Scriptures is the emphasis Paul was making. All Scripture is profitable in the field of doctrine and ethics and serves as moral equipment for the man of God. It is profitable for teaching by giving instructions in the things of God, and there is no portion of it which may not be found fit to furnish valuable lessons.

The Scriptures are valuable for use in rebuke or reproof for sin and lead to conviction and correction. They provide the remedy for sin and the way to rectify the past on the route to a righteous life.

The aim and purpose of these divinely inspired Scriptures and messages from God are that the man of God, being devoted to the Scriptures, will be made adequate or complete in character and life, equipped for every God-appointed task. Handley C.G. Moule exhorts us: "Let us betake ourselves afresh in our Bible, and let us never have done with it. It bears the proof of its own supernaturalness within it. . . . And the world is strewn with proofs, after a thousand criticisms, that this unique Book, manifold and one, is the divine vehicle of supernatural results in human souls" ("The Second Epistle to Timothy," *A Devotional Commentary*).

III. VICTORIOUS LIFE (2 Timothy 4:6-18)

In his volume *Notebook: Life*, William Ellery Channing wrote, "Life is a fragment, a moment between two eternities; influenced by all that has preceded, and to influence all that follows." To look at life in retrospect is natural when death is near. That is a special time of considering one's shortcomings and achievements during the life God has given him. Certainly it must be a real joy and satisfaction when one can feel that the work God led him or her into has been successfully completed. In earnest prayer, Jesus was able to say, "I have glorified thee on the earth: I have finished the work which thou gavest me to do" (John 17:4). Now we consider Paul one of Christ's dedicated servants who too had been faithful to fulfill the role God had given him.

A. Triumphant Testimony (vv. 6-8)

6. For I am now ready to be offered, and the time of my departure is at hand.

7. I have fought a good fight, I have finished my course, I have kept the faith:

8. Henceforth there is laid up for me a crown of righteousness, which the Lord, the righteous judge, shall give me at that day: and not to me only, but unto all them also that love his appearing.

The apostle Paul knew the end of his earthly life was near. The end which seemed a possibility at his first imprisonment now seemed a certainty. He considered his life to be an offering unto God (Romans 12:1) and his death a departure to be with the Lord (Philippians 1:21, 23). Donald Guthrie said, "What might have seemed like the end to Timothy appeared to the apostle as a glorious new era when he would be released from all the present restrictions" (*The Pastoral Epistles*).

Two interesting illustrations show Paul's victorious view of death. The first—"ready to be offered"—alludes to the Old Testament "drink offering," which was wine poured around the base of the altar as a sacrifice (Numbers 15:1-10). It is as if Paul were saying, "The day is ended, and it is time to rise and go. My life must be poured out as a sacrifice to God."

The second illustration is found in the word *departure*. It is the Greek word *analusis*, which literally means "loosing," as an animal from

its yoke or as a ship from its moorings. Loosing connotes freedom. Reflecting on Paul's departure, William Barclay says: "Many a time Paul had felt his ship leave the harbor for the deep waters. Now he is to launch out into the greatest deep of all, setting sail to cross the waters of death to arrive in the haven of eternity. So then, for the Christian, death is laying . . . aside shackles in order to be free; it is . . . casting off the ropes which bind us to this world in order to set sail on the voyage which ends in the presence of God. Who then shall fear it?" ("The Letters to Timothy, Titus, and Philemon," *The Daily Study Bible Series*).

In verse 7, the apostle in retrospect considered his ministerial life and used three metaphorical statements to describe his career:

"I have fought a good fight." This is by no means boastful language but the testimony of a good conscience. Paul had not been defeated by any opposition, but was victorious because God was on his side.

"I have finished my course" is again a metaphor tied to athletic games. As a runner hastens to the goal, so Paul had traversed the whole course of the missionary challenge that was impressed upon him to complete. Paul did not fall out on the last lap or the homestretch but finished the course.

Paul had demonstrated many times that the one thing necessary in the work of God was staying power—to "hang in there"—when the going was tough. The pages of history are indelibly marked with accounts of those who gave up early in the battles of life or who ran successfully up to the last mile and then gave up. But it is those who "endure to the end," who win the crown (see Matthew 10:22; 24:13).

"I have kept the faith" is Paul's affirmation that the gospel, which had been committed to him as a sacred trust, was carefully guarded up to the end. He had kept his faith in Christ and did not allow for perversions or the "watering down" of the truths of the message of Christ. "These are not the idle words of a braggart," says Roy S. Nicholson, "but the humble testimony of a man who has 'one foot in the grave and his heart already in heaven,' challenging his followers to new courage and daring" (*The Wesleyan Bible Commentary*, Vol. V).

What does it mean for us "to keep the faith"?

In verse 8, the apostle says, "Henceforth [Greek, *loipon*, meaning "from this time forward"] there is laid up [set aside] for me a crown of righteousness [a laurel wreath of honor]." Paul knew he would receive the crown at the time of Christ's appearing. But the Lord, the righteous Judge, will award a crown to everyone who has loved the truth and continues to cherish the thought of His appearing.

B. Appeal for Human Presence and Service (vv. 9-13)

(2 Timothy 4:9-13 is not included in the printed text.)

In verses 9-12, the apostle Paul made an appeal to Timothy to get there as quickly as he could, perhaps in view of the apparent shortness of time before Paul's death. He also gave Timothy an update regarding some of his helpers: (1) Demas had become enamored with "this present world" and had forsaken Paul when such a separation would have been especially painful. (2) Crescens and Titus are said to have gone to Galatia and Dalmatia respectively, but there is no indication whether that was by Paul's directive or their own choice. In any event, the apostle did not accuse them of deserting him. (3) Luke the "beloved physician" and faithful coworker of Paul still remained. Certainly Luke's presence must have meant a lot to Paul. His training as a physician enabled him to render professional service to the apostle, who suffered from a physical malady (2 Corinthians 12:7-10; Galatians 4:13). (4) Tychicus was a person whom Paul highly respected (Acts 20:4; Ephesians 6:21; Titus 3:12). Some scholars think Tychicus may have been the bearer of the letter and that he would fill in for Timothy while Timothy was with Paul.

Mark was also mentioned in the correspondence as the apostle asked Timothy to bring Mark with him when he came. Mark (also called John) was the person responsible for the separation of Paul and Barnabas in their ministry (Acts 13:5, 13; 15:37-40). Apparently that cause of separation had been settled, and the apostle now considered Mark a person "profitable" to him in the ministry.

In 2 Timothy 4:13, Paul made an appeal for service. He was confined to a cold, damp prison, and the cloak that he asked for certainly would provide some physical comfort. The books he requested were perhaps papyrus rolls, but the parchments were more costly vellum or dried skins of animals which were used for more valuable items. "Some think that Paul referred to the commentaries on the Hebrew Scriptures, his personal letters and manuscripts, notes on the life and sayings of Jesus and legal documents respecting his citizenship; and that he wished to have these personal effects to bequeath to Timothy as a trust for later transmission to the churches" (*The Wesleyan Bible Commentary*, Vol. V).

C. Warning About Opposition
   (vv. 14, 15)

(2 Timothy 4:14, 15 is not included in the printed text.)

The man Alexander, mentioned in verses 14 and 15, had to be further identified by adding a trade description—"coppersmith"—to distinguish him from other Alexanders in the New Testament.

The occasion when Alexander opposed Paul can only be speculated on; but in view of the verses which follow, it is easy to surmise that the opposition occurred at Paul's hearing before the courts. However, Alexander seems to have been at Ephesus, not Rome, for Timothy was warned to be on guard against him. It is reasonable to assume, therefore, that he was an opponent of the gospel and of Paul personally on many previous occasions.

Although Paul suffered from the opposition of Alexander, he knew that God would render him due reward for those malicious acts.

D. Strengthened by the Lord's
   Presence (vv. 16-18)

16. At my first answer no man stood with me, but all men forsook me: I pray God that it may not be laid to their charge.

17. Notwithstanding the Lord stood with me, and strengthened me; that by me the preaching might be fully known, and that all the Gentiles might hear: and I was delivered out of the mouth of the lion.

18. And the Lord shall deliver me from every evil work, and will preserve me unto his heavenly kingdom: to whom be glory for ever and ever. Amen.

Paul's first defense was apparently a preliminary hearing at which the charge was read and Paul had opportunity to make an initial statement. No one came to be beside Paul to vouch for his statements or act as his helper and advocate. The reference might mean that men of influence whose testimony would have strengthened his case could not be found. It may mean that none of his friends at all were there. Even Luke might not have arrived in Rome in time for the hearing. Whatever the reason, Paul felt abandoned, but not vengeful, and he prayed that God would not hold this failure against them.

In contrast to the absence of human representation, the Lord stood with Paul and gifted him with power. The purpose of this divine enabling was that the proclamation of the gospel might be fully made to this significant Roman audience. The Roman officials who heard Paul's defense were also made the recipients of an inspired recital of the gospel.

The apostle also indicates that he was "delivered out of the mouth of the lion." This well-known metaphor is found in Psalm 22:21. Paul's Roman citizenship would have secured him from being thrown to the wild beasts. The incident seems to have been a figure of extreme and immediate danger, and from this he was spared at that time.

Towering high above the immediate dreary circumstances was Paul's unshaken faith in the preserving power of the Lord. Just as Christ stood by him and delivered him from immediate death, so He would continue to deliver him "from every evil work." From all possibilities of evil works, the Lord would provide protection and deliverance. Nothing would prevent Paul's participation in the joys of Christ's heavenly kingdom.

Many of God's dear servants have been harassed by the forces of evil. At times it appears that the Enemy has gained the upper hand. But God's work will not be blotted out by the Enemy, nor will those who oppose God's work escape the consequences.

REVIEW QUESTIONS

1. What were the circumstances Paul was facing when he wrote the Second Epistle to Timothy?

2. What instructions did Paul give concerning Timothy's ministry?

3. Are there similarities between Paul's day and the present age in regard to opposition to the gospel?

4. How did Paul describe his readiness to die?

5. What is meant by the term "a crown of righteousness"?

GOLDEN TEXT HOMILY

"I HAVE FOUGHT A GOOD FIGHT, I HAVE FINISHED MY COURSE, I HAVE KEPT THE FAITH" (2 Timothy 4:7).

One of the cruelest theories presented by some ministers is that if you are a Christian there will never be problems—all will be sunshine and roses. God never promised it would be easy, but that He would be with us in all we face.

Multitudes have suffered for Christ, even martyrdom. However, few have had such severe difficulties while fulfilling God's will as did Paul.

Opposition to Paul's witness was on every side, but nothing deterred him. In spite of imprisonment, he fought on. In spite of the "perils among false brethren" (2 Corinthians 11:26), he fought on. In spite of his thorn in the flesh, he fought on. In spite of desertions, distrust, and mistrust, he fought on. What a testimony to the grace of God!

Now all that would detract from his ministry or destroy him was ending. There was a persistence within him to finish his race, the course God had set for him. Quickly the end would be a reality, coming at the hands of Nero's executioners. He did not flinch. From heaven and earth he was being cheered on. God's grace had seen him through.

Seeing ultimate victory, he acknowledged it was faith that had kept him, even as he had kept the faith. It wasn't just a faith of any kind or just any faith at all—but *the faith*—faith that Jehovah was his God, Jesus his redeemer, and the Holy Spirit his advocate.

The important issue for us when we face death will be this: In whom does our faith lie? (Acts 4:12). Sincerity is not enough.—**Fred H. Whisman, Chaplain (Lt. Col.), Group II Chaplain, Civil Air Patrol, Chattanooga, Tennessee**

SENTENCE SERMONS

THOSE WHO BELIEVE in Christ face death with the assurance of eternal life.

—**Selected**

BLESSED IS THE PERSON who can come to the end of life knowing he has done the will of God.

—**Anonymous**

OUR PIETY MUST be weak and imperfect if it does not conquer the fear of death.

—**Fénelon**

IN TIMES OF AFFLICTION we commonly meet with the sweetest experiences of the love of God.

—**John Bunyan**

EVANGELISM APPLICATION

A LIFE LIVED WITHOUT FAITH IN CHRIST RESULTS IN ETERNAL LOSS.

Death is not the end; it is only a beginning. Death is not the master of the house; he is only the porter at the King's lodge, appointed to open the gate and let the King's guests in to the realm of eternal day. And so shall we ever be with the Lord.

The range of our threescore years and ten is not the limit of our life. Our life is not a landlocked lake within the shoreline of 70 years. It is an arm of the sea. And so we must build for those larger waters. We are immortal! How, then, shall we live today in prospect of eternal tomorrow?—**J.W. Jowett,** *Knight's Masterbook of New Illustrations*

ILLUMINATING THE LESSON

Among the many thrilling stories told in connection with the search for gold in the Klondike is one which impressed me more than all the others. A prospecting party penetrating far into the country came upon a miner's hut. All without was as quiet as the grave. Entering the cabin, they found the skeletons of two men and a large quantity of gold. On a rough table was a letter telling of their successful search for the precious ore. In their eagerness to get it, they forgot the early coming of winter in that northern land. Each day, the gold was found in more abundance. One morning they awoke to find a great snowstorm upon them. For days the tempest raged, cutting off all hope of escape. Their little store of food was soon exhausted, and they lay down and died amidst abounding gold! Their folly was not in finding and gathering the gold, but in neglecting to provide against the inevitable winter. Neither are men to be classed as fools today who are diligent in business and successful in the accumulation of property. The folly is in permitting these to so occupy the attention that provision for the greater winter of death, so soon to fall, is entirely neglected.—**W.W. Weeks in** *The Heart of God*

DAILY BIBLE READINGS

M. Worship the Lord.
   Psalm 92:1-15

T. Seek God's Help.
   Proverbs 3:5-7

W. Press On Toward Jesus.
   Philippians 3:13-15

T. Proclaim God's Word.
   2 Timothy 4:1-5

F. Contend for the Faith.
   Jude 1-4

S. Receive Your Reward.
   Revelation 22:12-17

Use Life's Opportunities Wisely

Study Text: Ecclesiastes 11:1 through 12:1; 1 Peter 3:8-12

Objective: To understand that life is a precious gift of God and make the best of life by pleasing Him.

Time: The Book of Ecclesiastes was written between 940 and 935 B.C. The Book of 1 Peter was written around A.D. 63-64.

Place: The Book of Ecclesiastes was written at Jerusalem. The Book of 1 Peter was probably written at Rome.

Golden Text: "Walk circumspectly, not as fools, but as wise, redeeming the time, because the days are evil" (Ephesians 5:15, 16).

Central Truth: Life is filled with opportunities to serve God.

Evangelism Emphasis: Christians should use opportunities to lead the unsaved to Christ.

PRINTED TEXT

Ecclesiastes 11:1. Cast thy bread upon the waters: for thou shalt find it after many days.

2. Give a portion to seven, and also to eight; for thou knowest not what evil shall be upon the earth.

3. If the clouds be full of rain, they empty themselves upon the earth: and if the tree fall toward the south, or toward the north, in the place where the tree falleth, there it shall be.

4. He that observeth the wind shall not sow; and he that regardeth the clouds shall not reap.

5. As thou knowest not what is the way of the spirit, nor how the bones do grow in the womb of her that is with child: even so thou knowest not the works of God who maketh all.

6. In the morning sow thy seed, and in the evening with-hold not thine hand: for thou knowest not whether shall prosper, either this or that, or whether they both shall be alike good.

7. Truly the light is sweet, and a pleasant thing it is for the eyes to behold the sun:

8. But if a man live many years, and rejoice in them all; yet let him remember the days of darkness; for they shall be many. All that cometh is vanity.

9. Rejoice, O young man, in thy youth; and let thy heart cheer thee in the days of thy youth, and walk in the ways of thine heart, and in the sight of thine eyes: but know thou, that for all these things God will bring thee into judgment.

10. Therefore remove sorrow from thy heart, and put away evil from thy flesh: for childhood

and youth are vanity.

12:1. Remember now thy Creator in the days of thy youth, while the evil days come not, nor the years draw nigh, when thou shalt say, I have no pleasure in them.

1 Peter 3:10. For he that will love life, and see good days, let him refrain his tongue from evil, and his lips that they speak no guile:

11. Let him eschew evil, and do good; let him seek peace, and ensue it.

12. For the eyes of the Lord are over the righteous, and his ears are open unto their prayers: but the face of the Lord is against them that do evil.

LESSON OUTLINE

I. DO GOOD AT ALL TIMES
   A. Share
   B. Plant
II. BE RESPONSIBLE TO GOD
   A. Accountability
   B. Commitment
III. ENJOY LIFE IN PEACE
   A. Restraint
   B. Righteousness

LESSON EXPOSITION

INTRODUCTION

For several centuries the peoples of the world have been seeing the United States as the land of opportunity. Just the name speaks of chances previously withheld or unattainable. These opportunities take on varied forms—freedom from oppression, social and economic mobility, vocational change, and educational growth. If those people can just get to these shores, then a new life will appear. It's no wonder they are so willing to sacrifice and put forth the effort to come.

We are only too consciously aware that for many these dreams are never totally fulfilled. Oppression, economic hardship, and dead-end jobs are also part of the American scene. However, at least more choices are available. Then it becomes the responsibility of these individuals to use their skills and resources wisely.

The same is true in our spiritual lives. All of us—every single one of us—are given many and varied opportunities to serve God. Our responsibility is to use them wisely for the glory of God, for the edification of the church, and for the spread of the gospel—and for our personal spiritual growth as well.

Most of our lesson text is taken from the writings of Solomon in the Book of Ecclesiastes. He is our excellent example of how not to squander life's opportunities. Though blessed with personal abilities, divine wisdom, fame, and tremendous wealth, he made some "bad" choices. The other verses are from the writing of the apostle Peter. As we know so well, he too had spoken and acted on occasions in such a way that he later regretted. But not to be forgotten are those many times when he stood tall for truth and ministered in the power of the Holy Spirit.

The challenge facing us in today's lesson is one of wisely using our opportunities to do good, to be responsible, and to peaceably enjoy life.

I. DO GOOD AT ALL TIMES
(Ecclesiastes 11:1-6)

A. Share (vv. 1, 2)

1. Cast thy bread upon the waters: for thou shalt find it after many days.
2. Give a portion to seven, and also to eight; for thou knowest not what evil shall be upon the earth.

One of life's opportunities which occurs every year of our lifespan is that of doing good! No one—unless you live the life of a totally isolated hermit—is free from the chance to be charitable to another person.

Solomon previously had discussed the problems associated with loving money and selfishly clutching all of one's possessions (see 5:10-12; 6:1-6.) There is the problem of never being satisfied and the possibility of not living long enough to enjoy it. These first two verses of chapter 11 provide a total contrast. Solomon advocates a generosity to many.

There are several opinions as to what is meant by "casting bread upon the waters." One suggestion is that it refers to scattering rice seeds from a boat into the waters of a flooded field—a way of planting. A second suggestion is that it speaks of loading grain on a ship and sending it through treacherous shipping lanes for sale at other ports. In either case there is an eventual return. Planted seeds bear a crop. Sold grains bring a profit.

The encouragement to share isn't based on receiving a return. The motive for doing good should come from our renewed nature in Christ and our love for Him. But even if

you aren't desiring a return for your good deeds, it still comes. There is a return of satisfaction in knowing you have made it easier for someone. And not to be overlooked are the kindnesses which may come to members of your family even years later, simply because of your goodness.

In verse 2, Solomon's directives to give to seven or eight are not limitations. But rather they are an encouragement to go beyond an occasional good deed. Rather than selfishly storing our possessions, which can easily be destroyed by a single disaster, we are to generously share what we have. Not to be forgotten is the possibility of our not living long enough to enjoy it anyway. The story of the rich fool in Luke 12:13-21 demonstrates this so vividly.

When we have been blessed with a surplus of goods or money and come into contact with someone in need, that is one of life's opportunities. We can do good by sharing. We are not obligated to give away all of our surplus. That doesn't even enter the consideration. Of importance is seeing the needs and doing our very best to help.

B. Plant (vv. 3-6)

3. If the clouds be full of rain, they empty themselves upon the earth: and if the tree fall toward the south, or toward the north, in the place where the tree falleth, there it shall be.
4. He that observeth the wind shall not sow; and he that regardeth the clouds shall not reap.
5. As thou knowest not what is the way of the spirit, nor how the bones do grow in the womb of

her that is with child: even so thou knowest not the works of God who maketh all.

6. In the morning sow thy seed, and in the evening withhold not thine hand: for thou knowest not whether shall prosper, either this or that, or whether they both shall be alike good.

Verse 3 frequently is grouped with the first two verses of the chapter. However, since this section is a distinct emphasis on planting, it will be included with verses 4-6.

This verse emphasizes some of the fixed laws of nature that affect us. Water-laden clouds will release their moisture. It is the process or cycle by which the earth is watered. In the same way, when a tree falls it stays in the place where it fell. Its weight and the force of gravity keep it in place. These are predetermined events that God has placed in motion.

But in marked contrast, there are other areas which not only allow but demand adventurous action on our part. Unless we make a decision and then follow through, nothing will be accomplished.

In verse 4 the author provides us an example from farming. Now a good farmer takes the weather in consideration when planting and harvesting, but it never totally determines his action. Just because the wind blows doesn't keep him from planting! Yes, some seed will be blown away. Yes, some areas may not be seeded as properly as others. But waiting for the ideal weather very likely would result in the crop's being planted too late in the season and would either hinder or destroy the chances of harvesting in the fall.

The same holds true at harvest. If a farmer constantly allows threatening clouds to stop plans to cut the grain, the harvest will never be gathered. Now common sense keeps one from cutting at the immediate threat. To do so would soak the stalks and demand turning them repeatedly until dry. The modern farmer also knows there is an economic loss. Once the grain is cut and rain falls on it, there is a loss of color and weight which in turn lowers the price. However, there is another side. It is better for the grain to be cut and lying on the ground than to have it destroyed by a raging storm.

Verse 5 reminds us that we do not understand all the ways God chooses to work. But that lack of understanding isn't to keep us from doing what is right at that time. The author, Solomon, uses the illustration of a child developing in a mother's womb. It definitely was a mystery as to how bones, which later become hard and provide the skeleton, could grow in such an environment. But this lack of understanding didn't keep women from having children and men from desiring sons. Even today with all of our medical technology and factual information, the vast population doesn't understand the phenomena of conception and development, but children are still desired.

Keeping this in mind, Solomon exhorts all of us to continue planting the seeds of goodness and reaping the eventual harvest. We aren't to worry how much good may be accomplished. Our responsibility is to meet the needs with which we are confronted. We aren't to even concern ourselves with how our goodness is received by those we help. But rather, we are to use each of these opportunities wisely and fulfill God's desires for His children.

What are some reasons why we may not want to take advantage of our opportunities to do good?

II. BE RESPONSIBLE TO GOD (Ecclesiastes 11:7—12:1)

A. Accountability (11:7-9)

7. Truly the light is sweet, and a pleasant thing it is for the eyes to behold the sun:

8. But if a man live many years, and rejoice in them all; yet let him remember the days of darkness; for they shall be many. All that cometh is vanity.

9. Rejoice, O young man, in thy youth; and let thy heart cheer thee in the days of thy youth, and walk in the ways of thine heart, and in the sight of thine eyes: but know thou, that for all these things God will bring thee into judgment.

Using life's opportunities wisely becomes especially important when considering that we will not live forever. Solomon's views toward life and death varied. Early on he valued death over life (Ecclesiastes 4:2). Later, however, he discovered that life provides hope (9:4), and this positiveness continued (11:7). The light and sun are symbolic of life on this earth. And if a person is fortunate to live many years, life should be in an atmosphere of rejoicing for the opportunities afforded.

It is of special interest that Solomon offers no hope of life after death. Instead death appears as an

extended period of darkness. With such dismal contrast between life and death, it is no wonder he projects the need to enjoy life.

As believers we know this negative contrast is unnecessary. The words of the apostle Paul to the Philippians provide such a beautiful description: "For to me to live is Christ, and to die is gain . . . . For I am in a strait betwixt two, having a desire to depart, and to be with Christ; which is far better" (1:21, 23). He stated it differently in 2 Corinthians 5:6, 8: "Therefore we are always confident, knowing that, whilst we are at home in the body, we are absent from the Lord. . . . We are confident, I say, and willing rather to be absent from the body, and to be present with the Lord."

Though Solomon valued life and its actions so highly, he didn't overlook the need for accountability. He directed verse 9 and the accountability aspect to the younger individuals, especially the males. Along with the vitality of youth comes a recklessness due to the desire of pleasing personal wishes. Some of them originate within one's thought patterns. Others come through visually seeing and wanting to possess and enjoy. And not to be forgotten are some of the basic drives with which all are created.

Youth may fling aside constraints and controls for the sake of enjoyment. Life is sweet and seems like it will last forever. However, judgment awaits all. God will scrutinize our actions and words. There will be a time of giving an account for our actions.

The responsible person directs his/her life according to the principles of God shown through the

Scriptures. The irresponsible person emphasizes his/her own opinions.

How can we assist young people in understanding that they will be accountable to God for how they live their life?

B. Commitment (11:10; 12:1)

11:10. Therefore remove sorrow from thy heart, and put away evil from thy flesh: for childhood and youth are vanity.

12:1. Remember now thy Creator in the days of thy youth, while the evil days come not, nor the years draw nigh, when thou shalt say, I have no pleasure in them.

Knowing that judgment and accountability are inevitable, the author offers a positive approach. Judgment can be avoided by choosing the right lifestyle. The approach is that of putting away anything which will bring anxiety to our inner being and trouble to our outer being. What does that mean specifically? It means we are to choose a life of holiness before the Lord. We will do our very best to avoid the appearance of evil (1 Thessalonians 5:22) while striving to walk in the Spirit (Galatians 5:16).

This isn't a call to a dull, boring, unfulfilled life. In fact, it's just the opposite. When there is no fear of future judgment due to right actions now, a person lives a life of joy, contentment, and excitement. Jesus' words in John 10:10 apply here: "I am come that they might have life, and that they might have it more abundantly." *SEE OTHER*

Ecclesiastes 12:1 is frequently used in youth services. And rightly

so. It asks for a special commitment to God. The "evil days" refer to old age when we no longer are able to accomplish some of the aspects of youth. It also reminds us that the years of our later life cannot undo or even redo the deeds of our youth. So rather than finding ourselves despairing the folly and futility of earlier actions, we should just commit ourselves to God. Then actions of righteousness and wisdom will pervade. There will be no later regrets. Instead there will be memories of a life spent in service to God.

Verse 1 also reminds us of the aging process. Events or actions which were extremely pleasurable at one point in our lives may not only bring lesser satisfaction but also pain. For example, there comes a time when an athlete hangs up the glove, the cleats, and the uniform. Not only have some of the reactions slowed, but in certain parts of the body the pain becomes so great it drowns out all the pleasure from playing the game. But if he played as well as possible during his youth, those joys remain for the rest of his life.

The Biblical author definitely squashes the concept of sowing wild oats while we are young. He advocates sowing no wild oats so we won't reap its harvest later!

III. ENJOY LIFE IN PEACE
(1 Peter 3:8-12)

A. Restraint (vv. 8-10)

(1 Peter 3:8, 9 is not included in the printed text.)

10. For he that will love life, and see good days, let him refrain his tongue from evil, and his lips that they speak no guile.

Life can be filled with inner

peace. Salvation through Jesus Christ frees us from the turmoil of sin with its load of guilt. This peace is totally independent from our outward circumstances. Remember the words of Jesus to His disciples: "Peace I leave with you, my peace I give unto you: not as the world giveth, give I unto you. Let not your heart be troubled, neither let it be afraid" (John 14:27).

Not to be overlooked is the possibility of peace in outward relationships. Some we have no control over. Others are dependent on our choice of actions.

The apostle Peter wrote his first epistle to believers who were living in northern Asia Minor. They were being persecuted for their faith as believers in Jesus Christ. As Peter wrote to encourage and direct them, he provided some directives to help in this difficult situation. He asked these believers to strive for harmony among themselves. The pressure of persecution could have caused divisions among the believers unless there was concentrated effort to maintain harmony and peace.

He began by encouraging them to be very positive toward each other. First is the aspect of compassion, or sympathetic behavior. More than likely each of the believers and their families had not experienced all the same types of persecution. And even if they had, there may have been differences in their strength and ability to bear this burden. Surely those who were stronger and having an easier time were to demonstrate compassion for the less fortunate!

They were also reminded of the need to love each other. Love does more than simply make us feel good. Love causes us to remember our place in the family of God. We aren't standing alone but rather are circled by brothers and sisters. And as a result love empowers. There is a surge of strength in the face of evil.

Peter also called for humility. Pride can develop even in the middle of persecution. This sounds unusual initially. But it is possible for a person to be proud of his/her experiencing and enduring suffering. There is pride in the event rather than rejoicing in their being found worthy to suffer with Christ.

Following these positive qualities the apostle called for some specific restraints on their part. The emphasis of verses 9 and 10 centers on the verbal dimension. What were they tempted to say about their persecutors? This could possibly be answered by asking it very personally of ourselves. What might we be tempted to say about those who are physically, emotionally, and economically abusing us?

Peter begins by asking believers to restrain themselves from falling into the trap of becoming like their persecutors. If believers return evil for evil, then they are no different than the world. It also brings into question what difference salvation and empowerment through the baptism of the Holy Spirit makes in our lives. Plus, how can we forget Jesus' teaching that we are to love our enemies and pray for those who persecute us (Matthew 5:44)?

Verse 9 also introduces us to another one of those paradoxes which are so much a part of the Christian life. Instead of repaying evil and insults with the same actions, we are to bless those who pour forth these negatives. That doesn't mean to "bless them out" as some would like to. Instead it means to pray for their well-being—praying that God will prosper them physically, emotionally, and spiritually. It's an opportunity to demonstrate some of the very practical aspects of life in the Holy Spirit.

How is this action possible? First, it comes with being an obedient child of God desiring to follow His written Word. Second, it flows through the empowerment of being baptized in the Holy Spirit. Jesus stated very specifically that Spirit baptism would enable us to be His witness (Acts 1:8). And one important aspect of witnessing is to model the lifestyle of the Master we serve. In a previous chapter Peter reminds the believers of the importance of their actions: "Live such good lives among the pagans that, though they accuse you of doing wrong, they may see your good deeds and glorify God on the day he visits us" (1 Peter 2:12, *NIV*).

Of special importance in the peace process is how we speak. In verse 10 the apostle quoted from Psalm 34:12, 13. These original words from the pen of King David zero in on the power of the tongue and its types of communication. If we will strive to keep ourselves from speaking words which are evil and deceitful, we can expect a certain pleasantness to permeate our daily lives. However, if we are constantly gossiping, accusing, sharing half-truths, or speaking the worst about people, our inner peace will be destroyed.

By the way, speech problems aren't relegated to only one gender. Men as well as women need to guard their tongues. All of us possess this powerful member which can spread harmony and truth or deceit and dissension.

B. Righteousness (vv. 11, 12)

11. Let him eschew evil, and do good; let him seek peace, and ensue it.

12. For the eyes of the Lord are over the righteous, and his ears are open unto their prayers: but the face of the Lord is against them that do evil.

Righteousness is a choice. It doesn't appear in our actions without there being a conscious choice. This can be seen indirectly in the previous verses; however, in verse 11 the apostle states it very clearly. Peace with God and even with our fellowmen comes as we turn from evil and toward good. Just rejecting evil isn't sufficient. There must be a positive direction which receives our attention. Without this reduction it becomes very easy to simply slip back into our old ways.

Verse 11 further reminds us of the need to pursue peace. It tends not to come to us automatically or with very little effort. The opportunity for peace can loom on the horizon, but we have to strive toward it. Keep in mind the situation facing these believers. They were being persecuted for their faith. Some things could not be changed. The political and cultural climate appeared very hostile. They were unable to make the pagan unbelievers appreciate their stance as believers. Yet, that doesn't mean peace was impossible for them.

Furthermore, peace is attainable for believers today. First, there is the opportunity to be at peace within even though surrounded by unrest. That is one aspect of peace which comes from its being a virtue with the fruit of the Spirit (Galatians 5:22).

Second, a believer may need to make overtures of peace toward those who persist in evil. Offering kindness in the face of hostility as well as love in the presence of hatred are some of the ways to pursue peace and the final aspect of righteousness.

Verse 12 provides us with a very special view of God's care and concern for His children, the righteous. He is constantly watching over us and listening to our calls and communication. It's the picture of a mother who continues to be attentive to her children. She checks where they are and what they are doing. She carefully listens for any cry of distress or exclamation of joy.

In marked contrast is the relationship with those who pursue evil. He isn't attentively watching over them. But rather, He is in opposition to their ways. His face is turned from them. Now that doesn't mean He is oblivious to what they are doing. His omniscience keeps that from happening. God knows everything that is happening. Nothing escapes Him. He is open to the cries of the evil ones who are turning to Him for forgiveness and help. He desires for them to change their ways and be drawn to Him. However, as long as they persist in serving self in sin, there is a great division keeping them from God's parental care.

REVIEW QUESTIONS

1. What should be our motive for doing good?

2. How do the principles of farming apply to our using opportunities wisely?

3. Why are judgment and accountability inevitable?

4. What are some of the qualities which bring harmony during persecution?

5. How does God's relationship with the evildoers differ from that of the righteous?

GOLDEN TEXT HOMILY

"WALK CIRCUMSPECTLY, NOT AS FOOLS, BUT AS WISE, REDEEMING THE TIME, BECAUSE THE DAYS ARE EVIL" (Ephesians 5:15, 16).

Time is of high value, and those who "kill" time destroy one of the best resources God had given them. It is a sacred trust He has lent.

The apostle Paul urges us to "walk circumspectly, not as fools, but as wise [persons] redeeming the time." All time is not of the same value. There are moments of peculiar preciousness. Woe to him who through heedlessness or willful negligence allows them to slip by. The moment when the rope floats by the drowning man, it must be seized or he dies. Strike the iron while it is hot. Sow the seed in the spring if you would reap the harvest in autumn.

Youth has its golden opportunities that belong to no other age. Manhood has its time of vigor to work that will be beyond the strength of old age. Hence the wise person will watch for occasions of usefulness that his word may be "in season."

We must sacrifice our own pleasure in giving up time that we are tempted to expend on ourselves, our amusement, or our rest to the service of God. For he who gives to God only his leisure moments when he is worn and jaded with his own selfish work, he makes but a poor offering to a loving heavenly Father.—**Excerpts from *The Pulpit Commentary*, Vol. 20**

SENTENCE SERMONS

LIFE IS FILLED with opportunities to serve God.

—Selected

CHRISTIANS SHOULD use opportunities to lead the unsaved to Christ.

—Selected

AN OSTRICH with its head in the sand is just as blind to opportunity as to disaster.

—*Draper's Book of Quotations for the Christian World*

DO NOT WAIT for extraordinary circumstances to do good; try to use ordinary situations.

—Johann Paul Fredrick Richter

ILLUMINATING THE LESSON

The contrast of using life's opportunities wisely is demonstrated so clearly in the parable of the talents (Matthew 25:14-30). The three individuals had the same opportunity even though each one's was slightly different.

As the master left on a journey, he entrusted each servant with a portion of his goods. One received five talents. The second received two talents. And the third received one. The first two immediately went out and began to use their talents to produce a profit for their master. They were successful and doubled what had been given.

The third one simply hid his in the ground. Fearing the possibility of negative circumstances and failing results, he chose to do nothing. Not only did he miss the opportunity to excel in the eyes of his master, but missed the opportunity to be personally blessed. To make matters worse, upon his return, the master viewed these actions as signs of laziness and wickedness.

DAILY BIBLE READINGS

M. Accept Counsel.
   Exodus 18:13-24
T. Wait on God.
   1 Samuel 24:1-10
W. Decide Responsibly.
   Esther 4:10-16
T. Live Peaceably.
   Romans 12:14-21
F. Be Self-Disciplined.
   1 Corinthians 9:19-27
S. Build Good Relationships.
   Ephesians 4:25-32

Make Right Choices

Study Text: Matthew 7:13, 14; 19:16-29; John 3:36; Hebrews 11:24-27; 2 Peter 1:10, 11

Objective: To see that many choices have temporal and eternal consequences and determine to make right choices.

Golden Text: "I have set before you life and death, blessing and cursing: therefore choose life" (Deuteronomy 30:19).

Central Truth: Accepting Christ as personal Savior and Lord is the most important choice we can make.

Evangelism Emphasis: Accepting Christ as personal Savior and Lord is the most important choice we can make.

PRINTED TEXT

Matthew 19:16. And, behold, one came and said unto him, Good Master, what good thing shall I do, that I may have eternal life?

17. And he said unto him, Why callest thou me good? there is none good but one, that is, God: but if thou wilt enter into life, keep the commandments.

18. He saith unto him, Which? Jesus said, Thou shalt do no murder, Thou shalt not commit adultery, Thou shalt not steal, Thou shalt not bear false witness,

19. Honour thy father and thy mother: and, Thou shalt love thy neighbour as thyself.

20. The young man saith unto him, All these things have I kept from my youth up: what lack I yet?

21. Jesus said unto him, If thou wilt be perfect, go and sell that thou hast, and give to the poor, and thou shalt have treasure in heaven: and come and follow me.

29. And every one that hath forsaken houses, or brethren, or sisters, or father, or mother, or wife, or children, or lands, for my name's sake, shall receive an hundredfold, and shall inherit everlasting life.

Hebrews 11:24. By faith Moses, when he was come to years, refused to be called the son of Pharaoh's daughter;

25. Choosing rather to suffer affliction with the people of God, than to enjoy the pleasures of sin for a season;

26. Esteeming the reproach of Christ greater riches than the treasures in Egypt: for he had respect unto the recompence of the reward.

27. By faith he forsook Egypt, not fearing the wrath of the king: for he endured, as seeing him who is invisible.

Matthew 7:13. Enter ye in at the strait gate: for wide is the gate, and broad is the way, that leadeth to destruction, and many there be which go in

thereat:

14. Because strait is the gate, and narrow is the way, which leadeth unto life, and few there be that find it.

John 3:36. He that believeth on the Son hath everlasting life: and he that believeth not the Son shall not see life; but the wrath of God abideth on him.

2 Peter 1:10. Wherefore the rather, brethren, give diligence to make your calling and election sure: for if ye do these things, ye shall never fall:

11. For so an entrance shall be ministered unto you abundantly into the everlasting kingdom of our Lord and Saviour Jesus Christ.

LESSON OUTLINE

I. CHOICES EARLY IN LIFE
   A. The Desire
   B. The Decision
   C. The Reward

II. CHOICES LATER IN LIFE
   A. The Refusal
   B. The Choice
   C. The Faith

III. CHOOSE ETERNAL LIFE
   A. The Difference
   B. The Judgment
   C. The Assurance

LESSON EXPOSITION

INTRODUCTION

What would it be like if we never had to wrestle with any major decisions?

When we are in the middle of wrestling with a choice which has significant impact, we may be tempted to wish that we didn't have to make decisions. However, when we're not in that setting, most of us realize the value of having to make choices. First, it reminds us that we aren't programmed robots simply doing what has been completely predetermined. Second, decision making allows us to mature as individuals and as believers in Christ. Third, we begin to understand the consequences of our actions. And fourth, this process provides us with the opportunity to express our love and dedication to God, family, and other believers.

Throughout life we constantly face the challenge of making right choices. Some of the issues we face will be repeated in more than one decade of our lives. Others are faced again and again due to our vocation or health. And of course, as believers we daily choose either to be an obedient child of God following the principles of the Word and lifestyle of Jesus or to be independent and follow our own desires regardless of the consequences.

These are some of the basic choices that we face: Who should I marry? What type of work do I want to do? Should we move to another part of the country and take a new job? Which doctor will be the best for a particular physical problem? Should a major purchase be made such as a home or business? The list could be expanded to include many other personal situations, but all would very likely be within the same basic areas.

Each of us face the challenge of making the right choices for us physically, emotionally, and economically. However, the greatest challenge is in our spiritual beings; for here we are making choices which affect us both now and for eternity.

Today's lesson provides us with two examples of individuals who were facing decisions: (1) The young man who came to Jesus and wanted eternal life. (2) Moses desired to identify with his own people, the Hebrews. Each of these individuals had different positions and very possibly were at a different age. But one thing remained constant for each: There was a price to be paid. And they had to decide if what they desired was worth the cost.

I. CHOICES EARLY IN LIFE
(Matthew 19:16-22, 27-29)

A. The Desire (vv. 16-20)

16. And, behold, one came and said unto him, Good Master, what good thing shall I do, that I may have eternal life?

17. And he said unto him, Why callest thou me good? there is none good but one, that is, God: but if thou wilt enter into life, keep the commandments.

18. He saith unto him, Which? Jesus said, Thou shalt do no murder, Thou shalt not commit adultery, Thou shalt not steal, Thou shalt not bear false witness,

19. Honour thy father and thy mother: and, Thou shalt love thy neighbour as thyself.

20. The young man saith unto him, All these things have I kept from my youth up: what lack I yet?

What a significant situation! An apparently wealthy young man was so concerned about his future spiritual life that he came inquiring of Jesus. This type of behavior usually doesn't just happen instantly upon thinking about one's death. More than likely it was a subject which had been on his mind until he chose to take some direct action.

His addressing Christ as "Good Master" (v. 16) expressed the belief that Jesus not only had the position of One who leads but also possessed the desired qualities. This young man went directly to the very best person he knew to seek help in his desire.

In verse 17 Jesus responded first to the adjective *good*. Maybe He detected a weakness in the young man's perceptions. Or it could have been that Christ wanted to draw primary attention to His Father in heaven. Whatever the situation, we cannot overlook the emphasis on our understanding of God's righteousness and holiness. As humans we cannot compare or measure up to Him. We may speak of good men and women, but this goodness is a reflection of the best in human nature and action as empowered through salvation, sanctification, and the baptism of the Holy Spirit.

Jesus answered by stating the need to keep the Commandments. Why didn't He talk about faith, love, and repentance? Aren't these part of the salvation that brings eternal life? Yes! They are! But here was one of those situations where the Lord knew the real issue which might hinder this man's spiritual desire. Instead of dealing with peripheral areas, He charted a course which would run straight toward any hindrances to this

[handwritten: WILLINGNESS TO DO WHAT-EVER THE CALL NOT ALWAYS BUT CALLED IF?]

man's receiving his desire for eternal life.

The young man's question, "Which?" immediately indicated both his desire and position. Jesus' reply in verse 18 included four of the Ten Commandments. He provided a breadth of actions which included the preservation of life, marriage, personal property, and truth. But Jesus didn't stop there. Beginning with verse 19, He included a fifth one—the only command with a promise. Jesus wanted this young man to also be concerned about parental relationships, with the promise of long life as well as spiritually living forever.

Jesus still didn't stop there. He included the horizontal relationship with the rest of the population. There is an outreach motivated by love which goes beyond just being polite and courteous. In a similar passage in Luke 10:25-37, Jesus illustrated this concept with the story of the Good Samaritan. *[handwritten: No CHG NEEDED]*

In response to Jesus' answer, the young man replied, "No problem" (in today's language). Jesus' directives did not complicate this man's desire or stretch him beyond what had already been happening. This had been his practice for years. So logically he asked if there was any other weakness that needed improvement. *[handwritten: NO PROBLEM BEEN DOING FROM MY YOUTH]*

B. The Decision (vv. 21, 22)

(Matthew 19:22 is not included in the printed text.)

21. Jesus said unto him, If thou wilt be perfect, go and sell that thou hast, and give to the poor, and thou shalt have treasure in heaven: and come and follow me.

Here's the *real test* of the young

man's desire to inherit eternal life. Would he give up earthly possessions for heavenly treasure? And even if God didn't want him to follow that path, would he be willing to do so if required?

The issue at hand centers on being willing to forsake all material benefits and security in order to gain entrance to eternal life. Jesus didn't offer him the option of selling everything and putting the proceeds in a secure setting to draw interest. Instead He asked for the proceeds to be given to the poor. He asked the young man to forsake everything and in faith follow Him.

Apparently this individual didn't take too long to make a decision. He desired eternal life, but he valued his possessions much more. With a heavy, sorrowing heart he forsook the desire for eternal life so he could retain the immediate, temporal treasures which could be lost or stolen. And to make matters even worse, those possessions would stay behind when he died (see Job 1:21). *[handwritten: FORSOOK LIFE FOR PLEASE]*

What are some dangers of depending too greatly on personal wealth?

C. The Reward (vv. 27-29)

(Matthew 19:27, 28 is not included in the printed text.)

29. And every one that hath forsaken houses, or brethren, or sisters, or father, or mother, or wife, or children, or lands, for my name's sake, shall receive an hundredfold, and shall inherit everlasting life.

After the rich young man left, Jesus commented on the difficulty that riches present for those who desire heaven. This caused considerable concern for the disciples as they began to wonder who could be saved. They were in total contrast to the individual who had just left. Nothing had been withheld in their choosing to follow Christ. So then the logical consideration which followed was the reward. What could they expect for such sacrificial service?

In verse 28 Jesus responded with a brief statement of their future glorification. In His coming kingdom they would be given positions of honor and leadership. The current sacrifice and commitment in this life would not go unnoticed in the future life.

Jesus expanded the consideration beyond the borders of the 12 disciples. He made application to all believers and recognized that they have given up wealth, possessions, and even family. It is interesting to note how specific Jesus was in listing the individual family members whose influence and wishes may have to be disregarded for the cause of Christ. He started with siblings. The peer pressure of brothers and sisters can be tremendous since they have been your partners in so many areas. Through conflict and controversy they have known the real you.

The influence of parents needs very little discussion. We understand how difficult it can be to go against the wishes of a father whom you are trying to live up to, as well as the love of a mother who has always been there and sacrificed for your benefit. Jesus then proceeded to one's spouse and children. Since Christ's audience was a group of men, He only indicated the wife; however, the principle applies both ways. Some women have had to put Christ before their husbands. And of course there is also the interests and wishes of one's children regardless of their age.

It is important to remember that Jesus wasn't advocating the neglect of one's family. He wasn't allowing for their abuse or being pushed aside without regard of responsibilities. But He does strongly remind us that to serve Christ we must put Him first. And when we do, there is the assurance of His favor and care in all areas of our life—including the needs of our extended family.

II. CHOICES LATER IN LIFE
    (Hebrews 11:24-27)

A. The Refusal (v. 24)

24. By faith Moses, when he was come to years, refused to be called the son of Pharaoh's daughter.

The story behind this single verse is recorded in Exodus 2:11-15. These few verses share a limited perspective, yet they enable us to gain a perspective of what was involved. Moses was approximately 40 years old. For over 30 years his world had been in the environment of Pharaoh's court. He enjoyed the best education available, along with the luxuries of the elite, and it would have been so easy just to settle in and enjoy life.

But he didn't. In spite of all the outward coverings of being the son of Pharaoh's daughter, he knew his true identity. He was the son of Amram and Jochebed. He was a Hebrew. He was the result of being providentially saved from Pharaoh's decree of destruction (Exodus 1:22).

We aren't told the process by which Moses came to asserting his original identity as a Hebrew. However, there came a time when a decision was necessary. Would he continue life as usual, or would he make a dramatic break with monumental ramifications? How God worked in his life we aren't told. But we do know that during his initial years he was raised by Jochebed and taught by his father (see Exodus 2:7-10). Surely this provided a lasting impact! Yet the bottom line is, Moses had to make the right choice.

B. The Choice (vv. 25, 26) *Youth and Sexual activity*

25. Choosing rather to suffer affliction with the people of God, than to enjoy the pleasures of sin for a season;

26. Esteeming the reproach of Christ greater riches than the treasures in Egypt: for he had respect unto the recompence of the reward.

On the exterior, leaving pleasure for persecution isn't the most desirable choice. Why trade the positive environment of wealth and position for the painful circumstances of an outcast people? It's one thing to restrict ourselves occasionally, but another to move from indulgence to abstinence!

Verse 25 broadens the perspective. It's much more than simply a matter of material possessions. It goes beyond the perks of position and power. Moses was facing the matters of the heart and spirituality which please God. He must choose between what is temporary and fleeting or what is permanent and enduring. Though Moses must have been living a life consistent with his Jewish upbringing, his presence in the palace is symbolic of dwelling in the camp of sin. In God's sovereign will, Moses' being in Pharaoh's household was a part of the plan. But there came a time when he had to make the difficult choice of identifying with his own people in word and action.

This verse also reminds us that sin can be fun. Rebellion against God and His pattern for living does have its moments of enjoyment. Immorality, drunkenness, and other forms of wild living can bring temporary pleasure. However, there comes a day of reckoning when one faces the physical, emotional, economic, and spiritual results of this fling with fun.

Moses' choosing to suffer with his people is symbolic of the choice which believers through the ages have encountered—choosing the scoffing, laughter, and abuse for Christ's sake or succumbing to the patterns and philosophies of country and cultures. Aiding in this choice is the understanding of the values. Looking ahead to the reward which awaits those who believe and are faithful definitely changes the perspective. Moses knew of the riches of Egypt and Pharaoh's court. But they were of lesser value than his reward of faithfully serving God and enduring affliction with God's people.

Our commitment and service to Christ needs to stem from our love relationship with Him. It should stand foremost as the reason for service and making hard choices. But at the same time there is that added incentive of God's future reward for faithful servants. As Jesus taught the multitude in the Sermon on the Mount, He encouraged them to store up treasures in heaven rather than on this earth (Matthew 6:19-21).

WITHOUT PROMISE OF GREATNESS

What are some of the rewards from serving Christ here on earth even though experiencing the world's abuse?

C. The Faith (v. 27)

27. By faith he forsook Egypt, not fearing the wrath of the king: for he endured, as seeing him who is invisible.

Reading the story of Moses indicates that his fleeing from Egypt for the land of Midian didn't begin at the moment when Pharaoh attempted to kill him. It had already been developing when he chose to kill the Egyptian who was beating one of the Hebrews (Exodus 2:11, 12). We aren't told the full set of circumstances which would necessitate such drastic action. However, this does cause us to assume that Moses had become willing to pay a huge price to identify with and protect his brethren.

This verse reminds us how faith enables us to make decisions that are not only difficult but may also appear irrational to others. Leaving the luxury and finery of Pharaoh's court for the simplicity of a nomadic tent is a major step down. Plus, leaving a position of power to become a desert sheepherder seems ludicrous. But not in the eyes of faith as they are focused on God. Faith enables the greatness of the invisible to become a reality which supersedes the visible means of possessions and prestige. Faith can be summarized as commitment, confidence, and concentrated trust. Commitment is the beginning aspect, confidence is the enabling aspect, and concentrated trust is the sustaining aspect of our

faith. (See book by same author, Jerald Daffe, *In the Face of Evil You Can Find Faith*, pp. 26, 27.)

One other item needs to be noted. At this point in his life, Moses had no idea of God's future plans for him. This further emphasized his step of faith. He didn't escape to Midian with the knowledge that 40 years from then he would be returning. He didn't leave as a fugitive with the assurance of returning with authority and power. Without any special promises for his economic and political future, Moses stepped boldly in faith and rejected all that Egypt stood for and promoted.

III. CHOOSE ETERNAL LIFE (Matthew 7:13, 14; John 3:36; 2 Peter 1:10, 11)

A. The Difference (Matthew 7:13, 14)

13. Enter ye in at the strait gate: for wide is the gate, and broad is the way, that leadeth to destruction, and many there be which go in thereat:

14. Because strait is the gate, and narrow is the way, which leadeth unto life, and few there be that find it.

This third section of the lesson provides us with the heart of the matter. There are many important choices in life, but none of greater significance than choosing eternal life. It definitely isn't the easiest choice, due to the effort which it entails. Yet, on the other hand, we understand that once we make the choice, God is desiring to work through us to complete what has been initiated. Paul stated it this way: "Being confident of this, that he who began a good work in you will carry it on to completion until the day of Christ Jesus" (Philippians 1:6, *NIV*).

In the Sermon on the Mount, Jesus pointed out very graphically the difference in lifestyle and effort which the choice of eternal life necessitates. The picture is that of two paths each leading to a particular gate. The logical conclusion is that each gate leads to a city.

Immediately Jesus directs us to enter the narrow gate rather than the wide gate. The wide gate with a broad road appears inviting because of the initial ease in traveling. There is little effort and stress incurred on this path. One's choices are open. There are no required guidelines or cautions. Just continue as you like. However, the end result is destruction. What appears so safe is in reality dangerous. Destruction is the inevitable end.

Many individuals make this selection. They like the thought of doing things their way and being free from any restraint. They enjoy devising their own rules and guidelines. They glory in being the master of their life. Hidden to them is their eventual fate. Self-indulgence blinds them to the spiritual destruction toward which they are headed.

In contrast is the narrow road and gate which leads to the city of life. The topography of the area would suggest a scene in which a narrow winding path reaches the city set on a hill or mountain side. The path is steep and demands effort on the part of those who desire to attain this goal. Those who want pleasure and ease will immediately reject it in favor of a much less strenuous effort. But in doing so they fail to receive the reward of

life eternal which comes to all who enter the narrow gate.

Multitudes seek the broad road. Its temporary enjoyment appears so appealing. Only a minority of people select the life of commitment and extra effort. The difference at the end of life coincides with their choice here on earth.

List some of the specific items which draw people to follow the broad path to destruction.

B. The Judgment (John 3:36)

36. He that believeth on the Son hath everlasting life: and he that believeth not the Son shall not see life; but the wrath of God abideth on him.

This third chapter of John repeatedly shares the contrast between life and death. Those who believe in Christ and accept Him as Savior will be the recipients of eternal life. Through God's love and the sacrificial death of Jesus, salvation is offered to all of humankind. There are no qualifying tests or set requirements that each must meet prior to being allowed this privilege of life in Christ. John 1:12 states it so simply: "But as many as received him, to them gave he power to become the sons of God, even to them that believe on his name."

There is another reality that goes along with it: Those who reject this divine plan of life are going to receive the wrath of God. This aspect of God's relationship with the human race is frequently overlooked. Others do their best attempting to say it isn't so. One of the most common approaches is to ask how a loving God of mercy could bring such judgment on His creations.

What these individuals have overlooked or refused to acknowledge are some of God's other attributes. His love must be seen in light of His holiness. God hates sin. Therefore, anyone who persists in following sin removes himself from the influence and pull of God's desire—which is salvation for all.

God's mercy must also be seen in the light of His justice. Since God is just, there comes a point in which He will demand that this justice be served. Sin has to be punished. Rejection of God and His principles will not be allowed without retribution.

David's sin with Bathsheba provides us with an excellent example. At first, his adulterous act passed with no statement from God. Uriah was allowed to die by the command of David. Still no response. Nearly a year passed and then God held David accountable by sending the prophet Nathan to confront him (see 2 Samuel 12).

We should all be reminded of that classic scripture in Hebrews: "It is appointed unto men once to die, but after this the judgment" (9:27).

C. The Assurance
   (2 Peter 1:10, 11)

10. Wherefore the rather, brethren, give diligence to make your calling and election sure: for if ye do these things, ye shall never fall:

11. For so an entrance shall be ministered unto you abundantly into the everlasting kingdom of our Lord and Saviour Jesus Christ.

Can you know for sure that your name is written in the Lamb's Book of Life? Can you know without a shadow of doubt that you are on your way to heaven?

Yes! Emphatically, yes.

The apostle Peter offers tremendous reassurance to all believers. We can know without reservation that we are in a right relationship with our heavenly Father and that He is eagerly awaiting us. This assurance comes by our adopting a lifestyle of attitudes and actions which are consistent with the divine nature and Christ's teaching. This lifestyle is totally different from a "works" salvation, which consists of doing certain deeds and then receiving merit points.

In verses 5-7, Peter provided a partial list of these attitude/action principles which are indicative of being in a right relationship with our Lord. As we continue to love God and strive for mastery of these qualities, we can rest assured of our future welcome in His eternal kingdom.

Knowing the tremendous gift of life eternal which is being offered should be a stimulus for us to attain the assurance God wants us to have! Isn't it wonderful to know that we don't have to fail! We don't have to live in uncertainty! We don't have to wake up each morning and wonder if we are ready to meet the Lord!

That's how the apostle Paul could make such a final testimony: "I have fought a good fight, I have finished my course, I have kept the faith" (2 Timothy 4:7).

REVIEW QUESTIONS

1. How was it possible for the wealth of a man to override his desire for eternal life?

Time may pass with no apparent cost but!!!!

2. What is the reward for those who put Christ first?

3. What enabled Moses to make the decision to forsake the life in Egypt and Pharaoh's court?

4. How different are the paths of life and destruction?

5. How can we have the assurance of eternal life?

GOLDEN TEXT HOMILY

"I HAVE SET BEFORE YOU LIFE AND DEATH, BLESSING AND CURSING: THEREFORE CHOOSE LIFE" (Deuteronomy 30:19).

The primary theme of Deuteronomy is the renewal of God's covenant with Israel. Originally given at Sinai, the covenant was now reviewed by Moses with a new generation who was about to enter and possess the land of Canaan.

They had spent 40 years wandering in the wilderness, due to the unbelief and disobedience of their parents, who had all died along the way. They had traveled a trail of tears, heartbreak, and death during the past 40 years, but now a new day had dawned.

It was a new generation who stood at the gates of the new land—ready to go in and possess it. But before they would do so, they needed to know and understand the conditions they must meet to be successful. These conditions were contained in God's law. If they chose to obey His law, blessings would be the result. If they refused to obey, dire consequences (curses) would be the result. In Deuteronomy 28 these blessings and curses are set forth in clear and unmistakable language. In verses 1-14 the blessings for obedience are described in four areas: (1) military success (v. 7); (2) agricultural suc-

cess (v. 11); (3) financial success (v. 12); and (4) national greatness (v. 13).

In verses 15-68 the curses for disobedience are described. These curses included Israel's being thrust out from the land and scattered among the heathen nations with a trembling heart, the failing of eyes, sorrow of mind, and even life itself hanging in the balance day after day.

Thus, Moses stood before this new generation of Israel and declared that the choice was theirs to make. If they desired to live, to be blessed, to prosper, to be successful, to be great, then they must obey God's law, and so it would be with them.

But Moses warned them to make no mistake about it: if they refused to do all that God's law required, then they must be prepared to suffer the terrible consequences that would surely follow.

God was saying, "My will is that you choose life that you and your children may live, but the choice is yours to make."—**Excerpts from** *The Evangelical Sunday School Lesson Commentary*, **Vol. 38**

SENTENCE SERMONS

ACCEPTING CHRIST as personal Savior and Lord is the most important choice we can make.

—Selected

THE DIFFICULTY in life is the choice.

—George Moore

THE CHOICES OF TIME are binding in eternity.

—Jack MacArthur

GOD REGENERATES us and puts us in contact with all His

divine resources, but He cannot make us walk according to His will.
—**Oswald Chambers**

EVANGELISM APPLICATION

ACCEPTING CHRIST AS PERSONAL SAVIOR AND LORD IS THE MOST IMPORTANT CHOICE WE CAN MAKE.

Every day each one of us makes a large number of choices. Many of them happen so readily throughout the course of our work and other related activities that we fail to recognize them as such. For many that first decision comes when the alarm rings. *Do I shut it off and get up? Or do I hit the snooze button? How about just shutting it off and rolling over for another 20 minutes of sleep?* Other choices include which clothes to wear, what to eat, when to go or come, and where to buy.

Occasionally our general choices take on greater significance when we forget to do something, or happen to do it incorrectly, and thus suffer the consequences. Forgetting to fill the car with gas and consequently running out during rush-hour traffic is one example.

Other actions have greater importance because our choices impact to a greater degree and include longer consequences. The most important of these is our decision about Christ. For when we choose to recognize our sinfulness, repent before Christ, and ask Him to cleanse us and restore us to right fellowship, we inherit everlasting life in heaven. As we yield ourselves to Him as our Lord, He provides direction which will enable us to enjoy peace, joy, and fulfillment.

ILLUMINATING THE LESSON

Before the days of health clubs and specialized weight rooms, a college football player decided to spend the summer working on a farm. The strenuous work would be a great way to strengthen his muscles and build up endurance for the fall season.

After a number of intense workouts the farmer decided to give him an easier day. He was sent to the potato-seed barn with directions to sort them into three sizes—small, medium, and large.

Several hours passed before the farmer went to check on how the work was coming. Much to his surprise he saw the young man sitting on the floor surrounded by potatoes but with little done. His perplexed look suggested all wasn't well. Quickly in defense of his lack of accomplishment, the young man offered, "Sir, I can do hard work. But these decisions are killing me."

DAILY BIBLE READINGS

M. Serve God. Joshua 24:14-21
T. Ask for Understanding.
1 Kings 3:5-12
W. Seek Wisdom. Proverbs 2:1-11
T. Choose to Follow Christ.
Luke 9:57-62
F. Abstain From Sin.
1 Corinthians 10:7-13
S. Do Good.
1 Thessalonians 5:14-24

Accept Life's Responsibilities

Study Text: Genesis 18:17-19; Matthew 5:14-16; Romans 12:17, 18; Ephesians 6:4; Colossians 3:18, 19; 1 Thessalonians 4:11, 12; 2 Thessalonians 3:7-12; 1 Timothy 5:8; 1 Peter 2:11-15

Objective: To acknowledge the responsibilities that come with living and resolve to faithfully fulfill every obligation.

Golden Text: "Unto whomsoever much is given, of him shall be much required" (Luke 12:48).

Central Truth: God's Word commands us to live responsibly.

Evangelism Emphasis: Christians should demonstrate to the world that living for Christ is both responsible and wholesome.

PRINTED TEXT

1 Thessalonians 4:11. And that ye study to be quiet, and to do your own business, and to work with your own hands, as we commanded you;

12. That ye may walk honestly toward them that are without, and that ye may have lack of nothing.

2 Thessalonians 3:10. For even when we were with you, this we commanded you, that if any would not work, neither should he eat.

11. For we hear that there are some which walk among you disorderly, working not at all, but are busybodies.

12. Now them that are such we command and exhort by our Lord Jesus Christ, that with quietness they work, and eat their own bread.

Genesis 18:19. For I know him, that he will command his children and his household after him, and they shall keep the way of the Lord, to do justice and judgment; that the Lord may bring upon Abraham that which he hath spoken of him.

Colossians 3:18. Wives, submit yourselves unto your own husbands, as it is fit in the Lord.

19. Husbands, love your wives, and be not bitter against them.

Ephesians 6:4. And, ye fathers, provoke not your children to wrath: but bring them up in the nurture and admonition of the Lord.

1 Timothy 5:8. But if any provide not for his own, and specially for those of his own house, he hath denied the faith, and is worse than an infidel.

Matthew 5:14. Ye are the light of the world. A city that is set on a hill cannot be hid.

15. Neither do men light a candle, and put it under a bushel, but on a candlestick; and it giveth light unto all that are in the house.

16. Let your light so shine before men, that they may see your good works, and glorify

your Father which is in heaven.

Romans 12:17. Recompense to no man evil for evil. Provide things honest in the sight of all men.

18. If it be possible, as much as lieth in you, live peaceably with all men.

1 Peter 2:11. Dearly beloved, I beseech you as strangers and pilgrims, abstain from fleshly lusts, which war against the soul;

12. Having your conversation honest among the Gentiles: that, whereas they speak against you as evildoers, they may by your good works, which they shall behold, glorify God in the day of visitation.

15. For so is the will of God, that with well doing ye may put to silence the ignorance of foolish men.

LESSON OUTLINE

I. WORK
    A. The Ambition
    B. The Example
    C. The Role

II. FAMILY
    A. Father's Leadership
    B. Marital Relationship
    C. Extended Responsibility

III. CITIZENSHIP
    A. Witness
    B. Peace
    C. Submission

LESSON EXPOSITION

INTRODUCTION

Have you ever heard someone say, "Life's not all fun and games"? It's a simple way to convey several different concepts. When said to younger individuals, it is supposed to be a kind way of saying "grow up and take responsibility." To others, it is a reminder that certain areas of our lives demand and stretch us as we attempt to fulfill the requirements.

Today's lesson centers on three of those responsibilities—work, family, and citizenship. Responsible Christian living in any century and in any culture includes our following the Biblical directives for each area. In much the same way, God prescribed guidelines for His people, Israel. He has given us principles for living today. Failure to obey them not only places us in rebellion against God but also keeps us from experiencing the totality of what God has planned for us as individuals, as families, and as countries or nations.

There is another dimension which deserves our consideration. We are to be witnesses of our heavenly Father. We are to be the salt and the light of this world. In the darkness of sin, which seeks something for nothing and greedily accumulates for personal gain, we are to demonstrate honesty and to put forth an effort to earn what we possess. Our purpose isn't to make others feel inferior but to enlighten them by example as to what God expects. In the blandness of a world which simply recycles its own ineffective ideas century after century, God continues to offer a freshness which totally changes life. And we are to be the salt that provides that freshness. However, salt can't act unless it is allowed out of the saltshaker.

Our lesson today takes us into nine different books of the Bible. Most of the references are from the writings of the apostle Paul. One is from the Old Testament. Woven together they provide a picture of what God expects of us in the areas of our family, our work, and our civic responsibilities.

There is no doubt that some believers will find the requirements in one area easier than in another. Some of that is because of the guidance we received from our families when we were children. Not to be forgotten are our individual personalities, which also effect our initial success in given areas. Other factors are those habits we fall into without realizing how deeply they have become engrained. However, regardless of the ease or difficulty we may experience in any of these areas, all of them are ours to fulfill!

I. WORK (1 Thessalonians 4:11, 12; 2 Thessalonians 3:7-12)

A. The Ambition (1 Thessalonians 4:11, 12)

11. And that ye study to be quiet, and to do your own business, and to work with your own hands, as we commanded you;

12. That ye may walk honestly toward them that are without, and that ye may have lack of nothing.

This fourth chapter of Paul's first epistle to the Thessalonians begins with a section on living to please God. He begins with some direc-tives on holiness and human sexuality. Following are some verses on brotherly love. He then completes the section with these two verses on work.

Verse 11 begins with an admonition concerning a general attitude. It appears that this congregation may have been the source of some stir or unsettling among nearby churches. This may have come from their belief in the nearness of Christ's return. But regardless of the situation, Paul admonishes them to follow a different path. Instead of being instigators of strife and interference, they are to seek after their own affairs and well-being. It is easy to become so involved in the activities of someone else's household and belief structure that we neglect the important actions which should be evident in our lives.

One modern translation states the first part of this verse as follows: "Make it your ambition to lead a quiet life, to mind your own business . . ." (*NIV*). That states it very clearly!

The second part of verse 11 addresses the issue of working. Apparently, this wasn't a new topic for their discussion. More than likely the basic issues of the dignity of work and the need to responsibly provide for one's family would have been included in this discussion. Verse 12 adds the dimension of witnessing to unbelievers. Believers need to be respected for their work ethics and for caring for their family needs. They shouldn't be known for their dependence on others or for simply sitting around waiting for divine miracles of provision. Remember, God sent manna from heaven for the children of Israel only when no other source of food was available. Once they were in the Promised Land and a food source was at hand, the manna no longer came.

Paul's meaning is very clear. God's children shouldn't be known for their laziness and dependence. In fact, just the opposite should be true. Industriousness and helping the needy are to be our distinctives. These definitely fall under the category of loving one another.

Working to provide for oneself and the members of one's family isn't an option which can be accepted or rejected, but should be seen as the goal and obligation of every believer.

B. The Example (2 Thessalonians 3:7-9)

(2 Thessalonians 3:7-9 is not included in the printed text.)

One of the outstanding characteristics of the apostle Paul is that he never asked people to do what he hadn't already done as an example. It's easy to call people to accountability when you have already modeled for them the path they are to follow. Without going into any detail, he reminds them in verse 7 that he worked while ministering to them. His stay in Thessalonica had been very brief, but he didn't freeload or expect charity though he certainly deserved their care and provision. In verse 9 the reason is given. He wanted to provide a model for them. Having done so, he could now call them to accept responsibility in the same manner.

Verse 8 demonstrates the extent to which Paul had gone to provide an example. He personally paid for all of his own food. He worked long hours in order to be able to support himself and to minister. This is not unlike many ministers and their wives who through the years have worked days so they could preach the gospel at night and on Sunday. Not to be forgotten are the many men and women who are still doing this around the world.

The type of work Paul did isn't stated. However, we know from Acts 18:3 that he was a tentmaker and supported himself in ministry at Corinth through this vocation. All Jewish boys were taught a trade. Failure for a parent to train his son was considered the same as making him a thief.

In view of Paul's example, how do we also know it is correct to pay a pastor a regular salary?

C. The Rule (vv. 10-12)

10. For even when we were with you, this we commanded you, that if any would not work, neither should he eat.

11. For we hear that there are some which walk among you disorderly, working not at all, but are busybodies.

12. Now them that are such we command and exhort by our Lord Jesus Christ, that with quietness they work, and eat their own bread.

Paul here shares the requirement of work which all Christians are to follow. This is the nitty-gritty—where the rubber really meets the road. The bottom line is simply this: If you choose not to work, then you choose not to eat. No one is obligated to provide for the person who willfully chooses to be idle. No one has the right to eat when he purposefully chooses not to work at an available job! That's pretty straight talk. But remember the apostle is writing this under the inspiration of the Holy Spirit. Thus it is applicable to all of us, even at the end of the 20th century.

This rule of working to eat was not new to the Thessalonian believers. Verse 10 indicates that Paul shared it with them previously. However, it was necessary to emphatically bring it to their attention again due to the particular problem evident in their fellowship or church body. Some believers had stopped working altogether. Not only were they idle, but they interfered and caused difficulty in the lives of other believers. This sounds very similar to the verses shared in the first epistle.

Many Bible commentators believe the reason for this idleness stemmed from the Thessalonians' belief in Christ's imminent return. Apparently, they felt no need or motivation to work if the Lord was coming. Why spend time on such unspiritual activity as work, when they could instead be more heavenly minded? But that's where the apostle draws them up short. Instead of seeing them as spiritually-minded individuals seeking the better things, he indicates that they are disorderly. They aren't following the pattern of life in the Spirit, but in reality are leaning toward the works of the flesh.

This is another classic example of individuals trying to be so heavenly minded that they neglect God's Word and His principles while living on earth. There must be a balance! One cannot be neglected in favor of the other.

The situation which Paul de-scribes in the Thessalonian church isn't an isolated one. It is repeated in various centuries. One which comes to mind took place in the early 1970s in the state of Ohio. A small group of families became convinced the Lord was coming shortly. So they all quit their jobs and waited. Initially, they lived off their savings. When that source was exhausted, several of their homes were repossessed by the banks. Eventually they all ended up living in one house. The end of the story was never publicized, but the incident demonstrates how others have failed to follow the rule of working to eat even while waiting.

With firmness and authority based in Jesus Christ, Paul directs these individuals to do three things. First, they are to return to work. Second, they are to eat their own bread purchased with their own earnings. Third, they are to stop their pattern of disorderliness within the body (the church).

It seems only logical that this verse has broader application than to those who stop working to wait for the Lord. It applies to anyone who chooses not to work for any reason when a job, no matter how menial, is available. In God's sight, scrubbing floors or flipping burgers is far more acceptable than idleness.

II. FAMILY (Genesis 18:19; Colossians 3:18, 19; Ephesians 6:4; 1 Timothy 5:8)

A. Father's Leadership (Genesis 18:19; Ephesians 6:4)

Genesis 18:19. For I know him, that he will command his children and his household after him, and they shall keep the way

of the Lord, to do justice and judgment; that the Lord may bring upon Abraham that which he hath spoken of him.

Ephesians 6:4. And, ye fathers, provoke not your children to wrath: but bring them up in the nurture and admonition of the Lord.

This section on family begins with a specific emphasis on the role of the father. It points out the need for his leadership in spiritual matters and then follows with an admonition concerning personal relationships.

Genesis 18:19 is taken from the account of the three heavenly visitors coming to announce the birth of a son to Abraham and Sarah. As they begin to leave, Abraham walks with them in the direction of Sodom. At that point, God questions whether or not He should reveal His intentions toward Sodom and Gomorrah. God isn't obligated to explain but He reflects on the stature and future of this chosen man.

In verse 18, God reveals the future. The descendants of Abraham will become a powerful nation. Of even greater importance is the blessing for all nations which will come through Israel. This, of course, refers to the Messiah who will bring salvation to all who will believe.

It is at that point that God indicates the special role of Abraham. God will make the miraculous birth of a son possible. Then it will be Abraham's responsibility to mold and guide this child so God's promises can be fulfilled. Here we see that human involvement needs to accompany divine provision.

The thoughts given in verse 19

go beyond what is seen in Oriental culture to be the responsibilities of the patriarch of the family. Here is explained the responsibility of all men of every century in every culture to be spiritual leaders. Instruction in the way of the Lord is the father's or husband's duty. He is to take the lead in making sure the children and other members of his household receive training in the principles of Scripture and in Christian discipleship.

This training has to supply more than head knowledge. It must include encouragement to obey the truths which have been taught. Such encouragement may take the forms of personal example, family togetherness and, on occasion, even discipline.

The way of the Lord is not reflected in just any lifestyle. Rather, a godly lifestyle must be founded in justice and judgment. Only doing and saying what is right and just can qualify. This is true not only for the children and other members of the household, but it also applies to the father as well. That is why the verse from Ephesians 6 fits here so well.

Parents, but specifically fathers, have an obligation to be sensitive to their children as they lead them in the way of the Lord. The harshness of a father can be just as devastating to a family as the sins of the children. A balance must exist. The father's discipline and spiritual leadership must be bathed in love and understanding. Otherwise, the child or children may become so frustrated that in rebellion they choose the way of sin.

Training children and instructing them in the way of the Lord is not synonymous with teaching them a handbook of rules. You can have so many "thou shalt nots" surrounding a child that it becomes impossible for them to keep the major principles which God has declared. This form of legalism can be destructive. It destroys the very result one is trying to gain.

There are other ways fathers can provoke their children. Besides harshness and legalism, we must include partiality. Appearing to favor one child over the other not only separates child from parent, but also creates barriers between siblings.

B. Marital Relationship
   (Colossians 3:18, 19)

18. Wives, submit yourselves unto your own husbands, as it is fit in the Lord.

19. Husbands, love your wives, and be not bitter against them.

Another aspect of accepting life's responsibilities is to fulfill our roles in the marital relationship. Both the husband and the wife have specific actions which God requires of them.

Paul's directives in these two verses are also found in Ephesians 5. There he provides further expansion, but the concept remains the same.

The issue of submission creates some difficulty for those who do not understand the total overview. A wife's submission to her husband isn't due to any supposed inferiority or superiority. It isn't a sign of weakness, inability, defeat, or cowardliness! This submission doesn't even address the quality of man her husband is. It doesn't have anything to do with his sensitivity, abilities, character, or strength!

A wife's submission to her hus-band in marriage is first and foremost an act of obedience toward the Lord—a recognition of God's having ordained a divine order of headship. Thus her submission is based on love and service to God. This submission is one of function only and does not imply that they're unequal. There is still equality of essence. The bottom line is this—second in authority, but not second best.

This concept is described so well in 1 Peter 3:5, 6. In these verses Sarah and other holy women of the past are described as adorning themselves with submission. Sarah had physical beauty (Genesis 12:11-15), but her submission to her husband, Abraham, provided inner spiritual beauty.

Paul follows the directive of submission with a directive for husbands to love their wives. This isn't a suggestion or an option. This love isn't to be based on her appearance, qualities, or abilities. This love is to be a part of the husband's attitude toward his wife as a result of entering into the sacred covenant of marriage.

We know from Ephesians 5 that this love is to be patterned after Christ's love for the church (vv. 25-27), after the husband's care for his own body (vv. 28, 29), and after the husband's self love (v. 33). Studying these three dimensions indicates that this love is to be filled with words of endearment and actions of care. Anyone who truly loves in this manner would never stoop to actions of harshness or neglect.

The apostle reminds husbands in verse 19 that the love relationship in a marriage is the obligation or responsibility of the man. He is responsible for maintaining and growing this special relationship between husband and wife.

By the way, there is one observation which needs to be included. It's not difficult for the wife to submit to her husband when he really loves her as Christ does His bride, the church!

What are some contemporary views which hinder compliance with the Biblical directives of submission and love?

C. Extended Responsibility
   (1 Timothy 5:8)

8. But if any provide not for his own, and specially for those of his own house, he hath denied the faith, and is worse than an infidel.

Here we find some strong words! They must be seen in the context of the previous seven verses which deal with treatment of the older members of the congregation and of one's own family. Verse 4 needs special consideration. Here children and grandchildren are reminded of their responsibility to care for the elderly and widowed in their families.

In pagan culture families cared for their parents and grandparents. So if believers failed to do the very same, they would be in total disregard of divine commands as well as cultural standards. Honoring father and mother includes caring for their physical and economic needs personally rather than allowing a charitable or state organization to bear the responsibility.

This verse provides one of the strongest statements on the obligation of children to parents. It

implies that failure in this area is a sin equal to many of those which we usually list as the works of the flesh (Galatians 5:19-21). How can anyone claim to have the love of God dwelling within unless this love responds in ministry to the needs of his own parents? Paul declares very strongly that this claim must be seen as bogus or counterfeit when it does not.

Our current dependence on government support of the elderly allows many believers and the church in general to disregard this passage of Scripture. There's no doubt that our pattern of both husband and wife working makes it more difficult to fulfill some of the obligations; however, we need to take extreme care not to disregard the many areas of support which can be given to parents—physical, economic, and emotional.

III. CITIZENSHIP (Matthew 5:14-16; Romans 12:17, 18; 1 Peter 2:11-15)

A. Witness (Matthew 5:14-16)

14. Ye are the light of the world. A city that is set on a hill cannot be hid.

15. Neither do men light a candle, and put it under a bushel, but on a candlestick; and it giveth light unto all that are in the house.

16. Let your light so shine before men, that they may see your good works, and glorify your Father which is in heaven.

Our usual discussions on the Biblical view of citizenship do not begin with passages from the Sermon on the Mount. The normal pattern is to discuss paying our taxes, praying for the king or other leaders, and then to move on to submission. However, these three verses from Matthew 5 provide a foundation from which to launch a consideration of the believer's responsibilities in the area of citizenship.

Once again, believers are reminded of our position in a world of spiritual darkness. There is no light but ours. Our own spiritual darkness has been replaced by the light of Jesus Christ. We are to shine forth just like a city which is built on a hillside or better yet on the hilltop. At night the rays of its light can be seen for miles by those in valleys or on distant hillsides.

Verse 15 reminds us that candles aren't lit for the purpose of being covered and hidden from everyone's view. Instead, a candle, once lit, is placed on a candlestick, thus enabling its rays to spread outward and dispel as much darkness as possible. By doing this, all corners of the room or house benefit. Likewise, we haven't received the light of Jesus Christ just to hide in our own hearts. It must shine outward, helping those in darkness around us.

One aspect of letting our light shine is through doing good works. What we claim in words to be our experience should be transmitted into deeds which honor God. It isn't sufficient to pray that the hungry be fed. We must put legs to our prayers. There is no need to pray for God's intervention through a divine miracle when we have the means to supply someone's need. Why pray for manna when there is money in your pocket to buy the needed bread? Such visible needs being met by the actions of God's people brings glory to Him.

Furthermore, this concept applies to citizenship. If believers aren't active in civic affairs, how can the light of Christ shine forth? If believers don't run for office or vote, how can people of principle and Biblical belief be placed in office and make a difference? Of course this doesn't mean our churches are to become centers for political action. This would distort the purpose of the church. But there is no excuse for our not being in the forefront of determining local, state, and national policies.

B. Peace (Romans 12:17, 18)

17. Recompense to no man evil for evil. Provide things honest in the sight of all men.

18. If it be possible, as much as lieth in you, live peaceably with all men.

Here are some interesting challenges. The first is to refrain from retaliation. When angry or hurt, the old sinful nature so easily arises. It says, "Treat them just like you are being treated!" But that's not the way of Christ, and it definitely doesn't contribute to peace. In the Sermon on the Mount, Jesus teaches us to turn the other cheek, go two miles instead of one, and pray for those who persecute us (Matthew 5:38-48).

The second challenge is one of honest dealings. Believers are to be known for their honesty in business affairs. This includes paying a fair wage for a day's work, using quality materials and providing good workmanship for quality prices, and keeping your word even without a signed, notarized document! Honesty includes paying your bills. And during difficult economic times, it means going to your creditors, explaining your situation and paying a little, even if it isn't much.

It's amazing how much good can come from difficult situations, if the believer will be honest.

Then there's the third challenge to live peaceably (v. 18). This verse allows for the fact that some individuals make peace impossible; however, that impasse must be the result of their unreasonableness and desire for conflict. And we all know that there are such people! Some are our neighbors. Others are from groups who are in conflict with our Christian beliefs and lifestyle. These individuals make peace difficult and at times impossible, but we don't have the option of not trying.

Not to be forgotten is the beatitude, "Blessed are the peacemakers: for they shall be called the children of God" (Matthew 5:9).

How can Christians maintain peace while battling issues of morality which are contrary to Scripture?

C. Submission (1 Peter 2:11-15)

(1 Peter 2:13, 14 is not included in the printed text.)

11. Dearly beloved, I beseech you as strangers and pilgrims, abstain from fleshly lusts, which war against the soul;

12. Having your conversation honest among the Gentiles: that, whereas they speak against you as evildoers, they may by your good works, which they shall behold, glorify God in the day of visitation.

15. For so is the will of God, that with well doing ye may put to silence the ignorance of foolish men.

We begin this brief look at sub-

mission with an interesting view of our citizenship. Though our physical bodies are registered citizens of a country in this world, our spiritual beings are citizens of heaven. This provides us with two sets of responsibilities. We have the obligation to obey the laws and fulfill the responsibilities of earthly citizenship as long as they are not in conflict with our heavenly citizenship. Thus, any desires of the flesh which are either immoral or unlawful need to be pushed aside from our lifestyle. Those temptations need to be overcome through walking in the Holy Spirit.

As a result, our lifestyle (words, deeds, and attitudes) need to be of such Christian character that the world cannot realistically speak evil of us. And, once again, we see in verse 12 that by living in this manner we witness of Christ. We thus provide the opportunity for God to be glorified by our total being.

Part of such a lifestyle includes submission to political authorities. Verse 13 emphasizes the truth that authority is instituted by God. We are to honor and to abide by it where possible. It is true that some authorities misuse their power. Other individuals in leadership may be dominated by sinful thoughts and actions. But that doesn't give us the right to stop paying our taxes or respecting their office. At times it is hard to do! But God expects us as Christians to be good citizens and, in so doing, to convince unbelievers of the truth behind the consistency of our lives.

Special attention needs to be given to the setting of verse 15. It's God's will for us to live in such a manner as part of fulfilling the requirements of both our earthly and heavenly citizenship.

REVIEW QUESTIONS

1. How did the apostle Paul provide an example of the dignity of work?

2. What are the obligations each father is to fulfill as the leader of his family?

3. How is the believer to be a light to the world?

GOLDEN TEXT HOMILY

"UNTO WHOMSOEVER MUCH IS GIVEN, OF HIM SHALL BE MUCH REQUIRED" (Luke 12:48).

All that we are and all that we will ever be is a gift of God. The air we breathe, the food we eat, the clothes we wear are all provided by the hand of God. But even greater than the material gifts are the spiritual provisions. For He has provided grace, redemption, forgiveness, righteousness, eternal life, and the presence of the Holy Spirit. Truly we are a blessed people, for God has given us the opportunity to share in the abundance of His blessings.

Now the decision that mankind is faced with is, "How will I react to God's goodness to me?" Shall I serve, worship, and commit my life to Him, or will I only bless myself and feel I am my own provider? If we live a life committed to God, then we are living in accordance with His Word. To reject Him and live only for ourselves is the height of idolatry. Such a life results in worshiping the creature rather than the Creator (Romans 1:25).

The Bible teaches that when God created mankind, He placed a high calling for his life. Our highest purpose in life is to bring honor and glory to God our Creator. Man's dilemma on earth can be traced to the fact that he has failed in the primary purpose for which he was created. For it is God's purpose that we should use our talents, our faith, our worship, and our possessions to teach His Word to all nations. As a result God is glorified and many will come to the saving knowledge of Jesus Christ.

Truly we have received the abundance of God's blessings. But there also comes a responsibility: "Freely ye have received, freely give" (Matthew 10:8). Therefore all that God asks us to share with others is what He has already given to us. Romans 12:1 summarizes for us our responsibility to God: "Present your bodies a living sacrifice, holy, acceptable unto God, which is your reasonable service."—**Jerry Puckett, Customer Service Representative, Pathway Press, Cleveland, Tennessee**

SENTENCE SERMONS

GOD'S WORD commands us to live responsibly.

—Selected

NOT EVERYONE who seeks a job is looking for work; not everyone who wants a promotion is looking for more responsibility.

—Quotable Quotations

DAILY BIBLE READINGS

M. Work, a Gift of God.
   Genesis 2:8-15
T. Consecrate Your Family to God.
   Job 1:1-5
W. Conscientious Citizenship.
   Jeremiah 26:10-16
T. Responsibilities of Citizenship.
   Mark 12:13-17
F. Lead Your Family to Christ.
   Acts 16:25-34
S. Exemplary Worker.
   Acts 20:32-38

Avoid Hazards Along the Way

Study Text: Psalm 51:1-4; Ecclesiastes 2:15-17; Luke 22:31, 32; Galatians 6:7-9; 1 Thessalonians 4:3-7; Hebrews 3:12-14

Objective: To recognize and avoid the pitfalls that threaten our spiritual well-being.

Golden Text: "Enter not into the path of the wicked, and go not in the way of evil men" (Proverbs 4:14).

Central Truth: Spiritual alertness and determination are essential for right living.

Evangelism Emphasis: Perseverance in right living is essential to the Christian's witness.

PRINTED TEXT

Luke 22:31. And the Lord said, Simon, Simon, behold, Satan hath desired to have you, that he may sift you as wheat:

32. But I have prayed for thee, that thy faith fail not: and when thou art converted, strengthen thy brethren.

Hebrews 3:12. Take heed, brethren, lest there be in any of you an evil heart of unbelief, in departing from the living God.

13. But exhort one another daily, while it is called To day; lest any of you be hardened through the deceitfulness of sin.

14. For we are made partakers of Christ, if we hold the beginning of our confidence steadfast unto the end.

Ecclesiastes 2:15. Then said I in my heart, As it happeneth to the fool, so it happeneth even to me; and why was I then more wise? Then I said in my heart, that this also is vanity.

16. For there is no remembrance of the wise more than of the fool for ever; seeing that which now is in the days to come shall all be forgotten. And how dieth the wise man? as the fool.

17. Therefore I hated life; because the work that is wrought under the sun is grievous unto me: for all is vanity and vexation of spirit.

Galatians 6:7. Be not deceived; God is not mocked: for whatsoever a man soweth, that shall he also reap.

8. For he that soweth to his flesh shall of the flesh reap corruption; but he that soweth to the Spirit shall of the Spirit reap life everlasting.

9. And let us not be weary in well doing: for in due season we shall reap, if we faint not.

Psalm 51:1. Have mercy upon me, O God, according to thy lovingkindness: according unto the multitude of thy tender mercies blot out my transgressions.

2. Wash me throughly from mine iniquity, and cleanse me

from my sin.

3. For I acknowledge my transgressions: and my sin is ever before me.

4. Against thee, thee only, have I sinned, and done this evil in thy sight: that thou mightest be justified when thou speakest, and be clear when thou judgest.

1 Thessalonians 4:3. For this is the will of God, even your sanctification, that ye should abstain from fornication:

4. That every one of you should know how to possess his vessel in sanctification and honour;

7. For God hath not called us unto uncleanness, but unto holiness.

LESSON OUTLINE

I. KEEP FAITH
   A. Understand Satan's Sifting
   B. Encourage One Another

II. KEEP PURPOSE
   A. Avoid Foolishness
   B. Avoid Deception
   C. Avoid Weariness

III. KEEP VIRTUE
   A. Seek Forgiveness
   B. Follow Holiness

LESSON EXPOSITION

INTRODUCTION

No desirable path in life is without its hazards. The same holds true for our life in Christ. Our path to life eternal is strewed with many hazards intended not only to hinder but also to destroy. Not to be forgotten is that Satan is much more than a speed bump in the road of life. He is our adversary and desires not only to cause us to be ineffective but also to completely annihilate our relationship as blood-bought children of God.

There are several verses of Scripture which need to serve as a foundation for this lesson. First, from the writings of the apostle Peter: "Be sober, be vigilant; because your adversary the devil, as a roaring lion, walketh about, seeking whom he may devour" (1 Peter 5:8). And then from Paul's letter to the Galatians: "Ye did run well; who did hinder you that ye should not obey the truth?" (5:7).

Believers must recognize the hazards we face. It is equally vital that we be knowledgeable of how they can be overcome. We can live victoriously in Christ Jesus! We can be successful by walking in the power of the Holy Spirit! But it takes effort on our part.

Today's lesson provides us with three major areas for consideration. By carefully keeping our focus on each of them we can be successful in avoiding some of the basic hazards which every believer will face. Our study will emphasize keeping faith, purpose, and virtue.

The passages of Scripture for our consideration include writings from both the Old and New Testaments. This balance enables us to understand that the temptations and suggested detours of the Christian's life today are no different than those faced by individuals of centuries and even millennia ago.

It would seem extremely

beneficial for us to have one example to keep in mind. The life of Joseph demonstrates the concepts to be covered. For more than a decade he faced major hazards. Yet, every time he clung to what was right, avoided sin, and allowed God's will to be performed in his life.

Let's do a quick review. First, Joseph didn't allow his brothers hatred for him and their horrendous treatment of him to foster bitterness. After their father's death, the brothers worried about possible retribution. But Joseph assured them that there was no such plan in his heart. Second, he didn't allow the repeated sexual temptations by his master's wife to blind him to truth and virtue. He understood what was his to enjoy and what was to be shunned, even though he was falsely accused of raping her. Third, he didn't allow his imprisonment to dim or weaken his commitment to God. He continued to trust in the Lord and to be a vessel ready for service.

With the foundational verses and Joseph's example in mind, let's avoid the hazards which present themselves as problems to the believer in Christ.

I. KEEP FAITH (Luke 22:31, 32; Hebrews 3:12-14)

A. Understand Satan's Sifting (Luke 22:31, 32)

31. And the Lord said, Simon, Simon, behold, Satan hath desired to have you, that he may sift you as wheat:

32. But I have prayed for thee, that thy faith fail not: and when thou art converted, strengthen thy brethren.

Isn't it amazing that believers can become so carnal such a short time after a monumental spiritual experience? After having shared in the Last Supper and participated in Christ's institution of Communion, the disciples found themselves in another dispute. It's a very familiar topic—who among them will be greatest? Since this isn't the first occurrence of this discussion, it may be considered a sequel to the previous ones (see Luke 9:46). Other records of this strife are found in Matthew 18:1; 20:23; and Mark 9:34; 10:37.)

It's very possible that Jesus' own words about the kingdom may have spurred their thoughts about greatness. When presenting the Communion cup he said, "I will not drink of the fruit of the vine, until the kingdom of God shall come" (Luke 22:18). And just prior to that He had referred to the Passover meal by saying, "I will not any more eat thereof, until it be fulfilled in the kingdom of God" (v. 16).

In verses 25 through 30, Jesus addresses their discussion. Instead of rebuking them for their less than spiritual behavior, Jesus chooses to teach them about greatness and their future in the kingdom. And then He singles out Peter. There is no other hint that this aggressive disciple had been more adamant in the discussion than any of the others. However, in view of his outgoing personality and readiness to speak, it wouldn't be surprising if he had!

The Lord addresses Simon Peter by calling his name twice. This emphasizes the significance of what he is about to say as well as the importance of the events of the next few hours. It may also be evidence of the sadness Christ must feel as

He looks toward the events of the next 24 hours. There are some similarities here to Christ's addressing Martha by calling her name twice (see Luke 10:41).

Jesus knows how Satan desires to cause Peter to turn away from Christ (22:31, 32). He also knows this man's potential for God's kingdom. He uses the work at a threshing floor to illustrate what is going to happen to Peter in the spiritual realm. Harvested grain would be placed on the threshing floor, where oxen would walk on it, thus shelling the kernels from the stalks. After this is completed a large fan would blow the chaff and straw to the sides, away from the grain. This waste was collected and burned. Finally the grain kernels would remain alone in the middle of the floor and could easily be scooped up and stored.

Though Jesus specifically addresses Peter, His words are directed to all of the disciples. The pronoun, "you," is plural and thus includes all of them. Peter isn't the only target of Satan's devices. Knowing that, Jesus informs them that He has been praying for them so they will not fail spiritually when confronted by temptation and oppression.

This holds true for each believer today. We too are Christ's disciples and the target of Satan's attacks.

B. Encourage One Another
   (Hebrews 3:12-14)

12. Take heed, brethren, lest there be in any of you an evil heart of unbelief, in departing from the living God.

13. But exhort one another daily, while it is called To day; lest any of you be hardened

through the deceitfulness of sin.

14. For we are made partakers of Christ, if we hold the beginning of our confidence stedfast unto the end.

In writing to the believers, the author of Hebrews warns against the possibility of unbelief creeping into the heart of a believer. On the outside the person may appear the same as before and go through the motions of being a Christian, but within he may have lost his relationship with the Lord. Faith has been replaced by faithlessness.

Knowing of this possibility, the author calls believers to encourage one another on a regular basis. "Daily" isn't too often because we are bombarded by the oppression of a sinful society and the subtle temptations of evil. The exhortation mentioned here isn't of the type which lambasts, thereby emphasizing the power of the various sinful forces. Rather it encourages in the faith by emphasizing the promises of God's Word, the empowerment of the Holy Spirit, and the fellowship of the body of Christ. Guided by this trio of encouragements even the weakest can be renewed and strengthened to meet the challenge! However, this encouraging needs to take place while the opportunity is available. *NOT AFTER TOTALLY OVER WHELMED*

Verse 13 points out that daily encouragement can prevent believers from falling into the deceitfulness of sin. Not a single believer is exempt from drifting away. The principles and truth of life in Christ can become secondary. Sin may then start to become attractive. Or, we may allow those so-called "little" sins to remain until they appear normal to us. When that occurs, the deceitfulness of sin has become entrenched in our hearts.

The writer also reminds us of the means by which we preserve our salvation. It is faith which enables us to first experience forgiveness from sin and a restored relationship with our Lord. But not to be overlooked is the role of faith in continuing our salvation. We are to remain steadfast in that same faith if we expect to receive the fullness of eternal life. This is how we continue to be members of the family of God now and in the future.

Give some examples of how we believers can encourage each other on a daily basis.

II. KEEP PURPOSE (Ecclesiastes 2:15-17; Galatians 6:7-9)

A. Avoid Foolishness
(Ecclesiastes 2:15-17)

15. Then said I in my heart, As it happeneth to the fool, so it happeneth even to me; and why was I then more wise? Then I said in my heart, that this also is vanity.

16. For there is no remembrance of the wise more than of the fool for ever; seeing that which now is in the days to come shall all be forgotten. And how dieth the wise man? as the fool.

17. Therefore I hated life; because of the work that is wrought under the sun is grievous unto me: for all is vanity and vexation of spirit.

The second chapter of Ecclesiastes begins with a discussion of the various pleasures which the author has attempted. Beginning with verse 4 and continuing through verse 11, he lists all the activities and possessions he has either attempted or acquired. He includes construction projects for housing and beauty, enslaved subjects for work, treasures of silver and gold, along with some of the arts. However, when he reviews all that he has experienced and possessed, no satisfaction or meaning arises. He has lavished himself with everything his heart desired and his money could buy. Yet all these self-centered experiences have come up meaningless.

Beginning with verse 12, the author describes another pursuit to finding meaning. He chooses to review the relationship between wisdom and folly. How do they really compare? To begin with, he declares the superiority of wisdom to folly. In verse 13 he compares their difference to that between light and darkness. In verse 14 a wise man is seen as walking with intelligence, while a foolish man walks in ignorance.

But in verse 15 there is a marked change. The writer suddenly shows a loss of meaning. Maybe it would be better to say that a humanistic element begins to show. Comparing only the actual years of a person's lifespan he suggests there is little difference between the fool and the wise.

Beginning with verse 16 he suggests there is no greater remembrance of the wise man than of the foolish man when they die. There is an equality at the grave. Of course, this view totally overlooks the many examples of individuals whose legacy of righteousness and wisdom lives on through their children or even through their students and associates. But his assessment is a response to his realization that the lives of men and women are forgotten quickly. Someone steps into their positions and life goes on.

For that reason, the writer comes to the conclusion that he hates life. No matter how much one accomplishes, within a short time it will be forgotten or overlooked. However, that's where one of life's hazards enters the thought process. The author assumes that the purpose of living centers on men rather than on God. He emphasizes the temporal, overlooking the eternal. With such concentration on self and the "here and now," there is no satisfaction.

The individual with a higher perspective will always work to avoid foolishness and will cling to wisdom. Wisdom is pleasing to God and is itself fulfilling in this life.

B. Avoid Deception
(Galatians 6:7, 8)

7. Be not deceived; God is not mocked: for whatsoever a man soweth, that shall he also reap.

8. For he that soweth to his flesh shall of the flesh reap corruption; but he that soweth to the Spirit shall of the Spirit reap life everlasting.

The problem of deception is central to the Book of Galatians. It covers the entire book from beginning to end. Instead of continuing in the grace and freedom offered by Christ, Paul finds the Galatians accepting a legalistic pattern of doing works to obtain salvation. For that reason Paul rebukes them strongly in Galatians 3:1. He follows by pointing out how they have set aside the faith in God for the works of the law (v. 2).

It's easy to attempt to justify this lapse of faith by attributing it to spiritual immaturity. And there may be some merit in that defense. But at the same time these believers aren't ignorant of the truth. With this in mind, it becomes very clear that they have allowed themselves to follow a path of deception.

As the apostle Paul comes to the end of the epistle, he puts forth another strong admonition to avoid the trap of deception. Galatians 6:7 includes a metaphor which can also be found in 2 Corinthians 9:6. There it is used in relationship to liberally giving to charitably meet the needs of other believers. Here it is applied much more broadly to our actions on earth.

In the natural, we reap the harvest of the planted seed. Tomato seeds produce tomatoes, and in the same manner wheat seeds produce wheat grain. The same holds true spiritually. If we indulge in carnal actions, then we will reap their results. Initially there may be pleasure. But since these separate us from God, eventually there will be judgment and suffering. Not to be forgotten are the sufferings which come from drunkenness, drug abuse, and immorality.

But what a contrast when an individual chooses to sow to the Spirit! This brings life everlasting, as well as peace, joy, and comfort here on earth—even when one is surrounded by or encounters life's great struggles, persecutions, and disappointments.

The challenge for believers today, as in the previous ages, is to recognize the deception of temporal pleasure. We must also recognize that the natural desires of the body and mind can become so exaggerated that we believe nothing can be more important. In such a state a short-sightedness develops, and a desire for fulfilling the cravings of the flesh dominates.

So how do we deal with this and move on to the higher plain of sowing to the Spirit? The best possible answer is found in Galatians 5:16-25. In these verses the apostle Paul points out that living and walking in the Spirit keeps us from following the works of the flesh. And that is the best answer to avoiding the deceptions which come to all of us.

C. Avoid Weariness (Galatians 6:9)

9. And let us not be weary in well doing: for in due season we shall reap, if we faint not.

Physical, emotional, and mental fatigue come to all of us. Working very hard over a long period of time without proper rest or diet causes the body to become tired. When bombarded with emotional pressures from various crises, our inner being eventually can feel drained. At such times some of us become very sensitive emotionally. Others lapse into an unfeeling insensitivity and may even express a lack of care or concern. Constantly pressing the mind with huge amounts of information over an extended time of analysis causes thinking to become an effort. These are three forms of weariness.

The same type of fatigue may come into our spiritual lives as we live for Christ and minister to others. On occasion this weariness comes from striving so hard and seeing so few results. At other times it develops from the frustrations brought on by other believers who not only are careless in their own lives but also make it difficult for those striving to do God's will. Of course, other situations may

also bring on this weariness.

Knowing this, the apostle includes a short one-verse encouragement. To continue and fulfill their God-given purpose, believers must overcome weariness. It cannot be allowed to remain or to dominate their lives. So how can this be done?

Notice that the apostle Paul doesn't go into any lengthy discussion of the procedure. He doesn't offer a seven- or ten-step "how-to-plan." He simply reminds the Galatians of the future reward which awaits them. Continuing the metaphor of sowing and reaping, he indicates a harvest for those who do not give up or allow weakness to overcome them.

Our initial thoughts concerning this harvest are usually of the rewards awaiting the believer in heaven after he successfully completes life here on earth. However, we shouldn't overlook the blessings which come here on earth to those who persevere. They include new opportunities to share the gospel, answered prayers, special blessings through the ministry of the Holy Spirit, and continued fellowship with the saints in Christ's body, the church.

What are some ways individual believers can be of assistance to those who appear weary?

III. KEEP VIRTUE (Psalm 51:1-4; 1 Thessalonians 4:3-7)

A. Seek Forgiveness (Psalm 51: 1-4)

1. Have mercy upon me, O God, according to thy lovingkindness: according unto the multitude of thy tender mercies blot out my transgressions.

2. Wash me throughly from mine iniquity, and cleanse me from my sin.

3. For I acknowledge my transgressions: and my sin is ever before me.

4. Against thee, thee only, have I sinned, and done this evil in thy sight: that thou mightest be justified when thou speakest, and be clear when thou judgest.

This third segment of our lesson brings us to the hazard of losing virtue. This includes our sexual behavior, but isn't limited to it. Honesty and integrity in other areas of our lives also require virtue. The preferable state is for us not to break the bounds of virtue. But when that does happen, there should be only one course of action—that of seeking God's forgiveness and being restored to a right relationship with Him.

Psalm 51 records the plea of forgiveness from King David as he reaches out to be restored. The well-known events preceding this prayer are recorded in 2 Samuel 11 and 12: David succumbs to the lust of the flesh and commits adultery with Bathsheba, the wife of Uriah, a mighty warrior of Israel. When a pregnancy occurs, he plots to cover the sin by recalling Uriah from battle on the pretense of wanting information about the war. After the report David dismisses him, hoping that normal relations between husband and wife will cover his sin.

But his carefully crafted plan disintegrates in the face of Uriah's integrity. Even becoming drunk doesn't break his resolve to not enjoy the pleasures of home and his wife while the rest of the army is in the field (11:11). Rather than admit his personal sin, David chooses to have Uriah die. He sends a command by Uriah's own hand that Joab should put this mighty, faithful soldier in the hottest part of the battle and then withdraw from him (v. 15).

Uriah dies. After an appropriate period of mourning, Bathsheba becomes David's wife. The baby is born. The sin appears to be hidden. But then, the prophet Nathan appears before David with a story for him to judge. And through this, God reveals both His displeasure with David's sins and the punishment he will suffer (12:7-12). At this crucial point David acknowledges his sin. Recorded in Psalm 51, his repentance provides us with a pattern to follow if sin enters our lives.

With the deepest sense of guilt, David cries out to the Lord for mercy. He understands that there is no merit in himself. His immorality, deceit, and murder cannot be justified or excused. Also, being the king of God's chosen people, Israel, doesn't provide any special treatment. He is a sinner deserving God's punishment.

Knowing the situation, David throws himself on God's unfailing love and tender compassion. Only through God's mercy will there be forgiveness rather than justice. And only through God's cleansing can his sinful heart be cleansed and restored to righteousness.

Sin which is entrenched in one's nature and lifestyle doesn't come out easily. David's request to be washed is for much more than a warm, gentle shower which rinses off the dirt. This is nothing akin to a gentle wash on the delicate cycle of our washing machines. Instead, he uses a word which refers to washing garments by beating them. That's why in verse 8 he speaks of "the bones which thou hast broken."

In verse 3 we see David's honesty. He describes his actions as sins and transgressions. There is no attempt to minimize or soft-soap his actions. He doesn't portray them as errors or mistakes in judgment. They continue "ever before" him. That implies he knew all along the true nature of his actions, even before being confronted by God through the prophet Nathan.

As David seeks forgiveness, he turns his attention toward the One who had been wronged. When he says, "Against thee, thee only, have I sinned," there is no disregard for the individuals who have been wronged by his sins. He did sin against both Bathsheba and Uriah. However, the most important aspect of his wrongdoing is the breaking of his relationship with God. God's covenant has been broken. God's people are being led by a king who chose to be an adulterer, a liar, and a murderer. So when God comes on the scene to punish, He is responding to actions directed against Himself.

The scope of this lesson doesn't continue beyond these first four verses. However they sufficiently establish our need to seek forgiveness from God when we have sinned. Without such action and acknowledgment, there can be no restoration of virtuousness.

B. Follow Holiness
   (1 Thessalonians 4:3-7)

   (1 Thessalonians 4:5, 6 is not included in the printed text.)
   3. For this is the will of God, even your sanctification, that ye should abstain from fornication:
   4. That every one of you should know how to possess his vessel in sanctification and honour;
   7. For God hath not called us unto uncleanness, but unto holiness.

Keeping virtue is best accomplished by following a positive pattern of holy living. Understanding what God expects from us and what He expects regarding our sexuality and living according to those standards enables us to keep a virtuous heart and lifestyle. This lifestyle differs greatly from that of the world, which seeks after personal pleasure without regard for marital relationship.

Immediately we see God's will for us. We are to be holy—separated from sin. And in order to do so, each one of us must avoid all forms of sexual immorality, including sexual relationships before marriage. This was a novelty to the Greek mind. The wrongness or seriousness of adultery and incest was understood; however, fornication appears to have been acceptable to the heathen mind.

Paul wants the Thessalonian believers to understand that their cultural beliefs do not fit God's standard. There is no room for the argument of not being able to control themselves or of needing sexual expression prior to marriage. Verse 4 states very clearly that they are to control their own desires. It may not be easy. It may even necessitate prayer and fasting; however, abstinence is the means of maintaining personal holiness and of being a person of honor in God's sight.

The difference between the sexual control of the believer and unbeliever also needs to be considered. Instead of allowing lust to reign and dominate, we must take authority over this emotion by holiness and personal control. And when Christians do this, we set the example for other believers. We demonstrate that our God-given sexuality can be used within the boundaries which He intended. Our sexuality isn't to be a passion which rages, providing a negative example for others.

Verse 7 summarizes it all. The call to salvation is more than a call for repentance from one's past. It is a call to turn in an opposite direction. No longer do we seek the ways of the world, but rather the truths and principles of God. We turn from the uncleanness of sin to the holiness of life in the Spirit.

How can we encourage the standards of holiness in a world which encourages sexual freedom?

REVIEW QUESTIONS

1. What is the trio of encouragements which we should offer daily to every believer?

2. What were the various pleasures which the author of Ecclesiastes found unfulfilling?

3. How do we sow to the Spirit?

4. How did David approach God for forgiveness?

GOLDEN TEXT HOMILY

"ENTER NOT INTO THE PATH OF THE WICKED, AND GO NOT IN THE WAY OF EVIL MEN" (Proverbs 4:14).

Life is indeed a journey, and here the wise man attempts to give his son good guidance. In this case, good guidance comes in the form of a negative: "Don't do as the wicked do" (*TLB*).

Conversely, some of the best advice ever given to me was, "Be at the right place at the right time." As a lawyer, I once violated this rule by wandering aimlessly into a courtroom just to be a spectator at a court trial. I was quite embarrassed when the judge interrupted the entire proceeding to ask me why I was there!

Surely King David, Peter, and others in the Bible learned the lesson of "being in the wrong place at the wrong time."

Where is the "right place" and the "right time"? Daily we must seek God's face. Weekly we must worship in God's house. Annually we must review our walk with God. For a lifetime we must "pray without ceasing" (1 Thessalonians 5:17). The spiritual journey never ends!

Our lesson teaches us that sin is very delusive and that we must not wander, even briefly, from the right path of God!—**Dennis W. Watkins, Director of the Office of Legal Services for the Church of God, Cleveland, Tennessee**

DAILY BIBLE READINGS

M. Obey God. Genesis 12:1-9
T. Do Not Be Deceived.
   1 Kings 13:11-24
W. Watch Out for Pride.
   2 Kings 20:12-19
T. Heed the Words of Christ.
   Matthew 7:24-29
F. Examine Your Own Life.
   Luke 6:39-45
S. Be Faithful. Hebrews 10:19-25

Assurance for Senior Years

Study Text: Psalm 71:1-24

Objective: To realize that the senior years of life can be meaningful and productive and trust in God's help.

Time: Due to the many writers of Psalm, the time span reaches from 1450 to 450 B.C. However, the majority were written about 1,000 B.C.

Place: Numerous areas due to the many writers.

Golden Text: "When I am old and greyheaded, O God, forsake me not; until I have shewed thy strength unto this generation" (Psalm 71:18).

Central Truth: God is faithful to the end of life's journey.

Evangelism Emphasis: Trusting Christ as Savior is the best preparation for senior years.

PRINTED TEXT

Psalm 71:1. In thee, O Lord, do I put my trust: let me never be put to confusion.

2. Deliver me, in thy righteousness, and cause me to escape: incline thine ear unto me, and save me.

3. Be thou my strong habitation, whereunto I may continually resort: thou hast given commandment to save me; for thou art my rock and my fortress.

4. Deliver me, O my God, out of the hand of the wicked, out of the hand of the unrighteous and cruel man.

5. For thou art my hope, O Lord God: thou art my trust from my youth.

6. By thee have I been holden up from the womb: thou art he that took me out of my mother's bowels: my praise shall be continually of thee.

7. I am as a wonder unto many; but thou art my strong refuge.

8. Let my mouth be filled with thy praise and with thy honour all the day.

9. Cast me not off in the time of old age; forsake me not when my strength faileth.

15. My mouth shall shew forth thy righteousness and thy salvation all the day; for I know not the numbers thereof.

16. I will go in the strength of the Lord God: I will make mention of thy righteousness, even of thine only.

17. O God, thou hast taught me from my youth: and hitherto have I declared thy wondrous works.

18. Now also when I am old and grayheaded, O God, forsake me not; until I have shewed thy strength unto this generation, and thy power to every one that is to

come.

19. Thy righteousness also, O God, is very high, who hast done great things: O God, who is like unto thee!

20. Thou, which hast shewed me great and sore troubles, shalt quicken me again, and shalt bring me up again from the depths of the earth.

21. Thou shalt increase my greatness, and comfort me on every side.

22. I will also praise thee with the psaltery, even thy truth, O my God: unto thee will I sing with the harp, O thou Holy One of Israel.

23. My lips shall greatly rejoice when I sing unto thee; and my soul, which thou hast redeemed.

24. My tongue also shall talk of thy righteousness all the day long: for they are confounded, for they are brought unto shame, that seek my hurt.

LESSON OUTLINE

I. GOD IS OUR DELIVERER
   A. Fortress From The Wicked
   B. Fortress From Our Birth
   C. Fortress in Advancing Years

II. GOD IS OUR HOPE
   A. His Righteousness
   B. His Great Deeds

III. GOD IS FAITHFUL
   A. Restores Life
   B. Worthy of Praise

LESSON EXPOSITION

INTRODUCTION

Recently while browsing the shelves of used books at an antique store, I found one titled *Stop Aging Now*. It was subtitled, *The Ultimate Plan for Staying Young and Reversing the Aging Process*. Though it was filled with advice about proper diet and the use of vitamins, one truth still remains beyond all this advice: We cannot stop the aging process. Some may age slower by taking better care of themselves. But all of us will experience aging unless death or the Lord comes first. It is inevitable!

With a growing number of senior citizens becoming a vital part of American society, this lesson takes on added significance. The graying of our sociological landscape makes it increasingly important to understand the challenge which aging and the senior years present. At the same time it becomes vital for us as believers and for the church in general to realize what a wealth of knowledge, experience, and example seniors can offer us.

Our modern medical science is enabling individuals to enjoy longer lifespans. Just listen to NBC's *Morning News* and watch the parade of centenarians who are regularly highlighted each week. And if you follow the census trends, you frequently hear the estimates of how many individuals will live into their eighties and nineties. Extended life is desirable. But it offers its own set of problems which we as individual believers and the church in general need to consider.

Some of the challenges of aging and retirement include a certain amount of trauma and uncertainty. There comes a point of giving up an active, day-to-day, hands-on involvement in business and professional life. Some find their homes too large and taxing to care for and so they replace them with retirement homes. In some cases a nursing home or adult living home is needed. Health problems may appear which restrict or make impossible many normal activities and responsibilities of the aged.

Not to be overlooked are the separation and loneliness caused by the death of a spouse, child(ren) or even grandchildren. Some elderly question why they are given long life when younger family members may live only short lives. Another related problem is that of outliving friends or neighbors.

And then there is the feeling of being shelved. For some this is an inner-generated feeling evolving from their no longer having major responsibilities. Regrettably though, it may be fostered by those who assume that retirement and aging is to be a time of doing nothing.

Another reason for this lesson's significance is the emphasis on youth during the past 30 years. This continues to create difficulties and to cause a society to devalue individuals once they reach the point of being a senior citizen. Keep in mind that you can receive certain senior-citizen discounts at age 55. Members of the generation which disdained or distrusted anyone over 30 are currently entering their fifth decade. However, they now see their age as prime time. But, of course, they are fighting this aging process as hard as possible through diet, exercise, skin cremes, plastic surgery, and positive thinking. But the bottom line is still that youth continue to receive special emphasis in many areas of life. Notice that older employees are often the ones who are laid off when a company downsizes.

Psalm 71 provides a Biblical perspective on some of the issues faced in aging. The writer offers assurance to understanding God. When an individual knows and understands His character, he receives assurance during each of life's stages as well as help with the problems of growing older.

I. GOD IS OUR DELIVERER
    (Psalm 71:1-13)

A. Fortress From The Wicked
    (vv. 1-4)

    1. In thee, O Lord, do I put my trust: let me never be put to confusion.

    2. Deliver me in thy righteousness, and cause me to escape: incline thine ear unto me, and save me.

    3. Be thou my strong habitation, whereunto I may continually resort: thou hast given commandment to save me; for thou art my rock and my fortress.

    4. Deliver me, O my God, out of the hand of the wicked, out of the hand of the unrighteous and cruel man.

The writer of this psalm begins with a primary foundation. God is our deliverer. His power and concern for us, His children, know no limitation. It isn't greater when we are younger. Nor does it decline with our increasing age. Absolutely not! He continues to be the same. At issue isn't His ability or our age, but our trust.

Before going any further, a definition of trust needs to be given. It is taken from the book *In the Face of Evil:* "Trust . . . means we relinquish control. We take the backseat and let God do the driving. We become the private and let God be the sergeant. Regardless of what He asks or when He leads, our trust causes us to comply and confirm the direction."

When we trust in the Lord, we can be assured that He never fails. We will never be ashamed for having put our trust in Him. Of course, we must always remember that His deliverance may not take the exact form we expect or desire. However, we know from the many stories of the Old Testament that God does take care of His children.

Consider the story of Elijah. When God sends a drought to Israel, He provides for Elijah at the brook Cherith by having ravens bring him food twice daily. When the brook dries up, he is directed to the widow of Zarephath. At the time of his arrival she expects to make one more meal for her son and herself. After that they will die from starvation since all their food will be exhausted. But after she feeds Elijah, God miraculously provides a continuous supply of meal and oil (1 Kings 17:14).

Knowing the dangers he is encountering, the psalmist requests God's intervention in his situation. Verse 2 of the printed text asks for God to hear his plea and bring deliverance. Only through divine action will he be able to escape the problems and people who will do him harm.

The means of that deliverance may take various forms. In verse 3 he asks for a stronghold which will bring protection and safety on a continuing basis. The picture provided here is that of a high place which is easily protected from those who wish to attack and is difficult to scale by those who intend harm.

In the natural, Jerusalem was such a site. The Jebusites were so confident of this location they boasted that city could be successfully defended by the lame and the blind (2 Samuel 5:6). It would have been difficult for David and his armed men to overrun this site except for their finding the secret passage from an outside water source.

The unrighteous frequently are cruel. They disregard the rights of others in their attempt to achieve self-satisfaction. These individuals do not hesitate to prey on those who are weaker and are unable to defend themselves. We see this repeatedly. Sometimes it takes the form of forcibly taking the elders' possessions while physically abusing them. Others use extremely devious plans to deceive and bilk them out of life savings. We often wonder how anyone could be so wicked.

It is from this type of wickedness which the writer seeks deliverance. It is from this source of oppression that he seeks a protective fortress. And we have the assurance that God is able to provide that form of protection.

B. Fortress From Our Birth
(vv. 5-8)

5. For thou art my hope, O Lord God: thou art my trust from my youth.

6. By thee have I been holden up from the womb: thou art he that took me out of my mother's

bowels: my praise shall be continually of thee.

7. I am as a wonder unto many; but thou art my strong refuge.

8. Let my mouth be filled with thy praise and with thy honour all the day.

Since it is generally assumed that the author of this psalm is in the late years of his life, his reference to his youth provides a refreshing view. Instead of being a person who turns to God later in life, he demonstrates to us the individual who has trusted in the Lord since his youth. Along with this, the author reminds us of God's sovereignty. He is in control. By His will we are birthed from our mothers.

Beginning with verse 5 we immediately see that the author of this psalm has trusted in the Lord from his early years of life. His recognition of his need for God's intervention has not been due to a crisis or to the recognition of the nearness of death. Rather, the relationship has been constant over the span of many years, beginning as a child. The word *youth* makes us think of individuals in their teen years. However, in these cultures age 12 is the time of puberty and the assuming of adult responsibilities.

Concepts of both hope and trust are included in this passage. It can be understood in a combination of ways. One aspect is to wait passively for the Lord's intervention (Psalm 42:5). An opposite aspect is to actively anticipate His blessing and provision (Psalm 62:5). Trust understands that we accept whatever way God chooses to work.

In verse 6 we see the need for complete reliance on the Lord from

the time of our birth. It is God's sovereignty which enables a child to be born alive and ready to develop rather than to be stillborn or miscarried. For this reason each one of us should continually praise God. It is true that our conceptions occurred by action of our parents; however, it is only through God's sovereignty that each one of us was allowed to develop within our mother's womb. It was His will that each of us come into this world. Once again, we need to be reminded of Jeremiah's statement of God's call on his life. "Before I formed thee in the belly I knew thee; and before thou camest forth out of the womb I sanctified thee" (Jeremiah 1:5).

Verse 7 is more difficult to understand. One modern version translates the word *wonder* as "portent" (*NIV*). This carries with it the definition of being an omen of something about to occur. It also can be defined as "amazing" or as a "prodigy." Either word is acceptable as far as this psalmist is concerned. The important point continues to be the refuge found in God. His inclusion of the adjective *strong* emphasizes that this is no common shelter. No, this fortress defies the worst storms and the fiercest enemies.

It is only reasonable that praise should be a continuous part of the psalmist's response to God for this provision. Continual honor to God for who He is and what He does will flow from those who have this shelter at their disposal. Such speaking forth of praise and honor needs to be the practice of all believers, for all of us have the impenetrable shelter provided by God.

How does the believer enter God's fortress?

C. Fortress in Advancing Years
(vv. 9-13)

(Psalm 71:10-13 is not included in the printed text.)

9. Cast me not off in the time of old age; forsake me not when my strength faileth.

What a change between verses 8 and 9. And yet it really is a continuation. As this grey-haired gentleman enters his elderly years, he seeks the assurance of God's continued protection even as his personal strength fails. He desires God's deliverance which he has experienced in the past to continue into the future.

In verse 10 we see the problem he faces. Who these foes are isn't stated. But they appear to be plotting his harm and demise. In planning his fall, these individuals have come to the conclusion that God no longer offers His protection. There is no obstacle to their fulfilling their sordid wishes. Notice the assuredness they feel concerning his defenselessness.

While pouring out his problems, the writer of this psalm asks the Lord for some specific intervention. He asks for God's nearness and help. Then he requests that the wicked men who have planned his destruction be consumed themselves: Instead of victory, may they experience shame, scorn, and disgrace in the process of their own destruction.

Initially this may seem to be a request for revenge. But consider the whole picture. When God protects His children from evil, intruders cannot experience anything but defeat—and not just a casual loss! They are brought face-to-face with the impact of their opposition to God and one of His children.

II. GOD IS OUR HOPE
(Psalm 71:14-19)

A. His Righteousness (vv. 14, 15)

(Psalm 71:14 is not included in the printed text.)

15. My mouth shall shew forth thy righteousness and thy salvation all the day; for I know not the numbers thereof.

After sharing his problem and requesting God's intervention, the psalmist makes a marvelous statement. It is his testimony of personal intent. He declares his intent to be a person of hope and praise. Even when the shadows of life begin to hide the light, he intends to keep on hoping. Even when the situation appears bleak, he will continue to praise the Lord.

How is this type of behavior possible? Can it be the choice of any believer?

Let's answer the second question first. Yes, being a person of hope and praise regardless of the situation can be the choice of any believer. It becomes possible when we understand our relationship with God through Jesus Christ. He is our heavenly Father and is continuously concerned about our complete welfare. He never leaves us nor forsakes us! He is always by our side! This fact becomes obvious as we study the Scriptures. Not only are they filled with precious promises for each of us today, but also example after example is given of His fulfilling them. He is a God of His Word.

This leads us to the statement in verse 15. We have assurance at all ages of our lives due to God's righteousness. He is holy and just. He never treats anyone unjustly. He never says one thing and then does something else. Unlike individuals who fail to fulfill their obligations and declarations, God in His righteousness always completes His.

Remember the special promise God made to Israel, the promise first given to Moses and then reaffirmed to Joshua (Joshua 1:3)? God stated that everywhere they placed their foot it would be theirs. When in obedience they followed God's Word, this promise was fulfilled. However, when doubt or disobedience entered their ranks, they experienced frustration and defeat. A good example is the contrast between the attack on Jericho and the first attack against Ai. At Jericho the walls crumbled and the city was offered as a burnt sacrifice to the Lord. But at Ai the forces were routed, some men killed, and the people's hearts melted within them. Instead of assurance they experienced fear. What a change a few months can make. Once fearless conquerors, they have become fearful with all courage melted (Joshua 7:5).

B. His Great Deeds (vv. 16-19)

16. I will go in the strength of the Lord God: I will make mention of thy righteousness, even of thine only.

17. O God, thou hast taught me from my youth: and hitherto have I declared thy wondrous works.

18. Now also when I am old and grayheaded, O God, forsake me not; until I have shewed thy strength unto this generation, and thy power to every one that

is come.

19. Thy righteousness also, O God, is very high, who hast done great things: O God, who is like unto thee!

For the second time the writer makes a strong declaration of his intent to go forth testifying of God (see vv. 14, 15). He very specifically makes it known that his future actions will not be limited to the weakness of his own physical infirmities. Instead, this bold declaration will only be through the strengthening of God. As Pentecostals, we understand this very well since we see one dimension of the Holy Spirit's empowerment to be that of witnessing. However, the concept of the Lord being our strength is seen repeatedly in the various psalms.

Here are a few which need to be considered: "I will love thee, O Lord, my strength" (Psalm 18:1). "The Lord is my strength and my shield . . ." (28:7). "God is our refuge and strength, a very present help in trouble" (46:1). "My flesh and my heart faileth: but God is the strength of my heart, and my portion for ever" (73:26).

Thus strengthened, this individual makes it very plain that his witness will not be self-glorifying. Everything he shares will focus on God only. His righteousness will be the only focus of what is said.

Verse 17 continues the portrait of this writer's relationship with God. It isn't of recent origin. Ever since his childhood there has been an openness to the ways of the Lord. His teachableness is emphasized. But it has been more than that. On the one hand, he has been taught by God. On the other, he has actively witnessed all God has done. Thus, we see that his declaration to witness is a continuation of his previous pattern of life.

The writer repeats his request that the Lord not forsake him. But this request isn't selfish. He isn't seeking just his own good! He isn't wanting to live longer for his own purposes. No, he wants God's intervention on his behalf so the current generation can hear all that God has done. Everyone is to know of God's wondrous works and the many things He has done. Nothing and no one can compare!

This person's desire really should be replicated in each of our own lives. We too should desire that all people in our generation hear of God's marvelous interventions and His unsurpassed power. This is a story which needs to be told. Shouting it through the media would seem to be the most effective means. But what is most effective isn't broadcasting to the multitudes, but each of us sharing one-on-one what God does for us, as well as what He has done in the past.

Each of us has favorite stories of God's miraculous intervention as told in the Scriptures. One which needs to 'be included is of the beginning. His marvelous work of creation set the stage for everything else that has followed, even up to this very moment.

In verse 19 we are reminded that God's righteousness exceeds all others. He is beyond compare. This brings to mind the question asked by Isaiah: "To whom, then, will you compare God?" (Isaiah 40:18, *NIV*).

Make a list of some of God's glorious works which you believe your generation needs to know about.

III GOD IS FAITHFUL

(Psalm 71:20-24)

A. Restores Life (vv. 20, 21)

20. Thou, which hast shewed me great and sore troubles, shalt quicken me again, and shalt bring me up again from the depths of the earth.

21. Thou shalt increase my greatness, and comfort me on every side.

The final aspect of God which provides assurance is His faithfulness. By definition, *faithfulness* means "to be loyal." It involves firmly adhering to whatever you are bound to by duty or promise.

What a blessing and an assurance to know that the God we serve is faithful. He doesn't enter into a covenant relationship and then not fulfill it. He doesn't operate inconsistently, wanting to help one day and deciding not to the next. Our God faithfully follows through with all of His commitments.

A misconception needs to be addressed here. God's faithfulness isn't a guarantee against facing major difficulties. It doesn't keep us from facing the darkness as the shadows begin to envelop us. It doesn't keep us from falling into the clutches of our enemies. Keep in mind Psalm 23 points out that God meets us there. He walks through the shadows with us. He prepares a table for us to feast at, even when enemies surround us.

In verse 20 the writer of this psalm indicates his experience with difficult situations. He understands being brought low. The description is of being in the depths of the earth and needing to be raised up. When everything appears to be destroyed, God restores. When one's life seems to be ended, God resurrects it.

The Old Testament includes many examples which fit the description in verses 20 and 21. God intervenes at the right time. His faithfulness brings victory out of apparent defeat, restores truth when deception would reign, and provides protection when destruction threatens. Joseph, Job, and Daniel are superb examples of God's faithfulness.

Though loved by his father, Joseph suffered the jealously of his brothers. Sold into slavery, he became the top servant in Potiphar's household only to suffer the vengeance of a spurned, ungodly woman. He helped a fellow prisoner only to be forgotten for two years when that individual returned to Pharoah's court. But God was faithful and brought Joseph to power and prestige as the second in command of Egypt.

Then there's Job. God allowed Satan to attack this blameless, upright man. He allowed Job to be stripped of his possessions, family, and health. Yet God hadn't forsaken him! He was simply showing Satan Job's love for his God and his unwillingness to waver, regardless of how difficult situations became. But God is faithful. He restored Job's possessions a hundred fold. And he also restored his family.

Lastly, let's consider Daniel. As a young man he stood firm in his desire to drink water and eat vegetables rather than defile himself with the rich foods provided by the king. Then, as an old man, he disobeyed the king's decree forbidding the people to pray to anyone but the king himself. Continuing his practice of praying three times daily resulted in his being thrown into a den of lions. But God was faithful. He closed the mouths of the lions. Daniel did spend the night with the lions! But he spent the entire night in safety.

In each of these three examples, God was there. Each of these men experienced some difficult, stretching circumstances. However, God was faithful and restored them. Life suddenly flowed where previously death and destruction seemed very possible.

B. Worthy of Praise (vv. 22-24)

22. I will also praise thee with the psaltery, even thy truth, O my God: unto thee will I sing with the harp, O thou Holy One of Israel.

23. My lips shall greatly rejoice when I sing unto thee; and my soul, which thou hast redeemed.

24. My tongue also shall talk of thy righteousness all the day long: for they are confounded, for they are brought unto shame, that seek my hurt.

Simply talking about God's faithfulness isn't sufficient. There comes a point when bursting forth in praise is the only acceptable response. Coming to the end of this psalm, the author completes it with recognition of God's worthiness to be praised. He specifically points to God's faithfulness as the reason or motivating purpose.

Review how this psalm progresses. It begins with a request for God's deliverance and protection. Eventually the writer shares his desire to testify of God's righteousness and great works. How appropriate to conclude with praise and rejoicing!

Apparently this praise will take the form of songs sung with a musical accompaniment. The harp and lyre are specifically indicated. Verse 23 indicates that this praise will be more than lip service—it will not be the simple mouthing of words. It will spring from the soul. His praise will be an expression of his innermost being.

It's especially important to notice the reason for this praise. Yes, it includes recognition of God's sheltering protection. It includes recognition of all that God has done in the past. But the most important reason is his personal redemption. This reminds us that there is nothing more important that God can do for us than to provide salvation. His healing of our bodies, directing our lives, providing for our financial needs, and protecting us from harm are vitally important. Yet, not one or even a combination of several makes the same impact and far-reaching results as His provision for our soul's salvation.

The last line of verse 24 tells us the rest of the story. Those who plotted his ruin and demise have been overcome. Instead of successfully fulfilling all they planned, just the opposite has occurred. Shame and confusion have replaced their hoped-for victory.

What assurance this chapter offers! Regardless of our age, God doesn't change. He is always our deliverer and our hope. Plus, we can count on His being faithful!

List some specific actions of God in your life which deserve our praise of Him.

REVIEW QUESTIONS

1. What does it mean to trust?
2. How does God's sovereignty affect each of our lives?
3. What assurance comes to us based on God's righteousness?
4. How is the Lord our strength?
5. What are some of the reasons we should praise our God?

GOLDEN TEXT HOMILY

"WHEN I AM OLD AND GREY-HEADED, O GOD, FORSAKE ME NOT; UNTIL I HAVE SHEWED THY STRENGTH UNTO THIS GENERATION" (Psalm 71:18).

There are many great testimonies I could quote of how God has been faithful to so many of His well-known servants, but I believe my personal testimony is as valid as any of them. I don't have to say as the psalmist did, "When I am old and greyheaded"—I am old and grayheaded. By the time you read this, I'll be well into my 79th year, if I live till then—which I expect to do.

Having served for 35 years outside the United States as a foreign missionary, I saw the hand of God at work so many times that it would be impossible for me to doubt His loving care for young or old; but as time for retirement drew near, I did feel some misgivings about the future. One cannot save money on a foreign missionary's salary, so we faced a bleak future: no home, no furniture, no car, no savings. What were we going to do? I could not look to family—none of them belong to the church, and all have their own responsibilities. We had to depend on God!

"Forsake me not," I cried. "Now let me show Your strength to this generation!" Before we even reached the States, God had provided a nice large brick home—and a huge mortgage. As the need came, we were given practically all of our furniture free. Deacon Jones helped me get a nice car I could afford. Everything came at exactly the precise time of need.

It has been 11 years now and God has not forsaken us for even one minute. He is true and faithful. He has provided much more than just our needs. I could never praise Him enough!—**William R. McCall, Missionary, Church of God, Cleveland, Tennessee**

SENTENCE SERMONS

GOD GIVES His wrath by weight, but His mercy without measure.
—Sir Thomas Fuller

GOD'S LOVE for us is proclaimed with each sunrise.
—Draper's Book of Quotations for the Christian World

EVANGELISM APPLICATION

TRUSTING CHRIST AS SAVIOR IS THE BEST PREPARATION FOR SENIOR YEARS.

Prior to reaching one's late 40s, retiring and being a senior citizen appear far away. That time seems like a distant date on a far away calendar. However, except for the Lord's return or our early death, each one of us will reach a point at which some preparation will need to be made.

Financial preparation usually comes to the forefront of this consideration. Is there a plan for saving? Are long-term investments being made? Will Social Security still be available? Which tax-deferred savings plans should be started? The list could be expanded, but this is sufficient to make the point.

Health preparation enters some individuals' thinking. Hoping to push back the aging process and enter the latter portion of life in good health, they give new attention to diet and exercise and willingly spend thousands of dollars on exercise equipment and new medical prescriptions.

At the head of our list of preparations should be our spiritual preparation. The temptation for many is to attempt salvation by works. They do good deeds hoping each one provides spiritual merit that God will honor. Our actions are important, but they aren't the way to salvation. Only Jesus is. Remember He said, "I am the way, the truth, and the life: no man cometh unto the Father, but by me" (John 14:6).

The best preparation is to trust in God. Trust His redemptive work on Calvary. Trust His will for our lives. Trust His protection. Then we can have assurance regardless of the problems faced during the senior years.

DAILY BIBLE READINGS

M. God Proves His Faithfulness.
    Psalm 37:23-29
T. God's Mercy Endures Forever.
    Psalm 136:1-9
W. God Gives Strength.
    Isaiah 40:28-31
T. Blessed of the Lord.
    Matthew 5:1-9
F. Grace Is Sufficient.
    2 Corinthians 12:1-10
S. Victory Over the World.
    1 John 5:4-13

INTRODUCTION
TO WINTER
QUARTER

The lessons for the winter quarter (December, January, February) are presented in two units under the following themes: "God's Plan of Redemption" (lessons 1-8) and "Truths From the Tabernacle" (lessons 9-13).

Unit One provides an opportunity to make a comprehensive study of God's plan of redemption from both Old Testament and New Testament Scriptures. Lesson 3, however, is the Christmas lesson, but brings into focus the birth of the Redeemer.

Unit Two provides the student with a challenging series of lessons on the Tabernacle as God's sanctuary and its important place in the Judeo-Christian persuasion. Together the two units of study will enrich the understanding of the serious Bible scholar.

GOD'S PLAN OF REDEMPTION
(Map for General Use)

SCALE OF MILES

0   5   10   15   20

THE GREAT SEA

ISRAEL

CANAANITES

Jordan River

Shechem

Shiloh

Bethel

Ramah

Gibeah

Nab

Ekron

Jericho

Ashdod

Brook Elah

Jerusalem

Shochoh

Bethlehem

Azekah

Adullam

Gath

Keilah

Gaza

Hebron

Ziph

Engedi

SALT SEA

Ziklag

Carmel

Maon

JUDAH

PHILISTIA

Beer-Sheba

Hormah

Aroer

AMALEKITES

EDOM

Need for a Redeemer

Study Text: Genesis 3:1-24

Objective: To understand sin's destructive nature and accept God's offer of redemption.

Time: The Book of Genesis was probably written between 1450 and 1400 B.C.

Place: The Book of Genesis is believed to have been written by Moses following a revelation from God on Mount Sinai in the wilderness.

Golden Text: "I will put enmity between thee and the woman, and between thy seed and her seed; it shall bruise thy head, and thou shalt bruise his heel" (Genesis 3:15).

Central Truth: God has provided redemption for all people.

Evangelism Emphasis: God has provided redemption for all people.

PRINTED TEXT

Genesis 3:1. Now the serpent was more subtil than any beast of the field which the Lord God had made. And he said unto the woman, Yea, hath God said, Ye shall not eat of every tree of the garden?

4. And the serpent said unto the woman, Ye shall not surely die:

5. For God doth know that in the day ye eat thereof, then your eyes shall be opened, and ye shall be as gods, knowing good and evil.

6. And when the woman saw that the tree was good for food, and that it was pleasant to the eyes, and a tree to be desired to make one wise, she took of the fruit thereof, and did eat, and gave also unto her husband with her; and he did eat.

7. And the eyes of them both were opened, and they knew that they were naked; and they sewed fig leaves together, and made themselves aprons.

9. And the Lord God called unto Adam, and said unto him, Where art thou?

10. And he said, I heard thy voice in the garden, and I was afraid, because I was naked; and I hid myself.

11. And he said, Who told thee that thou wast naked? Hast thou eaten of the tree, whereof I commanded thee that thou shouldest not eat?

12. And the man said, The woman whom thou gavest to be with me, she gave me of the tree, and I did eat.

13. And the Lord God said unto the woman, What is this that thou hast done? And the woman said, The serpent

beguiled me, and I did eat.

14. And the Lord God said unto the serpent, Because thou hast done this, thou art cursed above all cattle, and above every beast of the field; upon thy belly shalt thou go, and dust shalt thou eat all the days of thy life:

15. And I will put enmity between thee and the woman, and between thy seed and her seed; it shall bruise thy head, and thou shalt bruise his heel.

22. And the Lord God said, Behold, the man is become as one of us, to know good and evil: and now, lest he put forth his hand, and take also of the tree of life, and eat, and live for ever:

23. Therefore the Lord God sent him forth from the garden of Eden, to till the ground from whence he was taken.

24. So he drove out the man; and he placed at the east of the garden of Eden Cherubims, and a flaming sword which turned every way, to keep the way of the tree of life.

LESSON OUTLINE

I.   TEMPTATION

    A. The Tempter

    B. The Tempted

    C. The Weapon

    D. The Transgression

II. THE COVER-UP

    A. The Flight

    B. The Shame

    C. The Rationalizing

III. CONSEQUENCES OF SIN

    A. The Tempter Judged

    B. The Transgressors' Penalty

    C. Mercy Displayed

    D. The Penalty Imposed

LESSON EXPOSITION

INTRODUCTION

Adam, the first man, was created a perfect being with responsibility for his words and moral accountability. He was given the power to choose. In his sinless situation he was free, and he was accountable. He chose in response to Satan's temptation to disobey God and eat of the Tree of Knowledge of Good and Evil. God had given him complete freedom in the Garden except for this one prohibition, a test of his continuing obedience.

According to the Genesis account, there was nothing in the Garden, in the covenant, or in the circumstances of his life that made it impossible for him to sin. Adam was an absolutely free being. He was in a covenant with God that required his obedience in refraining to eat of the fruit of the forbidden tree. He had been warned in advance by God of the consequences of disobedience—in the day that he should eat of that fruit, he would surely die.

When Adam sinned, he brought physical and spiritual death on himself and his descendants. The agent in Adam's fall was the devil, but Adam alone was responsible for the choice he made. He was not forced by God or the devil to do what he did. As a result of his sin, the whole earth, as well as all mankind, has been affected.

Adam's sin meant separation from God. This separation included eternal death. This actually meant exclusion from the presence of God forever. Man could do nothing in or of himself to bridge that gap that separated him from God. Whatever was to be done had to come from God. God had to provide the initiative.

The Biblical record is clear. Because God loved mankind, He chose to provide the plan of redemption. This plan involved the sending of His own Son to die on the cross (John 3:16). Man needed a redeemer, and Jesus Christ became that Redeemer.

I. THE TEMPTATION
(Genesis 3:1-7)

A. The Tempter (v. 1)

1. Now the serpent was more subtil than any beast of the field which the Lord God had made. And he said unto the woman, Yea, hath God said, Ye shall not eat of every tree of the garden?

The entrance of sin into the world began with the serpent's coming to the woman, Eve, to tempt her to eat the forbidden fruit. That the tempter was really Satan, using the physical body of a serpent, can be seen in the following passages of Scripture: John 8:44; Romans 16:20; 2 Corinthians 11:3; Revelation 12:9; 20:2. God permitted Satan to present the temptation in order to test Adam and Eve.

Although Satan approached Eve with the temptation, his goal was to entice both Adam and Eve into sin, thus condemning the whole human race. He was clever enough to realize that it would be easier to convince Adam to sin if he could first deceive Eve. Because of Adam's affection for his God-ordained helper, Eve was in an excellent position to influence and persuade him to follow her lead.

Satan began the temptation by challenging the command of God. With a half-interrogatory, half-exclamatory expression of astonishment, he insinuated that God had not been gracious, kind, or loving in His prohibitions. Moreover, Satan deliberately perverted what God had said. His question implied that God had forbidden the eating of fruit from any tree in the garden. However, God had actually commanded the couple to refrain from eating the fruit of only one tree. Satan's attack upon Eve involved the contradiction, denial, and twisting of the Word of God to suit his own purpose.

Satan has not changed his techniques in our day. His temptations still begin with an attempt to chip away at the foundation of man's trusting relationship with God. He questions; he unsettles; he confuses. He makes his first entry not by violent attack but by this undermining of the foundation. He endeavors to confuse and cloud the mind which afterward he plans to chain.

B. The Tempted (vv. 2, 3)

(Genesis 3:2, 3 is not included in the printed text.)

In responding to Satan, Eve made the mistake of arguing with him, suggesting that God's Word needs defending. She should have deliberately demanded that he leave her presence. She should have resisted him by obeying God's commandment. Obedience to the Word of God is the only way to overcome the subtle strategies of Satan.

It should be noted that not only Satan but also Eve altered what God had said. God had said that Adam and Eve could "freely eat" (Genesis 2:16) of every tree of the Garden except one (v. 17). Eve omitted the word *freely*. Moreover, she added to the prohibition God had given, "neither shall ye touch it" (3:3). In regard to the penalty for eating of the forbidden tree, she changed God's "thou shalt surely die" (2:17) to "lest ye die" (3:3)—a much weaker way of describing the penalty. In doing this, Eve minimized God's goodness, suggested a severeness on the part of God that did not exist, and weakened the certainty of punishment for disobedience. This compromise led her deeper into the trap of temptation designed for her destruction.

C. The Weapon (vv. 4, 5)

4. And the serpent said unto the woman, Ye shall not surely die:

5. For God doth know that in the day ye eat thereof, then your eyes shall be opened, and ye shall be as gods, knowing good and evil.

The first lie in human history was told by Satan (v. 4). Other lies were soon to follow. Satan gave false assurance to Eve that she would "not surely die." This was a brief and complete denial of what God had said. It was an absolute contradiction of God's Word.

In verse 5, Satan appealed to Eve's pride and, at the same time, led her almost to hate God for His having cheated her of what Satan purported to be life's highest privileges. He promised her two things if she would eat of the Tree of Knowledge of Good and Evil: her

eyes would be opened, and she would be as God, knowing good and evil.

D. The Transgression (vv. 6, 7)

6. And when the woman saw that the tree was good for food, and that it was pleasant to the eyes, and a tree to be desired to make one wise, she took of the fruit thereof, and did eat, and gave also unto her husband with her; and he did eat.

7. And the eyes of them both were opened, and they knew that they were naked; and they sewed fig leaves together, and made themselves aprons.

Satan appealed to the natural desires of Eve—desires not evil in themselves, but which became sinful when yielded to in disobedience to God. Eve's natural desire for food became the lust of the flesh when she saw the forbidden fruit as being "good for food" (v. 6). Her natural appreciation for beauty became the lust of the eyes when she saw the forbidden tree as being "pleasant to the eyes." Her God-given powers of reason were lifted up in pride against God when she saw that the forbidden tree was "to be desired to make one wise."

Eve's behavior should warn us that temptation and lust can cause us to see things as we wish to see them, not as God would have us see them. Adam and Eve had been warned by God to see the forbidden tree as something they should not desire for their own good. Eve saw only what she wanted to see—a tree to be desired.

Man's first temptation was a simple test of his obedience to God, virtually the only temptation possible in the Garden of Eden. The temptation of sexual immorality did not

appear in the first temptation—
Adam and Eve were the only couple, and they were husband and
wife. Eve could not be tempted to
envy her neighbors or to covet their
possessions—she had no neighbors. Adam could not be tempted
with greed or competition—he had
the whole world, and there was no
one with whom to compete. The
desires of the first couple were few
and simple. Because the many
vices now common among men
were absent from the Garden of
Eden, Adam and Eve could be
tempted only within the narrow
realm of their personal enjoyment,
appetite, and curiosity.

Eve yielded to the temptation,
disobeyed God, and ate the fruit of
the forbidden tree. She then gave it
to her husband, and he also disobeyed God and ate the forbidden
fruit. Both sinned. The deed was a
personal, willful act for which each
alone was responsible before God.

Sin brought the loss of innocence and the beginning of fear and
shame for mankind (v. 7). With sin
came the burden of guilt and a
sense of unworthiness in the presence of God. Afraid and ashamed
to be in the presence of their great
Creator, Adam and Eve tried to
hide from God. They made coverings for their bodies from fig leaves.
Man does not want God to see him
in his sin, but the truth is that he
is always "naked" before God and
cannot hide his sins from Him.

---

*Could Satan have tempted Eve
in some other way? Explain.*

II. THE COVER-UP
(Genesis 3:8-13)

A. The Flight (v. 8)

(Genesis 3:8 is not included in

the printed text.)

Adam and Eve hid themselves,
not as a result of a consultation but
as a result of their need to act
immediately to escape the presence
of the Lord. Undoubtedly two
motives determined their action—
fear and shame. God's greatness
was now the measure of their terror—the terror of the created who
had dared to disobey his Creator.

The awareness of sin also
brought the shame that followed.
Shame was an emotion absolutely
different from fear. The greatness
of God was the measure of Adam's
fear; but Adam's own lost greatness
was the measure of his shame.
There is no difficulty in characteriz-
ing the behavior of Adam and Eve
as foolish and irrational—they
attempted the impossible, and they
fled from their only hope. *Sin causes
us to run*

B. The Shame (vv. 9-11)

**9. And the Lord God called
unto Adam, and said unto him,
Where art thou?**

**10. And he said, I heard thy
voice in the garden, and I was
afraid, because I was naked; and I
hid myself.**

**11. And he said, Who told
thee that thou wast naked? Hast
thou eaten of the tree, whereof I
commanded thee that thou
shouldest not eat?**

Verse 9 is one of the saddest and
most inspiring verses in the Bible.
"Where art thou?" is God's first
recorded question in the Bible. It
was not asked because God did not
know where His sinning creatures
were, but because He was still
seeking a relationship with them.
God could have left Adam and Eve
to their own sin and misery, deepening darkness, and ultimate

death. Instead, He pursued them, seeking to redeem them from destruction and to bring them back into fellowship again.

Adam immediately responded to God by saying that he was afraid (v. 10). This is the first occurrence of fear in the Bible, but it has since been found again and again with the unfolding of human history. This should remind us of another thought that was to unfold. The thought was uttered by voices from heaven, often through angels and ultimately by the Lord Jesus Christ: "Fear not."

It is sad that the first recorded word to God, as far as the divine record goes, was a lie. Man did not hide himself because he was naked, for he was created naked and before this had often had fellowship with God without a thought of his nakedness. Furthermore, at this time Adam was not naked, for he had devised a covering for himself. The truth was that he hid himself because he had sinned and was afraid of God.

God immediately pointed Adam to the true cause of his shame and intimated His knowledge of Adam's transgression (v. 11). The question that God asked carried conviction to Adam's conscience and elicited an immediate confession.

C. The Rationalizing (vv. 12, 13)

12. And the man said, The woman whom thou gavest to be with me, she gave me of the tree, and I did eat.

13. And the Lord God said unto the woman, What is this that thou hast done? And the woman said, The serpent beguiled me, and I did eat.

Eve's response was to blame the serpent (v. 13). Her plea was that the serpent had deceived her. This was an attempt to find refuge from her guilt in the fact that she had been tricked by the devil. However, their disobedience could not be undone. They had allowed themselves to be lured into sin by failure to resist temptation.

How do people rationalize their failure to obey God today?

III.   CONSEQUENCES OF SIN
       (Genesis 3:14-24)

A.   The Tempter Judged
     (vv. 14, 15)

14. And the Lord said unto the serpent, Because thou hast done this, thou art cursed above all cattle, and above every beast of the field, upon thy belly shalt thou go, and dust shalt thou eat all the days of thy life:

15. And I will put enmity between thee and the woman, and between thy seed and her seed; it shall bruise thy head, and thou shalt bruise his heel.

The curse pronounced upon the serpent implies that the serpent had propelled himself in some other manner—possibly with legs or wings or both (v. 14). His altered manner of movement would be a severe handicap and a degradation of his status among the animals. Since the serpent had been used as an instrument of Satan, he also had to suffer the consequences of sin.

Verse 15 identifies the specific curse of God upon Satan. God said He would put enmity between the righteous descendants of Eve and Satan. Satan had pretended to be the friend of man, but the curse of God exposed him for what he really is—the great enemy of all mankind. Eventually, from the righteous line of Eve, there would come One who would bruise or crush the head of Satan. This is considered to be the first prophecy in the Bible of the coming of Christ to conquer the devil.

The terrible conflict between Satan and mankind came to a fearful crisis at the appearance of Jesus on earth. The prediction that Satan would bruise the heel of the seed of the woman was fulfilled when Satan motivated and drove men to put Jesus to death. At the same time, the seed of the woman, the Lord Jesus, bruised the head of Satan when He destroyed his powers. Jesus was victorious over Satan in His life and finally in His death and resurrection. He brought to naught all of Satan's power to bring death to man. Christ delivered those "who through fear of death were all their lifetime subject to bondage" (Hebrews 2:15).

Christ, wounded in the heel (not eternally or ultimately), overcame death in His resurrection; Satan, bruised in his head, received a mortal blow from which he has never recovered and which will be followed in the last days by his final defeat of being cast into the lake of fire and brimstone. There he will remain forever.

B. The Transgressors' Penalty (vv. 16-19)

(Genesis 3:16-19 is not included in the printed text.)

God told Eve that because of her transgression her pain would be greatly multiplied during childbirth and that her desire would be for her husband and that he would rule over her.

Adam was told that he would be compelled to toil and sweat all the days of his life on earth for his physical sustenance. Furthermore, the ground would be cursed with thorns and thistles, making Adam's labor all the more difficult.

Nature and man are always closely connected in Scripture, and here we are clearly told that nature was scarred, and would be allowed at times to exercise destructive influences because of the fall of man. When man is ultimately redeemed, the whole created universe will be redeemed from its present curse, and paradise will be restored.

Finally, Adam was told that he would return to the dust from which he was made. We must not draw the conclusion from this verse that the end of man's personality is physical dissolution in the dust. Death is only the end of man's earthly, physical life. Nothing is said here about his spirit, which will never perish and which cannot go back to the ground because it did not come from the ground.

C. Mercy Displayed (vv. 20, 21)

(Genesis 3:20, 21 is not included in the printed text.)

When Adam called his wife's name "Eve," which in the Hebrew is Havah, meaning "mother," he gave her a name indicating his own faith that she would be the mother of his own children.

God showed mercy and kindness to Adam and Eve in the midst of His judgment upon them. First, they would be granted a span of life before death should overtake them. Second, God gave them longer lasting clothing in the form of animal skins. The use of animal skins required the sacrifice of the animals, thus giving them an object lesson of the penalty of sin. This taught them the way in which they should approach God in worship for the forgiveness of their sins—"without shedding of blood is no remission [of sins]" (Hebrews 9:22).

D. The Penalty Imposed (vv. 22-24)

22. And the Lord God said, Behold, the man is become as one of us, to know good and evil: and now, lest he put forth his hand, and take also of the tree of life, and eat, and live for ever:
23. Therefore the Lord God sent him forth from the garden of Eden, to till the ground from whence he was taken.
24. So he drove out the man; and he placed at the east of the garden of Eden Cherubims, and a flaming sword which turned every way, to keep the way of the tree of life.

The terror of sin can be seen in these verses. Man had broken the perfect communion which had existed between him and his Creator. It was necessary, therefore, for the Creator to expel man from Paradise, preventing him from eating of the Tree of Life and living forever. God in this way pronounced the sentence of death upon the first man and all mankind to follow. Life was there impregnated with the seeds of the curse, about to spring forth into an awful growth of moral and physical evil.

How does Adam's sin affect man today?

REVIEW QUESTIONS

1. Was man created a sinner?
2. How long did man remain sinless?
3. What were the steps in the temptation?

4. Why did Adam and Eve hide in the Garden?
5. Why did God ask, "Where art thou?"

GOLDEN TEXT HOMILY

"I WILL PUT ENMITY BETWEEN THEE AND THE WOMAN, AND BETWEEN THY SEED AND HER SEED; IT SHALL BRUISE THY HEAD, AND THOU SHALT BRUISE HIS HEEL" (Genesis 3:15).

There is a certain sacred irony in the fact that the first intimation of redemption should have occurred in the context of the divine curse upon the serpent; that is, Satan. Genesis 3:15 is known as the *proto-evangelium*—the "first good news." That the verse is clearly Messianic has been the position of Jewish interpreters, of Paul, of Irenaeus and other early church fathers, as well as Luther and all other major Reformers.

Both the ultimate victory over Satan and the achievement of that victory by the seed of the woman are clearly referred to here. H.C. Leupold, in his *Exposition of Genesis*, suggests that "by leaving open the question of just what woman the Savior was to be born [of], God mocks the tempter, always leaving him in uncertainty [as to] which one would ultimately overthrow him, so that the devil had to live in continual dread of every woman's son that was born" (vol. 1).

In a manner of speaking, the rest of Holy Scripture is a commentary on Genesis 3:15, for it tells of the meticulous preparation and eventual emergence of Messiah. Genesis 3:15 and Galatians 4:4 are the poles between which the drama of redemption extends: God promised a Redeemer, and "when the fulness of the time was come, God sent forth his Son."

Paul referred directly and exultantly to the promise: "And the God of peace shall bruise Satan under your feet shortly" (Romans 16:20). Thank God for that final triumph over the Evil One!— **Excerpts from The *Evangelical Sunday School Lesson Commentary*, Vol. 28**

SENTENCE SERMONS

GOD HAS PROVIDED redemption for all people.

—**Selected**

TEMPTATIONS that find us dwelling in God are to our faith like winds that more firmly root the tree.

—**Anonymous**

EVERY MOMENT of resistance to temptation is a victory.

—**Fredrick W. Faber**

SIN IS man's declaration of independence of God.

—*The Encyclopedia of Religious Quotations*

EVANGELISM APPLICATION

GOD HAS PROVIDED REDEMPTION FOR ALL PEOPLE.

The words "Where art thou?" contain both a note of loneliness and a deep undertone of love. The words include a sense of divine justice which cannot overlook sin, as well as hints of the divine sorrow which grieves over the sinner and the divine love which offers redemption for sin. God's question "Where art thou?" still resonates loudly in the ears of every sinner.

ILLUMINATING THE LESSON

Adam and Eve, with no evil heritage, were placed in the best imaginable environment. They were placed in an environment that God himself said was very good. Yet even under these favorable circumstances they still believed the serpent rather than God. And they fell.

The tragic history that has characterized the family of man through all the centuries can be observed in this series of facts:

1. The woman saw the tree.
2. It was pleasant to the eye.
3. It was fruit to make one wise.
4. It was good to the taste.

At this instant, shame, wrath, and fear replaced sight, wisdom, and food. The curse of man in every age has been unsanctified knowledge. Sin has made man a creature of fear. It has brought a sense of shame to man.

Man did not know that he was naked before he sinned. The need for the first clothing shop was initiated in the Garden of Eden. The effort of man to use clothes to appear respectable in spite of his sin has given clothes a perverted meaning. It is perhaps significant that the best-dressed people are often the most difficult to convince of sin.

Thorns, thistles, sweat, toil, and a tired brow made work a drudgery. Before sin, Adam kept the Garden beautiful and enjoyed his work. After sin, work became irksome. A quick review of labor reveals that attitudes have not changed since the Garden experience.

DAILY BIBLE READINGS

M. Promise of Deliverance.
   Exodus 6:1-8
T. God Saves Sinners.
   Psalm 106:1-12
W. God Redeems His People.
   Isaiah 43:1-7
T. Sin Brings Bondage.
   John 8:31-38
F. No One Is Righteous.
   Romans 3:9-20
S. Power of God for Salvation.
   1 Corinthians 1:18-25

Looking for the Redeemer

Study Text: Luke 2:25-38; 7:18-23; John 1:29-36

Objective: To examine the responses of those who recognized Jesus as the promised Redeemer and find ways to tell others about Him.

Time: The Book of Luke was written between A.D. 58 and A.D. 70.

Place: The Book of Luke was probably written at Caesarea or Rome. The Book of John was probably written at Ephesus.

Golden Text: "Behold the Lamb of God, which taketh away the sin of the world" (John 1:29).

Central Truth: Jesus Christ fulfilled God's promise of redemption.

Evangelism Emphasis: Believers must tell others that Jesus Christ is the Savior.

PRINTED TEXT

Luke 2:25. And, behold, there was a man in Jerusalem, whose name was Simeon; and the same man was just and devout, waiting for the consolation of Israel: and the Holy Ghost was upon him.

26. And it was revealed unto him by the Holy Ghost, that he should not see death, before he had seen the Lord's Christ.

27. And he came by the Spirit into the temple: and when the parents brought in the child Jesus, to do for him after the custom of the law,

28. Then took he him up in his arms, and blessed God, and said,

29. Lord, now lettest thou thy servant depart in peace, according to thy word:

30. For mine eyes have seen thy salvation,

31. Which thou hast prepared before the face of all people;

32. A light to lighten the Gentiles, and the glory of thy people Israel.

7:19. And John calling unto him two of his disciples sent them to Jesus, saying, Art thou he that should come? or look we for another?

20. When the men were come unto him, they said, John Baptist hath sent us unto thee, saying, Art thou he that should come? or look we for another?

21. And in that same hour he cured many of their infirmities and plagues, and of evil spirits; and unto many that were blind he gave sight.

22. Then Jesus answering said unto them, Go your way, and tell John what things ye have seen and heard; how that the blind see, the lame walk,

the lepers are cleansed, the deaf hear, the dead are raised, to the poor the gospel is preached.

23. And blessed is he, whosoever shall not be offended in me.

John 1:29. The next day John seeth Jesus coming unto him, and saith, Behold the Lamb of God, which taketh away the sin of the world.

30. This is he of whom I said, After me cometh a man which is preferred before me: for he was before me.

31. And I knew him not: but that he should be made manifest to Israel, therefore am I come baptizing with water.

32. And John bare record, saying, I saw the Spirit descending from heaven like a dove, and it abode upon him.

LESSON OUTLINE

I. RECOGNIZED AS MESSIAH

  A. By Simeon

  B. By Anna

II. DECLARED THE SON OF GOD

  A. The Lamb of God

  B. The Baptizer with the Holy Spirit

  C. The Son of God

III. CONFIRMED BY MIRACULOUS SIGNS

  A. The Question

  B. The Response

LESSON EXPOSITION

INTRODUCTION

Jesus Christ is the Redeemer of prophecy. Knowing that man would sin and recognizing the awful consequences of sin, God prepared a plan to redeem man before the foundation of the world was laid. The New Testament declares that Jesus Christ was and is the Lamb of God slain before the foundation of the world. Throughout the history of God's people, the idea of this Redeemer was kept alive in many different ways.

The coats of skin with which the Lord God clothed the first pair in the Garden of Eden were a type and a shadow of the Redeemer to come. The firstlings of Abel's flock which he offered as a sacrifice to God were also a type and a shadow. The clean beasts, which Noah offered as a sacrifice upon the altar which he built on Mount Ararat after he came forth from the ark, were another type and a shadow.

The children of Israel had been in Egyptian bondage for 400 years when God sent Moses to deliver them. Nine great plagues were brought upon Egypt, but Pharaoh hardened his heart after each and refused to let them go.

Then one day Moses was told by God to take a lamb without blemish, kill it, then to take the blood and strike it on the two side posts and on the upper doorpost of every Hebrew house. God said, "I will pass through the land of Egypt this night, and will smite all the firstborn in the land of Egypt, both man and beast . . . and the blood shall be to you for a token . . . when I see the blood, I will pass over you" (Exodus 12:12, 13).

Moses and the children of Israel did as the Lord commanded, and that night the destroying angel passed through the land. There was tragedy, heartache, and death everywhere except in those homes covered by the blood. This was the first Passover; furthermore, it was a test of faith. This was an example of God's delivering power; but even more, it was a type and a shadow of One who would someday come into the world and deliver man from a greater bondage than that of Egypt. This One would deliver man from the bondage of sin and Satan.

I. RECOGNIZED AS MESSIAH
   (Luke 2:25-38)

A. By Simeon (vv. 25-35)

(Luke 2:33-35 is not included in the printed text.)

25. And, behold, there was a man in Jerusalem, whose name was Simeon; and the same man was just and devout, waiting for the consolation of Israel: and the Holy Ghost was upon him.
26. And it was revealed unto him by the Holy Ghost, that he should not see death, before he had seen the Lord's Christ.

Nothing is known of Simeon outside of what is recorded in these few verses in Luke. F. Godet makes an interesting observation concerning this man: "In times of spiritual degeneracy, when an official clergy no longer cultivates anything but the form of religion, its spirit retires among obscure members of the religious community and creates for itself unofficial organs often from the lowest classes. Simeon and Anna are representatives of this spontaneous priesthood" (*A Commentary on the Gospel of Luke*).

Luke describes Simeon as a man who was righteous in his dealings with others, and cautious and scrupulous in observing the commands of Jewish law.

He was among the many Jews looking for the Messiah. The word translated here "consolation" corresponds to the word translated "comforter" (John 14:16), and "Advocate" (1 John 2:1).

Luke is careful to note that the Holy Spirit was upon Simeon. In fact, it is rather significant that the Holy Spirit is mentioned three times in these verses in relation to this man.

Simeon had evidently been longing for the coming of the Messiah, and had been much in prayer concerning this. In response to his prayer and his longing, he was given a revelation that he would see the Messiah before he died. The term "the Lord's Christ" (v. 26) refers to "Jehovah's Anointed," the Messiah sent from God. Many believe that once he saw Christ he died soon after. They base this belief on verses 26 and 29. Tradition states that Simeon was 113 years old at the time.

27. And he came by the Spirit into the temple: and when the parents brought in the child Jesus, to do for him after the custom of the law,
28. Then took he him up in his arms, and blessed God, and said,
29. Lord, now lettest thou thy servant depart in peace, according to thy word:
30. For mine eyes have seen thy salvation,
31. Which thou hast prepared before the face of all people;
32. A light to lighten the

Gentiles, and the glory of thy people Israel.

Under the influence of the Holy Spirit Simeon entered the Temple just at the right time to receive the child Jesus and perform the appropriate ceremony according to Jewish law.

Alfred Edersheim writes concerning this ceremony: "The ceremony at the redemption of a firstborn son consisted of the formal presentation of the child to the priest, accompanied by two short 'benedictions'— the one for the law of redemption, the other for the gift of a firstborn son—after which the redemption money (about 10 or 12 shillings) was paid. Most solemn, as in such a place, and remembering its symbolic significance as the expression of God's claim over each family in Israel, must this rite have been" (*Life and Times of Jesus the Messiah*).

Standing with the infant Messiah in his arms, the aged Simeon has reached the apex of his long life, its glorious consummation, and is ready for death.

The salvation that Simeon refers to in verse 30 is that for which all men waited, and especially the Jewish people, the only salvation which God has ever provided, mediated through Jesus Christ our Savior.

B. By Anna (vv. 36-38)

(Luke 2:36-38 is not included in the printed text.)

F. Godet writes concerning Anna: "Anna was another inspired person waiting for the advent of the Messiah. An aged widow, she seems never to have left the temple, and to have risen as near the ideal of ceaseless service as one could in this life. She also gave thanks to God as with eager eye she gazed upon her Redeemer in the person of the holy Child. And to all who, like herself, were looking for redemption, she spoke of Jesus as the Redeemer promised and now given. There is the same melancholy tone about Anna as about Simeon. She speaks about redemption, and will wait for it, while Simeon seems inclined to reach it as speedily as possible by death" (*A Commentary on the Gospel of Luke*).

Why did Joseph and Mary marvel concerning the predictions of Simeon about Jesus?

II. DECLARED TO BE THE SON OF GOD (John 1:29-36)

A. The Lamb of God
  (vv. 29-31, 35, 36)

(John 1:35, 36 is not included in the printed text.)

29. The next day John seeth Jesus coming unto him, and saith, Behold the Lamb of God, which taketh away the sin of the world.

30. This is he of whom I said, After me cometh a man which is preferred before me: for he was before me.

31. And I knew him not: but that he should be made manifest to Israel, therefore am I come baptizing with water.

For 500 years there had not been a prophet in Israel. But suddenly a voice was heard in the wilderness. It was the voice of a prophet. This prophet made a great impression on the people in the surrounding villages. They were impressed by his appearance and by the things he said. With delight they quoted his stinging remarks to the Pharisees, the Roman soldiers, and to others. They soon discovered they could not be indifferent to his preaching. It was the type of preaching that stirred the hearts of all who heard him. Every one felt that a new day had dawned. A new preacher of righteousness had arisen in Israel.

Who was the new prophet? He was John the Baptist. He was the son of a priest, and his mother also came from a priestly family.

Why would a man from this background be dressed as he was and why would he be preaching in the wilderness?

A sense of sin drove John to the wilderness. Here he came face-to-face with God. To understand what sin is we need to be face-to-face with God. In the sight of His holiness and purity, we can see what our sin really is. Here we can recognize sin in all its hideousness and loathsomeness.

In the loneliness of the wilderness this prophet meditated upon God's revelation in the Old Testament until it was full of meaning to him. He must have read Isaiah's description of the coming Messiah many times. He was gripped by the thought of the suffering Messiah, of the One who bears other people's sins, of the One who suffers, of the Just One who dies for the unjust. Because of his wilderness experience he recognized Jesus when he saw Him coming, and he cried out, "Behold the Lamb of God, which taketh away the sin of the world."

John was thinking of death or sacrifice when he referred to Jesus as the Lamb of God. He was the Lamb of God because God both provided and accepted Him: "God so loved the world, that he gave his only begotten Son." This is the difference between Christianity and all other religions. In all other religions man provides the sacrifice for his god. In Christianity, God provides the sacrifice for man. If it cost Christ something to die, it cost the Father something to give Him up to death. The Father and the Son are in absolute unity in providing man's salvation.

John says the Lamb of God takes away the sin of the world. Such an action would seem to involve tremendous work. But it is not done in wholesale fashion. It is an individual matter. Each individual must have his own sin taken away. That is why John says, "Behold!" Every man must look for himself. When Moses lifted up the serpent in the wilderness, only those who looked were healed.

B. The Baptizer with the Holy
    Spirit (vv. 32, 33)

(John 1:33 is not included in the printed text.)

32. And John bare record, saying, I saw the Spirit descending from heaven like a dove, and it abode upon him.

John refers to two facts concerning the Holy Spirit in these verses: (1) the Holy Spirit descended upon Christ, and (2) the Holy Spirit was imparted to the believers.

The greatest gift of the New Testament was Jesus. The greatest gift of Jesus was the Holy Spirit. The Father sent the Son; the Son baptizes with the Spirit; and the Spirit brings both the Father and the Son into the heart and life of the believer.

Jesus is the giver of the Holy Spirit, inasmuch as He removes the hindrances to the coming of the Spirit into our hearts. The great hindrance is sin. The heart of man is not the temple of the Spirit until after Jesus finishes His work of atonement.

Jesus baptizes in the Holy Spirit in the sense that He distinctly sent Him on the Day of Pentecost. It was His promise that He would do so (John 14:16). And so Peter, speaking of the coming of the Spirit, says, "Jesus . . . having received of the Father the promise of the Holy Ghost, he hath shed forth this, which ye now see and hear" (Acts 2:32, 33). From that moment the residence of the Holy Spirit in this world has been in the hearts of Christ's people—His sanctuary, Christ's body, the church.

C. The Son of God (v. 34)

(John 1:34 is not included in the printed text.)

Jesus had lived among the people to whom John was speaking for about 30 years. He had existed in comparative oblivion during this time. Now He was about to step out of the shadows and onto the stage of public activity. When John announced that Jesus was "one among you" (v. 26), he meant it literally, for Jesus was standing in the crowd that had gathered on the banks of the Jordan. Having shaken the dust from His carpenter's tunic forever, He now stood as "one among" them, ready for the beginning for His redemptive mission.

Roy L. Laurin observes of this occasion: "Jesus stood unrecognized, for they knew Him not. Here were men whose life business was the recognition of and preparation for the coming Messiah, but they did not know Him. They were religious but spiritually blind.

"What may have been tragic for these religionists may be tragedy for us. We may be so busy running heavy religious juggernauts, spending millions, erecting buildings and directing organizations that we too, may not know the personal reality of God. It is possible today that 'there standeth one among you, whom ye know not' (v. 26).

"Perhaps it was at this moment that Jesus stepped out of the crowd and, approaching John, asked to be baptized. With characteristic humility, John declined, saying, 'I have need to be baptized of thee, and comest thou to me?' (Matthew 3:14). And when he baptized Jesus, he beheld the Holy Spirit, dovelike, descending on the Son of God, and he heard God say, 'This is my beloved Son, in whom I am well pleased' (Matthew 3:17).

"This was John's authentic identity of Jesus as the Son of God: 'He that sent me to baptize with water, the same said unto me, Upon who thou shalt see the Spirit descending, and remaining on him, the same is he which baptizeth with the Holy Ghost. And I saw, and bear record that this is the Son of God' (vv. 33, 34). Here are two important designations of Jesus: He is the Lamb of God (v. 29), and the Son of God (v. 34).

"As the Lamb of God He would 'take away the sin of the world'; as the Son of God He would 'baptize with the Holy Ghost.' As the Lamb of God He would redeem; as the Son of God He would sustain. As the Lamb of God the cleansing agent was blood; as the Son of God the enabling agent was the Spirit. As the Lamb of God it meant death; as the Son of God it meant life." (*John: Life Eternal*)

John did not identify Jesus as a teacher to pass on information or as a leader to pass on inspiration. He identified Him as the Divine Redeemer that He might communicate eternal life.

How can John's humility be recognized in his introduction of Jesus?

III.   CONFIRMED BY MIRACULOUS SIGNS (Luke 7:18-23)

A.   The Question (vv. 18-20)

(Luke 7:18 is not included in the printed text.)

7:19.   And John calling unto him two of his disciples sent them to Jesus, saying, Art thou he that should come? or look we for another?

20.   When the men were come unto him, they said, John Baptist hath sent us unto thee, saying, Art thou he that should come? or look we for another?

John was asking, Are you the Coming One? (see v. 19). This is a technical Hebrew term for the Messiah, based on Malachi 3:1. The term occurs as title in Luke 13:35; 19:38; John 1:15; 3:31; and Revelation 1:8. There was a time when John was certain that Jesus was the Coming One. But the time had come when John began to doubt, for the One he had proclaimed to be the Lamb of God was not what he expected him to be. As F.W. Farrar suggests, "He felt deep anguish at the calm and noiseless advance of a Kingdom for which, in his theocratic and Messianic hopes, he had imagined a very different proclamation. Doubtless his faith, like that of Elijah (1 Kings 19:4), of Job in his trials (Job 3:1), and of

Jeremiah in prison (Jeremiah 20:7), might be, for a moment, drowned by the tragic briefness and disastrous eclipse of his own career; and he might hope to alleviate, by this message, the anguish which he felt when he contrasted the joyful brightness of our Lord's Galilean ministry with the unalleviated gloom of his own fortress prison" *(The Gospel According to Luke).*

It should be noted that John brought his doubts to the Lord immediately.   This clearly reveals that he never questioned the sincerity of the Messiah.   If he had ever thought that he was an imposter, he would never have asked him the question he did.

John's experience should remind us that he was not the only worker who has had doubts and fears concerning his Master.   In the Bible, we read of David's being offended by God's severity (2 Samuel 6:8); Jonah's being offended by God's mercy (Jonah 4:1-3); and of Martha's offense at Christ's delay (John 11:21).

It would seem that the disciples of John who came to Jesus had no particular confidence themselves in the one to whom they had been sent (v. 20).   They were not the disciples of Jesus, but of the imprisoned John, and their sympathies were with him.

B. The Response (vv. 21-23)

21.   And in that same hour he cured many of their infirmities and plagues, and of evil spirits; and unto many that were blind he gave sight.

22.   Then Jesus answering said unto them, Go your way, and tell John what things ye have seen and heard; how that the blind

see, the lame walk, the lepers are cleansed, the deaf hear, the dead are raised, to the poor the gospel is preached.

23. And blessed is he, whosoever shall not be offended in me.

The word translated "plagues" (v. 21) means, literally, "distressing bodily diseases." Implied in the word is the idea that troubles are divine chastisements.

Jesus taught the truth to the disciples of John by their sight and hearing. They saw supernatural deeds of mercy. Thus Jesus gently reminded them of scriptures apparently overlooked, for example, Isaiah 29:18; 35:4-8; 61:1-3.

John needed much grace when his disciples came back and said: "Yes, He has all the power, and is all you thought him to be; but He did not say a word about taking you out of prison." No explanation; faith nourished; prison doors left closed; and then the message, 'Blessed is he whosoever shall not be offended in me.' That is all."

Christ will not explain Himself but instead He will reveal Himself as He did to David, to Jonah, to Martha, and to John.

How do you think you would have reacted to the response of Jesus if you had been John?

REVIEW QUESTIONS

1. Who was Simeon?
2. How would you describe Simeon's character?
3. Who was Anna?
4. How did John the Baptist characterize Jesus?
5. How did Jesus respond to the question of John the Baptist?

GOLDEN TEXT HOMILY

"BEHOLD THE LAMB OF GOD, WHICH TAKETH AWAY THE SIN OF THE WORLD!" (John 1:29).

When John the Baptist cried out, "Behold the Lamb," he was upsetting hundreds of years of Jewish philosophy. The Pharisees were looking for a prophet, and they desired a king who would deliver them from the Roman Yoke, but they had no yearnings for a Savior-priest. They revealed this when they questioned John asking him, "Art thou Elijah? Art thou that prophet?" When Jesus asked for the populace's opinion of Himself, some answered in a similar fashion.

No one asked whether Jesus was the One who would deliver them from the wrath to come. Surely the priests and the Levites were concerned about the sacrifice, but they apparently had no sense of sin! It was under these circumstances that the forerunner announced Jesus not as "the word of God" or as "the Christ of God" but as "the Lamb of God." Arthur W. Pink writes, "They would have welcomed Him on the throne, but they must first accept Him on the altar."

In Exodus 24:8 Moses sprinkled the people with the crimson lifestream and declared, "Behold the blood of the covenant." How forcibly he foreshadowed John's proclamation, "Behold the Lamb of God, which taketh away the sin of the world."

Pink declares, "Christ as an Elijah—a Social-Reformer—will be tolerated [today]; and Christ as a Prophet, as a Teacher of ethics will receive respect. But what the world needs first and foremost is the Christ of the Cross, where the Lamb of God offered Himself as a sacrifice for sin."—**Excerpts from** *The Evangelical Commentary*, **Vol. 28**

SENTENCE SERMONS

JESUS CHRIST fulfilled God's promise of redemption.

—**Selected**

THE PURPOSE of Christ's redeeming work is to make it possible for bad people to become good people—deeply, radically, and finally.

—**A.W. Tozer**

CHRIST IS the bread for men's souls. In Him the church has enough to feed the whole world.

—**Ian MacLaren**

JESUS CHRIST is the divine Physician and Pharmacist, and His prescriptions are never out of balance.

—**Vance Havner**

EVANGELISM APPLICATION

BELIEVERS MUST TELL OTHERS THAT JESUS CHRIST IS THE SAVIOR.

We never really know when we might be witnessing of Jesus. In 1857, a day or two before preaching at the Crystal Palace, Charles Spurgeon went to decide where the platform should be fixed; and, in order to test the acoustic properties of the building, he cried in a loud voice, "Behold the Lamb of God, which taketh away the sin of the world." In one of the galleries, a workman, who knew nothing of what was being done, heard the words, and they came like a message from heaven to his soul. He was smitten with conviction on account of his sin, put down his tools, went home, and there, after a season of spiritual struggling, found peace and life by beholding the Lamb of God. Years after, writes Spurgeon, he told this story to one who visited him on his deathbed.

ILLUMINATING THE LESSON

There is the story of a soldier with one arm who was standing in the streets one day when an acquaintance came up to him and said, "Well, old man, I see this war has taken it out of you." "Oh no," said the soldier, looking at his empty sleeve, "I gave it." That is the point of view from which we must begin to look at the death of Christ. Sin took Christ's life, but Christ gave it; and in that giving, He was more than master of the events. For it is the truth of the New Testament that the sin that put Him on the cross, signed with that very act, its own death warrant, putting into the hands of Christ the mightiest weapon against sin itself.

DAILY BIBLE READINGS

M. My Redeemer Lives.
   Job 19:23-27
T. Redeemed From Sin.
   Psalm 19:7-14
W. The Redeemer Will Come.
   Isaiah 59:20 through 60:3
T. Jesus Is the Messiah. Matthew 26:62-64
F. Praise God for Redemption.
   Luke 1:68-79
S. Christ Had to Suffer.
   Luke 24:17-27

The Joy Christ Brings (Christmas Lesson)

Study Text: Luke 2:1-20

Objective: To review the events surrounding Christ's birth and rejoice because of His coming.

Time: Probably 5 B.C. (It may seem strange to say that Christ was born four years before Christ, but this is due to a four-year error in our calendar. A monk by the name of Dionysius Exiguus made a mistake in calculating the date of the founding of Rome. He set the date at 754 B.C. It was later discovered that the true date was 750 B.C. Therefore, our calendar should have started four years before it did.)

Place: Bethlehem

Golden Text: "Unto you is born this day in the city of David a Saviour, which is Christ the Lord" (Luke 2:11).

Central Truth: Christ's birth is a special reason for the world to rejoice.

Evangelism Emphasis: We must take the good news to lost people everywhere.

PRINTED TEXT

Luke 2:1. And it came to pass in those days, that there went out a decree from Caesar Augustus, that all the world should be taxed.

2. (And this taxing was first made when Cyrenius was governor of Syria.)

3. And all went to be taxed, every one into his own city.

4. And Joseph also went up from Galilee, out of the city of Nazareth, into Judaea, unto the city of David, which is called Bethlehem; (because he was of the house and lineage of David:)

5. To be taxed with Mary his espoused wife, being great with child.

6. And so it was, that, while they were there, the days were accomplished that she should be delivered.

7. And she brought forth her firstborn son, and wrapped him in swaddling clothes, and laid him in a manger; because there was no room for them in the inn.

8. And there were in the same country shepherds abiding in the field, keeping watch over their flock by night.

9. And, lo, the angel of the Lord came upon them, and the glory of the Lord shone round about them: and they were sore afraid.

10. And the angel said unto them, Fear not: for, behold, I bring you good tidings of great joy, which shall be to all people.

11. For unto you is born this day in the city of David a Saviour,

which is Christ the Lord.

12. And this shall be a sign unto you; Ye shall find the babe wrapped in swaddling clothes, lying in a manger.

13. And suddenly there was with the angel a multitude of the heavenly host praising God, and saying,

14. Glory to God in the highest, and on earth peace, good will toward men.

20. And the shepherds returned, glorifying and praising God for all the things that they had heard and seen, as it was told unto them.

DICTIONARY

Caesar Augustus (SEE-zer aw-GUS-tus)—Luke 2:1—The Roman emperor.

Cyrenius (sigh-REE-ni-us)—Luke 2:2—Roman-appointed governor of the Syrian province of the eastern Mediterranean territory.

Syria (SEER-ee-uh)—Luke 2:2—A comparatively large country north of the Palestinian region that is now Israel, bordering on the Mediterranean Sea. The territorial boundaries of Bible lands were rather fluid.

LESSON OUTLINE

I. MIRACULOUS BIRTH

   A. The Circumstances

   B. The Event

II. ANGELIC ANNOUNCEMENT

   A. The Message

   B. The Song

III. JOYFUL RESPONSE

   A. The Reaction of the Shepherds

   B. The Response of Mary

   C. The Worship of the Shepherds

LESSON EXPOSITION

INTRODUCTION

The birth of Jesus has been called the most astonishing narrative in the world's literature. It is also the most blessed and unexpected. Who could have imagined that God would be born on earth as a human child? But now that the

event has occurred, it is seen as the most natural of happenings. What could be more inevitable than that the loving Creator of mankind, seeing His handiwork lost in sin, should assume mankind's humanity and die for their redemption? This is the wonderful and unparalleled event that we called the Incarnation.

The Incarnation was made emphatic when the angels said to the shepherds, "For unto you is born this day in the city of David a Saviour, which is Christ the Lord" (Luke 2:11). Christ was born "unto" those shepherds and, just as surely, "unto" us.

The essence of Christian theology can be summarized in these three titles: (1) "a Saviour, which is Christ the Lord." (2) "The Lamb slain from the foundation of the world" (Revelation 13:8). Christ was the Savior of men, the prophesied Messiah, the One to whom all sacrifices pointed, the atonement for our sins. (3) "The Anointed One" or "the Messiah"— these are the Greek and Hebrew meanings of the name *Christ*. By virtue of His obedience (Hebrews 12:2; Philippians 2:5-11) He is our Lord, our rightful ruler, the just master of our lives and owner of our possessions, of all that we have and are. For we are bought with a price (1 Corinthians 6:20), even His own precious blood.

I. MIRACULOUS BIRTH
(Luke 2:1-7)

A. The Circumstances (vv. 1-5)

1. And it came to pass in those days, that there went out a decree from Caesar Augustus, that all the world should be taxed.
2. (And this taxing was first made when Cyrenius was governor of Syria.)
3. And all went to be taxed, every one into his own city.
4. And Joseph also went up from Galilee, out of the city of Nazareth, into Judaea, unto the city of David, which is called Bethlehem; (because he was of the house and lineage of David:)
5. To be taxed with Mary his espoused wife, being great with child.

Undoubtedly the greatest event in the history of the world was the Incarnation. It was the coming into the world of God in human form— the God-man, Jesus Christ.

Cyrenius (Quirinius) was governor of Syria, and Herod the Great was the king of Judea. Augustus Caesar was the great Roman emperor at this time. His reign has been called the Golden Age of Latin literature. Augustus ruled over 120 million people. Half, about 60 million, were slaves; a third more were freedmen; only 20 million were full citizens. The population of Rome was about 6,000. There were about 6 million people in Palestine.

A universal census had been ordered by the Roman emperor. He wanted to determine the population of the empire. This first enrollment was followed by a second census to record property as a basis for taxation. The Roman plan was to register citizens in their places of residence, but the ancient Jewish custom was for everyone to go to the hometown of his respective family and be listed there.

Joseph, the village carpenter of Nazareth, in the northern Palestine province of Galilee, was compelled to travel southward 70 miles to Bethlehem, since he was descended from the great poet-king, David, who was born in Bethlehem (v. 4). This happening, which seems a mere matter of chance, was really ordered by Divine Providence, fulfilling the ancient but clear prophecy of Micah 5:2.

Joseph probably walked from Nazareth to Bethlehem, while Mary, his betrothed, rode a donkey. Mary was also descended from David, but it is unclear whether the law required her presence with Joseph for the taking of the census (v. 5).

Mary knew, as did all Jewish maidens, that one day the Messiah of promise would make glad the heart of the mother chosen for the high mission of bearing Him. But Mary did not clutch this high honor to herself. Her response to the angel of the annunciation was full of dignity and nobility: "Behold the handmaid of the Lord; be it unto me according to thy word" (Luke 1:38). She rose to the height of the promise of the Lord with all its wonder and mystery as she fully surrendered to the Lord's will. She probably understood only in a vague sense that she was to be the woman of destiny through whom the hopes of her people would be fulfilled.

B. The Event (vv. 6, 7)

6. And so it was, that, while they were there, the days were accomplished that she should be delivered.

7. And she brought forth her firstborn son, and wrapped him in swaddling clothes, and laid him in a manger; because there was no room for them in the inn.

Arriving in Bethlehem (six miles south of Jerusalem), worn with the long journey, Mary may have already been suffering her birth pangs. However, the pair found the little town so crowded with census visitors that there was no room for them in the rude inn. Joseph, anxiously inquiring, could find no shelter for Mary other than a stable. This stable was probably one of the many limestone caves of the vicinity. There the Son of God was born. It was a humble home for the King of Kings, but He came to earth for the very purpose of identifying Himself with the lot of the poorest and the lowliest. The manger of the stable was probably a stone trough hollowed out of the side of the cave, and this, filled with straw, served as the cradle for the Divine Babe, who was first, according to Jewish custom, wrapped in many long bands of cloth. Mary herself did this, for she was too poor to hire an attendant.

And so it was that the Son of God stooped to become a part of humanity. Literally, He took on flesh. The Word of God is explicit on this point. Mary asked the question, "How shall this be, seeing I know not a man?" (Luke 1:34). The angel answered, "The Holy Ghost shall come upon thee, and the power of the Highest shall overshadow thee: therefore also that holy thing which shall be born of thee shall be called the Son of God" (v. 35).

The Incarnation presupposes a true conception and a real birth. The Son whom God sent forth, the Person who took flesh, was born of a woman. It was a true acceptance of humanity with all its limitations, growth, and development.

It was the Godhead taking humanity, not humanity taking the Godhead. Paul said that Christ was in the "form of God" (that is, in His essential attributes) and that He was "equal with God" (Philippians 2:6) in honor, glory, and power and that He took the form of a servant (v. 7).

His incarnation meant, and means, that the preexistent Christ was embodied in human flesh, demonstrated in human life, exemplified in human action, crystalized in human form.

Christ as prophesied, stepped out of heaven to make history. He left his perfect existence to come to our imperfect one.

What was the nature of the incarnation?

III.   ANGELIC ANNOUNCEMENT
       (Luke 2:8-14)

A.   The Message (vv. 8-12)

8. And there were in the same country shepherds abiding in the

field, keeping watch over their flock by night.

9. And, lo, the angel of the Lord came upon them, and the glory of the Lord shone round about them: and they were sore afraid.

10. And the angel said unto them, Fear not: for, behold, I bring you good tidings of great joy, which shall be to all people.

11. For unto you is born this day in the city of David a Saviour, which is Christ the Lord.

12. And this shall be a sign unto you; Ye shall find the babe wrapped in swaddling clothes, lying in a manger.

In Palestine flocks were allowed to graze the land only while the fields were still unplowed. When they were out all night, the shepherds slept in their clothes in the midst of their flocks. The shepherds were able to find places that afforded a certain amount of protection until about December, when the torrential winter rains began. Then they were obliged to move into the valleys where the green pastures grew more quickly than above on the mountains. For those living in Bethlehem this meant wintering their sheep in the neighboring Judean desert. There, scarcely any snow fell in winter; and there, if necessary, flocks could remain at night in the open (v. 8).

These shepherds were simple, unsophisticated pastoral men. They were engaged in their common occupation when they received the wonderful revelation from heaven (v. 9-14). They were not simply gazing idly up into the sky, neglecting the work at hand.

The glory of the Lord was probably that wonderful light which accompanies the appearance of God and His angels, a light like the Shekinah that flamed above the mercy seat of the ark.

The shepherds should not be blamed for being afraid. The presence of supernatural beings, however lovely and loving they may be, overawes men with majesty, dazzles them with splendor, and terrifies them with strangeness.

The angel said unto the shepherds, "Fear not" (v. 10). That was heaven's first word to earth after the birth of Jesus. It was the voice of an angel sounding the keynote of the music of hope for sinful men. Christ often used the same comforting words during His ministry.

"I bring good tidings" is only one word in the Greek; literally it means "I evangelize." Why such words of comfort and hope? Well, it was a sad world to which Christ came, a world of slavery, of poverty, of outrageous sin, of dark idolatry and superstition, and of hopeless infidelity. Christ came as light, joy, and peace, precisely what the world needed.

Note to whom the message was given, "Which shall be to all people"—not only to Herod on the throne, not only to the high priest in the center of the Sanhedrin, not only to the famous rabbis, but to everyone, rich and poor, high and low, learned and ignorant, famous and obscure. "Whosoever will" may receive this "great joy."

What the angel was about to say explained why the shepherds did not need to be afraid. The message was in essence: You lowly shepherds, you toiling workers, you poor peasants, this radiant Messiah is all yours.

What a comprehensive

announcement the angel gave: "A Savior, who is Christ the Lord" (*NKJV*). *Jesus* means "Jehovah is salvation," the name given by the angel of the annunciation (Luke 1:31). *Christ* is from the Greek word meaning "Anointed," and the Hebrew *Messiah* means the same thing. *Lord* means "Jehovah." God himself was born in Bethlehem that day, to the shepherds and to each of us.

It should not be forgotten and cannot be overemphasized that it was a voice from heaven that declared these wonderful things about the Babe born in Bethlehem. These titles were not given to Jesus by His followers, or by Himself, or by later writers, but were announced as being His by the angel of the Lord, sent from heaven.

Christ in the manger meant that Deity had cradled itself in the midst of poverty and sorrow and suffering and sin (v. 12). When this Child wept, the world would behold God in tears. It would have harmonized with the previous expectations of these shepherds if some stately and celestial token had accompanied the infant Savior; but the ordinary and commonplace were chosen for Him by His Father. This continued in the lifestyle lived by Jesus. There was no straining after grandeur. The manger of Bethlehem symbolized the world's neglect of the obscure, its hardness to the needs of the suffering, and its scorn of the poor.

B. The Song (vv. 13, 14)

13. And suddenly there was with the angel a multitude of the heavenly host praising God, and saying,

14. Glory to God in the highest, and on earth peace, good will toward men.

While the shepherds gazed into the glorious light, they did not realize that the angel had a multitude of companions (v. 13). By *multitude* we understand a great number, and this host was part of a heavenly army. Thousands of angels appeared, filling the sky. All of this for a handful of shepherds.

Luke did not say the angels sang, but the angels' words were in poetic form, and the church has always assumed they were expressed in a song of praise.

The words "Glory to God" (v. 14) indicate a very important lesson. Because of the Babe, a world was to be redeemed. Millions and millions of human beings were to be rescued from everlasting death. Was this the thing uppermost in the angels' thoughts? No—it was second. The first thing was "Glory to God." Why so? Because God is the provider of this salvation. He himself provided the Savior in the person of His only begotten Son. Moreover in heavenly minds, God always occupies first place, and heavenly creatures consider Him first in everything.

The last part of the angels' song observes, "On earth, peace, good will toward men." This was the meaning of the coming of this Child—the meaning of the fact that He was and is the Savior, the Christ, the Lord.

The earth will experience peace only when men of the earth are become like the Prince of Peace. World peace talks will not bring peace. The population of the world is running everywhere crying for peace, yet always arming for war. Peace will never come that way. The Christ child came into the world that men who are displeasing to God because of their sins may be made pleasing to God.

Why do you think the shepherds were chosen for an angelic visitation?

III. JOYFUL RESPONSE
(Luke 2:15-20)

A. The Reaction of the Shepherds (vv. 15-18)

(Luke 2:15-18 is not included in the printed text.)

The angels left the shepherds, but they never left Jesus. P.W. Wilson writes: "As he went about His work, He was conscious of them, ascending and descending. In the wilderness, angels ministered to Him, when men neglected Him. In the garden, an angel strengthened Him, when His friends fell asleep. Twelve legions of them, more loyal than Israel's 12 tribes, were ever at His service, and by His empty tomb angels stood guard" (*The Christ We Forget*).

The shepherds did not reason or debate with themselves who should keep the wolf from the sheep, but did as they were commanded, committing their sheep to Him whose pleasure they obeyed. They did not go out of idle curiosity or in doubt of the angel, but in obedience. For the angel had said, "Ye shall find the babe" (v. 12).

The shepherds found Mary, Joseph, and the Babe. They found the sign given them by the angel. They, like other Jews, had expected that the Christ, or Anointed Savior, whom their prophets foretold, would come as a great King and Conqueror. It must, therefore, have been a trial to their faith to find Him in the lowest poverty laid in the manger in the inn's stable. Yet, like the apostle Paul, they were not disobedient to the heavenly vision, and they found Him who is eternal life.

The shepherds were not afraid of being disbelieved, scorned, ridiculed. The Lord had made a great revelation to them, and they felt it their duty to pass it on. So they excitedly communicated the wonderful news to everyone they passed on their way back to their flocks. Thus, to those humble shepherds was given the honor of being the first Christian preachers. Their words have gone to the ends of the earth. If they had been asleep, careless of their charge, or heedless of the foxes and jackals prowling about the fold, they would never have seen the angels or have heard the heavenly music, nor would they have made known abroad the saying which was told them concerning this Child.

Those who heard the story told by the shepherds did what too many of us do with the gospel. They wondered and went no further. A feeble ripple of astonishment ruffled the surface of their souls for a moment. But like the streaks on the sea made by a cat's paw of wind, it soon died out, leaving the depths unaffected.

B. The Response of Mary (v. 19)

(Luke 2:19 is not included in the printed text.)

Mary's response was different from that of the shepherds. She was astonished because she knew the significance of the Babe to which she had given birth because of the annunciations made to her and to Joseph. *Ponder* (v. 19) means "to bring together in one's mind, to consider." Mary had the words of the angel to her, the song of Elizabeth, the words of the angel to Joseph, and the message of the shepherds to put together, piece by piece, word by word, picture by picture. She had all of these sayings to help her see God in the Babe of Bethlehem.

C. The Worship of the Shepherds (v. 20)

20. And the shepherds returned, glorifying and praising God for all the things that they had heard and seen, as it was told unto them.

The shepherds were not distracted from their work even by these marvelous events. They returned glorifying and praising God for all they had seen and heard. This is the real climax of gospel preaching—when it motivates the audience to praise. This is represented as the chief responsibility and privilege of the redeemed. Experience is only perfected when God is praised.

What lessons are taught by the total reaction of the shepherds to their angelic experiences?

REVIEW QUESTIONS

1. What were the circumstances of the birth of Jesus?

2. Why was the birth of Jesus not announced to all of Bethlehem by the angels?

3. What was the message of the angels to the shepherds?

4. What did the shepherds do with the message of the angels?

5. How did Mary react to all that she had seen and heard concerning the birth of Jesus?

GOLDEN TEXT HOMILY

"UNTO YOU IS BORN THIS DAY IN THE CITY OF DAVID A SAVIOUR, WHICH IS CHRIST THE LORD" (Luke 2:11).

Oh, the greatness of the wisdom of God! Step-by-step throughout history God revealed a permanent answer to man's sinful dilemma—a Redeemer. This Redeemer would be born of a virgin in the city of Bethlehem under the direst of circumstances. This day had arrived!

The humble conditions of His birth would prove to be foolishness to some and a stumbling block to others. In light of this, we note those responsible for proclaiming the message: first, the heavenly angel, and then the humble shepherds. All are to be recipients of the message. Although He came first to His own—the Jewish nation—it is not His will that any should perish.

This Redeemer came as (1) Jesus the Savior, bringing deliverance for man's willful and innate sin; (2) Christ the Messiah, the Anointed One (In the house of worship, He explained explicitly why and for whom this anointing would be given—see Luke 4:16-21.); and (3) Lord. Daily tribute is paid Him as Lord of history by the calendar, which divides events by whether they happened before or after His birth. Whether willingly or unwillingly, every knee shall bow to Him.

Truly, it is great joy to experience and know that our deliverance has come and we have submitted our all to His ultimate will.—**Fred H. Whisman, Cost Analyst, Pathway Press, Cleveland, Tennessee**

SENTENCE SERMONS

CHRIST'S BIRTH is a special reason for the world to rejoice.

—**Selected**

CHRISTMAS BEGAN in the heart of God. It is complete only when it reaches the heart of man.

—*Draper's Book of Quotations for the Christian World*

THE SON OF GOD became a man to enable men to become the sons of God.

—**C.S. Lewis**

THE HINGE OF HISTORY is on the door of a Bethlehem stable.

—**Ralph W. Sockman**

EVANGELISM APPLICATION

WE MUST TAKE THE GOOD NEWS TO LOST PEOPLE EVERY-WHERE.

There was no reason why God should send His Son into the world for us except that He loved us. There was nothing in us to attract God; there was no glory which men could add to the glory of His Son. Indeed, the Son whom God sent into the world knew that He would be insulted, rejected, blasphemed, beaten, and put to death. But He also knew that without His coming men would be doomed to eternal death by their sin. Loving men in spite of all their transgressions and longing to impart eternal life to them, He undertook the only possible way to save those He loved from destruction; He sent His Son into the world for us.

ILLUMINATING THE LESSON

In Nashville, Tennessee, in the home of an Army chaplain, on the first Christmas Eve after World War II, the telephone rang. His wife answered. She was thrilled to hear the voice of her husband who after many months overseas had just returned to American shores. You can imagine her joy when she learned he would be home for Christmas. He would be able to get home sometime during the night. They decided to keep his homecoming a secret from the children so that he could surprise them on Christmas morning. The next morning when the children gathered around the tree to open their presents, the white sheet on which the presents had been placed suddenly stirred. Up from among the packages arose their father. It is easy to imagine the joy of that home when the little ones, expecting only presents, found their father himself.

This is a parable of the real meaning of Christmas. Up from the manger came no ordinary baby, but the Christ, the love of God himself incarnate.

DAILY BIBLE READINGS

M. God's Anointed Son.
    Psalm 2:1-12
T. Sure Prophecy. Isaiah 9:2-7
W. Source of Peace. Isaiah 53:1-5
T. Virgin Birth. Matthew 1:18-25
F. Cause for Rejoicing.
    Matthew 2:1-11
S. Miraculous Conception.
    Luke 1:26-35

Lamb Slain for Redemption

Study Text: Exodus 12:1-51; Romans 3:22-24; 1 Corinthians 5:7; 1 Peter 1:18, 19

Objective: To compare the Old Testament Passover lamb with Christ's perfect sacrifice and appreciate the redemption Christ provides.

Golden Text: "Christ our passover is sacrificed for us" (1 Corinthians 5:7).

Central Truth: Jesus Christ is the perfect sacrifice for our sins.

Evangelism Emphasis: Jesus Christ died to provide salvation for sinners.

PRINTED TEXT

Exodus 12:2. This month shall be unto you the beginning of months: it shall be the first month of the year to you.

6. And ye shall keep it up until the fourteenth day of the same month: and the whole assembly of the congregation of Israel shall kill it in the evening.

1 Peter 1:18. Forasmuch as ye know that ye were not redeemed with corruptible things, as silver and gold, from your vain conversation received by tradition from your fathers;

19. But with the precious blood of Christ, as of a lamb without blemish and without spot.

Exodus 12:7. And they shall take of the blood, and strike it on the two side posts and on the upper door post of the houses, wherein they shall eat it.

12. For I will pass through the land of Egypt this night, and will smite all the firstborn in the land of Egypt, both man and beast; and against all the gods of Egypt I will execute judgment: I am the Lord.

13. And the blood shall be to you for a token upon the houses where ye are: and when I see the blood, I will pass over you, and the plague shall not be upon you to destroy you, when I smite the land of Egypt.

1 Corinthians 5:7. Purge out therefore the old leaven, that ye may be a new lump, as ye are unleavened. For even Christ our passover is sacrificed for us.

Exodus 12:48. And when a stranger shall sojourn with thee, and will keep the passover to the Lord, let all his males be circumcised, and then let him come near and keep it; and he shall be as one that is born in the land: for no uncircumcised person shall eat thereof.

49. One law shall be to him that is homeborn, and unto the stranger that sojourneth among you.

50. Thus did all the children of Israel; as the Lord commanded Moses and Aaron, so did they.

Romans 3:22. Even the righteousness of God which is by faith of Jesus Christ unto all and upon all them that believe: for there is no difference:

23. For all have sinned, and come short of the glory of God;

24. Being justified freely by his grace through the redemption that is in Christ Jesus.

LESSON OUTLINE

I. SPOTLESS SACRIFICE
   A. The Passover Lamb
   B. The Costly Sacrifice

II. CHRIST, THE PASSOVER LAMB
   A. Application
   B. Protection
   C. Personal

III. REDEMPTION FOR ALL
   A. Provision for All
   B. Needed by All

LESSON EXPOSITION

INTRODUCTION

Redeemed is a word full of significance and meaning for the Christian. The word *redemption* is used in connection with the work of Christ on the cross. It expresses the wonderful deliverance effected by Christ for all who are under the guilt and bondage of sin. It involves two great truths: (1) that of purchase or buying back by the payment of a ransom and (2) deliverance from bondage by the ransom paid and by the power of God.

The Old Testament contains four different words in the original rendered by the English word *redeem*; in the New Testament the concept is expressed in different forms of two Greek words. One of the Old Testament words for *redeem* occurs only once (Psalm 136:24), and means "to break off" or "to separate." Another word for *redeem*, in Nehemiah 5:8, means "to buy" and so acquire for oneself or "to possess." It is the same word rendered *purchase* in Exodus 15:16; Psalms 74:2; 78:54; and the word *buy* in Ruth 4:4, 5, 8, 9. In the other two words, there is both the idea of purchase and of deliverance. From one of these we get the word *redeemer*.

The redeemer (*gaal*) had to be near a kinsman, so as to have the right to buy back that which had been sold and also have the authority to avenge or revenge the wronged one. In Numbers 35:12, 19, 21, 24, 25, 27, the word *avenger* or *revenger* is used, and it means the same as *redeemer*.

In redemption as a purchase, the basic idea is the price paid, but not its payment to any one person. In Psalm 49:6-9, the price paid in redemption is contrasted with all the wealth possessed by rich men, showing how utterly inadequate are all the riches they possess to pay the required ransom.

The New Testament words which speak of redemption as "purchase" are those used of men buying in the market or forum. Twice, believers are reminded that they "are bought with a price" (1 Corinthians 6:20; 7:23).

Redemption means not only purchase by payment of the ransom required, but it also means the deliverance or setting free of those who have been slaves and are in bondage. *Deliverance* is the prominent idea of redemption in both the Old and the New Testaments. In Egypt the redemption of Israel was effected by the sprinkling of the blood, which made them safe from the judgment of God; and then the passage at the Red Sea delivered them from the power of Pharaoh and his hosts. These find their fulfillment in the cross of Christ and His resurrection from the dead.

I. SPOTLESS SACRIFICE
   (Exodus 12:1-6; 1 Peter 1:18, 19)

A. The Passover Lamb
   (Exodus 12:1-6)

   (Exodus 12:1, 3-5 is not included in the printed text.)
   2. This month shall be unto you the beginning of months: it shall be the first month of the year to you.
   6. And ye shall keep it up until the fourteenth day of the same month: and the whole assembly of the congregation of Israel shall kill it in the evening.

   The institution of the Passover was so important that God ordained that the Hebrew people should date the beginning of the new year from the time of the Passover (v. 2). The Passover fell in the month of Abib,

also called Nisan in later Old Testament writings.

In giving the instructions to Moses concerning the Passover, God, for the first time in Hebrew history, called His people "the congregation of Israel" (vv. 3, 6). Four days before the night when the destroying angel was to pass over Egypt and the Israelites were to be permitted to leave, every Hebrew household was commanded to select a lamb. It was to be without blemish, a male, and one year old. There was to be one lamb for each home. If there were not enough members of a household to consume the lamb, they were to merge with another family. Later Jewish tradition stated that the number around the table for the Passover feast should be at least 10.

It should be noted that the first ordinance of the Jewish religion was a domestic service. This arrangement was divinely wise. No nation has ever been really prosperous or permanently strong that did not cherish the importance of the home. History records that ancient Rome failed to resist the enemy not because her discipline had degenerated, but because evil habits in the home had ruined her population. We cannot overlook the simple and obvious fact that God has built His nation upon families.

Why was the lamb to be kept four days? Probably to give the Israelites time enough to meditate upon the solemnity and significance of that divine event, and also it was an opportunity to prepare for their departure from Egypt.

B. The Costly Sacrifice
   (1 Peter 1:18, 19)
   18. Forasmuch as ye know

that ye were not redeemed with corruptible things, as silver and gold, from your vain conversation received by tradition from your fathers;

19. But with the precious blood of Christ, as of a lamb without blemish and without spot.

People with money are sometimes startled to discover how little their wealth can really do. It only touches the rim and circumference of life; but it fails utterly in questions that affect the heart of human existence. Money cannot compensate for broken vows, or unsay cruel words which eat into the soul like a cancer. Money cannot bring back the color to the pallid cheek of a loved one cold in death. Money cannot atone for the lack of love. Money can only buy things which are as corruptible as itself. But when it seeks to enter into the realm of souls—the eternal and incorruptible—its way is barred; its value will not be accepted; its claim will be denied.

An argument cannot be dissected with a knife. Love cannot be measured with a yardstick. A soul cannot be weighed with human scales. It is equally impossible to ransom a soul from sin by "corruptible things, as silver and gold" (v. 18). There is nothing in common between gold and silver, which, however long they may endure, must perish in the end; but the soul, which is of eternal value, is impervious to destruction and decay and is destined to survive the crash of matter and the wreck of worlds.

Things could not and cannot redeem souls. In the words of F.B. Meyer: "God could have given suns of gold, and stars of silver, constellations glowing with precious metals; but none of these would have been sufficient to free one soul from the curse or penalty of sin, or change it into a loyal and loving subject of His Kingdom. . . . Matter accounts for nothing in the weighing-in-chamber of eternity. And therefore the Creator must give not things, but life—not gifts, but Himself—ere He could redeem" (*Tried by Fire*).

The blood of Christ is the sole ground of forgiveness and acceptance with God. "Without shedding of blood is no remission" (Hebrews 9:22). Hebrews corresponds with Leviticus, where the truth of access to God by sacrifice is revealed and where a walk with God in sanctification is maintained by a God-appointed priesthood. In Romans 5, Ephesians 2, and Colossians 1, the believer is shown to have peace with God, being reconciled and having access into His presence through the blood. And from Hebrews 10:19, 20, we learn that the way into the Most Holy Place is by the blood, which gives boldness. No sinner could approach God in his sin, but by the blood of Christ forgiveness and cleansing is procured; and when accepted by faith, he has access with boldness into the very Holy of Holies. That was something quite unknown and utterly impossible to any Israelite, for until the veil was rent the way into God's presence in the Holy of Holies was closed. It was when the blood of Christ was shed on the cross that God himself rent the veil and opened the way for all who would come by faith in Christ. The action of the high priest in going into the Holiest on the great Day of Atonement once a year with the blood of the sin offering, which he sprinkled on and before the mercy seat, typified the action of Christ when He ascended to the right hand of God. And as the high priest acted as a representative, even so does Christ; and where He is, the believer may come by faith, that is, to the throne of grace with boldness. It is the blood of Christ that gives the believer this boldness.

Why did the Passover lamb have to be without blemish and without spot?

II. CHRIST, THE PASSOVER LAMB
(Exodus 12:7-13;
1 Corinthians 5:7)

A. Application (Exodus 12:7-11)

(Exodus 12:8-11 is not included in the printed text.)

7. And they shall take of the blood, and strike it on the two side posts and on the upper door post of the houses, wherein they shall eat it.

It should be noted that God did not leave the Israelites without some responsibility. They were, in the first place, to take the lamb, according to the instructions which He had given, and to slay the lamb on the night which He had appointed. They were to take the blood of the lamb and sprinkle it with hyssop on the two side posts and on the lintel of their houses. In doing this they were to understand that the blood was to be for them a token upon their houses.

B. Protection (vv. 12, 13)

12. For I will pass through the land of Egypt this night, and will smite all the firstborn in the land of Egypt, both man and beast; and against all the gods of Egypt I will execute judgment: I am the Lord.

13. And the blood shall be to you for a token upon the houses where ye are: and when I see the blood, I will pass over you, and the plague shall not be upon you to destroy you, when I smite the land of Egypt.

The blood was to be a token or sign that there had been death by sacrifice, so that when God saw it, He would pass over the door and not suffer the destroyer to enter. In every house where there was no blood, the death angel entered and the firstborn was killed as a result.

When the lamb was slain, a bunch of hyssop was dipped in the blood in the basin and struck on the lintel and two side posts of the door. The hyssop was a common weed which grew around their houses and speaks of the faith that is common to all of God's people. The word *passover*, referring to God's protection of the people, is not the word for "pass by" or "pass through," as the crossing of a river, or passing through a town or country. It occurs as "pass over" in Exodus 12:13, 23, 27, and is found in four other places as follows: "halt" (1 Kings 18:21); "leaped" (v. 26); "became lame" (2 Samuel 4:4); "passing over" (Isaiah 31:5). It means passing over from one foot to the other, or "hovering over"; and that meant that God stood over the houses and so came between His people and the destroying angel. He became their safety.

C. Personal (1 Corinthians 5:7)

7. Purge out therefore the old leaven, that ye may be a new lump, as ye are unleavened. For even Christ our passover is sacrificed for us.

"Christ died for the ungodly. . . . Christ died for us. . . . Christ died for our sins. . . . He died for all"

(Romans 5:6, 8; 1 Corinthians 15:3; 2 Corinthians 5:15). These statements show that Christ did not die for Himself; nor was it for any cause in Himself that He died, but on behalf of others. There was absolutely nothing in Him demanding death, or making it possible for death to touch Him. For death means sin, and "He did no sin . . . He knew no sin . . . and in Him was no sin" (see 1 Peter 2:22; 2 Corinthians 5:21; 1 John 3:5). He was ever perfectly sinless, never in any way being tainted by it, or having even the suspicion of it. He was holy, harmless, undefiled, and separate from sinners.

This sinless Christ became our Passover. He was sacrificed for us. His death was vicarious. There are 14 passages in the New Testament where the death of Christ is said to be vicarious, six of these being in the Gospel of John. In three of them we have His own words, saying that He would give His life "for the life of the world" (6:51); that "the good shepherd giveth his life for the sheep" (10:11); and "I lay down my life for the sheep" (10:15). The other three are in chapter 11. Caiaphas, the high priest, stated: "It is expedient . . . that one man should die for the people, and that the whole nation perish not" (v. 50). John further explained: "[Caiaphas] prophesied that Jesus should die for that nation; and not for that nation only, but that also he should gather together in one the children of God" (vv. 51, 52).

There are eight occurrences in the Epistles, as follows: "He that spared not his own Son, but delivered him up for us all" (Romans 8:32); "He hath made him to be sin for us" (2 Corinthians 5:21); "[He was] made a curse for us" (Galatians 3:13); "He by the grace of God should taste death for every man" (Hebrews 2:9); "Christ also suffered for us" (1 Peter 2:21); "Christ also hath once suffered for sins, the just for the unjust" (3:18); "Christ hath suffered for us in the flesh" (4:1); and "He laid down his life for us" (1 John 3:16).

Added to these 14 passages, there are seven others where the expression "died for" occurs, each one being connected with some particular doctrine relating to the Christian life. There are three in Romans, three in 2 Corinthians, and one in 1 Thessalonians. In between these is the great gospel statement of 1 Corinthians 15:3: "Christ died for our sins according to the scriptures." That is the great fundamental statement of the gospel, for apart from the atoning death of Christ on the cross, there is no gospel for lost sinners and no salvation to offer them. In Romans 5 we have the two statements "Christ died for the ungodly" and "Christ died for us" (vv. 6, 8). The first 11 verses of chapter 5 show the security of the position of the justified believer.

Is the blood of Christ emphasized enough in contemporary preaching? Explain.

III. REDEMPTION FOR ALL
      (Exodus 12:43-51; Romans 3:22-24)

A. Provision for All
    (Exodus 12:43-51)

(Exodus 12:43-47, 51 is not included in the printed text.)

48. And when a stranger shall sojourn with thee, and will keep the passover to the Lord, let all his males be circumcised, and then let him come near and keep it;

and he shall be as one that is born in the land: for no uncircumcised person shall eat thereof.

49. One law shall be to him that is homeborn, and unto the stranger that sojourneth among you.

50. Thus did all the children of Israel; as the Lord commanded Moses and Aaron, so did they.

The sojourning stranger who wished to keep the Passover had only to be circumcised—he and his males—to be admitted to the ordinance. He was then to be as one in the land.

B. Needed by All (Romans 3:22-24)

22. Even the righteousness of God which is by faith of Jesus Christ unto all and upon all them that believe: for there is no difference:

23. For all have sinned, and come short of the glory of God;

24. Being justified freely by his grace through the redemption that is in Christ Jesus.

The unanimous testimony of Scripture is that man outside of Jesus Christ is lost. This tragic fact cannot be denied by those who accept the Word of God as authoritative and valid.

There are only two classes of people, according to the Word of God—the saved and the lost. There is no middle ground. There is no halfway position. Each individual is in one or the other of these classes.

Man has difficulty in accepting this fact. He knows that he is not perfect; yet it is difficult for him to see his lostness. He believes there must be something in him or something he can do that will recommend him to God. There must be some other way to gain favor in God's sight. He often concludes that surely God is too merciful to cast him away altogether.

The only reliable source of knowledge we have on man's lost condition is the Word of God. We cannot depend on philosophy, science, ethics, and non-Biblical religions, because they tend to commend man rather than condemn him.

Man as a sinful creature has a depraved heart and a darkened mind; therefore, human consciousness and opinions are untrustworthy. It is impossible for man to form correct judgments about himself apart from divine revelation.

Man's lost condition points out his need for salvation. Biblical salvation is the greatest concept ever to be entertained by the mind of man. The word *salvation* as used in a comprehensive sense includes all that God does for man from eternity to eternity to deliver man from sin and its consequences. Salvation is what God does for and in man.

Paul's message concerning salvation is the message of the New Testament. The Word of God declares that "all [men] have sinned" and that "the wages of sin is death" (Romans 3:23; 6:23). This means that the consequence of sin is eternal separation from God. But the promise is given that anyone who believes in Jesus Christ will not perish. The word *anyone* in the Bible means "every individual." The word *believe* means "to put personal trust in Jesus Christ; to believe that Jesus Christ was the Sin-Bearer and died in the place of the sinner; to accept Christ and not have to pay the penalty for sin."

Why is it so difficult for man to accept his lost condition?

REVIEW QUESTIONS

1. What were God's instructions to Moses concerning the Passover feast?

2. What responsibility did the family have in getting ready to leave Egypt?

3. What did God promise to do when He saw the blood?

4. How does Christ become our Passover?

5. What is Paul's message for lost men?

GOLDEN TEXT HOMILY

"CHRIST OUR PASSOVER IS SACRIFICED FOR US" (1 Corinthians 5:7).

The connection of this illustration with the passage in which it occurs is obvious. The Jews commenced the Feast of Unleavened Bread with the slaying, roasting, and eating of the paschal lamb. Now, the apostle has been urging the Corinthians to moral purity, and has enjoined them to put away the leaven of wickedness, and keep the feast with the unleavened bread of sincerity and truth; and, as a motive to do this, he reminds them that the Christian dispensation is as a spiritual Passover, which commenced with the sacrifice of "the Lamb of God, which taketh away the sin of the world." The paschal lamb is regarded as a symbol of Christ.

The Israelites were reminded by the Passover feast of the bondage from which their ancestors had been delivered when they were brought out of Egypt "by a mighty hand, and by a stretched out arm." The nation had been emancipated from the tyranny of the pharaohs, and had been spared the doom of the firstborn of the people of the land. Christ's redemption set his people free from the tyranny, the bondage, the unrewarded toil, the darksome night, the dreary hopelessness of sin; and brought them out into the freedom, the light, the gracious privileges, the glorious hopes of the gospel.

Put to death by the head of the family, the lamb was taken to the priest, who sprinkled its blood upon the altar and burned its fat, according to the ordinance. Although the lamb was offered yearly, it was in the first instance that it was regarded most strictly as a sacrifice. Christ was offered once only; "There remaineth no more sacrifice for sin." Yet the Eucharist is a perpetual memorial of the great sacrifice of Calvary. It is by the willing, accepted, vicarious sacrifice of our Redeemer that mankind have been reconciled and consecrated unto God.

It was through participation in the paschal meal that every Hebrew family was reminded of its share in the covenant mercy and faithfulness of the Eternal. As they ate the lamb in the appointed way, and with the appointed observances and accompaniments, the children of Israel were led to appropriate, in faith and obedience, the spiritual provision which the God of their fathers had made for them. In like manner the members of the spiritual commonwealth of Israel "eat the flesh of the Son of man and drink his blood," taking Christ as the nourishment of their souls, and appropriating the strength, the wisdom, the grace of God himself. In the sacrament of the Supper, they who eat and drink in faith participate in the provisions of divine bounty and love.

In connection with the paschal meal, several circumstances may be noted. The lamb was without blemish; the house was freed from leaven; all were careful to avoid ceremonial defilement. These arrangements symbolized "holiness unto the Lord," and they remind us that those who regard the Christ of God as their Passover are bound by every sacred consideration to seek that purity of heart, that sanctification of nature, which can alone render a man and a society acceptable to a holy and heart-searching God.—**Excerpts from** *The Pulpit Commentary,* **Vol. 19**

SENTENCE SERMONS

JESUS CHRIST is the perfect sacrifice for our sins.

—Selected

JESUS CHRIST, God's Son, died for me, so no sacrifice can be too great for me to make for Him.

—Charles Thomas Studd

THE CROSS OF CHRIST does not make God love us; it is the outcome and measure of His love for us.

—Andrew Murray

CARRY THE CROSS patiently and with perfect submission, and in the end it will carry you.

—Thomas à Kempis

EVANGELISM APPLICATION

JESUS CHRIST DIED TO PROVIDE SALVATION FOR SINNERS.

Apart from Christ and His death on the cross there is no true life, for all men naturally are dead in sin. It is in Him that we have eternal life, for "he that hath the Son hath life; and he that hath not the Son of God hath not life" (1 John 5:12). He came to give life to the world, for He said, "I am come that they might have life, and that they might have it more abundantly" (John 10:10). "In him was life; and the life was the light of men" (John 1:4). These passages plainly show that it is in Christ alone that life is to be found, and that life is an abundant one.

ILLUMINATING THE LESSON

In Korea there is a large sign standing conspicuously by a railroad with the following message: "The precious blood of gallant officers and men of the Seventh Cavalry Regiment, First Cavalry Division, has made it possible for you to be here."

Heaven has no signboards, but everyone who enters will be conscious of the fact that the precious blood of Christ made it possible for him to be there.

Divine justice decreed that without shedding of blood there would be no remission of sins (Hebrews 9:22). The sinless Lord Jesus Christ willingly gave His blood at Calvary for the remission of sins. Nothing less would do; nothing more was required.

The apostle John declares: "The blood of Jesus Christ his Son cleanseth us from all sin" (1 John 1:7).

Personal faith in that divinely perfect and all-sufficient sacrifice of Christ is necessary. The writer of Acts says, "Whosoever believeth in him shall receive remission of sins" (10:43).

DAILY BIBLE READINGS

M. Everyone Can Partake.
   Numbers 9:9-14
T. Continual Observance.
   Deuteronomy 16:1-8
W. Reminder for Cleansing.
   2 Chronicles 30:13-22
T. Crucified Lamb.
   Luke 23:44-49
F. Jesus Is the Lamb.
   Acts 8:26-35
S. Eternal Sacrifice.
   Hebrews 10:11-14

Promised Redeemer

Study Text: Isaiah 52:13 through 53:12

Objective: To study Isaiah's prophecy about the crucifixion of Christ and give thanks for His sacrifice.

Time: The Book of Isaiah was written between 745 B.C. and 680 B.C.

Place: The Book of Isaiah was probably written at Jerusalem.

Golden Text: "All we like sheep have gone astray; we have turned every one to his own way; and the Lord hath laid on him the iniquity of us all" (Isaiah 53:6).

Central Truth: Christ suffered rejection, humiliation, and crucifixion to procure salvation for all people.

Evangelism Emphasis: Christ's suffering and death made salvation available for all people.

PRINTED TEXT

Isaiah 53:1. Who hath believed our report? and to whom is the arm of the Lord revealed?

2. For he shall grow up before him as a tender plant, and as a root out of a dry ground: he hath no form nor comeliness; and when we shal! see him, there is no beauty that we should desire him.

3. He is despised and rejected of men; a man of sorrows, and acquainted with grief: and we hid as it were our faces from him; he was despised, and we esteemed him not.

4. Surely he hath borne our griefs, and carried our sorrows: yet we did esteem him stricken, smitten of God, and afflicted.

5. But he was wounded for our transgressions, he was bruised for our iniquities: the chastisement of our peace was upon him; and with his stripes we are healed.

6. All we like sheep have gone astray; we have turned every one to his own way; and the Lord hath laid on him the iniquity of us all.

7. He was oppressed, and he was afflicted, yet he opened not his mouth: he is brought as a lamb to the slaughter, and as a sheep before her shearers is dumb, so he openeth not his mouth.

8. He was taken from prison and from judgment: and who shall declare his generation? for he was cut off out of the land of the living: for the transgression of my people was he stricken.

9. And he made his grave with the wicked, and with the rich in his death; because he had done no violence, neither was any deceit in his mouth.

10. Yet it pleased the Lord to bruise him; he hath put him to

grief: when thou shalt make his soul an offering for sin, he shall see his seed, he shall prolong his days, and the pleasure of the Lord shall prosper in his hand.

11. He shall see of the travail of his soul, and shall be satisfied: by his knowledge shall my righteous servant justify many; for he shall bear their iniquities.

12. Therefore will I divide him a portion with the great, and he shall divide the spoil with the strong; because he hath poured out his soul unto death: and he was numbered with the transgressors; and he bare the sin of many, and made intercession for the transgressors.

LESSON OUTLINE

I. REJECTED REDEEMER
  A. Exalted
  B. Marred
  C. Expiation
  D. Rejected
II. ABUSED REDEEMER
  A. Suffering
  B. Slain
III. VICTORIOUS REDEMPTION
  A. Sin Defeated
  B. Judgment Satisfied
  C. Victory

LESSON EXPOSITION

INTRODUCTION

Jesus Christ is the Redeemer of prophecy. When He had revealed Himself to Nathaniel as the omniscient Lord, Nathaniel said, "Thou art the Son of God; thou art the King of Israel" (John 1:49). This Israelite, "in whom [there was] no guile" (v. 47), belonged to that class of Jews of his day who waited faithfully for the accomplishment of the national expectations that God would send them the promised Messiah-King. The Lord Jesus Christ, the Virgin-born Son of God,

is that King; He came as the "minister of the circumcision for the truth of God, to confirm the promises made unto the fathers" (Romans 15:8). Before He was born, His mother, the Virgin of Nazareth, received the promise of God communicated by the angel Gabriel that her son, conceived by the Holy Spirit, should be King. "The Lord God shall give unto him the throne of his father David: and he shall reign over the house of Jacob for ever; and of his kingdom there shall be no end" (Luke 1:32, 33).

The promises to Israel had reached beyond their own nation; the Gentiles knew of it and therefore a caravan of learned men came from the East to Jerusalem asking direction to find "the newborn King of the Jews" (see Matthew 2:1, 2). John the Baptist heralded Him as the King in whose person the promised Kingdom had come near (see Matthew 3:2; Luke 10:9). Being of the seed of David He was a King, entitled to the throne, and as a King He manifested Himself in royal dignity and royal power, the power of God. The signs of the promised Kingdom attended Him every step of the way. The blind saw, the deaf heard, the lame leaped, the dead were raised (Isaiah 35; Matthew 11:5).

But it was not many days before the promised King was hanging on a cross. The Jews refused to acknowledge Him as their King; however, Pilate, the Gentile ruler, had a sign put above His cross; "Jesus of Nazareth the King of the Jews" (John 19:19).

All of this had been seen by the prophets, and they had written that this was the purpose of His coming to earth. It was through His death and resurrection He proved Himself to be the promised Redeemer.

I. REJECTED REDEEMER
(Isaiah 52:13-15; 53:1-3)

A. Exalted (52:13)

(Isaiah 52:13 is not included in the printed text.)

The Lord's Messiah is exalted because the Lord God views the Servant as divinely commissioned and qualified. He "shall deal prudently." Perhaps nothing shows more clearly the perfect wisdom of our Lord's life upon earth than the fact that, among all His detractors, not one has been able to point out any lack of wisdom in any part of it. Almost all men do unwise things— things they regret to have done, things which do them harm and which injure instead of protecting the objects that they have in view. But our Lord's whole course was guided by the most perfect wisdom in keeping with Isaiah 11:2: "And the spirit of the Lord shall rest upon him, the spirit of wisdom and understanding, the spirit of counsel and might, the spirit of knowledge and of the fear of the Lord."

B. Marred (52:14)

(Isaiah 52:14 is not included in the printed text.)

Verse 14 presents an awful picture of suffering. One scholar translates these words as "so disfigured, his appearance was not human, and his form not like that of the children of men." The word marred properly means "destruction," and here, "a disfigurement or defacement of the body, especially the face." Another writer states, "We have here the picture of a slave whose face has been disfigured and whose form has been distorted by heavy burdens and cruel blows."

C. Expiation (52:15)

(Isaiah 52:15 is not included in the printed text.)

The phrase "sprinkle many nations" probably refers to an act of expiation and cleansing (see Leviticus 14:7; Numbers 19:18). The idea is that Christ is the true High Priest, to whom the ordinary priesthood with its typical sprinklings typically pointed. The statement that "kings shall shut their mouths at him" is a reference to the involuntary effect of the overpowering impression, or the manifestation of their extreme amazement at one so suddenly brought out of the depths and lifted up to so great a height.

D. Rejected (Isaiah 53:1-3)

1. Who hath believed our report? and to whom is the arm of the Lord revealed?

So glorious and so unexpected is the prophet's message concerning the lowly-exalted Servant, that no one has believed it.

The "arm of the Lord [Jehovah]" refers to God's almighty power. God's holy arm had been "made bare . . . in the eyes of all the nations" (52:10), but they had not realized the wondrous workings of His providence. Thus also the workings of Jehovah in the life and death of Jesus Christ were not understood or believed by the men of His day, and these words from Isaiah are accordingly quoted in John 12:37, 38 and Romans 10:16.

2. For he shall grow up before him as a tender plant, and as a root out of a dry ground: he hath no form nor comeliness; and when we shall see him, there is no beauty that we should desire him.

According to the Gospel accounts of the life of Jesus, He grew up as any normal Jewish boy. His early life was one of obscurity and lowliness, not as a royal Prince on whom the hopes and eyes of a nation were fixed.

In commenting on the words "He hath no form nor comeliness; and when we shall see him, there is no beauty that we should desire him," James M. Gray writes: "A literal interpretation of these words would almost lead us to regard the Saviour as positively unattractive in appearance, but the prophet is referring rather to his state of moral abasement than to his outward aspect. In other words, he had no beauty in the way of external splendor, which it was expected the Jewish Messiah and the coming king of Israel would assume. There were no robes of royalty on his person, no diadems sparkled on his brow, and there was no spectacular retinue in his train. He was of humble rank, poor in the world's goods, and without eminent associates. He had disappointed the expectation of his nation and was not the Prince that they desired. How remarkable it is that the New Testament gives us not a particle of information as to our Lord's personal appearance! The Bible directs us to his moral beauty, his holiness,

his benevolence, never to his external form" *(Christology of the Old Testament).*

3. He is despised and rejected of men; a man of sorrows, and acquainted with grief: and we hid as it were our faces from him; he was despised, and we esteemed him not.

What all the prophets foresaw came to pass. No throne for Christ, but the cross! The Jews did not want this man to reign over them. They put Him into the hands of the Gentiles. When Pilate reminded the mob of His kingship, they answered, "We have no king but Caesar" (John 19:15). Then when Pilate asked Him, "Art thou a king then?" He answered, "Thou sayest that I am a king" (18:37). After that His own people demanded the release of Satan's man, Barabbas, and the crucifixion of their King. The awful choice was made. No throne for the King—the cross instead! And after that, the mockery of His kingship—the platted crown, the purple robe, the frail reed, the marred visage!

It was at the cross that sin found its full expression and showed itself in all its heinousness. All classes of men united at the cross in crucifying the Son of God; and their actions were a full manifestation of sin, exposing the utter depravity of the human heart and its revolt against all that is pure and holy and true. There, sin showed itself in taking that One who was perfectly pure and holy, ever meek and lowly, never injuring a creature, and nailing Him to a malefactor's cross as an object of shame and ignominy. Could there be any act more diabolical, or anything more fiendish? Sin surely gave vent to itself in all its fullness, and showed what an awful monster it is when unchecked and unrestrained.

It is important to remember that it was not the riffraff and the rabble who so acted, but the very highest in the land and those who were the religious leaders of the people. For the natural heart of man, even though religious and outwardly respectable and honest, is capable of the vilest and most heinous sin. There at the cross, sin showed itself in its envy, hatred, and malice toward the Son of God; and sin also showed itself in the scoffing, mocking, and jeering that were railed on Him when He was suffering the most intense agony. That surely was sin in all its fullness.

Is the Cross a crisis for man? Explain.

II. ABUSED REDEEMER
(Isaiah 53:4-9)

A. Suffering (vv. 4-6)

4. Surely he hath borne our griefs, and carried our sorrows: yet we did esteem him stricken, smitten of God, and afflicted.

The fact that Christ died is of the greatest importance to every Christian. But to really appreciate the fact that He died, we must also remember the manner in which He died. Paul told the Corinthians, "We preach Christ crucified" (1 Corinthians 1:23). That was the very first truth he emphasized when he brought them the gospel. The humbling of Christ and His condescension to the form of a servant, being made in the likeness of men, found its climax in His death on the cross (Philippians 2:6-8). Crucifixion was both cruel and shameful. It was the type of death meted out to criminals of the worst kind. The suffering was excruciating and prolonged. It often took days for death to occur. The Jews did not use this method of death—their law did not permit it. For that reason Jesus was handed over to the Romans, and His crucifixion by them was demanded by the Jewish leaders.

Both Psalm 22 and Psalm 69 emphasize the experiences through which the Lord Jesus passed in His sufferings on the cross. Psalm 22 has been called the "psalm of the sob." The first half of this psalm describes how intensely the Lord suffered when giving Himself up to death. He was not only forsaken by God, but mocked and taunted by His enemies and left alone by His followers. Psalm 69 emphasizes the aspect of reproach. Christ's death was the trespass offering that was presented, and it was an offering which showed sin to be wrong and injurious. Reproach and shame are the ideas stressed, and these are connected with sin.

5. But he was wounded for our transgressions, he was bruised for our iniquities: the chastisement of our peace was upon him; and with his stripes we are healed.

The cries which came from the lips of Christ while He was on the cross indicate the intensity of the sufferings He endured: "My God, my God, why hast thou forsaken me?" (Psalm 22:1; Matthew 27:46); and then shortly before He died, "I thirst" (John 19:28). The former indicates what the cross meant to Him as the Sin-Bearer, when it brought about separation from God even for a moment. For there He was made sin, and God cannot look upon sin, which He hates. And hence it was that He spared not His own Son. The cry of thirst signified something of the intense physical pain He was enduring, relieved somewhat by the vinegar given to Him.

All that sin meant to the sinner—as guilt, condemnation, judgment, and punishment—was borne by Christ. He took the place of the sinner and bore all that was against him fully, so that the sinner believing on Him is completely absolved from his sin and guilt and becomes the righteousness of God in Christ. Whether sin be represented as guilt or a debt or a burden or condemnation, all were put on Christ, and His death on the cross met all that was demanded by God because of sin.

6. All we like sheep have gone astray; we have turned every one to his own way; and the Lord hath laid on him the iniquity of us all.

It was when Christ hung on the cross that He became our substitute and not while He lived. "The Lord hath laid on him the iniquity of us all." Peter wrote, "Christ . . . suffered for sins, the just for the unjust" (1 Peter 3:18). He willingly took the place of the guilty sinner and bore the judgment of sin, so that the sinner who believes on Him might be both pardoned and cleared of his guilt and its judgment and also become the righteousness of God in Him.

B. Slain (vv. 7-9)

7. He was oppressed, and he was afflicted, yet he opened not his mouth: he is brought as a lamb to the slaughter, and as a sheep before her shearers is dumb, so he openeth not his mouth.

The word *oppressed* denotes harsh, cruel, and arbitrary treatment, such as that of a slave driver toward those who are under his supervision; however, this kind of action is not used by God toward men. When the average man is wrongly accused, he usually protests vehemently; but Christ's silence under false accusations at His trial caused His judge to marvel.

The prophet portrayed Jesus as a lamb led to the slaughter. John the Baptist called Jesus "the Lamb of God, which taketh away the sin of the world" (John 1:29). He was the Infinite Sacrifice to which the Paschal lamb through all the centuries had mutely pointed.

8. He was taken from prison and from judgment: and who shall declare his generation? for he was cut off out of the land of the living: for the transgression of my people was he stricken.

Through the use of oppressive judgment, Christ was condemned to the cross, by injustice cloaking itself under the forms of a judicial procedure. The word translated "taken" suggests the idea of being snatched or hurried away, and the word translated "prison" means generally "under violent constraint." Hostile oppression and judicial persecution were the circumstances under which Christ was carried away to death.

9. And he made his grave with the wicked, and with the rich in his death; because he had done no violence, neither was any deceit in his mouth.

If Joseph of Arimathea had not intervened, Jesus would have been buried with the two criminals who were crucified on either side of Him. The burial place would have been the cemetery for executed criminals. The Messiah had done nothing to warrant His execution, and His judges were without excuse for their actions. When His death was accomplished, His humiliation was ended, and no further indignity could be committed to His person. Thus, even in His burial, He was separated from sinners. The apostle Peter refers to this in 1 Peter 2:21-25.

What led the Son of God to endure the terrible sins He experienced for us?

III. VICTORIOUS REDEMPTION
      (Isaiah 53:10-12)

A.   Sin Defeated (v. 10)

10. Yet it pleased the Lord to bruise him; he hath put him to grief: when thou shalt make his soul an offering for sin, he shall see his seed, he shall prolong his days, and the pleasure of the Lord shall prosper in his hand.

At the cross of Christ every sin was met and answered fully and forever. "He hath made him to be sin for us" (2 Corinthians 5:21). There God searched out all that sin was and all that it deserved, and placed it on His Son. At the Cross sin was abolished, for "he appeared to put away sin by the sacrifice of himself" (Hebrews 9:26). The sacrifice of Christ on the cross is a full and complete remedy for all sin. The whole question of sin as guilt, demanding the judgment of God, was dealt with there; and that means that every sinner coming to the Cross, and by faith beholding Christ as a personal Savior, is fully forgiven for all sin and freed completely from its consequences. The salvation procured at the Cross is full, free, eternal, and absolutely complete from the moment it is received by faith.

B. Judgment Satisfied (v. 11)

11. He shall see of the travail of his soul, and shall be satisfied: by his knowledge shall my righteous servant justify many; for he shall bear their iniquities.

Finished, complete, full—these are words that come down to us from the Cross, telling so wondrously the fullness of the love of God, the awfulness and heinousness of sin, and exhibiting God's judgment upon it. These words also reveal to us the perfect salvation provided for every sinner who will but accept it as the free gift of God, and that by simple faith. The Cross makes it possible for God to save freely and fully every sinner who comes there by faith; but it also makes it impossible for God to save anyone, however good, any other way.

C. Victory (v. 12)

12. Therefore will I divide him a portion with the great, and he shall divide the spoil with the strong; because he hath poured out his soul unto death: and he was numbered with the transgressors; and he bare the sin of many, and made intercession for the transgressors.

We have here a final and glorious conclusion to the redemptive work which Christ accomplished by His own sacrifice. Not only was the sacrifice made once for all, providing atonement for sin, but it is continually efficacious. Atonement by the blood of Christ has not only put away past sins, but it has made atonement for all sin—past, present, and future. It puts the believer in a place of continual acceptance or continuous blessing. The word *continually* in Hebrews 7:3 and 10:1 is the same as in Hebrews 10:12, 14, rendered "for ever," and means uninterrupted continuance.

How would you define victorious redemption?

REVIEW QUESTIONS

1. Why did Isaiah portray Christ as a servant?

2. How did Isaiah describe Christ's humiliation?

3. What features of Christ's death did Isaiah predict?

4. What ideas of the Atonement are taught in today's lesson?

5. What did Isaiah say about Christ's final triumph?

GOLDEN TEXT HOMILY

"ALL WE LIKE SHEEP HAVE GONE ASTRAY; WE HAVE TURNED EVERY ONE TO HIS OWN WAY; AND THE LORD HATH LAID ON HIM THE INIQUITY OF US ALL" (Isaiah 53:6).

"Some chapters and verses of the Bible are so sacred to us that we almost fear to open and examine them; and yet those are the very portions that best reward a loving and reverent examination. This chapter is the gem of Isaiah's writings. This verse is the conclusion to which the prophet comes, and he here views the long sad story of the Savior's sufferings. 'The Lord hath laid on him the iniquity of us all.'

"*Man's iniquity.* The word means 'unequalness'; man is never quite the same, never quite steady, he does not keep the straight line, and this indicates a wrong state of mind and heart. Man's iniquity is affirmed in Scripture . . . and universally acknowledged, both by individuals and nations in moments of alarm. The apostle Paul, in Romans . . . convicts men of iniquity in view of the great, universal, natural laws of their own being and of human society. Personally, we are not prepared to deny this fact of human iniquity; though, to so many of us, it is only an intellectual conception without any moral power in it. We resort to various devices in order to keep off personal applications and convictions. We charge the evil on the race. We try to think of it as a mere disease or calamity. We procrastinate over the consideration of it. It would be altogether wiser to face it, and try to realize it and deal with it.

"*God bearing man's iniquity for him.* The person who bore man's iniquity was God's Christ, and so it was really God bearing. This expression should be viewed in the light of the figure used in the text— the figure of the shepherd laying on the under-shepherd the duty of bringing the wandering sheep back, and setting it, free of evil, self-willed propensities, in the fold again. That work was the "burden" which he was called to bear. So God laid on Christ the work of delivering men from their iniquity, from its consequences, and from itself. 'Himself bare our sicknesses, and carried our sorrows' [see Matthew 8:17; Isaiah 53:4]. He took on him man's deliverance from sin, and spent his time in illustrative healings of men's bodily infirmities, and gave his life in the endeavour to save men from their sins.

"In giving Christ, God proposed the saving of men from their sins, and therefore his Son was named the significant name of Jesus. God laid the sin on Christ, as if he had said, 'I charge you now with this supremely difficult, but most blessed work, of saving, everlastingly saving, sinful, willful, ruined men.'"

ROCK OF AGES
Could my tears forever flow,
Could my zeal no languor know,
These for sin could not atone;

Thou must save, and Thou alone;
In my hand no price I bring,
Simply to Thy cross I cling.

—**Excerpts from** *The Pulpit Commentary*, **Vol. 10**

SENTENCE SERMONS

CHRIST SUFFERED rejection, humiliation, and crucifixion to procure salvation for all people.

—**Selected**

THE CROSS OF CHRIST is the sweetest burden I ever bore; it is such a burden as wings are to a bird, or sails to a ship, to carry me forward to my harbor.

—**Samuel Rutherford**

ANYTHING that one imagines of God apart from Christ is only useless thinking and vain idolatry.

—**Martin Luther**

THE STRANGEST TRUTH of the gospel is that redemption comes through suffering.

—**Milo L. Chapman**

EVANGELISM APPLICATION

CHRIST'S SUFFERING AND DEATH MADE SALVATION AVAILABLE FOR ALL PEOPLE.

The greatest crisis that ever comes to any man or woman is the Cross. It means either life or death to everyone. To the sinner convinced of his sin, turning to the cross of Christ and believing on Him as a personal Savior means eternal life and eternal salvation; but to those who turn away from the Cross in unbelief and pride, it means eternal death or separation from God forever and ever. The Cross is therefore a crisis for everyone. For the believer in Christ it is surely a crisis, for there his sin was judged by God, and by the sacrifice

of Christ it is put away forever. There he is crucified to the world and the world to him.

ILLUMINATING THE LESSON

The cry of Jesus on the cross just before yielding up His spirit, "It is finished" (John 19:30), was one of His great utterances. It is full of wonderful significance. It was just one word—*finished* or *done*. This same Greek word is rendered in other passages by the following English words: *make an end, accomplish, fulfill, perform, fill up, pay, go over.* The word *finished,* therefore, has the meaning of "completeness, fullness, or of filling up."

By the sacrificial death of Christ on the cross, a full and complete salvation was provided for everyone who will accept it by faith. The death of Christ, which made atonement for sin, was therefore the one and only way of salvation provided by God for sinners, good and bad. The cry of Christ, "It is finished," was a triumphant one, announcing a work completely accomplished on behalf of a sinful world. And on the basis of that finished work and it alone, every sinner may find perfect and eternal acceptance with God.

DAILY BIBLE READINGS

M. A Prophet Like Moses.
   Deuteronomy 18:15-22
T. Kinsman-Redeemer.
   Ruth 4:1-10
W. The Son of David.
   2 Samuel 7:8-16
T. The Son of Man. Luke 18:31-34
F. Raised From the Dead.
   Acts 2:22-33
S. Exalted on High.
   Philippians 2:5-11

Redemption Through Faith in Christ

Study Text: Galatians 3:1 through 4:7

Objective: To realize that we are redeemed through faith in Christ Jesus and be confident of our position in Christ.

Golden Text: "The law was our schoolmaster to bring us unto Christ, that we might be justified by faith" (Galatians 3:24).

Central Truth: Faith in Christ is essential for a person to become a child of God.

Evangelism Emphasis: Faith in Christ sets people free from the bondage of sin.

PRINTED TEXT

Galatians 3:1. O foolish Galatians, who hath bewitched you, that ye should not obey the truth, before whose eyes Jesus Christ hath been evidently set forth, crucified among you?

2. This only would I learn of you, Received ye the Spirit by the works of the law, or by the hearing of faith?

3. Are ye so foolish? having begun in the Spirit, are ye now made perfect by the flesh?

4. Have ye suffered so many things in vain? if it be yet in vain.

5. He therefore that ministereth to you the Spirit, and worketh miracles among you, doeth he it by the works of the law, or by the hearing of faith?

10. For as many as are of the works of the law are under the curse: for it is written, Cursed is every one that continueth not in all things which are written in the book of the law to do them.

11. But that no man is justi-

fied by the law in the sight of God, it is evident: for, The just shall live by faith.

13. Christ hath redeemed us from the curse of the law, being made a curse for us: for it is written, Cursed is every one that hangeth on a tree:

14. That the blessing of Abraham might come on the Gentiles through Jesus Christ; that we might receive the promise of the Spirit through faith.

22. But the scripture hath concluded all under sin, that the promise by faith of Jesus Christ might be given to them that believe.

23. But before faith came, we were kept under the law, shut up unto the faith which should afterwards be revealed.

24. Wherefore the law was our schoolmaster to bring us unto Christ, that we might be justified by faith.

25. But after that faith is come, we are no longer under a schoolmaster.

26. For ye are all the children of God by faith in Christ Jesus.

27. For as many of you as have been baptized into Christ have put on Christ.

4:4. But when the fulness of the time was come, God sent forth his Son, made of a woman, made under the law,

5. To redeem them that were under the law, that we might receive the adoption of sons.

6. And because ye are sons, God hath sent forth the Spirit of his Son into your hearts, crying, Abba, Father.

7. Wherefore thou art no more a servant, but a son; and if a son, then an heir of God through Christ.

LESSON OUTLINE

I. FAILURE OF HUMAN EFFORT
  A. Reproof
  B. Argument
II. JUSTIFICATION BY FAITH
  A. Example
  B. Deliverance
  C. Promises
  D. Schoolmaster
III. HEIRS OF THE PROMISE
  A. Basis of Sonship
  B. Assurance of Sonship

LESSON EXPOSITION

INTRODUCTION

Martin Luther was correct when he said, "Faith alone *saves*." Man is saved by faith plus nothing else. This is the apostle Paul's position in answering the claims of the Judaizers in the Book of Galatians. The Judaizers taught that the Gentiles, in order to be saved, first had to become Jews. They challenged the truth of Paul's preaching by claiming that salvation is not by faith alone, but by obedience to the law of Moses. They also questioned Paul's right to preach the gospel. They argued that Paul was not a true apostle and that his teaching carried no authority.

Merrill Tenney observes that Galatians was written as a protest against corruption of the gospel of Christ. The essential truth of justification by faith rather than by the works of the law had been obscured by the Judaizers' insistence that believers in Christ must keep the law if they expected to be perfect before God. When Paul learned that this teaching had begun to penetrate the Galatian churches, and that it was beginning to alienate the new Christians from their newfound liberty, he could not refrain from writing.

Tenney sees the tone of Galatians as warlike. He writes: "It fairly crackles with indignation, though it is not the anger of personal pique but of spiritual principle. 'Though we, or an angel from heaven, should preach unto you any gospel other than that which we preached unto you, let him be anathema [accursed]' (1:8), cried Paul as he reproved the Galatians for their acceptance of legalistic error" (*New Testament Survey*).

It is true that the Book of

Galatians burns with the ardor of a conflict which Paul felt touched the continuance of the truth of the gospel. Galatians burst from the heart of the great apostle of liberty at an agonizing crisis of his conflict. Thus, the epistle has been the basis of liberty in every struggle of the church to assert the right of the sons of God. Christians will always revert to Galatians as their Magna Carta.

I. FAILURE OF HUMAN EFFORT (Galatians 3:1-5)

A. Reproof (v. 1)

1. O foolish Galatians, who hath bewitched you, that ye should not obey the truth, before whose eyes Jesus Christ hath been evidently set forth, crucified among you?

As spiritual father of the Galatians, Paul knew how they had come to know Christ and what transformation had been wrought in their lives. So, coming from him, the reference to past experiences should have been an effective reminder. He showed them that their present attitude was incongruent with the facts. They had been saved not by law, but by grace. This being so, were they attempting to perfect their experience by reverting to the law?

B. Argument (vv. 2-5)

2. This only would I learn of you, Received ye the Spirit by the works of the law, or by the hearing of faith?

3. Are ye so foolish? having begun in the Spirit, are ye now made perfect by the flesh?

4. Have ye suffered so many things in vain? if it be yet in vain.

5. He therefore that ministereth to you the Spirit, and worketh miracles among you, doeth he it by the works of the law, or by the hearing of faith?

There is a note of reproof in Paul's words in verse 2. There must have been some extraordinary power of delusion or of fascination at work to steer them so completely out of the way of true faith. Whatever, it was most effective in deluding them.

It is worth noting that by verse 3 the apostle had referred to the Galatians as foolish for the second time. These words indicate that their listening to the Judaizers was senseless and irrational. His tone here, however, exhibited more a sense of surprise and sadness than of harsh accusation. The Galatians were his children in the Lord.

The Galatian Christians had dared much, had risked much, and had suffered much by becoming believers in Christ (v. 4). By dropping back into the life pattern in which they had been reared, they had suffered in vain. By agreeing to circumcision, they were again putting the flesh, not Christ, at the center of their lives. For first-century Christians, the entire pattern of life was changed; becoming a Christian for them was almost a cosmic event. To be free from the flesh and threadbare traditions, many of them endured affliction and even death at the hands of men like Saul, the persecutor. If they fell back under the control of old laws, they lost their freedom and so had suffered in vain. Paul saw that his Galatian converts were not holding, they were surrendering.

Apparently, because of miracles occurring in their midst, the

Galatians had received the Holy Spirit (v. 5). On the surface, reception of supernatural power during a time of doctrinal error would seem impossible. Yet here it was. Furthermore, the Greek noun form of "ministereth" is translated a "supply of the Spirit" in Philippians 1:19. It is so rich that no exigency of life or death can exhaust it.

Is man a sinner because he sins, or does he sin because he is a sinner? Explain.

II. JUSTIFICATION BY FAITH
(Galatians 3:6-25)

A. Example (vv. 6-9)

(Galatians 3:6-9 is not included in the printed text.)

Paul cites Abraham as an example of faith. It was he, before and above any saint in the annals of his race, who represented the nature of faith and its power—faith, not as opposed to reason, but as opposed to sight. His faith was not perfect, but it was real; it rested on the simplest of virtues.

Abraham illustrates what it is like to walk by faith. Walking by faith and not by sight means a consistent endeavor to correlate our life with our convictions, so that what we are expresses what we believe.

The Bible repeatedly stresses the fact that faith and faith alone will save: "For by grace are ye saved through faith; and that not of yourselves: it is the gift of God: not of works, lest any man should boast" (Ephesians 2:8, 9). The Philippian jailer asked, "Sirs, what must I do to be saved?" Paul and Silas answered, "Believe on the Lord Jesus Christ, and thou shalt be saved, and thy house" (Acts 16:30,

31). "Without faith it is impossible to please him: for he that cometh to God must believe that he is, and that he is a rewarder of them that diligently seek him" (Hebrews 11:6).

B. Deliverance (vv. 10-14)

10. For as many as are of the works of the law are under the curse: for it is written, Cursed is every one that continueth not in all things which are written in the book of the law to do them.

11. But that no man is justified by the law in the sight of God, it is evident: for, The just shall live by faith.

Paul appeals to the ancient Deuteronomic writings by showing that the law can only bring men into condemnation. The Jewish rabbis taught that the common people who had no interest in the law were under God's curse. Here Paul taught that all persons who seek acceptance with God on the ground of obedience to the law are under God's curse. It is not possible for anyone to fulfill the requirement of the law.

The apostle emphasized the impossibility of justification by the law, and deliverance from the works of the law through Christ. He reminded the Jews who held that their submission to the law entitled them to special blessings as sons of Abraham: "As many as are of the works of the law are under a curse." Those who are under the law stand condemned rather than blessed or justified. Since Judaizers were under the curse, why should the Galatians share their fate? Since no one had kept the law fully, then all were condemned by the law. It is therefore evident that no one can be justified by keeping the law.

In verse 11 the apostle quoted Habakkuk 2:4 when he said, "The just shall live by faith." Faith in what Christ has done is the basis of justification. Theologians tell us that faith, justification (being declared righteous), and life are all simultaneous. As one exercises faith in Christ, he is justified and receives life. Then he goes on to live the Christian life by faith.

13. Christ hath redeemed us from the curse of the law, being made a curse for us: for it is written, Cursed is every one that hangeth on a tree:

14. That the blessing of Abraham might come on the Gentiles through Jesus Christ; that we might receive the promise of the Spirit through faith.

The word *redeem* means to pay the purchase price. It is as if Christ went to the slave market and paid the required number of Roman coins for the one in bondage.

Paul used the word *us* in the phrase "redeemed us" to refer to himself, as well as those with him at the time of writing, and those addressed—both Jews and Gentiles.

C. Promises (vv. 15-18)

(Galatians 3:15-18 is not included in the printed text.)

In his effort to show beyond a doubt the truth of justification by faith, Paul argued that the Sinaitic covenant, which came after the Abrahamic covenant, could not alter or destroy the unconditional covenant with Abraham. He observed that among men when a covenant is ratified, neither the author nor the second party can set it aside or amend it. If this is true

with men, how much more so with God! A second covenant, the Law, could not set aside the promise made to Abraham.

Paul's opponents might have argued that since the Law was given later than God's promise to Abraham, the Law was superior to, and superseded, the promise. But verses 15-18 teach that God's promise to Abraham and his posterity has permanent validity; its fulfillment can in no way be dependent on the keeping of a law that came centuries later.

D. Schoolmaster (vv. 19-25)

(Galatians 3:19-21 is not included in the printed text.)

22. But the scripture hath concluded all under sin, that the promise by faith of Jesus Christ might be given to them that believe.

23. But before faith came, we were kept under the law, shut up unto the faith which should afterwards be revealed.

24. Wherefore the law was our schoolmaster to bring us unto Christ, that we might be justified by faith.

The preparatory feature of the law is emphasized in these verses. In verse 22 the law shuts up all under sin and *paves* the way for the fulfillment of the promise. Here the law constrains or pushes men along unto faith. Reference is to faith in the person and work of Christ alluded to in the previous verses. God protected His children from the excesses of the heathen by controls of the law. "Shut up unto the faith which should afterwards be revealed" (v. 23) indicates that the aim of this protective function of the law was to constrain or urge or push men to faith. The law was certainly no refuge; there could be no real refuge in anything but faith. The law was given to prepare the way for Christ. In verse 24, Paul uses the child guardian as an illustration which was familiar to all his readers. In many Roman and Greek households, well-educated slaves took the children to and from school and watched over them during the day. Sometimes they would teach the children, sometimes they would protect and prohibit, and sometimes they would even discipline. This is what Paul meant by *schoolmaster*; however, we should not read into this our modern concept of a schoolteacher. The transliteration of the Greek would give us our word *pedagogue*, which literally means "a child conductor."

25. But after that faith is come, we are no longer under a schoolmaster.

Christ has come in the line of Abraham, fulfilling the promise to the "father of the faithful" and providing salvation by faith in His finished work. The law has done its work in showing the sinfulness of sin, in acting as a social control in Israel, in bringing men under condemnation and driving them to Christ. And Christ has fulfilled the law. Therefore we are no longer under this pedagogue; its office has ceased. The law in its preparatory ministry has not been against or contrary to promise (v. 21) and now will not be unless men insist on putting themselves under law after grace has come (Howard F. Vos, *Galatians: A Call to Christian Liberty*).

To what extent do believers today try to live under the law? Give some examples.

III.   HEIRS OF THE PROMISE
       (Galatians 3:26—4:7)

A.   Basis of Sonship
     (3:26-29; 4:1-5)

(Galatians 3:28, 29 and 4:1-3 are not included in the printed text.)

3:26. For ye are all the children of God by faith in Christ Jesus.

27. For as many of you as have been baptized into Christ have put on Christ.

4:4. But when the fulness of the time was come, God sent forth his Son, made of a woman, made under the law,

5. To redeem them that were under the law, that we might receive the adoption of sons.

When we become baptized into Christ's body, we become part of a spiritual unity in which the earthly distinctions of race, class, and sex have no significance. Such distinctions are part of our social system and do have significance, of course, in earthly matters. As long as we are on earth, these distinctions must be recognized and taken into account. Even the New Testament provides considerable regulation for the church in such things as the responsibilities of husbands and wives (Ephesians 5) and their relative positions in the functioning of the local church. But so far as the essential character of the body of Christ is concerned, we are all one in Christ Jesus (Galatians 3:28). All of us are in a vital union with Him whereby we share His life, His perfect righteousness, and His inheritance.

In 4:1, 2 mankind is presented as a child, in the sense of immaturity, until Christ's coming, when the guardian (law) was done away with. As was usually true in the testamentary systems of the Greeks and Romans, an heir, so long as he was a child, was no better off than a slave, though he was lord of the whole estate by title and birthright. But he was subject to tutors and governors for a specific amount of time appointed by the father. Tutors were the guardians of his person, and governors were the stewards in control of property and household management.

An application of this sociological arrangement is made by the apostle in verse 3. The word *we* refers primarily to Jews, but must include Gentiles (the Galatians) as well. The Jews were subject to the law of Moses, and the Gentiles to the universal law of holiness. Whether Jew or Gentile, all were under bondage until Christ came as emancipator. We too were spiritually children or minors, not adult sons referred to in the latter part of chapter 3, until a remarkable change was wrought by the gospel—from a position of spiritual minors to adult sons.

In verse 4 the words "but when" mark the beginning of a change in the state of affairs. "The fulness of the time" occurred when world conditions were most ready for the coming of Christ and at a time appointed by the Father. Perhaps at no other point in the history of the world could Christ and the church so effectively have swept onto the human stage.

The Greeks provided a culture and a language. The Romans contributed politically by uniting the Mediterranean world under one government. The Jewish contribution was their concept of monotheism. The philosophers also made a religious contribution by casting doubts on the old pagan systems of religion.

So in "the fulness of the time . . . God sent forth his Son." God took the initiative according to a divine plan and sent His Son on the divine mission of providing salvation. The fact that He sent forth His Son reveals that the Son was pre-incarnate. Taking on human flesh so He could identify with fallen humanity, the Son was born "of a woman, made under the law, to redeem them that were under the law" (vv. 4, 5).

B. Assurance of Sonship (4:6, 7)

6. And because ye are sons, God hath sent forth the Spirit of his Son into your hearts, crying, Abba, Father.

7. Wherefore thou art no more a servant, but a son; and if a son, then an heir of God through Christ.

It is one thing for God to assert that we are adopted to sonship in the family of God; it is another to give evidence of the fact. The evidence that God gives is the inner testimony of the Holy Spirit. The Holy Spirit is the witness of our sonship.

Because we are sons, God has sent into our hearts "the Spirit of his Son" (v. 6). This is another name for the Holy Spirit, who is also sometimes called "the Spirit of Christ" or "the Spirit of Jesus." The indwelling Spirit prompts the cry "Abba, Father."

A sure sign of adoption is the unerring leading of the Holy Spirit in all matters. Having the Spirit as the seal of adoption, we take on a likeness to God that marks us as His in this present evil world. We are God-directed and Godlike as His children.

Whom God adopts, He anoints; whom He makes sons, He makes

saints (v. 7). When a man adopts another for a son and heir, he may give him his name, but he cannot give him his own disposition and characteristics; but when God adopts, He sanctifies. He gives not only a new name, but a new nature. He turns the lion into a lamb. He works such a change as if another soul dwelt in the same body. According to 2 Corinthians 5:17 we become new creations.

What does it mean to be in the family of God?

REVIEW QUESTIONS

1. What term did the apostle use to describe the Galatians in 3:1?

2. What had the Galatians apparently done to warrant such a description?

3. What Old Testament personality did Paul use to illustrate justification by faith?

4. Why did Paul call the law a "schoolmaster"?

5. What are some signs of adoption into the family of God?

GOLDEN TEXT HOMILY

"THE LAW WAS OUR SCHOOLMASTER TO BRING US UNTO CHRIST, THAT WE MIGHT BE JUSTIFIED BY FAITH" (Galatians 3:24).

The term *schoolmaster* referred to a person, usually a slave, who was in charge of the moral welfare of the boys of the family. It was his duty to see that they acquired the qualities essential to true manhood. He was not their tutor, but was responsible for taking them to school, delivering them to the teacher, and bringing them home again.

Likewise, it was the function of the law to lead a man to Christ. The whole law was designed to accomplish this. The sacrifices and offerings pointed to the Savior. The moral aspects showed man his sin, and condemned him, and thus prepared him to receive the offer of pardon through the Redeemer.

Only through faith in Christ can a man be justified before God. Justification is the act or decree of God whereby any sinner, anywhere, through faith in Christ is cleared of all guilt before God. He is declared righteous by God and looked upon by God as though he had never sinned, as though he were altogether the righteousness of God: "For he hath made him to be sin for us, who knew no sin; that we might be made the righteousness of God in him" (2 Corinthians 5:21).— **Homer G. Rhea, Editor in Chief, Church of God Publications, Cleveland, Tennessee**

SENTENCE SERMONS

FAITH IN CHRIST is essential for a person to become a child of God.
—Selected

THE DOCTRINE of justification is the foundation that supports all of the other benefits we receive from Christ.
—Erwin W. Lutzer

A FAITH that cannot survive collision with truth is not worth many regrets.
—Arthur C. Clarke

FAITH IN GOD is a terrific venture in the dark.
—Oswald Chambers

EVANGELISM APPLICATION

FAITH IN CHRIST SETS PEOPLE FREE FROM THE BONDAGE OF SIN.

The experience of salvation means that in your actual life things are really altered—you no longer look at things as you used to; your desires are new, old things have lost their power. One of the touchstones of experience is—has God altered the thing that matters? If you still desire the old things, it is absurd to talk about being born from above—you are only kidding yourself. If you are born again, the Spirit of God makes the alteration manifest in your actual life and reasoning; and when the crisis comes, you are the most amazed person on earth at the wonderful difference there is in you. There is no possibility of imagining that you did it. It is this complete and amazing alteration that is the evidence you are a saved person.—**Oswald Chambers,** *My Utmost for His Highest*

ILLUMINATING THE LESSON

When we believe in Jesus Christ and appropriate the provisions of Calvary, we are adopted into the family of God. We are not stepchildren, but blood kin—heirs with the Elder Son. We are His treasure, His jewel, His joy. We are privileged to have angels as lifeguards. We are given His coat of arms—the lion for courage, the dove for meekness, the eagle for power and protection.

Belonging to the family of the Creator by physical birth is a matter with which we have nothing to do; belonging to the Father's family on the level of moral and spiritual choice is a personal matter. We all must make that choice.

DAILY BIBLE READINGS

M. Test of Faith.
    Genesis 22:9-18
T. Seek the Lord.
    Psalm 27:1-14
W. Live by Faith.
    Habakkuk 2:1-4
T. The True Light. John 1:9-14
F. Faith and the Law.
    Romans 3:21-31
S. Led by the Spirit.
    Romans 8:12-17

Blessings of Redemption

Study Text: Ephesians 2:11-22; Colossians 1:13-23; Titus 2:11-14

Objective: To explore and accept the benefits of the redemption Christ obtained for us.

Golden Text: "[Jesus Christ] gave himself for us, that he might redeem us from all iniquity, and purify unto himself a peculiar people, zealous of good works" (Titus 2:14).

Central Truth: Believers have been reconciled to God through Christ's atoning sacrifice.

Evangelism Emphasis: Sinners can be reconciled to God through Christ's atoning sacrifice.

PRINTED TEXT

Colossians 1:13. Who hath delivered us from the power of darkness, and hath translated us into the kingdom of his dear Son:

14. In whom we have redemption through his blood, even the forgiveness of sins.

19. For it pleased the Father that in him should all fulness dwell;

20. And, having made peace through the blood of his cross, by him to reconcile all things unto himself; by him, I say, whether they be things in earth, or things in heaven.

21. And you, that were sometime alienated and enemies in your mind by wicked works, yet now hath he reconciled

22. In the body of his flesh through death, to present you holy and unblameable and unreproveable in his sight:

23. If ye continue in the faith grounded and settled, and be not moved away from the hope of the gospel, which ye have heard, and which was preached to every creature which is under heaven; whereof I Paul am made a minister.

Titus 2:11. For the grace of God that bringeth salvation hath appeared to all men,

12. Teaching us that, denying ungodliness and worldly lusts, we should live soberly, righteously, and godly, in this present world;

13. Looking for that blessed hope, and the glorious appearing of the great God and our Saviour Jesus Christ;

14. Who gave himself for us, that he might redeem us from all iniquity, and purify unto himself a peculiar people, zealous of good works.

Ephesians 2:13. But now in Christ Jesus ye who sometimes were far off are made nigh by the blood of Christ.

14. For he is our peace, who hath made both one, and hath broken down the middle wall of partition between us;

15. Having abolished in his flesh the enmity, even the law of commandments contained in ordinances; for to make in himself of twain one new man, so making peace;

16. And that he might reconcile both unto God in one body by the cross, having slain the enmity thereby:

17. And came and preached peace to you which were afar off, and to them that were nigh.

18. For through him we both have access by one Spirit unto the Father.

19. Now therefore ye are no more strangers and foreigners, but fellowcitizens with the saints, and of the household of God.

LESSON OUTLINE

I. RESCUED FROM DARKNESS
   A. Delivered
   B. Forgiven
   C. Reconciled

II. SANCTIFIED BY CHRIST'S BLOOD
   A. Grace
   B. Instruction
   C. Hope
   D. Purity

III. BROUGHT NEAR TO GOD
   A. New Position
   B. Peace
   C. Access to God
   D. Fellow Citizens

LESSON EXPOSITION

INTRODUCTION

One of the greatest words in the Bible is the word *redeemed*, for it is so full of meaning and significance for the believer. *Redemption* is one of the great words connected with the work of Christ on the cross, expressing the blessed deliverance effected there for all under guilt and bondage of sin. It conveys two great truths: (1) that of purchase or buying back by the payment of a ransom and (2) deliverance from bondage by the ransom paid and by the power of God.

The New Testament Epistles present redemption as deliverance from sin and evil—committing the redeemed to holiness of life and to loving, devoted service—more than they do in the idea of purchase. In the Epistle to the Romans, redemption is the ground of justification, whereby the believer is cleared by God for all charges because of sin and is counted righteous by Him with the very righteousness of God. In Ephesians and Colossians, redemption procures for the believer the full forgiveness of all trespasses, meaning all that was entailed by the fall of man, and all the consequences flowing from it. In Titus, we are redeemed from all iniquity or lawlessness—that is, all that is contrary to the will of God—and made His peculiar people, or a peculiar treasure to Him, for His own possession, zealous of good works.

Redemption in 1 Peter has in view the taking of the people of Israel out of Egypt, and it means a change in the whole manner of life, as in their case. The change is from a state of slavery under sin to one of a holy people unto God. The Book of Revelation shows that the position of the redeemed in glory, with all its privileges and possibilities throughout eternity, is due entirely to redemption by the blood of Christ. Believers will then realize not only freedom from sin's guilt and power, and even its taint, but also in their redeemed bodies freedom from all tendency to sin, having full deliverance from all limitations and weaknesses, and so be unable to fail in any way whatever. That will be the complete emancipation from all the effects of the Fall, and the manifestation of the liberty and glory that belongs to the sons of God.

I. RESCUED FROM DARKNESS
(Colossians 1:13, 14, 19-23)

A. Delivered (v. 13)

13. Who hath delivered us from the power of darkness, and hath translated us into the kingdom of his dear Son.

There is a natural darkness that is seasonable, which, in the plan of nature, brings rest to man. The darkness Paul refers to in this verse is a spiritual one. It is the darkness of ignorance apart from "the light of life" (John 8:12; Ephesians 5:13). It is the darkness of sin (Romans 13:12), blinding men against the truth (2 Corinthians 3:14). It is the darkness of misery (Isaiah 8:22). It is the darkness of death (Psalm 88:10-12). It is the darkness of hell—"utter darkness."

The apostle is talking about the darkness organized for the ruin of man. It is the power of darkness—an arbitrary, usurped power, and not a "true kingdom." The prince of darkness is at the head of this realm of evil and strives to keep all his slaves in darkness, "lest the light of the glorious gospel of Christ, who is the image of God, should shine unto them" (2 Corinthians 4:4).

Paul says we have been rescued from this power of darkness. Only God can do this. How is this accomplished? He enlightens our minds in the knowledge of Christ, who is the true light (John 8:12). He persuades and enables us to embrace Christ as offered in the gospel (John 6:44). He renews our wills and causes us to "walk in the light, as he is in the light" (1 John 1:7). He clothes us with "the armour of light" (Romans 13:12).

We are delivered from the power of darkness and "translated," or transferred, into a new Kingdom. It is the kingdom of God's dear Son. It means separation from the world, from sin, and from the devil. It means the believer is a member of a new society—the Kingdom of grace; he is a fellow citizen with the saints (Ephesians 2:19); he is heir of the Kingdom of glory. He has a new name, new hopes, new friends, and works for a new heaven.

B. Forgiven (v. 14)

14. In whom we have redemption through his blood, even the forgiveness of sins.

The death of Christ so satisfied God's judgment upon sin that He not only can forgive the sinner but also clear the most guilty, and He can declare the believer righteous with the very righteousness of God. That is what *justified* means, and it is by faith alone. No sin has been overlooked by God, the guilt of sin has been removed, and every claim of God's holy law thereby answered. Regarding sin, the work of Christ has perfectly satisfied God, and He

has borne witness thereto by raising Christ from the dead. That fact
gives the believer true ground for
peace with God (Romans 5:1, 2).

C. Reconciled (vv. 19-23)

19. For it pleased the Father that in him should all fulness dwell;

20. And, having made peace through the blood of his cross, by him to reconcile all things unto himself; by him, I say, whether they be things in earth, or things in heaven.

21. And you, that were some-time alienated and enemies in your mind by wicked works, yet now hath he reconciled.

Reconciliation means a change from enmity to friendship; from estrangement and alienation to fellowship and nearness by bringing about a union. That is what the work of Christ on the cross effected. Sin is enmity with God; it estranges the sinner from God and hinders any communion or friendship with Him.

Hatred of God is one of the characteristics of sin, and sin is also hateful to God. Man naturally does not love God and trust Him with confidence, for that is the consequence of the fall through sin. Even God's own people, the children of Israel, became estranged from God by breaking His law and by giving way to idolatry. They therefore incurred the wrath of God and were sold into captivity to other nations.

Through the years, Israel so grievously departed from God that when the Lord Jesus came as their Messiah, they did not accept Him but rejected Him and called for His death. By this act they forfeited all

claim to blessing for themselves. Not only so, but at the cross the whole world took sides against God in rejecting His Son.

In giving Himself a willing offering and a sacrifice for sin, Christ met the wrath of God because of sin, appeasing that wrath. He made it possible for God to meet man in grace and to offer freely and abundantly every blessing He has to bestow. By rending the veil of the Temple, He bore witness to this purpose, for that meant the opening up of the way of access, as it had never been done before.

22. In the body of his flesh through death, to present you holy and unblameable and unreproveable in his sight:

23. If ye continue in the faith grounded and settled, and be not moved away from the hope of the gospel, which ye have heard, and which was preached to every creature which is under heaven; whereof I Paul am made a minister.

The death of Christ on the cross opened the way into the presence of God for any and every sinner, however bad he might be. The Cross removed all that was between man and God, making it possible for man to come to God and become a friend. "God was in Christ, reconciling the world unto himself, not imputing their trespasses unto them" (2 Corinthians 5:19). There He put to the account of Christ the offenses against men as sinners, so that now He can reckon or impute to the guilty sinner the righteousness of God. This is why Paul could show in the Epistle to the Romans the guilty sinner to be justified when he believes on Christ as Savior.

Why does man fight God's desire to rescue him from darkness?

II. SANCTIFIED BY CHRIST'S BLOOD (Titus 2:11-14)

A. Grace (v. 11)

11. For the grace of God that bringeth salvation hath appeared to all men.

Theologians define the grace of God as "His unmerited favor toward men, expressing itself in active love in procuring our redemption in Christ Jesus." It has also been called "the fountainhead of our salvation." The Bible says, "By grace are ye saved" (Ephesians 2:8). Because God is gracious, therefore sinful men are forgiven, converted, purified, and saved. It is not because of anything in them, or that ever can be in them, that they are saved; but it's because of the boundless love, goodness, pity, compassion, mercy, and grace of God.

Charles Spurgeon writes: "What an abyss is the grace of God! Who can measure its breadth? Who can fathom its depth? Like all the rest of the divine attributes, it is infinite. God is full of love, for God is love. God is full of goodness; the very name 'God' is short for 'good.' Unbounded goodness and love enter into the very essence of the Godhead. It is because His mercy endureth for ever that men are not destroyed; because His compassions fail not that sinners are brought to Him and forgiven" (*All of Grace*).

B. Instruction (v. 12)

12. Teaching us that, denying
ungodliness and worldly lusts, we should live soberly, righteously, and godly, in this present world.

Verse 12 provides a description of a man who lives a pure life. He denies some things and lives other things. *Purity* is the key to his life. God does not say of any men that they are at all times equally careful or punctual or scrupulous or amiable or even devout. He names a quality that is deeper and more comprehensive. Purity is not a single virtue, or a separate trait. It runs through the whole character, as blood does through the body. The root of it is faith in God. Place the pure man where you will, try him as you please, and he is the same man. Purity is not a thing of more or less, of seasons or opportunities, of rich or poor, of self-interest or respectability, of ornament or convenience. Principles never are, and purity is a principle. It is not to be measured or weighed, nor is it bought or sold at any price. You cannot dilute or half it or cut it into fractions. It is—or it is not. Whoever possesses it goes up among the high and strong souls, walks through the world trusting, tells the truth whatever it costs, is pure and temperate in the light and in the dark, never fails whatever he may lose, always succeeds with only real success, sits in heavenly places on the earth (though they may be hard or painful places), and he will live and reign with Christ forever.

C. Hope (v. 13)

13. Looking for that blessed hope, and the glorious appearing of the great God and our Saviour Jesus Christ.

Karl Menninger once said: "The

HOPE HIS COMING OUR GOING

best thing a psychiatrist can do for his patients is to light them a candle of hope."

The greatest thing a minister can do for his people is to light them a candle of hope. The people who sit in the pews, by and large, have rubbed shoulders with despair the previous hours. They enter the hour of worship needing a lot of things, but not so much as needing hope.

The greatest commodity the minister of the gospel can offer is hope. He proclaims good news to people who are faced with despair and frustrated with defeat. The minister can tell such a man that "across chaos, God stretches the rainbow of hope."

Years ago, a successful cosmetic manufacturer retired and was asked about his magic formula for such success. He refused to share his formula for achievement. However, on his 75th birthday, after much persuasion he decided to share his formula of success. The aged man began by saying: "You see, in addition to the formulas used by other manufacturers of cosmetics, I added the magic ingredient . . . I never promised a woman that my cosmetics would make her beautiful, but I always gave her hope."

When Billy Graham visited Sir Winston Churchill, the first words from Churchill were posed in the form of a question: "Do you have any hope?"

Congregations ask this every time they attend worship services. Paul provided the answer when he referred to the coming of Christ to claim His church and to vindicate her by a glorious display of power. This was Paul's blessed hope. He was looking to the culmination of salvation, which will occur when Christ and the Christian faith are finally vindicated by the visible display of glory evident to all the world.

D. Purity (v. 14)

14. Who gave himself for us, that he might redeem us from all iniquity, and purify unto himself a peculiar people, zealous of good works.

It was the self-sacrifice of Christ that provided redemption. "Who gave himself for us"—it was a definite, voluntary act on His part. It was an exhaustive act—"himself," His whole unique personality. It was substitutionary—"for us." Since He gave Himself to "redeem us," it is impossible to exclude the idea of substitution from verse 14. He "gave himself a ransom for all" to free us (1 Timothy 2:6).

Redemption is viewed both negatively and positively. Negatively— "that he might redeem us from all iniquity." Our condition of bondage in iniquity had to be undone. The redemption is viewed here as rescuing us from the power rather than the guilt of sin.

The redemptive purpose was also positive—"and purify unto himself a peculiar people [for his own possession]." The figure of purification presupposes a previous defilement by sin. Sin not only makes us guilty but also dirty. Those who have been cleansed are now "a people for His own possession" (*NASB*). "As redeemed and purified we belong to Christ as His special possession or treasure. The statement "a peculiar people" in the King James Version means that which is one's own private possession. It does not mean that Christians are

NOT TO BE

to be strange, odd, and ridiculous in their clothing, manners, and customs. But by character and behavior we are to reveal the fact that we are not our own but belong completely to Him. As such we must be characterized as being "zealous of good works." Every Christian should not be merely good, but be full of burning zeal in doing good. The believer who eagerly awaits the return of the Lord will involve himself in furthering the cause of his Lord (D. Edmond Hiebert, *Titus and Philemon*).

Why do believers have such a struggle with being pure?

III. BROUGHT NEAR TO GOD
(Ephesians 2:11-22)

A. New Position (vv. 11-13)

(Ephesians 2:11, 12 is not included in the printed text.)

13. But now in Christ Jesus ye who sometimes were far off are made nigh by the blood of Christ.

Once far off from salvation, without Christ, without the Old Testament promises, and without God, Gentiles now have been "made nigh" (brought near) to God. It was accomplished "in Christ Jesus," and specifically "by the blood of Christ." *Blood* suggests the sacrificial nature of Christ's death. It was not just His expiration, but the sacrificial shedding of His blood that brought salvation. Now Gentiles may enjoy salvation just as Jews, on the basis of the work of Christ at Calvary, made available by God to those who by faith are in vital union with His Son.

B. Peace (vv. 14-17)

14. For he is our peace, who

hath made both one, and hath broken down the middle wall of partition between us;

15. Having abolished in his flesh the enmity, even the law of commandments contained in ordinances; for to make in himself of twain one new man, so making peace;

16. And that he might reconcile both unto God in one body by the cross, having slain the enmity thereby:

17. And came and preached peace to you which were afar off, and to them that were nigh.

The justified believer is brought into peace with God, or oneness with Him; he has access into the grace in which he stands; and he can boast of the hope of the glory of God, having received the reconciliation. God has become his closest friend, is entirely on his side, and will not hear any charge or accusation made against him—everything of that nature having been put on the account of Christ on the cross. According to verse 15, "the enmity, even the law of commandments contained in ordinances," is abolished, and both Jew and Gentile are made one in Christ.

By the blood of Christ those who were far off and without God are brought near to Him, for Christ is our peace, and in Him believers are made one with God. All estrangement and all differences between man and man are done away by the reconciling work of the Cross, for all who believe in Christ are made one new body.

C. Access to God (v. 18)

18. For through him we both have access by one Spirit unto the Father.

The rending of the veil was the act of God by which He opened the way for any sinner to approach Him without fear, because of the blood of Christ. That was the new and living way made by God through the veil.

D. Fellow Citizens (vv. 19-22)

(Ephesians 2:20-22 is not included in the printed text.)

19. Now therefore ye are no more strangers and foreigners, but fellowcitizens with the saints, and of the household of God.

Gentile converts are on an equal footing with Jewish Christians in the church. Both are saints and thus members of the household of God. In Christ believers are formed into one body and building, in connection with the work of the Holy Spirit who regenerates and indwells, in order that we might form "an habitation of God" (v. 22).

What does it mean to be brought near to God?

REVIEW QUESTIONS

1. What does Paul mean by *darkness* in Colossians 1:13?

2. What does *reconciliation* mean?

3. Define *grace* in Titus 2:11.

4. What does Paul call the second coming of Christ in Titus 2:13?

5. How do believers experience peace with God?

GOLDEN TEXT HOMILY

"[JESUS CHRIST] GAVE HIMSELF FOR US, THAT HE MIGHT REDEEM US FROM ALL INIQUITY, AND PURIFY UNTO HIMSELF A PECULIAR PEOPLE, ZEALOUS OF GOOD WORKS" (Titus 2:14).

Here is the heart of the gospel: Christ "gave himself for us." As Savior of the world, Christ died on the cross, taking our place and bearing the consequences of our sins. Through the Cross the saving power of God came flooding into this world and is available to all who trust in Christ. The power of the Cross is more powerful than our strength and can do for us what we cannot do for ourselves. It sets us free from the bondage of sin and enables us to enter a life marked by good works.

We may not think that we are worth very much, but Christ's estimate of us was so high that He was willing to die for us so that we can become the special possession of God. The phrase "a peculiar people" reflects God's words to the Israelites in Exodus 19:5: "If ye will...keep my covenant, then ye shall be a peculiar treasure unto me above all people." After Israel's deliverance from Egyptian bondage, God made a covenant with them. Through the saving power of the Cross, God has made a new covenant and has brought together a new people—a people purified by the sanctifying work of the Holy Spirit and uniquely honored as God's own people.

The power of the Cross affords us a new life that identifies us as God's special people. It can set us free from ungodly desires and passions. It can set us free from the love of position and power and from scrambling for status. It can set us free from deceit and hypocrisy. It can set us free from bitterness, infighting, and divisiveness. But, on the other hand, the Cross should move us to be zealots for good works. It should move us to be steadfast in faith and to share the gospel with others. It should move us to serve others and to have a genuine concern about their needs. In short, the Cross should move us to bear the likeness of our Savior.—**French L. Arrington, Ph.D., Professor of New Testament Greek and Exegesis, Church of God School of Theology, Cleveland, Tennessee.**

SENTENCE SERMONS

BELIEVERS have been reconciled to God through Christ's atoning sacrifice.

—Selected

THE MORE WE COUNT the blessings we have, the less we crave the luxuries we haven't.

—William A. Ward

REFLECT UPON your present blessings, of which every man has many; not on your past misfortunes, of which all men have some.

—Charles Dickens

A YEAR of self-surrender to God will bring larger blessings than fourscore years of selfishness.

—*The Encyclopedia of Religious Quotations*

EVANGELISM APPLICATION

SINNERS CAN BE RECONCILED TO GOD THROUGH CHRIST'S ATONING SACRIFICE.

The Venerable Bede in his *Ecclesiastical History of England* describes the coming of some mis-sionaries to Britain. The kings, vassals, wise men, and pagan religious leaders were gathered in the hall of the stone castle. In the midst of the discussion a sparrow flew in at the open window, fluttered about the hall for a moment, and finding another open window, flew out. One wise man, a pagan sage observing the sparrow, got up and said words to this effect: "The life of man is like the flight of that bird through this hall—whence it comes, we know not. The life between the time he enters by the window of birth and time it leaves by the window of death, we can observe. What becomes of many beyond that window, we know not. If your religion can tell us something worthwhile about the life beyond that window—that is the religion we want."

This is the question men are still asking. What is the answer?

DAILY BIBLE READINGS

M. Redeemed by God.
   Deuteronomy 7:7-15
T. Forgiveness and Healing.
   Psalm 103:1-5
W. Bought With a Price.
   Hosea 3:1-5
T. Redemption Is at Hand.
   Luke 21:25-31
F. Heirs of God. Ephesians 3:1-6
S. Freedom From Fear.
   Hebrews 2:14-18

The Triumph of Redemption

Study Text: Romans 8:18-25; 1 Thessalonians 4:13-18; 2 Peter 3:13, 14; Revelation 22:1-7

Objective: To review end-time events as they relate to redemption and celebrate the hope we have in Christ.

Golden Text: "We, according to his promise, look for new heavens and a new earth, wherein dwelleth righteousness" (2 Peter 3:13).

Central Truth: The redeemed will live with God forever.

Evangelism Emphasis: Christ's imminent return should challenge believers to win the lost.

PRINTED TEXT

1 Thessalonians 4:16. For the Lord himself shall descend from heaven with a shout, with the voice of the archangel, and with the trump of God: and the dead in Christ shall rise first:

17. Then we which are alive and remain shall be caught up together with them in the clouds, to meet the Lord in the air: and so shall we ever be with the Lord.

18. Wherefore comfort one another with these words.

Romans 8:18. For I reckon that the sufferings of this present time are not worthy to be compared with the glory which shall be revealed in us.

22. For we know that the whole creation groaneth and travaileth in pain together until now.

23. And not only they, but ourselves also, which have the firstfruits of the Spirit, even we ourselves groan within ourselves, waiting for the adoption, to wit, the redemption of our body.

2 Peter 3:13. Nevertheless we, according to his promise, look for new heavens and a new earth, wherein dwelleth righteousness.

14. Wherefore, beloved, seeing that ye look for such things, be diligent that ye may be found of him in peace, without spot, and blameless.

Revelation 22:1. And he shewed me a pure river of water of life, clear as crystal, proceeding out of the throne of God and of the Lamb.

2. In the midst of the street of it, and on either side of the river, was there the tree of life, which bare twelve manner of fruits, and yielded her fruit every month: and the leaves of the tree were for the healing of the nations.

3. And there shall be no more curse: but the throne of God and of the Lamb shall be in it; and his servants shall serve him:

4. And they shall see his face; and his name shall be in their foreheads.

5. And there shall be no night there; and they need no candle, neither light of the sun; for the Lord God giveth them light: and they shall reign for ever and ever.

6. And he said unto me, These sayings are faithful and true: and the Lord God of the holy prophets sent his angel to shew unto his servants the things which must shortly be done.

7. Behold, I come quickly: blessed is he that keepeth the sayings of the prophecy of this book.

LESSON OUTLINE

I. HOPE OF CHRIST'S COMING
   A. Revelation
   B. Return
   C. Resurrection
   D. Rapture
   E. Reunion

II. NEW HEAVEN AND NEW EARTH
   A. Redemption Promised
   B. Motivation
   C. Anticipation

III. HOME AT LAST!
   A. Great Gifts
   B. A Great Promise

LESSON EXPOSITION

INTRODUCTION

A quick glance at any daily newspaper will suggest that we are living in a day when many of the things Jesus predicted would precede His second advent are coming true. Whenever signs of the times are mentioned today, many people rationalize that such signs have "always" been present. This is only partly true. Our age is the only one in which the universal preaching of the gospel has been possible. More important, however, although signs have been present in times past, they have never all been present at one and the same time. Let us note some of these individually:

1. *False Christs.* Jesus said, "Many shall come in my name, saying, I am Christ" (Matthew 24:5). It has been estimated by one Bible scholar that in the last 100 years, there have been no less than 1,100 leaders that have arisen who have claimed to be Christ. These have deluded and deceived many thousands of people throughout the world.

2. *Wars and rumors of wars.* Most of the world today is affected by the bondage of wars and rumors of wars. With the scientific achievements in modern warfare, the gravity of any war is multiplied beyond human imagination. Most of the world today is an armed camp. The slightest provocation by an egomaniac, posing as a leader, could lead to devastation.

3. *Famines and diseases.* Many ominous reports come daily from around the world telling of thousands of people who have died, or are suffering from starvation and pestilence. Most of the children of the world go to bed hungry every night. The majority of the world have never had a really satisfying meal.

4. *Earthquakes.* In the last 50

years, *earthquakes* has become a familiar word in our vocabulary, more so than in any corresponding period in history.

5. *Persecution of the Jews.* Jesus told His disciples, "Then shall they deliver you up to be afflicted . . . and ye shall be hated of all nations for my name's sake" (Matthew 24:9). These disciples were Jews, and at that time they were suffering under the heel of Roman bondage; but Jesus said that they, the Jews, would be hated of all nations. We have observed this in our own age. Think of the persecution of the Jews in Germany, in Russia, and in many other parts of the world. All the evils and misfortunes of the world have been blamed on the Jewish people.

6. *Wickedness and lack of love.* Jesus predicted, "Because iniquity shall abound, the love of many shall wax cold" (v. 12). This is perhaps more true today than at any other period in human history. In America we have departed from the simple faith of our forefathers, to the extent that Christ is almost entirely crowded out of our public schools and from our social and economic life. Christ is almost completely banned from our public schools, our national assemblies, our political meetings, our business life, and much of our society. The name of Christ is an offense to many.

7. *Preaching the gospel to the world.* Jesus also told His disciples that the gospel of the Kingdom would be preached in all the world (v. 14). For the first time in history it is possible to reach the whole world with the gospel. Through the use of radio and television, it is possible to send the message of salva-

tion to every corner of the globe.

It is generally agreed that many of these things will not be completely fulfilled until after the believers are raptured. In the Gospel of Luke, Jesus said: "And when these things begin to come to pass, then look up, and lift up your heads; for your redemption draweth nigh" (21:28).

I. HOPE OF CHRIST'S COMING (1 Thessalonians 4:13-18)

A. Revelation (v. 13)

(1 Thessalonians 4:13 is not included in the printed text.)

Ignorance of the truth often mars our spiritual comfort. Hopelessness characterizes heathen religions. There is no hope for the future life apart from the Lord Jesus Christ. But one of the great facts of faith in Christ is that we have faith when our loved ones precede us in death. Christians have the wonderful hope that when this life is completed, there is going to be a wonderful, unending life in the presence of God. We will be joined with our loved ones in joy and ecstasy. This is why Paul told the Thessalonians that he did not want them to adopt the attitude of the pagans who have no hope.

B. Return (v. 14)

(1 Thessalonians 4:14 is not included in the printed text.)

Notice how Paul links the return of Christ with the Cross. In the words of John F. Walvoord: "The precious truth concerning the coming of Christ for His own is as certain as the central doctrine of the death and resurrection of Christ. Unless we are absolutely certain concerning the death and resurrection of Christ, we are not certain in our Christian hope. The place to begin is at the cross of Christ. It is there that Christ died for our sins; it is there we learn that we had a substitute—one who was able to save us and one who provided a sufficient sacrifice for our sin. We do not progress in our Christian faith until we come to the cross. Linked with the cross is the resurrection of Christ which is God's seal and the evidence or the apologetic for our Christian faith. Here is the stamp of certainty: Christ rose from the dead. If we believe that Christ died for us, if we believe that Christ rose from the dead, and really believe it by receiving Jesus Christ as our Savior, then we have a ground for hope" (*The Thessalonian Epistles*).

C. Resurrection (vv. 15, 16)

(1 Thessalonians 4:15 is not included in the printed text.)

16. For the Lord himself shall descend from heaven with a shout, with the voice of the archangel, and with the trump of God: and the dead in Christ shall rise first.

Christians look past the sleep of physical death to physical resurrection, and thus glorious reunion; therefore, they are not "as others which have no hope" (v. 13). Those who sleep shall be raised, and the living shall not precede, or go before, those who sleep in Jesus (v. 15). Paul was emphasizing that the living shall in no way have an advantage over the dead in Christ. God will not send an angel for His saints. He shall come Himself, the same Lord who died and rose again (v. 16). No other will do to meet the Bride than the Bridegroom

himself, who has redeemed her.

Three unique sounds will be involved in this event: the Lord's shout, the voice of the archangel, and the sound of the trumpet. Jesus Christ will give "a shout of command," just as He did outside the tomb of Lazarus, and those in the graves will hear His voice.

D. Rapture (v. 17)

17. Then we which are alive and remain shall be caught up together with them in the clouds, to meet the Lord in the air: and so shall we ever be with the Lord.

The word *rapture* is not found in the New Testament, but that is the modern English term used for the literal meaning of "caught up." It comes from the Latin word *rapto* and means "to seize, to carry off."

The Greek word translated "meet" carries with it the concept of meeting a person of royalty or an important person. Christians have walked with Christ by faith on earth, but in the air He shall be seen as He is and we will become like Him. What a meeting to anticipate!

E. Reunion (v. 18)

18. Wherefore comfort one another with these words.

The Thessalonians were having a difficult time dealing with the death of their loved ones. So Paul presented the wonderful truth of the coming of the Lord, the resurrection of their loved ones, and their being gathered together with them to be with the Lord forever. "Together with them" (v. 17) is a great statement of encouragement. So in verse 18, Paul admonished them to comfort each other with this message.

I IMPORTANCE OF EVENT

Death is the great separator, but Jesus Christ is the great Reconciler.

How did Paul attempt to encourage the Thessalonian Christians? Is there a need for this today? Explain.

II. NEW HEAVEN AND NEW
EARTH (Romans 8:18-25;
2 Peter 3:13, 14)

A. Redemption Promised
(Romans 8:18-23)

(Romans 8:19-21 is not included in the printed text.)

18. For I reckon that the sufferings of this present time are not worthy to be compared with the glory which shall be revealed in us.

22. For we know that the whole creation groaneth and travaileth in pain together until now.

23. And not only they, but ourselves also, which have the firstfruits of the Spirit, even we ourselves groan within ourselves, waiting for the adoption, to wit, the redemption of our body.

Christians are the most blessed people upon the earth. However, we are also subject to some of the greatest sorrows known to man. This only says that it is not in this world, but in the future world, that we are to enjoy perfect uninterrupted joy.

Paul, therefore, encouraged afflicted believers to endure trials patiently, all the while living in expectation of a rich reward (v. 18).

According to Paul, creation was reduced to a deplorable condition by the fall of man. The material world underwent an awful change.

The atmosphere was turned over to storms, tempests, and pestilences. The animal world, originally subjected to man's control and being innocuous in habit, became predatory and hostile. Man, universally and without exception, no longer retained his divine image. He was corrupted in all of his faculties, both mind and body, and subjected to innumerable diseases, miseries, and death.

In verses 22 and 23 the apostle indicates there is a time coming when the sentence against the whole creation will be reversed. Then, every creature, according to its capacity, may partake in universal blessedness. The material world will become again what it was at first—beautiful in all its parts and suited to all of man's needs. The animal world will have all its venomous and hostile propensities removed, according to the prophet Isaiah (11:6-9).

Believers already have a foretaste of future joy in their souls. Paul refers to this as "the firstfruits" (v. 23). The firstfruits were a part of any produce devoted to God as an acknowledgment that the whole was from Him (Exodus 22:29; 23:19; Deuteronomy 26:2). The harvest of the Spirit is that abundant effusion of holiness and happiness that God will give us at the latter day. And of this Spirit we now have the firstfruits. We are renewed in spirit after the very image of our God in righteousness and true holiness. And with this renewal of our nature, we are filled with the joy of the Holy Ghost, even a joy that is unspeakable and full of glory.

It might be supposed by some that because of these present

attainments, we would be less anxious for the promised blessings. But just the reverse is true. Paul says, "Ourselves also, which have the firstfruits of the Spirit, even we ourselves, groan within ourselves, waiting for the adoption . . . the redemption of our body" (v. 23).

B. Motivation (Romans 8:24, 25)

(Romans 8:24, 25 is not included in the printed text.)

Paul represented the effect of hope under the term *salvation*: "We are saved by hope." How does hope effect salvation? First, we are comforted in our affliction (2 Corinthians 1:4). Afflictions are part of the human condition, but especially the Lord's people (see Hebrews 11:25). But afflictions are our "appointed" way to the kingdom of heaven (1 Thessalonians 3:3). After the most careful investigation, however, Paul reckoned (computed by accurate calculation) that "the sufferings of this present time are not worthy to be compared with the glory which shall be revealed in us" (Romans 8:18).

Paul also stated that we are supported by this hope in all of our conflicts. To all true Christians there are, on some occasions, "conflicts without, fears within" (2 Corinthians 7:5, *NASB*). But the hope of salvation, and the grace of God, serves as a helmet to protect us from the stroke of the most powerful enemy (1 Thessalonians 5:8). We know that God is for us and that we are more than conquerors through Him who loved us (Romans 8:37).

C. Anticipation (2 Peter 3:13, 14)

13. Nevertheless we, according to his promise, look for new heav-ens and a new earth, wherein dwelleth righteousness.

14. Wherefore, beloved, seeing that ye look for such things, be diligent that ye may be found of him in peace, without spot, and blameless.

In verse 13 Peter identifies the Christian's hope for the future. This agrees with John's experience in Revelation 21:1: "And I saw a new heaven and a new earth: for the first heaven and the first earth were passed away." This promise cited by Peter is also recorded in Isaiah 65:17: "For, behold, I create new heavens and a new earth: and the former shall not be remembered, nor come into mind."

The catastrophe at the end will introduce new heavens and earth. Our concern, Peter says in verse 14, must be to be found in peace with God—to be the friends of God, so that the trouble shall not reach us, and so that the new heavens and new earth shall be our blessed and eternal abode. We can expect this only if we are "without spot, and blameless." The spots and blemishes of sin attract the fire of divine judgment. We must give diligence to have all spots and blemishes of sin removed by the cleansing blood of Christ.

How does Paul attempt to motivate believers to be faithful?

III. HOME AT LAST!
(Revelation 22:1-7)

A. Great Gifts (vv. 1-5)

1. And he shewed me a pure river of water of life, clear as crystal, proceeding out of the throne of God and of the Lamb.

2. In the midst of the street of

it, and on either side of the river, was there the tree of life, which bare twelve manner of fruits, and yielded her fruit every month: and the leaves of the tree were for the healing of the nations.

3. And there shall be no more curse: but the throne of God and of the Lamb shall be in it; and his servants shall serve him:

4. And they shall see his face; and his name shall be in their foreheads.

5. And there shall be no night there; and they need no candle, neither light of the sun; for the Lord God giveth them light: and they shall reign for ever and ever.

The Bible does not give a detailed and systematic account of life in the kingdom of God; however, there are some indications of what it will be like.

It will be a life of fellowship with Christ. "For now we see through a glass, darkly; but then face to face" (1 Corinthians 13:12).

"Beloved, now are we the sons of God, and it doth not yet appear what we shall be: but we know that, when he shall appear, we shall be like him; for we shall see him as he is" (1 John 3:2).

"I will come again, and receive you unto myself; that where I am, there ye may be also" (John 14:3).

It will be a life of rest. "And I heard a voice from heaven saying unto me, Write, Blessed are the dead which die in the Lord from henceforth: Yea, saith the Spirit, that they may rest from their labours; and their works do follow them" (Revelation 14:13).

It is a life full of knowledge. "Now I know in part; but then shall I know even as also I am known" (1 Corinthians 13:12).

It will be a life of holiness. "And there shall in no wise enter into it any thing that defileth, neither whatsoever worketh abomination, or maketh a lie: but they which are written in the Lamb's book of life" (Revelation 21:27).

It will be a life of joy. "And God shall wipe away all tears from their eyes; and there shall be no more death, neither sorrow, nor crying, neither shall there be any more pain: for the former things are passed away" (Revelation 21:4).

It will be a life of service. "And there shall be no more curse: but the throne of God and of the Lamb shall be in it; and his servants shall serve him" (Revelation 22:3).

It will be a life of abundance. "I will give unto him that is athirst of the fountain of the water of life freely" (Revelation 21:6).

It will be a life of glory. "For our light affliction, which is but for a moment, worketh for us a far more exceeding and eternal weight of glory" (2 Corinthians 4:17).

It will be a life of worship. "And after these things I heard a great voice of much people in heaven, saying, Alleluia; Salvation, and glory, and honour, and power, unto the Lord our God" (Revelation 19:1).

Perhaps the best way of thinking about our future with Christ is to use the words of John: "We know that, when he shall appear, we shall be like him" (1 John 3:2).

B. A Great Promise (vv. 6, 7)

6. And he said unto me, These sayings are faithful and true: and the Lord God of the holy prophets sent his angel to shew unto his servants the things which must shortly be done.

7. Behold, I come quickly:

blessed is he that keepeth the sayings of the prophecy of this book.

The hope of the second coming of Christ is one of the greatest incentives to the church for vitality of service and holiness of life that we have in the Bible. In all ages of the church it has been a source of inspiration and cheer. Exhortations to purity, fidelity, holiness, and hope are based on it.

Do you think Christians you know are really eager to get to their new heavenly home? Explain.

REVIEW QUESTIONS

1. What did Paul tell the Thessalonians about their dead friends and relatives?

2. What does the word *rapture* mean?

3. What kind of redemption is promised in Romans 8:18-23?

4. What can the believer anticipate according to 2 Peter 3:13, 14?

5. What great promise is given in Revelation 22:6, 7?

GOLDEN TEXT HOMILY

"WE, ACCORDING TO HIS PROMISE, LOOK FOR NEW HEAVENS AND A NEW EARTH, WHEREIN DWELLETH RIGHTEOUSNESS" (2 Peter 3:13).

Peter was talking to believers in the earlier part of this book about false teachers, apostates, scoffers, and the willfully ignorant. Now he says, "Nevertheless [in spite of these people] we [those of us "that have obtained like precious faith . . . through the righteousness of God

and our Saviour Jesus Christ" (1:1)] . . . look for new heavens and a new earth."

As we look about us at our present heavens and earth, our heavens are full of smog, acid rain, and all kinds of pollutants. The earth has become so contaminated that there is no longer space available to dump our trash. Our hospitals overflow with the sick, our mental institutions bulge at the seams, and our prisons overflow. No wonder we look forward to a new heaven and a new earth.

But what gives us hope of these? Peter says that it is "according to his promise." God told Isaiah about it some 750 years before Christ and said this promise was for His people. There, their former troubles would be forgotten and God's people should be glad and rejoice forever (Isaiah 65:17, 18). In John 14:2, 3, Jesus promised to prepare us a place and to return to take us there. Therefore, we should be as confident of His promises as Abraham, who was "fully persuaded that, what he [God] promised, he was able also to perform" (Romans 4:21). In our lesson, John testifies that he saw the new heaven and the new earth. God promised it, John saw it in a vision, and Jesus promised to come back and take us there. What more could we desire?

The most important part is that there will be no unrighteousness there. Justice will reign supreme. Sin cannot enter. Death and sorrow will have been banished. Sickness and pain will have been abolished. Why shouldn't we rejoice evermore?**—William R. McCall, Missionary, Church of God, Cleveland, Tennessee**

SENTENCE SERMONS

THE REDEEMED will live with God forever.

—**Selected**

HE THAT WILL ENTER into paradise must come with the right key.

—**Sir Thomas Fuller**

HEAVEN IS a place prepared for those who are prepared for it.

—*Draper's Book of Quotations for the Christian World*

HEAVEN IS NOT a reward for "being a good boy," but is the continuation and expansion of a quality of life which begins when a person's central confidence is transferred from himself to God.

—**J.B. Phillips**

EVANGELISM APPLICATION

CHRIST'S IMMINENT RETURN SHOULD CHALLENGE BELIEVERS TO WIN THE LOST.

We do not know when Christ will come, and so it is our responsibility to be ready. Jesus will come in the air, the dead in Christ will be raised incorruptible, the living saints will be changed and made like Him, and then we shall all be caught up together to meet Him in the air. The unsaved will be left here to go through the Tribulation that will overtake a godless world.

What will be your condition on that day? What you do for Christ now will determine that.

ILLUMINATING THE LESSON

Christians should remember that in studying the teaching of the second coming of Christ, the main theme and center of attraction should be Christ himself, and not merely a human desire to escape difficulties. Jesus Christ is the central theme of the Bible. He is the One of whom prophets and apostles wrote and to whom angels and redeemed hosts ascribe praise and glory and honor. Our hope should not be the glory of the coming, nor the joy and benefit that His coming will bring. Christ alone must be our hope.

DAILY BIBLE READINGS

M. Redeemed by God's Power.
   Psalm 111:1-10
T. Abundant Redemption.
   Psalm 130:1-7
W. Redeemed From Our
   Enemies. Psalm 136:23-26
T. Christ Is Our Redemption.
   1 Corinthians 1:26-31
F. Delivered From the World.
   Galatians 1:1-5
S. Sealed Unto Redemption.
   Ephesians 4:25-32

The Tabernacle: God's Sanctuary

Study Text: Exodus 25:1-9; 40:1-15, 34-38; Deuteronomy 12:10-14; John 4:19-24; Hebrews 8:1-5; 9:6-12

Objective: To introduce the typology of the Tabernacle and appreciate its significance for Christians today.

Golden Text: "True worshippers shall worship the Father in spirit and in truth: for the Father seeketh such to worship him" (John 4:23).

Central Truth: A study of the Tabernacle offers glimpses of Christ and how believers can worship Him.

Evangelism Emphasis: The Tabernacle is a divine pattern of Christ's sacrifice for sinners.

PRINTED TEXT

Exodus 25:8. And let them make me a sanctuary; that I may dwell among them.

9. According to all that I shew thee, after the pattern of the tabernacle, and the pattern of all the instruments thereof, even so shall ye make it.

40:34. Then a cloud covered the tent of the congregation, and the glory of the Lord filled the tabernacle.

35. And Moses was not able to enter into the tent of the congregation, because the cloud abode thereon, and the glory of the Lord filled the tabernacle.

Deuteronomy 12:10. But when ye go over Jordan, and dwell in the land which the Lord your God giveth you to inherit, and when he giveth you rest from all your enemies round about, so that ye dwell in safety;

11. Then there shall be a place which the Lord your God shall choose to cause his name to dwell there; thither shall ye bring all that I command you; your burnt-offerings, and your sacrifices, your tithes, and the heave-offering of your hand, and all your choice vows which ye vow unto the Lord.

John 4:23. But the hour cometh, and now is, when the true worshippers shall worship the Father in spirit and in truth: for the Father seeketh such to worship him.

24. God is a Spirit: and they that worship him must worship him in spirit and in truth.

Hebrews 8:1. Now of the things which we have spoken this is the sum: We have such an high priest, who is set on the right hand of the throne of the Majesty in the heavens;

2. A minister of the sanctuary, and of the true tabernacle, which the Lord pitched, and not man.

9:6. Now when these things were thus ordained, the priests went always into the first tabernacle, accomplishing the service of God.

11. But Christ being come an high priest of good things to come, by a greater and more perfect tabernacle, not made with hands, that is to say, not of this building;

12. Neither by the blood of goats and calves, but by his own blood he entered in once into the holy place, having obtained eternal redemption for us.

LESSON OUTLINE

I. PATTERN OF THE TABERNACLE
   A. The Pattern of Giving
   B. The Pattern of Worship
   C. The Pattern of God's Presence

II. PLACE TO WORSHIP GOD
   A. A Particular Place
   B. A Separate Place
   C. Places of the Heart

III. CHRIST AND THE TABERNACLE
   A. The Excellency of Christ's Priesthood
   B. The Superiority of Christ's Sacrifice

LESSON EXPOSITION
INTRODUCTION

Within months of the Exodus, which began around 1450 B.C., God called Moses to the peak of Mount Sinai where He promised to make Israel "a peculiar nation." Here God gave Moses the Ten Commandments and the charge to build the Tabernacle according to the pattern which God showed him.

The Tabernacle is an important Old Testament type in that it prefigures the ministry of Christ. Concerning *typology*, A. Berkeley Mickelsen says that although the Greek word for *type* (*tupos*) has several meanings, the word has only two basic ideas: (1) pattern and (2) that which is produced from the pattern.

Through the study of types, we look for a correspondence in one or more respects between a person, event, or thing in the Old Testament and a person, event, or thing in the New Testament (*Interpreting the Bible*).

In God's divine plan, types represent certain ideas that God wished to impress on us which foreshadow many teachings of the Christian faith. Two other significant terms are as follows:

1. *Antitype*—meaning "that which corresponds to something that has gone before." Jesus, for example, is the antitype of the Tabernacle.

2. *Prototype* (or *archetype*)—meaning "first or primary type of anything, the original or model after which something is formed." The heavenly tabernacle that God pitched and not man (Hebrews 8:2) can be seen as the prototype for the earthly Tabernacle.

Through this figurative method of interpretation, we can better appreciate the Tabernacle as a divine pattern of Christ's ministry in our lives today.

I. PATTERN OF THE TABERNACLE (Exodus 25:1-9; 40:1-15, 34-38)

A. The Pattern of Giving (25:1-9)
   (Exodus 25:1-7 is not included in

the printed text.)

That the pattern of the Tabernacle included freewill offerings is indicative of the personal relationship God desires to have with His people.

The principle of giving to God that which He has provided reminds me of the way my father used to lay out a Sunday school offering for my two brothers and me each Sunday morning. Without fail, Daddy would place three quarters (and three pennies for the Penny March) on the top of the chest of drawers, which we had to pass on our way out the door for church.

It was our responsibility to pick up our money and get it safely to church and into the offering. It was important to Daddy that we had something to give.

And so it was on leaving Egypt, God gave His people the spoils of Egypt—"jewels of silver, and jewels of gold, and raiment" (12:35). And so it is today, the Lord himself sees to it that we have a part in the divine fellowship of giving and receiving.

"The materials for the Tabernacle were to be contributed by Israelites only. Three metals were needed: gold, silver, and brass. Three kinds of skins were acceptable: goats' skins, rams' skins, and badgers' or sealskins. Other materials were linen, acacia wood, oil, spices, onyx, and other precious stones. The colors were to be purple, scarlet, blue, and white" (*Exploring the Old Testament*).

8. And let them make me a sanctuary; that I may dwell among them.

9. According to all that I shew thee, after the pattern of the tabernacle, and the pattern of all the instruments thereof, even so shall ye make it.

God's pitching His tent among the tents of men, making His home among a people who were themselves homeless, and revealing His presence—all that the pattern of the Tabernacle and its services typified—foreshadowed God's making His home, through His Son, in the heart of the believer.

B. The Pattern of Worship
(40:1-15)

(Exodus 40:1-15 is not included in the printed text.)

Setting up the Tabernacle, and setting in order its symbolic articles of furniture and its ministers, teaches us some important lessons about worship. Consider the following, for instance:

1. *Getting ready to worship*. All that went into setting up the Tabernacle as a place of worship suggests the importance of preparing our hearts to worship God. Worship focuses our attention on God and His goodness to the children of men.

2. *Sharing the life of Christ*. The six movable articles in the Tabernacle typify important truths connected with the Christian faith. The altar of burnt offering represents sacrifice; the laver, cleansing; the table of shewbread, the Bread of Life; the candlestick, the Light; the altar of incense, prayer and praise; the ark of the covenant, the power and presence of God.

3. *Affirming what is holy*. What God had set apart for sacred use was already holy. The act of anointing these things with oil enabled Moses to make a formal, judicial declaration that what God calls holy is, indeed, holy.

4. *Affirming the custodians of worship.* How blessed we are in having ministers to lead us in worship and service unto God. Not only do they minister to us but also to God. The priesthood, which was established by God through Aaron and his sons, is important to us today in that it serves as a type of the priesthood of the Lord.

C. The Pattern of God's Presence (40:34-38)

(Exodus 40:36-38 is not included in the printed text.)

34. Then a cloud covered the tent of the congregation, and the glory of the Lord filled the tabernacle.

35. And Moses was not able to enter into the tent of the congregation, because the cloud abode thereon, and the glory of the Lord filled the tabernacle.

The cloud that covered the newly erected sanctuary was more than a mass of visible vapor having to do with weather conditions. The glory that filled the Tabernacle was more than that of polished silver, gold, or brass; more than that of the precious stones in Aaron's breastplate.

This was the cloud of God's presence. This glory was the Shekinah radiance forming the visible manisfestation of the divine presence. This cloud both revealed and veiled the presence of God. This glory reflected the majesty and splendor of God, the sufferings of the Lamb of God, and the guidance of the Holy Spirit.

In what ways does God reveal His presence to us today?

II. PLACE TO WORSHIP GOD (Deuteronomy 12:10-14; John 4:19-24)

A. A Particular Place (Deuteronomy 12:10, 11)

10. But when ye go over Jordan, and dwell in the land which the Lord your God giveth you to inherit, and when he giveth you rest from all your enemies round about, so that ye dwell in safety;

11. Then there shall be a place which the Lord your God shall choose to cause his name to dwell there; thither shall ye bring all that I command you; your burnt-offerings, and your sacrifices, your tithes, and the heave-offering of your hand, and all your choice vows which ye vow unto the Lord.

At this time the children of Israel were about to cross Jordan and enter Canaan. Forty years have passed since the beginning of the Exodus. And to secure the unity and the purity of Tabernacle worship that was instituted during that first year out of Egyptian bondage, God reminded them that the geographical location of their place of worship would not be their concern but His.

That God would, indeed, choose the place of worship is mentioned five times in this one chapter (Deuteronomy 12). Through repetition the Holy Spirit impressed upon their hearts, and ours, the importance of worshiping God in ways that are pleasing to Him.

That there should be one national center for the religion of the Jews, one religious and civil rallying point, was essential to the eternal purposes of God to be fulfilled by the earthly ministry of Jesus.

Where the Jews were headed, it was not unusual to find mountains, valleys, and districts named after the gods worshiped there. The Canaanites worshiped the local fertility deity, "the Baal," but the people of each community had their own Baal, as is evidenced by place names such as Baal-peor and Baal-hermon. The names of these gods were engraved in the stones of the place and cut into the trees. Thus God, by divine initiative, declared He would choose the place in which His honor and His name would dwell.

The place is not named. And while over the years the Tabernacle would come to rest at such places as Kadesh and Shiloh, the one place name that bespeaks the Hebrew religion of one God is Jerusalem. Most importantly, there would always be a God-chosen meeting place.

B. A Separate Place
(Deuteronomy 12:12-14)

(Deuteronomy 12:12-14 is not included in the printed text.)

The place of worship was to be a place apart—a separate place for a separate people. It was never God's desire that the Jews live a separated life. Here they were cautioned not to be influenced by the pagan religious practices they would see on every hand—groves of wooden images in the form of tree trunks and poles.

All the places upon the mountains and hills and under the trees where false gods were served were to be destroyed. The altars, pillars, groves, images, and the names of them were to be torn down and burned.

That this was carried out only in part is a sad commentary on the periodic lapses into idolatry recorded in the history of the Jews.

In what ways does 2 Corinthians 6:17, "Come out from among them, and be ye separate, saith the Lord" apply to the lesson?

C. Places of the Heart
(John 4:19-24)

(John 4:19-22 is not included in the printed text.)

To help relate our Tabernacle studies to lessons Christ taught on true worship, we will consider His encounter with the woman at the well in Samaria.

Among the things that make this an interesting study is that the Jews customarily had no dealings with the Samaritans.

"The Samaritans were descendants of the Jews who remained in Palestine after the Assyrians defeated Israel. They came from mixed marriages between Jews and Assyrian settlers who entered the Promised Land, so their very existence was a violation of God's Law. They worshiped God on Mount Gerizim, where they built their own temple and sacrificed animals. The Samaritans were despised by the Jews who returned from the Exile" (*Everyday Life in the Bible*).

In the time of Jesus, Samaria was the natural route between Galilee and Judea. But the pure-blooded Jews would go out of their way rather than go through Samaria. As Jesus' ministry at one point was primarily to the lost house of Israel, He himself had told His disciples to stay away from the Gentiles and the cities of Samaria

(Matthew 10:5-7).

And so it is of special interest that we read, "And he must needs go through Samaria" (John 4:4). Apparently led by the Spirit, Jesus—on going through, and not around, that dreaded place—met a Samaritan woman who had come to draw water from Jacob's well. In a dialogue initiated by Jesus' request for a drink of water, the conversation inevitably came around to the age-old controversy between Jews and Samaritans about the place for the central worship and sacrifice of the religion of Israel.

The quarrel had started with the building of a temple on Mount Gerizim in Shechem as a rival to the Temple at Jerusalem.

Perceiving that Jesus was a prophet, the woman of Samaria stated her case for worshiping on Mount Gerizim rather than on Mount Zion. This opened up the way for Jesus' discourse on true worship—the essence being that the time would come when the place of worship would be neither here nor there, but in the heart.

23. But the hour cometh, and now is, when the true worshippers shall worship the Father in spirit and in truth: for the Father seeketh such to worship him.

24. God is a Spirit: and they that worship him must worship him in spirit and in truth.

That God seeks or desires believers to worship Him in spirit and in truth should make us all the more eager to worship Him with all our hearts. That God in times of worship is seeking us more ardently than we are seeking Him should make us all the more eager to come before His presence with a joyful heart. It is good to know that when

we come to God we are met by an expectancy greater than our own.

"Really to worship, one must get past the symbols to the realities they typify, and of which they are meant to remind us; past conventions and the formal or thoughtless putting through of the accepted rites in the accepted manner, to an open vision of God, breathlessly real and near, or at least to a sure knowledge that whether we see and feel it or do not, he is here, in this place now, and we are in his presence, and he is stooping to listen and take action, *is* taking action upon our behalf, if we will give his gracious purposes toward us a chance to mature" (*The Interpreter's Bible*, Volume 8).

III. CHRIST AND THE TABERNACLE (Hebrews 8:1-5; 9:6-12)

A. The Excellency of Christ's Priesthood (8:1-5)

(Hebrews 8:3-5 is not included in the printed text.)

1. Now of the things which we have spoken this is the sum: We have such an high priest, who is set on the right hand of the throne of the Majesty in the heavens;

2. A minister of the sanctuary, and of the true tabernacle, which the Lord pitched, and not man.

In this passage from Hebrews, our study of Christ and the Tabernacle focuses on the ways in which the priestly ministry of Christ fulfills, and enlarges upon, that prefigured by the Levitical priesthood. In truth, Christ's is "a more excellent" ministry, based on a "better covenant," established upon "better promises" (v. 6).

The main point, says the writer to the Hebrews, is this: Yes, we do have such a High Priest whose excellency is indicated, in part, by His exalted position at the right hand of God's throne. Our heavenly High Priest is not come "into the holy places made with hands, which are the figures of the true; but into heaven itself, now to appear in the presence of God for us" (9:24).

Christ was never a minister of the earthly Tabernacle. But He is ever a minister of the heavenly. Praise God! We do have a High Priest—not after the order of Levi, but of Melchisedec, the king of Salem and priest of the Most High God. "For that after the similitude of Melchisedec there ariseth another priest, who is made, not after the law of a carnal commandment, but after the power of an endless life. For he testifieth, Thou art a priest for ever after the order of Melchisedec" (7:15-17).

What is meant by the phrase "the true tabernacle"?

B. The Superiority of Christ's Sacrifice (9:6-12)

(Hebrews 9:7-10 is not included in the printed text.)

6. Now when these things were thus ordained, the priests went always into the first tabernacle, accomplishing the service of God.

The daily, weekly (Sabbath), monthly, and yearly (feast day) offerings kept the priests, who no doubt served on a rotating basis, busy in the outer court of the Tabernacle and in the Holy Place. But only once a year, on the Day of Atonement, did the high priest go into the room behind the veil called the "holiest of all" (v. 8).

Observance of the Day of Atonement, a solemn time of fasting and strict conformity to the law, emphasized man's inability to offer atonement for his sins. In *Christ in the Tabernacle,* Louis T. Talbot says: "In our English Old Testament, *atonement* suggests 'at-one-ment' with God for the guilty sinner who brought the sacrifice in anticipation of Calvary's cross. On the merit of the one perfect sacrifice of the promised Redeemer, God 'covered,' or 'passed over,' the sins done aforetime—from Adam to Christ."

In verse 8 we read, "The Holy Spirit was showing by this that the way into the Most Holy Place had not yet been disclosed as long as the first tabernacle was still standing" (*NIV*).

Our Lord's everlasting priesthood stands in sharp contrast to the "figure," or the representative plan of salvation, "for the time then present" (v. 9). Unlike the blood of Christ which clears the conscience of the guilt of sin, the Tabernacle sacrifices served to keep sin in remembrance.

Compared to the gospel of Christ, the law—with its sacrifices, its ceremonial washings, and its external rules and regulations—was a necessary imposition that passed with the passing of the Tabernacle and the earthly priesthood.

11. But Christ being come an high priest of good things to come, by a greater and more perfect tabernacle, not made with hands, that is to say, not of this building;

12. Neither by the blood of goats and calves, but by his own blood he entered in once into the

holy place, having obtained eternal redemption for us.

It is interesting to note that Jesus is both the antitype and the prototype of the ministry of the Tabernacle and its ministers.

As the antitype, Jesus fulfills all that the Tabernacle prefigures. And as pointed out earlier, Jesus actually goes beyond the type in that He, himself, is the minister of realities whereas the priests were ministers of types and shadows. As the prototype, Jesus is the primary or original sacrifice "slain from the foundation of the world" (Revelation 13:8).

The heavenly sanctuary which represented Him, and which He came to represent, was a greater and more perfect tabernacle than that which is the object of our study. The superiority of Christ's sacrifice is evidenced by the fact that it was not the substitutionary blood of goats and calves that He brought into the Holy of Holies, but His own life's blood.

For over 500 years, blood sacrifices were offered in the Holy of Holies. But Christ "entered the Most Holy Place once for all by his own blood, having obtained eternal redemption" (Hebrews 9:12, *NIV*).

REVIEW QUESTIONS

1. What is meant by "the cloud of God's presence"?

2. Why did God command the Israelites to destroy the groves where the gods of the Canaanites worshiped?

3. On what mountain did the Samaritans worship?

4. What is the significance of Christ sitting "on the right hand of the throne of the Majesty in the heavens" (Hebrews 8:1)?

5. On what feast day did the high priest offer sacrifices in the Holy of Holies?

GOLDEN TEXT HOMILY

"TRUE WORSHIPPERS SHALL WORSHIP THE FATHER IN SPIRIT AND IN TRUTH: FOR THE FATHER SEEKETH SUCH TO WORSHIP HIM" (John 4:23).

The word *true* means "consistent with fact or reality."

Worshipers denote those reverencing God. Man has to reverence God to be a true worshiper. To be a true worshiper of God, we must believe there is but one God. The Bible expresses this truth—the Godhead consists of Father, Son, and Holy Ghost.

In spirit means with strength, loyalty, and dedication to this one God. Man has to worship God with a strong desire to please Him, and man must be loyal to God's Word and commandments to be a true worshiper.

Dedication is a must for the Christian worshiper. So many things can draw our attention away from true worship, including world conditions, personal cares, and the religious failures of man.

To *seek* means "to reach out or reach after." God is seeking individuals who are also reaching out for Him and who will become true worshipers.

God sent His Son, Jesus Christ, to be born of the Virgin Mary, to come to this earth as a Savior to express His love for man so that man could worship Him in spirit and truth.

Jesus ministered on the earth, seeking the sinner, healing the sick, dying on the cross for man's sins, training disciples, and ordaining the church to go into all the world and preach the gospel in order to seek and win the sinner.

Jesus told the Samaritan woman at the well that a time was coming—and indeed, it had already come—when worshipers would worship neither on a certain mountain nor in Jerusalem. True worshipers now worship God in all parts of the world, meeting in the name of Jesus Christ, His Son.—**Charles G. Wiley, Pastor, New Boston, Texas**

SENTENCE SERMONS

A STUDY of the tabernacle offers glimpses of Christ and how believers can worship Him.
—Selected

THE TABERNACLE IS a divine pattern of Christ's sacrifice for sinners.
—Selected

THE CHURCH with no great anguish on its heart has no great music on its lips.
—Karl Barth

IN THE SANCTUARY of God two opposite dangers are to be recognized and avoided: they are a COLD HEART and a HOT HEAD.
—A.W. Tozer

EVANGELISM APPLICATION

THE TABERNACLE IS A DIVINE PATTERN OF CHRIST'S SACRIFICE FOR SINNERS.

Writing about the principles of worship based on the *Tabernacle of Moses*, Doug Small says: "In the Most Holy Place, we found 'home.' In his presence, we were earthbound in body, but our spirit touched heaven. We realize, that deep inside us, we have a longing now for another world.

"Yet, he has chosen to leave us here. So, we will live in transit between his tent and our tent, between heaven and earth, between the Most Holy Place of his presence and the most unholy world.

"As we leave the Most Holy Place, we do so conscious of the fact that we are missionaries to our world. As we were touched by each piece of furniture in preparation for his presence, we are now touched by each piece of furniture in preparation for his service" ("Principles of Worship").

ILLUMINATING THE LESSON

SO THIS IS WHERE?

So this is where the Lord has pitched His tent—
I am God's secret place and He is mine!
The veil of separation now is rent,
And this is where the Lord has pitched His tent!
The mountains are no more His tenement,
Nor is an earthly dwelling place His shrine.
My heart is where the Lord has pitched His tent—
I am His secret place and He is mine!
—Betty Spence

DAILY BIBLE READINGS

M. Spirit-Filled Workers.
Exodus 35:30 through 36:1
T. A Place of Sacrifice.
Leviticus 8:14-21
W. A Place of Worship.
1 Chronicles 16:37-43
T. God's Dwelling Place.
1 Corinthians 3:10-17
F. Temple of the Living God.
2 Corinthians 6:14-18
S. A Place of God's Power.
Revelation 15:5-8

Court of the Congregation

Study Text: Exodus 27:1-19; 30:17-21; 38:8; Leviticus 9:7; Numbers 28:1-8; Psalm 27:4-8; John 10:7-9; 15:3; Ephesians 5:25-27; Titus 3:5; Hebrews 10:5-10

Objective: To consider the relationship of the outer court to Israel's worship of God and draw near to Him.

Golden Text: "According to his mercy he saved us, by the washing of regeneration, and renewing of the Holy Ghost" (Titus 3:5).

Central Truth: Spiritual cleansing is available to all who come to God through Christ.

Evangelism Emphasis: Spiritual cleansing is available to all who come to God through Christ.

PRINTED TEXT

John 10:9. I am the door: by me if any man enter in, he shall be saved, and shall go in and out, and find pasture.

Exodus 27:1. And thou shalt make an altar of shittim wood, five cubits long, and five cubits broad; the altar shall be foursquare: and the height thereof shall be three cubits.

2. And thou shalt make the horns of it upon the four corners thereof: his horns shall be of the same: and thou shalt overlay it with brass.

Leviticus 9:7. And Moses said unto Aaron, Go unto the altar, and offer thy sin-offering, and thy burnt-offering, and make an atonement for thyself, and for the people: and offer the offering of the people, and make an atonement for them; as the Lord commanded.

Numbers 28:2. Command the children of Israel, and say unto them, My offering, and my bread for my sacrifices made by fire, for a sweet savour unto me, shall ye observe to offer unto me in their due season.

3. And thou shalt say unto them, This is the offering made by fire which ye shall offer unto the Lord; two lambs of the first year without spot day by day, for a continual burnt-offering.

4. The one lamb shalt thou offer in the morning, and the other lamb shalt thou offer at even.

Hebrews 10:9. Then said he, Lo, I come to do thy will, O God. He taketh away the first, that he may establish the second.

10. By the which will we are sanctified through the offering of the body of Jesus Christ once for all.

Exodus 30:18. Thou shalt also make a laver of brass, and his foot also of brass, to wash withal: and thou shalt put it between the tabernacle of the congregation and the altar, and thou shalt put water therein.

19. For Aaron and his sons shall wash their hands and their feet thereat:

20. When they go into the tabernacle of the congregation, they shall wash with water, that they die not; or when they come near to the altar to minister, to burn offering made by fire unto the Lord.

John 15:3. Now ye are clean through the word which I have spoken unto you.

Ephesians 5:25. Husbands, love your wives, even as Christ also loved the church, and gave himself for it;

26. That he might sanctify and cleanse it with the washing of water by the word.

LESSON OUTLINE

I. ACCESS TO GOD
   A. The Court
   B. The Gate
   C. The Door

II. FORGIVENESS FOR SIN
   A. The Altar
   B. The Sacrificial System
   C. The Sweet-Smelling Sacrifice
   D. The Sacrifice of Christ

III. DAILY CLEANSING
   A. The Laver
   B. The Mirror of God's Word
   C. The Pruning of the Branches
   D. A Glorious Church
   E. The Washing of Regeneration

LESSON EXPOSITION

INTRODUCTION

Just how much the Israelites initially related the ritual of Tabernacle worship to the doctrine of Christ is uncertain. Later the Jews did have the Scriptures which prophesied the coming of the Messiah; but it is doubtful that when the worshiper in the Temple offered up his lamb on the brazen altar, he pictured Jesus dying on the cross as the Lamb of God.

But one of the special joys today of being a Christian is that it has been "given unto [us] to know the mysteries of the kingdom of heaven" (Matthew 13:11). It is our joyous privilege to draw truths from the age-old Tabernacle by studying it in the light of the New Testament, the Book of Hebrews in particular.

On the other hand, some modern readers accustomed to quick access of factual information find figures of speech tedious. And we must admit that a Christological approach to our studies discloses a multiplicity of poetic figures. But when we consider that the typological minefield in which we dig contains the "unsearchable riches of Christ," we should be all the more diligent in studying the doctrine of Christ as it is revealed in the Old Testament.

In Old Testament typology, the New Testament correspondences are there because God controls history and He embodies characteristics in the types which are meaningful for time and eternity. Keep in mind, however, that studying figures is not an end in itself. In this lesson on the "Court of the Congregation," for instance, our main objective is to consider the relationship of the outer court to Israel's worship of God and draw near to Him in true worship.

I. ACCESS TO GOD (Exodus 27:9-19; Psalm 27:4-8; John 10:7-9)

A. The Court (Exodus 27:9-15)

(Exodus 27:9-15 is not included in the printed text.)

Coming into the court of the congregation suggests that a wayfaring pilgrim at long last had arrived at the end of his weary pilgrimage. Coming into the court, he moves from the circumference to the center, from the outside to the inside, from who he was to the person his passage has made him.

The court sets limits and defines borders that say, "Here, not there, is where you are to worship Jehovah, the one true God." It was, in fact, the white linen fence that gave the court its sense of place. And what a place it was!

Whereas the Tabernacle itself was covered with layers of hangings, the rectangular-shaped outer court was open to the heavens. According to the ancient Hebrew measurement, the court measured about 150 feet in length and 75 feet in width.

The "fine twined linen" fence (v. 9) which was about 7 1/2 feet tall, represents Christ's righteousness and reminds us that God's dwelling place is holy. That the linen threads were finely woven together for added strength and beauty is suggestive of the way grape branches wind themselves around the vine. And once we make the connection with Christ's metaphor of the Vine and the branches in John 15, we see in a new way the importance of winding our very lives around the very life of Christ.

Consider also that the brass of the 60 pillars and sockets on which the linen curtains were hung speaks of the judgment of God; the silver of the hooks and tops of the pillars speaks of redemption. Silver reminded the Israelites of the atonement or ransom money that was required as an offering to the Lord for the service of the Tabernacle (Exodus 30:11-16).

Louis T. Talbot says, "It must have been an impressive sight—to behold the brass pillars in brass sockets, the white linen hangings fastened by silver hooks, and the ornamental silver chapiters above—all glistening in the sunlight. But how much more impressive is the sight of the God of glory, the spotless Lamb of Calvary, bearing our sins in His own body on the tree—Christ, our Righteousness, our Sin-Bearer, our Redeemer" (*Christ in the Tabernacle*).

B. The Gate (Exodus 27:16-19; Psalm 27:4-8)

(Exodus 27:16-19 and Psalm 27:4-8 are not included in the printed text.)

The gate of the courtyard was a "hanging" curtain of blue, purple, and scarlet (Exodus 27:16). With blue standing for deity, purple for royalty, and scarlet for redemption, the embroidered white linen gate of the court beautifully represents our Lord Jesus Christ as the Way, the Truth, and the Life (John 14:6).

Inside the gate the Hebrew found his purpose, his destiny as a Jew and spiritual son of Abraham. The gate was a passage from the profane to the sacred. This one and only way into the dwelling place of God—this gate that opened to the rising sun—offered a respite from the wilderness and ever-present enemies.

The psalmist David sang of the gates of the Lord and the joys of entering and dwelling in God's house. In Psalm 27:4-8 he expresses his desire to spend his days gazing upon the beauty of the Lord and seeking Him in His temple. He says, "Therefore will I offer in his tabernacle sacrifices of joy; I will sing, yea, I will sing praises unto the Lord" (v. 6).

Why do you think that praise has been called the gateway into the presence of the Lord?

C. The Door (John 10:7-9)

(John 10:7, 8 is not included in the printed text.)

9. I am the door: by me if any man enter in, he shall be saved, and shall go in and out, and find pasture.

Someone has said that a doorknob is symbolic of the fact that the next move is in one's own hands. When we think about Christ as the way to God, we realize, indeed, that it is the seeker's privilege and responsibilty to ask, seek, and knock—thereby having the door opened to him, to cross over the threshold.

Unlike the entrance to the Tabernacle courtyard which was open only to Jews (and more specifically to Jews bearing gifts and sacrifices), the entrance to the kingdom of heaven is opened to "whosoever will"—whoever will believe that the sacrifice of Christ opens up the way into the presence of God.

II. FORGIVENESS FOR SIN
(Exodus 27:1-8; Leviticus 9:7; Numbers 28:1-8; Hebrews 10:5-10)

A. The Altar (Exodus 27:1-8)

(Exodus 27:3-8 is not included in the printed text.)

1. And thou shalt make an altar of shittim wood, five cubits long, and five cubits broad; the altar shall be foursquare: and the height thereof shall be three cubits.

2. And thou shalt make the horns of it upon the four corners thereof: his horns shall be of the same: and thou shalt overlay it with brass.

The focal point in the outer court was the great altar used for daily burnt offerings and meal offerings. Once inside the gate the Israelite was confronted with the 7 1/2 feet square, 4 1/2 feet high, brazen altar. Made of shittim (acacia) wood and overlaid with brass (bronze), the brazen altar was a symbol of access to God through atonement by blood. The four corners of the altar had hornlike projections seen to represent divine strength and power as well as refuge for those taking hold of them upon fleeing an enemy.

The fire of the altar on which sacrifices for the sins of the people were placed was kindled by God and maintained by the priests. While it is true the altar was made by man, God gave the plan—the pattern and the purpose. That God ordered that it be made of valuable wood and metal indicates that true worship requires man's best and that God initiates worship.

I.M. Haldeman says, "Since our Lord is the announced antitype of the burnt offering and that was offered on the Brazen Altar, the Brazen Altar is the symbol of the cross on which He died and demonstrates it to be, not merely the instrument of a Roman judicial death, but the divinely ordained and definite, chosen Altar of Sacrifice" (*The Tabernacle*

Priesthood and Offerings).

B. The Sacrificial System
(Leviticus 9:7)

7. And Moses said unto Aaron, Go unto the altar, and offer thy sin-offering, and thy burnt-offering, and make an atonement for thyself, and for the people: and offer the offering of the people, and make an atonement for them; as the Lord commanded.

A central idea in the ritual and worship of the Tabernacle was that sin had cut Israel off from God's presence. Through disobedience Israel had broken covenant with God. But through the sacrificial system, God showed that He would accept a substitute—the blood of an animal, instead of the offender.

In the case of the burnt offering the whole animal was burned, thus symbolizing the worshiper's reverence and total dedication to God. "In laying his hand on the animal he identified himself completely with the sacrifice. The offering had to cost him something—one of his herd of cattle or flock of sheep and goats (a bird was permitted for the poor), and it had to be of the best—'a male without blemish'" (Philip Budd, *Eerdmans' Handbook to the Bible*).

C. The Sweet-Smelling Sacrifice
(Numbers 28:1-8)

(Numbers 28:1, 5-8 is not included in the printed text.)

2. Command the children of Israel, and say unto them, My offering, and my bread for my sacrifices made by fire, for a sweet savour unto me, shall ye observe to offer unto me in their due season.
3. And thou shalt say unto them, This is the offering made by fire which ye shall offer unto the Lord; two lambs of the first year without spot day by day, for a continual burnt-offering.
4. The one lamb shalt thou offer in the morning, and the other lamb shalt thou offer at even.

To God the scent of the offerings made by fire was an agreeable odor. "It is a continual burnt-offering, which was ordained in mount Sinai for a sweet savour, a sacrifice made by fire unto the Lord" (v. 6).

In the Scriptures there are numerous references to the sweet aroma accompanying an acceptable sacrifice. And because scent is symbolic of memories, I would like to think that when God smelled the sweet odor of the essence of faith and obedience, He remembered His covenant promises to make of Israel a great nation from which the Messiah would come.

And in view of Ephesians 5:2, which says that Christ has "given himself for us an offering and a sacrifice to God for a sweetsmelling savour," the sweet fragrance proves to be that which ascends to God through the person making the sacrifice.

It follows then that as disciples of Christ, "we are unto God a sweet savour of Christ" (2 Corinthians 2:15). As we daily make of our lives "a living sacrifice, holy, acceptable unto God" (Romans 12:1), the sweet fragrance of Christ's sacrifice is made to linger still.

How can a sweet and agreeable spirit be a witness for Christ?

D. The Sacrifice of Christ (Hebrews 10:5-10)

(Hebrews 10:5-8 is not included in the printed text.)

9. Then said he, Lo, I come to do thy will, O God. He taketh away the first, that he may establish the second.

10. By the which will we are sanctified through the offering of the body of Jesus Christ once for all.

Because the sacrificial system was "a shadow of good things to come" (v. 1), because it was a reminder of sin and an instrument of guilt, because it could not take away sins, and because it did not fully please God, Jesus said, "Lo, I come to do thy will, O God."

Don Brandeis, in *The Gospel in the Old Testament*, says, "The Saviour's death made redemption an accomplished fact. Type met antitype; substance took the place of the shadows. All who long for power to obey the law of God, whether they be Jew or Gentile, must receive help in God's appointed way through the Saviour."

III. DAILY CLEANSING (Exodus 30:17-21; 38:8; John 15:3; Ephesians 5:25-27; Titus 3:5).

A. The Laver (Exodus 30:17- 21)

(Exodus 30:17, 21 is not included in the printed text.)

18. Thou shalt also make a laver of brass, and his foot also of brass, to wash withal: and thou shalt put it between the tabernacle of the congregation and the altar, and thou shalt put water therein.

19. For Aaron and his sons shall wash their hands and their feet thereat:

20. When they go into the tabernacle of the congregation, they shall wash with water, that they die not; or when they come near to the altar to minister, to burn offering made by fire unto the Lord.

Between the brazen altar and the entrance to the Holy Place stood the brazen (bronze or copper) laver. With a bowl and a base which formed a smaller basin, the laver provided a place for the priests to wash their hands and feet before entering the Holy Place and offering sacrifices at the brazen altar.

"There was no bloodshedding at the laver, yet the priests dared not worship without its cleansing. Again, the lesson is plain. We cannot approach God except with clean hands and a clean heart. If we want to know His quickening power, we must confess our sins so that He may cleanse us from all unrighteousness" (Louis T. Talbot, *Christ in the Tabernacle*).

B. The Mirror of God's Word (Exodus 38:8)

(Exodus 38:8 is not included in the printed text.)

The brass mirrors that went into the construction of the laver, contributed by the women who served at the door of the Tent of Meeting, have several associations worthy of notice. Let's consider the laver as an instrument that reflects the plan of salvation as well as the inner life of the believer:

The mirror of God's Word. From the earliest times, mirror symbolism is linked with water as a reflector. And in James 1:23 the Word is figuratively compared to a mirror. The hearer who disobeys is like a person who, having looked into the Word, forgets what he has read after turning away. The person who obeys is like one who gazes into the mirror of God's Word and retains the reflection of what he should be.

The mirror of testimony. In the same way that God's Word mirrors His will and His way, the life of the believer reflects his or her resemblance to the heavenly Father.

In literary symbolism, hand mirrors, in particular, are emblems of truth. Let us so live that our lives will reflect both the Truth and the Light.

What is the significance of the brass mirrors being used in the construction of the laver?

C. The Pruning of the Branches (John 15:3)

3. Now ye are clean through the word which I have spoken unto you.

Cleansing in still another context is drawn from the passage in John 15, in which Christ declares that He is the Vine and His disciples are the branches. The metaphor for cleansing here deals with the act of purging or pruning. For the sake of fruit, the heavenly Father, as the gardener, cuts off the unfruitful branch. But the fruit-bearing branch, He cuts back. When there is no fruit on a fruit tree, something is wrong.

In light of Hebrews 9:14, which deals with Christ's purging the conscience of works that produce death and not life, we get the idea that an expanding list of things to do may not indicate we are being effective in serving the Lord. That what appears to us to be growth in our spiritual life may be nothing more than "dead works."

When a too-full agenda leaves no place for prayer and Bible study, we might as well look to have our activities cut back. To undergo spiritual pruning is always a traumatic experience. But in some cases fruit is produced only on new

wood. Sometimes when we persist in doing what is not effective, God takes the initiative in cleaning off our desks and freeing up our calendar of events. And while the cutting back may appear at first to be a set-back, if we are faithful and abide in the Vine, new growth will come and with it fruit.

D. A Glorious Church (Ephesians 5:25-27)

(Ephesians 5:27 is not included in the printed text.)

25. Husbands, love your wives, even as Christ also loved the church, and gave himself for it;

26. That he might sanctify and cleanse it with the washing of water by the word.

Still another illustration of the laver, and its association with washing through the Word, is in the doctrine of Christ's giving Himself for the church.

The various images of sanctification in this passage begin to come together when we consider that the primary use of the Biblical *wash* related to the washing of clothes both for ordinary cleansing and ritual cleansing.

The points of similarity in the ritual of ceremonial washings are expressed in Christ's purpose of cleansing the church in order to present her to Himself as the bride of Christ without spot or wrinkle. It is only through the sanctifying power of the Word that we, as believers, can be a part of that radiant, glorious church, "holy and without blemish" (v. 27).

E. The Washing of Regeneration (Titus 3:5)

(Titus 3:5 is not included in the

printed text.)

Water as an agent in natural birth gives us an interesting point of reference in studying "the washing of regeneration, and renewing of the Holy Ghost." Regeneration presupposes generation or birth, as well as degeneration or death. While the heavenly Father and the Son are active powers in the "washing of regeneration," it is the blessed Holy Spirit who renews our spiritual life.

"From the nature of the act of new birth, spiritual resurrection, and creation, it is clear that regeneration is not accomplished by any good work of man. It is not an act of the human will in itself, and it is not produced by any ordinance of the church such as water baptism. It is entirely a supernatural act of God in response to the faith of man" (Lewis Sperry Chafer and John F. Walvoord, *Major Bible Themes*).

REVIEW QUESTIONS

1. What is the spiritual significance of coming into the courts of the Lord?

2. What does the gate of the court represent?

3. Discuss the symbolism of the brazen altar located in the outer court of the Tabernacle?

4. What does the brass laver represent?

5. What is the connection between cleansing and pruning?

GOLDEN TEXT HOMILY

"ACCORDING TO HIS MERCY HE SAVED US, BY THE WASHING OF REGENERATION, AND RENEWING OF THE HOLY GHOST" (Titus 3:5).

Ever since Adam and Eve sinned and thought their works of self-righteousness would serve as a sin covering, all people have been born in innate rebellion against God. Cain missed God's will because he wanted his way—to sacrifice farm produce, not an animal as God had commanded.

No doubt self-righteousness is part of the reason that God said, "All our righteousnesses are as filthy rags" (Isaiah 64:6). Christ's death on the cross would have been unnecessary if our own deeds were the basis of our title to eternal life. Whatever we have done, when we come to receive salvation from the hands of God, no element is involved but mercy. It is not by our repentance and faith, not by all our tears, sighs, and prayers, but salvation is by the favor of God. We are not saved by the works of righteousness, even though they should be done in obedience to God's Word. Ephesians 2:8, 9 explains, "For by grace are ye saved through faith; and that not of yourselves: it is the gift of God: Not of works, lest any man should boast."

Washing by regeneration means that God sanctifies and cleanses our hearts with the water of the Word. New life commences through the Word's being applied and allows us to become new creatures in Christ Jesus.

The Holy Spirit convicts us of our sins and helps us to understand that we need salvation, that Christ died and rose from the grave for us, thereby making salvation available to us. We must accept that gift by repenting and confessing our sins; then through God's mercy we are accepted by the Holy Spirit to become children of God. The Holy Spirit makes us over anew—new in our views, feelings, desires, happiness, plans, and purposes. Man is so different from what he was before that it can be said he has entered a new life. We were dead in our sins before accepting Christ, but upon receiving Christ, we have the Holy Spirit to begin and continue the spiritual process in our new lives (1 Corinthians 4:16).—**Willie F. Lawrence, D.D., Pastor, Church of God, Danville, Illinois**

SENTENCE SERMONS

SPIRITUAL CLEANSING is available to all who come to God through Christ.

—Selected

SIN IS A SOVEREIGN till sovereign grace dethrones it.

—Charles Haddon Spurgeon

THE OTHER FELLOW'S SINS, like the other fellow's car lights, always seem more glaring than our own.

—The Encyclopedia of Religious Quotations

THOSE WHO ARE WISE consider how God responds to their worship.

—David Mains

EVANGELISM APPLICATION

SPIRITUAL CLEANSING IS AVAILABLE TO ALL WHO COME TO GOD THROUGH CHRIST.

When Robert Moffat, the great missionary was about 20, he wrote this:

"Living alone in an extensive garden, my leisure was my own. While poring over the Epistle to the Romans, I could not help wondering over a number of passages which I had read many times before. They appeared altogether different. I exclaimed with a heart nearly broken, 'Can it be possible that I have never understood what I have been reading?' turning from one passage to another, each sending light into my darkened soul. The Book of God seemed to be laid open, and I saw at once what God had done for the sinner. I felt that, being justified by faith, I had peace with God through the Lord Jesus Christ."

—Knight's Illustrations for Today

ILLUMINATING THE LESSON

Sarah Hornsby, in her book *At the Name of Jesus*, said:

"Jesus is a Sweet Savour. It is Jesus' total gift of Himself to God which is a delight, a pleasure to God. It is the distinctive aroma of the sacrificial love which God himself had for us in giving us His Son.

"Jesus says . . . 'You are the salt in the stew of the earth's peoples. You are the flavoring which is essential, which makes life bearable, even enjoyable. When others recognize in you the sweetness of My Presence, they will respond. They will taste and see that I am good.'"

DAILY BIBLE READINGS

M. Rebellion of Korah.
    Numbers 16:1-12
T. Reminder of Judgment.
    Numbers 16:28-40
W. Praise God in His Courts.
    Psalm 100:1-5
T. Cleansing the Temple Courts.
    Matthew 21:12-16
F. Rejoicing in the Temple
    Courts. Acts 3:1-10
S. Preaching in the Temple
    Courts. Acts 5:12-21

The Holy Place

Study Text: Exodus 25:23-40; 30:1-10, 34-38; Leviticus 24:1-9; Psalm 141:2; John 1:4-9; 6:32-35, 44-51; 8:12; 1 Corinthians 11:17-34; Revelation 5:8; 8:3, 4

Objective: To understand how the objects in the Holy Place relate to Christ's provision of eternal life and pray for unbelievers to be saved.

Golden Text: "I am the light of the world: he that followeth me shall not walk in darkness, but shall have the light of life" (John 8:12).

Central Truth: The objects of the Holy Place picture Christ's ministry for the believer.

Evangelism Emphasis: Jesus Christ sets sinners free from the power of darkness.

PRINTED TEXT

Leviticus 24:2. Command the children of Israel, that they bring unto thee pure oil olive beaten for the light, to cause the lamps to burn continually.

3. Without the vail of the testimony, in the tabernacle of the congregation, shall Aaron order it from the evening unto the morning before the Lord continually: it shall be a statute for ever in your generations.

John 1:4. In him was life; and the life was the light of men.

Exodus 25:23. Thou shalt also make a table of shittim wood: two cubits shall be the length thereof, and a cubit the breadth thereof, and a cubit and a half the height thereof.

30. And thou shalt set upon the table shewbread before me alway.

John 6:48. I am that bread of life.

49. Your fathers did eat manna in the wilderness, and are dead.

50. This is the bread which cometh down from heaven, that a man may eat thereof, and not die.

51. I am the living bread which came down from heaven: if any man eat of this bread, he shall live for ever: and the bread that I will give is my flesh, which I will give for the life of the world.

1 Corinthians 11:23. For I have received of the Lord that which also I delivered unto you, That the Lord Jesus the same night in which he was betrayed took bread:

24. And when he had given thanks, he brake it, and said, Take, eat: this is my body, which is broken for you: this do in remembrance of me.

25. After the same manner also he took the cup, when he

had supped, saying, This cup is the new testament in my blood: this do ye, as oft as ye drink it, in remembrance of me.

26. For as often as ye eat this bread, and drink this cup, ye do shew the Lord's death till he come.

Exodus 30:1. And thou shalt make an altar to burn incense upon: of shittim wood shalt thou make it.

7. And Aaron shall burn thereon sweet incense every morning: when he dresseth the lamps, he shall burn incense upon it.

Revelation 8:3. And another angel came and stood at the altar, having a golden censer; and there was given unto him much incense, that he should offer it with the prayers of all saints upon the golden altar which was before the throne.

LESSON OUTLINE

I. LIGHT FOR THE WORLD
   A. The Candlestick
   B. The Eternal Flame
   C. The True Light
   D. The Light of the World

II. BREAD OF LIFE
   A. The Table of Shewbread
   B. The Bread of Communion
   C. The Bread of God
   D. The Living Bread
   E. The Bread of Remembrance

III. PRAYERS OF THE SAINTS
   A. The Golden Altar
   B. Perfume, Pure and Holy
   C. Prayers
   D. The Golden Censer

LESSON EXPOSITION

INTRODUCTION

The Tabernacle was in the form of a tent measuring 15 feet wide and 45 feet long. Its only entrance faced the east. It had a wooden framework of shittim (acacia) wood overlaid with gold. The roof consisted of four coverings. The first, in colors of blue, red, and purple, was linen embroidered with cherubim. The second was of white goats' hair. The third was of rams' skins dyed red. The outermost covering was badgers' skins. Since the badger as we know it was supposedly not found in Bible lands, some have suggested the outer covering was made of porpoise skins or possibly other leather.

The first room in the sacred tent was the Holy Place and the second, the Holy of Holies. The Holy Place was entered through blue, scarlet, and purple linen curtains which served as a door. The Holy of Holies could only be entered through a veil and then only by the high priest one time a year.

Three objects in the Holy Place—the candlestick, the table of shewbread, and the altar of incense—their functions, what they represent in the life of the believer, and their fulfillments in the New Testament are the focus of this lesson.

I. LIGHT FOR THE WORLD
   (Exodus 25:31-40; Leviticus 24:1-4; John 1:4-9; 8:12)

   A. The Candlestick (Exodus 25:31-40)

   (Exodus 25:31-40 is not included in the printed text.)

   Two important aspects of the

candlestick are the material out of which it was made and its design. In contrast to the brazen altar and the laver of the court, the furnishings of the Holy Place were made of pure gold. The candlestick in particular was made of hand-hammered gold as were its accessories.

Gold is symbolic of all that is superior. Furthermore, the gold of the seven-branched candlestick reflected the glory of its substance as the one source of light in the Tabernacle. Both a light and a light-bearer, the golden candlestick was a divine symbol of our Lord Jesus Christ.

The design of the candlestick, which was made according to the pattern shown Moses on Mount Sinai, featured a central branch out of which sprang six other branches. All of the branches were decorated with sepals and petals of the blossoms of the almond tree, traditionally known as a symbol of sweetness and delicacy. The bowls that held the olive oil for the lamps were almond-shaped as well.

B. The Eternal Flame
(Leviticus 24:1-4)

(Leviticus 24:1, 4 is not included in the printed text.)

2. Command the children of Israel, that they bring unto thee pure oil olive beaten for the light, to cause the lamps to burn continually.

3. Without the vail of the testimony, in the tabernacle of the congregation, shall Aaron order it from the evening unto the morning before the Lord continually: it shall be a statute for ever in your generations.

Two distinguishing features of the maintenance of the candlestick were that the olive oil for the lamps was to be provided by the people and the lampstand itself was to be tended by the priests. In this we see the ever important element of man's being allowed to participate in the plan of salvation.

Turning our attention to the oil that lit the golden lamps of the candlestick, we see that the word translated "Candlestick" might be better translated "lampstand" since oil and not candles was used. And just as the hammering of the gold was the work of the goldsmith's hands, the extraction of the oil was the handiwork of the people.

The olive tree was an invaluable resource to the Israelites. Its fruit was used for food and medicine, and the best virgin oil was kept for liturgical purposes. A staple in the homes of ancient peoples, the olive was a symbol of strength and health. Today oil is a familiar symbol of the Holy Spirit.

The believers bringing pure olive oil to the Tabernacle for the candlestick were as much a part of the lasting ordinance of light in God's dwelling place as were the priests tending the lamps so that they would burn before the Lord continually.

The typical lamp in Bible times was a simple, shallow, saucer-like bowl with one side pinched to hold the wick. To light the house and keep a ready fire, it was customary to keep a lamp burning at all times.

In the Tabernacle too the priests had to keep the wicks trimmed and the light burning. Today we can keep the light burning in our hearts by daily walking in accordance with God's will. In a manner of speaking, we let our light shine by trusting in the guidance of the Holy Spirit and by continually renewing our relationship with Christ.

C. The True Light (John 1:4-9)

(John 1:5-9 is not included in the printed text.)

4. In him was life; and the life was the light of men.

For an overview of some of the main ideas in this passage, consider the following key words and their antonyms.

Being/Non-being. In John's hymn of light, we are reminded that Jesus was with God from the beginning and that nothing was created without Him. For "in him was life" (John 1:4).

We were given a world to live in and a body. But until God breathed into us the breath of life, we were not living souls. The life of Christ gave us existence for the present time—and for eternity. "And the life was the light of men" (v. 4). This living Light gave us both the light of reason and of faith. This Light gave us a conscious existence. You are, because He is. In Him you move and live and have your being (Acts 17:28).

Light/Darkness. Light is ever the enemy of darkness. Understanding is always in conflict with ignorance. In verse 5 we read: "And the light shineth in darkness; and the darkness comprehended it not." While this verse is often explained as meaning that spiritual darkness cannot hold back or put out the light of Christ—and surely this is true, praise God, for the light goes on shining—but it implies as well that the darkness in the unregenerate heart will not admit, accept, or appropriate the light. The sin-darkened heart and mind has no sensitivity to or awareness of the Light.

True/False. John was a true witness of the true Light. John well knew that Jesus was the message and that he, John, was the messenger. As a witness, John was a

beholder. In a flash of spiritual insight, John, upon seeing Jesus coming down the road, cried out, "Behold the Lamb of God, which taketh away the sin of the world" (v. 29).

John's witness presents Jesus as the antitype of the candlestick, the revealer of God. Jesus, not John, is the real and lasting light, not merely the fading reflection of the type.

D. The Light of the World (John 8:12)

(John 8:12 is not included in the printed text.)

The words of Jesus "I am the light of the world" were emphatic. The claim was both superlative and inclusive. Just as there was light in the wilderness to direct the wandering Israelites, there is a Light for believers of Christ to follow, and that light is Jesus. He is the Light of the World, but only those who follow Him walk not in darkness.

In reference to the effect of this Light, Jesus said that His followers were "the light of the world" (Matthew 5:14). Jesus had also spoken of living water that would flow from one's innermost being (John 7:38), and now emphasized the light that His followers could have from Him to give to others.

What could be called a false light today?

II. BREAD OF LIFE (Exodus 25:23-30; Leviticus 24:5-9; John 6:32-35, 44-51; 1 Corinthians 11:23-26)

A. The Table of Shewbread (Exodus 25:23-30)

(Exodus 25:24-29 is not included in the printed text.)

23. Thou shalt also make a table of shittim wood: two cubits shall be the length thereof, and a

cubit the breadth thereof, and a cubit and a half the height thereof.

30. And thou shalt set upon the table shewbread before me alway.

The golden table situated on the north side of the Holy Place opposite the candlestick suggests the idea that at God's house the table is always set. Made of acacia wood and overlaid with gold, the table was 2 1/4 feet high, 3 feet long, and 18 inches wide. It featured a gold rim and double molding. On the four corners were gold rings which held the poles used in carrying the table. The serving pieces for the table were also made of gold.

Associated with the idea of a gathering and fellowship, the table of shewbread signifies that God wishes to have communion with His people. A table in and of itself has many meaningful associations. But in this case, that which is placed on the table is especially significant. In this case it is the "shewbread," or "the bread of Presence" (NIV).

B. The Bread of Communion
(Leviticus 24:5-9)

(Leviticus 24:5-9 is not included in the printed text.)

True religion has been defined as the communion between two persons: God and man. Nothing is more expressive of a personal relationship between God and man than the ritual of the table of shewbread. Initially, the fellowship of giving and receiving is expressed by the people's offering of flour for the bread to be "set . . . before the Lord" (v. 6). The principle is that everything we have is a gift of God, and the only way we can really say thanks is to give back to God a portion of what He has so freely given us.

The ritual of the priest's eating the week-old bread each Sabbath represents the believer-priest feeding on the bread of God. Matthew Henry says that when the bread was removed and given to the priest, the frankincense that crowned the 12 loaves was burned upon the golden altar and that this was for a memorial instead of the bread—an offering made by fire.

Today we can partake of the bread of Presence by reading and seeking to understand God's Word.

C. The Bread of God
(John 6:32-35)

(John 6:32-35 is not included in the printed text.)

In the events leading up to Jesus' discourse on the bread of life, we see the manner in which hearing and believing relate to everlasting life. There were those among the 5,000 fed by the loaves and fish who failed to discern the spiritual significance of the miracle. As if this were not sign enough, they wanted more.

"Jesus must show a sign on a far grander scale if He wanted them to believe Him greater than Moses. The Master replied, correcting their false conception of religion: 'It was not Moses who gave you the bread from heaven (a blunt denial), but it is my Father (mine in a peculiar sense) who is giving you the true bread out of heaven.'

"The manna gave nourishment to the Jews; the genuine bread gives life to all. True life must come from more than material bread and faith must be founded on deeper foundations than mere signs and miracles" (J.W. Shepard, *The Christ of the Gospels*).

Today, to appropriate the blessings of Christ as the Bread of God come down from heaven, we must acknowledge that He alone can satisfy the spiritual hunger that sets man apart from all of God's creatures. Just how fully we discern who Jesus is, and how He relates to us now and forever, will be manifested in the time we spend each day feeding on His Word and enjoying His presence. If we really believe that Jesus is the Bread of God we will never go hungry.

D. The Living Bread (John 6:44-51)

(John 6:44-47 is not included in the printed text.)

48. I am that bread of life.

49. Your fathers did eat manna in the wilderness, and are dead.

50. This is the bread which cometh down from heaven, that a man may eat thereof, and not die.

51. I am the living bread which came down from heaven: if any man eat of this bread, he shall live for ever: and the bread that I will give is my flesh, which I will give for the life of the world.

Even as Jesus revealed Himself as living water to the woman at the well, he tells the unbelieving Jews that He is the Bread of Life, the living bread that gives eternal life. The picture of living bread stands out in bold relief among other divinely ordained provisions such as the Pascal Lamb of the Passover, the manna of the wilderness, the showbread of the Holy Place, and the miraculous bread and fish of the Gospels. Each was for a specific time and purpose. But the "living bread" is everlasting and of eternal value. This bread is Christ's own flesh, His own body which He will give as a sacrifice for the sins of the world.

How can we assimilate Christ, the living bread, into our lives?

E. The Bread of Remembrance (1 Corinthians 11:23-26)

23. For I have received of the Lord that which also I delivered unto you, That the Lord Jesus the same night in which he was betrayed took bread:

24. And when he had given thanks, he brake it, and said, Take, eat: this is my body, which is broken for you: this do in remembrance of me.

25. After the same manner also he took the cup, when he had supped, saying, This cup is the new testament in my blood: this do ye, as oft as ye drink it, in remembrance of me.

26. For as often as ye eat this bread, and drink this cup, ye do shew the Lord's death till he come.

Eating, as a metaphor for receiving spiritual food and the benefits thereof, was familiar to the Jews. Instruction was called bread, and those who received it were said to have eaten it. This being true, it should not have come as a surprise to the disciples at the Last Supper to have the Lord use a piece of bread and a cup of wine to symbolize His soon-to-be broken body and shed blood.

Shepard points out that much has been written about the meaning and character of the Memorial Supper but that it is important to keep in mind that the bread and wine are symbols with no spiritual grace conferred in either.

"It is in the atoning blood of

Jesus that the power for the remission of sins resides. The bread does not become the body of Christ in the Supper, much less His soul and divinity. In no sense is the bread changed in nature. The fruit of the vine (probably grape juice) was in no sense changed in nature by its use in the Supper" (*The Christ of the Gospels*).

The greater significance of the bread and wine is that they are to be partaken of until He comes again in remembrance of Christ and His sacrifice on the cross. Today the ordinance of Holy Communion is a memorial supper in which we rally around the cross in expectation of the soon return of the Christ of Calvary.

III. PRAYERS OF THE SAINTS
(Exodus 30:1-10, 34-37; Psalm 141:2; Revelation 5:8; 8:3, 4)

A. The Golden Altar
(Exodus 30:1-10)

(Exodus 30:2-6, 8-10 is not included in the printed text.)

1. And thou shalt make an altar to burn incense upon: of shittim wood shalt thou make it.

7. And Aaron shall burn thereon sweet incense every morning: when he dresseth the lamps, he shall burn incense upon it.

The Physical Properties of the Golden Altar. Three feet tall and 1 1/2 feet square, the incense altar featured a crown under which were rings and staves for carrying. Like the brazen altar, it had at the four corners horns on which blood was sprinkled once a year as a sign of atonement.

This third piece of symbolic furniture in the Holy Place—the place of personal relationship with God—

was made of wood produced by the shittim, or acacia, tree and overlaid with gold. Harder than our oak, acacia is insect repellent and its fine-grained wood is sweet-smelling.

In natural symbolism, the suppleness of wood, which allows it to be bent and straightened, suggests new possibilities—something constructive about to happen. As a religious symbol, wood, by way of association with the tree, is reminiscent of the cross and the humanity of Christ.

The Placement of the Altar of Incense. "Nowhere in all the Hebrew tabernacle did the glories of Christ shine forth with more radiance and beauty than in the golden altar of incense that stood before the veil in the Holy Place. It was directly in front of the Ark of the Covenant and Mercy Seat, which stood within the veil in the Holy of Holies. Only the beautiful hanging of fine-twined linen separated it from the Shekinah glory. On the left of the golden altar of incense, the candlestick shed its light upon everything in the Holy Place; to the right, just opposite the candlestick, stood the table of shewbread. Thus the altar, before which Aaron offered sweet incense to God as he prayed for the people, became another important link in 'the shadow of the cross' formed by the six pieces of furniture in the Hebrew tabernacle and outer court" (Louis T. Talbot, *Christ in the Tabernacle*).

The Particulars of the Use of the Altar of Incense. On coals taken from the brazen altar in the outer court, Aaron burned incense on the golden altar morning and evening. Once a year on the Day of Atonement, blood of the sin offering was sprinkled on the horns of the incense altar and some of the burning coals were taken by the high priest in a golden censer into the Holy of Holies.

In that the golden altar and its services were holy unto the Lord, no incense other than that specified by God was to be offered upon it, and no other kind of offering. Improperly compounded incense would speak of insincere or purely formal worship.

Like the other articles of the Holy Place which foreshadowed the person and ministry of Christ, the altar and its precious materials symbolize Christ as our altar and priest and intercessor. It is through and by Him that our prayers rise up to God as a sweet-smelling savor.

B. Perfume, Pure and Holy
(Exodus 30:34-37)

(Exodus 30:34-37 is not included in the printed text.)

Offering of incense was common in the religious ceremonies of nearly all ancient nations. The orientals loved sweet odors and burned incense to those they wished to honor. However, the incense for Tabernacle worship was unlike any other because its ingredients were distinctly and plainly set forth by God, and as such it was set apart for sacred use.

Three sweet spices and frankincense went into this holy perfume. Nothing could be substituted, nothing imitated. The purity of the formula suggests that in true worship no person or thing can be substituted for Christ as the object of our devotion.

Make a spiritual application of the holy perfume based on the availability today of inexpensive imitations of costly designer perfumes.

C. Prayers (Psalm 141:2; Revelation 5:8)

(Psalm 141:2; Revelation 5:8 are not included in the printed text.)

"The golden vials or bowls filled with sacred perfume or incense represent the prayers of the saints according to the text. Here in heaven the importance of prayer in the earthly scene is inferred. Later in the book testimony is made to the continued witness on earth of those who trust in Christ during the time of dreadful tribulation. Their prayers are said to be as sweet incense before the throne of God. The symbolism of bowls of incense representing the prayers of the saints is reflected in Psalm 141:2 where David cried to the Lord, 'Let my prayer be set forth before thee as incense; and the lifting up of my hands as the evening sacrifice'" (John F. Walvoord, *The Revelation of Jesus Christ*).

Vials filled with the prayers of the saints bring to mind another of David's psalms in which he asks God to put his tears into God's bottle (Psalm 56:8). That David wanted his tears to be remembered in this way alludes to the Eastern custom of collecting tears shed in a time of trouble and sorrow, and keeping them in a small, tear bottle. In his notes on the Book of Psalms, Albert Barnes says, "It cannot be wrong to weep if our eye 'poureth out' its tears 'unto God' (Job 16:20); that is, if in our sorrow we look to God with submission and with earnest supplication."

D. The Golden Censer
(Revelation 8:3, 4)

(Revelation 8:4 is not included in the printed text.)

3. And another angel came and stood at the altar, having a golden censer; and there was given unto

him much incense, that he should offer it with the prayers of all saints upon the golden altar which was before the throne.

At the golden altar in heaven, an angel—which many Bible scholars believe is Christ in His work as High Priest—stands with a golden censer presenting incense and the prayers of the saints before the throne. In view of verse 5, the censer, apparently corresponding to that used to offer incense in the Most Holy Place, appears to be a symbol of judgment cast out on the earth in response to the intercession and prayers of the suffering saints.

To see the part the prayers of the saints play in the final judgment of sin should encourage us today to pray without ceasing and to know that though all of our prayers may not be answered in our lifetime, the "effectual fervent prayer of a righteous man availeth much" (James 5:16).

REVIEW QUESTIONS

1. Name the three pieces of furniture in the Holy Place. Explain the symbolism of each.

2. What is the significance of the people's furnishing the oil for the golden candlestick?

3. What does the table of shewbread represent to us today?

4. What does offering incense symbolize?

5. Explain how this lesson teaches that God remembers our prayers?

SENTENCE SERMONS

JESUS CHRIST sets sinners free from the power of darkness.

—Selected

ALL THAT I AM, I owe to Jesus

Christ, revealed to me in His divine Book.

—David Livingstone

JESUS CHRIST IS GOD'S everything for man's total need.

—Richard Halverson

CHRIST DIED FOR US. Now He, and we, live for others.

—Malcolm Cronk

EVANGELISM APPLICATION

Brown bag luminaries consisting of candles placed in sand-filled bags provide us with a beautiful analogy to letting our lights shine for Christ. For the festive glow of each such luminary belies the fact that the humble source is a light shining through an ordinary paper sack.

Likewise, as Christians, we shine not by our own power, but by our Lord's. According to Paul, we have this treasure of light "in earthen vessels, that the excellency of the power may be of God, and not of us" (2 Corinthians 4:7).

And just as darkness manifests light, dark times show up the light of Christ in the life of the believer. When we feel the least like shining, we can shine and glorify Jesus, the Light of the World.

DAILY BIBLE READINGS

M. Faithful Service.
2 Chronicles 13:10-12
T. "By My Spirit."
Zechariah 4:1-10
W. Pure Incense. Malachi 1:6-11
T. Offering of Incense.
Luke 1:8-17
F. Bread of Fellowship.
1 Corinthians 10:14-17
S. Light for the Church.
Revelation 1:12-20

The Holy of Holies

Study Text: Exodus 25:10-22; 26:31-34; Leviticus 16:1-34; Matthew 27:50, 51; Hebrews 4:14-16; 9:2-7, 16-28; 10:19-22; 1 John 2:1, 2

Objective: To realize how Christ's sacrifice fulfills the symbolism of the Holy of Holies and the Day of Atonement, and come into God's presence with boldness and joy.

Golden Text: "Let us draw near with a true heart in full assurance of faith, having our hearts sprinkled from an evil conscience, and our bodies washed with pure water" (Hebrews 10:22).

Central Truth: All people can have access to God through the blood of Christ.

Evangelism Emphasis: All people can have access to God through the blood of Christ.

PRINTED TEXT

Exodus 25:21. And thou shalt put the mercy seat above upon the ark; and in the ark thou shalt put the testimony that I shall give thee.

22. And there I will meet with thee, and I will commune with thee from above the mercy seat, from between the two cherubims which are upon the ark of the testimony, of all things which I will give thee in commandment unto the children of Israel.

26:33. And thou shalt hang up the vail under the taches, that thou mayest bring in thither within the vail the ark of the testimony: and the vail shall divide unto you between the holy place and the most holy.

Matthew 27:50. Jesus, when he had cried again with a loud voice, yielded up the ghost.

51. And, behold, the veil of the temple was rent in twain from the top to the bottom; and the earth did quake, and the rocks rent.

Hebrews 10:19. Having therefore, brethren, boldness to enter into the holiest by the blood of Jesus,

22. Let us draw near with a true heart in full assurance of faith, having our hearts sprinkled from an evil conscience, and our bodies washed with pure water.

Leviticus 16:30. For on that day shall the priest make atonement for you, to cleanse you, that ye may be clean from all your sins before the Lord.

33. And he shall make an atonement for the holy sanctuary, and he shall make an atonement for the tabernacle of the congregation, and for the altar, and he shall make an atonement for the priests, and for all the people of the congregation.

34. And this shall be an everlasting statute unto you, to

make an atonement for the
children of Israel for all their
sins once a year. And he did as
the Lord commanded Moses.

Hebrews 9:24. For Christ is
not entered into the holy places
made with hands, which are the
figures of the true; but into heaven
itself, now to appear in the
presence of God for us:

**28. So Christ was once
offered to bear the sins of
many; and unto them that look**
for him shall he appear the second
time without sin unto salvation.

1 John 2:1. My little children,
these things write I unto you, that
ye sin not. And if any man sin,
we have an advocate with the
Father, Jesus Christ the righteous:

**2. And he is the propitiation
for our sins: and not for our's
only, but also for the sins of the
whole world.**

LESSON OUTLINE

I.   MEETING WITH GOD
  A. The Ark of the Covenant
  B. The Veil
  C. The Torn Veil
  D. The New and Living Way
II. COMPLETE ATONEMENT
  A. The Day of Atonement
  B. The Great High Priest
  C. A Better Sacrifice
  D. Our Advocate and
       Propitiation

LESSON EXPOSITION

INTRODUCTION

Reviewing the steps that have
led us to the study of the Most Holy
Place, we are reminded that as the
Israelite entered the gate of the
outer court, he brought his animal
sacrifice to be offered up on the
brazen altar. Then as the priest
went on toward the Holy Place he
washed his hands and feet at the
brazen laver. Inside the sanctuary,
the priest saw on his left the beautiful
golden candlestick, and on the
right he saw the gold-covered table
of showbread. Before him, just in
front of the veil, the priest saw the
golden altar where Aaron burned
the fragrant incense. And inside
the veil in the Holy of Holies, the
high priest beheld the glory of God
above the mercy seat, between the
gold cherubim. There God's holiness
was satisfied because the
blood of sacrifice, typified by the
shed blood of Christ, was sprinkled
upon the mercy seat.

Studying the Tabernacle in the
light of the New Testament, perhaps
we get the whole picture more
clearly than did Israel some 1,500
years before Christ's birth. And
because we have the indwelling of
the Holy Spirit as a guide who
leads us into all truth, we can more
fully realize how Christ's sacrifice
fulfills the symbolism of the Holy of
Holies and the closely related ritual
of the Day of Atonement, thereby
we ourselves come into God's presence
with boldness and joy.

I. MEETING WITH GOD (Exodus
   25:10-22; 26:31-34; Matthew
   27:50, 51; Hebrews 9:2-7;
   10:19-22)

A The Ark of the Covenant
   (Exodus 25:10-22)
   (Exodus 25:10-20 is not includ-

ed in the printed text.)

21. And thou shalt put the mercy seat above upon the ark; and in the ark thou shalt put the testimony that I shall give thee.

22. And there I will meet with thee, and I will commune with thee from above the mercy seat, from between the two cherubims which are upon the ark of the testimony, of all things which I will give thee in commandment unto the children of Israel.

Description. The ark was approximately 27 by 27 by 45 inches. Made of acacia wood and covered with gold, inside and out, it had four rings of gold through which carrying poles were inserted. These poles were never to be removed from the rings, which suggests that the children of Israel's spiritual pilgrimage was not over (see vv. 10-15).

Forming a lid that fit within the gold molding of the top edge of the ark was the mercy seat. Of one piece with the cherubim that stood facing each other with wings outstretched and faces bowed, the mercy seat marked God's dwelling place (see vv. 17-20).

Contents. Inside the ark were the two stone tablets containing the Ten Commandments (vv. 16, 21). The Law hidden away in the ark typifies the Word of God hidden away in the heart of the believer. The golden pot of manna, which God preserved as a testimony, was also in the ark as was Aaron's rod that budded (Hebrews 9:4).

History. During the wilderness wanderings the ark was carried by the sons of Levi. Upon being carried into the Jordan River, the waters parted so Israel could cross on dry ground. Over the years the ark was found at different places.

For a time the ark was at Shiloh.

Before David brought the ark to Jerusalem, it had been at Kirjath Jearim. While at some point in time the ark came to contain only the Ten Commandments, the ark of the covenant remained a part of the ritual of Temple worship. After the destruction of Jerusalem in 586 B.C. it is not known what became of the ark.

B. The Veil (Exodus 26:31-34)

(Exodus 26:31, 32, 34 is not included in the printed text.)

33. And thou shalt hang up the vail under the taches, that thou mayest bring in thither within the vail the ark of the testimony: and the vail shall divide unto you between the holy place and the most holy.

Color. As one of the most universal types of symbolism, color has long been associated with the language of religion. In verse 31, God instructed Moses to make a veil of blue, purple, and scarlet.

- Blue is the color of the sky—and by association, heaven; so blue stands for religious feelings. Representing truth and spiritual fulfillment, blue was featured in liturgical garments and Tabernacle tapestries.

- Purple is made by using equal portions of red and blue; therefore, this royal color may be seen to symbolize the loving fusion of the marriage of our Lord and the church. It is more commonly seen as a symbol of Christ's passion and kingship.

- Scarlet (red) speaks to us of the blood of Christ. An interesting commentary on this color of redemption is expressed in the ancient custom of staining with blood any object which one wished to bring to life.

Form. The cherubim-decorated veil was attached by golden hooks to four pillars made of acacia wood overlaid with gold and set in sockets of silver (v. 32). The phrase "cunning work" (v. 31) in reference to the inner veil is seen by some to indicate the colors were woven in by weavers rather than sewn in by embroiderers, as was the case of the work of the gate to the outer court and the door to the Tabernacle.

The use of both embroidery and weaving was widespread among the cultures of the ancient world. And while the art of weaving and needlework may have been learned in Egypt, the Tabernacle craftsmen were set apart by God for this sacred service. God gave them the heart to do the work and to teach their skills to others.

Even so, God will bless the work of our hands and our hearts when we dedicate our talents to Him. Through the experience of sanctification, we are as much set apart for sacred use as was "Bezaleel and Aholiab, and every wise hearted man, in whom the Lord put wisdom and understanding to know how to work all manner of work for the service of the sanctuary, according to all that the Lord had commanded" (36:1).

Function. The veil, which divided the Holy Place from the Holy of Holies, was a partition that prohibited entrance or view into the dwelling place of God (26:33, 34). In one sense of the word, during the dispensation of the law, grace was veiled. The veil of separation reminds us that sin keeps man at a distance from a holy God.

C. The Torn Veil
(Matthew 27:50, 51)

50. Jesus, when he had cried again with a loud voice, yielded up the ghost.

51. And, behold, the veil of the temple was rent in twain from the top to the bottom; and the earth did quake, and the rocks rent.

At the time of Christ, the Holy of Holies with its ark and its dividing veil was still an important ordinance in the Temple worship. And of particular interest in Matthew's report of the miracles and mysteries attending Christ's death was the rending of the veil.

While the torn veil was obviously a sign of judgment upon errant Temple leaders, the broader significance is that the way was opened up to the throne of God.

In Ephesians 2:13-18 Paul explains the access we now have to God through the death of Christ, who has broken down the middle wall of partition between Gentiles and Jews.

D. The New and Living Way
(Hebrews 9:2-7; 10:19-22)

(Hebrews 9:2-7 and 10:20, 21 are not included in the printed text.)

10:19. Having therefore, brethren, boldness to enter into the holiest by the blood of Jesus,

22. Let us draw near with a true heart in full assurance of faith, having our hearts sprinkled from an evil conscience, and our bodies washed with pure water.

Written before the destruction of Jerusalem and the Temple in A.D.

70, the Book of Hebrews shows the relationship of Christianity to Judaism. That Christ is superior to prophets and angels, to Moses and Joshua, and to the old covenant is the theme of this book, which was generally believed to have been penned by Paul to Jewish Christians whose faith needed strengthening.

In Hebrews 9:2-7, the ministry of the priests is described in relation to the furniture in the Holy Place and the Most Holy Place of the earthly Tabernacle. The purpose was to show the typical nature of the old covenant as it relates to Christ, His person, and ministry.

The following key words from Hebrews 10:19-22 will help us better understand how we, as modern-day followers of Christ, can come into God's presence with boldness and joy:

Boldness (v. 19). To come boldly to God is to come with confidence and certainty. Such an attitude does not imply impudence or brazenness. But neither is shame-facedness, doubt, or dread implied. Having "boldness to enter into the holiest" implies having one's heart fixed on God.

The blood of Jesus (v. 19). This boldness of which we speak is neither based on self-confidence nor self-esteem. It stems from faith in the blood of Jesus—faith in the atoning work of the sacrifice of our Lord and Savior, Jesus Christ. Even as a blood sacrifice allowed the high priest to draw aside the veil and come before the mercy seat, so the blood of Christ, our High Priest, gives access into God's presence.

A new and living way (v. 20). The "new and living way" into the throne room of God has been consecrated for us through the veil of Christ's flesh. The veil of the Temple and the bodily sacrifice of Christ are seen to be alike in that they gave access to God.

Let us draw near with a true heart (v. 22). True worship demands sincerity and full assurance of faith. The analogy of the symbolic sprinkling of blood and the ceremonial washing associated with Tabernacle worship denote the power of Christ's blood to cleanse from the guilt of sin.

Discuss the significance of the rending of the veil.

II. COMPLETE ATONEMENT
(Leviticus 16:1-34; Hebrews 4:14-16; 9:16-28; 1 John 2:1, 2)

A. The Day of Atonement
(Leviticus 16:1-34)

(Leviticus 16:1-29, 31, 32 is not included in the printed text.)

30. For on that day shall the priest make atonement for you, to cleanse you, that ye may be clean from all your sins before the Lord.

33. And he shall make an atonement for the holy sanctuary, and he shall make an atonement for the tabernacle of the congregation, and for the altar, and he shall make an atonement for the priests, and for all the people of the congregation.

34. And this shall be an everlasting statute unto you, to make an atonement for the children of Israel for all their sins once a year. And he did as the Lord commanded Moses.

While the entire 16th chapter of

Leviticus concerns the Day of Atonement and its services, verses 29-34 summarize the particulars of this annual fast of the people of Israel. On this day only, the "tenth of the [seventh] month"—corresponding to our October—the high priest entered into the Holy of Holies to make atonement for himself and his family, the Tabernacle itself, and the people.

On this day sin was brought to remembrance and the appropriate response was godly sorrow expressed through ceasing to work, fasting, and mourning.

The ordinances of the Day of Atonement touches on at least three great doctrines of the Bible: the sinfulness of man, the holiness of God, and the atonement for sin (salvation). A brief look at these precepts will help us make the spiritual connections developed in the New Testament—and particularly in Hebrews.

The sinfulness of man. In the first verse of our study text we are confronted with the sinful nature of man. Two of Aaron's sons, Nadab and Abihu, had died as a result of intruding into a sacred office that did not belong to them and by offering incense with "strange fire" (Leviticus 10). In a manner of speaking, they proceeded to worship in the flesh and not in the spirit. They had "the fire," but it was not that which God had kindled. Through this we are reminded that those who worship God must worship Him in spirit and in truth (John 4:24).

Even among the priests whom God had set apart for sacred service, there was "none righteous, no, not one. . . . For all have sinned, and come short of the glory of God"

(Romans 3:10, 23). On the Day of Atonement even Aaron had first to offer sacrifices for his own sins. Before he could offer up the sweet-savor offerings of prayer and praise and perform his priestly duties, he had to deal with the sin in his own life and that of his family.

Even the Tabernacle—or we might say, especially the earthly tabernacle (the human body), which sinful man had corrupted—had to be covered by the blood. The only way God could dwell at all among sinners was to have the place of His presence purified with fire and cleansed by the blood.

The children of Israel were saved from the curse of sin and the wrath of God through obedience to the rituals representing the saving works of the promised Messiah. In a special sense, for them faith was "the substance of things hoped for, the evidence of things not seen" (Hebrews 11:1).

The holiness of God. The holiness of God is what atonement is all about. The reality and awfulness of sin that so characterizes our world today stands in sharp contrast with the reality and awesomeness of a holy God. In Leviticus 10, which deals with the incident of the fire of the Lord devouring Aaron's sons who offered "strange fire before the Lord," Moses declared God's word to Aaron: "I will be sanctified in them that come nigh me, and before all the people I will be glorified" (v. 3).

William Evans, in *The Great Doctrines of the Bible*, says it is God's holiness by which He desires to be remembered, as that is the attribute which most glorifies Him. Evans adds, "Our view of the necessity of the atonement will depend very largely upon our view of the holiness of God. Light views of God and His holiness will produce light views of sin and the atonement."

What is the one attribute which God would have His people remember Him by more than any other? Why?

Atonement for sin. The sinful condition of man and the holiness of God demand some means of overcoming the enmity that separates the two. Especially in the Old Testament, atonement is seen to be the reconciling factor in bringing man and God into agreement. The word *atone* means "to cover over" or "to propitiate." The concept of "covering over" with the blood of a sacrifice in order to atone for some sin goes all the way back to the Garden of Eden, when the life of an animal was taken in order to cover the nakedness of Adam and Eve with its skin.

Thereafter the life's blood of a living creature came to be recognized as an atonement for sin. And with this, God established the vicarious work of redemption, involving a person or thing taking the blame or punishment for another.

An interesting type of placing one's guilt upon another is seen in the atonement ritual of the two goats: "The one goat 'for Jehovah' was sacrificed as a sin offering and its blood sprinkled on (that is, in the front of) the mercy seat (as with the bullocks). The other goat was 'for Azazel,' the scapegoat. On his head the high priest laid his hands, confessing over it the sins of the people. Then this goat was led by a chosen man into the wilderness (a land uninhabited) and there let loose. These goats have been held

to typify: the slain one, the atoning and vicarious sacrifice of Christ in bearing 'our sins in his own body on the tree' (1 Peter 2:24). The freed one typifies the complete removal of our sin out of sight" (*Vine's Expository Dictionary of Old and New Testament Words*).

B. The Great High Priest
    (Hebrews 4:14-16)

(Hebrews 4:14-16 is not included in the printed text.)

At the time of the early church, the Jewish religion still had its high priests, its rituals and traditions of the law. And while many Jews were converting to Christianity, there were some who were tempted to turn back to the traditions of the law. The Hebrews are thusly exhorted in verse 14 to hold fast to their "profession" (confession) of Jesus as the Son of God, as He fulfills the law—and further, having no need to atone for His own sins. The greatness of Jesus as our High Priest is seen in His heavenly office, His sympathy, and His mercy and grace.

Jesus at the Father's right hand. Even as the high priest passed through the veil into the presence of God, Jesus passed into the heavens where He "ever liveth to make intercession" (7:25). His greatness is described in Hebrews 1:3: "Who being the brightness of his glory, and the express image of his person, and upholding all things by the word of his power, when he had by himself purged our sins, sat down on the right hand of the Majesty on high."

What is the significance of Christ's being at the Father's right hand?

The sympathizing Jesus. That Jesus is touched with our moral weaknesses and flaws (4:15) indicates He has a "fellow feeling" that puts Him in touch with the joys and sorrows of the human condition. Being Himself a man of sorrows, He suffers with us. Such compassion brings Him in contact with the feelings that are an important part of our lives. Thus, in and through Christ, there is this coming together of man and God that puts us in touch with a caring and loving heavenly Father. Surely, Jesus is the consolation of Israel—and of us all.

Mercy at the throne of grace. Through the mediation of Jesus the throne of judgment has been made to us a throne of grace. The mercy seat in the Holy of Holies was a reminder that mercy indeed precedes judgment. But having witnessed God's wrath poured out upon errant priests and Levites, there probably was a healthy awareness of judgment among the Israelites.

Today, complete atonement through Jesus Christ, whose blood covers our sins, allows us to "come boldly unto the throne of grace, that we may obtain mercy, and find grace to help in time of need" (v. 16)

C. A Better Sacrifice
   (Hebrews 9:16-28)

   (Hebrews 9:16-23, 25-27, is not included in the printed text.)

   24. For Christ is not entered into the holy places made with hands, which are the figures of the true; but into heaven itself, now to appear in the presence of God for us:

   28. So Christ was once offered to bear the sins of many; and

unto them that look for him shall he appear the second time without sin unto salvation.

A fundamental element in the superiority of Christ's sacrifice is the efficacy of His shed blood. It is by the blood of Christ that we are justified, freed from guilt of sin, and made righteous in God's eyes. The Biblical key to unlocking the mystery of complete atonement is found in the last part of Hebrews 9:22: "Without shedding of blood is no remission." That the "blood" no longer finds such a prominent place in preaching and teaching is a sad commentary on what one writer has called "casual Christianity."

The sum and substance of all that has thus far been presented is that once for all, Christ through the sacrifice of His own dear blood has entered, not into the earthly symbols of the Tabernacle but into the tabernacle of heaven itself, where He continues to intercede for us. And this is not all. The same Lord who came to earth to die for us— this same Jesus who died for us and was resurrected and who ascended to the Father for us—is coming again. For those who look for Him, He shall appear. At His coming, we who hold fast our confession of faith will realize to the fullest the effects of complete atonement.

D. Our Advocate and Propitiation
   (1 John 2:1, 2)

   1. My little children, these things write I unto you, that ye sin not. And if any man sin, we have an advocate with the Father, Jesus Christ the righteous:

   2. And he is the propitiation for our sins: and not for our's

266   The Holy of Holies

only, but also for the sins of the whole world.

As we have already learned, the priests were to act as mediators between God and the people. Man, through the transgression of God's holy laws, separated himself from God. For this reason man needs a sympathetic intercessor, not to reconcile God to man, but man to God. The mediatorial work of the Levitical priesthood prefigured the mediation of our Advocate, Jesus Christ, whose shed blood covers the enmity that separates sinners from a holy God.

Closely associated with Christ's role as advocate is the part He plays as propitiator. Through the propitiatory sacrifice of Christ, the believer is brought into a right relationship with God. The expiatory work, or restoration of communion, of the Cross is therefore the means whereby the barrier which sin puts between God and man is broken down.

REVIEW QUESTIONS

1. What three articles of testimony did the ark of the covenant contain?

2. What is the significance of the torn veil?

3. What is meant by the word *atone*?

4. What is meant when we say that Jesus is "touched with the feeling of our infirmities" (Hebrews 4:15)?

5. Why does man need an intercessor between himself and God?

GOLDEN TEXT HOMILY

"LET US DRAW NEAR WITH A TRUE HEART IN FULL ASSURANCE OF FAITH, HAVING OUR HEARTS SPRINKLED FROM AN EVIL CONSCIENCE, AND OUR BODIES WASHED WITH PURE WATER" (Hebrews 10:22).

Today, as we speed toward the 21st century, there is a floodgate of untold suffering, unchecked hatred among peoples and nations. Amidst all this turmoil, people look with desperation into the future.

Many individuals live a hopeless existence. They mistrust their governments and have even lost faith in God. Understanding these conditions, let's look once again at Hebrews 10:22. Our High Priest, Jesus Christ, allows us into the Holy of Holies—what a privilege!

We have available to us the power of Christ the King, as God, and as the God-man. By right of conquest, Jesus is exercising His full kingly power. By the shedding of His most precious blood, He ransomed man. By His glorious resurrection from the dead, Jesus vindicated every claim that He made of Himself. Thus, we can enter into a relationship with Him and have access to God, the Father. Through Jesus the Son, God is willing to dwell with mankind on earth, and to have mankind dwell with Him in heaven, but not without a High Priest. His sacrifice allows us to free ourselves from this troubled world. We can enter into an unrestrained familiarity of warmest friendships, face-to-face, no longer the awful Lord with thunder and lightning; rather, we see Him radiant, mild, and with inviting love. God, through Jesus, removes from us the scourges and judgments we deserved, and He shows us mercy, giving us His gifts.—**James L. Durel, Captain, The Salvation Army, Vacaville, California**

SENTENCE SERMONS

ALL PEOPLE can have access to God through the blood of Christ.

—Selected

HE LEFT His Father's throne above / So free, so infinite His grace! / Emptied Himself of all but love, / And bled for Adam's helpless race.

—Charles Wesley

WHEN JESUS CHRIST shed His blood on the cross, it was not the blood of a martyr, or the blood of one man for another; it was the life of God poured out to redeem the world.

—Oswald Chambers

GOD IS the light in my darkness, the voice in my silence.

—Helen Keller

EVANGELISM APPLICATION

ALL PEOPLE CAN HAVE ACCESS TO GOD THROUGH THE BLOOD OF CHRIST.

Just as the Tabernacle services were an object lesson to the surrounding nations about God and the way in which He related to the people who were called by His name, the worship services of our churches today witness in one way or the other to the unbeliever about our relationship with God.

In a day when there seems to be less and less distinction between what is secular and what is sacred in the presentation of the gospel, we would do well to remember that Aaron's sons lost their lives when they lost their appreciation for the holiness of God. May we not compromise today what is sacred in the guise of making the gospel attractive. For, indeed, there is nothing very alluring about Jesus dying on a rugged cross to save us. There's nothing very appealing about bleeding and dying and bearing sins away. And yet, Jesus said, "And I, if I be lifted up from the earth, will draw all men unto me" (John 12:32).

ILLUMINATING THE LESSON

Our Savior is on the eternal throne of God. He looks upon every soul that turns to Him as personal Savior. He knows by experience what are the weaknesses of humanity, what are our wants, and what are our temptations; for He was in all points tempted as we are, yet without sin. He is watching over you, trembling child of earth. Are you tempted? He will deliver. Are you weak? He will strengthen. . . . The weaker and more helpless you know yourself to be, the stronger will you become in His strength. The heavier your burdens, the more blessed the rest in casting them upon the Sin Bearer.**—Don Brandeis,** *The Gospel in the Old Testament*

DAILY BIBLE READINGS

M. Tent of Meeting.
   Exodus 33:7-11
T. Cleansing From Sin.
   Psalm 51:1-12
W. Return to God. Hosea 14:1-9
T. Which Is Easier?
   Mark 2:1-12
F. The Intercessor.
   Romans 8:31-39
S. Perfect High Priest.
   Hebrews 7:20-28

Tabernacle Sacrifices and Offerings

Study Text: Leviticus 1:1 through 5:19; Luke 22:19; Ephesians 1:7; 2:13-16; 5:2; Revelation 1:5

Objective: To study the requirements and purposes of the tabernacle offerings and appropriate their spiritual benefits for us today.

Golden Text: "Walk in love, as Christ also hath loved us, and hath given himself for us an offering and a sacrifice to God for a sweetsmelling savor" (Ephesians 5:2).

Central Truth: Old Testament sacrifices foreshadowed Christ's perfect sacrifice.

Evangelism Emphasis: Christ's sacrifice removes the guilt of sin.

PRINTED TEXT

Leviticus 1:2. Speak unto the children of Israel, and say unto them, If any man of you bring an offering unto the Lord, ye shall bring your offering of the cattle, even of the herd, and of the flock.

3. If his offering be a burnt-sacrifice of the herd, let him offer a male without blemish: he shall offer it of his own voluntary will at the door of the tabernacle of the congregation before the Lord.

Ephesians 5:2. And walk in love, as Christ also hath loved us, and hath given himself for us an offering and a sacrifice to God for a sweetsmelling savour.

Ephesians 1:7. In whom we have redemption through his blood, the forgiveness of sins, according to the riches of his grace.

Revelation 1:5. And from Jesus Christ, who is the faithful witness, and the first begotten of the dead, and the prince of the kings of the earth. Unto him that loved us, and washed us from our sins in his own blood.

Leviticus 2:1. And when any will offer a meat-offering unto the Lord, his offering shall be of fine flour; and he shall pour oil upon it, and put frankincense thereon:

2. And he shall bring it to Aaron's sons the priests: and he shall take thereout his handful of the flour thereof, and of the oil thereof, with all the frankincense thereof; and the priest shall burn the memorial of it upon the altar, to be an offering made by fire, of a sweet savour unto the Lord.

Luke 22:19. And he took bread, and gave thanks, and brake it, and gave unto them, saying, This is my body which is given for you: this do in remembrance of me.

Leviticus 3:1. And if his oblation be a sacrifice of peace-offering, if he offer it of the herd;

whether it be a male or female, he shall offer it without blemish before the Lord.

2. And he shall lay his hand upon the head of his offering, and kill it at the door of the tabernacle of the congregation:

and Aaron's sons the priests shall sprinkle the blood upon the altar round about.

Ephesians 2:13. But now in Christ Jesus ye who sometimes were far off are made nigh by the blood of Christ.

LESSON OUTLINE

I. SACRIFICES FOR CLEANSING
    A. Burnt Offering
    B. Sin Offering
    C. Guilt Offering
II. OFFERINGS FOR THANKSGIVING
    A. Grain Offering
    B. Peace Offering

LESSON EXPOSITION

INTRODUCTION

As we have already learned, once inside the gate of the outer court of the Tabernacle, the worshiper was confronted with the brazen altar. Having the meaning of "place of slaughter," the altar represents the cross of Christ. It was to the brazen altar that offerings and sacrifices were first brought.

To offer up a sacrifice is to choose spiritual goods over material ones. A sacrifice may also involve the exchange of the physical life of a substitute for that of the worshiper. To sacrifice what one esteems is to sacrifice a part of oneself. To give out of one's abundance shows feelings befitting a man. However, giving out of one's own need shows feelings befitting the Son of Man.

To the pioneers of our churches, giving sacrificially meant "giving until it hurt." The preciousness of such, first expressed so beautifully in God's gift of His only Son, is also exemplified in the words of David. Refusing a free threshing floor on which to offer sacrifices, he said, "Nay; but I will surely buy it of thee at a price: neither will I offer burnt-offerings unto the Lord my God of that which doth cost me nothing" (2 Samuel 24:24).

In this, the last of our tabernacle studies, we will examine the five main types of offerings.

The *burnt offering* was the only voluntary offering. As an expression of devotion and a symbol of consecration to God, the burnt offering gave off a sweet savor in which God took delight.

The *sin offering* was an acknowledgment that "all have sinned, and come short of the glory of God" (Romans 3:23). Ignorance of sin did not excuse the sinner. The offerer, priest, ruler, or other individual presented his sacrificial animal and confessed his sins.

The *guilt offering*, also called the trespass offering, was for an intentional offender, especially one who had sinned against another. In addition to offering the sacrifice, the guilty one had to make restitution, as well as to additionally compensate the one wronged.

The *grain offering* was an offering of cakes or wafers presented to God as an expression of thanksgiving and dedication to the service of God.

The *peace offering* denoted fellowship with God and man. A portion of the peace offering was offered to God, and the remainder was eaten by the priests and the offerer.

As we look more closely at the requirements and purposes of the tabernacle offerings in order to appropriate their spiritual benefits for us today, let us remember that the sacrifices were "gifts brought to a holy God, serving the twofold purpose of illustrating the need of atonement for sin and consecration to God. They were object lessons in holiness, given to the people during a stage in their spiritual development when they could best learn by having the abstract concepts of righteousness and purity acted out before them in beautiful ceremony and symbolism" (*Exploring the Old Testament*).

I. SACRIFICES FOR CLEANSING (Leviticus 1:1-17; 4:1—5:19; Ephesians 1:7; 5:2; Revelation 1:5)

A. Burnt Offering (Leviticus 1:1-17; Ephesians 5:2)

(Leviticus 1:1, 4-17 is not included in the printed text.)

Leviticus 1:2. Speak unto the children of Israel, and say unto them, If any man of you bring an offering unto the Lord, ye shall bring your offering of the cattle, even of the herd, and of the flock.

3. If his offering be a burnt-sacrifice of the herd, let him offer a male without blemish: he shall

offer it of his own voluntary will at the door of the tabernacle of the congregation before the Lord.

Ephesians 5:2. And walk in love, as Christ also hath loved us, and hath given himself for us an offering and a sacrifice to God for a sweetsmelling savour.

Here God calls to Moses, not from Mount Sinai but from the Tabernacle. At this point, God is in the midst of His people. The next step—by way of Calvary—would make it possible for God to tabernacle in the heart of man and to speak to him through the Word, Jesus Christ.

Today God speaks to us directly through His Word which was verified and spoken by our Lord, who is Himself called the Word or Logos of God. Through the perfect sacrifice of Christ we have thus become living letters of Christ, "written not with ink, but with the Spirit of the living God; not in tables of stone, but in fleshy tables of the heart" (2 Corinthians 3:3).

In Leviticus the message of God to Moses concerns access to God through offerings and sacrifices. And while the first, the burnt offering, typified the offering of the blood of Christ which washes sin away, did not necessarily come first in practice. It is good, however, to examine it first since it presents various elements that apply to the other offerings and sacrifices for cleansing and for thanksgiving. One approach to an overview of the burnt offering is to think in terms of the sacrificer, the sacrifice, and the priests who minister the sacrifice.

The sacrificer brought his animal or fowl of his own free will to the door of the tabernacle and presented it as a sacrificial gift to the Lord. He put his hands on the head of the sacrifice, thereby confessing his sins and transferring his guilt onto the innocent substitute.

Finis Jennings Dake, in *Dake's Annotated Reference Bible*, points out seven things this act of the offerer signified: (1) The sacrifice was the offerer's own. (2) It was offered to atone for sins. (3) The offerer was worthy of death. (4) He had broken the law, thereby incurring the death penalty. (5) He hereby sought forgiveness. (6) He accepted the substitute of an innocent victim in his place. (7) He had faith in the coming Redeemer who would take his place and die in his stead.

The offerer himself killed his offering and with some assistance cut it up. Paul said in Galatians 2:20, "I am crucified with Christ: nevertheless I live; yet not I, but Christ liveth in me." Through the sanctifying power of the blood of Christ, the old man—the carnal nature—is crucified. Out of Jesus' death comes life, service, and commitment on the part of the sanctified believer.

The sacrifice for the burnt offering (as well as for the other offerings except the grain offering) could be one or more of five different animals or birds. In writing about the creatures used in the offerings and the way in which they typified Christ, Louis T. Talbot lists them as follows: (1) a bullock or ox, (2) a sheep or a lamb, (3) a goat, (4) a turtledove, (5) a young pigeon.

"The bullock speaks to us of Christ the strong One, patient and faithful as the servant of God, 'obedient unto death' (Philippians 2:8). The sheep and the lamb remind us of Isaiah's description of our Lord's meekness and submission to His Father's will, for He was led 'as a lamb to the slaughter, and as a sheep before her shearers is dumb, so He openeth not his mouth' (Isaiah 53:7). Jesus was the Passover Lamb 'without blemish and without spot' (1 Peter 1:19). The goat is a picture of Christ, the sinner's substitute, bearing 'the iniquity of us all' (Isaiah 53:6). The turtledove and pigeon symbolize mourning innocency and are associated with poverty. The fowls of the heavens also speak to us of the heavenly One who came down to offer Himself as our Sacrifice upon the altar" (*Christ in the Tabernacle*).

Because of the variety of acceptable creatures, no one, regardless of how poor, would be unable to bring a gift to God. In fact, if the offerer could not afford to bring a bird, he could bring a handful of flour. The central issue was to make a gift of something that was one's own. In the broadest sense, God was more interested in the giver than the gift.

The priest's job was to receive the blood of the sacrifice and sprinkle it around the brazen altar. The sons of Aaron also put fire upon the altar. To keep the fire burning was a solemn duty of the priesthood. When the Tabernacle was en route, live coals from off the brazen altar were carried in fire pans. And when the Tabernacle was set up once more and the rituals were begun again, this God-kindled fire was put upon the altar.

The eternal flame of the brazen altar speaks of the fiery tongues of Pentecost burning out the impurities of the soul, illuminating the understanding, and empowering the believer with the Holy Spirit to witness for God.

Upon the altar fire, the priests laid the wood in a certain order, and on the wood was laid in certain order the parts of the "offering made by fire, of a sweet savour unto the Lord" (Leviticus 1:9; see also vv. 7, 8).

Thus in the Tabernacle sacrifices and offerings we see Christ's perfect sacrifice. The unchanging priesthood of Christ was the substance of which the Levitical priesthood was only the shadow of good things to come.

As an act of consecration, the burnt offering was "a sweet savour unto the Lord." This means that it was pleasing to God. In Ephesians 5:2, Paul exhorts Christians to "walk in love, as Christ also has loved us" (*NKJV*). Christ has set the perfect example in giving Himself for us. Taking our blame, dying in our place, He became the sacrifice that God finds pleasing.

What is the significance of the offerer laying his hand on the head of his sacrifice?

B. Sin Offering (Leviticus 4:1 through 5:13; Ephesians 1:7; Revelation 1:5)

(Leviticus 4:1—5:13 are not included in the printed text.)

Ephesians 1:7. In whom we have redemption through his blood, the forgiveness of sins, according to the riches of his grace.

Revelation 1:5. And from Jesus Christ, who is the faithful witness, and the first begotten of the dead, and the prince of the kings of the earth. Unto him that loved us, and washed us

from our sins in his own blood.

As pertains to the sin offering, ignorance of sin did not excuse the sinner. The whole message is that all have sinned, and need a Savior. The priest had to bring his own sin offering, as well as that of the whole congregation of Israel, the rulers, and the common people.

While people of different rank and position brought different types of sacrifices, the ritual was practically the same. The sinner presented his own offering, thus acknowledging his guilt that, in type, was being placed upon the head of his substitute sin-bearer. The priest sprinkled the shed blood seven times before the veil of the sanctuary and upon the horns of the altar of incense and poured all the blood out around the base of the brazen altar.

Of particular import here is that nothing but the fat of the sacrifice was offered upon the altar of burnt offering. The slain animal, except for its fat, was carried outside the camp and burned. The prophetic echo "outside the camp" (Hebrews 13:11, 13, *NKJV*) resounded hundreds of years and thousands of sacrifices later on a hill called Calvary, outside the gate of Jerusalem, when ritual became reality.

The fat that covered the "inwards, and all the fat that is upon the inwards" represented the richest part of the animal (Leviticus 4:8). It is said that in the ancient world, the fatty portions of the animal were eaten as a delicacy. And that in Old Testament times, being fat was considered a sign of personal success and abundance. As such, the fat represented the best part of the sacrifice being given to God.

That the fat protected the internal parts—the entrails and

intestines of the animal, the "innards"—suggests the thoughts and feelings which belong to the inner life. David must have had this in mind when he prayed for forgiveness saying, "Behold, thou desirest truth in the inward parts: and in the hidden part thou shalt make me to know wisdom" (Psalm 51:6).

"Who can understand his errors? cleanse thou me from secret faults" is the prayer of David in Psalm 19:12. How meaningful this prayer is in light of what we have studied about the sin offering: "Keep back thy servant also from presumptuous sins; let them not have dominion over me: then shall I be upright, and I shall be innocent from the great transgression" (v. 13).

In the first four verses of Leviticus 5 we have a description of four types of sins that needed atonement through the sin offering. In some pulpits today sin is not a popular topic, and naming sin is not considered to be wise. But this was not the case during the time of Tabernacle worship.

Here the silent witness to wrongdoing is charged with the moral failure of the person for whom he is covering. Also, an individual who has come into contact with unclean things in his environment is himself ceremonially unclean. Furthermore, personal uncleanness can be transferred from one man to another, and the loss of personal integrity due to the failure of keeping one's word or commitment constitutes guilt.

In comparison with modern practices such as homosexuality, drug abuse, murder, abortion, and involvement in the occult; social and environmental sins, breakdowns in relationships and morals

may seem at first to be of little consequence. But after a closer look, we see that at the heart of the worst of sins is disregard for God and fellowmen.

Only God knows where self-will leads. Sin, however big or small, misses the mark where God is concerned. When we consider how, because of our ignorance of God's Word, we have often failed to receive all that Christ has provided for us through His Word; when we realize the number of opportunities to do good that we have let slip, the divine appointments we have missed by failing to pray and meditate on the goodness of God; when we are made aware by the Holy Spirit of our sins of omission, we will know that nothing can present us faultless before God—nothing but the atoning blood of Jesus.

What is the significance of burning the fat of the bullock in the sin offering?

C. Guilt Offering
(Leviticus 5:14-19)

(Leviticus 5:14-19 is not included in the printed text.)

The guilt or trespass offering is similar to the sin offering in that it represents Christ as the substitute for the guilty sinner. Although the rituals of the guilt offering and the sin offering may be seen to overlap, the sin offering focuses on the penalty of sin, and the latter emphasizes the consequences of breaking faith in relationships with God and with man.

In this case, a trespass might concern the unwitting eating of animals that were to be set apart for Jehovah. At other times it had to do with neglecting the tithe or with dealing falsely with a fellow Israelite. To be faithless to one's neighbor was to be faithless to God. The person committing a violation and an unintentional sin was "to bring to the Lord as a penalty a ram from the flock, one without defect and of the proper value in silver, according to the sanctuary shekel" (v. 15, *NIV*).

The guilt offering featured confession and restitution plus an added 20 percent. The restitution money had nothing to do with atonement, but giving it showed the repentant attitude of the guilty person. To trespass has the implication of acting unfaithfully. The difference then between offending and pleasing God is the difference between faithfulness and faithlessness. It also follows that not to act in faith is to commit a trespass. Not to do whatever we do to the glory of God is to be guilty of trespassing against the holy things of the Lord.

Put another way, to trespass is to act in bad faith. Bad faith has as its object the wrong thing or the wrong person. It goes without saying that God and God alone is ever to be the object of our hope and our trust. When taken to extremes, positive thinking can produce faith in oneself rather than in God. There comes a point when mere affirmation is ineffective. True faith and faithfulness, however, are always effective and actually bring God and man together.

II. OFFERINGS FOR THANKSGIVING (Leviticus 2:1-16; Luke 22:19; Leviticus 3:1-17; Ephesians 2:13-16)

A. Grain Offering (Leviticus 2:1-16; Luke 22:19)

(Leviticus 2:3-16 is not included in the printed text.)

Leviticus 2:1. And when any will offer a meat-offering unto the Lord, his offering shall be of fine flour; and he shall pour oil upon it, and put frankincense thereon:

2. And he shall bring it to Aaron's sons the priests: and he shall take thereout his handful of the flour thereof, and of the oil thereof, with all the frankincense thereof; and the priest shall burn the memorial of it upon the altar, to be an offering made by fire, of a sweet savour unto the Lord.

Luke 22:19. And he took bread, and gave thanks, and brake it, and gave unto them, saying, This is my body which is given for you: this do in remembrance of me.

The grain offering is called "the meat-offering," *meat* meaning "food." Consisting of fine flour, oil, frankincense, salt, and sometimes green ears of corn dried and offered with oil, it foreshadows the perfect humanity of Christ.

Fine flour speaks to us of our Lord's sinless life. The oil that was mingled with or poured on the flour is a symbol of the Holy Spirit. Frankincense, said to become most fragrant when burned, reminds us of the divine fragrance of the life of Christ as He was tested by the fires of suffering. That salt was a necessary ingredient reminds us that believers are the salt of the earth.

Absent from the grain offering were yeast and honey, both of which ferment and become corrupted when burned. While obviously no blood was involved in the grain offering, the shed blood of Christ is symbolized by a libation of wine poured out at the foot of the altar.

Sometimes the grain offering was in the form of cakes baked in a pan or on a griddle. Sometimes it was flour kneaded with oil. In whatever form, only a memorial portion of the offering made by fire was burned upon the altar; the rest was given to the priests. According to Numbers 18, such offerings were designated as food for the priests (v. 9) in the "covenant of salt"—so called because the covenant was sealed with salt (v. 19). The fulfillment of the symbolic grain offering is beautifully expressed in the Passover bread which Christ gave His disciples at the Last Supper saying, "This is my body which is given for you: this do in remembrance of me" (Luke 22:19).

Explain why yeast and honey were not to be a part of the grain offering.

B. Peace Offering (Leviticus 3:1-17; Ephesians 2:13-16)

(Leviticus 3:3-17 and Ephesians 2:14-16 are not included in the printed text.)

Leviticus 3:1. And if his oblation be a sacrifice of peace-offering, if he offer it of the herd; whether it be a male or female, he shall offer it without blemish before the Lord.

2. And he shall lay his hand upon the head of his offering, and kill it at the door of the tabernacle of the congregation: and Aaron's sons the priests shall sprinkle the blood upon the altar round about.

Ephesians 2:13. But now in Christ Jesus ye who sometimes were far off are made nigh by the blood of Christ.

The main point in the law of the peace offering was fellowship with God as the result of atonement. Customarily offered in conjunction with the grain and burnt offering, various forms of the peace offering were shared by God, the priests, and the offerer. The latter is implied in the fact that a large animal such as a bullock or lamb could not have been eaten by the lone offerer. The flesh of the thanksgiving offering had to be eaten the same day it was offered (Leviticus 7:15). But if the peace offering was a vow or voluntary offering, the meat had to be eaten within two days. These requirements prevented the possibility of eating spoiled meat. But it is also likely that God wanted the memory of the sacrifice made by fire to be fresh in the mind of the offerer, who in the midst of the festivities might otherwise lose sight of the true meaning of it all.

As in the other offerings, different animals could be used, and the ritual of laying hands on the head of the sacrifice further perpetuated the sinner's identification with his sin— and the sin-bearer/substitute whose life had to be given as a sacrifice.

The basic idea that peace implies wholeness is expressed in Ephesians 2:13-16. In showing how Christ's sacrifice broke down the wall of partition between Jews and Gentiles, Paul speaks of Christ as "our peace." And as was foreshadowed in the Hebrew peace offering, the believer, through the Prince of Peace, is brought into a relationship with God marked by harmony and wholeness.

REVIEW QUESTIONS

1. Name the three sacrifices for cleansing.

2. Why did the burnt offering have to be wholly consumed upon the altar?

3. What might an Israelite offer as a sacrifice if he could not afford a lamb?

4. What were the two offerings of thanksgiving?

5. Which of the offerings is sometimes called the "salvation offering"?

GOLDEN TEXT HOMILY

"WALK IN LOVE, AS CHRIST ALSO HATH LOVED US, AND HATH GIVEN HIMSELF FOR US AN OFFERING AND A SACRIFICE TO GOD FOR A SWEETSMELLING SAVOUR" (Ephesians 5:2).

There is an obvious allusion in our Golden Text to the various kinds of sacrifices prescribed by the law of Moses. Paul calls these sacrifices collectively "an offering and a sacrifice to God."

A striking fact about Christ's self-offerings is that Paul describes them as "an offering and a sacrifice to God for a sweetsmelling savour," or, as the *Revised Standard Version* and the *New International Version* render it, "a fragrant offering and sacrifice to God."

We may well ask, "Is there not a contradiction here?" When we contemplate *sacrifice*, how can it be described as "a sweetsmelling savour," a "fragrant offering and sacrifice," or, as it can be literally translated from the Greek, "an odor of sweet smell"? How could the stench and filth and smell of burning animals, in Old Testament days,

be a sweet smell to God; and in reference to the death of Christ on the cross, how could the oozing blood and open wounds of Jesus in the full blaze of the noonday sun be like a sweet perfume to God?

Francis Foulkes quotes Dr. F.B. Meyer: "To our eyes the Cross can only present an awful horror." Nevertheless, he goes on to say: "In love so measureless, so reckless of cost, for those who were naturally unworthy of it, there was an action that filled heaven with fragrance" (*Tyndale New Testament Commentaries, Ephesians*).

It is this wonderful love which makes the glory scene so appealing and fragrant to God—and also to the believer. It is the quality of the sacrifice, the nobility of the purpose, the sublime significance of the cross of Christ which turns it into a thing of wonder and glory. And it will be so throughout the ages of eternity.—**Noel Brooks, D.D. (Retired), Avon, England, Writer, *Adult Sunday School Teacher Quarterly,* International Pentecostal Holiness Church, Oklahoma City, Oklahoma**

DAILY BIBLE READINGS

M. Acceptable Offerings.
Genesis 4:1-7

T. Costly Offerings.
2 Samuel 24:18-25

W. Worship With Offerings.
1 Chronicles 16:1-6

T. Offer Yourself to God.
Romans 12:1-8

F. Offer Your Resources.
1 Corinthians 16:1-4

S. Offer Your Praise.
Hebrews 13:10-15

INTRODUCTION
TO SPRING
QUARTER

The month of March begins the spring quarter series of lessons, which is divided into two distinct units. Unit One (lessons 1-7) is presented under the theme "People Who Met Jesus." As the title implies, this series of lessons deals with experiences and reactions of those who had the privilege of meeting Jesus face-to-face.

Unit Two (lessons 8-13) is presented under the theme "Personal Evangelism." The series of lessons are reminders of the service God's children should provide to the unredeemed.

Both the Easter lesson (5) and Pentecost lesson (12) fall in this quarter. These lessons, however, serve to strengthen the units of study.

Nicodemus, a Curious Seeker

Study Text: John 3:1-21

Objective: To understand the necessity of the new birth and believe in Jesus for salvation.

Time: The Gospel According to John was probably written near the end of the 1st century, between A.D. 85 and A.D. 96.

Place: The Gospel According to John was probably written at Ephesus.

Golden Text: "Except a man be born again, he cannot see the kingdom of God" (John 3: 3).

Central Truth: The new birth that comes through faith in Jesus Christ is necessary for salvation.

Evangelism Emphasis: The new birth that comes through faith in Jesus Christ is necessary for salvation.

PRINTED TEXT

John 3:1. There was a man of the Pharisees, named Nicodemus, a ruler of the Jews:

2. The same came to Jesus by night, and said unto him, Rabbi, we know that thou art a teacher come from God: for no man can do these miracles that thou doest, except God be with him.

3. Jesus answered and said unto him, Verily, verily, I say unto thee, Except a man be born again, he cannot see the kingdom of God.

4. Nicodemus saith unto him, How can a man be born when he is old? can he enter the second time into his mother's womb, and be born?

5. Jesus answered, Verily, verily, I say unto thee, Except a man be born of water and of the Spirit, he cannot enter into the kingdom of God.

6. That which is born of the flesh is flesh; and that which is born of the Spirit is spirit.

7. Marvel not that I said unto thee, Ye must be born again.

8. The wind bloweth where it listeth, and thou hearest the sound thereof, but canst not tell whence it cometh, and whither it goeth: so is every one that is born of the Spirit.

9. Nicodemus answered and said unto him, How can these things be?

10. Jesus answered and said unto him, Art thou a master of Israel, and knowest not these things?

11. Verily, verily, I say unto thee, We speak that we do know, and testify that we have seen; and ye receive not our witness.

12. If I have told you earthly things, and ye believe not, how shall ye believe, if I tell you of

heavenly things?

13. And no man hath ascended up to heaven, but he that came down from heaven, even the Son of man which is in heaven.

14. And as Moses lifted up the serpent in the wilderness, even so must the Son of man be lifted up:

15. That whosoever believeth in him should not perish, but have eternal life.

16. For God so loved the world, that he gave his only begotten Son, that whosoever believeth in him should not perish, but have everlasting life.

DICTIONARY

Pharisees (FARE-ih-seez)—John 3:1—"The separate people." They followed the Jewish religious laws and customs very strictly.

Nicodemus (nick-uh-DEE-mus)—John 3:1—An important Jewish leader and teacher.

LESSON OUTLINE

  I. DESIRE TO KNOW JESUS

     A. The Seeker

     B. The Curiosity

     C. The Conversation

  II. RECEIVE INSTRUCTION

     A. The Question

     B. The Response

  III. BELIEVE IN GOD'S SON

     A. The Offer

     B. The Contrasts

LESSON EXPOSITION

INTRODUCTION

John presents a striking contrast between the personalities participating in the night conference described in John 3. Jesus had just come up from the little village of Nazareth, where He had lived in near obscurity with His mother, His foster father (the carpenter), and His brothers. It had not been long since He had been baptized by John in Jordan and had attracted a few followers: John, Philip, Andrew, Peter, and Nathanael. He had been invited to a marriage feast in Cana and had performed a miracle. Now He had come up to Jerusalem for the Passover. He had no official position, no ecclesiastical standing. He was an unknown young man who had no property. On the other hand, Nicodemus was a member of the Sanhedrin, a teacher in Israel, and a man of considerable wealth and influence. He belonged to the very strict sect known as the Pharisees. They were sticklers for the exact observance of all of the ceremonial rituals of the Jewish religion, even to the most minute. They constantly disputed with the Sadducees—the modernists of the day. They were strict disciplinarians, lived clean lives, and were zealous for their faith. Jesus said that they would move heaven and earth to make one proselyte. As a teacher, Nicodemus was trained in the Law and the Prophets. He knew the Talmud and the mass of tradition that had grown up around the Scripture. The meeting of Jesus with Nicodemus has been compared to a great theological teacher from a seminary coming to a young man just beginning his ministry and asking him for instruction.

I. DESIRE TO KNOW JESUS (John 3:1-8)

A. The Seeker (v. 1)

1. There was a man of the Pharisees, named Nicodemus, a ruler of the Jews.

The only New Testament writer who mentions Nicodemus is the apostle John. In his gospel he mentions him three times. We first find Nicodemus as a seeker after truth in chapter 3. Then in chapter 7 he is a witness, and in chapter 19 he is a disciple. In order to appreciate the account of John in this chapter, it is important to understand the position of Nicodemus. He was held in high esteem by his fellowmen. He was a man of the Pharisees who was looked upon as honorable and righteous. He was not only a man of education and blameless character, but was also one who had such excellent ability that he had been chosen a member of the Sanhedrin. This was the highest civil and ecclesiastical court of the Jews. He was a scholar with a passion for truth, even though at times his thinking as a Pharisee was undoubtedly somewhat narrow in range.

Candor was the dominant and distinguishing characteristic of Nicodemus. He was the one great exception in the Sanhedrin. The rest of the scribes and Pharisees had condemned Christ without taking time to investigate Him. Knowing that He came from Nazareth was enough for them. They dismissed Him and His mighty works with the statement that He had a devil. But with Nicodemus it was a little different. He was a seeker of truth, and he was intellectually honest. He refused to form a judgment before he examined the facts. He had become interested by what he had seen and heard of Jesus. Christ had raised questions that he could not answer; therefore, to be honest with himself, he decided to go see Jesus. He must have gone in the spirit of a scholar—with an open mind and a receptive attitude. He was concerned with knowing the truth, even though it came through One from Nazareth.

B. The Curiosity (v. 2)

2. The same came to Jesus by night, and said unto him, Rabbi, we know that thou art a teacher come from God: for no man can do these miracles that thou doest, except God be with him.

Many preachers and Bible commentators have given Nicodemus bad press. They have accused him of being timid and of acting cowardly because he came to Jesus by night and did not identify himself publicly with Jesus Christ until His crucifixion and death. Norman V. Hope quotes Clovis G. Chappell as saying that "his timidity was at least part of the reason for coming by night." He also refers to A. Leonard Griffith's statement, "We cannot escape the conclusion that for obvious reasons Nicodemus did not want to be seen either by the common people or by his colleagues of the Sanhedrin." But perhaps the most interesting quote comes from J. D. Grey, who speaks of Nicodemus and Joseph of Arimathea as "two outstanding men [who] having failed to stand up for Christ during his life, came to shed their tears too late after his death" (*Christianity Today*).

Why did Nicodemus choose the darkness of night for his visit? We may do him an injustice if we place emphasis on timidity as some have done. Several things combined to make him cautious. He did not know what to think of Christ. He was not sure of himself. The conversation does not support the idea that he was a secret disciple at this time. He was considering, but not convinced. Some of the people, upon seeing the miracles of Jesus, jumped to the conclusion that He was the Messiah. But Nicodemus was not a man to jump to conclusions. He was a teacher in Israel. He was a man of authority and responsibility. The people looked up to him and depended on him. As such a man, he had to be careful in his attitude.

It has been suggested by William Barclay that Nicodemus may have had another reason for coming to Jesus at night. The rabbis declared that the best time to study the law was at night when a man was undisturbed. Throughout the day, Jesus was surrounded by crowds of people all the time. It could be that Nicodemus came to Jesus by night because he wanted a completely private interview with Him. He may have come to Jesus at night because he wanted Jesus to himself in a way that would not have been possible during the crowded hours of the day (*The Daily Study Bible*).

Undoubtedly Nicodemus was a concerned man. He was a man with many honors, but there was yet a great void in his life. He came

to Jesus at night for a talk that might help him come to the light of the truth.

Nicodemus called Jesus, *Rabbi*. This was a courteous term applied to a recognized teacher of religion. He not only recognized Jesus as a teacher, but also as "a teacher come from God." It would seem that Nicodemus believed that Jesus came from God in a way different from that of any other man. Note that he also confessed that the miracles which Christ was performing testified to divine approval upon his life. As a teacher of the law himself, Nicodemus revealed true sincerity and open-mindedness in his search for the truth, because he was eager to hear what this greater teacher might say.

C. The Conversation (vv. 3-8)

3. Jesus answered and said unto him, Verily, verily, I say unto thee, Except a man be born again, he cannot see the kingdom of God.

4. Nicodemus saith unto him, How can a man be born when he is old? can he enter the second time into his mother's womb, and be born?

5. Jesus answered, Verily, verily, I say unto thee, Except a man be born of water and of the Spirit, he cannot enter into the kingdom of God.

6. That which is born of the flesh is flesh; and that which is born of the Spirit is spirit.

7. Marvel not that I said unto thee, Ye must be born again.

8. The wind bloweth where it listeth, and thou hearest the sound thereof, but canst not tell whence it cometh, and whither it goeth: so is every one that is

born of the Spirit.

The repetition of the word "verily" (v. 3) by Jesus shows the earnestness and importance of what He was about to say. The word *verily* is translated from the Greek word *amen* meaning "so be it." Essentially, Nicodemus was told that unless he was supernaturally changed or divinely transformed, he could not see the kingdom of God.

The idea of seeing the Kingdom involves partaking of it, becoming a citizen of it, or being incorporated into God's realm of peace, love, and righteousness. The experience of entering into the kingdom of God is called the new birth and comes from above. It is the impartation of new life from God himself.

It is important to note that these words emphasizing the necessity of the new birth were not spoken to one who might be called a great sinner, an adulterer, or a thief. They were spoken to Nicodemus, a ruler of the Jews and a teacher of the law.

There is disagreement among Bible scholars concerning the meaning of the question posed by Nicodemus in verse 4. Some see it as a perfectly natural question. They interpret it as being not so much the result of unbelief as of astonishment. Others see in it the natural ignorance of man in spiritual matters. Just as the Samaritan woman in John 4 took literally the meaning of the words of Jesus about "living water," and just as the Jews in John 6 thought literally of Christ's being the "bread of God," so Nicodemus understood literally the words "born again."

Jesus wanted Nicodemus to understand that no one could become His disciple unless his inward man was as thoroughly cleansed and renewed by the Spirit as the outward man is cleansed by water (3:5). To possess the privileges of Judaism, a man needed to be born of the seed of Abraham after the flesh. To possess the privileges of Christ's kingdom, a man has to be born again of the Holy Spirit.

Christ's terminology here is evidence that the change essential to salvation is no slight or superficial one. It is not merely reformation, amendment, moral change, or outward alteration of life. It is a thorough change of heart, will, and character. It is a resurrection. It is a new creation. It is a passing from death to life. It is the implanting in our dead hearts of a new principle from above.

The Pharisees lay great emphasis on outward conformity to the law, but Jesus said in essence, "Outward conformity to either ceremonial or moral requirement is insufficient. Regeneration alone can meet the need of man and the requirement of God" (see v. 6). The former is of the flesh, but the latter of the spirit. Outward conformity is the will of men, but the new birth is the will of God.

In the religious circles of Jerusalem the people were talking of nothing except the kingdom of God, which John the Baptist had declared to be at hand. When Jesus told Nicodemus that in order to enter this kingdom he must be born again (v. 7), He told him exactly what John had been telling the people.

The movements of God's Spirit upon the soul of man are mysterious, and we cannot expect to predict them, understand them, or control them (v. 8). But they are nonetheless real, nonetheless certain and sure—the fundamental reality in the universe.

Do you think Nicodemus believed in Jesus at the time of his visit? Explain.

II. RECEIVE INSTRUCTION
   (John 3:9-15)

A. The Question (v. 9)

9. Nicodemus answered and said unto him, How can these things be?

The emphasis should be on the word *how*. Nicodemus was a Pharisee. His religion was a matter of strict rule, prescribed paths, definite duties, and predetermined observance. However, here was One who described the working of the Spirit of God as absolute liberty combined with profound mystery. No wonder Nicodemus was bewildered.

Jesus demanded that Nicodemus should enter into an entirely new relationship with God. In the world of Nicodemus there were two classes of people, the righteous and the sinners. The difference between them had to do with their attitude toward the Law. The righteous knew the Law, and so counted themselves right with God; the sinners did not know the Law, and the righteous pronounced judgment upon them: "This people who knoweth not the law are cursed" (7:49).

When Nicodemus came to Jesus, instead of being confirmed for his righteousness or perhaps being told what omissions he had to make in order for his obedience to the Law to be perfect, he was informed by

Christ that the whole framework of his life was wrong. His relation had been to the Law, not to the person of God. He had obeyed God as a servant would; he had not loved Him as a son. The whole structure of self-righteousness which he had built up by rigid observance of the precepts of the Law therefore had to be taken down. He had to begin at the beginning again. To use the words of Jesus, he had to be born again.

B. The Response (vv. 10-15)

10. Jesus answered and said unto him, Art thou a master of Israel, and knowest not these things?

11. Verily, verily, I say unto thee, We speak that we do know, and testify that we have seen; and ye receive not our witness.

12. If I have told you earthly things, and ye believe not, how shall ye believe, if I tell you of heavenly things?

13. And no man hath ascended up to heaven, but he that came down from heaven, even the Son of man which is in heaven.

14. And as Moses lifted up the serpent in the wilderness, even so must the Son of man be lifted up:

15. That whosoever believeth in him should not perish, but have eternal life.

Many see verse 10 as a rebuke to Nicodemus. The things which the Lord had just mentioned should have been known and understood by him. He professed to be a religious teacher. He professed to know the Old Testament Scriptures. Therefore, the doctrine of the necessity of a new birth should not have seemed so strange to him. "A clean heart," "circumcision of the heart," "a new heart," "a heart of stone instead of a heart of flesh," were expressions and ideas he must have read in the Prophets; all pointed toward the new birth.

Most Bible scholars see the plural pronouns of verse 11 as rhetorical. Christ knew the Father and testified of Him. He came to bear witness of the Father and of all the great spiritual truths that relate to God. Yet as He was expounding one of these great truths, this teacher in Israel did not receive His testimony.

The "earthly things" Christ explained involved such matters as repentance and regeneration (v. 12). He did not specify the heavenly things relating to the next world, to God's plan for the salvation of men. As Neil Anderson writes, "How were men ever to be brought to a knowledge of these and belief in them if they—even their religious leaders—could not understand the simpler matters of life on earth? Many men have open minds for God. They are blind to the greatest of all facts, the grace and power of the present Christ, transforming and remaking souls about them every day" (*God's World and Word*).

A.B. Bruce paraphrases verse 13 as follows: "No one has gone up to heaven and by dwelling there gained a knowledge of heavenly things: One only has dwelt there and is able to communicate that knowledge—He, viz., who has come down from heaven" (*The Expositor's Greek Testament*).

The brazen serpent was lifted up before the dying people of Israel that they might simply look on it and be saved (v. 14). They were not saved by anything in themselves, but by simply doing what the Lord said, by looking at that which he had lifted up before them, a type of their sin. So was Christ lifted up on the cross in the midst of dying humanity. The One who became sin for us—upon whose body on the tree our sins were placed—was crucified that we, looking to Him, might be saved.

Eternal life is God's life, the fullest life possible, a life of holiness, a life of peace and joy, a life that has no end (v. 15). It is not simply life that endures forever, but life in God and with God.

How would you describe the new birth?

III. BELIEVE IN GOD'S SON
(John 3:16-21)

A. The Offer (vv. 16-18)

(John 3:17, 18 is not included in the printed text.)

16. For God so loved the world, that he gave his only begotten Son, that whosoever believeth in him should not perish, but have everlasting life.

Verse 16 has been reduced to an acrostic:

G od so loved the world, that He gave his
O nly begotten
S on, that whosoever believeth in him should not
P erish, but have
E verlasting
L ife.

Robert F. Horton writes, "This acrostic tells us the whole gospel or good news of Jesus Christ. Eternal life comes, and can only come through a vital relationship with the ever-living God, and the reason why this believing in Jesus brings eternal life is that this believing in Jesus brings you into a vital fellowship with God. It is called eternal life, which does not mean that it is life in a future world; but it is called eternal life here and now because here and now this life which means vital fellowship with God is established, and begins to run on into eternity" (*The Triumphant Life*).

Man is perishing and will continue to do so unless he believes in Christ. The word *perish* means "to become destroyed" or "ruined." It is often translated "lost" in the New Testament. This can be seen in the three parables of Luke 15 and in John 6:12. The same word is translated "lost" in other New Testament passages. The process of perishing begins in this life and will continue throughout eternity. Man will never cease to exist. However, he will exist in a state of separation from God, in eternal death, if he does not accept Christ as Savior.

B. The Contrasts (vv. 19-21)

(John 3:19-21 is not included in the printed text.)

The alternative to salvation is condemnation. He who believes in Christ escapes condemnation. He who does not believe is already condemned. This is the natural condition of the spiritual life just as surely as the state of physical life into which we were born eventually ends in death.

The phrase "every one that doeth evil" refers to all unsaved people (v. 20). Included is every individual whose heart is not right and honest in the sight of God. It refers to all people who are evil and ungodly. These are the ones who will not

come to Christ because they do not want their wicked ways discovered. They shrink from the light because they want to keep their ungodliness a secret.

The words "he that doeth truth" identify the person whose heart is right and honest in the sight of God. He has nothing to hide. His past is forgiven, his present is protected by the power of God, and his future is bright with hope in Christ.

Is God's plan of salvation for man reasonable? Explain.

REVIEW QUESTIONS

1. Describe the religion of Nicodemus.

2. How did Nicodemus begin the conversation with Jesus?

3. Why did Nicodemus come to Jesus?

4. What did Jesus mean by the new birth?

5. What Old Testament event did Jesus use to illustrate the concept of atonement?

GOLDEN TEXT HOMILY

"EXCEPT A MAN BE BORN AGAIN, HE CANNOT SEE THE KINGDOM OF GOD" (John 3:3).

Jesus used a double "verily" to show the earnestness and importance of what He was about to say. The word *verily* is translated from the Greek word *amen* and means "so be it." Essentially, Nicodemus was told that unless he was supernaturally changed or divinely transformed, he could not see the kingdom of God.

The word *see* in this verse means to partake of the kingdom of God. The experience of entering into the kingdom of God is called the new birth and comes from above. It is the impartation of new life from God himself.

It is important to note that these words emphasizing the necessity of the new birth were not spoken to one who might be called a great sinner, an adulterer, or a thief. They were spoken to Nicodemus, a ruler of the Jews and a doctor of the law.—**Eugene C. Christenbury, Ed.D., Senior Adjunct Professor of Education, Lee University, Cleveland, Tennessee**

SENTENCE SERMONS

THE NEW BIRTH that comes through faith in Jesus Christ is necessary for salvation.

—**Selected**

NO HUMAN BIRTH can compare to the supernatural birth of a child of God.

—**James Montgomery Boice**

IN THE NATURAL WORLD it is impossible to be made all over again, but in the spiritual world it is exactly what Jesus Christ makes possible.

—**Oswald Chambers**

AT THE ROOT of the Christian life lies belief in the invisible. The object of the Christian's faith is unseen reality.

—**A.W. Tozer**

EVANGELISM APPLICATION

THE NEW BIRTH THAT COMES THROUGH FAITH IN JESUS CHRIST IS NECESSARY FOR SALVATION.

The world was condemned and should have been judged, but before He permitted judgment to take place, God first sent His Son to save the world. Man cannot experience salvation from sin or deliverance from the wrath of God except through Jesus Christ. This is the purpose for which God sent Him. He is the Savior of the world, and without Him the world will never be saved.

ILLUMINATING THE LESSON

I remember reading a tract with the title "The Gospel in Three Colors." Apart from the title page, it contained not a single word, only three pages—black, red, and white. The dark page stands for sin. The red page represents the atoning blood of Christ. The white page symbolizes cleansing. In the marvels of God's grace, nothing is so wonderful as this: the darkness of sin, by the washing of blood, is made white as the driven snow.

DAILY BIBLE READINGS

M. Folly of Denying God.
Psalm 14:1-7
T. Benefits of Seeking God.
Psalm 34:4-14
W. Seek Treasure in Heaven.
Matthew 6:19-24
T. Seek Rest in Jesus.
Matthew 11:25-30
F. Keep Seeking.
Luke 11:1-13
S. Seek Right Priorities.
Luke 18:18-30

Forgiveness for an Adulterous Woman

Study Text: John 8:1-11; Romans 5:12-21

Objective: To discover and embrace Christ's power to forgive and deliver from sin.

Time: The Gospel According to John was probably written between A.D. 85 and 96. The Book of Romans was written between A.D. 56 and A.D. 58.

Place: The Gospel According to John was probably written at Ephesus. The Book of Romans was written at the city of Corinth in Greece.

Golden Text: "As sin hath reigned unto death, even so might grace reign through righteousness unto eternal life by Jesus Christ our Lord" (Romans 5:21).

Central Truth: Christ will forgive anyone who comes to Him in repentance.

Evangelism Emphasis: Christ will forgive anyone who comes to Him in repentance.

PRINTED TEXT

John 8:1. Jesus went unto the mount of Olives.

2. And early in the morning he came again into the temple, and all the people came unto him; and he sat down, and taught them.

3. And the scribes and Pharisees brought unto him a woman taken in adultery; and when they had set her in the midst,

4. They say unto him, Master, this woman was taken in adultery, in the very act.

5. Now Moses in the law commanded us, that such should be stoned: but what sayest thou?

6. This they said, tempting him, that they might have to accuse him. But Jesus stooped down, and with his finger wrote on the ground, as though he heard them not.

7. So when they continued asking him, he lifted up himself, and said unto them, He that is without sin among you, let him first cast a stone at her.

8. And again he stooped down, and wrote on the ground.

9. And they which heard it, being convicted by their own conscience, went out one by one, beginning at the eldest, even unto the last: and Jesus was left alone, and the woman standing in the midst.

10. When Jesus had lifted up himself, and saw none but the woman, he said unto her, Woman, where are those thine accusers? hath no man condemned thee?

11. She said, No man, Lord. And Jesus said unto her, Neither do I condemn thee: go, and sin no more.

Romans 5:18. Therefore as by the offence of one judgment came upon all men to condemnation; even so by the righteousness of one the free gift came upon all men unto justification of life.

19. For as by one man's disobedience many were made sinners, so by the obedience of one shall many be made righteous.

20. Moreover the law entered, that the offence might abound. But where sin abounded, grace did much more abound:

21. That as sin hath reigned unto death, even so might grace reign through righteousness unto eternal life by Jesus Christ our Lord.

LESSON OUTLINE

I. CONDEMNED BY THE LAW
  A. The Plot
  B. The Punishment

II. DELIVERED BY CHRIST
  A. The Advocate
  B. The Restoration

III. MADE RIGHTEOUS BY GRACE
  A. The Illumination
  B. The Abundance

LESSON EXPOSITION

INTRODUCTION

Jesus came to seek and save the lost, and He never avoided close association with sinners. He ate and drank with them in order to win them to Himself. The New Testament records at least three conversations He had with women who had been guilty of adultery—the woman of Samaria, the woman who came to Him in the house of Simon, and the woman in John 8. His dealings with each of them are characterized by His loving-kindness and tender mercy. The circumstances leading up to the exposure of the woman taken in adultery in John 8 are interesting. Jesus had spent the night on the Mount of Olives. He woke up early and made His way to the Temple. There He found a large group of people coming together to hear Him teach. Apparently, while He was teaching, the enemies of Jesus brought before Him a woman guilty of adultery and asked what punishment she deserved. John distinctly tells us that they asked the question, "tempting him" (v. 6). They hoped to entrap Him into saying something for which they might accuse Him. They thought perhaps He who preached pardon and salvation to publicans and harlots might be trapped into saying something which would contradict either the law of Moses or His own words. Observe how Jesus handled the situation.

I. CONDEMNED BY THE LAW
(John 8:1-5; Romans 5:12-14)

A. The Plot (John 8:1-5)

1. Jesus went unto the mount of Olives.

2. And early in the morning he came again into the temple,

and all the people came unto him; and he sat down, and taught them.

3. And the scribes and Pharisees brought unto him a woman taken in adultery; and when they had set her in the midst,

4. They say unto him, Master, this woman was taken in adultery, in the very act.

5. Now Moses in the law commanded us, that such should be stoned: but what sayest thou?

Dr. Wilbur M. Smith writes that in going to the Mount of Olives, Jesus went to the place where He could privately commune with His Father, the place where strength for the next day could be found, the place where His soul would know perfect peace, the place where God would reveal to Him exactly what the next step was that should be taken (v. 1). The One who went to the Mount of Olives that day while His followers slept was the One who, the next day, knew how to meet the temptations which came His way.

Jesus came to the outer courts of the Temple, where it was customary for the Jews to assemble and listen to teachers of religion (v. 2). Both in Eastern countries and during the time before the advent of printing, much instruction was given in this way. Open air addresses and conversations were the normal ways of sharing information. For example, Socrates taught this way at Athens.

It was common for the teacher to sit and the hearers to stand during instructional periods. This can be seen in other places in the New Testament. "I sat daily with you teaching in the temple" (Matthew 26:55). In the synagogues of Nazareth when Jesus began to preach, He first "gave [the book] again to the minister, and sat down. And the eyes of all them that were in the synagogue were fastened on him" (Luke 4:20). "He sat down, and taught the people out of the ship" (Luke 5:3). The practice was also used in the early church. Paul states in Acts 16:13, "We sat down, and spake unto the women."

The ability to pierce the secrets of the human heart and to find out its sin is Christ's alone. An example of this power in operation can be seen in His dealing with the scribes and Pharisees who came to Him as He sat in the Temple, bringing the woman taken in adultery (John 8:3). As they placed her before Him, they boldly declared, "Master, this woman was taken in adultery, in the very act" (v. 4). They settled at once any doubt regarding her guilt. "Now Moses in the law commanded us, that such should be stoned: but what sayest thou?" (v. 5). In other words, they were saying, "You claim to be a teacher with authority; what do you say about it?" They desired to appear to be innocent, as if they were simply seeking to deal with a sinner as she should be dealt with.

It was a curious custom among the Jews to consult distinguished rabbis in cases of difficulty. But there was no difficulty here. The Law spelled out clearly what the punishment was to be in a case like this.

B. The Punishment
   (Romans 5:12-14)

(Romans 5:12-14 is not included in the printed text.)

Paul made a frightening and realistic statement in these verses when he said that sin entered the world and by it death entered also. Sin is the tragedy of the universe. Sin, like disease, is debilitating, deadening, deforming, and dooming. Sin is a God-resisting disposition because of which man in self-sufficiency and pride opposes God, thereby withdrawing from the active ministry of God's life and love. That God-resisting disposition is anarchy. Sin, a breach in the moral order and harmony of the universe, works disintegration and confusion. Every step into sin is a step backward and downward. Sin, a conspiracy against the sovereignty of God, is a contradiction of His nature, an insult to His holiness. There is no term, expressive of reproach, shame, or misery that cannot be used to describe the terror of sin. There is no image that can produce aversion or fear that may not be employed to represent sin. Paul said the law condemned sin.

How does the law condemn sin?

II. DELIVERED BY CHRIST
   (John 8:6-9; Romans 5:15-17)

A. The Advocate (John 8:6-9)

**6. This they said, tempting him, that they might have to accuse him. But Jesus stooped down, and with his finger wrote on the ground, as though he heard them not.
7. So when they continued asking him, he lifted up himself, and said unto them, He that is without sin among you, let him first cast a stone at her.
8. And again he stooped down, and wrote on the ground.
9. And they which heard it,**

being convicted by their own conscience, went out one by one, beginning at the eldest, even unto the last: and Jesus was left alone, and the woman standing in the midst.

John informs us in verse 6 that the scribes and Pharisees were tempting Jesus. In other words, they were laying what they thought to be a clever trap. If He should confirm the letter of the Law and let the execution take its course, they would censure Him for being inconsistent in His message of mercy and compassion. But should He acquit the adulteress and declare that the sentence should not be carried out, it would be told everywhere that He was an enemy of the Law of Moses. However, they did not realize that the evil in men's hearts could not be hidden from Christ and that He did not come just to reveal and condemn, but that He came to seek and to save.

Again, we have to ask why the scribes and Pharisees brought the woman to Jesus and why they continued to insist that He respond to their questions (v. 7). The probable answer is that it occurred to the religious leaders that this case afforded a good opportunity to experiment with Christ. They could use the incident to discover how He regarded the Mosaic Law. They had reason to believe that He was heterodox on this subject. To satisfy themselves and the people on this point, they asked Christ whether or not He agreed with Moses on the subject of adultery. He gave them a judgment, but it was not what they had expected. In thinking of the case, they had forgotten the woman and even the deed. What became of the criminal became unimportant to them. Toward her crime or her character they had no feeling whatsoever.

What did Jesus write on the ground (v. 8)? It has been suggested that this was a common method of signifying intentional disregard. Jesus certainly acted as if He had not heard the woman's accusers. What He actually wrote we are not told. It was the divine finger that wrote the Law (Exodus 31:18), and perhaps Jesus reflected on this fact as He wrote on the ground.

The judgment of Christ was upon the religious leaders (v. 9). The shame of the deed itself, and the brazen hardness of the prosecutors, the legality which had no justice and did not pretend to have mercy, the religious malice that could make its advantage out of the fall and ignominious death of a fellow creature—all this was thrust upon His mind at once. The effect on Him was such as might have been produced on anyone. "He that is without sin . . . let him first cast a stone," said Jesus. Suddenly, a new realization of their condition and conduct astonished the religious leaders, and they began to slip away. The crowd soon dissolved and left Christ alone with the woman.

B. The Restoration
   (Romans 5:15-17)

(Romans 5:15-17 is not included in the printed text.)

Sin, in the course of the ages, multiplied, abounded, exceeded, and overflowed. There are many instances of this in the history of man. The abundance of sin occasioned the Flood. The exceeding sinfulness of Sodom brought the overthrow of the cities of the plain.

The sins of Israel preceded the captivity of God's people.

As for the Gentile world, Paul, in the beginning of the Roman epistle, portrays the crimes, vices, and horrible sins of the nations in such an appalling manner that we do not wonder at his declaration of the wrath of God against those who do such things.

The sin of humanity culminated when it brought the Lord Jesus Christ to the cross. The crucifixion shows the exceeding sinfulness of sin. The greatness of the ransom paid proved the terrible nature of the captivity from which men could only at such a price be delivered.

It should be noted, as Paul asserted, that the sin of Adam was the sole cause of death among men. On the other hand, however, the gift of righteousness through Christ abounds unto many. The apostle's argument was this: If the many were condemned by the sin of one, then it is just as certain that the righteousness of the One abounds unto many.

How does Paul describe the effects of sin?

III. MADE RIGHTEOUS BY GRACE (John 8:10, 11; Romans 5:18-21)

A. The Illumination (John 8:10, 11)

10. When Jesus had lifted up himself, and saw none but the woman, he said unto her, Woman, where are those thine accusers? hath no man condemned thee?

11. She said, No man, Lord. And Jesus said unto her, Neither do I condemn thee: go, and sin

no more.

F.B. Meyer once declared: "There are three ways of dealing with sin: the sinner's way—to expose sin, to scandalously and unforgivingly criticize the sinner, and to almost rejoice in the guilt of one's shame; the law's way of treating the sinner—to condemn and to put to death; and the Savior's way of treating sin—to forgive, to cleanse the heart that has sinned, and to deliver from the power of that sin through the days that follow."

The Savior's way was to seek and to save that which was lost. Mercy is justice in the case of the woman brought to Christ in John 8. Christ proposed the true test: Let the one without sin cast the first stone. No one was eligible to do that. But He interposed with His more excellent way of hope and new life. He said to the woman, "Go, and sin no more." Thereby, He condemned sin while pardoning the sinner.

The statement of Jesus to this woman involved a second chance. It was as though Jesus said to her, "I know you have made a mess of things, but life is not finished yet. I am going to give you another chance, the chance to help yourself." In Jesus, there is the gospel of the second chance. Jesus was always intensely interested not only in what a person had been, but also in what a person could become. He did not say that what they had done did not matter. Broken laws and broken hearts always matter, but Jesus was sure that everyone has a future as well as a past.

The challenge with which Jesus confronted the woman was the challenge of the sinless life. He did not say, "It's all right. Don't worry about it. Just go on doing as you are doing." He said, "It's all wrong. Go out and fight to change your life; go and sin no more." Here was no easy forgiveness. Here was a challenge which pointed the sinner to heights of goodness of which she had never dreamed. Still today Jesus confronts the bad life with the challenge of the good life.

True relief from sin is found only in Christ. It cannot be found in rationalization. It does not help to say that sin is not real, that it is simply a figment of one's imagination. It does not satisfy to say that sin is only an attitude and that sin is therefore not real and guilt is not true. It is true that sin is sometimes a result of an attitude and that thoughts are sometimes sin. It is also true that many sins are sins whether anyone thought about it or not.

Christ has the answer to the sin problem. The answer is found in Christ's provision which allows men to shift their sin to Him. In the Old Testament days, men came to the altar of the Temple and confessed their sins to God, left the required sacrifice, and went away feeling forgiven because they had complied with the requirements of God. They had shifted their sin to God through the sacrificial system that God had established. They felt forgiven because God had said that those who offered their sacrifices, confessed their sins, repented of those sins, and believed Him would have their sins forgiven.

In the New Testament, Christ became the sin offering. The writer of Hebrews illustrated this fact by saying, "This man, after he had offered one sacrifice for sins for ever, sat down on the right hand of

God" (Hebrews 10:12). Again the writer of Hebrews wrote, "Neither by the blood of goats and calves, but by his own blood he entered . . . into the holy place, having obtained eternal redemption for us" (Hebrews 9:12). It means that when one becomes aware of the cross as a symbol of redemption, and recognizes that God allowed Christ to go to the cross to show forth His great love for mankind; when one realizes that forgiveness is offered freely to anyone who will come with a full recognition of his sin and ask for forgiveness, it is then that the individual can find real relief from guilt (W. Maurice Hurley, "Ouch . . .! My Conscience").

B. The Abundance
    (Romans 5:18-21)

18. Therefore as by the offence of one judgment came upon all men to condemnation; even so by the righteousness of one the free gift came upon all men unto justification of life.

19. For as by one man's disobedience many were made sinners, so by the obedience of one shall many be made righteous.

The purpose of Christ was to make all men free. He observed around Him servitude in every form—man in slavery to man, and race to race; His own countrymen in bondage to Rome; men trembling before priestcraft; and men who were slaves to their own passions. Conscious of His own deity and of His Father's intentions, He—with neither the hurry, nor the rebellious excitement which accompanies an earthly liberator—calmly said, "Ye shall be free" (John 8:36). Before man can be free, he must face the fact that he is in bondage. The gospel must first become "bad news" before it can become good news. The Jews felt acutely their political position. They suffered under foreign domination. Many times they tried rebellion—seeking to throw off the hated yoke of the Romans. It was unthinkable to them to be thought of as slaves of Caesar. The purpose of Jesus was to convince them of an underlying slavery which accounted for their political servitude, and to confer upon them the spiritual liberty which contains the power and promise of all freedoms. Real slavery is interior. Political coercion may imprison the body. Intellectual error may degrade the mind. But, by far, the most abject and fatal bondage is that of the soul under the dominion of ignorance, passion, and sin.

20. Moreover the law entered, that the offence might abound. But where sin abounded, grace did much more abound:

21. That as sin hath reigned unto death, even so might grace reign through righteousness unto eternal life by Jesus Christ our Lord.

In thinking of the abundance of sin, it is necessary to think of the various forms which sin assumes; of the reproductive power with which, as a principle of action, it is endowed; of its widespread dominion; and of its power over mankind. Sin is disobedience, rebellion, treason, murder—the work of Satan. Sin is ignorance, folly, madness. Sin is blindness, deafness, dumbness, sickness. Sin is poison, plague, slavery. Sin is death. Sin built hell. Sin kindled the fire that shall never be quenched (Mark

9:44). Sin made the outer darkness where no ray of light ever enters (Matthew 8:12).

Although sin is mighty, the grace of God is stronger. God's grace is as a breeze which overflows the pestilential air of a city. It is as the tide of a mighty ocean which enters the vast harbor and overflows and sweeps away the accumulated pollution. Its victorious superabundance must be explained by referring to its omnipotent Author and Bestower, God; to its Divine channel, Christ, the Mediator; to its appointed means, the gospel, at once the wisdom and the power of God; and to its Agent, the Holy Spirit of God.

How would you define the righteousness of God?

REVIEW QUESTIONS

1. How did the scribes and Pharisees approach Jesus in John 8?

2. What question was Jesus asked by the scribes and Pharisees?

3. How did Jesus react to the question from the scribes and Pharisees?

4. What does Paul say about condemnation by the Law?

5. What was the attitude of Jesus toward the woman accused of adultery?

GOLDEN TEXT HOMILY

"AS SIN HATH REIGNED UNTO DEATH, EVEN SO MIGHT GRACE REIGN THROUGH RIGHTEOUSNESS UNTO ETERNAL LIFE BY JESUS CHRIST OUR LORD" (Romans 5:21).

The greatest and most important decision people make in this life is whether they will live in sin and be lost eternally, or accept Christ as their Savior and live eternally with Him.

Have you ever thought what life would be like for us if Christ had not come and given Himself for us on Calvary? Anyone who will accept Him as Savior and will serve Him will make it to heaven. Those who do not accept Him as their Redeemer will miss the joy of living for Him here on earth and will be lost eternally.

I will always be very thankful I made that important choice 65 years ago when, as a boy of 12 years of age, I accepted Christ as my Savior. I have never been sorry; in fact, as I grow older, I continue to become even more grateful that I accepted Christ as Lord of my life when I did.

There is a great contrast between Adam and Christ. Adam brought sin and death into the world, but Christ brought righteousness and life.

For man to be vitally in touch with his spiritual environments is spiritual life; to be out of touch with them is spiritual death.

When we Christians come in touch with people who have made the wrong decision and are living sinful lives, we should do our best to persuade them to make the right decision—to accept Christ, who brought righteousness and life to this world, as their Savior.—**O.W. Polen, D.D., (Retired) Former Editor in Chief, Church of God Publishing House, Cleveland, Tennessee**

SENTENCE SERMONS

CHRIST WILL FORGIVE anyone who comes to Him in repentance.
—Selected

BEFORE GOD can forgive us, we must undeceive ourselves.

—**St. Augustine**

YOU CANNOT repent too soon, because you do not know how soon it will be too late.

—**Thomas Fuller**

THE LAW detects, grace alone conquers sin.

—**St. Augustine**

EVANGELISM APPLICATION

CHRIST WILL FORGIVE ANYONE WHO COMES TO HIM IN REPENTANCE.

If a man really wants forgiveness for his sins, he must actually come to Christ. Jesus said, to let him come. It is not sufficient just to wish or even to talk, to intend, to resolve, or to hope. There must be action on the part of the individual. He must come in a personal way. He cannot have others to come for him. Salvation is very personal. It is a relationship between the individual and Christ.

ILLUMINATING THE LESSON

Paul's message concerning salvation is the message of the New Testament. The Word of God declares that all men have sinned and that the "wages of sin is death"

(Romans 6:23). This means that the consequences of sin is eternal separation from God. But the promise is given that anyone who believes in Jesus Christ will not perish. The word *anyone* means "every individual." The word *believe* means "to believe that Jesus Christ was the sin-bearer and died in the place of the sinner." It means that "those who accept Christ do not have to pay the penalty for sin."

The New Testament portrays Jesus Christ as standing at the door of the heart of the sinner. The responsibility of the sinner is to open the door, through prayer and faith, and invite Him in, just as anyone else would be invited into his home. When this is done, Christ will come in because of the faith exercised by the individual.

DAILY BIBLE READINGS

M. Request for Forgiveness.
   2 Chronicles 6:22-27
T. A Forgiving God.
   Nehemiah 9:13-21
W. Joy of Being Forgiven.
   Psalm 32:1-7
T. Commanded to Forgive.
   Matthew 6:9-15
F. Undeserved Forgiveness.
   Romans 5:6-11
S. Price of Forgiveness.
   Hebrews 9:11-16

Zacchaeus, Changed by Christ

Study Text: Luke 19:1-10; 2 Corinthians 5:16-19

Objective: To know and demonstrate that a personal encounter with Christ results in change.

Time: The Gospel According to Luke was written between A.D. 58 and 70. The Book of 2 Corinthians was written between A.D. 55 and 57.

Place: The Gospel According to Luke was probably written at Caesarea or Rome. The Book of 2 Corinthians was probably written at the Macedonian city of Philippi.

Golden Text: "If any man be in Christ, he is a new creature: old things are passed away; behold, all things are become new" (2 Corinthians 5:17).

Central Truth: Accepting Christ as Savior results in a changed life.

Evangelism Emphasis: A life changed by Christ witnesses to the lost of His saving power.

PRINTED TEXT

Luke 19:1. And Jesus entered and passed through Jericho.

2. And, behold, there was a man named Zacchaeus, which was the chief among the publicans, and he was rich.

3. And he sought to see Jesus who he was; and could not for the press, because he was little of stature.

4. And he ran before, and climbed up into a sycomore tree to see him: for he was to pass that way.

5. And when Jesus came to the place, he looked up, and saw him, and said unto him, Zacchaeus, make haste, and come down; for to day I must abide at thy house.

6. And he made haste, and came down, and received him joyfully.

7. And when they saw it, they all murmured, saying, That he was gone to be guest with a man that is a sinner.

8. And Zacchaeus stood, and said unto the Lord; Behold, Lord, the half of my goods I give to the poor; and if I have taken any thing from any man by false accusation, I restore him fourfold.

9. And Jesus said unto him, This day is salvation come to this house, forsomuch as he also is a son of Abraham.

10. For the Son of man is come to seek and to save that which was lost.

2 Corinthians 5:16. Wherefore henceforth know we no man after the flesh: yea, though we have known Christ after the flesh, yet now henceforth know we him no more.

17. Therefore if any man be in Christ, he is a new creature: old things are passed away; behold, all things are become new.

18. And all things are of God, who hath reconciled us to himself by Jesus Christ, and hath given to us the ministry of reconciliation;

19. To wit, that God was in Christ, reconciling the world unto himself, not imputing their trespasses unto them; and hath committed unto us the word of reconciliation.

DICTIONARY

Jericho (JEHR-ih-ko)—Luke 19:1—Probably the world's oldest city. It is located five miles west of the Jordan River and seven miles north of the Dead Sea.

Zacchaeus (za-KEE-us)—Luke 19:2—A Jewish tax collector in the city of Jericho.

LESSON OUTLINE

I. SEEKING TO SEE JESUS
   A. The Man
   B. The Desire
   C. The Resourcefulness

II. JESUS SEEKS A SINNER
   A. The Honor
   B. The Scorn

III. JESUS SAVES SINNERS
   A. The Repentance
   B. The New Creature

LESSON EXPOSITION

INTRODUCTION

On February 11, 1847, the great American Thomas A. Edison was born in Milan, Ohio. His inventions have changed the entire pattern of civilization. Edison's ideas have invaded almost every phase of our daily life. We pick up a telephone and his handiwork is there. We push a switch and Edison's idea illuminates the room. We put a record on a stereo and Edison makes it come to life. He helped create the electrical age and began the world of motion pictures. Edison has made our world a more convenient, a more interesting, and a much better place in which to live.

Because of the variety and number of Edison's inventions, we are inclined to think that these things came easily to him—that they were just flashes of genius. Nothing could be further from the truth.

One story illustrates his hard work, determination, and tenacity of purpose. He was searching for the best filament material for his incandescent lamp. For 18 to 20 hours a day he experimented with all kinds of materials—from human hair to plant fiber from the South Seas—until one day he found that carbonized bamboo fiber gave the best results. Most people would have stopped there, but not Edison—he had to find the best type of fiber. As one writer put it, "He ransacked the earth from the

Malay Peninsula to the jungles of the Amazon. He tried 6,000 varieties and it cost him over one hundred thousand dollars until he found the ideal type in the South American jungle." His determination paid off.

In his desire to see Jesus, Zacchaeus illustrates determination. The odds were against him. He was small of stature. The crowd was large. The attitude of the people was unfavorable. But this little man knew what he wanted to do, and he was determined to reach his goal.

I. SEEKING TO SEE JESUS
(Luke 19:1-4)

A. The Man (vv. 1, 2)

1. And Jesus entered and passed through Jericho.

2. And, behold, there was a man named Zacchaeus, which was the chief among the publicans, and he was rich.

The city of Jericho was called "the city of palm trees" (Deuteronomy 34:3; Judges 1:16). It was about five miles west of the Jordan River and about 15 miles from Jerusalem.

Jericho was a notoriously wicked city. In the words of Dr. William M. Thomson, a student of the Holy Land, "Not only was Jericho, because of its location far below the level of the sea, the nearest city, geographically speaking, to hell, but also in the morals of its people, nearer hell than any other city of late Bible times."

The name Zacchaeus (v. 2) means "pure." It is a Jewish name (Ezra 2:9; Nehemiah 7:14) and identifies this man as a member of the Jewish race. Luke calls him a chief publican. This is undoubtedly an official title and means that he was what we would call a commissioner of taxes. Since Jericho was a large frontier city through which much commerce passed and which had a large trade in balsams, it would be an appropriate place for a commissioner of taxes.

Zacchaeus was a very rich man. He was a servant of the government and had agreed to pass along to the Romans certain sums of money. He was allowed to collect from the oppressed people that amount and as much more through his subordinates as he could, to supply their profit and his own. It was an iniquitous system, productive of great wealth for the publicans and much misery for the poor people.

B. The Desire (v. 3)

3. And he sought to see Jesus who he was; and could not for the press, because he was little of stature.

Why did this publican and rich man want to see Jesus? A.B. Bruce gives his answer to this question in the following words: "There is in the minds of people, generally, a very great reverence for any eminent servant of God, and, when he makes his appearance in any place, men hear him, not out of curiosity altogether, but, with a sort of dim desire and hope that he whom God has so blessed to others, may also bring some message to them. For, at the bottom, we all feel our need; and, with a kind of reverential submissiveness, we would put ourselves in the way of good when we have an opportunity. Such considerations as these may account for the conduct of Zacchaeus here" (*Expositor's Greek Testament*).

Luke describes Zacchaeus as being "little of stature." The word for *little* or *small* is *mikros* in Greek. He was not merely slightly under the average in height—it was a physical characteristic noticeable enough for Dr. Luke to mention in his Gospel. Some Bible scholars think he was almost, if not quite, a dwarf. Such characteristics may sometimes cause an individual to develop an inferiority complex. Some think this happened to Zacchaeus.

It is possible that Zacchaeus may have possessed feelings of inferiority. So, denied the normal human fellowship his more fortunate fellows enjoyed, he could have compensated by accumulating wealth. At first the getting of wealth may have been a means to an end—to secure the respect and friendship of his neighbors. But in order to get wealth quickly, he became a publican, and so he was doubly despised.

C. The Resourcefulness (v. 4)

4. And he ran before, and climbed up into a sycamore tree to see him: for he was to pass that way.

The sycamore tree in this verse is probably what is known as a fig-mulberry tree, whose fruit is like the fig and whose leaf is like the mulberry.

Why did Zacchaeus climb a tree to see Jesus? Probably not just out of mere curiosity. No doubt he had heard a great deal about Jesus. He had heard of His unusual teachings, His compassionate understanding of and sympathy with human need, and His popularity with the masses. Here was a man who must be supremely happy;

without wealth, without office, He was loved. The multitudes followed Him; they listened to His every word, followed Him wherever He went, and came to Him with praise and pleas for help. Zacchaeus, whom nobody loved, whom everybody either hated or despised, though he had both wealth and power, wanted to see such a man. He could endure neither the press of the crowd nor the jeers shouted at him, so he climbed a tree from which, unobserved, he might see Jesus.

Why do you think Zacchaeus was so determined to see Jesus?

II. JESUS SEEKS A SINNER
    (Luke 19:5-7)

A. The Honor (vv. 5, 6)

5. And when Jesus came to the place, he looked up, and saw him, and said unto him, Zacchaeus, make haste, and come down; for to day I must abide at thy house.

6. And he made haste, and came down, and received him joyfully.

Jesus knew what He would see when He looked up into the sycamore tree beneath which He was passing. It was no haphazard glance. It was as when, three years before, the Lord said to Nathanael, "Before that Philip called thee, when thou wast under the fig tree, I saw thee" (John 1:48).

One of the most remarkable characteristics of Jesus—one of the many evidences of His divinity—was His ability to see into the depths of the souls of men. His was more than the ability to read the mind; He could read the heart. It was the apostle John who wrote: "And [He] needed not that any should testify of man: for he knew what was in man" (John 2:25). There is a key to every human heart. There is in every individual soul some chord that will respond to the right touch. To find the hidden key—to discover the right touch that will be an opening wedge to a soul deeply hidden beneath a layer of protective hardness—is the task of all who would help others.

Arriving at the tree and looking up, Jesus saw the little man sitting in a tree and read his mind and heart with instant compassion and understanding. He knew the right approach. So He said, "Zacchaeus, hurry and come down, for I am going home with you today."

Those pleasant words may well have been the only kind words the publican had received for many years. This was an unbelievable honor. That the great Rabbi should condescend to speak to him was great, but that He should actually seek the hospitality of a despised tax collector must have totally amazed Zacchaeus and the crowd.

Zacchaeus could not believe his own eyes and ears. This great Prophet, whose face he had been determined to see, actually stopped, called his name, invited Himself to his house, and was walking with him back to his house. Zacchaeus must have been almost beside himself with amazement and delight.

B. The Scorn (v. 7)

7. And when they saw it, they all murmured, saying, That he was gone to be guest with a man that is a sinner.

A gasp of dismay went up from the crowd. It was followed by a babble of conjecture. The neighbors of Zacchaeus saw him as a man with scarcely a redeeming trait. To them he was a traitor, a despised publican, a Jew who had sold his birthright. They saw him as being greedy, dishonest, hard, cruel, and miserly. He had used his office to enrich himself at the expense of his oppressed neighbors. He had risen to a place of prominence among his fellow publicans—perhaps because he was known as a conscienceless and merciless collector of taxes. He was a man without friends, unloving and unloved.

Charles R. Brown writes of this verse: "The Master heard their murmuring but was undisturbed. He was always ready to pay the full price of doing good in his own way. There never was an hour from the time when he faced the devil in the wilderness until he hung upon the cross when he was not willing to be wounded for the transgressions of others, to be bruised by their iniquities that by his stripes they might be healed. He was ready to incur suspicion, ridicule, hatred in order to put himself in open alliance with the better nature of that man whom he would help" (*The Master's Way*).

Can you identify with Zacchaeus in verses 6 and 7? How?

III. JESUS SAVES SINNERS (Luke 19:8-10; 2 Corinthians 5:16-19)

A. The Repentance (Luke 19:8-10)

8. And Zacchaeus stood, and said unto the Lord; Behold, Lord, the half of my goods I give to the poor; and if I have taken any

thing from any man by false accusation, I restore him four-fold.

9. And Jesus said unto him, This day is salvation come to this house, forsomuch as he also is a son of Abraham.

10. For the Son of man is come to seek and to save that which was lost.

With this confession Zacchaeus freed himself from his major sin—that of miserliness. Jesus, not wealth, and God, not gold, from now on were to be his masters. Here is true repentance: the substitution of the corresponding virtue for the corroding sin. This was not mere turning from sin in theory but in fact.

This man was determined to start a new life with as clean a slate as possible. Grace creates a new heart that is not content to leave old wrongs unrighted wherever restitution is possible.

Some imagine and teach that repentance is easy. This is not always so, as can be seen in the case of Zacchaeus. It is more than saying merely, "I am sorry; I won't do it anymore. Please forgive me." How much did it cost this publican? How much would he have left after he gave half to the poor and then restored fourfold that which he had taken by fraud? It made little difference to him now. He had found something better than all the wealth in the world.

This was a case of sudden conversion. The change in Zacchaeus was radical and complete. Anyone but Jesus would probably have said, "Wait awhile; see whether he holds out." But Christ could read the heart and knew that Zacchaeus had been saved from his old life and

had entered into eternal life. It is interesting that Zacchaeus did not say that he would give up his business, but indicated that he would redeem it. Jesus saw that the salvation of Zacchaeus would also involve his entire household.

Why did Jesus refer to Zacchaeus as "also . . . a son of Abraham?" J.D. Jones responds to this question in the following statement: "He also, as well as Christ and his disciples and all other Jews in the room. It was a special factor in the hatred felt toward Zacchaeus that he, a Jew, should take service under the hated Romans and oppress his own countrymen; our Lord transforms this fact into an element of hopefulness. Christ saw something in the little man's soul that convinced him that he belonged to the spiritual family of the father of the faithful. The Pharisees thought of Zacchaeus as a bit of sterile and waste ground, Jesus saw in him the possibility and promise of rich and blessed fruitage; the Pharisees saw him as a sinner, Jesus saw him as a son of Abraham. We are saved by hope says Paul, and that is true. And the hope that saves is not our hope, but Christ's hope for us" (*The Gospel of the Sovereignty*).

"Son of Man" was evidently Christ's favorite name for Himself, asserting His complete union with man, that loving connection between deity and humanity which He came to establish. It was a well-known title of the prophesied Messiah in the Old Testament.

Verse 10 is one of the greatest sentences ever written. It identifies the essence of Christ's mission. It has been called the summing up of Christianity. It means four things:

that mankind is lost without Christ; that Christ came from heaven to earth; that He is constantly seeking men and is ready to respond to any seeking soul; and that when a human soul meets the divine soul in Christ, the human soul is saved. It has been said that all of theology is wrapped up in this one verse.

C.R. Scarborough said, "*Lost* is the darkest word in the history of languages. It means separation from God. It means no peace. It means no joy, no happiness. It means all there is in the punishment of sin" (*Prepare to Meet God*).

Perhaps the greatest lack in modern man is a sense of sin. The natural man recoils from considering his lost condition. He knows that he is not perfect, far from it, but he can hardly think that the situation amounts to lostness. He believes there must be something in him, something he can do, which will commend him to God and will gain him acceptance in God's sight.

B. The New Creature
(2 Corinthians 5:16-19)

16. Wherefore henceforth know we no man after the flesh: yea, though we have known Christ after the flesh, yet now henceforth know we him no more.

17. Therefore if any man be in Christ, he is a new creature: old things are passed away; behold, all things are become new.

H.A. Ironside writes: "We now look out upon the world through altogether different eyes from those we used when we belonged to it. When men of the world, we made much of the flesh, and all that was linked with it. We thought of men

as great, or as rich, or as powerful, talented or able, as superior to one another. Some men we despised because they were poor and ignorant, and degraded, with little intelligence, and less talented, but now all that has changed. . . . We look now out upon this world, not thinking of the different distinctions between man and man, but as seeing a world of sinners for whom Christ died, and we realize that all men, whether rich or poor, foolish or wise, whether barbarian or civilized, whether morons or highly talented, are dear to the heart of God" (*Addresses on the Second Epistle to the Corinthians*).

A man is said to be "in Christ" (v. 17) when he is engrafted into Him as a branch of the living vine, or, in other words, when he truly believes in Christ. He is then a Christian. But in order to show what a change every man experiences when he becomes a Christian, the apostle says of him that he is "a new creation" (*NKJV*). In this term there is a reference to the creation of the world, which may be considered as a type or pattern of that work which God performs in the hearts of His people. The correspondence between them may be seen in the manner, the order, and the end of their formation (Charles Simeon, *Expository Outlines on the Whole Bible*).

18. And all things are of God, who hath reconciled us to himself by Jesus Christ, and hath given to us the ministry of reconciliation;

19. To wit, that God was in Christ, reconciling the world unto himself, not imputing their trespasses unto them; and hath committed unto us the word of

THE CROSS

reconciliation.

The cost of reconciliation was of staggering proportions. Sin had contaminated every area of man's life. It had brought him into complete slavery. This bondage affected all men.

Reconciliation came through the work of Christ on Calvary. In the wisdom and compassion of God, the price was available. Nothing less than the blood of Jesus Christ would suffice. This was the price of redemption that made possible reconciliation.

Reconciliation means that once we belonged to sin and Satan, but now we belong to God. Now there is no gulf between God and men, and we are in a position now to be called the children of God. Reconciliation means that our life's supreme duty is now to glorify the One who bought us. We are to magnify Him in thought, word, and deed and to make known His name to the ends of the earth.

To what extent is man lost? Explain.

REVIEW QUESTIONS

1. Why did Zacchaeus want to see Jesus?

2. How was he hindered?

3. What promises did Zacchaeus make?

4. How did Christ sum up His mission?

5. What is meant by reconciliation?

GOLDEN TEXT HOMILY

"IF ANY MAN BE IN CHRIST, HE IS A NEW CREATURE: OLD THINGS ARE PASSED AWAY; BEHOLD, ALL THINGS ARE BECOME NEW" (2 Corinthians 5:17).

The greatest beginning in life is also the greatest opportunity in life. Life begins in Christ, who redeems and makes an individual a new creation through the power of the gospel. How exciting to a person whose life is marked by sin to have a new beginning, a new start in life! How wonderful to be free from the darkness of sin and the burden and guilt that sin gives!

The person who experiences this new beginning gains the greatest opportunity of life. This person can allow God to work His perfect will in his life. How is this done? Scriptures answer this question. Note Psalm 81:10-13: "I am the Lord thy God, which brought thee out of the land of Egypt: open thy mouth wide, and I will fill it. But my people would not hearken to my voice; and Israel would none of me. So I gave them up unto their own hearts' lust: and they walked in their own counsels. Oh that my people had hearkened unto me, and Israel had walked in my ways!"

These verses point out the importance of one's willingness to allow God access to his life. Jesus told believers in John 8:31, 32, "If ye continue in my word, then are ye my disciples indeed; and ye shall know the truth, and the truth shall make you free."

If we allow God, by opening wide our life, then He can minister His Word in us by the Spirit of Truth to lead us into all truth. Thus we will experience the perfect will of God and the promise of John 10:10—abundant life!**—Levy E. Moore, Mayor, City of Franklin Springs, Franklin Springs, Georgia**

SENTENCE SERMONS

ACCEPTING CHRIST as Savior results in a changed life.

—Selected

THE STRANGE THING about Jesus is that you can never get away from Him.

—A Japanese Student

THE DYING JESUS is the evidence of God's anger toward sin; but the living Jesus is the proof of God's love and forgiveness.

—Lorenz Eifert

CHRIST IS NOT valued at all unless He is valued above all.

—St. Augustine

EVANGELISM APPLICATION

A LIFE CHANGED BY CHRIST WITNESSES TO THE LOST OF HIS SAVING POWER.

Charles R. Brown writes of Zacchaeus: "We find in the action of Zacchaeus a full-page, life-size picture of old-fashioned, thorough-going repentance. Where repentance is genuine, it costs. Tears are cheap—there are those who shed bucketfuls of them and they have no more worth or significance than so much rain water. Remorse is cheap—it may be merely the pain of being found out, not involving any serious change of purpose. Repentance, where it is real, is more precious than diamonds and rubies. It foretells the upward movement of a soul which will outlast and outshine them all. Repentance means an about-face, the putting away of dishonest purpose, the actual movement of the life toward that light where there is not darkness at all" (*These Twelve*).

ILLUMINATING THE LESSON

God's provision for man's salvation centers in Jesus Christ. At the birth of Jesus it was announced twice that He was the Anointed of God to save men from sin. The announcement was made by the angel of the Lord to Joseph, and it was also announced to the shepherds.

Strictly speaking, a *Savior* is one who "delivers" another, or others, from an impending danger or from disaster and destruction.

In referring to Christ, the word *Savior* means that Christ has delivered us from the power of death, and has communicated to us His own eternal life. As a Savior, He also saves us now, day-by-day, and for all eternity from the bondage of sin.

DAILY BIBLE READINGS

M. New Song.
   Psalm 40:1-5
T. New Heart.
   Ezekiel 36:25-28
W. New Commandment.
   John 13:31-35
T. New Life.
   Colossians 3:1-10
F. New and Living Way.
   Hebrews 10:16-25
S. New Name.
   Revelation 3:7-13

A Demoniac Delivered

Study Text: Mark 5:1-20

Objective: To know that Jesus brings deliverance and believe that He will set free those who are bound.

Time: The Gospel According to Mark was probably written between A.D. 50 and 70.

Place: There is uncertainty about where the Gospel of Mark was written. Rome is a likelihood.

Golden Text: "They cried unto the Lord in their trouble, and he delivered them out of their distresses" (Psalm 107:6).

Central Truth: Christ's power breaks the bondage of sin.

Evangelism Emphasis: Those whom Christ has freed from sin must share the good news of deliverance.

PRINTED TEXT

Mark 5:1. And they came over unto the other side of the sea, into the country of the Gadarenes.

2. And when he was come out of the ship, immediately there met him out of the tombs a man with an unclean spirit,

3. Who had his dwelling among the tombs; and no man could bind him, no, not with chains:

4. Because that he had been often bound with fetters and chains, and the chains had been plucked asunder by him, and the fetters broken in pieces: neither could any man tame him.

5. And always, night and day, he was in the mountains, and in the tombs, crying, and cutting himself with stones.

6. But when he saw Jesus afar off, he ran and worshipped him,

7. And cried with a loud voice, and said, What have I to do with thee, Jesus, thou Son of the most high God? I adjure thee by God, that thou torment me not.

8. For he said unto him, Come out of the man, thou unclean spirit.

9. And he asked him, What is thy name? And he answered, saying, My name is Legion: for we are many.

14. And they that fed the swine fled, and told it in the city, and in the country. And they went out to see what it was that was done.

15. And they come to Jesus, and see him that was possessed with the devil, and had the legion, sitting, and clothed, and in his right mind: and they were afraid.

16. And they that saw it told them how it befell to him that was possessed with the devil, and also concerning the swine.

17. And they began to pray

him to depart out of their coasts.

18. And when he was come into the ship, he that had been possessed with the devil prayed him that he might be with him.

19. Howbeit Jesus suffered him not, but saith unto him, Go home to thy friends, and tell them how great things the Lord hath done for thee, and hath had compassion on thee.

20. And he departed, and began to publish in Decapolis how great things Jesus had done for him: and all men did marvel.

DICTIONARY

Gadarenes (gad-uh-REENZ)—Mark 5:1—People who lived in Gadara, southeast of Lake Galilee.

Decapolis (dee-KAP-oh-lis)—Mark 5:20—Ten towns in an area southeast of Lake Galilee.

LESSON OUTLINE

I. HELD IN BONDAGE

    A. Description

    B. Self-Destruction

II. SET FREE

    A. Question

    B. Response

    C. Appeal

III. SHARE THE GOOD NEWS

    A. Curiosity

    B. Request

    C. Instructions

LESSON EXPOSITION

INTRODUCTION

The visit of Jesus to the Gadarenes, or Gergesenes, was a striking one. Only in Gadara for a few hours, He found a demoniac and left behind a great example of His power as God's messenger to the people. Most Bible scholars see no contradiction between the demoniacs Mark and Luke refer to, and the two of Matthew's account (Matthew 8:28). Matthew Henry said, "If there were two, there was one." The plausible explanation is that one was more prominent, more violent, more worthy of notice than the other.

The Bible recognizes that evil spirits do exist and do take possession of men's bodies. Sometimes men invited them to do so and became friendly with them. They are then called "familiar spirits" (Leviticus 19:31; 20:6-27). Those who did so were put to death. Moral depravity might precede demon possession, but once the possession is effected, sensuality and violence become more apparent. Once Satan enters, then surrender to his will is hard to resist. Physical and mental disorders follow which are more or less related to the evil spirits.

The Bible clearly maintains that not all human disorders are the result of demon possession (Matthew 4:23, 24; 10:1; 11:5, and others). Insanity, blindness, dumbness, fevers, and so forth were frequent accompaniments and symptoms of demon possession (Matthew 12:22; 9:32; Mark 9:17;

Luke 11:14) but were not necessarily identified with it. However, these diseases were often aggravated by these powers. Ancient beliefs held that these diseases were caused by demon possession and that the demons had to be cast out before the possessed could be healed.

Many Bible scholars believe that the demoniac in Mark 5 was suffering from some form of mental illness. The symptoms given are those cited by medical writers in connection with certain forms of mental illness. But demon possession and lunacy are expressly distinguished (Matthew 4:24). It is, therefore, incorrect to say that demon possession is just another name for mental illness. With the Gadarene demoniac, his disease was the result of his own wickedness. Added to his illness was the demoniac element in its extreme form. Trench says, "It may well be a question, moreover, if an apostle, or one gifted with apostolic discernment of spirits, were to enter a madhouse now, he might not recognize some of the sufferers there as 'possessed.' Certainly in many cases of mania . . . there is a condition very analogous to that of the demoniacs" (Herbert Lockyer, *All the Miracles of the Bible*).

I. HELD IN BONDAGE
    (Mark 5:1-5)

A. The Description (vv. 1-4)

1. And they came over unto the other side of the sea, into the country of the Gadarenes.

2. And when he was come out of the ship, immediately there met him out of the tombs a man with an unclean spirit,

3. Who had his dwelling among the tombs; and no man could bind him, no, not with chains:

4. Because that he had been often bound with fetters and chains, and the chains had been plucked asunder by him, and the fetters broken in pieces: neither could any man tame him.

Arriving on the east side of the lake, Jesus and His disciples expected to find a quiet place of rest. Instead, they found a raging maniac. Jesus had to perform another miracle. This time He had to cast out the demons that possessed the man. He had to still the raging storm in the deranged man's mind.

Demonology is a difficult subject to deal with. The study of demons has been and still is one of the main problems of theology. There is a tendency today to dismiss the idea of demon possession as a superstitious way of explaining the phenomenon of mental illness. It is true that demon possession and some forms of mental illness are often linked together in the Gospels. However, this does not explain all mental illness. Many people feel that all the evil happenings in our world can be explained as being the work of unseen destructive forces. The Bible calls these forces demons. The evidence of their existence is obvious and abundant.

Honest students who study the Bible with an open mind cannot deny the fact that Jesus Christ recognized the existence of the devil and demons. He also believed in their evil influence on human beings. If He had not believed in the dreadful powers of darkness, He would not have spoken as earnestly, profoundly, and courageously about these hideous forces as He did. He vividly portrayed the manifestation of evil in the bodies and souls of men as coming from an evil source.

To avoid being defiled, the Jews did not have their burial places in their cities. Therefore, they buried their dead in the fields or mountains outside the gates of the cities. Sepulchers were frequently hewn out of the rock in the sides of the limestone hills. They were lofty and spacious so the living could enter them, as they would enter a vault. The demoniac in Mark 5 dwelt in a field of tombs. He had been driven there by unclean spirits. The associations of the place were in keeping with his malady.

The author of the Gospel of Matthew spoke of two demoniacs. He described them as "exceedingly fierce, so that no one could pass that way" (8:28, *NKJV*). The demoniac mentioned by Mark is also described as having extraordinary muscular strength, which so often occurs in maniacs. All efforts to bind and restrain him had been ineffective. Chains and fetters had often been tried, but in vain.

B. Self-Destruction (v. 5)

5. And always, night and day, he was in the mountains, and in the tombs, crying, and cutting himself with stones.

There is no doubt that the man was suffering from some form of mania or lunacy. Matthew states there were two men (Matthew 8:28). Luke, like Mark, mentions only one man "which had devils" (Luke 8:27). Undoubtedly there were many in the land suffering from conditions similar to that of the man mentioned by Mark and Luke. The latter two writers had one man in mind. Matthew's writing is more inclusive. One man was probably more verbal and active and thus more likely remembered.

Some people attempt to explain the fact that demon possession occurs in the Gospels by attributing it to Babylonian and Persian beliefs or superstitions that had become part of the beliefs of the Jews. They claim that the Jews attributed physical and mental disorders to some sort of weird personality.

Other people reject the reality of demon possession by saying that Jesus simply accommodated His language to the ideas prominent in His time. They emphasize that as part of His divine mission He assumed the role of a corrector of popular beliefs by commanding the supposed evil spirits to come out of the possessed.

There is ample evidence in the Bible to support belief in the reality of demons. They are former angelic beings who rebelled against God and were expelled from heaven with their leader—now known as Satan. Man's entanglement with this power is the result of the Fall. Sin is a terrible reality. It must not be underemphasized. The Bible clearly and unmistakably teaches that the devil and evil spirits are real beings. It teaches that the power of the devil is exercised in a threefold way: directly, indirectly through demons who are subject to him, and through human beings he has influenced and possessed.

How do evil spirits work today?

II. SET FREE (Mark 5:6-14)

A. Question (vv. 6, 7)

6. But when he saw Jesus afar off, he ran and worshipped him,

7. And cried with a loud voice, and said, What have I to do with thee, Jesus, thou Son of the most high God? I adjure thee by God, that thou torment me not.

The possessed man, from his cave high up in the hills, had probably seen Jesus' boat nearing the shore. He ran and worshiped Jesus; he felt the power of His presence and was constrained through fear to reverence Him.

Using the voice of the man they possessed, the evil spirits cried out. Note their words: "What have I to do with thee, Jesus, thou Son of the most high God." The evil spirits recognized that Christ was no ordinary man daring to set foot on their domain. The demoniac seems to have been conscious of the fact that an awful gulf divided him from Christ and that in his degraded condition he could have nothing to do with Him. Yet, he recognized the deity of Christ.

This is the first occurrence in the New Testament of the designation of Christ as the "Son of the most high God." It is a divine title going back to the patriarchal worship of the one supreme deity.

The torment which they would suffer after expulsion was dreaded by the evil spirits. Luke tells us that the evil spirits entreated Jesus that He would not command them to go into "the deep" (8:31), "the abyss" (*NKJV*), or "the bottomless pit" (Revelation 20:3).

E. Bickersmith writes: "Great as this mystery of evil is, we may believe that the evil spirits are in misery even while they roam about on this earth. Still, it was by some alleviation that they were not yet shut up in the prison house of hell, but were allowed to wander about

and find their depraved pleasure in tempting men. Therefore, if possible, they would at least drag their victims down with them into the abyss. Demons are full of hatred of God and envy of man. They find a miserable satisfaction in attempting to keep man out of the heavenly mansions from which, through pride, they are themselves excluded forever" (*Pulpit Commentary*).

B. Response (vv. 8, 9)

8. For he said unto him, Come out of the man, thou unclean spirit.

9. And he asked him, What is thy name? And he answered, saying, My name is Legion: for we are many.

Note the difference between Christ's dealings with this poor man and the treatment he received from his fellowmen. They had tried to chain and fetter him and, failing in that, had driven him away, to live in nakedness and hunger among the tombs. However, Christ went to the root of the problem and spoke a quiet word to take care of his troubles by ridding him of the evil spirits.

Jesus, in order to awaken in the man memories of his days before he became a demoniac, asked him his name; but the evil spirits in him promptly replied for him. Why did Jesus ask this question? Many Bible scholars state that it was to elicit from the demon speaker an answer that would reveal a multitude of the evil spirits and so make His own power over them fully known.

The demon speaker replied to the question of Jesus with the words: "My name is Legion: for we are many." The Roman legion consisted of 6,000 soldiers. But this word is here used to represent an indefinitely large number. Luke explains it thus: "And he said, Legion: because many devils were entered into him" (8:30). This revelation is probably designed to teach us how great is the number as well as the malignity of the evil spirits.

This should cause us to think that if one human being can be possessed by so many evil spirits, then how vast must be the host of those who are permitted to have access to the souls of men and, if possible, to lead them to destruction. Satan here imitated Him who is the Lord of Hosts. Satan too marshals his hosts that he may fight against God and His people, but "for this purpose the Son of God was manifested, that he might destroy the works of the devil" (1 John 3:8).

C. Appeal (vv. 10-14)

(Mark 5:10-13 is not included in the printed text.)

Before being cast out, the demons made a strange request of Christ. They asked to be allowed to enter a herd of swine. It appears that the evil spirits felt that if they were driven from their present dwelling place, their condition would be changed for the worst. Apparently they felt that until the time should come when they would be cast into hell their best relief was to enter into what was, according to Jewish thought, the lowest species of animal life, the swine—to occupy at least flesh and blood. Even the swine would be better than nothing.

We are told by Mark that the herd of swine, 2,000 strong, was feeding on the slopes of the mountain. The Jews were not permitted to eat the flesh of swine, but Jews were not the only ones living in this area. It had been colonized, at least in part, by the Romans immediately after the conquest of Syria, about 60 years before Christ. In this district the 10 cities are said to have been rebuilt by the Romans. This is where the area got the name Decapolis. And though the Jews were forbidden to eat swine meat, they were not forbidden to raise it for other uses, such as to sell it to the Roman army.

Jesus gave His permission for the demons to enter the herd of swine. This is important to note. They could not even enter into the swine without Christ's permission. It should be said that Christ did not send the demons into the swine; He merely drove them out of the man. All beyond that was merely permissive. Augustine said that the swine's being driven into the sea was no work of divine miracle, but was the work of the demons by divine permission.

14. And they that fed the swine fled, and told it in the city, and in the country. And they went out to see what it was that was done.

Mark's record of the reaction of those who fed the swine is interesting. No doubt many of them lived in the various districts. Therefore, the fame of the miracle spread very quickly. The swineherders took care that those who owned the swine understood that the swine perished through no carelessness on their part. They let it be known that this was caused by a power over which they had no control.

The owners of the swine came to see what had happened. Their first concern was the extent of their loss.

They must have seen the carcasses of the swine floating in the peaceful sea. This must have been quite a shock.

How would the current media react to an event such as the one described by Mark?

III. SHARE THE GOOD NEWS (Mark 5:15-20)

A. Curiosity (vv. 15-17)

15. And they come to Jesus, and see him that was possessed with the devil, and had the legion, sitting, and clothed, and in his right mind: and they were afraid.

16. And they that saw it told them how it befell to him that was possessed with the devil, and also concerning the swine.

17. And they began to pray him to depart out of their coasts.

What a change they saw in the man. The features were the same, but no longer distorted. The eyes were the same, but in them no longer burned the pain of fire. His form was unchanged, but it was no longer racked with convulsive shaking. It was his own voice, but it spoke in quiet tones and uttered words that could be understood.

The healing of the demoniac was so strange that it would not have been believed except on the testimony of eye witnesses. The change was evident. Instead of wild, terrifying restlessness, he was clothed and sitting peacefully at the feet of Jesus. The disciples had probably provided the necessities to cover his body. He was now in his right mind—Christ-possessed instead of demon-possessed. This certainly illustrates the transformation Christ makes possible. Through

Him, we are at His feet, clothed with the garments of salvation, and having His mind within.

The owners of the swine were afraid when they saw what had happened. They dreaded Christ's power. They saw that He was almighty, but they did not seek to know His love or to receive that love which can cast out fear.

The Gadarenes, with fatal short-sightedness and fear of the supernatural, entreated Jesus to depart out of their coasts, not so much because he had healed the demoniac, but because through His marvelous powers the swine had been lost. They feared further loss by the same means. Touch a man's money and he is usually moved.

B. Request (v. 18)

18. And when he was come into the ship, he that had been possessed with the devil prayed him that he might be with him.

Perhaps the healed man was afraid the demons would return to him if he did not remain with the Healer. Certainly his gratitude led him to desire to attach himself to his benefactor, and he wished to see more of the great Teacher and learn of Him. Worldly selfishness had requested Jesus depart; humble gratitude desired to continue with Him.

C. Instructions (vv. 19, 20)

19. Howbeit Jesus suffered him not, but saith unto him, Go home to thy friends, and tell them how great things the Lord hath done for thee, and hath had compassion on thee.

20. And he departed, and began to publish in Decapolis

how great things Jesus had done for him: and all men did marvel.

As Jesus sent His 12 disciples away that they might help Him to do His work, so He sent the healed man back to his family and friends. He told him in effect to go to those who knew him best, and to testify of all the fearful circumstances from which he had been saved. His first task was to tell the good news to his own household. This is what Lydia and Cornelius and the Philippian jailer did.

Prior to this, Christ had told those He healed to keep silent concerning it, but that was in the part of Palestine where Christ's enemies dwelled, where He intended to continue working, and where the people were ready to make Him a leader and to rise against the Romans. In the country east of the lake, there were none of these reasons for secrecy as to Christ's miracles, and moreover, this healed man was the only agent for evangelizing the region.

The healed demoniac obeyed Jesus (v. 20). He went all over Decapolis, the region east and southeast of the Sea of Galilee. His message was simple but glorious. He told "how great things Jesus had done for him," and he told it with such loving compassion that "all men did marvel."

Is it ever appropriate for Christians to keep quiet about what Christ has done for them?

REVIEW QUESTIONS

1. What marked the case of demon possession as extreme?
2. What was the plea of the evil spirits?
3. How was the plea granted?
4. Why did Christ leave the region?
5. What injunction did He give to the healed man?

SENTENCE SERMONS

CHRIST'S POWER breaks the bondage of sin.

—Selected

THOSE WHOM CHRIST has freed from sin must share the good news of deliverance.

—Selected

MAN IS really free only in God, the source of his freedom.

—Sherwood Eddy

EVANGELISM APPLICATION

THOSE WHOM CHRIST HAS FREED FROM SIN MUST SHARE THE GOOD NEWS OF DELIVERANCE.

As John B. Gough was reeling through the streets of Newburyport, a humble cobbler, noting the desperate condition of the poor drunkard, laid a hand upon his shoulder and said kindly, pointing upward, "John, there is One that can help thee." That marked the turning point of his life. He gave up every other reliance and threw himself upon the omnipotent help of God.— **David Burrell,** *The Unaccountable Man*

DAILY BIBLE READINGS

M. Promise of Deliverance. Exodus 3:1-10
T. Great Deliverance. Exodus 14:13-22
W. Deliverance From Trouble. Isaiah 43:1-3
T. Delivered From Death. Daniel 3:16-26
F. Delivered From Bonds. Acts 12:1-11
S. Comfort in Deliverance. 2 Corinthians 1:3-11

Authority of the Risen Christ (Easter Lesson)

Study Text: Matthew 27:57-66; 28:1-20

Objective: To understand the significance of Christ's resurrection and tell others that He is alive.

Time: A.D. 30

Place: Jerusalem

Golden Text: "He is not here: for he is risen" (Matthew 28:6).

Central Truth: Jesus Christ rose from the dead and lives forever.

Evangelism Emphasis: The resurrected Christ gives eternal life to all who believe in Him.

PRINTED TEXT

Matthew 27:57. When the even was come, there came a rich man of Arimathaea, named Joseph, who also himself was Jesus' disciple:

58. He went to Pilate, and begged the body of Jesus. Then Pilate commanded the body to be delivered.

59. And when Joseph had taken the body, he wrapped it in a clean linen cloth,

60. And laid it in his own new tomb, which he had hewn out in the rock: and he rolled a great stone to the door of the sepulchre, and departed.

28:1. In the end of the sabbath, as it began to dawn toward the first day of the week, came Mary Magdalene and the other Mary to see the sepulchre.

2. And, behold, there was a great earthquake: for the angel of the Lord descended from heaven, and came and rolled back the stone from the door, and sat upon it.

3. His countenance was like lightning, and his raiment white as snow:

4. And for fear of him the keepers did shake, and became as dead men.

5. And the angel answered and said unto the women, Fear not ye: for I know that ye seek Jesus, which was crucified.

6. He is not here: for he is risen, as he said. Come, see the place where the Lord lay.

7. And go quickly, and tell his disciples that he is risen from the dead; and, behold, he goeth before you into Galilee; there shall ye see him: lo, I have told you.

8. And they departed quickly from the sepulchre with fear and great joy; and did run to bring his disciples word.

9. And as they went to tell his disciples, behold, Jesus met them, saying, All hail. And they came and held him by the feet, and worshipped him.

10. Then said Jesus unto

them, Be not afraid: go tell my brethren that they go into Galilee, and there shall they see me.

18. And Jesus came and spake unto them, saying, All power is given unto me in heaven and in earth.

19. Go ye therefore, and teach all nations, baptizing them in the name of the Father, and of the Son, and of the Holy Ghost:

20. Teaching them to observe all things whatsoever I have commanded you: and, lo, I am with you alway, even unto the end of the world. Amen.

DICTIONARY

Arimathaea (AYR-ih-ma-THE-ah)—Matthew 27:57—The location of this city is in doubt, but it is possibly the Ramah of Samuel's day in the hill country of Ephraim.

Mary Magdalene (MAG-duh-lean)—Matthew 28:1—A woman out of whom Jesus cast seven devils (Mark 16:9). She was from the town of Magdala, located on the shore of the Sea of Galilee.

Galilee (GAL-i-lee)—Matthew 28:7—The northernmost of the three provinces of Palestine in the days of Jesus.

LESSON OUTLINE

I.   THE BURIAL OF CHRIST

   A. The Burial

   B. The Sealing and the Guard

II. THE RESURRECTION OF CHRIST

   A. The Miracle

   B. The Message

   C. The Master

   D. The Misrepresentation

III. THE COMMAND OF CHRIST

   A. The Meeting

   B. The Commission

LESSON EXPOSITION

INTRODUCTION

Resurrection is the word most characteristic of the Christian religion. It is the one word that can focus and express the very essence of Christianity. Christianity is essentially the religion of resurrection. The church is the community of those who believe in resurrection. The gospel is the power of resurrection.

It is true that the Cross must stand at the very heart of God's program of redemption, but many gaze at the Cross for a lifetime and yet miss the gospel that saves. Such a man is on the wrong side of Easter. The cross is not the symbol of Christianity, but rather a risen Savior.

The resurrection of Christ is regarded by too many people as an epilogue to the gospel. Many consider it to be an addendum to the scheme of salvation; to others it is a codicil to the divine last will and testament. But these attitudes misrepresent the whole emphasis of the Word of God; if there had been no resurrection, there would have been no New Testament. It was with a burning certainty in the resurrection of Christ that men were motivated to pen the gospel record. They knew that the One about whom they were writing had conquered death and was alive forevermore. The Resurrection was no mere appendix to their faith; it was their faith. It was the seal of victory—Christ had defeated the Enemy.

Resurrection had become a reality in their hearts. Such is the authentic Christian faith—they knew that nothing in life or in death could separate them from the love of God, which they had experienced in Christ the Lord.

This is what Easter is all about. Christ is alive and dwells in the heart of the Christian.

I. THE BURIAL OF CHRIST
   (Matthew 27:57-66)

A. The Burial (vv. 57-61)

(Matthew 27:61 is not included in the printed text.)

57. When the even was come, there came a rich man of Arimathaea, named Joseph, who also himself was Jesus' disciple:

58. He went to Pilate, and begged the body of Jesus. Then Pilate commanded the body to be delivered.

59. And when Joseph had taken the body, he wrapped it in a clean linen cloth,

60. And laid it in his own new tomb, which he had hewn out in the rock: and he rolled a great stone to the door of the sepulchre, and departed.

It is believed by some that the Jews intended to bury Jesus beside Judas in the plot of ground pur-chased with the price of treachery, but if this was their aim, it was frustrated by God. The moment Christ suffered death, God allowed no further insults to be cast upon His Son. From the moment of His expiration until the hour of His resurrection, the body of Jesus was in the hands of loving friends.

Joseph of Arimathea was a member of the Sanhedrin, but he had not voted for the death of Jesus. He was a man of social position and of wealth. He was a good and righteous man, a secret disciple of Christ. But throwing off his timidity, he went boldly to Pilate and asked for the body of Jesus so he could bury Him in a new, unused, rock-hewn tomb near Jerusalem. Pilate readily granted permission, and he was joined by another member of the Sanhedrin, the same Nicodemus who held the night conference with Jesus early in our Lord's ministry.

Joseph and Nicodemus took the body of Jesus, put preservative spices around it, wrapped it in a linen cloth, and placed it in the tomb. The tomb was closed with a large circular stone which rolled into a groove. Fastening it thus, they left the body in the grave.

B. The Sealing and the Guard
   (vv. 62-66)

(Matthew 27:62-66 is not included in the printed text.)

The day after Jesus was buried, the chief priests and Pharisees remembered Christ's words of prophecy concerning His resurrection on the third day. They went to Pilate and asked him to prevent the possibility of the disciples stealing the body of Jesus and then asserting that He had risen from the dead. In their words, "The last error [would] be worse than the first" (v. 64). Agreeing, Pilate gave them a detail of Roman soldiers to keep watch over the tomb.

The chief priests and Pharisees, with double caution, put cords across the stone door and sealed both ends to the stone and to the entrance. This made it impossible to tamper with the grave without discovery.

What was the significance of the stone at the door of the tomb of Jesus?

II. THE RESURRECTION OF CHRIST (Matthew 28:1-15)

A. The Miracle (vv. 1-5)

1. In the end of the sabbath, as it began to dawn toward the first day of the week, came Mary Magdalene and the other Mary to see the sepulchre.

2. And, behold, there was a great earthquake: for the angel of the Lord descended from heaven, and came and rolled back the stone from the door, and sat upon it.

3. His countenance was like lightning, and his raiment white as snow:

4. And for fear of him the keepers did shake, and became as dead men.

5. And the angel answered and said unto the women, Fear not ye: for I know that ye seek Jesus, which was crucified.

The credibility of Jesus' claims to be the Messiah rested on the fact of His resurrection. It should be remembered that at the beginning of His ministry He said, "Destroy this temple, and in three days I will raise it up" (John 2:19). These words were not understood at the time, although His enemies used them as a charge against Him at the close of His life. After His resurrection, the mysterious statement was recalled by his friends as a prediction of the event which had just taken place.

On another occasion, when urged by the unbelieving Pharisees to give some sign greater than those they had already seen, He told them that no sign would be given them other than that of the prophet Jonah: "For as Jonas was three days and three nights in the whale's belly; so shall the Son of man be three days and three nights in the heart of the earth" (Matthew 12:40).

On several other occasions He had spoken of His resurrection as the destined evidence of His messiahship. The great stone at the entrance to the tomb was the foundation of all the precautions that were used against any attempt of the disciples of Jesus to practice some fraud on the people. It was feared by some that the disciples might actually attempt to steal the body from the tomb and then say that He had risen from the dead. To prevent any such happening, the tomb was sealed with Pilate's seal and guarded by a band of soldiers.

We are told by Matthew that when Jesus arose from the dead there was a great earthquake. We are also told that the angel of the Lord descended from heaven and rolled back the stone from the door of the tomb and sat upon it. We do not need to suppose that Jesus needed the help of an angel when He came forth from the grave; we need not doubt that He rose again by His own power. But it pleased

God that Christ's resurrection should be accompanied and followed by signs and wonders. It seemed good that the earth should shake and that a glorious angel should appear when the Son of God arose from the dead as a conqueror.

We are also informed by Matthew that the Roman soldiers shook with fear and became like dead men at the time of Christ's resurrection. It should be kept in mind that these soldiers were above average men. They were trained soldiers and not unused to dreadful sights; however, on this occasion they saw a sight which surpassed all others in its fearfulness to them. Their courage melted at the sight of one angel from the Lord.

The words "Fear not ye: for I know that ye seek Jesus, which was crucified" (v. 5) were meant to cheer the hearts of believers in every age. They were intended to remind every Christian that there is no cause for alarm, regardless of what may come along life's way. The Lord shall appear in the clouds of glory; the graves shall give up the dead that are in them; the judgment shall be set; and the books shall be opened. But clothed in the righteousness of Christ, the believer shall be found blameless and without spot.

B. The Message (vv. 6-8)

6. He is not here: for he is risen, as he said. Come, see the place where the Lord lay.

7. And go quickly, and tell his disciples that he is risen from the dead; and, behold, he goeth before you into Galilee; there shall ye see him: lo, I have told you.

8. And they departed quickly from the sepulchre with fear and great joy; and did run to bring his disciples word.

The visit of the women to the tomb of Christ revealed their strong love for Him. The Gospel of Mark records that they brought sweet spices to anoint our Lord and that very early in the morning, the first day of the week, they came to the tomb at the rising of the sun.

Think of the courage it took to do what the women did. To visit a grave in the dim twilight of daybreak would be difficult for many people, under any circumstance. But to visit the grave of One who had been put to death as a criminal, and to rise early to show honor to One whom the nation had despised, would take boldness on the part of anyone.

Are not these the kind of acts which show the difference between weak faith and strong faith? These women had been touched by our Lord's pardoning mercies. Their hearts were full of gratitude to Him for light, hope, comfort, and peace. They were willing to risk any consequence to testify of their love for Christ.

The angel said to the women, "He is risen." This is the most momentous announcement ever made. It is the proof of Christianity. It is the evidence of immortality. It affects the soul of man more deeply than any other announcement possibly could.

It was Matthew who reported: "He is risen, as he said" (v. 6). These words were a reminder to the women, for they must have known of our Lord's repeated prophecies concerning His resurrection. Luke implied a reproach when he stated,

"Why seek ye the living among the dead?" (24:5). The angel further said, "Behold the place where they laid him" (Mark 16:6). This statement emphasized that the empty grave, even without any appearance of the risen Lord, was proof that He had risen.

The angel gave the women a message for the disciples—and Peter—from the Lord. It has been construed from this particular detail that Peter, after his denial, had no longer been considered a disciple. The words "tell his disciples and Peter" (v. 7) reveal that Christ, after His resurrection, was quick and eager to bring peace to the soul of that disciple who had lived in an agony of remorse and shame ever since his denial in the judgment hall. Christ's first message was to him. It was a message that emphasized the assurance of pardon and abiding love.

C. The Master (vv. 9, 10)

9. And as they went to tell his disciples, behold, Jesus met them, saying, All hail. And they came and held him by the feet, and worshipped him.

10. Then said Jesus unto them, Be not afraid: go tell my brethren that they go into Galilee, and there shall they see me.

Jesus appeared in person to the women who had come to honor His body. Those who were last at the cross were first at the tomb and first to see the risen Lord. To them He gave a commission to carry tidings to His disciples: "Go tell my brethren," was the message. It is characteristic that His first thought was for His little scattered flock.

There is something significant in

these words "my brethren." These men were weak, frail, and erring, and yet Jesus still called them "brethren." Though they had come short of their profession, they were still His brethren; though they had sadly yielded to fear, they were still His brethren.

Glorious as He was in Himself—a conqueror over death, hell, and the grave—the Son of God is still meek and lowly of heart. He still calls His disciples "brethren."

D. The Misrepresentation (vv. 11-15)

(Matthew 28:11-15 is not included in the printed text.)

These verses give us the report of Christ's resurrection made to the chief priests by the Roman guard, the dismayed meeting of the Sanhedrin, and the bribing of the soldiers. The priests paid them to say that while they (the soldiers) slept, the disciples came and stole the body of Jesus. The Sanhedrin agreed to protect the soldiers if Pilate should threaten to punish them, for it was death for a sentinel to sleep on duty! It was inconceivable in the first place that the soldiers would be asleep and, in the second place, that they would confess it if they were, since such a confession meant death. In the third place, the disciples would never have done such a thing. The disciples were honest men. They eventually died for their faith in Christ, based on His resurrection. Men do not voluntarily die for an impostor or for a scam they have perpetrated. And if they had stolen the body, what did they do with it? It would have been easy for the foes of Christ to hunt and discover it. This attempt to explain away

Christianity is absolutely impossible to believe.

What do the words "He is risen" mean to the world today?

III. THE COMMAND OF CHRIST
(Matthew 28:16-20)

A. The Meeting (vv. 16, 17)

(Matthew 28:16, 17 is not included in the printed text.)

The message to the disciples was to meet Jesus in Galilee. This was His home province and the scene of most of His work and that of the disciples also. The place was probably some retreat among the hills with which the disciples were so familiar as to need no more definite directions. Some believe it was the hill where the Sermon on the Mount was delivered. Some have suggested that verse 16 includes the meeting mentioned by Paul (1 Corinthians 15:6) at which Christ was seen by "above five hundred brethren at once." This is not out of the question, for Galilee was where most of the followers of Christ lived and where those who attended would be safest from any interference or attack.

Matthew, being among those who revered Jesus as the Son of God, states that when they saw Jesus they worshiped Him. They had had time to think matters over and realized that the risen Lord could be no one else but the Son of God—God manifest in human form to the world.

Note Matthew's absolute honesty in the words "But some doubted." If he had been writing a false narrative, he would never have included a statement of the doubt of some of the witnesses. These people were not credulous, the easy victims of hallucinations, or self-deceived visionaries. They were intelligent, keen, critical investigators, as well they should have been, since their reputations, their possessions, and even their lives depended on the truth of Christ's actual appearance to them. And 500 is a very large number of eyewitnesses.

B. The Commission (vv. 18-20)

18. And Jesus came and spake unto them, saying, All power is given unto me in heaven and in earth.

19. Go ye therefore, and teach all nations, baptizing them in the name of the Father, and of the Son, and of the Holy Ghost:

20. Teaching them to observe all things whatsoever I have commanded you: and, lo, I am with you alway, even unto the end of the world. Amen.

In these verses we have what is called the Great Commission of our Lord. This has also been called the marching orders of the church. It is an unparalleled incentive to missionary effort. The words "All authority has been given to Me in heaven and on earth" (*NKJV*) give us a staggering assertion that almost takes our breath away. We are familiar with authority in piecemeal fashion—authority over a nation, an institution, a department. But this is authority over all things, seen or unseen. It is the unifying authority for which human life had been waiting.

Christianity is an ever-advancing, forward-pushing, missionary religion. And this is because of Christ's authority; therefore, it could not be so with anything less than infinite power and authority in back of it. It is significant that the first two letters of *gospel* spell *go*. Jesus says, "Because I command you to go forth, I will empower you to go. Because there is no other way to get the gospel to all the world, therefore go."

The Great Commission is not a command to civilize; it is not to educate; it is not to heal; it is not to make converts to any special creed, or to propagate any special dogma. It is to make disciples or Christians of all nations. But it should be said that where the gospel is preached, people become civilized, they become educated, and many are healed.

The command of Christ includes "baptizing them in the name of the Father, and of the Son, and of the Holy Ghost." With the inward reality of discipleship must go the outward rite of baptism. Baptism is to be done in the name of the triune God.

Jesus fearlessly bids His disciples to teach the nations "whatsoever I have commanded you." He reigns in both the moral and the intellectual world. He is certain of the authority of the commission which He gives to teach.

Jesus assured the disciples He would be with them all their days, even unto the consummation of the age. Without this assurance, the disciples could not have faced life or the martyrs have faced death. So it is with us; without it we cannot live, but we dare not die.

Do you think the church takes seriously the promise of Jesus to the disciples? Explain.

REVIEW QUESTIONS

1. Identify some of the events that occurred in connection with the resurrection of Christ.

2. What was the purpose of the words spoken by the angel to the friends of Christ at the tomb?

3. What was the message to the first people in the world who were confronted with the empty tomb?

4. What message did Jesus send to His disciples?

5. What is involved in the Great Commission?

SENTENCE SERMONS

JESUS CHRIST rose from the dead and lives forever.

—**Selected**

CHRIST'S RESURRECTION is the foundation stone of the believer's new life.

—**Ralph W. Harris**

THE STONE over Christ's grave was rolled away from the door, not to permit Christ to come out, but to enable the disciples to go in.

—*Draper's Book of Quotations for the Christian World*

THE RESURRECTION is a true sunrising, the inbursting of a cloudless sky on all the righteous dead.

—**Horace Bushnell**

EVANGELISM APPLICATION

THE RESURRECTED CHRIST GIVES ETERNAL LIFE TO ALL WHO BELIEVE IN HIM.

Because we have a living Savior, we can come to Him for help. He is not just a Savior to take us to heaven, but He is also One who can help us down here. He came that we might enjoy life more abundantly. He has walked the way through life, and He can help us. He knows what temptation, sorrow, and heartbreak mean, and He can assist us when these come our way. If we remember Him in our time of need, He will help us.

ILLUMINATING THE LESSON

The Resurrection, like the virgin birth of Jesus Christ, is questioned as a fact. Either He did arise, or He did not arise. Whatever the doubters and skeptics may say, the apostles and the early church taught and believed that He arose from the dead. Without the Resurrection one cannot explain the existence of the church at all. The church would not have lasted one week if the truth of the Resurrection had not revitalized the disciples. Immediately after the experience of Calvary, they were about to separate; their fellowship was disintegrating. The birth and growth of the church is one tremendous evidence of the resurrection of Jesus Christ.

DAILY BIBLE READINGS

M. Resurrection Song.
   Psalm 16:1-11
T. Resurrection Promise.
   Daniel 12:1-3
W. Resurrection Message.
   Romans 1:1-6
T. Resurrection Life.
   Romans 6:1-11
F. Resurrection Hope.
   1 Corinthians 15:1-11
S. Resurrection Power.
   Ephesians 2:1-10

People Who Showed Gratitude

Study Text: Mark 14:1-9; Luke 17:11-19; Colossians 3:15-17; 1 Thessalonians 5:18

Objective: To recognize Jesus for who He is and express gratitude for His many blessings.

Golden Text: "Whatsoever ye do in word or deed, do all in the name of the Lord Jesus, giving thanks to God and the Father by him" (Colossians 3:17).

Central Truth: A Christian shows a grateful heart by not taking for granted the blessings of God.

Evangelism Emphasis: Believers demonstrate their gratitude for salvation by witnessing to the lost.

PRINTED TEXT

Luke 17:11. And it came to pass, as he went to Jerusalem, that he passed through the midst of Samaria and Galilee.

12. And as he entered into a certain village, there met him ten men that were lepers, which stood afar off:

13. And they lifted up their voices, and said, Jesus, Master, have mercy on us.

14. And when he saw them, he said unto them, Go shew yourselves unto the priests. And it came to pass, that, as they went, they were cleansed.

15. And one of them, when he saw that he was healed, turned back, and with a loud voice glorified God,

16. And fell down on his face at his feet, giving him thanks: and he was a Samaritan.

17. And Jesus answering said, Were there not ten cleansed? but where are the nine?

18. There are not found that returned to give glory to God, save this stranger.

Mark 14:6. And Jesus said, Let her alone; why trouble ye her? she hath wrought a good work on me.

7. For ye have the poor with you always, and whensoever ye will ye may do them good: but me ye have not always.

8. She hath done what she could: she is come aforehand to anoint my body to the burying.

9. Verily I say unto you, Wheresoever this gospel shall be preached throughout the whole world, this also that she hath done shall be spoken of for a memorial of her.

Colossians 3:17. And whatsoever ye do in word or deed, do all in the name of the Lord Jesus, giving thanks to God and the Father by him.

1 Thessalonians 5:18. In every thing give thanks: for this is the will of God in Christ Jesus concerning you.

DICTIONARY

Samaria (sah-MEHR-ih-ah)—Luke 17:11—A country north of Jerusalem occupied by people only partly Jewish, and hated by orthodox Jews.

Galilee (GAL-i-lee)—Luke 17:11—The country between the Jordan River and the Mediterranean Sea.

LESSON OUTLINE

LESSON EXPOSITION

INTRODUCTION

The heart of the redeemed always has room for gratitude. While the spirit of gratitude is always timely, there are special occasions to provide us opportunities to express our gratitude in adoration to God.

The word *gratitude* means to show thanks or to be thankful. The word *thankful* is, in its derivation, allied with the Anglo-Saxon word *thinkful.* To think is to thank. Pathetic indeed are the words of Jesus to the single leper who returned to say thanks for healing him of his leprosy. He asked, "But where are the nine?" How deeply significant that the one who did return was a Samaritan—a religious outcast, a foreigner. There is no more deadly attitude than that which takes for granted life's unearned blessings. In prophetic sadness Isaiah exclaimed: "The ox knoweth his owner, and the ass his master's crib: but Israel doth not know, my people doth not consider" (1:3). Shakespeare wrote: "Ingratitude, thou marble-hearted fiend."

As Christians we may well be thankful for the day in which we live. True, we have our problems, our injustices, inequalities, prejudices, and innumerable crimes of sordid nature—but how great is our opportunity! Just what other day would you have chosen to live in? Read the Epistles of the New Testament and sense the depth of problems existing in those days. Nothing but the grace and sovereignty of God, coupled with the profound sense of His providence, could possibly have held those congregations together.

In spite of any problems we may have and because of all the blessings we enjoy from the hands of God, let us join with the healed leper and the psalmist and say: "I will offer to thee the sacrifice of thanksgiving, and will call upon the name of the Lord" (Psalm 116:17).

I. FAILURE TO GIVE THANKS (Luke 17:11-19)

A. The Cry for Mercy (vv. 11-13)

11. And it came to pass, as he

went to Jerusalem, that he passed through the midst of Samaria and Galilee.

12. And as he entered into a certain village, there met him ten men that were lepers, which stood afar off:

13. And they lifted up their voices, and said, Jesus, Master, have mercy on us.

In verse 12 the account of the healing of the lepers is original with Luke. He also recorded the healing of a leper early in the ministry of Jesus (5:12-14).

History records that in the ancient world, leprosy was the most terrible of all diseases. It is reported that no other disease reduced a human being for so many years to such a hideous wreck. *PROGRESSIVE*

From ancient writers we learn that it might begin with little nodules which become ulcerated. The ulcers develop a foul discharge; the eyebrows fall out; the eyes become staring; the vocal cords become ulcerated, causing the voice to become hoarse and the breath to wheeze. The hands and feet always ulcerate. Slowly the sufferer becomes a mass of ulcerated growths. The average course of this type of leprosy is nine years, and it ends in mental decay, coma, and ultimate death.

Another type of leprosy might begin with the loss of all sensation in some parts of the body—the nerve trunks are affected, the muscles waste away, and the tendons contract until the hands are like claws. This is followed by ulceration of the hands and feet. Then comes the progressive loss of fingers and toes, until in the end a whole hand or a whole foot may drop off. The duration of this type

of leprosy is from 20 to 30 years. It is a kind of terrible progressive death in which a person dies by inches.

There was good reason for Luke to state that the men "stood afar off." The historian Josephus tells us that lepers in Bible times were treated as if they were, in effect, dead men. When leprosy was diagnosed, the leper was immediately banished from human society. This banishment was absolute and complete. The leper had to go with torn clothes, disheveled hair, with a covering upon his upper lip; and wherever he went, he had to cry, "Unclean, unclean!"

During the time of Jesus, the leper was barred from Jerusalem and from all walled towns. In the synagogue there was provided for him a little isolated chamber, 10 feet high and 6 feet wide, which was called the *Mechitsah*.

The Law listed 61 different contacts which could defile a man, and the defilement caused by contact with a leper was listed second only to the defilement caused by contact with a dead body.

If the wind were blowing toward a person from where a leper was, the leper must stand at least 150 feet away. It is said that one rabbi would not even eat an egg that was bought in a street where a leper had passed by. History records no other disease which so separated a man from his fellowmen as leprosy did.

The word translated "Master" (v. 13) is one that only Luke uses when the intimate circle of disciples (8:24), especially Peter (5:5; 9:33) and John 9:49) refer to Jesus. According to Lonsdale Ragg, "It seems to be a loose equivalent for *Rabbi*, which Luke never uses, with something more of the idea of 'one who has a right to command'" (*Westminster Commentary*).

Their prayer for mercy seems to indicate, on their part, some faith in Christ and His power to heal.

B. The Cleansing (v. 14)

14. And when he saw them, he said unto them, Go shew yourselves unto the priests. And it came to pass, that, as they went, they were cleansed.

According to the Law, the priest was the person to examine the leper and see whether he was suffering from true leprosy. He was given the authority to pronounce him clean if he was clean. The Jews would go to the priests in Jerusalem for this examination or, perhaps, to the priests near their own homes. A Samaritan would go to a priest of the temple on Mount Gerizim.

In a previous account of cleansing a leper, Christ first healed the leper of his disease and then sent him to a priest. Here He commanded the lepers to go to the priest, and healed them afterward. Here the healing followed obedience to His command. It was their faith that brought their healing.

C. The Response (vv. 15-19)

(Luke 17:19 is not included in the printed text.)

15. And one of them, when he saw that he was healed, turned back, and with a loud voice glorified God,

16. And fell down on his face at his feet, giving him thanks: and he was a Samaritan.

17. And Jesus answering said, Were there not ten cleansed? but where are the nine?

18. There are not found that returned to give glory to God, save this stranger.

To glorify God means to acknowledge His power, love, grace, and holiness. Here was a man experiencing joy because he knew he was no longer a leper.

G.H. Knight writes: "The nine had thought only of His wonderful power. The poor, despised Samaritan thought also of His deep compassionate love, a love that pitted and healed even him, and it is love alone that ever leads to thankfulness. If there is one thing more than another that must make me return to give glory to God, it is the remembrance of what a loathsome, hopeless leper I was before He healed me. This purging from my old sins, I must never forget. It will keep me humble, but it will keep me praising Him too. All that I have ever done is worthy of sorrow and shame; but what God has done for me is worthy of an endless song" (*The Master's Questions to His Disciples*).

Luke is very direct in identifying the man of gratitude as a Samaritan. Alfred Plummer observes: "It is strange to find this Samaritan mingling with the other Jews, for 'the Jews have no dealings with the Samaritans' (John 4:9). Apparently, their dreadful malady had broken down the barrier between them" (*A Critical and Exegetical Commentary on the Gospel According to Saint Luke*).

Christ was actually hurt by the ingratitude of the nine (vv. 17, 18). It seems that they had already concluded that, as Jews, sons of Abraham, they were entitled to every favor God could possibly bestow upon them, while the

Samaritan realized that his cleansing had been completely an act of grace. Yet, he was a stranger to the covenants and promises that belonged to the Jews.

In verse 19 Jesus told the Samaritan, "Arise, and go thy way: thy faith hath made thee whole." The Lord was here bestowing upon the cleansed Samaritan an added blessing.

How can gratitude be most effectively expressed?

II. GRATITUDE EXPRESSED
   (Mark 14:1-9)

A. The Plot (vv. 1, 2)

(Mark 14:1, 2 is not included in the printed text.)

The triumphal entry of Christ had convinced the members of the Sanhedrin that their influence would end if they did not take steps to put Him out of the way. They held a meeting soon after Jesus' arrival and determined to put Him to death, but decided to arrest Him quietly for fear of causing a riot among the common people. A riot could cause intervention by the Romans, who loved to enforce the law.

It was also only two days before the Passover, the feast commemorating the escape of the Israelites from Egyptian bondage. This feast always aroused hopes in the Jews of deliverance from the hated Roman bondage. Anticipating trouble at that time, with so many hundreds of thousands of Jews in Jerusalem from all parts of the world, Pontius Pilate, the Roman governor, had come to his capital, Caesarea, and kept a double garrison in the tower of Antonia next to the Temple area. For these reasons, although Jesus taught openly day by day in the Temple, the Jewish leaders did not dare attempt to arrest Him there.

B. The Grateful Love (vv. 3-9)

(Mark 14:3-5 is not included in the printed text.)

6. And Jesus said, Let her alone; why trouble ye her? she hath wrought a good work on me.

7. For ye have the poor with you always, and whensoever ye will ye may do them good: but me ye have not always.

8. She hath done what she could: she is come aforehand to anoint my body to the burying.

9. Verily I say unto you, Wheresoever this gospel shall be preached throughout the whole world, this also that she hath done shall be spoken of for a memorial of her. *DEAD But he ALIVE*

Jesus and His disciples were in Bethany, where they were gladly received by Mary, Martha, and Lazarus whom Jesus had recently raised from the dead. It seems that the house of these friends was the headquarters for Jesus when He was in this area. Since Bethany was about two miles from Jerusalem, Jesus would be relatively safe from His enemies.

On this occasion Jesus was visiting in the home of Simon the leper. It is believed that he had been a leper but had been healed by Christ. Some believe Simon was the husband of Martha because John tells us she had charge of the household arrangements for the meal. Others think he was Mary's husband. Some believe him to have been the brother of Mary, Martha, and Lazarus.

MONEY HIS GOD

Mark records that as Jesus sat at the meal, a woman came in (v. 3). Mark does not give her name, and neither does Matthew (26:6-13); but John (12:3) tells us it was Mary. It should be remembered that the active attempt to kill Jesus began with the raising of Lazarus from the dead (John 11:53). Therefore, it would have been dangerous for any of the Bethany family to be mentioned at this time. So John alone, writing after the fall of Jerusalem and probably after the deaths of Lazarus and his sisters, could name them in his Gospel and give an account of the resurrection miracle.

At the feast Mary performed a deed which, as Christ prophesied, has echoed down through the ages to her praise. She brought with her "an alabaster box of ointment of spikenard." This was probably the most precious possession she had. It was an oily, fragrant perfume that the ancients were fond of using. John 12:3 says there was "a pound" of it—a Roman pound of 12 ounces. Spikenard was made of a plant from India. It was so expensive that only the rich could afford it. Mary had a pound of it, which was more than 300 denarii (John 12:5, NKJV). The value of it can be seen when it is remembered that the denarius was the day's wage for an ordinary laborer.

Breaking off the narrow neck of the flask, Mary came to Jesus as He lay stretched out on the low couch at the table, and poured out all the perfume, starting with His head. John tells us that she even anointed the feet of Jesus, tenderly wiping them with her long, flowing hair (12:3).

Mary's deed of love was criticized by some of those attending the feast. Judas Iscariot took the lead in this criticism. He strenuously objected to the "waste" of the ointment, hypocritically reminding those present that the spikenard, if sold, would have provided money to feed the poor (see John 12:4-6). In commenting on the attitude of Judas, Dinsdale T. Young writes: "Judas' notion of 'waste' was crude and materialistic in the extreme. Love is never 'waste.' Generosity is never 'waste.' Sacrifice is never 'waste.' No poetic thought or deed is ever 'waste'" (*Ephesians*).

Frederick Lynch has written that Mary was "purchasing a joy for the lonely Jesus, and an eternal satisfaction for herself, that were worth all the spikenard in Palestine" (*The Enlargement of Life*).

The word translated "good" (Mark 14:6) is the strongest adjective of admiration the Greek language contains. It is a word which carried the idea of virtue clothed in beauty. William Wright suggests we could understand the whole scene better if instead of "She hath wrought a good work" we read, "She hath done a superb, a magnificent, a heroic deed" (*The Heart of the Master*).

Jesus did not mean that poverty was a necessary condition of some people and that to expect it to be completely eliminated would be foolish. Those who interpret Christ's words this way may sound very heartless. Jesus was simply stating a fact regarding Palestine and many other countries of that time. Many people experienced wretched poverty in Palestine then as do many people today in countries around the world. The implication of the words of Jesus is that Judas, and others who criticized

Mary's action, would do well to do what they could to improve the condition of the poor.

The words "But me ye have not always" (v. 7) echo the prophecies of His rapidly approaching death which Christ had been making during the preceding weeks.

What a statement from the lips of the King of kings! Material possessions are often given from the wrong motives. But it is the person who loves and honors Jesus himself who really "does good works."

No stronger statement of commendation could have possibly been used than this: "She hath done what she could" (v. 8). She did her best. When we do our best, angels can't do any better.

In verse 9, Christ affirmed the greatness of Mary's gift. The message resulting from Mary's action is that all goodness and kindness are immortal in results, that every real sacrifice bears fruit throughout the years, and that no accurate history can ever be written without including the "widow's mite" and the "cup of cold water."

Compare the criticism by Judas of Mary's action with how the church is criticized today.

III. GIVE THANKS TO GOD
(Colossians 3:15-17;
1 Thessalonians 5:18)

A. When to Give Thanks
(Colossians 3:15-17)

(Colossians 3:15, 16 is not included in the printed text.)

17. And whatsoever ye do in word or deed, do all in the name of the Lord Jesus, giving thanks to God and the Father by him.

In Colossians 3:12, 13, Paul gives a list of Christian graces that

the follower of Jesus Christ must exemplify: A Christian must have a heart of compassion; he must understand the sufferings of others. He must show kindness to his fellowman. This must be done in a spirit of humility and gentleness. And this will require patience, forebearance, and forgiveness. These characteristics are not automatic for the Christian. He must allow the Holy Spirit to develop them in his heart.

Paul indicates that the crowning characteristic of the Christian is the perfect bond of love (v. 14). This is the binding power which holds Christianity together in unbreakable fellowship.

When these characteristics prevail in the life of the Christian, then the peace of God will be the decision maker, or umpire, in his heart. When there is peace in the heart, there will be praise on the lips: "And be ye thankful" (v. 15).

B. Why Give Thanks
(1 Thessalonians 5:18)

18. In every thing give thanks: for this is the will of God in Christ Jesus concerning you.

There are untold mysteries in the human adventure. Some walk through the long labyrinth of human sorrow. The good do suffer. There is no easy or final answer for us in the universal problem of pain. It is only as we go to the very heart of suffering and see God's own Son on His cross and hear His cry, "My God, my God, why hast thou forsaken me?" that we realize how deeply we can be shaken. Here at the Cross we see how far God was willing to go on our behalf, and it is also here that we witness the triumph of faith and love. "The Light shines on in the darkness, for the darkness has never overpowered it" (John 1:5, *Amp.*). Thank God that we do not need to stumble through a meaningless universe; but rather, in the hour of our greatest need, as we reach through the maze of tears, a hand clasps ours and, behold . . . it has a scar! Words then are unnecessary. "Nevertheless the foundation of God standeth sure" (2 Timothy 2:19).

REVIEW QUESTIONS

1. How were lepers treated during the time of Jesus?

2. How did Jesus react to the cry of the 10 lepers?

3. How did the one leper show his gratitude to Jesus?

4. Why did Judas and others object to Mary's act of love?

5. Why is it the will of God for the Christian to give thanks to God?

SENTENCE SERMONS

A CHRISTIAN shows a grateful heart by not taking for granted the blessings of God.

—Selected

BELIEVERS demonstrate their gratitude for salvation by witnessing to the lost.

—Selected

GRATITUDE IS not only the memory but the homage of the heart—rendered to God for His goodness.

—Nathaniel Parker Willis

GRATITUDE IS the heart's memory.

—*The Encyclopedia of Religious Quotations*

EVANGELISM APPLICATION

BELIEVERS DEMONSTRATE THEIR GRATITUDE FOR SALVATION BY WITNESSING TO THE LOST.

Evangelism is at the heart of the victorious life. The best defense is offense. There is an organization called Alcoholics Anonymous. One of the secrets of their successful reclamation of many drunkards is that they immediately undertake to rescue someone else from alcoholism. The best way to be victorious over sin is to go to the rescue of another sinner.

ILLUMINATING THE LESSON

Works do not save, but they provide evidence of salvation. If there is a new work of grace, there must be an outward manifestation. This is emphasized throughout the New Testament. "If any man be in Christ, he is a new creature: old things are passed away; behold, all things are become new" (2 Corinthians 5:17). Has there been a change? Have old things passed away and all things become new? Is there a difference? If so, that will prove to others the genuineness of my experience. If I have really been saved, I will bear fruit. My life will be different.**—Oswald J. Smith, *The Consuming Fire***

DAILY BIBLE READINGS

M. Song of Gratitude.
Exodus 15:1-11

T. Remember God's Benefits.
Psalm 77:11-14

W. Express Gratitude.
Psalm 105:1-7

T. Refusal to Give Thanks.
Romans 1:18-22

F. Gratitude for Others.
Philippians 1:2-11

S. Pray With Gratitude.
Philippians 4:4-9

Simon Peter, a Failure Restored

Study Text: Luke 22:31-34, 54-62; John 21:15-22

Objective: To see that failure is not final and believe that Christ restores those who fail.

Time: The Gospel According to Luke was written between A.D. 58 and A.D. 70. The Gospel According to John was probably written between A.D. 85 and A.D. 96.

Place: The Gospel According to Luke was probably written at Caesarea or Rome. The Gospel According to John was probably written at Ephesus.

Golden Text: "If any man sin, we have an advocate with the Father, Jesus Christ the righteous" (1 John 2:1).

Central Truth: Christ restores fallen believers who turn to Him.

Evangelism Emphasis: Christ reconciles sinners and restores fallen believers who turn to Him.

PRINTED TEXT

Luke 22:33. And he said unto him, Lord, I am ready to go with thee, both into prison, and to death.

34. And he said, I tell thee, Peter, the cock shall not crow this day, before that thou shalt thrice deny that thou knowest me.

56. But a certain maid beheld him as he sat by the fire, and earnestly looked upon him, and said, This man was also with him.

57. And he denied him, saying, Woman, I know him not.

58. And after a little while another saw him, and said, Thou art also of them. And Peter said, Man, I am not.

59. And about the space of one hour after another confidently affirmed, saying, Of a truth this fellow also was with him: for he is a Galilaean.

60. And Peter said, Man, I know not what thou sayest. And immediately, while he yet spake, the cock crew.

61. And the Lord turned, and looked upon Peter. And Peter remembered the word of the Lord, how he had said unto him, Before the cock crow, thou shalt deny me thrice.

62. And Peter went out, and wept bitterly.

John 21:15. So when they had dined, Jesus saith to Simon Peter, Simon, son of Jonas, lovest thou me more than these? He saith unto him, Yea, Lord; thou knowest that I love thee. He saith unto him, Feed my lambs.

16. He saith to him again the second time, Simon, son of Jonas, lovest thou me? He saith unto him, Yea, Lord; thou knowest that

I love thee. He saith unto him, Feed my sheep.

17. He saith unto him the third time, Simon, son of Jonas, lovest thou me? Peter was grieved because he said unto him the third time, Lovest thou me? And he said unto him, Lord, thou knowest all things; thou knowest that I love thee. Jesus saith unto him, Feed my sheep.

LESSON OUTLINE

I. PRESUMPTUOUS SELF-CONFIDENCE
   A. The Temptation
   B. The Intercession
   C. The Presumption
   D. The Exhortation

II. BITTER FAILURE
   A. Distant Discipleship
   B. Real Denials
   C. Real Repentance

III. RESTORED BY CHRIST
   A. Probing Love
   B. Foretelling the Future
   C. Checking Curiosity

LESSON EXPOSITION

INTRODUCTION

All the cards were stacked in his favor. He was intelligent, talented, well-adjusted. He was without physical and moral defects. He had a perfect heredity. His marriage was made in heaven. He lived in a perfect environment. He began life with every advantage desirable. Yet, he is known as the worst failure in the history of humanity. His name is Adam.

Because Adam failed—sinned, if you will—every human being born since his day is capable of indescribable evil. The potential for every sin lies within each human being. But the good news is that God has the remedy for failure if we will only accept it.

Erwin W. Lutzer writes: "God is well aware of the pitfalls along our path. Sin did not take Him by surprise. Long before Adam and Eve were created, God planned to turn our failure into success. With a detailed knowledge of all the facts, God provided a remedy that would not fail—if it was seriously applied" (*Failure: The Backdoor to Success*).

God is our Maker, not only as our Creator but the molder of our lives and the divine mender of our errors, mistakes, failures, and even our sins. The rough ax eventually gets into His hand as a graving tool. God does not create the afflictions and adversities that men encounter. Ignorance, error, and sin are partly responsible. The flywheels of natural law—which produce our power, blessings, and our general good—are sure to do some damage. But even difficult circumstances can be turned to good. To illustrate, a basket is not a transport for passengers, but Paul used it as an elevator "going down" from the Damascus wall and escaped with his life. A roof is a shelter, but the friends of the paralytic made a door of it, and through the opening, the sick man was healed. The cross is an instrument of punishment and shame, but by a divine usage it was turned into an emblem of everlasting glory and a key to the kingdom of God.

The ax that rough-hewed Peter, bruised and bled him, was ever in the eye of the nearby God who had dreamed his dream in him; and when the tempters cast it aside, quite satisfied they had hacked the design to pieces, the Divine Sculptor took it in His hand and fashioned for Himself a first-rate man who would provide great leadership in the early church.

I. PRESUMPTUOUS SELF-CONFIDENCE (Luke 22:31-34)

A. The Temptation (v. 31)

(Luke 22:31 is not included in the printed text.)

Jesus verified the personality, activity, and power of the devil in verse 31 when He said, "Simon, Simon, behold, Satan hath desired to have you, that he may sift you as wheat." This is the same devil who brought sin into the world by tempting Eve. He is the same devil described in the Book of Job as "going to and fro in the earth, and . . . walking up and down in it" (1:7; 2:2). This is he whom Jesus called "the prince of this world" (John 12:31; 14:30; 16:11), a "murderer" and a "liar" (8:44). This is the same devil whom Peter compared to "a roaring lion . . . seeking whom he may devour" (1 Peter 5:8). This is he whom John spoke of as "the accuser of the brethren" (see Revelation 12:10). He is the same devil who is constantly working evil in the church, stealing the seed of the Word from the hearts of hearers, sowing tares amid the wheat, stirring up strife, suggesting false doctrine, and fomenting divisions.

Someone has said that the world is a snare to the believer. The flesh is a burden and a clog. But there is no enemy so dangerous as that restless, invisible, experienced enemy, the devil. He wanted Peter, and he wants every believer in Christ.

The repetition of Simon's name implies the importance of the statement of Jesus concerning the devil. It also shows the deep concern of Jesus on behalf of Simon's soul. It is like the statement to Martha, when she was "careful and troubled about many things" (Luke 10:41), and to Saul, when he was persecuting disciples (Acts 9:4).

Believers must be constantly on guard against the devices of the devil. The Enemy who overthrew David and Peter, and assaulted Christ himself, is not an enemy to take lightly. He is very subtle. He has studied the human heart for thousands of years. He can approach us disguised as an "angel of light" (2 Corinthians 11:14). We must watch and pray and put on the whole armor of God. But we have the blessed promise that if we resist him he will flee from us (James 4:7). We also have the assurance that when the Lord comes, He will bruise Satan under our feet and bind him in chains (Romans 16:20).

B. The Intercession (v. 32)

(Luke 22:32 is not included in the printed text.)

The great secret of the believer's perseverance in the faith is found in verse 32. Jesus told Peter, "I have prayed for thee, that thy faith fail not." It was because of Christ's intercession that Peter did not fail utterly and entirely.

In dealing with Jesus' statement to Peter in Luke 22:32, J.C. Ryle writes: "The continued existence of grace in a believer's heart is a great standing miracle. His enemies are so mighty, and his strength is so small, the world is so full of snares, and his heart is so weak, that it seems at first sight impossible for him to reach heaven. The passage before us explains his safety. He has a mighty Friend at the right hand of God, who ever lives to make intercession for him. There is a watchful Advocate, who is daily pleading for him, seeing all his necessities, and obtaining daily supplies of mercy and grace for his soul. His grace never altogether dies, because Christ always lives to intercede (Hebrews 7:25)" (*Expository Thoughts on the Gospels*).

C. The Presumption (v. 33)

33. And he said unto him, Lord, I am ready to go with thee, both into prison, and to death.

Peter's words were the statement of a self-confident, inexperienced disciple who had not yet discovered the weakness of his own faith and the deceitfulness of his own heart. People do not know what they will really do until the time of temptation actually comes.

Peter's overconfidence led to his failure in the hour of temptation. To be sure, he did emphasize "with thee," but he was too certain of his own ability. Thus when Peter thought he could walk on the waves as Christ did, he said, with seeming humility, "Lord, if it be thou, bid me come unto thee on the water"; but his faith was incomplete, and after a few steps he sank into the sea (see Matthew 14:28-31). Thus Peter, during the first part of his life, was a "waveman," up and down.

D. The Exhortation (v. 34)

34. And he said, I tell thee, Peter, the cock shall not crow this day, before that thou shalt thrice deny that thou knowest me.

This is the only place in which Jesus addressed Peter by his name, the name which signified "stone." It was meant to remind him how weak even the strongest disciples can be.

The prediction of Jesus that Peter would deny Him is striking evidence of His foreknowledge. Matthew and Mark also record Peter's indignant denial that he could do such a dreadful thing, a denial in which all the other disciples joined; yet in a short while, at Christ's arrest, they all forsook Him and fled.

James Hastings writes: "There was in Peter one great defect—a large amount of self-confidence, which made him quick at speaking and acting; and self-confidence in the New Testament is always treated in one way, as that which shuts out confidence in God. It is the enemy of faith. Faith is insight, and self-confidence is a blinding influence" (*Great Texts of the Bible*).

What contributes to overconfidence as exhibited by Peter?

II. BITTER FAILURE
(Luke 22:54-62)

A. Distant Discipleship (v. 54)

(Luke 22:54 is not included in the printed text.)

Even though Peter followed "afar off," much courage was required under the circumstances. John was with Jesus and as an acquaintance of the high priest had no difficulty in obtaining entrance with the Savior and the soldiers; Peter, however, was forbidden entrance until John spoke to the portress and brought him in. John, following his usual custom, does not name himself in his account, but calls himself merely "another disciple" (John 18:15, 16).

B. Real Denials (vv. 55-60)

(Luke 22:55 is not included in the printed text.)

56. But a certain maid beheld him as he sat by the fire, and earnestly looked upon him, and said, This man was also with him.

57. And he denied him, saying, Woman, I know him not.

58. And after a little while another saw him, and said, Thou art also of them. And Peter said, Man, I am not.

59. And about the space of one hour after another confidently affirmed, saying, Of a truth this fellow also was with him: for he is a Galilaean.

60. And Peter said, Man, I know not what thou sayest. And immediately, while he yet spake, the cock crew.

Peter's denial of Jesus is one of the most shameful events recorded in the New Testament. It is perhaps one of the most natural also. Wilbur M. Smith says it is shameful for three reasons: "In the first place, everything that Peter was and everything that Peter had came from his fellowship with Jesus; his fullness of life, his knowledge, his change of character, his position among the disciples, all the promises that he had received, were entirely of grace. What he was, the Lord had made him, from a blustering, irresponsible fisherman in Galilee. In the second place, the Lord Jesus was, at this time, going through the greatest crisis of His life. If ever friendship is to be truly revealed, it should be when our friends are in danger or suffering; Peter forsook the Lord in the very hour when he should have been faithful to Him. In the third place, Peter actually repudiated his relationship to the only holy and sinless man the world has ever seen; he thought more of his own preservation than he did of the honor of his Lord; and with his denial, which was a lie, blasphemy and cursing kept company. Thus did the man who boasted most of his own strength and courage, fall into the deepest sin of all the apostles, except Judas" (*Select Notes*).

C. Real Repentance (vv. 61, 62)

61. And the Lord turned, and looked upon Peter. And Peter remembered the word of the Lord, how he had said unto him, Before the cock crow, thou shalt deny me thrice.

62. And Peter went out, and wept bitterly.

Someone has said there is one exquisite touch in the story of Peter's denial of Jesus. If we were left to ourselves, our sins would make everything black and hopeless, but whenever Jesus enters, a ray of light penetrates. It is He alone who can deliver us from the power of darkness; it is He alone who can break our hearts; it is He alone who can give us a new beginning. So it was here. The record reads simply, "The Lord turned, and looked upon Peter." And because of that look, "Peter remembered the word of the Lord...and

[he] went out, and wept bitterly."

James Stalker observes: "Jesus did not speak; for a single syllable of surprise would have betrayed his disciple, nor could he linger, for the soldiers were hurrying him on. But, for a single instant, their eyes met, and soul looked into soul. The look of Jesus was a tailsman dissolving the spell in which Peter was held. The look of Jesus brought him to himself. The look of Jesus was the mirror in which Peter saw himself. He saw what Christ thought of him. The past came rushing back, but there was more than this in the look of Christ. It was a rescuing look. Had it been an angry look he saw on Christ's face when their eyes met, Peter might have rushed to the precipice over which Judas plunged himself not many hours afterward. But there was not a spark of anger in the look. There was pain, and there was disappointment, but, deeper than these, there was the Savior's instinct, that instinct which made him reach out and grasp Peter when he was sinking in the sea. In that look of an instant, Peter saw forgiveness and unutterable love. If he saw himself in it, he saw more of the Savior—such a revelation of the heart of Christ as he had never yet known. He saw now what kind of Master he had denied; and it broke his heart. It is this that always breaks the heart. It is not our sin that makes us weep, it is when we see the kind of Savior we have sinned against. The Savior threw into that look such a world of kindness and of love that, in an instant, it lifted the falling disciple from the gulf and set him on the rock, where he ever afterward stood, himself a rock in the constancy of his faith and the vigor of his testimony" (*The Suffering Savior*).

How do Christians deny their Lord?

III. RESTORED BY CHRIST
      (John 21:15-22)

A. Probing Love (vv. 15-17)

15. So when they had dined, Jesus saith to Simon Peter, Simon, son of Jonas, lovest thou me more than these? He saith unto him, Yea, Lord; thou knowest that I love thee. He saith unto him, Feed my lambs.

16. He saith to him again the second time, Simon, son of Jonas, lovest thou me? He saith unto him, Yea, Lord; thou knowest that I love thee. He saith unto him, Feed my sheep.

17. He saith unto him the third time, Simon, son of Jonas, lovest thou me? Peter was grieved because he said unto him the third time, Lovest thou me? And he said unto him, Lord, thou knowest all things; thou knowest that I love thee. Jesus saith unto him, Feed my sheep.

"Simon, son of Jonas, lovest thou me?" (v. 15). This question by the Lord Jesus was aimed at probing Peter's love. Jesus' use of the old name Simon is very suggestive. It does not imply that Peter had forfeited the right to the new name, but it perhaps was a gentle reminder of the weakness that had led to the denial. Peter had boasted that he would, if need arose, die for his Lord; and yet he had not been able, for Christ's sake, to endure the questioning of a serving maid. He had boasted that he at least would not deny Jesus, even though all the other disciples should deny Him. Jesus asked him this question to see whether he had learned humility from his sad experience. "[Peter] saith unto him, Yea, Lord; thou knowest that I love thee." This entire situation is very beautiful and very true to life. It is plainly John's clear memory of the very words that were uttered. Peter, deeply ashamed of his past, made no more prophecy of the future, made no more comparison of himself with others, did not even dare assert his love for Christ, but humbly threw himself on Christ's knowledge of that love.

Peter used another word for *love* than the one used by the Master. Christ had used an exalted word (*agapao*) implying the higher, well-reasoned affection, or godly love. Peter used a warmer word (*phileo*) of lowlier significance—the affection of the emotions rather than the intellect, or brotherly love. That is all he would dare to claim. "[Jesus] saith unto him, Feed my lambs" (v. 15). Here is Peter's new commission. He had been called at the first to be a fisher of men; now he was called to be a shepherd of lambs. He was given lowly work to do—to care for the young while others gathered the great flock, led it to green pastures, and defended off the wolves and the robbers. Undoubtedly Peter felt that this was more than he deserved.

In verses 16 and 17, Christ no longer inserted the phrase "more than these," the humiliating reminder of Peter's boast: "Although all shall be offended, yet will not I" (Mark 14:29). Nevertheless, the disciple had not yet learned his lesson, so Jesus asked him again.

D.L. Moody used to say that the Lord spent 40 years in teaching Moses to be something, another 40 years in teaching him to be nothing, and still another 40 years in showing the world what God could do with a man who had learned these two great lessons. Jesus dealt with Peter in much the same way. He first taught him by the grace of God to be something and then to be nothing, and after this he was ready for the Holy Spirit and Pentecost. "[Peter] saith unto him, Yea, Lord; thou knowest that I love thee." Peter had said it all before, and did not even venture to add a word for fear that it might be the wrong word. The second time Jesus "saith unto him, Feed my sheep" (v. 16). The Greek uses another word for *feed*, implying not only feeding the sheep but also guiding and protecting them. Peter had won promotion as to his task, and also as to the objects of his work—it was *sheep* now and no longer *lambs*. Jesus Christ was eager to promote His disciples as fast as they could take promotion.

The third time (v. 17) Christ used Peter's own word for *love*—the lowlier, the more familiar word—and questioned even that degree of love in His disciple. It was a searching test of Peter's humility. Peter was grieved this time, and it might be significant that he was only grieved and not angry. This shows progress on the part of Peter.

Peter was summoned from fishing to shepherding. This was a strange new calling for a rough old Galilean. It required a struggle to leave self and serve others, to forget the nets and to become a shepherd.

Why do you think Christ asked Peter three consecutive times whether or not he loved Him?

B. Foretelling the Future
   (vv. 18, 19)

(John 21:18, 19 is not included in the printed text.)

Jesus told Peter, "When thou shalt be old, thou shalt stretch forth thy hands, and another shall gird thee, and carry thee whither thou wouldest not." These words were a prediction of the manner of the apostle's death. They were fulfilled later, it is commonly accepted, when Peter was crucified as a martyr for Christ's sake.

C. Checking Curiosity (vv. 20-22)

(John 21:20-22 is not included in the printed text.)

Jesus Christ had a separate experience for each of His followers. Concerning John the Beloved, Peter asked, "Lord, and what shall this man do?" (v. 21). Jesus replied, "If I will that he tarry till I come, what is that to thee?" (v. 22). By these words Jesus emphatically told Peter that he should follow in his own way and leave John's case to Christ. The one was to labor, the other was to wait. There was to be a difference in the future for these two men who had followed Christ side by side. John could not lead the life of Peter. Peter could not fulfill the destiny of John. Tradition tells us that Peter was martyred about A.D. 64. The apostle John lived about 30 years longer than this. What Christ really said to Peter was that he should leave the destiny of other men in His hands and simply continue to do his own work for God.

REVIEW QUESTIONS

1. What solemn warning did Christ give Peter?
2. How did Peter deny his Lord?
3. How was he restored?
4. How did Peter react to Christ's questions concerning his love for Him?
5. What did Peter want to know about John's future?

GOLDEN TEXT HOMILY

"IF ANY MAN SIN, WE HAVE AN ADVOCATE WITH THE FATHER, JESUS CHRIST THE RIGHTEOUS" (1 John 2:1).

If we should sin and grieve our heavenly Father—through ignorance, inexperience, the subtleness of temptation, carelessness, or anything else—we need not continue in sin or despair of receiving forgiveness and being restored to favor. We have an Advocate—the One who died for our offenses, rose again for our justification, and now makes intercession for us. He is the righteous, who "suffered for sins, the just for the unjust, that he might bring us to God" (1 Peter 3:18). Therefore, we have immediate recourse to God through Him.

God is pure, holy, and transcendent. He has revealed His commandments and His will to us through the Holy Scriptures. If we fail to live in accordance with His commandments, we are guilty and subject to punishment. However, if we confess our sin and ask forgiveness, Jesus is there before the throne to plead our case. He knows what we go through because He lived on earth as a man. He knows our weaknesses and frailties. And

He knows our temptations, because He was tempted in all points as we are (Hebrews 4:15). With such an Advocate, we should not remain under the guilt of sin but experience forgiveness and restoration.— **Richard Y. Bershon, Ph.D., Chaplain, State Veterans Home, Hot Springs, South Dakota**

SENTENCE SERMONS

CHRIST RESTORES fallen believers who turn to Him.

—Selected

SELF-CONFIDENCE is a plant of slow growth requiring some pruning.

—H. Bert Ames

A FAILURE IS a person who has blundered but is not able to cash in on the experience.

—Elbert Green Hubbard

CHRIST RECONCILES sinners who turn to Him.

—Selected

EVANGELISM APPLICATION

CHRIST RECONCILES SINNERS AND RESTORES FALLEN BELIEVERS WHO TURN TO HIM.

When the child of God is overtaken, he rises again by true repentance, and by the grace of God amends his life. Let no man flatter himself that he can sin with impunity, just because David committed adultery and because Peter denied his Lord. These men sinned greatly. But they did not continue in sin. They repented greatly. They mourned over their falls. They loathed and abhorred their own wickedness. Well would it be for many, if they would imitate them in their repentance. Too many are acquainted with their fall, but not with their recovery. Like David and Peter, they have sinned, but they have not, like David and Peter, repented. Let us remember that the Savior of Peter still lives. There is mercy, if we would find it. Let us turn to God, and He will turn to us. His compassions fail not.—**J.C. Ryle, *Expository Thoughts on the Gospels***

DAILY BIBLE READINGS

M. Presumption Punished.
   Numbers 14:40-45
T. Acknowledge Sin.
   2 Samuel 12:1-13
W. Promise of Restoration.
   Jeremiah 33:12-16
T. Doubt Removed.
   John 20:24-29
F. A Brother Restored.
   Philemon 8-17
S. Call to Repentance.
   Revelation 3:14-22

Example of Evangelism

Study Text: John 4:1-42

Objective: To examine the pattern of evangelism that Christ demonstrated and seek to lead others to Him.

Time: The Gospel According to John was probably written near the end of the first century between A.D. 85 and A.D. 96.

Place: The Gospel According to John was probably written at Ephesus.

Golden Text: "Lift up your eyes, and look on the fields; for they are white already to harvest" (John 4:35).

Central Truth: Christ's pattern of evangelism is the believer's example for winning the lost.

Evangelism Emphasis: Christ's pattern of evangelism is the believer's example for winning the lost.

PRINTED TEXT

John 4:3. He left Judaea, and departed again into Galilee.

4. And he must needs go through Samaria.

7. There cometh a woman of Samaria to draw water: Jesus saith unto her, Give me to drink.

8. (For his disciples were gone away unto the city to buy meat.)

9. Then saith the woman of Samaria unto him, How is it that thou, being a Jew, askest drink of me, which am a woman of Samaria? for the Jews have no dealings with the Samaritans.

10. Jesus answered and said unto her, If thou knewest the gift of God, and who it is that saith to thee, Give me to drink; thou wouldest have asked of him, and he would have given thee living water.

11. The woman saith unto him, Sir, thou hast nothing to draw with, and the well is deep: from whence then hast thou that living water?

12. Art thou greater than our father Jacob, which gave us the well, and drank thereof himself, and his children, and his cattle?

13. Jesus answered and said unto her, Whosoever drinketh of this water shall thirst again:

14. But whosoever drinketh of the water that I shall give him shall never thirst; but the water that I shall give him shall be in him a well of water springing up into everlasting life.

15. The woman saith unto him, Sir, give me this water, that I thirst not, neither come hither to draw.

27. And upon this came his disciples, and marvelled that he talked with the woman: yet no man said, What seekest thou?

or, Why talkest thou with her?

28. The woman then left her waterpot, and went her way into the city, and saith to the men,

29. Come, see a man, which told me all things that ever I did: is not this the Christ?

30. Then they went out of the city, and came unto him.

DICTIONARY

Judaea (joo-DEE-uh)—John 4:3—The land of the Jews.

Galilee (GAL-i-lee)—John 4:3—The country between the Jordan River and the Mediterranean Sea.

Samaria (sah-MEHR-ih-ah)—John 4:4—A country north of Jerusalem occupied by people only partly Jewish. So the orthodox Jews hated them.

LESSON OUTLINE

I. USE PERSONAL ENCOUNTERS

  A. Back to Galilee

  B. At Jacob's Well

  C. Asking a Favor

II. RECOGNIZE THE NEED

  A. The Obstacle

  B. The Offer

  C. The Questions

  D. The Answer

  E. The Request

III. POINT OTHERS TO CHRIST

  A. The Confession

  B. The Surprise

  C. The Report

  D. The White Harvest

LESSON EXPOSITION

INTRODUCTION

Jesus gave personal evangelism high priority in His ministry. The Gospels record many examples of His ministering personally to individuals. In some cases He dealt only with the spiritual needs of individuals, but in other cases He dealt with both physical and spiritual needs, while in a few situations the physical needs alone received His attention.

G. Campbell Morgan did a study of 50 examples of personal evangelism in the New Testament. He summarized some of the general principles of personal evangelism used by Jesus: "He was keenly conscious of human need. He purposely went among the needy. He used an infinite variety of methods. In His universal recognitions He always approached the human soul the same way; but in methods He never approached two souls in the same way, and He never employed the exact same method twice over. He knew all men individually and universally, and He knew humanity generically. He treated all as spiritual in essence, but as sinning in experience and savable by grace. He always sought to compel men to think" (*The Great Physician*).

In his book, *Taking Men Alive*, Dr. Charles G. Trumbull cites the following principles in the personal work of Jesus: (1) He sought to win men, not to drive them away; (2) He commended the good in men rather than criticizing the evil; (3)

He gave the present interests of men a prominent place; (4) He sought to find points of agreement with those whom He would win; (5) He led men to think most about what they believed, not what they doubted; (6) He refused to offer proof to the insincere, but was always ready to furnish it to those who wished to believe; (7) if the Scriptures were prominent in the interest of the other person, He quoted Scripture; but if some other interest was more prominent, He began with it.

Dr. F.V. McFatridge identifies four characteristics of the personal evangelism of Jesus: (1) His infinite tenderness and compassion for all the victims of sin; (2) His quick and accurate insight into the tangled morass of sinful human nature; (3) His great boldness in making His subjects aware of their true spiritual and moral condition; (4) His ability to help without having to grope for a remedy. He never manifested the least uncertainty or unpreparedness (*The Personal Evangelism of Jesus*).

I. USE PERSONAL ENCOUNTERS (John 4:1-8)

A. Back to Galilee (vv. 1-4)

(John 4:1, 2 is not included in the printed text.)

3. He left Judaea, and departed again into Galilee.

4. And he must needs go through Samaria.

Some Bible scholars say if John the Baptist had not been a true child of God, it would have been easy for him to become jealous of Christ's success and by harsh and critical words to have hindered the opening ministry of Jesus. For Christ spent His first months preaching in Judea, not far from where John was preaching. He instantly became more popular than John, and, though Jesus himself did not baptize, He had at least six disciples who performed that rite. But John had a noble soul. He said of Jesus, "He must increase, but I must decrease" (John 3:30), and he rejoiced in the growing success of Jesus.

The Pharisees in Jerusalem took a completely different attitude toward Jesus. They saw in His popularity danger for themselves and their positions as leaders. They observed how the people received this young prophet of Galilee, with His ideas of spiritual freedom and of inner peace as opposed to merely external religion. They saw their influence becoming less important to the people. They began to show their jealousy in many different ways.

To escape the hostility of the Pharisees, Jesus decided to go northward with His little band of chosen followers, returning to His own Galilee. Most Jews going northward often crossed the Jordan into Perea, and traveled up along the east bank of the river to avoid the insults of the Samaritans. But Jesus was fleeing from persecution in Judea and so probably felt that the Samaritans would be friendlier.

B. At Jacob's Well (vv. 5, 6)

(John 4:5, 6 is not included in the printed text.)

The route chosen by Jesus took Him through the Samaritan village of Sychar. Here was located Jacob's well. Being weary with the long walk, He sent His disciples into Sychar to buy food, while He sat alone on the well curb to rest. The white road, steep and dusty, was one broad glare beneath the sun. Over the well, no doubt, palm trees cast their shadow, and around it the grass was abundant as in an oasis. This would be an ideal spot to rest.

C. Asking a Favor (vv. 7, 8)

7. There cometh a woman of Samaria to draw water: Jesus saith unto her, Give me to drink.

8. (For his disciples were gone away unto the city to buy meat.)

While Jesus sat by the well, a woman of Sychar came to draw water. She came to draw water because this was the ordinary and toilsome duty of women in that period of Jewish history.

The "sixth hour" (v. 6) was approximately 12 o'clock midday. This, of course, was when the heat from the sun was at its greatest. Why she came at this particular time we do not know. As she was a woman of questionable character, she may have come at that unusual time to avoid the slights and sneers that would have assailed her had she come at the same time as the other women customarily came. Jesus knew her evil doings, but He nevertheless entered into conversation with her.

Jesus made a simple request for a drink of water. But in this request there are several things worthy of consideration. This was a gracious act of spiritual aggression toward a sinner. He did not wait for the woman to speak to Him, but He began the conversation. This was also an act of marvelous condescension. He by whom all things were made—the Creator of the fountains, the brooks, the springs, the rivers—

was not ashamed to ask for a drink of water from the hands of one of His sinful creatures. It was an act full of wisdom and tact. He did not immediately attempt to force spiritual ideas on the woman and rebuke her for her sins. He began with a subject that the woman was thinking about at the moment. He asked her for a drink of water. It was an act illustrating His perfect knowledge of the human mind. He asked for a favor and put Himself under an obligation.

The Lord Jesus followed a general rule not to perform miracles in order to supply His own needs. He who could feed five thousand with a few loaves and fishes, when He willed, was satisfied to buy food like any other man. The Creator of all things, though rich, for our sakes became poor. It should teach Christians that they are not meant to be so spiritual that they neglect the normal everyday affairs of life. It should also teach us that we are responsible for using our money to provide for the necessities of life. God could feed Christians as He fed Elijah, by a daily miracle, but He knows it is better for us if we think and work and do the things that we are able to do. There is no real spirituality in being careless or indifferent to our daily needs.

Should Christians attempt to escape the hostility of the world? Why?

II. RECOGNIZE THE NEED

(John 4:9-15)

A. The Obstacle (v. 9)

9. Then saith the woman of Samaria unto him, How is it that

thou, being a Jew, askest drink of me, which am a woman of Samaria? for the Jews have no dealings with the Samaritans.

The woman responded to the request of Jesus by referring to an old quarrel between the Jews and the Samaritans. It dated back to the fall of the northern kingdom, when Sargon carried off into captivity the chief inhabitants and introduced, in their place, idolatrous colonists from Babylonia, Hamath, and Arabia. As a result of this, a mongrel population arose whom the Jews would not allow to join with them in the rebuilding of their Temple. In retaliation, the Samaritans delayed the rebuilding of the walls of Jerusalem. The Samaritans erected their own rival temple on the summit of Mount Gerizim, which, however, was destroyed about 129 B.C. by John Hyrcanus, so that in Christ's day the Samaritans merely worshiped on the site of their former temple.

B. The Offer (v. 10)

10. Jesus answered and said unto her, If thou knewest the gift of God, and who it is that saith to thee, Give me to drink; thou wouldest have asked of him, and he would have given thee living water.

Jesus did not answer the woman's question. He was not, at that moment, interested in the trivial quarrels of Jews and Samaritans. But He told the woman that if conditions were reversed and she were asking water from Him, He would have given it to her quickly and gladly; it would not have been from a well, but it would have been "living water."

"If thou knewest . . . ." The woman of Samaria did not know. She failed, as yet, to realize her opportunity. She was on the edge of the supreme moment in her life, and apparently she could find nothing better to talk about than her ancestors. But Jesus met this attitude by revealing His own personality. "If thou knewest the gift of God, and who it is that is speaking to thee . . . ." The free gift of God is simply God giving, and giving of Himself in Jesus Christ. God spared not His Son, and the Son spared not Himself, to make the gift real to men.

C. The Questions (vv. 11, 12)

11. The woman saith unto him, Sir, thou hast nothing to draw with, and the well is deep: from whence then hast thou that living water?

12. Art thou greater than our father Jacob, which gave us the well, and drank thereof himself, and his children, and his cattle?

"Living water" might mean spring water, or flowing water, as distinct from stagnant water, and the woman may have thus taken His words literally. She found it impossible to grasp the spiritual aspects of our Lord's statement, and, for the most part, confined her attention to the matter of drawing water from the well immediately before them; yet, in her next question, "From whence then hast thou that living water?" (v. 11), she seemed to acknowledge that Christ was talking about something greater and more satisfying than the water which this well would provide, and went so far as to ask Him where He could possibly have living water.

If Christ presumed to have water with greater virtue than that which

[handwritten marginal note: WHY THE HATE?]

the well provided, then He must presume to be a greater person than Jacob, the one who had dug the well.

D. The Answer (vv. 13, 14)

13. Jesus answered and said unto her, Whosoever drinketh of this water shall thirst again:

14. But whosoever drinketh of the water that I shall give him shall never thirst; but the water that I shall give him shall be in him a well of water springing up into everlasting life.

Jesus ignored her question. He did not stop to compare Himself with Jacob, but He did state a truth which she could not deny—that the water in this well could only temporarily quench the thirst of any who drink from it. That is true with everything in the world. Nothing, if it is of earthly origin, ever really permanently satisfies our deeper needs.

Christ imparts life that absolutely satisfies. We no longer must seek here and there for something to quench our spiritual thirst. We continue to drink, but we no longer find ourselves with unsatisfied needs in the soul. A person without Christ can go on thirsting for years, trying everything to satisfy that thirst, without success. A Christian can be continually satisfied with Christ.

E. The Request (v. 15)

15. The woman saith unto him, Sir, give me this water, that I thirst not, neither come hither to draw.

Not only had the curiosity of the woman been aroused, but Christ had created within her heart a deep longing for this living water of which He had been speaking, though she did not understand fully what He had been saying. There was a groping for that which is the better, a recognition of a deep craving in her own heart. The woman seemed now to be somewhat confused. The gift offered to her by Christ appeared to have two virtues—it would satisfy her own personal wants and it would eliminate from her life the great need of continually coming down the long, dusty path to the well and tediously drawing up vessel after vessel of water.

Are there people whom we should not bother to speak to about Christ? Why?

III. POINT OTHERS TO CHRIST (John 4:25-42)

A. The Confession (v. 25)

(John 4:25 is not included in the printed text.)

The Samaritan woman was confused. She was not able to rise to the height of Christ's sublime statements; but she had faith to believe that the coming Messiah would make it all clear to her. The word *Messiah* means "the Anointed One." Priests, prophets, and kings were anointed in the Old Testament. Christ is for all men who believe in Him, the Great High Priest, the final Prophet from God, and the King of kings. It is believed the Samaritan woman emphasized the prophetic office of Christ because the Samaritans had only the Pentateuch, in which the only aspect of the Messiah referred to was the prophetic (Deuteronomy 18:15-19).

B. The Surprise (v. 26)

(John 4:26 is not included in the printed text.)

Jesus concluded His conversation with the Samaritan woman by telling her openly and unreservedly that He was the Savior of the world. He said, "I that speak unto thee am he [the Messiah]." Nowhere in all the Gospels do we find the Lord making such a complete declaration of His messiahship as He does in this place. This declaration was not made to the scribes and Pharisees, but to one who had been an ignorant, thoughtless, and immoral person. At last the woman had obtained an answer to one of her first questions.

C. The Report (vv. 27-30)

27. And upon this came his disciples, and marvelled that he talked with the woman: yet no man said, What seekest thou? or, Why talkest thou with her?
28. The woman then left her waterpot, and went her way into the city, and saith to the men,
29. Come, see a man, which told me all things that ever I did: is not this the Christ?
30. Then they went out of the city, and came unto him.

The attitude of the disciples upon returning gives us one of those indirect, unexpected, and vivid testimonies to the absolute purity and spotlessness of the life of Christ (v. 27). For any other man to have been found speaking with this woman would have meant the arousing of suspicion concerning his motives in the minds of those who observed him, but none of the disciples, knowing Jesus as they did, could ever suspect anything

else but the absolute sincerity of any act of His.

There can be no doubt this woman was really convinced that Christ was the Messiah, and that she was experiencing that day a revolutionary change in her life. This was evidenced by the fact that she was so absorbed in these matters which pertained to God and the Messiah that she actually forgot her errand at the well. She left her water jar and hurried back to the city to invite all her fellow townsmen to come and see One who must be the Christ.

Observe in verse 29 what she told them about Christ—not that He had taught her about the water of life, but that He had shown her the wickedness of her life. She had pretended not to heed, but Christ's arrow had struck home. It was as one convicted of her sins that she sought to lead other sinners to the Savior. She had learned the first duty of a Christian—to be an evangelist.

D. The White Harvest (vv. 31-42)

(John 4:31-42 is not included in the printed text.)

Frederick A. Noble writes of these verses:

"There is hardly a stranger or more beautiful picture in all the New Testament than of Christ, born of the flesh of David, the king of the Jews, abiding for two days in this Samaritan village, all because of the testimony of the woman. Many of the people of this village now came to believe on Christ, first because of the testimony of the woman herself, and, later, because they heard from Christ's own lips the teachings which had won her to acknowledge him as the Messiah. This great revival had been brought about by this one woman because she herself had been radically changed in character by the power of Christ and filled with a high enthusiasm for souls. This one woman, this Samaritan woman, regenerated, brought over from the fellowship of the world to the fellowship of the Christ, by her simple timeliness and activity in witnessing, set a marked religious movement on foot, and led, nobody knows how many souls out of darkness into light and out of death into life" (*Typical New Testament Conversions*).

Would you have believed this woman's testimony? Why?

REVIEW QUESTIONS

1. Why did Jesus leave Judea?

2. How did the woman respond to Jesus' request for a drink of water?

3. How did Jesus probe the conscience of the Samaritan woman?

4. How did the woman try to change the conversation?

5. How did the woman prove her conversion?

SENTENCE SERMONS

CHRIST'S PATTERN of evangelism is the believer's example for winning the lost.

—Selected

BE TO THE WORLD a sign that while we as Christians do not have all the answers, we do know and care about questions.

—Billy Graham

EVANGELISM applies a super-natural remedy for the need of the world.

—Faris Whitesell

MEN LOOK FOR better methods of evangelism, but God looks for better men.

—Erwin W. Lutzer

EVANGELISM APPLICATION

CHRIST'S PATTERN OF EVANGELISM IS THE BELIEVER'S EXAMPLE FOR WINNING THE LOST.

Most of us have forgotten the very name of the man who spoke to a clerk named Dwight L. Moody, who set the bells of heaven ringing, and kept them ringing, with the news of the salvation of tens of thousands of souls. Not one of us, perhaps, can recall the ignorant country preacher whose message touched young Spurgeon's heart as he was going up to London. Maybe he never knew about it himself. We go to Sunday school and find just one little, towheaded boy on a rainy day, and we say to the superintendent, "What's the use of teaching this class?" Yet that little boy might, by the grace of God, become a Moody or a Spurgeon.**—Neal L. Anderson, *God's World and Word***

DAILY BIBLE READINGS

M. Reluctant Witness.
Jonah 1:1-17

T. Repentant Witness.
Jonah 2:1-10

W. A City Repents.
Jonah 3:1-10

T. Great Commission.
Matthew 28:16-20

F. Ripe Harvest.
Luke 10:1-9

S. Power Promised.
Acts 1:1-8

Leading a Person to Christ

Study Text: Romans 3:21-26; 5:6-8; 6:23; 10:9-13; Ephesians 2:8, 9

Objective: To examine the steps involved in leading a person to Christ and commit to winning the lost.

Time: The Book of Romans was written between A.D. 56 and A.D. 58. The Book of Ephesians was probably written between A.D. 60 and A.D. 61.

Place: The Book of Romans was written at the city of Corinth in Greece. The Book of Ephesians was written from a Roman prison.

Golden Text: "God commendeth his love toward us, in that, while we were yet sinners, Christ died for us" (Romans 5:8).

Central Truth: The Bible is the best resource for knowing how to lead others to Christ.

Evangelism Emphasis: Christians need to make the gospel known to everyone.

PRINTED TEXT

Romans 3:21. But now the righteousness of God without the law is manifested, being witnessed by the law and the prophets;

22. Even the righteousness of God which is by faith of Jesus Christ unto all and upon all them that believe: for there is no difference.

23. For all have sinned, and come short of the glory of God.

5:6. For when we were yet without strength, in due time Christ died for the ungodly.

7. For scarcely for a righteous man will one die: yet peradventure for a good man some would even dare to die.

8. But God commendeth his love toward us, in that, while we were yet sinners, Christ died for us.

10:9. That if thou shalt confess with thy mouth the Lord Jesus, and shalt believe in thine heart that God hath raised him from the dead, thou shalt be saved.

10. For with the heart man believeth unto righteousness; and with the mouth confession is made unto salvation.

Ephesians 2:8. For by grace are ye saved through faith; and that not of yourselves: it is the gift of God:

9. Not of works, lest any man should boast.

Romans 3:24. Being justified freely by his grace through the redemption that is in Christ Jesus:

25. Whom God hath set forth

to be a propitiation through faith in his blood, to declare his righteousness for the remission of sins that are past, through the forbearance of God;

26. To declare, I say, at this time his righteousness: that he might be just, and the justifier of him which believeth in Jesus.

6:23. For the wages of sin is death; but the gift of God is eternal life through Jesus Christ our Lord.

LESSON OUTLINE

I. ALL HAVE SINNED
   A. Plenty
   B. Problem
   C. Plan
   D. Possibility
   E. Personality

II. ALL MUST CONFESS
   A. Proof
   B. Pleasure
   C. People

III. SAVED BY GRACE
   A. Provision
   B. Pardon
   C. Propitiation
   D. Power
   E. Payment

LESSON EXPOSITION

INTRODUCTION

When Dr. Lyman Beecher lay dying, a ministerial friend said to the aged man of God: "Dr. Beecher, you know a great deal. Tell me what is the greatest of all things." His reply was, "It is not theology, it is not controversy, it is to save souls."

David Brainerd, apostle to the Indians, wrote, "I cared not where or how I lived, or what hardship I went through, so that I could but gain souls for Christ."

Christians cannot engage in a wiser or more beneficial work than winning souls. Soulwinning is different from anything else we can do in that it is eternal in its issues. Its results travel beyond the grave. A person may be successful in a profession, but that success ends with death; its worth and influence are only for time. Soulwinning, however, is not only for time, but for eternity. The soulwinner is the only person who can shine in heaven. The honors and successes of a mere business career are not remembered above.

William Evans writes "Every Christian should consider it the highest honor, and the greatest privilege to assist in the growth of the kingdom of God, by personal effort in individual soulwinning. He should realize, too, that it is not only his privilege to thus work for God, but that a most solemn responsibility rests upon him to do so.

"The supreme business of the Christian is to individualize the gospel. No distinction, such as clergy and laity, is here recognized. As followers of Christ we are called to be personal soulwinners. Every Christian layman is 'ordained' to go and bring forth fruit, and is a 'minister' in so far as every man who has received a gift—and every

Christian has received one—is
called upon to minister therewith
(John 15:16; 1 Peter 4:10, 11)"
(*Personal Soulwinning*).

I. ALL HAVE SINNED (Romans 3:21-23; 5:6-8)

A. Plenty (3:21, 22)

**21. But now the righteousness
of God without the law is manifested, being witnessed by the
law and the prophets;
22. Even the righteousness of
God which is by faith of Jesus
Christ unto all and upon all them
that believe: for there is no difference.**

The "righteousness of God" in
these verses means the believer's
status of being approved by God,
having been acquitted of sin and
declared righteous—a blessing only
God can confer on an individual.
Man could never achieve this righteousness on his own. Nevertheless,
God has made it available to all.
The only condition is faith—"upon
all them that believe." And it is only
logical that since all have sinned, all
need it.

This righteousness is apart from
the law; however, Paul was quick to
point out that both the Law and the
Prophets bear witness to it. Paul's
reference to "the law" here does not
indicate the revelation of God
through the Law in the Old
Testament. Rather it stands for a
rigid religion that had become
merely a set of statutes and ordinances which must be strictly
obeyed.

This by no means implies we are
not to keep God's laws. It simply
means we cannot depend on our
good needs—our righteousness—for
salvation. That can come only

through our faith in Jesus Christ.
It is truly a gift from God.

B. Problem (v. 23)

**23. For all have sinned, and
come short of the glory of God.**

Sin has been defined as "a three-
letter word that spells the difference
between happiness and misery,
freedom and bondage, heaven and
hell." Men may deny its existence,
minimize its influence, or try to
evade its consequences. But it
remains a cold, stubborn reality,
separating the soul from Almighty
God.

The Biblical concept of sin is
indicated in the words used to portray it. The Hebrew term means "to
deviate from the way"; the Greek
terms imply a "missing of the
mark," a "going aside from." The
very existence of sin reveals that
there is a norm or standard against
which the acts of men may be measured. Paul puts it bluntly: "The law
worketh wrath: for where no law is,
there is no transgression" (Romans
4:15). And John defines sin as
"lawlessness" (1 John 3:4, *NKJV*)—
that is, a breach of the law.

Adam represented the entire race
of men without distinction as to
color, condition, circumstance,
clime, or culture. Sin is the great
leveler. All men everywhere, and in
every age, are confronted with the
ghastly specter of iniquity. The
heart of the untutored savage, like
the heart of the intellectual, condemns him.

Of sin in relation to men, the
Bible declares that no one escapes
its guilt: "All we like sheep have
gone astray; we have turned every
one to his own way" (Isaiah 53:6).
Sin is no "respecter" of age. David
exclaimed, "Behold, I was shapen in

iniquity; and in sin did my mother conceive me" (Psalm 51:5). Sin embraces each because it embraces all. This means that it includes you and me. We can refuse to acknowledge it; we can try to explain it away, or condone it. But the best thing we can do is confess it, forsake it, and, as David did, plead the mercy of God for pardon and cleansing (Lindsell and Woodbridge, *A Handbook of Christian Truth*).

C. Plan (5:6)

6. For when we were yet without strength, in due time Christ died for the ungodly.

The sinner is powerless to deliver himself from sin. We discover how weak we are when we try to get rid of our besetting sins without Christ's help. Knowing how helpless man was, Christ came at the time appointed by the Father, which was when mankind most desperately needed the advent of a Savior.

Paul declares that Christ died for all men, for all are ungodly. We can, to an extent, understand that God would die for the good, the righteous, the pure, the godly; but that the infinitely Holy One should love the unholy, and give His Son for their redemption, becomes the wonder of all wonders to us. But the apostle says that He died for them, in their stead, suffering the death they deserved to die. This is the heart of the gospel.

D. Possibility (v. 7)

7. For scarcely for a righteous man will one die: yet peradventure for a good man some would even dare to die.

It is rare for us to observe death on behalf of another. When it does happen, we make much of it. Those who make such sacrifices become heroes and receive praise for decades and even centuries. And this rare deed is always performed on behalf of a good man, not a bad man. It is always a friend, not an enemy.

E. Personality (v. 8)

8. But God commendeth his love toward us, in that, while we were yet sinners, Christ died for us.

The word *commendeth* literally means "to place together," and hence "to teach by combining and comparing" and so "to prove, establish, exhibit." H.C.G. Moule writes: "Infinite condescension lies in this simple word. We look at the cross, or rather we look at the crucified Lord Jesus in His resurrection; we read at His feet these words of His apostle; and we go away to take God at His assurance that we, unlovely, are beloved" (*Commentary on Romans*).

Why do men so readily reject the fact that they are sinners?

II. ALL MUST CONFESS (Romans 10:9-13)

A. Proof (vv. 9, 10)

9. That if thou shalt confess with thy mouth the Lord Jesus, and shalt believe in thine heart that God hath raised him from the dead, thou shalt be saved.

The Lord Jesus Christ was sent from God to be the Savior of the world. He accomplished all that was necessary for man's salvation on the cross and by His resurrection. All we have to do to be saved is to exercise faith in Christ as our crucified and risen Savior.

To show that we have faith in Christ, we must publicly confess Him as Lord. No confession of man can add anything to the finished work of Christ; yet we are required to confess Him openly. This is because His glory and the good of man demand it. If we should conceal our faith in Him, who would be benefited? In what respect would He be glorified? Jesus himself required that all who would be benefited by Him should take up their cross daily and follow Him. And if we fail to do this, He will not acknowledge us as disciples.

Paul declared that whoever believes in Christ and confesses Him shall be saved. This statement is plain, positive, and unequivocal. Christ wrought a righteousness for sinful man. It is a righteousness fully commensurate with the most stringent demands of law and justice. This righteousness is received by faith.

10. For with the heart man believeth unto righteousness; and with the mouth confession is made unto salvation.

If we were able to purchase an interest in righteousness by any works of our own, salvation would be by works. We are continually told that righteousness comes by faith and by faith alone.

Deeply rooted in the heart of every man is self-righteousness. Its workings are numerous and subtle; and its dangers, far-reaching. It subverts the foundations of the gospel. It usurps the office of the Savior. It robs God of His glory.

Each individual needs to search his heart and analyze the basis of his hope. Each one needs to see

whether he is willing to accept himself as a sinner or whether he is, rather, wishing to find some worthiness in himself that might serve as a basis of confidence in his approach to God.

As believers, we can face the world of evil unafraid and unashamed. We have more than a set of religious precepts. We are related to the living God. He is with us. We need only to give Him complete control.

B. Pleasure (v. 11)

(Romans 10:11 is not included in the printed text.)

The Christian need never be disappointed in accepting Christ as Savior, Lord, and Master. Paul quoted from Isaiah 28:16 and 49:23 and said, "Whosoever believeth on him shall not be ashamed." R.M. Edgar writes of this verse: "Faith in a risen Saviour who is waiting to be found of us must prove its genuineness by the confession of his name. It is when we take the Lord's side deliberately that we have tested the reality of our faith. There is a cowardly tendency to believe, but not confess; to get the benefits of salvation without running a single risk for our Saviour. But such a selfish, easy-going faith is mere delusion. Whoever really believes in Jesus will not be ashamed to confess him. And consequently we are encouraged first to believe that God raised Jesus from the dead, and then to confess him as our risen Saviour before men" (*Pulpit Commentary*).

C. People (vv. 12, 13)

(Romans 10:12, 13 is not included in the printed text.)

The same Lord is for both Jew and Gentile. Note the wonderful word *whosoever*. Salvation is free to all. There is no difference between the Jew and the Greek. This way of salvation existed before there were Jews in the world. The Jews' only advantage is that the way of salvation was revealed to them in types and shadows before other people were aware of salvation. This distinguishing mercy, however, makes no difference as to the way Jews are to be saved. Their national status does not afford them special privileges any more than it excludes Gentiles. If any person fears God and looks to Christ the Savior, he will be saved.

Is it possible to be a secret disciple of Jesus? Explain.

III. SAVED BY GRACE
(Ephesians 2:8, 9;
Romans 3:24-26; 6:23)

A. Provision (Ephesians 2:8, 9)

8. For by grace are ye saved through faith; and that not of yourselves: it is the gift of God:
9. Not of works, lest any man should boast.

Paul reminds his readers that they have been saved by God's grace. The original Greek text uses the article "the" with *grace* in verse 8, meaning that particular grace of God which has been under discussion in the passage. "Are saved" is in the same form as in verse 5, depicting the present state resultant from a past action. Here (v. 8) he adds the expression "through faith," to name the channel through which man receives the salvation God provides. It must not be supposed, however, that faith is in any

sense causative. Salvation is not a cooperative venture in which both God and man contribute their parts. It is entirely God's work. Man either receives it or rejects it. "Faith" names the response of those who receive it.

"And that not of yourselves" emphasizes this truth that salvation is in no sense man's work. Salvation is the gift of God from beginning to end, from planning to accomplishment. When Paul said it is "not of works" (v. 9), he was giving a further elaboration of "not of yourselves." Not even deeds of righteousness can effect salvation. There can never be the slightest reason for man's personal glorying. Faith is the opposite of works, for it offers no works to God but rather accepts that work of redemption that God has done. Thus Paul wrote in Romans 3:27 that God's plan of providing salvation through faith excludes all human boasting, for man has contributed nothing to it. Because fallen human nature is so prone to boast of its accomplishments and to take credit where there is even the slightest occasion, God devised a plan to save men in their hopelessness which allows no grounds whatever for human pride to operate (Homer Kent Jr., *Ephesians: The Glory of the Church*).

B. Pardon (Romans 3:24)

24. Being justified freely by his grace through the redemption that is in Christ Jesus.

One of the most important words in the Bible is the word *redeemed*, for it is so full of meaning and significance to the believer. *Redemption* is one of the great words connected with the work of Christ on the cross, expressing the deliverance effected there for all under the guilt and bondage of sin. It conveys two great truths: (1) the purchase or buying back by the payment of a ransom and (2) deliverance from bondage by the ransom paid and by the power of God.

In redemption as a purchase, the prominent thought is the price paid, but not its payment to any person. In Psalm 49, the price paid in redemption is contrasted with all the wealth possessed by rich men, showing how utterly inadequate are all the riches they possess to pay the required ransom. "For the redemption of their soul is precious [costly], and it ceaseth for ever" (v. 8). And this last clause may be rendered, "It must be let alone forever." It is far too costly for man to face, even if he possessed all the wealth the world had to give. Redemption cannot be effected by silver or gold or any other material wealth, but only by "the precious blood of Christ" (1 Peter 1:18, 19).

The New Testament words which speak of redemption as a purchase are those used of men buying in the market or forum. Twice, believers are reminded that they "are bought with a price" (1 Corinthians 6:20; 7:23), while false teachers are said to be "denying the Lord that bought them" (2 Peter 2:1). In the Book of Revelation the great company seen about the throne of God is said to have been "redeemed," or bought (5:9; 14:4). A stronger word is used in Galatians 3:13 and 4:5, where redemption by Christ is from the law and its curse, and it means "to buy out from under, or to buy up."

The price paid for anything determines its value to the purchaser; and the greater the cost, so much more is the article prized by its owner. No greater price could have been paid than that paid by God for our redemption, for it was the precious blood of Christ, His only begotten Son. There can be nothing in the world, then, so precious in His sight as those who have been purchased by the payment of that great price, and it is that which makes it so very blessed to be a child of God. "Ye are not your own . . . ye are bought with a price" (1 Corinthians 6:19, 20).

Redemption means not only purchase by payment of the ransom required, but it has in view particularly the deliverance, or setting free, of those who have been slaves and are in bondage. Deliverance is the prominent idea of redemption in both Old and New Testaments.

C. Propitiation (3:25)

25. Whom God hath set forth to be a propitiation through faith in his blood, to declare his righteousness for the remission of sins that are past, through the forbearance of God.

Propitiation means "to appease or satisfy wrath." God's righteous wrath against sin has been met and satisfied by the atoning work of Christ on the cross, for "He is [made] the propitiation for our sins: and not for our's only, but also for the sins of the whole world" (1 John 2:2). God can never be indifferent to sin, nor can He pass over it lightly, for He is holy. Sin must be met and put away by death, if the blessing of God is to be received.

The first three chapters of Romans show that all men are under sin and are guilty before God, deserving judgment, and that man therefore has no righteousness of his own. Then in 3:21 "the righteousness of God" is proclaimed, which is a faith righteousness apart from works altogether, for it is a righteousness of God bestowed by Him on the believer. That righteousness can only be given after sin has been atoned for and put away, is the ground on which redemption by Christ is based.

D. Power (3:26)

26. To declare, I say, at this time his righteousness: that he might be just, and the justifier of him which believeth in Jesus.

Justification is a legal act. It originates in the loving will of God. It is the basis on which the believer is pardoned and declared righteous in God's sight. This powerful act relates to the sending of Christ Jesus, the Son of God, into the world to bear the sinner's guilt and death and to bring him back to God.

E. Payment (6:23)

23. For the wages of sin is death; but the gift of God is eternal life through Jesus Christ our Lord.

The distribution of rewards and punishments in the Day of Judgment will be in perfect agreement with the works of men: the righteous will be exalted to happiness; the wicked, doomed to misery. The gospel makes no difference with respect to this: it provides relief for the penitent, but rather aggravates than removes the condemnation of the impenitent. However, it shows us an important fact—namely, that the punishment of the ungodly is the proper fruit and deserved recompense of their own works, whereas the reward bestowed upon the godly is a free unmerited gift of God for Christ's sake.

What does propitiation mean?

REVIEW QUESTIONS

1. According to Romans 3:23, who has sinned?
2. When did Christ die for the ungodly?
3. When did God "commend" His love to us?
4. Define *redemption*.
5. Does the church put enough emphasis on personal witnessing?

SENTENCE SERMONS

THE BIBLE IS the best resource for knowing how to lead others to Christ.
—Selected

CHRISTIANS need to make the gospel known to everyone.
—Selected

NO MAN is ever more than four steps from God: conviction, repentance, consecration, and faith.
—Roy L. Smith

GRACE is given not because we have done good works, but in order that we may be able to do them.
—Saint Augustine

DAILY BIBLE READINGS

M. The Fall of Man. Genesis 3:1-7
T. Confronted by God.
   Genesis 3:8-19
W. Invitation to Seek God.
   Isaiah 55:1-7
T. Restore Those Who Fall.
   Galatians 6:1-10
F. Confess Christ.
   Philippians 2:9-16
S. Christ Came to Save.
   1 Timothy 1:12-17

Reaching Family and Friends

Study Text: John 1:35-51; 2 Timothy 1:1-5

Objective: To recognize the need to reach your family and friends for Christ and look for opportunities to share your faith.

Time: The Gospel According to John was probably written near the end of the first century between A.D. 85 and A.D. 96. The Book of 2 Timothy was written between A.D. 66 and A.D. 67.

Place: The Gospel According to John was probably written at Ephesus. The Book of 2 Timothy was probably written from a Roman prison.

Golden Text: "From a child thou hast known the holy scriptures, which are able to make thee wise unto salvation through faith which is in Christ Jesus" (2 Timothy 3:15).

Central Truth: Christians must seek opportunities to share Christ with family and friends.

Evangelism Emphasis: Christians must not neglect sharing Christ with family and friends.

PRINTED TEXT

John 1:35. Again the next day after John stood, and two of his disciples;

36. And looking upon Jesus as he walked, he saith, Behold the Lamb of God!

37. And the two disciples heard him speak, and they followed Jesus.

38. Then Jesus turned, and saw them following, and saith unto them, What seek ye? They said unto him, Rabbi, (which is to say, being interpreted, Master,) where dwellest thou?

39. He saith unto them, Come and see. They came and saw where he dwelt, and abode with him that day: for it was about the tenth hour.

40. One of the two which heard John speak, and followed him, was Andrew, Simon Peter's brother.

41. He first findeth his own brother Simon, and saith unto him, We have found the Messias, which is, being interpreted, the Christ.

42. And he brought him to Jesus. And when Jesus beheld him, he said, Thou art Simon the son of Jona: thou shalt be called Cephas, which is by interpretation, A stone.

43. The day following Jesus would go forth into Galilee, and findeth Philip, and saith unto him, Follow me.

44. Now Philip was of Bethsaida, the city of Andrew and Peter.

45. Philip findeth Nathanael,

and saith unto him, We have found him, of whom Moses in the law, and the prophets, did write, Jesus of Nazareth, the son of Joseph.

46. And Nathanael said unto him, Can there any good thing come out of Nazareth? Philip saith unto him, Come and see.

47. Jesus saw Nathanael coming to him, and saith of him, Behold an Israelite indeed, in whom is no guile!

48. Nathanael saith unto him, Whence knowest thou me?

Jesus answered and said unto him, Before that Philip called thee, when thou wast under the fig tree, I saw thee.

49. Nathanael answered and saith unto him, Rabbi, thou art the Son of God; thou art the King of Israel.

2 Timothy 1:5. When I call to remembrance the unfeigned faith that is in thee, which dwelt first in thy grandmother Lois, and thy mother Eunice; and I am persuaded that in thee also.

DICTIONARY

Cephas (SEE-fuss)—John 1:42—The Aramaic name for "rock"; in Greek, "Peter." Jesus gave this name to the apostle Simon.

Galilee (GAL-i-lee)—John 1:43—The country between the Jordan River and the Mediterranean Sea.

Bethsaida (beth-SAY-ih-duh)—John 1:44—A city in Galilee and home of Peter, Andrew, and Philip.

Nathanael (nuh-THAN-yul)—John 1:45—One of Jesus' 12 apostles, probably called "Bartholomew."

Israelite (IZ-ree-ul-lite)—John 1:47—A person from the nation of Israel.

Eunice (YOU-nis)—2 Timothy 1:5—Mother of Timothy.

LESSON OUTLINE

I. WIN YOUR FAMILY
   A. The Announcement
   B. The Unique Discovery
   C. Unselfish Service

II. TELL A FRIEND
   A. Philip
   B. Nathanael

III. LEAVE A LEGACY OF FAITH
   A. Salutation
   B. Gratitude
   C. Yearning
   D. Reminder

LESSON EXPOSITION

INTRODUCTION

It is interesting to study how different groups and individuals came to be followers of Jesus. Andrew and John the apostle, two disciples of John the Baptist, were introduced by John the Baptist himself. Nothing shows the greatness of John the Baptist more than this— that he introduced his own devoted followers to One whom they were now to follow exclusively. Simon Peter was brought to Jesus by his own brother, Andrew. Philip came into the company of Christ's followers by being sought after by Jesus himself. Nathanael was introduced to Christ by his friend Philip. Thus, in different ways the Holy Spirit brings men to Christ.

It is also interesting to note how differently Christ received each group. Of the two disciples of John the Baptist, who were already devout Jews, Christ asked a question; and to them He extended an invitation. The question was, "What seek ye?" (John 1:38) as though He would have them to be clear in their own minds as to why they were following Him. Jesus wanted them to confess that they were seeking in Christ that completion of their spiritual life which neither John the Baptist nor any other man could ever give them. The invitation to them was a very gracious one: "Come and see."

There is no conversation recorded between Philip and Jesus, but undoubtedly, words were exchanged. To Simon Peter, the Lord gave a great promise: "Thou shalt be called Cephas" (v. 42), which means that he was to be called "a rock."

Nathanael was a student of the Scriptures, a worshiper of Jehovah, looking for the Messiah. To this man, Jesus paid a high compliment. Jesus said of him, "Behold an Israelite indeed, in whom is no guile!" (v. 47). To Nathanael He also made two definite statements: (1) that before Philip had called him, the Lord had seen him, indicating Christ's supernatural knowledge, and (2) that in the future Nathanael would "see heaven open, and the angels of God ascending and descending upon the Son of man" (v. 51).

One thing these men had in common was that each of them left all to follow Christ. The Lord Jesus Christ knows us deeply and intimately—all of our weaknesses, all of our sins, all of our needs—yet, He promises to every man a fulfillment of his deepest longings. Therefore, Andrew and John found in the Lamb of God the One who could take away the sins which their master, John the Baptist, had exposed. Simon Peter found in Christ the One who could give him fullness of life and make him what he ought to be. Philip found in Christ the One of whom Moses and all the prophets had written, the One for whom all the world was looking. Nathanael found in Christ the One who could reveal the past and unveil the future, the King of Israel. Thus, Christ becomes to every man what that man needs spiritually.

I. WIN YOUR FAMILY
    (John 1:35-42)

A. The Announcement (vv. 35, 36)

35. Again the next day after John stood, and two of his disciples;

36. And looking upon Jesus as he walked, he saith, Behold the Lamb of God!

No prophet had been heard in Israel for five long centuries. Suddenly a voice was heard in the wilderness. It was the voice of a prophet. It made a great impression upon the people. They were attracted, first of all, by his appearance. But they were still more astonished by the things he said. It became their joy and delight to quote the things he said to the Pharisees and the Roman soldiers. His preaching was such that no one could be indifferent to it. His words have echoed down to the present time. It was preaching that was mighty, and it stirred the hearts of men. They felt that a new day had come for Israel (see vv. 15-34).

Who was this preacher . . . this John the Baptist? His family was a religious family. His father was a priest, and his mother belonged to a priestly family. What sent him into the wilderness? It was his sense of sin.

This sense of sin drove John into the wilderness, and it was here that he came face-to-face with God. This was the only way he could really understand sin—that is, to come face-to-face with God. We can understand and see sin for what it really is when its only background is God's holiness and purity.

It was in the wilderness that John became saturated with the revelation of God. Moved upon by the Holy Spirit, John, when he first saw Jesus coming, recognized Him as the Messiah and cried out, "Behold the Lamb of God, which taketh away the sin of the world" (v. 29).

"The Lamb of God" means sacrifice; it suggests an altar; it foreshadows the cross. The Lamb is a suffering Savior who takes away the sin of the world. Because He is provided by God and accepted by God, He is able to save to the uttermost. What a ministry! He "taketh away the sin of the world."

B. The Unique Discovery
   (vv. 37-39)

37. And the two disciples heard him speak, and they followed Jesus.

38. Then Jesus turned, and saw them following, and saith unto them, What seek ye? They said unto him, Rabbi, (which is to say, being interpreted, Master,) where dwellest thou?

39. He saith unto them, Come and see. They came and saw where he dwelt, and abode with him that day: for it was about the tenth hour.

In the experience of Andrew and John, we have an interesting study in spiritual development. It is the record of their spiritual pilgrimage from John to Jesus. They had been attracted by the great prophet of the wilderness, and they had joined themselves to the number of disciples that were following him. However, the day came when the ministry of John reached its climax and consummation in the baptism of Jesus, about whom John had made the great prophetic declaration. It was then that the two disciples began to follow Jesus.

Their action was not to be construed as a desertion of John the Baptist. Rather, it was a response to the deeper significance of John's own teaching. Their going from him was really a tribute to him. It showed that they had caught some glimpse of the deeper significance of his message and ministry. Nevertheless, it was a great venture of faith. On the one hand was the famous prophet, the man who had the ear of the nation, the most prominent figure in the national life. On the other hand was a humble unknown Galilean peasant, with, as yet, no credentials beyond the testimony of John. But they made the venture—they left John and followed Jesus. In doing this they made a unique discovery. In the words of Andrew, "We have found the Messiah" (see v. 41). They had been looking for Him. The Jews were the nation of hope. Andrew, we may be sure, had heard of the Messiah, the hope of Israel, all his life. Now in this dramatic moment of his life, he discovered that what he had been seeking was a present reality.

C. Unselfish Service (vv. 40-42)

40. One of the two which heard John speak, and followed him, was Andrew, Simon Peter's brother.

41. He first findeth his own brother Simon, and saith unto him, We have found the Messias, which is, being interpreted, the Christ.

42. And he brought him to Jesus. And when Jesus beheld him, he said, Thou art Simon the son of Jona: thou shalt be called Cephas, which is by interpretation, A stone.

Andrew did not think of keeping the discovery of the Messiah to himself. He immediately thought of telling his brother Simon. He was full of the experience which he had just been blessed with. He could think of nothing else. He could talk of nothing else but Jesus. "He first findeth his own brother Simon" (v. 41). His eyes sparkled, his face shone, his voice was vibrant with emotion as he exclaimed, "Simon, we have found the Christ!" There is no joy to a human heart like the discovery that your sins have been forgiven and that the joy of Jesus Christ is yours.

It is important to observe that Andrew started at once to share the good news. The day after his conversion he became a soulwinner. Nobody said to Andrew, "Go and look for your brother." It was instinctive. It was a natural impulse. He had found the Christ, and he felt that he simply had to share the experience. It is always that way. If a man has a real depth of conviction, he cannot rest until he shares it with somebody else.

It is interesting to note that Andrew did not wait until he was fully equipped and had been fully trained by the Master. He started with what he knew. In a few hours he had seen enough in Jesus to be awed, attracted, and won. He had seen enough to realize that here was the One who could be loved and trusted, and he wanted to share this with his brother.

"He brought him to Jesus" (v. 42). This is the best service that any human being could ever do for any other. Look at the man who did this. He was an ordinary man. There is no record that he was a genius. He does not even play a conspicuous role in the gospel story. We know him a little better than some of the other disciples, but not nearly as well as the one whom he brought to Jesus.

Andrew had just come from communion with Christ. He had spent a night with the Messiah, and his entire life had been changed. He had seen and found the Christ. This is the secret of success—communion with Christ. It is the indispensable qualification for every Christian worker. As someone has said, "It makes of the dwarf a giant, and without it the giant becomes a dwarf." In the work of the church we can influence others for Christ only as we have been influenced by Christ.

We are not told that Andrew ever preached a sermon in his life; but he never did a better day's work in his life than when he brought Peter to Jesus. This brother, whom he brought to Jesus, preached a sermon that led 3,000 people to Jesus in one day. Dr. R.A. Torrey calculated that if each of the 2,000 individuals in his audience were to lead to Christ only one person a year, and the ones thus brought to Jesus should each bring to Him only one person a year, and so on, at the end of 35 years every man, woman, and child on the face of the earth would have heard the gospel.

The Reverend Warren Hathaway writes: "There is nothing we can do so great, so far-reaching in its influence, so blessed in its results, so immortal, so divine, as bringing a soul to Christ" (*Living Questions*).

Jesus looked at Simon and said, "Thou art Simon the son of Jona: thou shalt be called Cephas, which is by interpretation, A Stone [Peter]" (v. 42). *Cephas* (or *Kephas*) is Aramaic, and *Peter* is Greek and Latin for "stone," or "rock," from which we get our English word *petrified*. This change of name, which Christ was here foretelling occurred later at Caesarea Philippi, on the occasion of Simon's bold confession of Jesus as the Messiah, the Son of God (Matthew 16:13-18). A.B. Bruce says: "The reason of this utterance to Simon is understood when it is considered that the name he as yet bore was identified with a character full of impulsiveness; which might well lead him to suppose that he would bring mischief to the Messiah's kingdom. But, says Christ, thou shalt be called Rock. Those who enter Christ's kingdom, believing in Him, receive a character fitting them to be of service" (*The Expositor's Greek Testament*).

What role should the church play in helping individuals win their family to Christ?

II. TELL A FRIEND (John 1:43-51)

A. Philip (vv. 43-45)

43. The day following Jesus would go forth into Galilee, and findeth Philip, and saith unto him, Follow me.

44. Now Philip was of Bethsaida, the city of Andrew and Peter.

45. Philip findeth Nathanael, and saith unto him, We have found him, of whom Moses in the law, and the prophets, did write, Jesus of Nazareth, the son of Joseph.

We can see in the experience of Philip how the Holy Spirit acts sovereignly in calling individuals as He wills. This man was apparently not moved by the testimony of John the Baptist, as Andrew and his companions were. He was not drawn, like Simon Peter, through the personal witnessing of an outspoken brother. He was called directly by Jesus himself, without the assistance of human agency. Yet he was accepted without question by those who had become disciples before him.

The experience of Philip is important because it illustrates that God is not confined to any particular method of saving souls. All true Christians are led by one Spirit and washed in the same blood. They serve the same Lord, believe in the same Savior, accept one truth, and live by one Book. But all are not brought into fellowship with God in the same manner.

We have very little information

about Philip and Nathanael. Philip has been described as a man whose intellect was practical and prompt in its decisions, but whose spiritual perception was dull. His mind was precise, methodical, and almost mechanical—but with no originality. We see these characteristics in the references to him which John alone, of the four evangelists, makes: the matter-of-fact way in which he summoned Nathanael; his prosaic reckoning of how much it would take to feed the 5,000 (6:7); his requiring the aid of Andrew before he would bring the Greeks to Jesus (12:20-22); and especially his impatient demand, "Lord, shew us the Father, and it sufficeth us" (14:8).

Whatever else we may say about Philip, he had a prompt heart. He was quicker than most Christians are to act on the principle of soul-winning. After Jesus had called him, then Philip found Nathanael and reported to him that he had found the One about whom Moses and the prophets had written.

B. Nathanael (vv. 46-51)

(John 1:50, 51 is not included in the printed text.)

46. And Nathanael said unto him, Can there any good thing come out of Nazareth? Philip saith unto him, Come and see.

47. Jesus saw Nathanael coming to him, and saith of him, Behold an Israelite indeed, in whom is no guile!

48. Nathanael saith unto him, Whence knowest thou me? Jesus answered and said unto him, Before that Philip called thee, when thou wast under the fig tree, I saw thee.

49. Nathanael answered and saith unto him, Rabbi, thou art the Son of God; thou art the King of Israel.

We know very little about Nathanael. His name is not mentioned by the Synoptic writers, but it is generally accepted that he is the same as Bartholomew and is generally associated with Philip in their lists.

Apparently Nathanael was not a man in the habit of accepting every opinion that was offered him. He had his own ideas of the Messiah and they did not fit in with any local personality. Nazareth was hardly the place he would look for the Messiah. Nathanael asked Philip the question, "Can . . . any good thing come out of Nazareth?" (v. 46).

The infinite tact of Jesus can be seen in His opening sentence in verse 47. He was quick to acknowledge and recognize the honesty and sincerity of Nathanael in very flattering terms: "Behold an Israelite indeed, in [whose heart there] is no guile!"

The purpose of Jesus, of course, was to reveal to Nathanael His own supernatural powers, which were to awaken faith in His messiahship. He answered Philip's question by saying, in effect, "Why, just before Philip met you, while you were under the fig tree praying, I saw you" (v. 48). Now, no mere man had seen Nathanael praying.

The victory of Jesus over Nathanael was complete. John described the meeting in an interesting way. The man who had questioned whether any good thing could come out of Nazareth recognized Jesus, the prophet of Nazareth, as the One who was Rabbi, Son of God, and King of

Israel. "Can . . . any good thing come out of Nazareth?" was his first utterance. "Rabbi, thou art the Son of God; thou art the King of Israel" (v. 49) was his declaration after he had seen, met, and talked with Jesus.

Jesus did not end His conversation with Nathanael abruptly. He knew this newfound faith must be confirmed. He promised deeper and more profound spiritual experiences than Nathanael had just experienced. He said, "Because I said unto thee, I saw thee under the fig tree, believest thou? Thou shalt see greater things than these . . . . Hereafter ye shall see heaven open, and the angels of God ascending and descending upon the Son of man" (vv. 50, 51).

Jesus used wonderful spiritual psychology on this occasion. Nathanael, deeply religious and cautious, needed to know that his experience was not just enthusiasm, a passing emotional storm, but a deep spiritual reality that could be confirmed by greater experiences as he walked with Christ.

How did Jesus reveal to Nathanael that he was never alone?

III. LEAVE A LEGACY OF FAITH
  (2 Timothy 1:1-5)

A. Salutation (vv. 1, 2)

(2 Timothy 1:1, 2 is not included in the printed text.)

Paul's position was an apostle of Jesus Christ. Timothy had no doubts about Paul's position and authority. In fact, this letter was official as well as personal, and thus the full title was in order. Paul's apostleship was a responsibility which he exercised through the will of God. This will of God, which had constituted him an apostle, was also leading him at the time of writing as a doomed prisoner in Rome to the end of his earthly career. Yet Paul had no misgivings about the will of God for his life. Just because suffering enters one's life, it is no indication that the individual is out of God's will.

The standard by which Paul's ministry can be measured and evaluated is given in the phrase "according to the promise of life" (v. 1). God who gave men life in Christ is the One who set up the apostles to testify of this life. The promise of eternal life made the need for apostles to announce the message.

Timothy's position was that of a beloved child. This suggests the affection which bound Timothy and Paul together.

The blessing pronounced upon Timothy consisted of "grace, mercy, and peace" (v. 2). These three terms summarize all that Paul could possibly wish for Timothy, for time and eternity (Homer A. Kent Jr., *The Pastoral Epistles*).

B. Gratitude (v. 3)

(2 Timothy 1:3 is not included in the printed text.)

Paul's gratitude to God was evoked on this occasion by the happy memories he had of others whose lives had meant much to him. He was thankful for his own godly heritage. The God whom he now served was the same God in whom he had been taught to trust by his ancestors. Though his parents had not taught him to be a Christian, they had reared him in the ancestral faith in the true God.

C. Yearning (v. 4)

(2 Timothy 1:4 is not included in the printed text.)

Paul desired to see Timothy again. He remembered Timothy's tears shed at their last parting. Now he anticipated joy if they should meet again.

D. Reminder (v. 5)

5. When I call to remembrance the unfeigned faith that is in thee, which dwelt first in thy grandmother Lois, and thy mother Eunice; and I am persuaded that in thee also.

When Paul thought of Timothy he was reminded of his godly ancestry. This genuine faith which Timothy possessed was first the possession of his grandmother Lois and then his mother Eunice. Lois and Eunice were godly Jewesses who reared young Timothy in the Old Testament and true faith in the God of Israel. Paul and Barnabas advanced this faith to the receiving of Christ as the Messiah. Paul was grateful for the genuine faith of this godly family, and he was convinced that Timothy was a worthy example of this faith.

How does a godly heritage help children in a family?

REVIEW QUESTIONS

1. What witness did John the Baptist bear to Jesus?
2. Which two of his disciples did he turn to Jesus?
3. What message did Andrew bring to Simon?
4. Whom did Philip find?
5. What was Paul thankful for?

GOLDEN TEXT HOMILY

"FROM A CHILD THOU HAST KNOWN THE HOLY SCRIPTURES, WHICH ARE ABLE TO MAKE THEE WISE UNTO SALVATION THROUGH FAITH WHICH IS IN CHRIST JESUS" (2 Timothy 3:15).

From a personal witness I can say for certainty that proper Biblical education during early childhood is effective in establishing one's faith—especially if it is directed toward Christ, who has brought us salvation. From a very early age I can remember the instructions, guidance, and education from the Scriptures. Church, Sunday school, and revivals are most important and fulfilling memories that I have of my youth. Even though the apostle Paul was referring to the young evangelist Timothy, somehow I am personally overwhelmed with the excitement and gratitude that I received early religious education from my parents and church family.

I have often heard excuses from those who take a shallow view from Proverbs 22:6: "Train up a child in the way he should go: and when he is old, he will not depart from it." Some will philosophize that he or she may not ever come to salvation, but children certainly will not forget what they are taught about it. Personally, I detest such weak confidence in the divine revelation of God's Word. Solomon was not just writing a book of Eastern culture philosophy. He was writing God's holy, divine will. If God's Word is powerful enough to convert someone who never heard the Word during his early childhood, then I believe that Proverbs 22:6 means what it says.

I am saved, sanctified, and filled with the baptism of the Holy Ghost today because it was taught to me when I was a child. My parents firmly believed in these precepts: "For the promise is unto you, and to your children, and to all that are afar off, even as many as the Lord our God shall call" (Acts 2:39); "Whom shall he teach knowledge? and whom shall he make to understand doctrine? them that are weaned from the milk, and drawn from the breasts" (Isaiah 28:9); "Wherewithal shall a young man cleanse his way? by taking heed thereto according to thy word" (Psalm 119:9).

Psalm 19:7 says: "The law of the Lord is perfect, converting the soul: the testimony of the Lord is sure, making wise the simple." It is a great happiness for me to have known the Holy Scriptures from my childhood. The age of children is the learning age, and those who would get true learning must get it out of the Scriptures. "Remember now thy Creator in the days of thy youth, while the evil days come not, nor the years draw nigh, when thou shalt say, I have no pleasure in them" (Ecclesiastes 12:1). Those who would acquaint themselves with the things of God, and be assured of them, must know the Holy Scriptures, for these are the summary of divine revelation. And oh, how wonderful and divine it would be if all could say that of this scripture: "That from a child I have known the Holy Scriptures, which have made me wise for salvation" (see 1 Timothy 3:15).

Parents, please don't fail to educate your children in the knowledge of the divine Word of God. "And, ye fathers, provoke not your children to wrath: but bring them up in the nurture and admonition of the Lord" (Ephesians 6:4).—**Aaron D. Mize, Chaplain I, Mississippi State Prison, Parchman, Mississippi**

SENTENCE SERMONS

CHRISTIANS must seek opportunities to share Christ with family and friends.

—Selected

THE CHRISTIAN HOME is the Master's workshop where the silent work of character molding is going on.

—Richard Milnes

INSOMUCH as anyone pushes you nearer to God, he or she is a friend.

—Anonymous

DAILY BIBLE READINGS

M. Leadership in the Home.
   Genesis 18:16-22
T. Teach Your Children.
   Deuteronomy 6:1-9
W. Choice for the Family.
   Joshua 24:14-21
T. Committed to the Family.
   Ruth 1:8-18
F. Intercede for Family.
   Luke 8:40-42, 49-56
S. Gather Family and Friends.
   Acts 10:23-27, 44-48

A Ready Witness

Study Text: Acts 8:26-40

Objective: To discover how the Holy Spirit can direct us in our witness and determine to follow His leading.

Time: The Book of Acts was written between A.D. 61 and A.D. 63.

Place: The Book of Acts was probably written at Caesarea or Rome.

Golden Text: "Be ready always to give an answer to every man that asketh you a reason of the hope that is in you with meekness and fear" (1 Peter 3:15).

Central Truth: Christians must be sensitive and obedient to the Holy Spirit in witnessing to sinners.

Evangelism Emphasis: Christians must depend on the Holy Spirit to make their witness effective.

PRINTED TEXT

Acts 8:26. And the angel of the Lord spake unto Philip, saying, Arise, and go toward the south unto the way that goeth down from Jerusalem unto Gaza, which is desert.

27. And he arose and went: and, behold, a man of Ethiopia, an eunuch of great authority under Candace queen of the Ethiopians, who had the charge of all her treasure, and had come to Jerusalem for to worship,

28. Was returning, and sitting in his chariot read Esaias the prophet.

29. Then the Spirit said unto Philip, Go near, and join thyself to this chariot.

30. And Philip ran thither to him, and heard him read the prophet Esaias, and said, Understandest thou what thou readest?

31. And he said, How can I, except some man should guide me? And he desired Philip that he would come up and sit with him.

32. The place of the scripture which he read was this, He was led as a sheep to the slaughter; and like a lamb dumb before his shearer, so opened he not his mouth:

33. In his humiliation his judgment was taken away: and who shall declare his generation? for his life is taken from the earth.

34. And the eunuch answered Philip, and said, I pray thee, of whom speaketh the prophet this? of himself, or of some other man?

35. Then Philip opened his

mouth, and began at the same scripture, and preached unto him Jesus.

36. And as they went on their way, they came unto a certain water: and the eunuch said, See, here is water; what doth hinder me to be baptized?

37. And Philip said, If thou believest with all thine heart, thou mayest. And he answered and said, I believe that Jesus Christ is the Son of God.

38. And he commanded the chariot to stand still: and they went down both into the water, both Philip and the eunuch; and he baptized him.

39. And when they were come up out of the water, the Spirit of the Lord caught away Philip, that the eunuch saw him no more: and he went on his way rejoicing.

40. But Philip was found at Azotus: and passing through he preached in all the cities, till he came to Caesarea.

DICTIONARY

Gaza (GAY-zuh)—Acts 8:26—One of the five chief Philistine cities located three miles inland from the Mediterranean coast of the Gaza Strip.

Eunuch (YOU-nuk)—Acts 8:27—A castrated male.

Candace (CAN-dah-see)—Acts 8:27—The queen of Ethiopia.

Azotus (ah-ZOH-tus)—Acts 8:40—The Old Testament city of Ashdod.

Caesarea (SES-uh-REE-uh)—Acts 8:40—A city on the Mediterranean coast northwest of Jerusalem.

Have you ever met a Christian who seems to have no real...

LESSON OUTLINE

I. BE LED BY THE SPIRIT
   A. Angelic Direction
   B. An Earnest Inquirer
   C. A Divine Errand

II. BE READY TO ANSWER
   A. Asking a Question
   B. Awaiting an Answer

III. MAKE JESUS KNOWN
   A. Using the Word
   B. Removing the Hindrances
   C. Continuing to Witness

LESSON EXPOSITION

INTRODUCTION

Psalm 126:6 is one of the most important verses in the Bible on soulwinning. It reads: "He that goeth forth and weepeth, bearing precious seed, shall doubtless come again with rejoicing, bringing his sheaves with him."

Dr. Horace F. Dean makes the following suggestion: "Nothing can keep the Christian warm, fresh, and vibrant like personal soulwinning. Witnessing daily gives the child of God a radiance to be had in no other way. Soulwinning is the great safeguard against dead and fruitless orthodoxy. The continuous growth of every believer and the expansion of any church depends upon a living pulsating and consistent soulwinning program without which no church can survive. No Christian can remain

strong and effective as a representative of Jesus Christ who fails constantly to witness for Him"
(*Operation Evangelism*).

The newly formed church in the
Book of Acts considered its one
uppermost task to be the winning of
others, the saving of souls, with
every believer a witness.

In the Gospels and the Book of
Acts, the early Christians were constantly reaching out to others with
the message of Christ. Andrew
brings Peter; Philip finds Nathanael;
Philip later reaches the Ethiopian
eunuch. Most experts on evangelism say the church, as well as the
individual, which loses its evangelistic passion loses out with the
Lord. There may be the retention of
some form of religion—the saying of
prayers, the recitation of creed—but
the real manifestations of power
and fruitbearing are absent.

Dean believes that every real
child of God has a desire to see others won to Christ. He writes: "This
desire is implanted in the heart of
every Christian at the time of conversion. Here is a sort of paternal
desire or maternal longing which
God puts into our hearts as believers, a yearning to see the family of
God increase."

Dean also thinks that most
Christians have the feeling that
they cannot do the work of the soulwinner. They will faithfully and regularly attend church, they will even
live separated lives and avoid all
forms of worldliness. They will give
generously to support the work of
the gospel and be faithful in praying
and reading of the Bible.

Dean says: "Many are willing to
sing in the choirs of the church or
to teach Sunday school classes, and
fill other responsibilities, but some-

how, they just feel that they cannot
win souls. Satan wants to keep
them thinking this way and thus be
able to rob them of the joy and to
keep them from fulfilling this definite responsibility" (*Operation
Evangelism*).

Dr. R.A. Torrey, in his book
Personal Work, emphasizes the
advantages of personal evangelism.
He points out: "All can do it; it can
be done anywhere; it can be done
anytime; it reaches all classes; it
meets the definite need and every
need of the person dealt with; it hits
the mark; it avails where other
methods fail; it produces large
results."

Dr. E.J. Daniels emphasizes that
great talent is not required to win
souls: "Many hesitate to attempt to
win souls because they feel they
have little talent for this work.
Actually, a sincere love for the lost,
a willingness to do your best and to
improve every opportunity is the
'best talent' for winning lost souls.
Sometimes an untrained, stammer-
ing, unlearned soulwinner can do
what skilled preachers cannot do in
winning the lost" (*Techniques of
Torchbearing*).

I. BE LED BY THE SPIRIT
    (Acts 8:26-29)

A. Angelic Direction (v. 26)

**26. And the angel of the Lord
spake unto Philip, saying, Arise,
and go toward the south unto the
way that goeth down from
Jerusalem unto Gaza, which is
desert.**

Philip the deacon has been called
the apostle to Samaria. He was evidently a Greek-speaking Jew; his
name is Greek and means "horse
lover." Like all of the seven deacons

of Acts 6, he was a man "of good reputation, full of the Spirit and of wisdom" (v. 3, *NASB*). As a good executive he did not omit any of the poor Christians in the distribution of money and food. But when persecution came, these Christians were driven from Jerusalem, and Philip's job was complete there. So he followed the fleeing Christians to Samaria ministering to their needs (8:1-8).

While in Samaria, Philip preached about the Redeemer. The people eagerly accepted his message and a revival broke out. Demons were driven out of their wretched victims, and many sufferers of palsy and many cripples were restored to health. Luke says "there was great joy in that city" (v. 8)

It was in the midst of this revival that Philip was directed by an angel to go south to the desert (v. 26). He was not told what to do or what to expect. Sometimes God sends His servants forth in the dark, bidding them go out as Abraham went, "not knowing whither he went" (Hebrews 11:8). He often does this to strengthen their faith and prove their courage. Others may be led by an angel. We must leave the method of guidance to God, who knows our hearts and our abilities, and who, if we yield ourselves to His guidance, will always get us to the desired place on time.

B. An Earnest Inquirer (vv. 27, 28)

27. And he arose and went: and, behold, a man of Ethiopia, an eunuch of great authority under Candace queen of the Ethiopians, who had the charge of all her treasure, and had come to Jerusalem for to worship,
28. Was returning, and sitting
in his chariot read Esaias the prophet.

Philip obeyed promptly. He did not say he had much work yet to do in Samaria. He did not ask for additional information about the journey or for more time to prepare. He did not suggest that Peter or John or one of the other apostles would be more suitable for the task. He simply arose and went.

Luke does not waste any time in getting to the essentials of his story. He tells us that Philip met an Ethiopian who was a eunuch and was the treasurer for Candace, queen of the Ethiopians. He was also a Jewish proselyte who had been attending a feast in Jerusalem.

The feast was over and he was on his way back to his home by way of Gaza. As he traveled he was reading from the Book of Isaiah. Horatio B. Hackett, in his *Commentary on Acts*, suggests: "It is not improbable that the eunuch had heard, at Jerusalem, of the death of Jesus, and of the wonderful events connected with it, of his claim to be the Messiah, and the existence of a numerous party who acknowledged him in that character. Hence he may have been examining the prophecies at the time Philip approached him, with reference to the question how far they had been accomplished in the history of the person concerning whom such reports had reached him."

C. A Divine Errand (v. 29)

29. Then the Spirit said unto Philip, Go near, and join thyself to this chariot.

Probably by an inner divine prompting, the Spirit told Philip to join the chariot. This would be natural for a lone traveler to do in this kind of situation. An important person like the eunuch would be traveling with a large retinue. This would provide protection for Philip as well as companionship for both of them.

Do you think believers today are as prompt to respond to God's call as Philip? Explain.

II. BE READY TO ANSWER
(Acts 8:30-34)

A. Asking a Question (v. 30)

30. And Philip ran thither to him, and heard him read the prophet Esaias, and said, Understandest thou what thou readest?

Again there was no hesitation on the part of Philip. Perhaps he remembered the words of the psalmist, "I will run the way of thy commandments" (Psalm 119:32). As he approached he heard the eunuch reading. According to Cunningham Geikie, "Orientals are accustomed to read aloud, even when they are alone, and it was usual for a Jew, or one who had virtually become so, to read from the Scriptures when traveling, to beguile the way; for the sacred writings, in some part of them, were, we may say, the one book a Jew of that age would open; all others being proscribed as heathen, or concerned with subjects related to heathen studies" (*New Testament Hours*).

Philip had a real concern for those whom he met. He also had a love for souls and a knowledge of the Word of God. So he asked the eunuch if he understood what he was reading.

B. Awaiting an Answer (vv. 31-34)

31. And he said, How can I, except some man should guide me? And he desired Philip that he would come up and sit with him.

32. The place of the scripture which he read was this, He was led as a sheep to the slaughter; and like a lamb dumb before his shearer, so opened he not his mouth:

33. In his humiliation his judgment was taken away: and who shall declare his generation? for his life is taken from the earth.

34. And the eunuch answered Philip, and said, I pray thee, of whom speaketh the prophet this? of himself, or of some other man?

The eunuch was a man of influence, accustomed to guide others, but humble as a child in matters of the Spirit. All believers need assistance in understanding the Scriptures. Someone has said that only a fool will reject such assistance when it is offered in the right spirit.

The word translated "guide" (v. 31) is the same word used by Jesus when He promised the disciples that the Holy Spirit would "guide you into all truth" (John 16:13).

Without doubt the Holy Spirit had guided the eunuch to the prophecy of Isaiah. He was reading Isaiah 53:7, 8, the crowning prophecy of the Messiah, extending from 52:13 to the end of chapter 53.

The verses quoted are not from the Hebrew Bible but from the Septuagint, the translation of the Old Testament into Greek. Philip, being a Grecian, would be familiar with that version, and since it was made in Egypt, the Ethiopian was probably reading it. The expressions in this version are somewhat different, but the message is the same.

The eunuch wanted Philip to explain the entire passage from Isaiah. The statement "He was led as a sheep to the slaughter" (Acts 8:32) refers to the Lamb of God, who died as a sacrifice for the sins of the world. This occurred at the time when the Passover lamb was offered in memory of the preservation of all the firstborn of the Hebrews in Egypt. The Jews expected a coming Messiah who would be a great conqueror and a political ruler with power. They could not conceive of Him as a sheep led to the slaughter.

The reference to the "lamb dumb [being silent] before his shearer" refers to the trial of Jesus. Pilate was amazed at the reaction of Jesus before His accusers. Jesus refused to answer His accusers even though their charges were unjust. His status was considered so insignificant that the laws of both the Jews and the Romans were completely disregarded. In fact, many Bible scholars reefer to it as a lynching.

In verse 34 the eunuch was responding to the question of Philip concerning his understanding of what he was reading. He wanted to know if the prophet was referring to himself. Thomas M. Lindsay has an interesting observation on this question: "The Jews did not apply these words to the Messiah; their Messiah was a conquering captain, not a suffering Saviour. There was a tradition that Isaiah was sawn asunder by Manasseh. The treasurer may have been acquainted with this tradition and conjectured that Isaiah was foretelling his own sufferings" (Handbook for Bible Classes).

Evaluate Philip's approach to the eunuch.

III. MAKE JESUS KNOWN
      (Acts 8:35-40)

A. Using the Word (v. 35)

35. Then Philip opened his mouth, and began at the same scripture, and preached unto him Jesus.

The eunuch had certainly not heard the name of Jesus in Jerusalem, at least not from the Jewish people. It is possible that he had never heard of the name until Philip began to tell him of the One whose sufferings and death were the perfect fulfillment of Isaiah's great prophecies. The heart of this man must have been moved as he discovered all the phrases of Isaiah's prophecy to be, as it were, the very lines of a portrait that characterized perfectly the humiliation and death of the Messiah.

Dr. Wilbur M. Smith says, "This is perfect preaching, preaching to the human heart, preaching with enthusiasm and passion—when the Word of God, be it Old or New Testament, is made to lead up to Christ Jesus our Lord."

It is important to remember that Jesus and His apostles made much use of the Word of God in their evangelistic ministries. They were constantly referring to the Old Testament Scriptures as being fulfilled, or as giving them a "thus saith the Lord" basis for their speaking. They did not once question any truth of the Old Testament. They were intimately acquainted with the Old Testament and used it freely.

Dr. Faris Daniel Whitesell has some valuable words on the use of the Bible in witnessing to people: "The record of world evangelization in the Book of Acts is one of spreading the Word of God, honoring the Word of God, and explaining the Word of God.

"The New Testament method of evangelizing is to rely upon the Word of God and the Spirit of God. The Word of God must constitute our message and our authority. On the authority of God's Word we know that men are lost and need Christ. That Word clearly shows us our responsibility to seek and to save the lost, and gives us the right principles of procedure. The Word of God gives us our message, a message which is 'the power of God unto salvation to every one that believeth' (Romans 1:16). To neglect the Word of God, or to substitute anything else for the Word of God, is sheer folly.

"The winner of men must live by the same Word which he preaches to others. He must be so saturated with the Scriptures that they can perform their function of cleansing, rebuking, refreshing, inspiring, informing, and empowering him. He should read the Bible . . . not merely for sermonic material, but for spiritual knowledge and growth" (*Basic New Testament Evangelism*).

B. Removing the Hindrances
   (vv. 36-39)

36. And as they went on their way, they came unto a certain water: and the eunuch said, See, here is water; what doth hinder me to be baptized?

37. And Philip said, If thou believest with all thine heart, thou mayest. And he answered and said, I believe that Jesus Christ is the Son of God.

38. And he commanded the chariot to stand still: and they went down both into the water, both Philip and the eunuch; and he baptized him.

39. And when they were come up out of the water, the Spirit of the Lord caught away Philip, that the eunuch saw him no more: and he went on his way rejoicing.

It must be assumed that Philip spent a considerable amount of time with the eunuch, for he had much to tell him and the eunuch had much he wanted to learn. The fact that Philip's teaching included baptism shows that he was thorough. The treasurer had been converted, and proved it by his desire to be obedient to what he had heard, for Philip had evidently told him that Christ commanded baptism as an outward sign of allegiance to Him. Nothing more accurately reveals the true Christian than his eager desire to be obedient to his Savior. Jesus said, "Ye are my friends, if ye do whatsoever I command you" (John 15:14).

The statement by the eunuch in verse 37 shows that he believed in the deity of Christ before he was baptized. He was baptized as the follower not of a mere man but of the glorified Son of God, Redeemer of the world. Without such a belief, baptism and church membership are both meaningless and fruitless.

The Jews followed the custom of baptizing in rivers (v. 38). Thus John the Baptist baptized in the river Jordan. The duty and privilege of baptism is based on the command of Christ in Matthew

28:19. Christians generally agree that baptism represents the washing away of our sins in the blood of Christ and the entering into a new life in Him. Christians should consider it a joy to show faith in baptism.

Leonard Bacon makes an interesting observation on this verse: "As you read this story—in fact, as you read the whole New Testament—you get the impression that the way into the kingdom of heaven, in the days of our Lord Christ and his apostles, was a very obvious and straightforward way to any who was willing to enter it. What a simple business they seemed to make of it" (*The Simplicity That Is in Christ*).

The implication of a supernatural carrying away of Philip is clear (v. 39), and such a departure would seal upon the eunuch's mind the truths that Philip had been teaching. Luke, it must be remembered, had ample opportunity to learn these facts from Philip himself.

The eunuch went his way rejoicing. He was not rejoicing because Philip was gone; he was rejoicing because the Lord was with him. Tradition says this man took the gospel to many places in Africa.

C. Continuing to Witness (v. 40)

40. But Philip was found at Azotus: and passing through he preached in all the cities, till he came to Caesarea.

"Azotus" (v. 40) is another name for Ashdod, one of the old cities of the Philistines, about 30 miles from Gaza, midway between it and Joppa. Caesarea was an important city. It was the Roman capital of Palestine and the seat of the governor. We find Philip here 20 years later, with his four daughters,

entertaining Paul and Luke (21:8, 9).

Evaluate Philip's witnessing to the eunuch.

REVIEW QUESTIONS

1. Who was Philip?
2. How was Philip sent to the desert?
3. Whom did Philip meet in the desert?
4. What Scripture passage did Philip explain to the eunuch?
5. What was the result of the conversation between Philip and the eunuch?

SENTENCE SERMONS

CHRISTIANS MUST BE sensitive and obedient to the Holy Spirit in witnessing to sinners.

—Selected

A CANDLE loses nothing by lighting another candle.

—Selected

GOD does not do anything with us, only through us.

—Oswald Chambers

OBEDIENCE IS the key to every door of opportunity.

—George McDonald

DAILY BIBLE READINGS

M. God Commissions.
　　Exodus 4:10-17
T. God Draws People to Himself.
　　Jeremiah 31:1-9
W. The Spirit Convicts.
　　John 16:5-14
T. The Spirit Gives Life.
　　Romans 8:1-11
F. God Gives Boldness.
　　2 Timothy 1:6-12
S. The Faithful Witness.
　　Revelation 1:1-8

Pentecostal Power (Pentecost)

Study Text: Joel 2:32; Acts 1:1-8; 2:1-41

Objective: To appreciate the power of the Holy Spirit and receive His power in our lives.

Time: The Book of Joel was written between 835 and 800 B.C. The Book of Acts was written between A.D. 61 and 63.

Place: The Book of Joel was probably written at Jerusalem. The Book of Acts was probably written at Caesarea or Rome.

Golden Text: "Ye shall receive power, after that the Holy Ghost is come upon you" (Acts 1:8).

Central Truth: The Holy Spirit empowers believers for effective service.

Evangelism Emphasis: The Holy Spirit leads sinners to repentance and faith in Christ.

PRINTED TEXT

Acts 1:5. For John truly baptized with water; but ye shall be baptized with the Holy Ghost not many days hence.

6. When they therefore were come together, they asked of him, saying, Lord, wilt thou at this time restore again the kingdom to Israel?

7. And he said unto them, It is not for you to know the times or the seasons, which the Father hath put in his own power.

8. But ye shall receive power, after that the Holy Ghost is come upon you: and ye shall be witnesses unto me both in Jerusalem, and in all Judaea, and in Samaria, and unto the uttermost part of the earth.

2:1. And when the day of Pentecost was fully come, they were all with one accord in one place.

2. And suddenly there came a sound from heaven as of a rushing mighty wind, and it filled all the house where they were sitting.

3. And there appeared unto them cloven tongues like as of fire, and it sat upon each of them.

4. And they were all filled with the Holy Ghost, and began to speak with other tongues, as the Spirit gave them utterance.

13. Others mocking said, These men are full of new wine.

14. But Peter, standing up with the eleven, lifted up his voice, and said unto them, Ye men of Judaea, and all ye that dwell at Jerusalem, be this known unto you, and hearken to my words:

15. For these are not drunken, as ye suppose, seeing it is but the third hour of the day.

16. But this is that which was spoken by the prophet Joel;

21. And it shall come to pass, that whosoever shall call on the name of the Lord shall be saved.

40. And with many other words did he testify and exhort, saying, Save yourselves from this untoward generation.

41. Then they that gladly received his word were baptized: and the same day there were added unto them about three thousand souls.

LESSON OUTLINE
I. POWER PROMISED
   A. The Earthly Ministry
   B. The Parting Words
II. POWER RECEIVED
   A. The Description
   B. The Reception
III. POWER MISUNDERSTOOD
   A. The Astonishment
   B. The Mocking
IV. POWER FOR SALVATION
   A. Negative Confutation
   B. Positive Confutation
   C. Instruction
   D. Results

LESSON EXPOSITION

INTRODUCTION

One of the most distinctive aspects of the life of Christ is the perfect calmness He manifested in regard to the future course and fate of the disciples, whom He had gathered around Him, and of the work which He had begun. He set His face forward. He did not permit any weight of disappointment for His own career cut short to dull His apprehension of what lay beyond the time of His departure. He discerned the actual relation between His departure from His disciples and the future, divine visitations which His disciples would know. He could see that for their perfection in grace, it was expedient that He should go away.

Jesus called His disciples from their contemplation of their own impending loss to the great gift which should follow His going away. The disciples did not understand it, and they were grief-stricken and bewildered. All they knew was that they were going to lose Jesus. But Jesus told them that in the end this was all for the best; because when He went away, the Holy Spirit, the Helper, would come.

In John 16:1 Jesus told them, "These things have I spoken unto you, that ye should not be offended." Well did our Lord know that nothing is so dangerous to our comfort as to indulge false expectations. He therefore prepared His disciples for what they must expect to meet with in His service. They must not look for a smooth course and a peaceful journey. They must make up their minds to face battles, conflicts, opposition, persecutions, perhaps even death. Like a wise army officer, He did not conceal from His soldiers the nature of the battle which they were beginning. He told them all that was before them. How true this prediction turned out to be. Indeed, "All that will live godly in Christ Jesus shall suffer persecution" (2 Timothy 3:12).

Jesus, following this warning, promised to send the Holy Spirit to assist the apostles and all Christians in all areas of life. True to His word, Christ has sent the Holy Spirit to work in and through the believer.

I. POWER PROMISED (Acts 1:1-8)

A. The Earthly Ministry (vv. 1-3)

(Acts 1:1-3 is not included in the printed text.)

In the opening verses of Acts we find a reiteration of a promise given by Jesus to the disciples. This time it is in a new context. Jesus had been crucified, and resurrected, but He awaited ascension. He again gave the promise of the coming Spirit—this time to empower His followers for witnessing at home, abroad, and to the uttermost parts of the earth.

The statement "until the day in which he was taken up" (v. 2) defines the terminus of the Gospels and the point of beginning for Acts. The word *commandments* is interpreted by some as a reference to the Great Commission; others see it as pointing to the command to wait for enduement of power by the Spirit. The context may be general enough to include both ideas.

The period between the Resurrection and the Ascension was important to the disciples. The apostles needed three things if they were to accomplish the task assigned them by their Lord: (1) assurance that Jesus was alive; (2) instruction concerning what was expected of them as His followers; and (3) the spiritual power necessary to accomplish the task assigned them. The activity of the risen Christ was designed to meet these needs and thus to prepare the apostles for their mission in the world.

B. The Parting Words (vv. 4-8)

(Acts 1:4 is not included in the printed text.)

5. For John truly baptized with water; but ye shall be baptized with the Holy Ghost not many days hence.

6. When they therefore were come together, they asked of him, saying, Lord, wilt thou at this time restore again the kingdom to Israel?

7. And he said unto them, It is not for you to know the times or the seasons, which the Father hath put in his own power.

8. But ye shall receive power, after that the Holy Ghost is come upon you: and ye shall be witnesses unto me both in Jerusalem, and in all Judaea, and in Samaria, and unto the uttermost part of the earth.

Verses 4 and 5 record an event that took place during one of the appearances of Jesus. Being assembled with the disciples, He charged them not to leave Jerusalem until they had received "the promise of the Father," and until they were "endued with power from on high" (see also Luke 24:49).

This commandment to wait for the promise is often taken out of context and imposed upon modern believers as a condition for being baptized in the Holy Ghost. However, the stress of the command is on the words "in Jerusalem." The charge to the disciples is not as much concerned with the waiting (with spiritual preparation) as with geographical direction (in Jerusalem) and with the certainty that God would fulfill His promise of a new Spirit experience.

Luke refers to the Holy Spirit as the "promise of the Father" (Acts 1:4). The phrase is repeated from Luke 24:49, and is distinctive to these two passages. The promise of the gift of the Holy Spirit is prominent in the Old Testament (Isaiah 32:15; Joel 2:28-32), and is often confirmed and explained in the New Testament (John 7:38, 39; 14:16-18, 26; 15:26; 16:7, 13). To Luke, the sacred gift bore the idea that it is the heavenly Father's gift to His believing children, and so to invite their faith. No obedient child of God need fear to seek and claim his Father's special promise.

The baptism in the Holy Ghost is expressly promised in all four Gospels. This fact alone shows the importance of the subject. We must remember also that in connection with the promise of the Spirit baptism, the office of Christ as baptizer was thus announced. It is clear, therefore, that the New Testament attaches importance to the experience of baptism in the Holy Spirit.

These apostles recognized in Christ the Messiah of God, and they naturally asked if it were not time for Christ to set up such a kingdom as they hoped for (Acts 1:6).

Jesus did not rebuke the supposed ignorance of the disciples, nor did He tell them that they were mistaken. His answer approved of the subject of the question. The kingdom was to be restored, but the times and the seasons were not to be revealed (v. 7).

The preeminent task of the disciples was to witness to the facts concerning the Lord Jesus Christ, so that, through this witnessing, men might be convicted of their sins and brought to an acceptance of Christ as their Savior. Sinners are bound in their sins—by the power of their own flesh, by the power of the world they live in, and by the power of the devil. There is no power resident in any man sufficient to overcome these three powers in the life of another. As A.B. Bruce has written: "If men are to be delivered from their sins, if men are to emancipate from the bonds of this world, then a supernatural power is indispensable. Something more than eloquence, intellect, money, and organization is required; true spiritual power cannot be produced like electric sparks by the friction of excitement, but must come sovereignly and graciously down from on high" (*The Training of the Twelve*).

Luke gives us an actual outline of the Book of Acts in verse 8: Jerusalem is the center of the events recorded in 1:1 to 8:3; Judea and Samaria witness the events recorded in 8:4-25; while the events occurring in the rest of the Book of Acts may be described as taking place in "the uttermost part of the earth."

Is it possible to witness for Christ without the power of the Holy Spirit? Explain.

II. POWER RECEIVED (Acts 2:1-4)

A. The Description (vv. 1-3)

1. And when the day of Pentecost was fully come, they were all with one accord in one place.

2. And suddenly there came a sound from heaven as of a rushing mighty wind, and it filled all the house where they were sitting.

3. And there appeared unto them cloven tongues like as of fire, and it sat upon each of them.

The Greek word *Pentecost* (v. 1) means "fiftieth," having reference to the fact that the long-standing Feast of Pentecost was celebrated on the 50th day after the offering of the barley sheaf on the day following the Passover Sabbath. The feast was the second of three annual Jewish feasts, occurring between the Passover and the Feast of Tabernacles. In the Old Testament it bears the names of "Feast of Weeks," "Feast of Harvest," and "Day of Firstfruits."

The word *all* (v. 1) refers back to Acts 1:15, which speaks of all the disciples assembled in Jerusalem, men and women, particularly the 120, and not the apostles only. The expression of "all with one accord in one place" is most striking because it points to a perfect unity of heart, thought, and purpose among the disciples.

According to Luke this mighty work of God occurred suddenly and unexpectedly. There is no evidence that the disciples experienced a storm, but only that they heard a tempestuous wind. The word *wind* (v. 2) is translated from a word that means "blowing, blast, breath." The literal translation is that the disciples heard "a sound as of a mighty blast borne along."

The general interpretation of verse 2 is that the sound, not a wind, filled the house. Just as the phenomena of light and sound indicate the presence of invisible energy, so the sound of wind in this instance told of the coming of the Divine Spirit.

Each of the disciples experienced the visible phenomenon of "cloven tongues"—tongues parting asunder—as of fire, and sitting upon each of them (v. 3). Here again, it is not said that they experienced actual tongues of fire, but that the tongues had the semblance of fire.

One scholar made this interesting interpretation of the symbol of the tongues of fire. The emblem of the tongue implied that the witnesses were to speak to their fellowmen the things of God. The emblem of the fire indicated the power of their message was the burning power of the Holy Ghost. Thus, this symbol has come to represent the Holy Spirit.

B. The Reception (v. 4)

4. And they were all filled with the Holy Ghost, and began to speak with other tongues, as the Spirit gave them utterance.

All the disciples in the room were filled with the Holy Ghost. And what a significant difference the coming of the Spirit in His fullness made to those first disciples! The weak became strong; the timid became bold; the carnal became spiritual.

How did the disciples know they had received the Holy Spirit? Luke states they spoke with tongues. Speaking in tongues is but an evidence of Spirit baptism, and not Spirit baptism itself. When we speak of being filled with the Spirit, we must remember that the Holy Spirit is a person. The baptism in the Spirit cannot be separated from the person of the Spirit. We may understand this to mean that when the disciples were baptized in the Spirit, the Spirit himself took entire possession of them. This makes something more of Spirit baptism than a surface or purely emotional experience.

Luke states that the disciples "began to speak with other tongues." R. Hollis Gause writes: "A careful study of the language of Acts 2:4 shows a causative relationship between being filled with the Spirit and speaking in tongues: 'And they were all filled with the Holy Spirit, and they began to speak with other tongues because [*kathos*: because] the Spirit was giving them inspiration to speak.' When they were filled with the Spirit, the Spirit became the agent and origin of their speech. They were not empowered to speak before the Holy Spirit filled them" (*Living in the Spirit: The Way of Salvation*).

Do the same signs accompany the reception of the Holy Spirit today? Explain.

III. POWER MISUNDERSTOOD (Acts 2:5-13)

A. The Astonishment (vv. 5-12)

(Acts 2:5-12 is not included in the printed text.)

All that happened in the place of the outpouring of the Holy Spirit attracted the attention of Jews gathered in Jerusalem. The new Spirit-empowered men and women did not take calmly the experience they had just received. Theirs had been no ordinary experience. They were gripped by a power which strongly possessed them. They recognized the sublime fulfillment of the promise of the Father and gave vent to the Holy Ghost.

A multitude of Jews from various nations and cultures gathered to see what was happening. They were bewildered because each one heard the disciples speak in his own language. From lands beyond the Jordan, from Asia, from Egypt, from Italy—they all heard "the wonderful works of God" in their own tongues (v. 11).

B. The Mocking (v. 13)

13. Others mocking said, These men are full of new wine.

The curious onlookers marveled at first at what they saw and heard. Apparently they understood basic Jewish traditions and were acquainted with the Old Testament. Hearing strange words in their native tongues may have reminded them of the powers of ancient prophets. However, they were not used to seeing and hearing 120 people speaking simultaneously like prophets. They were amazed and perplexed at first, asking, "What does this mean?" (see v. 12). Some of them mocked. Some of them said, "These men are full of new wine."

Evaluate the reactions of the onlookers on the Day of Pentecost.

IV. POWER FOR SALVATION (Acts 2:14-16, 21, 40, 41)

A. Negative Confutation (vv. 14, 15)

14. But Peter, standing up with the eleven, lifted up his voice, and said unto them, Ye men of Judaea, and all ye that dwell at Jerusalem, be this known unto you, and hearken to my words:

15. For these are not drunken, as ye suppose, seeing it is but the third hour of the day.

In response to the questions and

accusations of the crowd, Peter disposed of the false accusation that his brethren, who were heard speaking with tongues, were drunk. The fact that it was only 9 o'clock in the morning made these critics' explanation ridiculous, for wine was drunk by the Jews with meat only; and basing the custom on Exodus 16:8, they ate bread in the morning and meat in the evening, and so they took no wine until late in the day.

B. Positive Confutation (vv. 16, 21)

(Acts 2:17-20, 22-36 is not included in the printed text.)

16. But this is that which was spoken by the prophet Joel;

21. And it shall come to pass, that whosoever shall call on the name of the Lord shall be saved.

Having told his expectant audience that what they had heard was not true, Peter proceeded to tell them what it was—"But this is that which was spoken by the prophet Joel" (v. 16). The quotation is from Joel 2:28-32 and, for the most part, from the Greek (Septuagint) version.

The prophet Joel had declared that in the last days God would pour out His Spirit upon all flesh— both young and old, upon men and women, upon privileged and unprivileged.

At least part of Joel's prophecy had been fulfilled on that memorable Pentecost. Peter drove home his point that a new day had dawned in God's relationship with His people.

Peter then proceeded in sermon to show that Jesus of Nazareth is the exalted Lord on whom men and women must call in order to be

saved. First, there must be repentance and water baptism; then there is Holy Ghost baptism. And as it was for all present on the Day of Pentecost, nearly two millenniums ago, so it has been every day since. And no less so today.

After speaking of judgments that would follow the outpouring of the Spirit, Joel's thoughts were drawn back to reflect upon the blessing of salvation implied in the outpouring of the Spirit upon all mankind. Such a diffusion of the Spirit would of necessity mean that salvation (deliverance) would be offered to all who call upon the name of the Lord. The promise that the Spirit would be poured out "upon all flesh" presupposes that all who call on the name of the Lord in faith and repentance will be saved (v. 21).

In verses 22-36, Peter concluded his sermon, which was based on the Word of God. He stated the Jews had crucified the Lord as a blasphemer and a false Messiah. God had recognized and exalted Jesus as the true Messiah. Then Peter emphasized it was time for the Jews to acknowledge their error, and to accept God's verdict and believe in Him.

C. Instruction (v. 40)

(Acts 2:37-39 is not included in the printed text.)

40. And with many other words did he testify and exhort, saying, Save yourselves from this untoward generation.

Some of the Jews present may have sneered at the claims of Jesus, or kept silent when His foes abused Him. Others may have had a chance to influence the authorities in His favor but had been too cowardly to do it. All of them as Jews felt the shame for what their people had done and for fear of the consequences of falling into the hands of an angry God. By addressing the apostles as brethren, they were in a way seeking admission to their fellowship as believers in Jesus. They virtually admitted their guilt and wanted to know what they could do to escape the penalties.

Peter began—as John the Baptist began, as Christ himself began—with the exhortation to repentance, to a change of heart and life, not mere regret for the past. First, there was to be an inward change and then submission to the external rite. Baptism is a sign and a symbol of the washing away of our sins. What clean water does with the stains we have accumulated on our hands and bodies, from contact with the physical world, the precious blood of Christ does with the stains from sin in our hearts.

D. Results (v. 41)

41. Then they that gladly received his word were baptized: and the same day there were added unto them about three thousand souls.

Receiving Peter's word means accepting it, acknowledging its truth, and acting on the advice of the apostle. The day had begun with 120 Christians in the little community in Jerusalem, and then 3,000 were added to them. What a sermon Peter preached! And yet the ingathering, like all ingatherings, was the work of the Holy Spirit alone. All through the ages He has accomplished similar wonders, and never more notably than in our day through the work of the church around the world.

REVIEW QUESTIONS

1. Explain how Acts 1:8 can be considered an outline for the Book of Acts.

2. Explain the symbolism of the tongues of fire which came on the disciples on the Day of Pentecost.

3. What did Joel say God will do in the last days and what signs will accompany them?

4. How did the crowd react to the 120 receiving the Holy Spirit on the Day of Pentecost and what was Peter's response?

5. What did Peter tell the inquirers they must do to receive the promise of the Holy Spirit?

GOLDEN TEXT HOMILY

"YE SHALL RECEIVE POWER, AFTER THAT THE HOLY GHOST IS COME UPON YOU" (Acts 1:8).

Jesus cared so much for His followers that He would not leave them until He had equipped them with the full message of the gospel. In the wake of His ascension, He first corrected His disciples about their concern whether the kingdom would be immediately restored to Israel. In His last words on earth, He told them to have nothing to do with the times or seasons, of dates or predictions, but their care was to be His witnesses.

What then were they to do? Instead of forecasting the future or seeking political power, Jesus offered them the assurance of heavenly power. They were to await the power from on high which would fill their service and their preaching with the power of God. Jesus told them again of their dependency upon the Holy Spirit.

It is this promise that our Lord extends to each of us, His disciples. We will never be alone, without comfort or without hope. Although Jesus was bodily received up into a higher life, a life not made with human hands or limits of materialism, He did not go away! Jesus is even with us now as the Holy Spirit takes what belongs to Him and testifies of His presence. It is the Holy Spirit who fills the life of the believer and gives power to be His witness.

Several New Testament principles are revealed in this scene of Christ and His disciples: (1) Witnessing is a universal obligation—Jesus has gathered the whole earth into His declaration of purpose. (2) Witnessing is centered in the fact and meaning of the earthly ministry of Christ—His "will be done on earth as it is in heaven." (3) Witnessing depends on the saving grace of what Christ has done in the life of the believer—the child of God has only to tell the truth of what God has done. (4) Finally, as Christian witnesses we are to be faithful regardless of the circumstances that confront us.

It is necessary for the Christian church to realize that Christ has commissioned His followers to be witnesses; this is their purpose, their mission. Effective witnessing will always find power in being dependent on and being led by the Spirit of God.

How effective is your witness? Do you see yourself dependent on the Holy Spirit? Let Him give you daily guidance. Wait each day until you know the power from on high has refreshed your soul for this day's task of being a witness for Christ's sake.—**Florie Brown Wigelsworth, M.Div., Elizabeth City, North Carolina**

SENTENCE SERMONS

THE HOLY SPIRIT empowers believers for effective service.
—Selected

WE MUST NOT be content to be cleansed from sin; we must be filled with the Holy Spirit.
—John Fletcher

THE BAPTISM in the Holy Spirit is promised to every believer.
—Selected

ILLUMINATING THE LESSON

The soulwinner must know the Holy Spirit as a reality in his own life. He should be born of the Spirit in regeneration, filled with the Spirit, led by the Spirit, taught by the Spirit, and empowered by the Spirit. As recorded in John's Gospel, Jesus taught much about the work of the Holy Spirit in the life of the believer. For example: the new birth (3:5, 6); rivers of living water issuing from him by the Spirit (7:38, 39); the Spirit as Comforter (14:16; 16:7); the Spirit as teacher (14:26; 16:13-15); the Spirit as guiding into all truth about Christ and glorifying Him (14:26; 15:26; 16:13, 14); and the Spirit through believers convicting the world of sin (16:7-11).

DAILY BIBLE READINGS

M. Power at Creation.
    Genesis 1:1-10
T. Power for Service.
    Exodus 31:1-11
W. Power of Wisdom.
    Proverbs 9:1-10
T. Power Upon Christ.
    Matthew 3:13-17
F. Power for Praise.
    Luke 1:67-75
S. Powerful Presence.
    John 14:15-27

God Uses Circumstances

Study Text: Acts 16:16-34

Objective: To understand that God can use adverse circumstances to reach the lost and be sensitive to these opportunities.

Time: The Book of Acts was written between A.D. 61 and 63.

Place: The Book of Acts was probably written at Caesarea or Rome.

Golden Text: "Believe on the Lord Jesus Christ, and thou shalt be saved" (Acts 16:31).

Central Truth: Circumstances in life often bring opportunities to accept Christ as Savior.

Evangelism Emphasis: Believers need to share their personal testimony in leading others to Christ.

PRINTED TEXT

Acts 16:16. And it came to pass, as we went to prayer, a certain damsel possessed with a spirit of divination met us, which brought her masters much gain by soothsaying:

17. The same followed Paul and us, and cried, saying, These men are the servants of the most high God, which shew unto us the way of salvation.

18. And this did she many days. But Paul, being grieved, turned and said to the spirit, I command thee in the name of Jesus Christ to come out of her. And he came out the same hour.

19. And when her masters saw that the hope of their gains was gone, they caught Paul and Silas, and drew them into the marketplace unto the rulers,

20. And brought them to the magistrates, saying, These men, being Jews, do exceedingly trouble our city,

21. And teach customs, which are not lawful for us to receive, neither to observe, being Romans.

22. And the multitude rose up together against them: and the magistrates rent off their clothes, and commanded to beat them.

23. And when they had laid many stripes upon them, they cast them into prison, charging the jailor to keep them safely:

24. Who, having received such a charge, thrust them into the inner prison, and made their feet fast in the stocks.

25. And at midnight Paul and Silas prayed, and sang praises unto God: and the prisoners heard them.

26. And suddenly there was a great earthquake, so that the foundations of the prison were shaken: and immediately all the doors were opened, and every one's bands were loosed.

27. And the keeper of the prison awaking out of his sleep, and seeing the prison doors open, he drew out his sword, and would have killed himself, supposing that the prisoners had been fled.

28. But Paul cried with a loud voice, saying, Do thyself no harm: for we are all here.

29. Then he called for a light, and sprang in, and came trembling, and fell down before Paul and Silas,

30. And brought them out, and said, Sirs, what must I do to be saved?

31. And they said, Believe on the Lord Jesus Christ, and thou shalt be saved, and thy house.

LESSON OUTLINE

I.   ADVERSE CIRCUMSTANCES
  A. A Slave Girl Healed
  B. The Power of Greed
  C. Beaten and Imprisoned

II. UNSEEN OPPORTUNITIES
  A. Songs in the Night
  B. A Great Earthquake
  C. Preventing Disaster

III. WONDERFUL RESULTS
  A. Conviction
  B. Proclaiming the Gospel
  C. Accepting the Gospel

LESSON EXPOSITION

INTRODUCTION

All God's children experience difficult circumstances—days that are desperate. The Bible is full of such days. Its record is made up of them, its songs are inspired by them, its prophecy is concerned with them, and its revelation has come through them.

Difficult circumstances are the stepping-stones in the path of light. They seem to have been God's opportunity and man's school of wisdom.

Often the "wit's end" of despera-tion has been the beginning of God's power. Recall the promise of seed as the stars of heaven, and as the sands of the sea, to a couple as good as dead. Ponder again the story of the Red Sea and its deliverance, and of the river Jordan with its ark standing midstream. Study once more the prayers of Asa, Jehoshaphat, and Hezekiah, when they were facing difficult times and did not know what to do. Look again at the history of Nehemiah, Daniel, Hosea, and Habakkuk. Stand with awe in the darkness of Gethsemane, and linger by the tomb in Joseph's garden through those terrible days.

In the lesson today God shows how He can use difficult circumstances to bring about positive results. Paul and Silas were facing desperate circumstances, but they were not in despair. Their faith had not created their desperate situation, but it worked to sustain them and to solve their problem. The only alternative to a desperate faith is despair, and faith holds on and prevails.

I. ADVERSE CIRCUMSTANCES
    (Acts 16:16-24)

A. A Slave Girl Healed (vv. 16-18)

16. And it came to pass, as we went to prayer, a certain damsel

possessed with a spirit of divination met us, which brought her masters much gain by soothsaying:

17. The same followed Paul and us, and cried, saying, These men are the servants of the most high God, which shew unto us the way of salvation.

18. And this did she many days. But Paul, being grieved, turned and said to the spirit, I command thee in the name of Jesus Christ to come out of her. And he came out the same hour.

Luke does not tell us how long Paul and Silas had been in Philippi, but they were there probably long enough to establish the beginning of what was to become a strong Christian church. One day as they were going to the place of prayer, a certain girl having "a spirit of divination" met them (v. 16). The literal meaning here is that she had "a spirit of a python." Python, in Greek mythology, was the serpent which guarded Delphi. According to the myth, Apollo descended from Mount Olympus in order to select a site for his shrine and oracle. Having decided upon a spot on the southern side of Mount Parnassus, He found it guarded by a serpent, which he slew with an arrow, and allowed its body to rot in the sun. Hence the name of the serpent, Python (meaning "rotting"). The name Python was subsequently used to denote a prophetic demon, and was also used by soothsayers who practiced ventriloquism, or "speaking from the belly." The pagan inhabitants of Philippi regarded the woman as inspired by Python. Luke used the term, *a Python spirit*, which would naturally suggest itself to a physician, pre-

senting phenomena identical with the convulsive movements and wild cries of the Pythian priestess of Delphi.

The poor girl was a slave, controlled by her masters, to whom she had proved so popular and profitable that more than one person had charge of her. The gold miners came to her for advice as to where to find nuggets, or to have thieves pointed out who had robbed them of their treasure. Mothers whose sons were about to cross the Aegean Sea anxiously inquired of her what kind of weather there would be, and if their sons would return in good health. Merchants desired news of their convoys, and politicians even sought to know beforehand the outcome of elections.

The demon-possessed girl followed Paul and his companions, shouting out to them and about them. In spite of her demon possession, she could not but speak the truth. Weymouth translates her cry as "These men are the bondservants of the Most High God, and are proclaiming to you the way of salvation" (v. 17). She had heard the apostles preach, and had caught up in her confused mind some of their often-repeated statements. Thus the evil spirits in her, even as the evil spirits in the days of Christ (Mark 1:24; Luke 4:41), were led to testify of Christ.

Paul finally reached the end of his patience in this matter. Being greatly annoyed and troubled at the poor girl's cries, he decided to do something about it. He, like Christ, would not receive the testimony of a demon. Therefore he turned upon the raving girl and, in the name of Jesus Christ, solemnly ordered the evil spirit to come out of her. At once her frenzy left her; her shoutings were silenced and she came into her right mind.

G. Campbell Morgan has an interesting comment on verse 18: "A grave error in the history of the Christian church has been that she has been content, again and again, to admit the testimony of evil men because the testimony in itself was true. Alliance with evil is the most subtle peril that confronts the church at any time" (*The Westminster Pulpit*).

B. The Power of Greed (vv. 19-21)

19. And when her masters saw that the hope of their gains was gone, they caught Paul and Silas, and drew them into the marketplace unto the rulers,

20. And brought them to the magistrates, saying, These men, being Jews, do exceedingly trouble our city,

21. And teach customs, which are not lawful for us to receive, neither to observe, being Romans.

The slave girl who had been a lucrative possession suddenly became valueless to her owners. W.J. Conybeare and J.S. Howson explain: "The law had no remedy for property depreciated by exorcism. The true state of the case was therefore concealed, and an accusation was laid before the praetors [or magistrates] in the following form: 'These men are throwing the whole city into confusion; moreover, they are Jews, and they are attempting to introduce new religious observances, which we, being Roman citizens, cannot legally receive and adopt.' The accusation was partly true and partly false. It

was quite false that Paul and Silas were disturbing the colony; for nothing could have been more calm and orderly than their worship and teaching at the house of Lydia or by the waterside. In the other part of the indictment there was a certain amount of truth. The letter of the Roman law . . . was opposed to the introduction of foreign religions; and though exceptions were allowed, as in the case of the Jews themselves, yet the spirit of the law entirely condemned such changes in worship as were likely to unsettle the minds of the citizens or to produce any tumultuous uproar. . . . Thus, Paul and Silas had undoubtedly been doing some things that in some degree exposed them to legal penalties, and were beginning a change which tended to bring down—and ultimately did bring down—the whole weight of the Roman law on the martyrs of Christianity. The force of another part of the accusation, which was adroitly introduced—namely, that the men were 'Jews to begin with'—will be fully apprehended, if we remember, not only that the Jews were generally hated, suspected, and despised, but that they had lately been driven out of Rome in consequence of an uproar, and that it was incumbent on Philippi, as a colony, to copy the indignation of the mother city" (*The Life and Epistles of the Apostle Paul*).

C. Beaten and Imprisoned (vv. 22-24)

22. And the multitude rose up together against them: and the magistrates rent off their clothes, and commanded to beat them.

23. And when they had laid

many stripes upon them, they cast them into prison, charging the jailor to keep them safely:

24. Who, having received such a charge, thrust them into the inner prison, and made their feet fast in the stocks.

The rabble of the marketplace joined in the attack on Paul and Silas. The magistrates, accepting without question the accusers' statement that Paul and Silas were Jews (v. 20) and forgetting or ignoring the possibility of their possessing Roman citizenship, ordered them to be scourged and then to be thrown into prison.

Paul and Silas were severely beaten. And as if they were the worst of criminals, they were placed in the most secure part of the prison—the inner prison. Conybeare and Howson state: "The inner prisons of which we read in the ancient world were like that 'dungeon in the court of the prison,' into which Jeremiah was let down with cords, and where 'he sank in the mire.' They were pestilential cells, damp and cold, from which the light was excluded, and where the chains rusted on the limbs of the prisoners" (*The Life and Epistles of the Apostle Paul*).

Are contemporary Christians prepared to suffer as Paul and Silas did? Explain.

II. UNSEEN OPPORTUNITIES
   (Acts 16:25-28)

A. Songs in the Night (v. 25)

25. And at midnight Paul and Silas prayed, and sang praises unto God: and the prisoners heard them.

The jailer had placed many men in his prison, but never before any like Paul and Silas. Instead of groaning and moaning and mumbling in their pain and fear, Paul and Silas talked to God and sang praises to Him. This is surely what Job meant when he spoke of "songs in the night" (35:10). The missionaries sang because they counted it all joy to suffer for the name of Christ. *LINGER ON PROBLEMS THEY GET WORSE*

B. A Great Earthquake (v. 26)

26. And suddenly there was a great earthquake, so that the foundations of the prison were shaken: and immediately all the doors were opened, and every one's bands were loosed.

A fearful earthquake as the world's Redeemer hung dead on the cross testified to the earth's sympathy with its Creator (Matthew 27:50-54). In the early days of the church, when Peter and John had been warned by the Sanhedrin not to preach or teach any longer in the name of Christ, the prayer meeting of the disciples which followed received God's witness in the form of an earthquake (Acts 4:31). Another earthquake came as a result of prayer and praise. This time the prayers came from Paul and Silas who were imprisoned at Philippi. Luke himself felt the effects of the earthquake, though not in the prison, and knew that it was "great."

Eastern prisons were built of stone or brick on a stone foundation, and such buildings crumbled easily in an earthquake. The rending of the stone or brick walls would twist the doors from their hinges and thrust loose their bolts. The prisoners' chains were fastened to staples in the walls, and these staples were loosened as the walls cracked, and fell out, so that the prisoners were completely free to leave the prison.

C. Preventing Disaster (vv. 27, 28)

27. And the keeper of the prison awaking out of his sleep, and seeing the prison doors open, he drew out his sword, and would have killed himself, supposing that the prisoners had been fled.

28. But Paul cried with a loud voice, saying, Do thyself no harm: for we are all here.

Startled from sleep, and catching sight of the prison doors standing open, the jailer instantly drew his sword and was on the verge of killing himself, thinking that the prisoners had escaped. A jailer was responsible with his life for the safe-keeping of his prisoners, and this man preferred to kill himself rather than suffer the humiliation of a public execution. Suicide was not regarded as a sin in those days, and some of the noblest of Romans took their own lives. In fact, after their defeat in the great battle near Philippi, Brutus killed himself and Cassius compelled his freed man to kill him. The sanctity of human life is one of the teachings of Christianity, since the Son of God died to bring eternal life to all.

Paul kept his head in all that confusion and terror, with the building seeming to be falling upon him. There was probably a light in the outer prison, and that's how Paul could see from the inner prison what was happening there, though he himself could not be seen.

Paul shouted to the jailer, "Do thyself no harm: for we are all here" (v. 28). The brutal treatment which he had received from the hands of this jailer would have left bitter resentment in the mind of Paul, if he had been an ordinary man; but since he was not an ordinary man, his heart was full of the Spirit of Christ. He had probably been praying for his enemies, and now here was an enemy whose life he was glad to save.

In response to the question "How could Paul have been so kind to the jailer?" Alfred Lee writes: "The Christian may be a prisoner in the chamber of sickness or a mourner in the house of death, a captive in a dungeon of the enemy or a bond-man under the lash—whatever the weight of the burden or the thickness of the gloom, God can infuse joy, and consolation, and peace, and hope, and sweet submission, and unwavering trust" (*Eventful Nights in Bible History*).

Are contemporary Christians prepared to endure persecution as the early Christians did? Explain.

III. WONDERFUL RESULTS
(Acts 16:29-34)

A. Conviction (vv. 29, 30)

29. Then he called for a light, and sprang in, and came trembling, and fell down before Paul and Silas,

30. And brought them out, and said, Sirs, what must I do to be saved?

The jailer's call for torches was for the purpose of making a thorough examination, and also to summon aid, since each torch would mean a torchbearer.

The jailer probably had heard of the demoniac slave girl who had been delivered. This event had been closely connected with the incarceration of Paul and Silas. His mind instantly connected the earthquake with the Wonder-worker—their God, who was so powerful, was thus freeing them from prison. He fell down and worshiped them as the messengers of a god, or perhaps as gods themselves.

The jailer could safely take Paul and Silas from the horrible inner prison into the praetorium, for they had proved they would not run away.

The jailer's question is the most important question that can be asked by a human being in this world. D.L. Moody said it is not "What must my brother do?" or "What must my friends do?" but "What must I do to be saved?"

It is possible the jailer had heard Paul preach about the salvation which is in Christ, or he may have heard the slave girl crying after them and shouting that the strangers could show men the way of salvation.

Note the drastic attitude change that occurred in the jailer. He now called them "Sirs." This word in Greek is a title of great respect, almost equal to "Lords." They were no longer prisoners, they were now his superiors.

B. Proclaiming the Gospel
   (vv. 31, 32)

(Acts 16:32 is not included in the printed text.)

31. And they said, Believe on the Lord Jesus Christ, and thou shalt be saved, and thy house.

There are some single verses in the New Testament which contain the whole Way of Life. The best known of these is John 3:16. In Acts 16:31 there is another conden-

sation of divine truth only second in power and splendor—the human side of the great truth of which John 3:16 is the Godward side.

Paul and Silas answered the jailer's question by giving him the essence of Christianity. Here is all we need to know for our eternal happiness and safety. Peter at Pentecost made a very comprehensive answer to basically the same question (Acts 2:38); but though his was a wonderful summary, Paul's simpler reply had the essentials. Everyone can understand what believing on the Lord Jesus means: simply accepting what Christ says about Himself and what He asks us to do. All who do this will be saved from their sins.

C. Accepting the Gospel
   (vv. 33, 34)

(Acts 16:33, 34 is not included in the printed text.)

The next event of the night was the baptism of the jailer and his household. The final event of this exciting night was a meal in the jailer's house. The jailer "set meat" before Paul and Silas, "and rejoiced, believing in God with all his house" (v. 34). The night which had begun in a manner so conducive to discouragement for Paul and Silas turned out to be a happy one, not only for them but for the Philippian jailer and his household. What rejoicing there must have been among all of those present for that meal at the jailer's house that night in Philippi.

How would you evaluate the attitude of Paul and Silas toward persecution?

REVIEW QUESTIONS

1. What miracle did Paul work?
2. What was the result of the slave girl's being delivered?
3. What great question did the jailer ask?
4. How did Paul and Silas answer the question of the jailer?
5. How did the jailer respond to the answer to his question?

GOLDEN TEXT HOMILY

"BELIEVE ON THE LORD JESUS CHRIST, AND THOU SHALT BE SAVED" (Acts 16:31).

In this particular passage of Scripture the Greek word for salvation, *soteria*, means specifically that God saves fallen man, both body and soul. So man is saved from sin and its nature. Sin results in spiritual death. "For the wages of sin is death" (Romans 6:23). The curse of sin has brought destruction to the body as well. Therefore man needs to be saved from physical illness (see Matthew 9:21, 22), from lostness (18:11), from sin (1:21), and from the wrath of God (Romans 5:9).

The study of God's plan for man's deliverance from sin is *soteriology*, which deals with the provisions of salvation through Christ and the application of it through the Holy Spirit. The Bible teaches that since Adam and Eve's sin, every man is by nature depraved, guilty before God, and under the penalty of death.

It was God's promise from the first fallen man that He would provide through the seed of a woman the way of redemption. And He did—through His Son Jesus Christ. God has only one plan of salvation, but He has dealt with man in various ways concerning it. The Scripture tells us that God had prepared what was needful over a period of time. "But when the fullness of the time had come, God sent forth His Son, born of a woman, born under the law" (Galatians 4:4, *NKJV*).

With an earthquake God arrested the attention of the jailer and alerted him to the fact of his need of salvation. God sometimes uses peculiar ways to attract an individual's attention to bring about his conviction. The jailer would have been under penalty of death if he had allowed the prisoners to escape. He was about to take his own life when Paul called out to him, "Don't take your life; we are all here" (see Acts 16:24-34). The jailer's situation was apparently hopeless, but God had provided a better way. If the jailer had taken his own life, he might have escaped the judgment of man; but then he would have had to face God, who would judge him for taking his own life. What could he do to be saved—completely delivered from all unrighteousness? After Paul and Silas had given him the answer (v. 31), the Scripture says, "They spoke the word of the Lord to him and to all who were in his house" (v. 32, *NKJV*).

There are people in this world today who do not believe in the promise of the Lord for complete deliverance from sin. This negative doctrine is not in agreement with the whole Word of God. Paul said, "Knowing this, that our old man is crucified with [Christ], that the body of sin might be destroyed, that henceforth we should not serve sin. . . . Now if we be dead with Christ, we believe that we shall also live with him" (Romans 6:6, 8).

If you need deliverance from sin, you can have it in Christ Jesus. If you need healing for your body, Jesus can heal you. As Scripture says, "By whose stripes ye were healed" (1 Peter 2:24). To believe on the Lord Jesus Christ unto salvation, you must believe the whole complete record God gave of His Son (see 1 John 5:10, 11).—**Aaron D. Mize, Chaplain I, Parchman, Mississippi**

SENTENCE SERMONS

CIRCUMSTANCES IN LIFE often bring opportunities to accept Christ as Savior.

—**Selected**

WE ARE ALL FACED with a series of great opportunities brilliantly disguised as impossible situations.

—**Charles Swindoll**

ADVERSITY is the perfect glass wherein we truly see and know ourselves.

—**Sir William Davenant**

EVANGELISM APPLICATION

BELIEVERS NEED TO SHARE THEIR PERSONAL TESTIMONY IN LEADING OTHERS TO CHRIST.

Walford Davies was known as a composer and radio personality. He was a versatile popularizer of classical music whose talks were listened to and appreciated by many who would make no claim to be highbrow in their musical tastes.

When Davies discovered that he had this gift of exposition, he had to make up his mind whether he was to keep it to himself and lead the secluded life of a composer, dispensing his knowledge and experi-ence to the few. But instead he felt the call to take a message to the people. He became an interpreter of all that was best in the realm of music to the man on the street. In the words of Vaughn Williams, he chose "to go down to the world of men and show them what he had learned about eternity and beauty." He determined to share his insights with every man. He believed that music was meant to speak not just to the long-haired, but to the masses of the people, and that conviction led him to undertake the program of popularization with which his name was eventually associated.

That is the decision every Christian has to make in relation to the music of the gospel. We who are believers have been privileged to hear and respond to the good tidings of salvation. We have tasted that the Lord is good. Now we are faced with a critical choice. Either we hug this experience to ourselves, like a child with its teddy bear refusing to let anyone else play with it; or we go down into the world of men and seek to pass on what we have learned about Christ.—**A. Skevington Wood,** *Evangelism: Its Theology and Practice*

DAILY BIBLE READINGS

M. Providence of God.
   Genesis 45:1-8
T. Tested by God.
   Job 2:1-10
W. Humbled by God.
   Daniel 4:28-37
T. Declaration of Deliverance.
   Daniel 6:16-27
F. Positive Attitude.
   2 Corinthians 4:7-14
S. Contentment in Christ.
   Philippians 4:10-13

INTRODUCTION
TO SUMMER
QUARTER

The lessons for the summer quarter (June, July, August) are presented under two distinct units of study. Lessons 1-9 come under the theme "Revelation." Lessons 10-13 are given the theme title "Mission of the Church."

Unit One provides an opportunity to study the Book of Revelation—an often neglected book. But it is a portion of God's Word that brings His blessing and a valuable understanding of future events.

Unit Two provides a review of what the church is to be doing as it awaits the return of the Lord. The two units of this quarter of study tie together effectively to help us focus on Christ—the Alpha and Omega—the Lord who will return to catch away His bride.

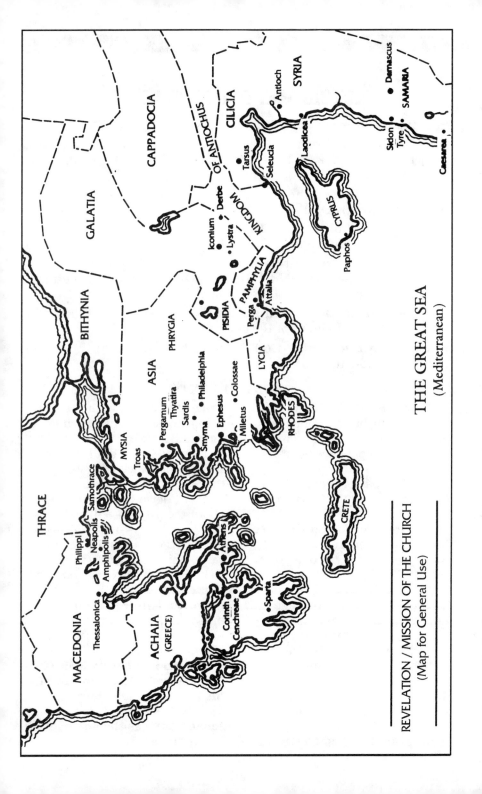

THE GREAT SEA
(Mediterranean)

REVELATION / MISSION OF THE CHURCH
(Map for General Use)

Revelation of Jesus Christ

Study Text: Revelation 1:9-20

Objective: To recognize that Jesus Christ is the author and subject of the Book of Revelation and embrace the future with confidence.

Time: The time of the writing of the Book of Revelation was probably about A.D. 96.

Place: The Book of Revelation was written on the island of Patmos in the Aegean Sea.

Golden Text: "I am Alpha and Omega, the beginning and the ending, saith the Lord, which is, and which was, and which is to come, the Almighty" (Revelation 1:8).

Central Truth: Jesus Christ reveals Himself to be the author and subject of the Book of Revelation.

Evangelism Emphasis: God reveals His salvation in the person and work of Jesus Christ.

PRINTED TEXT

Revelation 1:9. I John, who also am your brother, and companion in tribulation, and in the kingdom and patience of Jesus Christ, was in the isle that is called Patmos, for the word of God, and for the testimony of Jesus Christ.

10. I was in the Spirit on the Lord's day, and heard behind me a great voice, as of a trumpet,

11. Saying, I am Alpha and Omega, the first and the last: and, What thou seest, write in a book, and send it unto the seven churches which are in Asia; unto Ephesus, and unto Smyrna, and unto Pergamos, and unto Thyatira, and unto Sardis, and unto Philadelphia, and unto Laodicea.

12. And I turned to see the voice that spake with me. And being turned, I saw seven golden candlesticks;

13. And in the midst of the seven candlesticks one like unto the Son of man, clothed with a garment down to the foot, and girt about the paps with a golden girdle.

14. His head and his hairs were white like wool, as white as snow; and his eyes were as a flame of fire;

15. And his feet like unto fine brass, as if they burned in a furnace; and his voice as the sound of many waters.

16. And he had in his right hand seven stars: and out of his mouth went a sharp twoedged sword: and his countenance was as the sun shineth in his strength.

17. And when I saw him, I fell at his feet as dead. And he laid his right hand upon me, saying unto me, Fear not; I am the first and the last:

18. I am he that liveth, and was dead; and, behold, I am alive for evermore, Amen; and have the keys of hell and of death.

19. Write the things which thou hast seen, and the things which are, and the things which shall be hereafter;

20. The mystery of the seven stars which thou sawest in my right hand, and the seven golden candlesticks. The seven stars are the angels of the seven churches: and the seven candlesticks which thou sawest are the seven churches.

DICTIONARY

Patmos (PAT-mus)—Revelation 1:9—A small rocky island in the Aegean Sea.

Ephesus (EF-eh-sus) . . . Smyrna (SMUR-nuh) . . . Pergamos (PER-guh-mus) . . . Thyatira (THIGH-ah-TIE-rah) . . . Sardis (SAR-dis) . . . Philadelphia (fill-uh-DEL-fee-uh) . . . Laodicea (lay-ah-deh-SEE-uh)—Revelation 1:11—These were the names of seven principal towns in Asia Minor (now Turkey) in which there were Christian congregations. These churches were probably under the jurisdiction of the apostle John at the time he wrote the Book of Revelation.

LESSON OUTLINE

I. FIRST AND LAST

   A. Identity of the Author

   B. The Lord's Day

   C. Alpha and Omega

II. MAJESTY AND POWER

III. LIFE AND DOMINION

LESSON EXPOSITION

INTRODUCTION

Editor's Note: For those seeking additional information on the Book of Revelation, the following books are recommended: *The Book of Revelation* by Clarence Larkin, published by the Clarence Larkin Estate, P.O. Box 334, Glendale, PA 19038; *The Vision of His Glory*, by Anne Graham Lotz, published by Word, Nashville; *What on Earth is Going to Happen*, by Ray C. Stedman (out of print); and *The Revelation of Jesus Christ* by John F. Walvoord, published by Moody Press, Chicago.

Just as Genesis is a book of beginnings, Revelation is about endings. Although the casual reader might find it intimidating and incomprehensible, the full message of God's Word would be lost without it. Revelation brings all the themes of the Bible into focus. Someone has said that Genesis and Revelation are like bookends holding the Bible together. Genesis gives the origins of civilization and the beginning of recorded history; Revelation gives the destruction of civilization and the end of history. In Genesis we see the initiation of God's judgment on man for his sin; in Revelation we see the culmination of it.

Perhaps it is this ultimate indictment of sin that keeps many from reading and studying Revelation. It is certainly the most frightening book of the Bible. Containing fearsome pictures of plagues, earthquakes, wars, and strange creatures, it can easily cause the most faithful Christian to wonder about his or her own survival.

Revelation is also different from other New Testament books in that it is *apocalyptic*. This comes from a Greek word (*apokalupsis*) meaning "an unveiling." Apocalyptic literature by its nature is written to reveal divine mysteries that would otherwise remain concealed. However, even as it unveils hidden secrets, it is often couched in symbolism and metaphor. This makes the casual reader wary. However, we should not be deterred. The prologue says, "Blessed is the one who reads the words of this prophecy, and blessed are those who hear it and take to heart what is written in it, because the time is near" (v. 3, *NIV*). Obviously, we are encouraged to study Revelation, relying on the Lord to open our hearts to its meaning. If we take its message seriously, we will be guided through the barrage of conflicting ideas and philosophies thrown at us.

We don't know why John used such mystical imagery and symbols, but there are several possibilities. Apocalyptic writings tended to be given during periods of great danger for God's people. Writers would select words that only their intended readers would understand. Revelation was written at a time when Rome was becoming increasingly hostile to Christians (see 1:9; 2:10, 13). Certainly the body of Christ in the first century had developed a sense of language of its own, using terms and expressions the secular world of the time would not understand. With this in mind, the language and imagery used in Revelation was not so strange to its initial readers. They were probably accustomed to abstract terms clothed in visual images. For example, *evil* is a word we understand; however, it comes across much stronger when John describes it as a "woman drunken with the blood of the saints" (17:6).

Also, John was trying to accurately convey the visions he had seen. Heavenly realities were difficult to put in earthly terms. For instance, how could he possibly describe nuclear warfare, modern aircraft, or artillery that had never been seen by man at that time? Only through symbolic imagery could he paint a vivid picture for his readers.

What must be remembered when reading Revelation is that it is a book of hope. God is sovereign—greater than any power in the universe. No government, leaders, or religion can compare with Him. He controls history and its outcome—all for the purpose of uniting the faithful into a full, loving fellowship with Himself. Although Satan may exert a temporary power over the earth, true followers of Christ will not be deceived. They know that God is in control. He will bring the believer to eternal life.

Much of what is revealed in the book can be detected from the very first three verses, the prologue: "The revelation of Jesus Christ, which God gave him to show his servants what must soon take place. He made it known by sending his angel to his servant John, who testifies to everything he saw—that is, the word of God and the testimony of Jesus Christ. Blessed is the one who reads the words of this prophecy, and blessed are those who hear it and take to heart what is written in it, because the time is near" (NIV). We have already discussed the fact that this is an apocalypse, or unveiling. Also, we know it is Christ himself who is unveiled. Jesus sent an angel to give the message to John. The Greek word for "made it known" (v. 1, NIV) is translated "signified" in the King James Version. This might better be stated as "sign-ified"; in other words, everything is made known by signs or symbols. Beasts and scorpions, weird personages, and animals are symbols of things that are real and literal.

Actually, the author of the book was not the apostle John, but God himself. John was simply the recipient—the scribe who wrote it down. The book began in the Godhead. The Father revealed it to the Son, who passed it to an angel to reveal to John. In verse 4 we see the term "seven Spirits." This is another name for the Holy Spirit. The Trinity—the Father, the Son, and the Holy Spirit—is the ultimate source of truth.

The interpreting of Revelation has taken a number of directions over the centuries. Basically there are four major views:

1. The *symbolist* or *idealist* viewpoint maintains that Revelation is not a predictive book at all, but rather a symbolic picture of the cosmic conflict between good and evil. Therefore, history and prophecy are ruled out.

2. The *preterist* view also denies the prophetic value of the book, limiting it exclusively to the events of the first century. It is only a symbolic description of the Roman persecution of the early church, emperor worship, and God's judgment of the ancient Roman Empire.

3. The *historicist* view sees Revelation as an allegorical panoramic view of history from the first century to the Second Coming. The difficulty with this is that its adherents in every age tend to see the book as climaxing in their own generation.

4. The *futurist* view acknowledges the influence that the first-century conflict between Roman power and the church had upon the themes of the book. However, it also accepts the bulk of Revelation (chs. 4-22) as a prophetic look into the time just prior to the Second Advent—the Tribulation, seen as seven years (chs. 4-18) and the return of Christ to the creation of the new heaven and earth (chs. 19-22). According to this interpretation, the Apocalypse centers on the second advent of Christ, who will return in power and glory as the Judge of all who rejected His offer of salvation. Futurists watch for

literal meanings behind the symbolism of Revelation.

Adherents of the first three views are generally postmillennial or amillennial, while futurists are premillennial. *Postmillennialists* believe that the spread of the gospel will lead to a golden age of peace on earth followed by the return of Christ; *amillennialists* believe that the Christian's present spiritual position in Christ is the true "millennium"; *premillennialists* believe that the thousand-year reign (20:2-7) should be taken literally as the earthly kingdom that Christ will establish between the Second Coming and the creation of the new universe.

The one thing everyone agrees on is that Revelation was written to encourage believers. Christ will ultimately triumph over all who rise up against Him and His saints. First-century readers were facing terrible times. They needed to be encouraged to stand firm in Christ. Those who were weak in their faith were challenged to stop compromising with the world.

In our lessons we will take the *futurist* viewpoint. This writer believes that the Bible, both Old and New Testaments, have relevance to every age. And, while some of the events spoken of in Revelation likely had an immediate fulfillment in the early church age, an ultimate fulfillment is yet to come. We will search with an open mind and a prayerful spirit to "rightly divide" God's Word.

In taking the futurist viewpoint, however, we must adhere to two principles. The first is that the symbols found in Revelation are not introduced just to us. They were all seen in earlier books of the Bible. You cannot read the last section of the book first. In order to understand Revelation, we must garner knowledge and bits of prophecy from the earlier books. Not only symbols but events too will line up with descriptions given earlier. For example, 1:7: "Look, he is coming with the clouds, and every eye will see him, even those who pierced him; and all the peoples of the earth will mourn because of him. So shall it be! Amen" (*NIV*). The glorious second coming of Christ is one of the key themes of Revelation. To understand it, we look back at a number of scriptures. Jesus said in Matthew 24:30: "At that time the sign of the Son of Man will appear in the sky, and all the nations of the earth will mourn. They will see the Son of Man coming on the clouds of the sky, with power and great glory" (*NIV*). This is reiterated in Matthew 26:64: "In the future you will see the Son of Man sitting at the right hand of the Mighty One and coming on the clouds of heaven" (*NIV*; see also Mark 13:36; 14:62; Luke 21:27). We learn that in the Ascension, clouds removed Jesus from sight (Acts 1:9-11), but at His second coming "every eye shall see him" (Revelation 1:7).

However, there is no indication that the world as a whole will see Jesus at the time of the rapture of the church. For example, some passages of Scripture suggest this is a different appearance of Christ from the one just mentioned:

• "For the Lord Himself will descend from heaven with a shout, with the voice of an archangel, and with the trumpet of God. And the dead in Christ will rise first. Then we who are alive and remain shall be caught up together with them in the clouds to meet the Lord in the air. And thus we shall always be with the Lord. Therefore comfort one another with these words" (1 Thessalonians 4:16-18, NKJV).

• "For as the lightning comes from the east and flashes to the west, so also will the coming of the Son of Man be" (Matthew 24:27, NKJV).

• "Behold, I tell you a mystery: We shall not all sleep, but we shall all be changed—in a moment, in the twinkling of an eye, at the last trumpet. For the trumpet will sound, and the dead will be raised incorruptible, and we shall be changed" (1 Corinthians 15:51, 52, NKJV).

• "Watch therefore, and pray always that you may be counted worthy to escape all these things that will come to pass, and to stand before the Son of Man" (Luke 21:36, NKJV).

• "The end of all things is at hand; therefore be serious and watchful in your prayers" (1 Peter 4:7, NKJV).

We might even mention the parable of the five wise virgins and the five foolish virgins. Here Jesus urges us to be watchful and ready for the appearance of the Bridegroom (see Matthew 25:1-13).

By putting the pieces together from a variety of prophecies in Scripture, the doctrine of the Rapture (or "catching away of the church") has been concluded, but we must study the entire Bible to fully understand Revelation. This is the way the futurist interprets this book.

The other principle is to divide the Book of Revelation into three distinct parts. John was instructed in 1:19: "Write the things which thou hast seen, and the things which are, and the things which shall be hereafter." Thus, the three divisions may be seen as follows: (1) "things which thou hast seen" (ch. 1), the vision John saw; (2) "the things which are" (chs. 2, 3), the things which existed in John's day; and (3) "the things which shall be hereafter" (chs. 4-22), things which deal with the hereafter.

I. FIRST AND LAST (Revelation 1:9-11)

A. Identity of the Author (v. 9)

9. I John, who also am your brother, and companion in tribulation, and in the kingdom and patience of Jesus Christ, was in the isle that is called Patmos, for the word of God, and for the testimony of Jesus Christ.

Though John's name has been mentioned twice in the earlier verses, this is the first time he said "I John." He described himself as a brother and a companion to the churches he was addressing. He was certainly well known to most early believers. His own exile to the island of Patmos provides a story of dedication to spreading the gospel. Patmos is an island about 37 miles southwest of Miletus, in the Aegean Sea. It was used as a penal institution by the Romans. Only six miles wide and 10 miles long, Patmos contained mines and quarries where prisoners were forced to work. This indicates that John was writing during the A.D. 90s. Apparently,

John was released in A.D. 96 at Domitian's death, and allowed to return to Ephesus when Emperor Nerva was in power.

These were dire circumstances for the old apostle. Shut off from friends and fellowship, he was blessed with the "most extensive revelation of future things shown to any writer of the New Testament" (John F. Walvoord, *The Revelation of Jesus Christ*).

B. The Lord's Day (v. 10)

10. I was in the Spirit on the Lord's day, and heard behind me a great voice, as of a trumpet.

Soon after the church was established, the early Christians began to meet on Sunday as a day of worship. John's incarceration did not stop his zeal for serving. In saying that he was "in the Spirit" did not mean that John was in some high ecstatic state. He was simply worshiping—through prayers, praise, and paying tribute to God's majesty and power. His worship was a fulfillment of Jesus' prophetic words to the woman at the well of Sychar: "Yet a time is coming and has now come when the true worshipers will worship the Father in spirit and truth, for they are the kind of worshipers the Father seeks" (John 4:23, *NIV*). For any believer to truly hear from the Lord, he or she must establish a regular lifestyle of worship. John's heart was prepared for what God would reveal to him by a disciplined homage.

This is the only time the phrase "the Lord's day" appears in the Bible. John was writing to the seven churches located in Asia Minor, where many people cele-

brated the first day of each month as "Emperor's Day." A regular day of the week might also have been set aside for this name. "Thus, by calling the first day of the week the Lord's Day, John may have been making a direct challenge to emperor worship, as he does elsewhere in the book" (*The Word in Life Study Bible*, note on Revelation 1:10).

C. Alpha and Omega (v. 11)

11. Saying, I am Alpha and Omega, the first and the last: and, What thou seest, write in a book, and send it unto the seven churches which are in Asia; unto Ephesus, and unto Smyrna, and unto Pergamos, and unto Thyatira, and unto Sardis, and unto Philadelphia, and unto Laodicea.

The voice John heard behind him was like a trumpet in its power and intensity (v. 10). The voice was that of Jesus himself. He gave John a command to write "what thou seest." This command to write is found 12 times in the book, indicating that John was to write after each vision. The entire message was then sent to the seven churches, along with an individual message to each church.

Just as He had done in verse 8, Jesus identified Himself as the Alpha and Omega—the beginning and the ending. Jesus is the ruler of all things past, present, and future (see also 4:8; Isaiah 44:6; 48:12-15).

Can any significance be drawn from the fact that John's vision occurred on "the Lord's Day?"

II. MAJESTY AND POWER
(Revelation 1:12-16)

12. And I turned to see the voice that spake with me. And being turned, I saw seven golden candlesticks;

13. And in the midst of the seven candlesticks one like unto the Son of man, clothed with a garment down to the foot, and girt about the paps with a golden girdle.

14. His head and his hairs were white like wool, as white as snow; and his eyes were as a flame of fire;

15. And his feet like unto fine brass, as if they burned in a furnace; and his voice as the sound of many waters.

16. And he had in his right hand seven stars: and out of his mouth went a sharp twoedged sword: and his countenance was as the sun shineth in his strength.

At the sound of the loud voice, John instinctively turned to its source, and before him was the Lord standing among seven golden lampstands. He was holding seven stars in His hand and was dressed in priestly garments. As High Priest, Jesus ministers among His churches. This ministry can be seen in the symbolism of His appearance. The long robe and golden sash speak of deity in Scripture. His white head and hair speak of wisdom and purity (see Daniel 7:9). His eyes blazed like fire, and nothing could be hid from them. His face was as brilliant as looking directly into the sun. His feet were like the glow of bronze in a hot furnace. This intensity speaks of undeniable truth, while the fire indicates judgment. The voice that sounded like "rushing waters" (Revelation 1:15, NIV) can be compared to the massive strength of Niagara Falls and indicates God's ultimate power and sovereignty. In giving a description of the personage he saw, John used words "drawn almost entirely from imagery used in Daniel, Ezekiel, and Isaiah of God's majesty and power" (NIV Bible Commentary).

John was probably reminded of an experience that took place many years before where he, his brother James, and Peter were with Jesus, high on a mountain, when the Transfiguration took place (Matthew 17:1-8; Mark 9:2-8; Luke 9:28-36). Peter spoke of the same encounter as being a preview of Christ's second coming (2 Peter 1:16-19). Now John is given another opportunity to see the majesty and power of the glorified Lord.

An interesting speculation can be made here, tying these two experiences together. At the end of the Gospel of John, while Jesus was speaking to Peter, he alluded to the possibility that John might still be alive when He returned: "If I want him to remain alive until I return, what is that to you? You must follow me" (21:22, NIV). Although tradition says that John returned to Ephesus after his exile on Patmos and died as a very old man, yet he did in a sense see the Second Coming. The vision granted John was a preview of what has yet to take place. He saw in the spiritual realm what will ultimately be seen by all who are alive.

The seven stars in Jesus' right hand represent the seven angels of the seven churches in Asia (v. 20). The sword in His mouth indicates the power and force of the message being given. His words were sharp as swords in their judgment, yet came from love, not anger and criticism. God's message to His people is always based on love. Correction is given for the sake of restoring life and relationship.

Does Jesus ever forget any of His churches? What can be seen in the fact that He was standing among the seven candlesticks?

III. LIFE AND DOMINION
(Revelation 1:17-20)

17. And when I saw him, I fell at his feet as dead. And he laid his right hand upon me, saying unto me, Fear not; I am the first and the last:

18. I am he that liveth, and was dead; and, behold, I am alive for evermore, Amen; and have the keys of hell and of death.

19. Write the things which thou hast seen, and the things which are, and the things which shall be hereafter;

20. The mystery of the seven stars which thou sawest in my right hand, and the seven golden candlesticks. The seven stars are the angels of the seven churches: and the seven candlesticks which thou sawest are the seven churches.

John's reaction to the powerful vision was much the same as others in the Bible. An easy comparison can be made to Isaiah (ch. 6). Any real encounter with God will produce awe and worship. The only bodily position to assume when in the presence of God is on one's face in total surrender. The phrase "fear not" appears frequently in Scripture, indicating the reaction God's presence initiates.

Jesus assured John that there was safety within this majesty. Fear should not overwhelm us when we willingly place our lives in the Master's care. This had to be reassuring to the aged apostle. As Roman persecution increased, so did apprehension for the churches' survival. Knowing that the One who has "the keys of hell and of death" is reaching out in love, gives strength to face any trial.

Since Jesus holds the keys of hell and death, should the Christian have any fear for facing the future?

REVIEW QUESTIONS

1. Did John see and describe real things, or were the things he described purely symbolic?

2. What did the "seven Spirits" (v. 4) represent?

3. How was John's vision like the one Isaiah saw in the Temple?

4. Describe John's vision of Jesus, standing among the seven golden candlesticks.

5. What did the seven stars and seven candlesticks of verse 20 represent?

GOLDEN TEXT HOMILY

"I AM ALPHA AND OMEGA, THE BEGINNING AND THE ENDING, SAITH THE LORD, WHICH IS, AND WHICH WAS, AND WHICH IS TO COME, THE ALMIGHTY" (Revelation 1:8).

The eternity of God is clearly

expressed in this passage of Scripture. In the Greek alphabet the first and last characters are *alpha* and *omega*, signifying a completeness. Jesus declares that He is the completeness of all things—He is now, He was always, and He will be in the future.

Without entering into the presumptuousness of predestination, we conclude by Christ's own testimony that He existed for all time. He was present when God the Father, He himself, and the Holy Ghost devised the plan of Creation. He was present when man failed. He was present during the existence of time until now, and He will be present forever, because He is the Almighty.

Because of this proclamation of Christ by His own lips, we can live the remainder of our lives knowing that we have a captain who is our Savior forevermore. All the promises of God are ours forever. He has promised He will never leave us or forsake us. His promise to us is that nothing will separate us from God's love and that Satan will not be able to tempt us beyond our breaking point. In essence, when we come to Him, we are eternal and we have eternal life. We now look to the future with Him and to the new body that is ours forever, as a result of this promise: "Because I live, ye shall live also" (John 14:19).

It is all right to get excited and hope for the time when we will live in heaven. Sure, we will face troubles and heartaches here, but the glory we shall see there will make all of this life's problems disappear from our memories. We look for a future whose planning and presentation is by the truly Eternal One, Jesus Christ, our Lord and King.—**Marion H. Starr, Pastor, Marion, South Carolina**

SENTENCE SERMONS

JESUS CHRIST reveals Himself to be the author and subject of the Book of Revelation.
—Selected

CHRIST IS the aperture through which the immensity and magnificence of God can be seen.
—J.B. Phillips

CHRIST IS not one of many ways to approach God, nor is He the best of several ways; He is the only way.
—A.W. Tozer

JESUS CHRIST will be Lord of all or He will not be Lord at all.
—Saint Augustine

DAILY BIBLE READINGS

M. The Messiah Revealed.
    Psalm 2:1-12
T. A Mystery Revealed.
    Daniel 2:30-35
W. The Kingdom Foretold.
    Micah 4:1-8
T. A Promise Kept. Luke 1:67-79
F. Resurrection and Life.
    John 11:17-27
S. Power and Glory Revealed.
    Ephesians 1:15-23

Challenge to Overcome

Study Text: Revelation 2:1 through 3:22

Objective: To hear Christ's message of the need for significant change and accept His challenge to be overcomers.

Time: The Book of Revelation was probably written around A.D. 96.

Place: The Book of Revelation was written on the island of Patmos in the Aegean Sea.

Golden Text: "He that overcometh, the same shall be clothed in white raiment; and I will not blot out his name out of the book of life" (Revelation 3:5).

Central Truth: Jesus Christ challenges believers to be obedient to His purpose and plan.

Evangelism Emphasis: Victorious believers will witness to the lost.

PRINTED TEXT

Revelation 2:1. Unto the angel of the church of Ephesus write; These things saith he that holdeth the seven stars in his right hand, who walketh in the midst of the seven golden candlesticks;

2. I know thy works, and thy labour, and thy patience, and how thou canst not bear them which are evil: and thou hast tried them which say they are apostles, and are not, and hast found them liars:

3. And hast borne, and hast patience, and for my name's sake hast laboured, and hast not fainted.

19. I know thy works, and charity, and service, and faith, and thy patience, and thy works; and the last to be more than the first.

3:2. Be watchful, and strengthen the things which remain, that are ready to die: for I have not found thy works perfect before God.

3. Remember therefore how thou hast received and heard, and hold fast, and repent. If therefore thou shalt not watch, I will come on thee as a thief, and thou shalt not know what hour I will come upon thee.

15. I know thy works, that thou art neither cold nor hot: I would thou wert cold or hot.

16. So then because thou art lukewarm, and neither cold nor hot, I will spue thee out of my mouth.

17. Because thou sayest, I am rich, and increased with goods, and have need of nothing; and knowest not that thou art

wretched, and miserable, and poor, and blind, and naked:

18. I counsel thee to buy of me gold tried in the fire, that thou mayest be rich; and white raiment, that thou mayest be clothed, and that the shame of thy nakedness do not appear; and anoint thine eyes with eyesalve, that thou mayest see.

19. As many as I love, I rebuke and chasten: be zealous therefore, and repent.

20. Behold, I stand at the door, and knock: if any man hear my voice, and open the door, I will come in to him, and will sup with him, and he with me.

21. To him that overcometh will I grant to sit with me in my throne, even as I also overcame, and am set down with my Father in his throne.

22. He that hath an ear, let him hear what the Spirit saith unto the churches.

DICTIONARY

Ephesus (EF-eh-sus)—Revelation 2:1—The capital city in the Roman state of Asia.

LESSON OUTLINE

I. STRENGTHS ASSESSED

   A. Attributes of the Ephesus Church

   B. Thyatira's Strengths and Faults

II. WEAKNESSES EXPOSED

   A. Sardis—The Lifeless Church

   B. Laodicea—The Lukewarm Church

III. VICTORY PROMISED

LESSON EXPOSITION

INTRODUCTION

Revelation 2 and 3 present a remarkable series of letters to seven ancient churches. Why only seven? Certainly there were many other churches in Asia, perhaps larger and more important, and some even more well known. These churches were representative of the entire church at the time of the writing, as they have been throughout the last 2000 years. Perhaps these particular examples show different conditions at different times in church history. As such, they give us a preview of the entire panorama of the church from its inception on the Day of Pentecost to its final consummation sometime still in the future. God's message in His Word is often multifaceted so that a fresh message is always coming from a passage of Scripture, even when we think we have exhausted its meaning.

So it is true with the entire church age. It is not yet completed. Christ has not returned. Are we living in a time that might be called the Laodicean Age? While this is quite possible, we don't have the full view of God's plans.

We can only see as one in the middle of a forest. We see only the trees, not the entire forest.

Still, it is interesting and applicable to our lives to study the seven churches. Look back at Revelation 1:3: "Blessed is he that readeth, and they that hear the words of this prophecy, and keep those things which are written therein: for the time is at hand." The letters to the churches were part of this prophecy and should be regarded as useful in any age.

To summarize the above, we can look at the seven churches in the following ways:

1. *Seven types of churches that exist at all times.* Most of us know of churches within our own experience that appear to have lost their first love, that are compromising with the world, and so forth.

2. *Seven phases any church might go through.* Just like there are phases of recovery from grief, there are phases of love and dedication a church goes through.

3. *Seven periods of church history.* Seven is seen as the number of completeness. These, then, give a preview of the entire church throughout history as it moves through the various stages of development.

4. *Seven views of our individual spiritual condition.* Have we lost our first love? Are we compromising with the world? Does our present relationship with the Lord match that of one of the churches?

One thing is certain: "The messages to the seven churches . . . embody admonition suitable to churches with different spiritual needs. Along with the messages

to the churches were exhortations, personal in character, constituting instruction and warning to the individual Christian. Each of the messages given to the churches therefore ends in personal exhortation beginning with the phrase, 'He that hath an ear, let him hear" (John Walvoord, *The Revelation of Jesus Christ*).

If we are ever inclined to think God doesn't care about our church or that maybe He has forgotten us, we can look at these letters to the churches. The Lord knew each of them and each situation. Jesus told John to write about specific people, places, and events. He praised the successes of the churches before declaring their faults. His criticisms were for correction, not for destruction, and were sent from a loving Father.

I. STRENGTHS ASSESSED (Revelation 2:1-3, 18, 19)

A. Attributes of the Ephesus Church (vv. 1-3)

1. Unto the angel of the church of Ephesus write; These things saith he that holdeth the seven stars in his right hand, who walketh in the midst of the seven golden candlesticks;

2. I know thy works, and thy labour, and thy patience, and how thou canst not bear them which are evil: and thou hast tried them which say they are apostles, and are not, and hast found them liars:

3. And hast borne, and hast patience, and for my name's sake hast laboured, and hast not fainted.

The Ephesus church had a

record of intolerance to sin among its members. This city was difficult to live in, especially with all the sexual deviations associated with the goddess Diana. "It is popular to be open-minded toward many types of sin," calling them 'personal choices' or 'alternative lifestyles.' But when the body of believers begins to tolerate sin in the church, the standards are lowered and the church's witness is compromised. Remember, God's approval is infinitely more important than the world's" (*Life Application Bible*). The Ephesus church was commended for (1) working hard, (2) being patient, (3) resisting sin, (4) critically examining the claims of false prophets, and (5) suffering patiently without quitting.

All of these qualities must, however, stem from a love for Jesus Christ, not from a false sense of self-righteousness. The Ephesians had lost their first love (v. 4)—or perhaps were slipping into legalism (obedience without love). They were guilty of disobeying the greatest commandment: "'Love the Lord your God with all your heart and with all your soul and with all your mind.' This is the first and greatest commandment" (Matthew 22:37, 38, *NIV*).

Part of the problem at Ephesus was that it was now a second-generation church. Many of its founders had died, and younger leaders had emerged. Though they had the heritage of their fathers, their own experience with Jesus Christ was not as vital. They were still active believers, doing much to benefit the congregation and the community, but they were acting for the wrong

reasons. Service in God's kingdom has no merit unless it flows from a heart of love for God.

There are preventative measures for not losing our first love. We can find them in Peter's second letter: "For this very reason, make every effort to add to your faith goodness; and to goodness, knowledge; and to knowledge, self-control; and to self-control, perseverance; and to perseverance, godliness; and to godliness, brotherly kindness; and to brotherly kindness, love. For if you possess these qualities in increasing measure, they will keep you from being ineffective and unproductive in your knowledge of our Lord Jesus Christ" (2 Peter 1:5-8, *NIV*).

New believers experience joy and enthusiasm unparalleled to any other emotion when they first come to Christ. The early converts in Ephesus sat under the leadership of Paul and then Timothy. Their instruction in the faith was powerful. After a time, however, that initial joy had been tempered by years of hard work and service. They knew God's Word and had a great record of service, but their love and enthusiasm had waned.

The Ephesian believers knew how to recognize error and would not tolerate it. They were commended for rejecting the heresy of the Nicolaitans (Revelation 2:6), who compromised their faith to include lustful practices. "When we want to take part in something we know is wrong, we often make excuses to justify our behavior, saying that it isn't as bad as it seems or it won't hurt our faith" (*Life Application Bible*). However, despite their discernment and moral character, the church seemed to be operating on head knowledge alone. Their hearts had grown cold. They had lost their first love.

B. Thyatira's Strengths and Faults (vv. 18, 19)

(Revelation 2:18 is not included in the printed text.)

19. I know thy works, and charity, and service, and faith, and thy patience, and thy works; and the last to be more than the first.

Situated 35-40 miles southeast of Pergamos was the city of Thyatira (the modern name today is Akhisar, meaning "white castle"), a small metropolis, but still a busy commercial center. It was located on a major road of the Roman Empire known for the many trade unions that had settled there. Membership in one of the guilds was necessary for any real financial success. The city was especially known for its cloth production and bronze manufacture. Included among these trades were carpenters, dyers, tentmakers, cloth weavers, and so forth. Lydia, the seller of purple, was from this city (see Acts 16:14).

This is the only time in Revelation the title "Son of God" is used (v. 18). Though Jesus usually referred to His role as that of the Son of Man, He asserted His deity a number of times during His earthly ministry. This is one of the incidences. As the Son of God, He has omniscient "eyes like unto a flame of fire" which can burn through the hardest facades and disguises. His feet "like fine brass" can trample sin and punish sinners. Apparently both of these divine characteristics—fiery discernment and stern judgment—were needed in Thyatira, the most corrupt of the seven churches.

Nevertheless, there were positive words for the believers in Thyatira. They were praised for their love, service, faith, and patience. All of these qualities are interrelated. Love leads to faithful service, faith leads to patience, or perseverance. Also, they had apparently become more faithful in their service than they had been earlier in their history. On the surface this was an impressive church—faithful Christians busy in the ministry.

One would think, *How could extreme problems exist in a church with such excellent commendations?* The problem rested in a self-proclaimed prophetess (symbolically named Jezebel) who was leading some of the members into spiritual and physical fornication (v. 20). Outside the church, the trade guilds in Thyatira practiced pagan worship that included animal sacrifice and illicit sex. To make a successful living here, membership in the guilds was viewed as a must. Also, the best meats available for purchase had been offered to pagan idols. Jezebel apparently insisted on accepting the world's customs and ways as harmless, claiming this would be the sensible thing to do. The leadership of the church did not have the fortitude to deal sternly with her error.

This is paralleled today in those churches accepting the gross sexuality and loss of absolute standards our society condones. When Christians permit homosexual practices, adultery and fornication, approve of pornography, and refuse to discipline or challenge those who practice these sins, they are just as guilty as Thyatira in tolerating Jezebel.

We must never be guilty of thinking our good works (faith, love, service, and patience) can offset sin. The Christian life is not a balancing of good and bad. Any violation of God's Word violates God's authority in our lives—and ultimately leads to destruction.

Is there ever any room for sin in the Christian life?

II. WEAKNESSES EXPOSED
(Revelation 3:1-3, 14-19)

A. Sardis—The Lifeless Church
(vv. 1-3)

(Revelation 3:1 is not included in the printed text.)

2. Be watchful, and strengthen the things which remain, that are ready to die: for I have not found thy works perfect before God.
3. Remember therefore how thou hast received and heard, and hold fast, and repent. If therefore thou shalt not watch, I will come on thee as a thief, and thou shalt not know what hour I will come upon thee.

Seven hundred years before John's letters were written to the churches, Sardis reigned as one of the greatest cities in the ancient world. Built on an excellent site—sitting 1500 feet high—it was almost impregnable by enemy invaders. Croesus, the greatest of the Sardian kings, was said to have invited Solon, the Greek wise man, to view his riches. Solon, dismayed by the king's pride, tried to warn him of softness and complacency, but Croesus was blinded by his success.

Croesus launched an invasion against Cyrus of Persia, only to be easily routed. The stunned king quickly returned to what he thought was the safety of the citadel of Sardis. However, King Cyrus then began a siege of Sardis.

Even though Sardis appeared invulnerable, the plateau had developed faults and cracks. One day a Sardian soldier accidentally dropped his helmet into one of these. He quickly lowered himself into the crevice to recover it. Watching this, a Persian soldier reasoned that there might be a way to enter the city by following these faults. That night a group of soldiers reached the top of Sardis and found the city completely unguarded. Sardis then fell to Cyrus because her defenders had become complacent. Croesus lost his city because he didn't think he needed to post guards.

Now, 700 years later, the Sardis church was much like its namesake. It was a degenerate church in a degenerate city. The words "you are dead" (v. 1, *NIV*) describe the situation. As certain as if it had been bitten by a deadly snake, death was imminent unless an antidote was given. Jesus declared this church dead unless other measures were quickly initiated.

The members of the Sardis church were carrying out their Christian activities in order to "build a portfolio." They were working to impress others—

perhaps even God himself. They were believers in name alone. Sardis is typical of churches that worship their past glories and deeds, concerned more with forms than with life. They loved their "system" more than they loved Jesus.

It is interesting to note that this church had fewer struggles going on within it than the other churches. There were no Judaizers, no Nicolaitans, no Jezebels, because Satan didn't have to fight them. The Sardis church was like many in our cities today. We pass them daily, but they have no effect whatever on our lives. Their existence means nothing to our communities. They simply exist, dead and lifeless.

Sardis was warned to do five things. These are aptly translated in the *New International Version*:

1. "Wake up!" (v. 2). Ask these sobering questions: Why do we do the things we do? Are our lives representing Christ?

2. "Strengthen what remains" (v. 2). Help it to come alive again. Find the people in the church who still love the Lord and encourage them in their faith. Motivate them to follow Christ.

3. "Remember . . . what you have received" (v. 3). In the same way that the church at Ephesus was encouraged to return to its first love, the Sardian members were told to look back to the time when they had a vital experience with the Lord. The King James rendition says to remember how they received. They had received the gospel with joy. They had been vibrant. They had to find that same exhilaration.

4. "Repent" (v. 3). Every stim-ulus invites a response. Every action requires a reaction. God's message of correction requires repentance as its response. The people of Sardis would not find life until they repented of their sins of neglect and complacency.

5. "If you do not wake up . . ." (v. 3). The phrase "wake up" is repeated. This church had lost its expectation and hope of the Lord's coming. The warning was that if it did not recover that hope, it would be caught like the five foolish virgins described in Matthew 25:1-13. They would miss the hope of being caught away with Christ as Paul described in 1 Corinthians 15.

B. Laodicea—The Lukewarm Church (vv. 14-19)

(Revelation 3:14 is not included in the printed text.)

15. I know thy works, that thou art neither cold nor hot: I would thou wert cold or hot.

16. So then because thou art lukewarm, and neither cold nor hot, I will spue thee out of my mouth.

17. Because thou sayest, I am rich, and increased with goods, and have need of nothing; and knowest not that thou art wretched, and miserable, and poor, and blind, and naked:

18. I counsel thee to buy of me gold tried in the fire, that thou mayest be rich; and white raiment, that thou mayest be clothed, and that the shame of thy nakedness do not appear; and anoint thine eyes with eye-salve, that thou mayest see.

19. As many as I love, I rebuke and chasten: be zealous therefore, and repent.

In the first century, Laodicea was listed as one of the wealthiest cities of the world. The people lacked nothing. With all of its wealth, however, it is interesting that the city had no natural water supply of its own. Water was brought from six miles away at Hierapolis by aqueduct from hot springs. By the time the water reached Laodicea, it was lukewarm—just like the church that drank of it.

The city was known for three things: its banking industry, its cloth manufacture, and its medical school (famous for eyesalve). The wealth obtained from these three areas gave the church a false assumption of spiritual blessing. Luxury made them comfortable and complacent. In verse 18, Jesus counseled them to buy three spiritual things—*gold, white raiment,* and *eyesalve.* These parallel the three things they had mistakenly put their trust in. "Gold tried in the fire" represents faith. Peter described this: "These have come so that your faith—of greater worth than gold, which perishes even though refined by fire—may be proved genuine and may result in praise, glory and honor when Jesus Christ is revealed" (1 Peter 1:7, *NIV*). True faith comes from confidence in God, not in material possessions. All through Scripture "white raiment" represents a changed character—righteousness imparted from the risen Christ. Human self-righteousness is as filthy rags in the sight of God (Isaiah 64:6). The salve they needed to clear their eyes was the truths of God. The anointing of the Spirit is the agent

for doing such: "As for you, the anointing you received from him remains in you, and you do not need anyone to teach you. But as his anointing teaches you about all things and as that anointing is real, not counterfeit—just as it has taught you, remain in him" (1 John 2:27, *NIV*).

To receive this true gold, white clothing, and eyesalve, the Laodiceans had to be willing to submit to holy rebuke and discipline. Despite their condition, Jesus loved them and wanted to restore them. We too must be ready to remove the spiritual blinders from our eyes, and then accept the change and discipline to make us true servants of the living God.

How do you evaluate your own church to see what type of church it is? Are there elements of all seven churches in your church?

III. VICTORY PROMISED
(Revelation 3:20-22)

20. Behold, I stand at the door, and knock: if any man hear my voice, and open the door, I will come in to him, and will sup with him, and he with me.

21. To him that overcometh will I grant to sit with me in my throne, even as I also overcame, and am set down with my Father in his throne.

22. He that hath an ear, let him hear what the Spirit saith unto the churches.

In all situations God promises us potential victory if we turn our hearts toward Him. Even with the faults and shortcomings found in the churches, including Laodicea, there was still hope. To anyone who overcomes by walking in faith (see Galatians 3:2-5), Christ promises that he will sit with Him upon His throne. The assurance that we can rule with Christ (at present in a spiritual sense, but in a more literal way during the Millennium) was especially meaningful to the people of Laodicea who had just received a severe tongue-lashing. As always, God's intent is to draw His people back to Himself.

All the churches of Revelation 2 and 3 are represented in the world today. We have Ephesian churches that have lost their first love, Smyrnan churches that are suffering terribly, Pergamon and Thyatiran churches which allow false doctrines and immoral practices, Sardian churches that are dead, Philadelphian churches that are full of love, and Laodicean churches that teeter on the lukewarm fence, being neither hot nor cold. Let us search our hearts to make sure we hear the word that the Spirit has for us in each of them.

How do we know there was hope for the Laodicean church, despite its lukewarm condition?

REVIEW QUESTIONS

1. How can we stand guard over our "first love" to make sure we don't lose our joy and excitement in the Lord?

2. The Thyatira church had several good commendations, but were heavily condemned for their weaknesses. Can we ever allow ourselves to be deluded by our weaknesses?

3. How can we best assess ourselves as Christians and as churches? How do we expose our weaknesses?

4. If you were Jesus and were dictating a letter to John to send to your church, what kind of message would it include?

5. What must we do to overcome and be assured of victory?

GOLDEN TEXT HOMILY

"HE THAT OVERCOMETH, THE SAME SHALL BE CLOTHED IN WHITE RAIMENT; AND I WILL NOT BLOT OUT HIS NAME OUT OF THE BOOK OF LIFE" (Revelation 3:5).

To be an overcomer is to utterly defeat the enemy, to put him underfoot (Malachi 4:3; Luke 10:19). In this passage, the promise for one who overcomes is threefold: (1) he will be clothed in white raiment; (2) his name will not be blotted out of the Book of Life; (3) the Son will confess his name before the Father.

In ancient cities the name of a citizen was recorded in a book of the living until his death. At death his name would be erased or marked out of the book. There is some evidence that a person's name could be removed from the book before death if he were convicted of a crime. Early Christians who were loyal to Christ were under constant threat of being branded as political or social rebels, then stripped of their citizenship and their names removed from the book of the living. Christ offers those who overcome a more secure, safe, and eternal citizenship in His kingdom. To be accepted into His kingdom, one must remain faithful to God and His call. Jesus said in our text, "He that overcometh, the same shall be clothed in white raiment."

Not only will the overcomer be clothed in white raiment, but he will also receive the promise of Christ that his name will not be blotted out of the Book of Life. A person whose name has been recorded in the Book of Life remains in it by faithfulness to the commandments of God and can be erased only by disloyalty to those commandments.

The Word of God in 1 Timothy 2:5 tells us we have "one mediator between God and men, the man Christ Jesus." Jesus reached up to heaven, took God by the hand, then He reached down to earth and took man by the hand. On the cross He hung suspended between heaven and earth, interceding for our sins. He stands today at the side of God, still interceding for us, acting as our advocate, One who pleads our case before God the righteous Judge. In Hebrews, the Bible refers to Christ as being the mediator of a *better covenant* (8:6), the mediator of the *new testament* (9:15), and the mediator of the *new covenant* (12:24). Whatever position we give Him in our lives, we know we have an Advocate with the Father. We have His word that we can come boldly to the throne of grace. In whatever life situation we find ourselves in, we know His grace is sufficient to meet all our needs.—**Ronald M. Padgett, Chaplain, Director of Religious Programs, Mississippi Department of Corrections, Parchman, Mississippi**

SENTENCE SERMONS

JESUS CHRIST challenges believers to be obedient to His purpose and plan.

—Selected

GOD comes in where my acknowledged helplessness begins.

—Oswald Chambers

OUR WEARINESS makes us appreciate God's strength.

—Erwin W. Lutzer

GOD has not called me to be successful; He has called me to be faithful.

—Mother Teresa of Calcutta

DAILY BIBLE READINGS

M. Strength to Overcome.
   Judges 15:9-15
T Defeated by Immorality.
   Judges 16:15-21
W. Victory Over Enemies.
   Judges 16:22-30
T. Overcoming by the Word.
   Psalm 119:105-112
F. Challenge to Persevere.
   Matthew 24:3-13
S. Reward for Perseverance.
   Galatians 6:7-9

Worship in Heaven

Study Text: Revelation 4:1 through 5:14

Objective: To examine and apply the Biblical revelation of heavenly worship as a model for our worship.

Time: The Book of Revelation was probably written around A.D. 96.

Place: The Book of Revelation was written on the island of Patmos in the Aegean Sea.

Golden Text: "Thou art worthy to take the book, and to open the seals thereof: for thou wast slain, and hast redeemed us to God by thy blood" (Revelation 5:9).

Central Truth: The Lamb of God is worthy of all praise and worship.

Evangelism Emphasis: Through praise and worship, believers discover God's desire to save the lost.

PRINTED TEXT

Revelation 4:2. And immediately I was in the spirit: and, behold, a throne was set in heaven, and one sat on the throne.

3. And he that sat was to look upon like a jasper and a sardine stone: and there was a rainbow round about the throne, in sight like unto an emerald.

5. And out of the throne proceeded lightnings and thunderings and voices: and there were seven lamps of fire burning before the throne, which are the seven Spirits of God.

6. And before the throne there was a sea of glass like unto crystal: and in the midst of the throne, and round about the throne, were four beasts full of eyes before and behind.

8. And the four beasts had each of them six wings about him; and they were full of eyes within: and they rest not day and night, saying, Holy, holy, holy, Lord God Almighty, which was, and is, and is to come.

5:1. And I saw in the right hand of him that sat on the throne a book written within and on the backside, sealed with seven seals.

2. And I saw a strong angel proclaiming with a loud voice, Who is worthy to open the book, and to loose the seals thereof?

3. And no man in heaven, nor in earth, neither under the earth, was able to open the book, neither to look thereon.

4. And I wept much, because no man was found worthy to open and to read the book, neither to look thereon.

5. And one of the elders saith unto me, Weep not: behold, the Lion of the tribe of Juda, the Root of David, hath prevailed to open the book, and to loose the seven seals thereof.

9. And they sung a new song, saying, Thou art worthy to take the book, and to open the seals thereof: for thou wast slain, and hast redeemed us to God by thy blood out of every kindred, and tongue, and people, and nation;

10. And hast made us unto our God kings and priests: and we shall reign on the earth.

11. And I beheld, and I heard the voice of many angels round about the throne and the beasts and the elders: and the number of them was ten thousand times ten thousand, and thousands of thousands;

12. Saying with a loud voice, Worthy is the Lamb that was slain to receive power, and riches, and wisdom, and strength, and honour, and glory, and blessing.

DICTIONARY

jasper (JAS-pur) and sardine (SAR-den) stone—Revelation 4:3— Items of adornment at the throne of God which John saw in his vision.

LESSON OUTLINE

I. GOD'S HOLY PRESENCE

    A. The Throne of Heaven

    B. Surrounding the Throne

II. THE TRIUMPHANT LAMB

    A. He Who Sits on the Throne

    B. Who Is Worthy to Open the Book?

    C. The Lion of the Tribe of Judah, the Root of David

    D. The Lamb Who Takes the Scroll

III. RESPONSE OF PRAISE

    A. A New Song

    B. The Multitudes of Angels Around the Throne

    C. The Praise of All Heaven

LESSON EXPOSITION

INTRODUCTION

Revelation 4 begins with a dramatic change in John's vision. This initiates the third division of the book (see introduction to lesson 1). In 1:19, the apostle was charged, "Write the things which thou hast seen, and the things which are, and the things which shall be hereafter." "The things which thou hast seen" covers chapter 1; "the things which are" covers the seven churches of chapters 2 and 3; and finally, "the things which shall be hereafter" takes us through those things that will occur in the future after the church age.

The phrases "after this" at the beginning of 4:1 and "hereafter" at the close of the verse possibly tell us twice that the church age has been completed, and that the saints have been caught away to be with the Lord. The "first voice" is none other than the one John heard before in 1:10, 11—the voice of Jesus himself. The apostle was summoned upward to catch a view of heaven. He was the first Biblical character to be caught up as such. The prophets Isaiah, Ezekiel, and Daniel were privileged to look into the heavenlies, but only from an earthly stance. And now John is privileged, through a vision, to view heaven and future events.

The words of 4:1 have a strong similarity to the description of the catching away of the saints in 1 Thessalonians 4:13-18. This leads many of us to conclude that the church is represented by John here, and is caught up to be with Christ before the beginning of Tribulation. There are many, however, who feel that the similarities are only superficial. For instance, the *New International Version Commentary* says, "There is no good reason for seeing the invitation for John to come up into the opened heaven as a symbol of the rapture of the church." The writers go on to state that, even though the word *church* is missing from chapter 4 until chapter 22, this does not give credibility to the Rapture theory, since that word *church* or (*churches*) is always used in reference to the historic Asian churches. For purposes of this commentary, however, we will assume that what John saw was the same as what the church will see when it is raptured to heaven. Thus, from this point on in Revelation, all things are viewed from the standpoint of eternity.

To come to the deduction that the church has already been raptured at this point in Revelation, we look at the following reasoning:

Since 1 Thessalonians 5:9, "For God did not appoint us to suffer wrath but to receive salvation through our Lord Jesus Christ" (*NIV*), promises that God's wrath will not fall upon believers of this age; and since God was always careful to remove the faithful from divine judgment (Noah and his family in Genesis 6—8, and Lot in Genesis 19); and since the Great Tribulation (Revelation 6—19) is a time of God's wrath upon the world; therefore the conclusion is drawn that Christ will catch the church up to be with Him (1 Thessalonians 4:13-18) before the events of Revelation 4—19 begin.

We must remember that these studies and our ideas on prophecy are still speculative. The Jews before Christ's birth studied diligently to determine the circumstances of His first coming—and they still missed Him. No doubt, our ideas today can be just as flawed. What is certain is that John's reaction to seeing heaven was much the same as other prophets. In reading Isaiah 6 and Ezekiel 1, we see that these men were stimulated to worship. Also, what John experienced gives us not so much a visual view of heaven, but rather one of its character. The unmistakable conclusion is that everything in creation centers on the heavenly throne and the One who sits on it. The only appropriate response to the majesty of God is absolute praise and worship.

I. GOD'S HOLY PRESENCE
   (Revelation 4:1-11)

A. The Throne of Heaven (vv. 1-3)

   (Revelation 4:1 is not included in the printed text.)

   2. And immediately I was in the spirit: and, behold, a throne

was set in heaven, and one sat on the throne.

3. And he that sat was to look upon like a jasper and a sardine stone: and there was a rainbow round about the throne, in sight like unto an emerald.

John has now been called up from earth into the realm of the spirit. What he sees is the celestial headquarters of God. This is the place where the judgments of the Tribulation will be pronounced. The wrath of the One on the throne is about to be poured out in vehemence upon a rebellious world.

The minerals "jasper" and "sardine stone" (v. 3) portray the glorious splendor of God's presence, while the rainbow conveys the idea of His "encircling brilliance" (*NIV Commentary*). Ezekiel's vision also included a rainbow (Ezekiel 1:28). The most notable appearance of a rainbow was after the Flood (Genesis 9:13-17), when God made a covenant with Noah that the earth would never again be destroyed by a flood. Thus the rainbow represented God's unchanging mercy.

The appearance around the throne in Revelation possibly indicates mercy even in the midst of terrible judgment during the Tribulation period. Revelation 7 indicates that great multitudes will turn to Christ during the Judgment era. It is interesting to note that the Great White Throne (Revelation 20:11-15) does not include a rainbow, telling us that there will be no mercy for the unrepentant after that point. They will be cast into the lake of fire.

B. Surrounding the Throne
  (vv. 4-11)

(Revelation 4:4, 7, 9-11 is not included in the printed text.)

5. And out of the throne proceeded lightnings and thunderings and voices: and there were seven lamps of fire burning before the throne, which are the seven Spirits of God.

6. And before the throne there was a sea of glass like unto crystal: and in the midst of the throne, and round about the throne, were four beasts full of eyes before and behind.

8. And the four beasts had each of them six wings about him; and they were full of eyes within: and they rest not day and night, saying, Holy, holy, holy, Lord God Almighty, which was, and is, and is to come.

It is possible that the 24 elders (v. 4) represent the redeemed saints of all time, both before and after Christ's death. Including Jews and Gentiles, they may be symbolic of the 12 tribes of Israel and the 12 apostles. The fact that they are sitting in heaven in white garments indicates that they are finished with their earthly labor. Their crowns of gold show they have received a glorified and rewarded state, having overcome "by the blood of the Lamb, and by the word of their testimony; and they loved not their lives unto the death" (12:11).

The lightning and thunder here (4:5), as well as in other portions of Revelation, signify an important event is about to happen. The same phenomena occurred when God gave the Law at Sinai (Exodus 19:16). God's presence is coming near for judgment and wrath. The seven lamps before the throne indicate the omniscient and omnipresent Holy Spirit, who testifies against the world's sin and forecasts the justice of the wrath that is about to begin.

The "sea of glass" (Revelation 4:6) does not mean that John was actually speaking about a body of water or glass. Rather, he describes in symbolic language the appearance of the surface before the throne. *PURE GOLD?*

The four beasts were creatures proclaiming God's glory, possibly representing God's government over the four corners of the earth. They appeared much like those of Ezekiel's vision (Ezekiel 1:5-10), but with some differences. Their six wings were much the same as Isaiah's vision (Isaiah 6:2). An important point can be made here. The Old Testament is a prerequisite study in understanding the New Testament. So much of what John saw had an earlier prototype by at least one of the prophets.

Do these weird creatures actually exist in heaven, or are they only manifestations of a vision? There is certainly nothing to prevent God from having such beings around His throne, praising Him at all times. If we look at the vast array of species on earth, we can understand that divine creative energy for further variety is certainly possible.

The four faces on the beasts (Revelation 4:7) fall in line with the traditions given to the four Gospels. Matthew wrote to the Jews, and often spoke of Christ as the *Lion* of Judah. Mark wrote to a pragmatic Roman audience, portraying the Savior as the perfect servant, much like the *ox*. Luke wrote in a polished style to the sophisticated Greek mind. He portrayed the Lord as the perfect *Man*. Finally, John wrote of the deity of Christ, and thus shows Him soaring like an *eagle*.

Are the similarities between John's vision and those of Ezekiel, Daniel and Isaiah coincidental, or are they essentially the same?

II. THE TRIUMPHANT LAMB
(Revelation 5:1-8)

A. He Who Sits on the Throne (vv. 1-3)

1. And I saw in the right hand of him that sat on the throne a book written within and on the backside, sealed with seven seals.

2. And I saw a strong angel proclaiming with a loud voice, Who is worthy to open the book, and to loose the seals thereof?

3. And no man in heaven, nor in earth, neither under the earth, was able to open the book, neither to look thereon.

It is obvious from the final three verses of chapter 4 that He "that sat on the throne" of heaven is God the Father—the Creator. Now, 5:6, 7 reveals that it is Jesus, the Son, who receives and opens the seven-sealed scroll from the Father. Who knows the scroll's contents? Both the Father and the Son. It is apparent from the Olivet Discourse (Matthew 24) that Jesus was describing events that would occur in the end, especially those relating to the seven seals. The only detail Jesus does not know is the timing of its initiation. Matthew 24:36 tells us, "No one knows about that day or hour, not even the angels in heaven, nor the Son, but only the Father" (*NIV*).

We can find hope in the knowledge that God does sit on the throne in heaven, in total control of all that happens. Even when He seems to be silent during the everyday affairs of life, He is not disinterested. He is not inactive.

He has the big picture in mind, orchestrating His will for our lives.

B. Who Is Worthy to Open the Book? (v. 4)

4. And I wept much, because no man was found worthy to open and to read the book, neither to look thereon.

The scroll reveals "the mystery of God" that Old Testament prophets foretold centuries earlier (see Revelation 10:7). It sheds light on the entire puzzle of the universe, and how history will end for the earth and its inhabitants. It is the unfolding of God's ultimate work in renewing creation—making once again a perfect state for man to live in fellowship with the Creator. Christ alone is worthy to open this document. He earned this right by His substitutionary death on the cross. Finally, there is Someone who can rectify all the wrongs ever committed, give total justice to the oppressed, and reverse the evils that began with the fall of man.

Throughout history there have been many who thought they were capable of "opening the scroll." All failed miserably. Nebuchadnezzar, Alexander the Great, the Caesars of Rome, Charlemagne, Napoleon, Hitler—all had ambition and plans to rule the world. What they really had, however, was a thirst for power and glory, much the same hunger for power that brought about Lucifer's fall. Even good men who struggled to bring justice were incapable of solving the human condition. Men like George Washington, Abraham Lincoln, and Winston Churchill; spiritual giants like Martin Luther, the Wesley brothers, Charles Finney, and Dwight L.

Moody, all left their mark but were unable to reverse the downward spiral of sin on the planet. After 50 years of ministry, Billy Graham was asked if he was pleased with his success as an evangelist. His reply was an honest statement of inadequacy: "I don't think of myself as successful at all. I feel like a failure." The great man of God went on to say, "The world is worse today than when I began my ministry" (Anne Graham Lotz, *Vision of His Glory*).

It is no wonder that John was moved to tears. The weight of all the wrongs and injustices of history caused him to sink momentarily in despair. It was only when one of the elders told him to "weep not" (v. 5) that he realized all hope was not gone. He quickly learned that the problem does, after all, have a solution. There *is* One who is worthy to open the scroll.

C. The Lion of the Tribe of Judah, the Root of David (v. 5)

5. And one of the elders saith unto me, Weep not: behold, the Lion of the tribe of Juda, the Root of David, hath prevailed to open the book, and to loose the seven seals thereof.

Exhausted by his own weeping, John takes his eyes off the throne momentarily. Then, the voice of one of the elders tells him, "Behold, the Lion of the tribe of Juda, the Root of David." John turns, expecting to see a great King of the Jews. The "Lion of the tribe of Judah" came from Jacob's prophecy in Genesis 49:9, 10. Here it was predicted that the Messiah would come from Judah. The "Root of David" was a promise that the Messiah would come from David's lineage (Isaiah 11:1, 10). John's ears must have perked up as he heard these familiar titles. He fully expected to see a triumphant "Lion" as he lifted his eyes.

D. The Lamb Who Takes the Scroll (vv. 6-8)

(Revelation 5:6-8 is not included in the printed text.)

Instead of a conquering Lion, John saw a slain Lamb with the marks of death still written on His body. These marks will remain on the Lamb for all eternity. It has been said that the only one throughout the ages who will have a less than perfect body will be the eternally perfect One himself. The Lion is a symbol of majesty, power, and authority. The Lamb is a symbol of submission. Here John saw the Conqueror who conquers by submitting. The Lamb of God is filled with mercy and grace, but those who defy and reject that grace will find that the Lamb is also a Lion.

Christ comes with seven horns (representing complete omnipotent power) and seven eyes (complete omniscience) to receive the scroll. The beasts and the 24 elders fall down in adoration and worship. Revelation 19:10 says that only God may be worshiped. Thus, the deity of Christ as coequal with the Father is manifest in the heavenly realm.

The "prayers of the saints" (5:8) are never lost. Their answers may be postponed, but God keeps them and will ultimately answer every one of them. The prayers of the saints are the vials of incense in heaven. "Just imagine . . . you and I kneel or stand or sit down to pray, really opening our hearts to God—and what we say is so precious to Him that He keeps it like a treasure" (Jim Cymbala, *Fresh Wind, Fresh Fire*).

Do you see your prayers as important to God? Or, in your frustrations and problems, do you see them as never getting God's attention?

III. RESPONSE OF PRAISE (Revelation 5:9-14)

A. A New Song (vv. 9, 10)

9. And they sung a new song, saying, Thou art worthy to take the book, and to open the seals thereof: for thou wast slain, and hast redeemed us to God by thy blood out of every kindred, and tongue, and people, and nation;
10. And hast made us unto our God kings and priests: and we shall reign on the earth.

The song John heard being sung was a new one. It recounts all the work of Christ for which He is to be praised. He was slain, redeeming with His blood those who believe on Him. He brings them into His kingdom, makes them priests, and appoints them to reign upon the earth. No matter what faces Christians today, they should always worship God for what has been done for them. As the four beasts and the 24 elders fell down to worship the Lamb in verse 8, they each had a harp. When the people of Judah were carried off to captivity in Babylon, they hung up their harps (Psalm 137:1-4), signifying that they no longer had anything to sing about. They had lost their song. Here in John's vision of the throne, we see that we always have a reason to sing. "When we realize the glorious future that awaits us, we will find the strength to face present difficulties" (*Life Application Bible*).

The song gave all the glory to the Lamb. He is the only One worthy of praise. Believers should remember this, making sure they are ever aware that no credit can be reserved for themselves. "If Jesus alone is worthy of praise— and He is!—why do we seek praise for ourselves? Why are we offended when others don't give us credit for what we have done?" (Lotz).

B. The Multitudes of Angels
Around the Throne (v. 11)

11. And I beheld, and I heard the voice of many angels round about the throne and the beasts and the elders: and the number of them was ten thousand times ten thousand, and thousands of thousands.

As the Lamb takes the scroll from the Father, the angelic hosts break out into spontaneous praise. The time has finally come for evil men to be judged and their dominion taken away. The numbers of angels present are staggering—10,000 times 10,000 plus 1,000 times 1,000. Angels are spiritual creatures who help carry out God's work on earth. Their great numbers indicate the unbelievable grandeur of what John witnessed. This was a man who had seen Jesus beaten, stripped, flogged, and crucified. Now he sees millions encircling Him with worship and adoration.

C. The Praise of All Heaven
(vv. 12-14)

(Revelation 5:13, 14 is not included in the printed text.)

12. Saying with a loud voice, Worthy is the Lamb that was slain to receive power, and riches, and wisdom, and strength, and honour, and glory, and blessing.

The praise to the Lamb spreads out in successive circles around the throne before John's eyes. The four creatures, the 24 elders, the numberless angels, and now all the creatures of the universe are glorifying the Father on the throne and the Lamb who was slain. Again it is seen that Christ is coequal with God the Father and deserves equal glory.

Do you sing praise to God in the midst of your troubles? Have you laid down your "harp" because of the pressures of daily life?

REVIEW QUESTIONS

1. Describe the four beasts John saw around the throne. What is their purpose? Explain the symbolism of each of the four faces?

2. Are any of our prayers ever forgotten in heaven? Explain.

3. What evidences do we see in the picture of the throne of heaven that show Christ as equal to God the Father?

4. Why should the Christian life be one of constant praise and worship of God? What has Christ done for us to deserve our praise?

5. What is the primary role of the angels in heaven?

GOLDEN TEXT HOMILY

"THOU ART WORTHY TO TAKE THE BOOK, AND TO OPEN THE SEALS THEREOF: FOR THOU WAST SLAIN, AND HAST REDEEMED US TO GOD BY THY BLOOD" (Revelation 5:9).

This is a glorious scene which John the Revelator shares with the worshipers of the Lord on earth. Since Calvary, people in all generations who worship the Lord may look at this heavenly scene and understand the style of worship which is pleasing to the heavenly Father, and which is beneficial to those on earth.

Jesus, while on earth, gave a preview of the type of worship which is pleasing to the heavenly Father. He spoke these words to the woman by the well in Samaria: "But the hour cometh, and now is, when the true worshippers shall worship the Father in spirit and in truth" (John 4:23). We would do well to observe this type of worship in which these heavenly beings were involved and to follow this pattern. First, there were the heavenly singers who were singing a new song. It is evident that when people on earth adopt this worship procedure, every song, whether old or new, will sound like a new song.

Second, these heavenly worshipers were committed to exuberant worship. When people on earth abandon themselves to this kind of worship, tremendous blessings are received from heaven. Someone has said, "Heaven must be in us before we can be in heaven."

Here is evidence that when following this heavenly procedure of worship, saints on earth will receive tremendous blessings.— **Wayne S. Proctor, Coordinator, Church of God Autumn Ministries of Illinois, Harrisburg, Illinois**

SENTENCE SERMONS

THE LAMB OF GOD is worthy of all praise and worship.
                        —Selected

THEY ARE WISE who consider God's response to their worship.
                        —Selected

ILLUMINATING THE LESSON

Do you sometimes experience moments when you feel hopeless—that nothing will ever change the tide of evil on this planet? Surely the people who lost friends and loved ones in the Oklahoma City bombing feel this. As this commentary is being written, the court trials of the bombing suspects are being carried out. However, even a guilty verdict will not change the horrible events on that awful day in 1995; it will not bring back the innocent who were killed; it will do nothing to prevent future crimes men perpetrate against each other.

The one thing that the "scroll" of Revelation tells us is that God is still on the throne. There will be a "final justice." It has been said that the wheels of God's justice grind very slowly, but they grind so very fine. Whether or not we understand the events that unfold in Revelation is unimportant. What matters is that we have grounds to trust the One who created us to ultimately bring about good, eliminate evil, and dry the tears that have been shed over the centuries.

DAILY BIBLE READINGS

M. Praise From the Heart.
    Psalm 138:1-8
T. Song of Praise. Isaiah 12:1-6
W. Vision of God's Glory.
    Ezekiel 43:1-6
T. Behold the Lamb of God.
    John 1:29-34
F. A Worshiping Church.
    Acts 2:41-47
S. Orderly Worship.
    1 Corinthians 14:26-33

End-Time Conditions

Study Text: Revelation 6:1 through 7:17

Objective: To understand that God controls end-time events and trust Him with our future.

Time: The Book of Revelation was probably written around A.D. 96.

Place: The Book of Revelation was written on the island of Patmos in the Aegean Sea.

Golden Text: "When these things begin to come to pass, then look up, and lift up your heads; for your redemption draweth nigh" (Luke 21:28).

Central Truth: God warns of disastrous conditions and promises hope to His people.

Evangelism Emphasis: Sinners can be saved from God's wrath through faith in Jesus Christ.

PRINTED TEXT

Revelation 6:1. And I saw when the Lamb opened one of the seals, and I heard, as it were the noise of thunder, one of the four beasts saying, Come and see.

2. And I saw, and behold a white horse: and he that sat on him had a bow; and a crown was given unto him: and he went forth conquering, and to conquer.

3. And when he had opened the second seal, I heard the second beast say, Come and see.

4. And there went out another horse that was red: and power was given to him that sat thereon to take peace from the earth, and that they should kill one another: and there was given unto him a great sword.

5. And when he had opened the third seal, I heard the third beast say, Come and see. And I beheld, and lo a black horse; and he that sat on him had a pair of balances in his hand.

7. And when he had opened the fourth seal, I heard the voice of the fourth beast say, Come and see.

8. And I looked, and behold a pale horse: and his name that sat on him was Death, and Hell followed with him. And power was given unto them over the fourth part of the earth, to kill with sword, and with hunger, and with death, and with the beasts of the earth.

11. And white robes were given unto every one of them; and it was said unto them, that they should rest yet for a little season, until their fellowservants also and their brethren, that should be killed as they

were, should be fulfilled.

12. And I beheld when he had opened the sixth seal, and, lo, there was a great earthquake; and the sun became black as sackcloth of hair, and the moon became as blood;

13. And the stars of heaven fell unto the earth, even as a fig tree casteth her untimely figs, when she is shaken of a mighty wind.

14. And the heaven departed as a scroll when it is rolled together; and every mountain and island were moved out of their places.

7:9. After this I beheld, and, lo, a great multitude, which no man could number, of all nations, and kindreds, and people, and tongues, stood before the throne, and before the Lamb, clothed with white robes, and palms in their hands;

10. And cried with a loud voice, saying, Salvation to our God which sitteth upon the throne, and unto the Lamb.

LESSON OUTLINE

I. WAR AND VIOLENCE
   A. The White Horse
   B. The Red Horse

II. ECONOMIC AND COSMIC UPHEAVAL
   A. The Black Horse
   B. The Pale Horse
   C. The Sixth Seal

III. PERSECUTION AND HOPE
   A. Martyrdom of the Saints
   B. A Great Multitude Before the Throne
   C. White-Robed Saints

LESSON EXPOSITION

INTRODUCTION

The Tribulation period begins when Christ pulls the first seal away from the scroll of judgments in chapter 6. To gather an understanding of this seven-year horror, we refer to Daniel 9. Over 500 years before John, the prophet Daniel had a vision outlining history through its final days (9:24-27). There would be a distinct period of 70 weeks of years. "The 70 weeks are divided into three periods of 7 weeks, 62 weeks, and 1 week. They cover the time from the going forth of the commandment to restore and to build Jerusalem, which was the 14th day of the month Nisan (March 445 B.C.), to the second stage (the revelation of the second coming of Christ. The first period, 7 weeks, refers to the time required to rebuild the walls of Jerusalem, which was 49 years, thus giving us the key to the meaning of the word week; for if 7 weeks are equal to 49 years, then 1 week is equal to 7 years. Now we are told that 'from the going forth of the commandment to restore and to build Jerusalem [445 B.C.] unto the Messiah the Prince shall be seven weeks, and threescore and two weeks,' or 69 weeks, or if 1 week is equal to 7 years, 7 x 69 or 483 years" (Clarence Larkin, *The Book of Revelation*). From a *futurist* perspective, this took place the day

Jesus rode into Jerusalem on a donkey to the adulation of throngs of common people. Shortly after this, the Messiah would be "cut off" (v. 26), which obviously refers to His crucifixion.

Daniel was then told of events that would take place during the 70th week, or last seven years of the 490-year period. Most futurist commentators believe this week is yet to be fulfilled, and is the same period referred to by Jesus in the Olivet Discourse (Matthew 24). As He sat looking over Jerusalem from the Mount of Olives, Jesus told His disciples that many strange things would happen on earth. He referred to Daniel's prophecy (see Daniel 9:27) of the "abomination of desolation" (Matthew 24:15). To gain a full understanding of the tribulation described in Revelation 6 through the remainder of the book, we must consider both Daniel's vision and Jesus' very own words.

Before proceeding with a study of the opening of the seals, it is wise to recognize that true prophetic study should not be simply an exercise in solving riddles, looking for timetables, and searching for the order of events to come. God's prophets were more interested in revealing the nature of God than in trying to foretell the future. This is demonstrated by the life of Daniel. Daniel had been a captive in Babylon for many years when the Persians overthrew the Babylonians. God quickened Daniel's heart to understand that this was more than a political power change. He had access to a letter from Jeremiah predicting a 70-year captivity (Jeremiah 29:10). As Daniel reflected on Jeremiah's words, he could have been excited because the captivity was about to end. He might have been tempted to forget his duties. Like many today who anticipate the rapture of the church, he might have become so "heavenly minded" that he might have forgotten to "occupy till [He comes]" (Luke 19:13).

However, Daniel did none of these things. His response to the prophecy was to repent and worship. He was certainly more concerned with why the captivity had taken place than with the imminent end of it. "The question for him was not 'When are we going to return?' but 'Are we ready to return?'" (Notes on Daniel 9, *Word In Life Study Bible*).

Jeremiah told the captives to put down roots and expect a full 70 years in Babylon. He also told them to "seek the peace and prosperity of the city to which I [God] have carried you into exile. Pray to the Lord for it, because if it prospers, you too will prosper" (Jeremiah 29:7, *NIV*). These were not pleasant words to the captives who had been taken from their homeland, because they revealed that their own well-being was tied to that of their captors.

The same message is true for us today when studying prophecy. We must search for peace from God and pray for our leaders— even as we see events unfolding toward the end times described in Revelation. God's peace (*shalom*) is a just peace, a peace that includes justice. As we pray and study God's Word to understand His nature, we show others that

He is in us. This provides a witness to a dying world. James described it like this: "But the wisdom that comes from heaven is first of all pure; then peace-loving, considerate, submissive, full of mercy and good fruit, impartial and sincere. Peacemakers who sow in peace raise a harvest of righteousness" (James 3:17, 18, *NIV*).

We must look at the opening of the seals, not just with curiosity but with a perspective of understanding God's nature . . . His righteousness . . . His holiness . . . and His justice.

I. WAR AND VIOLENCE
   (Revelation 6:1-4)

A. The White Horse (vv. 1, 2)

1. And I saw when the Lamb opened one of the seals, and I heard, as it were the noise of thunder, one of the four beasts saying, Come and see.

2. And I saw, and behold a white horse: and he that sat on him had a bow; and a crown was given unto him: and he went forth conquering, and to conquer.

The seven years of Tribulation begin in chapter 6. As the Lamb breaks the seals, we see a series of four horses and their riders. The first of these, the rider of the white horse, comes as a conqueror. Although a white horse speaks of peace, holiness, majesty, and righteousness, it is not likely that Christ is the rider. Christ comes as conqueror at Armageddon (Revelation 19:11-16), but this rider in 6:2 is holding a bow with no arrows and is handed a crown. Many scholars

believe this is the Antichrist, deceptively riding a white horse. The absence of arrows with his bow may be because he pretends to stand for peace during his early years of rule. Satan once told Christ that all the kingdoms of the world were his to give (Luke 4:6). Christ refused Satan's offer, but the Antichrist will accept it willingly. Daniel labels this rider as the "prince that shall come" (Daniel 9:26). He is Satan's master counterfeit of Christ, the same individual described as the "beast . . . out of the sea" in Revelation 13:1.

B. The Red Horse (vv. 3, 4)

3. And when he had opened the second seal, I heard the second beast say, Come and see.

4. And there went out another horse that was red: and power was given to him that sat thereon to take peace from the earth, and that they should kill one another: and there was given unto him a great sword.

The fiery red color of this horse represents the bloodshed of a war that is unparalleled in earth's history. Although there have always been "wars and rumours of wars" (see Matthew 24:6), this warfare is on a scale that is almost impossible to imagine. Ray Stedman sees the "great sword" as possibly being a nuclear war. Only in recent decades has the scale of death and destruction described in the Bible become possible. Civil wars, organized crime, regional feuds, and so forth, might all be included in this seal.

The fact that horses are used symbolically in the first four seals is significant. Throughout history, horses have indicated fast movement, covering much ground very quickly. The judgments represented here take place in quick succession and spread over the earth.

Although white represents victory, why would the rider of the white horse not likely be Christ?

II. ECONOMIC AND COSMIC UPHEAVAL (Revelation 6:5-8, 12-17)

A. The Black Horse (vv. 5, 6)

(Revelation 6:6 is not included in the printed text.)

5. And when he had opened the third seal, I heard the third beast say, Come and see. And I beheld, and lo a black horse; and he that sat on him had a pair of balances in his hand.

The rider of the black horse carries a set of balances. In the ancient world the method of selling food was to balance it with a set of weights. Proverbs 11:1 reflects this custom by saying, "The Lord abhors dishonest scales, but accurate weights are his delight" (*NIV*). Famine is illustrated by the rider having the scales. Food is so scarce that it has to be carefully portioned out. This situation is likely the result of the war which will come with the red horseman. The unsettling conditions of war prevent farmers from planting crops, and destroying existing crops and livestock.

Man's daily needs in ancient times were approximately one pound and 3 ounces of wheat, and a denarius was a day's salary for the common laborer. The information that it would con-

sume a day's wages to buy a day's supply of food is given in verse 6. Some scholars interpret the statement "hurt not the oil and the wine" to mean that some will still live in luxury. We are all aware of the power and influence the very rich have in our world. The decisions of a small number of powerful people who control a large percentage of the earth's wealth affect the lives of millions of people daily.

B. The Pale Horse (vv. 7, 8)

7. And when he had opened the fourth seal, I heard the voice of the fourth beast say, Come and see.

8. And I looked, and behold a pale horse: and his name that sat on him was Death, and Hell followed with him. And power was given unto them over the fourth part of the earth, to kill with sword, and with hunger, and with death, and with the beasts of the earth.

With the appearance of the pale horse we find that death is rampant. Havoc covers the earth, and one-fourth of the population is destroyed either by war, starvation, deadly disease, and so forth. The Greek word for *pale* is *chloros*, the root of the modern word *chlorophyll*. Thus, the actual color is a yellow-green, portraying a picture of dying and rotting human flesh.

The "fourth part of the earth" could mean that death is to pervade over a fourth of the earth through war, famine, and with death by demonic forces and wild beasts. (Beasts will be greatly increased because of the existence of carcasses to feed on, just as they have increased in times past following wars and the presence of dead bodies.

At the same time, it must be noted that this is controlled judgment. "The limited punishment not only demonstrates God's wrath on sin, but also his merciful love in giving people yet another opportunity to turn to him before he brings final judgment" (*Life Application Bible*).

C. The Sixth Seal (vv. 12-17)

(Revelation 6:15-17 is not included in the printed text.)

12. And I beheld when he had opened the sixth seal, and, lo, there was a great earthquake; and the sun became black as sackcloth of hair, and the moon became as blood;

13. And the stars of heaven fell unto the earth, even as a fig tree casteth her untimely figs, when she is shaken of a mighty wind.

14. And the heaven departed as a scroll when it is rolled together; and every mountain and island were moved out of their places.

In response to the terrible bloodshed of the forces of the Antichrist, the sixth seal is opened (vv. 12-17). The earth quakes, the sun blackens, the moon turns red, and meteors fall from the sky, spreading terror on the planet. By the end of this seal, the world finally realizes that God is bringing judgment. However, instead of repenting, the people run and try to hide. In their hardened hearts, death is preferable to submission to the Lamb. They call to the rocks and mountains to fall on them (v. 16).

They have rebelled to the point of no return.

This should warn anyone who indulges in sinful behavior—especially in the use of drugs, pornography, alcohol, and so forth. Sin is addictive. Just as may happen to the drug junkie, a time comes when there is no turning back. Although God still reaches out in mercy, it becomes ever more difficult to exercise the will to accept that mercy.

Why are the four horsemen given control of only a fourth of the earth?

III. PERSECUTION AND HOPE
   (Revelation 6:11; 7:9-14)

A. Martyrdom of the Saints (6:11)

11. And white robes were given unto every one of them; and it was said unto them, that they should rest yet for a little season, until their fellowservants also and their brethren, that should be killed as they were, should be fulfilled.

Following the four horsemen (the Antichrist, war, famine, and death), comes the fifth seal—martyrdom of the saints. If we make a comparison of the horsemen (Revelation 6:1-11) with Jesus' prophetic words in the Olivet Discourse (Matthew 24:5-9), we can see several similarities. The first seal that was broken revealed the Antichrist; in Matthew 24:5, Jesus predicted that there would be many false christs appearing. Both the second seal and Jesus revealed that there would be wars and rumors of wars; likewise, both the third seal and Jesus' words predicted famines. The fourth seal showed much death; Jesus declared that there would be pestilence and earthquakes in various places. Finally, in the fifth seal of Revelation, it is revealed that there will be many people martyred; Jesus also spoke of the saints being killed for His sake. Thus, we can conclude that there will be much sorrow and suffering in the end times.

If this comparison is accurate, then we notice that the first four seals are "the beginning of sorrows" (Matthew 24:8). Although these things have occurred throughout the last 2,000 years (false christs, wars, famines, earthquakes, etc.), they will increase as the end times draw near. In reviewing the 1980s and 1990s, we see the dramatic rise in natural disasters around the globe. The terrible hurricanes, floods, earthquakes, and tornadoes occurring the last few years seem to be accelerating in ferocity and frequency. However, the loss of life has not been high. This can certainly be attributed to God's mercy. He is patient with men, "not wanting anyone to perish, but everyone to come to repentance" (2 Peter 3:9, NIV). He is patient because "He understands how long eternity is! He knows that when an unbeliever dies, that person is not only separated from God and barred from heaven, he or she is condemned to live for all eternity in hell, a place of physical, emotional, mental, and spiritual torment that lasts forever and ever and ever and ever" (Anne Graham Lotz, *The Vision of His Glory*).

The fifth seal is martyrdom and apparently has two phases. First, there are those who are told to rest for a little longer. These are the ones who died for their faith and their witness over the centuries. They are eager to see justice brought to earth, but are told to wait. They did not die in vain, but are singled out for special honor, indicated by the white robes they are given.

Millions of saints died for their faith during the church age. Stephen was the first martyr (Acts 7). Nero set fire to Rome and then blamed the Christians for it, sentencing many to horrible deaths. Paul saw himself as a willing martyr for the faith, and paid the supreme sacrifice: "For I am already being poured out like a drink offering, and the time has come for my departure" (2 Timothy 4:6, NIV). Although it has been little publicized, more Christians have been persecuted and martyred for their faith in the 20th century than at any other time. According to the Manila Conference on World Evangelism, over 10 million believers have lost their lives since 1950 (Lotz). The late 1990s show an alarming increase in the persecution and martyrdom of believers, especially in countries ruled by radical Muslims.

The fifth seal indicates that the saints must wait for their fellow servants and brethren who are yet to be martyred. This is the second phase of the seal. The persecution and deaths of believers before the Rapture, as well as of those who come to faith during the Tribulation, will make all past horrors pale by comparison.

B. A Great Multitude Before the Throne (7:9-12)

(Revelation 7:11, 12 is not

included in the printed text.)

9. After this I beheld, and, lo, a great multitude, which no man could number, of all nations, and kindreds, and people, and tongues, stood before the throne, and before the Lamb, clothed with white robes, and palms in their hands;

10. And cried with a loud voice, saying, Salvation to our God which sitteth upon the throne, and unto the Lamb.

Revelation 7 begins with a pause in God's judgments on the earth. The phrase "after these things" (v. 1) refers to the first six seals. This chapter apparently contains two parenthetical visions, or asides, taking place at the same time as the first six seals. The first of these (vv. 1-8) shows that a multitude of Jews (144,000) will be sealed, meaning they turn to Christ during the Tribulation. Four angels of destruction are restrained as the members from the 12 tribes are sealed. These are four of the seven who will blow trumpets in the coming chapters. Afterward a fifth angel ascends to seal the witnesses. The "seal of the living God" (v. 2) is the Holy Spirit (Ephesians 4:30). Paul wrote in Romans 8:16 that "the Spirit himself testifies with our spirit that we are God's children" (NIV). The presence of the Holy Spirit in a life is the true sign of God's ownership.

The 144,000 apparently carry a visible mark (v. 3). They are called "servants of our God" and willingly give their lives for others. Some might say the Spirit departed when the church was raptured. However, the Holy Spirit is a member of the Trinity and is

still everywhere, even in this unique relationship with the church. He still calls those to faith, just as in the days before Pentecost.

Then, beginning in verse 9 (the second of the parenthetic happenings), John sees an innumerable multitude gathered, clothed in white, and standing before the throne of God. I believe these are the people who were won to the Lord and martyred for their faith during the last half of the Tribulation.

In Matthew 24:14, Jesus said, "This gospel of the kingdom will be preached in the whole world as a testimony to all nations, and then the end will come" (NIV). The phrase "of the kingdom" refers specifically to Israel. Both Jesus and John the Baptist preached the "gospel of the kingdom" to Israel. They announced that the long-prophesied messianic kingdom was at hand. On the Sunday before His crucifixion, Jesus fulfilled the prophecy of Zechariah: "See, your king comes to you, righteous and having salvation, gentle and riding on a donkey, on a colt, the foal of a donkey" (Zechariah 9:9, NIV). However, as history proves, the Jews refused to accept Him as their king. Did this bring an end to the promise of a restored Jewish kingdom? Let us look further.

When Jesus sent His disciples out to preach in Matthew 10, He instructed them not to go to the Gentiles, but only to the "lost sheep of Israel" (vv. 5, 6). He warned them of many dangers and persecutions that would follow. What eventually happened to the disciples in the early church days is certainly a fulfillment of Jesus' words. They too were persecuted and rejected by the Jews. However, Jesus could have been speaking prophetically (in Matthew 10 and 24) of a fulfillment during the Great Tribulation. The gospel will again be preached to Israel. In other words, Jesus commissioned His disciples and, at the same time, prophesied that a future group of disciples would go out to preach the Kingdom.

What John views at this point occurs apparently at the close of the seven-year period. Great multitudes came out of the Tribulation through martyrdom, their robes washed white in the blood of the Lamb. They have lost their lives at the hands of the Antichrist, who massacres anyone not having the mark of the Beast. They hold palm branches in their hands. The greatest harvest of souls will come during earth's darkest hours.

The fact that this multitude, including millions of Gentiles, carry palm branches is significant. They have no crowns, but their palm branches signify rejoicing and gladness as they stand "before the throne" (Revelation 7:9).

C. White-Robed Saints (vv. 13, 14)

(Revelation 7:13, 14 is not included in the printed text.)

One of the elders asks John who these saints are who stand before the throne. The *Living Bible* states verse 13 succinctly: "Do you know who these are, who are clothed in white, and where they come from?" John obviously does not know, but is anxious to learn.

The elder then tells him that they are the ones who have come through the Great Tribulation. How could their garments be washed white with blood? "The blood of Jesus Christ is the world's greatest purifier because it removes the stain of sin. White symbolizes sinless perfection or holiness, which can be given to people only by the sacrifice and shed blood of the sinless lamb of God" (*Life Application Bible*).

In the past, some questioned John's view of this "great multitude, which no man could number" (v. 9). How could so many be martyred during the Tribulation if one-fourth of earth's population has already been destroyed by the first four horsemen? We must take into account the enormous growth of the world's population. It has been projected that by the year 2000, China alone will have 1 billion people. As we move closer to the end, the reality of John's visions become more and more feasible.

The Great Tribulation is the last "week of years" that will end this age—Daniel's 70th week. A great number from all the tribes and nations will be saved during this horrible time. Jesus prophesied it in His Olivet Discourse, saying, "For then shall be great tribulation, such as was not since the beginning of the world to this time, no, nor ever shall be" (Matthew 24:21).

REVIEW QUESTIONS

1. Who is the rider of the white horse in the first seal?

2. What do the absence of arrows and the presence of a crown indicate about the rider of the white horse?

3. Is there any unfulfilled prophecy holding back Christ's rapture of the church?

4. Will the Holy Spirit still operate on earth during the Tribulation?

GOLDEN TEXT HOMILY

"WHEN THESE THINGS BEGIN TO COME TO PASS, THEN LOOK UP, AND LIFT UP YOUR HEADS; FOR YOUR REDEMPTION DRAWETH NIGH" (Luke 21:28).

Jesus spoke of many calamities that would take place before His return. His instruction to Christians was that they not be overly concerned or anxious when these things occur. Rather, we should look up and consider them as signs that our redemption is drawing near.

As we look around at the conditions in the world today, we can see many of the things of which Jesus spoke. These may bring terror to the hearts of many, but they should not cause Christians to be fearful. They involve only earthly things, and our citizenship is in heaven.

Jesus said when we begin to see these things come to pass, we should look up. To look up is to look above the horizon. It is to look toward heaven. We need to look up to Jesus. Our Lord ascended into heaven; He is now in heaven, seated at the right hand of the Father, as our Intercessor. And it is from heaven that He will come to receive us unto Himself. When we look up, we get our eyes off the difficulties, distractions, and distresses of this world and focus our attention on Jesus.

We need a horizontal vision to see the problems around us and to see our need to help others. We also need a vertical vision to look up to Jesus, who has promised to return and redeem us.—**Richard Y. Bershon, Ph.D., Chaplain, State Veterans Home, Hot Springs, South Dakota**

SENTENCE SERMONS

GOD WARNS of disastrous conditions and promises hope to His people.

—Selected

LIFE WITH CHRIST is an endless hope; without Him, a hopeless end.

—Anonymous

A RELIGIOUS HOPE does not only bear up the mind under her sufferings, but makes her rejoice in them.

—Joseph Addison

"IF THOU FAINT in the day of adversity, thy strength is small."

—Proverbs 24:10

DAILY BIBLE READINGS

M. Day of the Lord. Joel 2:1-11
T. Call on the Lord. Joel 2:28-32
W. Empty Rituals Rejected.
Amos 5:21-27
T. Be Spiritually Alert.
Mark 13:5-13
F. Prepare for Hard Times.
1 Thessalonians 5:1-11
S. Remain True to God's Word.
1 Timothy 4:1-6

Judgment Is Coming

Study Text: Revelation 8:1 through 11:19

Objective: To comprehend that God will judge sin and heed His warning.

Time: The time of the writing of the Book of Revelation was probably about A.D. 96.

Place: The Book of Revelation was written on the island of Patmos in the Aegean Sea.

Golden Text: "The kingdoms of this world are become the kingdoms of our Lord, and of his Christ; and he shall reign for ever and ever" (Revelation 11:15).

Central Truth: God's judgment exposes and destroys sin and establishes the kingdom of Christ.

Evangelism Emphasis: Believers are commissioned to intercede for the lost.

PRINTED TEXT

Revelation 8:1. And when he had opened the seventh seal, there was silence in heaven about the space of half an hour.

2. And I saw the seven angels which stood before God; and to them were given seven trumpets.

3. And another angel came and stood at the altar, having a golden censer; and there was given unto him much incense, that he should offer it with the prayers of all saints upon the golden altar which was before the throne.

4. And the smoke of the incense, which came with the prayers of the saints, ascended up before God out of the angel's hand.

5. And the angel took the censer, and filled it with fire of the altar, and cast it into the earth: and there were voices, and thunderings, and lightnings, and an earthquake.

6. And the seven angels which had the seven trumpets prepared themselves to sound.

13. And I beheld, and heard an angel flying through the midst of heaven, saying with a loud voice, Woe, woe, woe, to the inhabiters of the earth by reason of the other voices of the trumpet of the three angels, which are yet to sound!

9:20. And the rest of the men which were not killed by these plagues yet repented not of the works of their hands, that they should not worship devils, and idols of gold, and silver, and brass, and stone, and of wood: which neither can see, nor hear, nor walk:

21. Neither repented they of their murders, nor of their sorceries, nor of their fornication, nor of their thefts.

11:14. The second woe is past; and, behold, the third woe cometh quickly.

15. And the seventh angel sounded; and there were great voices in heaven, saying, The kingdoms of this world are become the kingdoms of our Lord, and of his Christ; and he shall reign for ever and ever.

18. And the nations were angry, and thy wrath is come, and the time of the dead, that they should be judged, and that thou shouldest give reward unto thy servants the prophets, and to the saints, and them that fear thy name, small and great; and shouldest destroy them which destroy the earth.

LESSON OUTLINE

LESSON EXPOSITION

INTRODUCTION

Revelation 6 ended with the opening of the sixth seal. In chapter 7, we saw two concurrent happenings (or parenthetical visions). One was the sealing of the 144,000 witnesses, and the other was the gathering of the multitudes before the throne in heaven. Thus, during the Tribulation's greatest fury, God still reaches out to men, wooing both Jews and Gentiles to come to Christ.

In one sense, the first six seals are the result of God's removing all restraints on mankind and letting human evil find its ultimate expression. By the time of the Tribulation, there appears to be no moral check on the depths to which men will sink. This leads to war, death, plague, and so forth. There is an important principle here for believers to understand. Where Christianity flourishes, there is morality, decency, equitable government, and progress. The Judeo-Christian system of values and ethics produces stability in the nations where it is embraced. It is when God's Word is abandoned that nations disintegrate. The Judeo-Christian ethic is responsible for much good that has been accomplished on this earth. We today must maintain a solid witness, exemplified by consistent Christian character. Otherwise, there is no moral restriction to the depth to which men will sink.

With chapter 8, the judgments on earth continue. We now see the seventh seal opened. John watches as this seal is broken, and a silence of one-half hour occurs. This silence represents "a dramatic pause preceding the new set of calamities that are to ensue." Man's sin demands absolute punishment. Ray Stedman says this moment is much like the pause before the last "hallelujah" of Handel's "Hallelujah Chorus."

Seven angels, representing seven trumpets, are revealed to John. Each of these trumpets will bring frightening plagues to the earth. The plagues are the answer to millions of prayers prayed by saints through the ages. Though God may have seemed slow to hear the pleading cries of His people, He has recorded every prayer. Their petitions are now vindicated.

I. INTERCESSION FOR RIGHTEOUSNESS (Revelation 8:1-6)

A. The Concept of Time (v. 1)

1. And when he had opened the seventh seal, there was silence in heaven about the space of half an hour.

The fact that there is silence for a specific period of time in heaven indicates that there is a timetable. Time is merely the progression of "a before, a during, and an after." Even in eternity we will be aware of a certain sense of time. Those who refuse to accept Christ will surely be aware of it: "Then he will say to those on his left, 'Depart from me, you who are cursed, into the eternal fire prepared for the devil and his angels'" (Matthew 25:41, *NIV*). For the believer, time will simply lose its importance, since there is no end to it: "There will be no more night. They will not need the light of a lamp or the light of the sun, for the Lord God will give them light. And they will reign for ever and ever" (Revelation 22:5, *NIV*). On earth we have been limited by the confines of time schedules. In heaven, time will cease to have any effect on us.

B. Seven Angels and Another Angel (vv. 2-6)

2. And I saw the seven angels which stood before God; and to them were given seven trumpets.

3. And another angel came and stood at the altar, having a golden censer; and there was given unto him much incense, that he should offer it with the prayers of all saints upon the golden altar which was before the throne.

4. And the smoke of the incense, which came with the prayers of the saints, ascended up before God out of the angel's hand.

5. And the angel took the censer, and filled it with fire of the altar, and cast it into the earth: and there were voices, and thunderings, and lightnings, and an earthquake.

6. And the seven angels which had the seven trumpets prepared themselves to sound.

The contents of the seventh seal appear in the form of seven angels bearing seven trumpets. The plagues these trumpets bring upon the earth will be devastating. Many will be humbled to their knees and brought to faith. Many more will harden their hearts and face eventual judgment.

In verse 3 we see the appearance of another angel standing before the altar. He holds a golden censer and is given much incense that he should offer, along with the prayers of the saints, upon the golden altar. Some identify this angel as Jesus himself because He appeared as the "Angel of the Lord" in a preincarnate form (a theophany) in the Old Testament (Genesis 16:10-13; Exodus 3:2-6; 23:20; Judges 6:11). Also, the New Testament teaches that Jesus is the Great High Priest for His people. The Book of Hebrews (and also Romans 8:34) tells us that Jesus is now a High Priest who "is able to save completely those who come to God through him, because he always lives to intercede for them" (Hebrews 7:25, *NIV*).

The prayers of the saints are like a fragrance to God. This was seen earlier in chapter 5 when the 24 elders fell before the throne, "holding golden bowls full of incense, which are the prayers of the saints" (v. 8, *NIV*). As the prayers of the saints in 8:4 are mingled with the fragrance of the incense, God is delighted and moved to action.

If the saints' prayers implore God to action, then what is seen next (v. 5) is the result of their prayers. The returning of fire to earth symbolizes answered prayer. The time has come for the accumulated cries of millions of believers to be answered. Countless Christians who suffered over the centuries at the hands of those who hated Christ and His kingdom prayed for a day when they would be vindicated. The thunders of judgment are now swift for those whose "feet are

swift to shed blood" (Romans 3:15, *NIV*).

The trumpets bring more devastating plagues on the earth, which has already been hounded by the judgments opened in the seals. False prophets, wars, revolutions, famine, death, and strange signs in the heavens have made their frightening presence known. Judgment now escalates.

How is the other angel standing before the altar like the high priest of the Old Testament?

II. IMMINENT DOOM (Revelation 8:7-13; 9:20, 21)

A. The First Two Trumpets (8:7-9)

(Revelation 8:7-9 is not included in the printed text.)

The striking aspect of these first trumpets is the precision of their targets. The first trumpet sounds, and hail and fire destroy one-third of the green plant life on earth. The second sounds, and a huge blazing mountain is thrown into the sea, destroying one-third of marine life there, as well as one-third of the ships. The third and fourth trumpets will also produce a one-third ratio of destruction. The trumpets announce a carefully controlled series intended to let the world know they are not mere random events but the precise judgments of God.

We can look at the natural disasters of the last few years in the United States alone and see a similar message. Hurricanes, floods, earthquakes, and so forth, have brought minimum loss of life. These have been environmental disasters more so than human ones. Anne Graham Lotz compares this to the Old Testament where God first warned the people through the prophets by sending environmental events: "He sought their attention by sending a plague of locusts or a drought or a flood, warning them in precise judgments that if they did not repent of their sin and turn to Him, they would come under His wrath!" (*The Vision of His Glory*)

In all of the first four trumpet plagues, fire is an integral element. Fire is the light and heat that comes from burning. Fire is also a symbolic word, indicating torture, judgment, anguish, and torment. These are all elements of the results of the trumpet judgments.

B. The Second Two Trumpets (8:10-12)

(Revelation 8:10-12 is not included in the printed text.)

The Greek word for "star" (aster) indicates any heavenly body emitting light. A burning meteor is possibly what is described by the third trumpet. It could also refer to some type of nuclear bomb, with destruction of the rivers and fountains coming from its radiation. A strange portent of this has already been seen in our lifetime. The terrible nuclear accident that occurred in Russia was in the city of Chernobyl. *Chernobyl* is the Russian word for "Wormwood."

In the Old Testament, wormwood was any of a number of plants that produce a dark green, bitter, poisonous oil. It symbolized bitterness and gall in men. The effect it has in our present text is to cause the death of many people. They die, apparently from consuming poisoned water or from thirst because of the lack of clean drinking water.

With the fourth trumpet comes a supernatural darkness, much like that of the ninth plague in Egypt (Exodus 10:21-23), and again like that at the crucifixion of Christ (Matthew 27:45). These were literal happenings, so there is no reason to believe that the darkness coming with this trumpet will not be just as literal. Whether it is caused by some type of man-made nuclear explosion, or purely by a divine disaster, we cannot tell. However, the effect is the same. There will be chaos and death.

There is a great environmental movement at work today. Men seem to instinctively know that we have been poor stewards of the planet. In Genesis 1, God gave man dominion over the earth, but instead of having dominion, man has abused the earth for selfish and greedy gain. However, many environmentalists are also missing the mark. They want to preserve the earth because they believe it is all they will ever have. They see "Mother Earth" as their sole home and deny the reality of a future life. What they don't understand is that the only real future for humanity will come from surrendering to Christ. The greatest threat to our environment is not fluorocarbons, carbon monoxide, chemical plants, nuclear reactors, bulldozers, or arsonists. The greatest threat to our environment is *sin!*

C. An Angel Cries Out (8:13)

13. And I beheld, and heard

an angel flying through the midst of heaven, saying with a loud voice, Woe, woe, woe, to the inhabiters of the earth by reason of the other voices of the trumpet of the three angels, which are yet to sound!

Ray Stedman, in his studies of Revelation, says that the phrase "inhabiters of the earth" is more accurately translated "those who make their home on earth." This verifies the point just made about environmentalists. If we insist that earth is to be our home, then we are doomed to hear the words "Woe, woe, woe." People who live selfishly and are concerned only about the cares of this life are the objects of the trumpet judgments.

The first four seals (ch. 6) were distinct from the last three because they were represented by four horses, indicating swiftness of judgment. The last three trumpets (chs. 9, 11) are called "woes" because their judgments are so severe. As we progress from the seals to the bowls ("vials," ch. 16), the destruction intensifies greatly. We can draw from this that the seals, trumpets, and bowls are not the same events described in different manners. However, they may be happening concurrently. To illustrate this, we can use the Olympic coverage on television every four years. Many athletic events take place at the same time, but in different locations. The network tapes these, showing them one after another so that the viewer can see them all. Perhaps this is the way John's vision occurred. He was shown things one after another, although they may overlap in time sequence.

With each of the first four trumpets there is a partial destruction—one-third of each entity. This shows the continual mercy of God. By limiting the destruction from the trumpets, man still has opportunity to repent. We see in the next verses his refusal to do so.

D. Men Refuse to Repent (9:20, 21)

20. And the rest of the men which were not killed by these plagues yet repented not of the works of their hands, that they should not worship devils, and idols of gold, and silver, and brass, and stone, and of wood: which neither can see, nor hear, nor walk:

21. Neither repented they of their murders, nor of their sorceries, nor of their fornication, nor of their thefts.

In one sense, one might say that all God has to do to begin the Tribulation is take away human restraint. By permitting the full expression of the evil that man invents, God will allow man to destroy himself with his own self-centered indulgence in sin. If the church has been raptured when the Tribulation begins, much of that restraint will indeed be gone. Sin breaks down the moral defenses of people. If the defenses are gone, man will act like he has a spiritual AIDS disease—he will have no immunity left.

What we see in these verses is humanity with no restraint, so engrossed in sin that moral judgment has been suffocated. We are certainly seeing the beginnings of this in our own generation. The believer must constantly remind himself of this scripture: "You are not your own; you were bought at a price. Therefore honor God with your body" (1 Corinthians 6:19, 20, *NIV*). We cannot have the mind-set of the culture around us that preaches a hedonistic, self-centered view of life.

What does fire represent in the first four trumpets?

III. JUDGMENT AND REWARDS (Revelation 11:14-18)

(Revelation 11:16, 17 is not included in the printed text.)

14. The second woe is past; and, behold, the third woe cometh quickly.

15. And the seventh angel sounded; and there were great voices in heaven, saying, The kingdoms of this world are become the kingdoms of our Lord, and of his Christ; and he shall reign for ever and ever.

18. And the nations were angry, and thy wrath is come, and the time of the dead, that they should be judged, and that thou shouldest give reward unto thy servants the prophets, and to the saints, and them that fear thy name, small and great; and shouldest destroy them which destroy the earth.

One prayer that saints through the ages have prayed has yet to be visibly realized. Jesus taught it as part of the model prayer when He said, "Thy kingdom come. Thy will be done in earth, as it is in heaven" (Matthew 6:10). Invisibly, the Kingdom has existed in the church, as well as in God's overall control of man's affairs. With the blowing of the seventh trumpet, the ultimate fulfillment of Christ's kingdom is finally accomplished.

The question is, "Why here?" There are still the seven bowls of judgment left. One explanation is that although there are still judgments coming, the end is in sight. The inhabitants of heaven plainly see that God is in total control, holding ultimate power over the affairs of men. The announcement of the reign of the King occurs here, but the final breaking of the enemies' hold over the world does not occur until the return of Christ" (see 19:11, *NIV*).

Where does the kingdom of Christ exist on earth today?

REVIEW QUESTIONS

1. Who was the "Angel of the Lord" in the Old Testament?

2. How does the destruction of only one-third of the entities by each of the first four trumpets indicate God's mercy?

3. When will Christ's kingdom be fully realized on earth?

4. What do the inhabitants of heaven see with the blowing of the seventh trumpet?

5. Do the plagues cause men to repent? Why or why not?

GOLDEN TEXT HOMILY

"THE KINGDOMS OF THIS WORLD ARE BECOME THE KINGDOMS OF OUR LORD, AND OF HIS CHRIST; AND HE SHALL REIGN FOR EVER AND EVER" (Revelation 11:15).

After Jesus was baptized by John the Baptist, He was led into the wilderness to be tempted of the devil. Let us look at the last of the three temptations recorded in the Bible: "The devil taketh him up into an exceeding high mountain, and sheweth him all the kingdoms of the world, and the glory of them; and saith unto him, All these things will I give thee, if thou wilt fall down and worship me" (Matthew 4:8, 9). Jesus knew that the kingdoms of this world would one day be under His control, but He also knew that this was not the time or the method for achieving that control. His Father had a plan, and that was the one He would follow.

Jesus said to the devil: "Get thee hence, Satan: for it is written, Thou shalt worship the Lord thy God, and him only shalt thou serve" (v. 10).

At this moment, the kingdoms of this world are not the kingdoms of Christ. Satan and evil men have tremendous influence and power in today's society, but it will not always be that way. Thank God, the day will come—and it may be very soon—when every knee shall bow to Christ (Isaiah 45:22, 23; Romans 14:10, 11; Philippians 2:9-11). During our times of difficulty when the forces of evil seem to almost overpower us in the world, let us remember that our suffering will cease. Evil power one day will be cut off because Jesus Christ, the Son of God, is coming again to this earth. The world will be under His control.—**Excerpts from the**

Evangelical Sunday School Lesson Commentary, **Vol. 27**

SENTENCE SERMONS

GOD'S JUDGMENT exposes and destroys sin and establishes the kingdom of Christ.

—Selected

GOD JUDGES persons not by the point they have reached, but by the way they are facing; not by distance but by direction.

—James S. Stewart

IN THE DAY when all men will stand before God, the significant question for each of us will no longer be what we think of Christ, but what He thinks of us.

—Elva J. Hoover

YOU MAY JUGGLE human laws, you may fool human courts, but there is a judgment to come, and from it there is no appeal.

—Orin Philip Gifford

DAILY BIBLE READINGS

M. Interceding for Sinful Society.
Genesis 18:16-25
T. Righteous Intercession.
Psalm 106:28-31
W. Responsibility of Watchmen.
Ezekiel 3:17-21
T. Judgment Is Certain.
Luke 12:16-21
F. Impartial Judgment.
Romans 2:1-11
S. Judgment on Ungodliness.
2 Peter 2:4-11

War Against the Righteous

Study Text: Revelation 12:1 through 13:18

Objective: To preview the endtime conflict between good and evil and serve God in all circumstances.

Time: The Book of Revelation was probably written about A.D. 96.

Place: The Book of Revelation was written on the island of Patmos in the Aegean Sea.

Golden Text: "Be sober, be vigilant; because your adversary the devil, as a roaring lion, walketh about, seeking whom he may devour" (1 Peter 5:8).

Central Truth: The reign of the Antichrist will be a period of unprecedented apostasy and rebellion against righteousness.

Evangelism Emphasis: Christians must warn sinners to repent and avoid eternal damnation.

PRINTED TEXT

Revelation 12:9. And the great dragon was cast out, that old serpent, called the Devil, and Satan, which deceiveth the whole world: he was cast out into the earth, and his angels were cast out with him.

10. And I heard a loud voice saying in heaven, Now is come salvation, and strength, and the kingdom of our God, and the power of his Christ: for the accuser of our brethren is cast down, which accused them before our God day and night.

11. And they overcame him by the blood of the Lamb, and by the word of their testimony; and they loved not their lives unto the death.

13:4. And they worshipped the dragon which gave power unto the beast: and they worshipped the beast, saying, Who

is like unto the beast? who is able to make war with him?

5. And there was given unto him a mouth speaking great things and blasphemies; and power was given unto him to continue forty and two months.

6. And he opened his mouth in blasphemy against God, to blaspheme his name, and his tabernacle, and them that dwell in heaven.

7. And it was given unto him to make war with the saints, and to overcome them: and power was given him over all kindreds, and tongues, and nations.

8. And all that dwell upon the earth shall worship him, whose names are not written in the book of life of the Lamb slain from the foundation of the world.

9. If any man have an ear, let him hear.

11. And I beheld another beast coming up out of the earth; and he had two horns like a lamb, and he spake as a dragon.

12. And he exerciseth all the power of the first beast before him, and causeth the earth and them which dwell therein to worship the first beast, whose deadly wound was healed.

16. And he causeth all, both small and great, rich and poor, free and bond, to receive a mark in their right hand, or in their foreheads:

17. And that no man might buy or sell, save he that had the mark, or the name of the beast, or the number of his name.

18. Here is wisdom. Let him that hath understanding count the number of the beast: for it is the number of a man; and his number is Six hundred three score and six.

LESSON OUTLINE

I. PERSEVERANCE IN PERSECUTION
   A. Who Is the Woman?
   B. Who Is the Child?
   C. Who Is the Dragon?
   D. Heavenly View of Conflict on Earth
   E. War in the Heavens
   F. Overcomers

II. BLASPHEMY AGAINST GOD
   A. The Beast From the Sea
   B. War With the Saints

III. THE MARK OF THE BEAST

LESSON EXPOSITION

INTRODUCTION

Editor's Note: There are many opinions and interpretations of chapters 12 and 13 of the Book of Revelation. The exposition of Scriptures used in this lesson is based on the published works of John F. Walvoord, Clarence Larkin, Ray C. Stedman, and H.A. Ironside. (See lesson 1 for additional information on these sources.) Refer also to *The Interpretation of St. John's Revelation* by R.C.H. Lenski, *The Broadman Bible Commentary*, Vol. 12, *The Pulpit Commentary*, Vol. 22, and *The Daily Bible Series*—"The Revelation of John," Vol. 2, by William Barclay.

Our last lesson dealt primarily with the first four trumpets. To bring us to this lesson we should first view the last three of the trumpet plagues:

Fifth trumpet (9:1). With the fifth trumpet John sees a light descending from heaven. When it reaches the ground it takes on a personage who is given the key to the bottomless pit. He opens the pit and out pours smoke filled with locusts. These have the power of scorpions. For five months they torture all who do not have the seal of God on their foreheads. This is somewhat like the fourth plague of flies in Egypt (Exodus 8) that swarmed only on the Egyptians and not the Israelites.

Sixth trumpet (9:13). With the sixth trumpet comes an army of 200 million warriors (v. 16) that have been held back at the Euphrates River. At their release they kill one-third of all mankind. The horses in this army have breastplates of fire, heads like lions, with smoke and fire pouring from their mouths. Steven Gregg writes: "Whether these are symbols or the best description John can give of modern warfare, this is an awesome picture of an almost irresistible military force destroying all that oppose it" (*Revelation—Four Views*). The nationality of this army has been debated for centuries. Until recently no one nation could boast of such large numbers. However, China now has 1 billion people and could mobilize a militia this size.

After the sixth trumpet, chapter 11 deals with the two witnesses, their powerful testimonies, their defeat by the beast, and their miraculous resurrection and ascension.

Seventh trumpet (11:15). The second woe ends when the seventh trumpet sounds, and voices in heaven proclaim that the kingdoms of the world have become the kingdoms of Christ. Although the seven bowls of judgment are not yet seen, the heavenly inhabitants rejoice in seeing God in total control. This brings us to the present lesson.

Revelation 12 through 14 has been called a book of signs (symbols). Up to this point there have been no signs. We will look at three of the signs in this lesson. Two of these take place in heaven (12:1, 3), and one on earth (13:13, 14). This book of signs gives us

another parenthetical vision (or simultaneous occurrence) we studied in earlier chapters. This vision precedes the final bowl judgments and further describes the persecution God's people will endure. Chapter 12 gives a visionary glimpse of Satan, symbolized as the "great red dragon," waging war on the woman and her children. Chapter 13 continues this theme, portraying the beasts who are the puppets of the Dragon. Chapter 14 shows the 144,000 as they triumph over the Beast.

Who is the woman? Who is the child? Who is the dragon? These are the questions we look at in reading chapter 12. There are also three vivid scenes portrayed: the birth of the child (vv. 1-6), the expulsion of the Dragon (vv. 7-12), and the Dragon's attack on the woman and her children (vv. 13-17).

In Revelation women are used symbolically. Four different women are portrayed, two evil and two good. The first was Jezebel (2:20-23). Later we will see the great harlot, Babylon (14:8; 17:1-6, 15-18; 18:1-24). Since Eve offered the forbidden fruit to Adam in Genesis, women are sometimes pictured as being responsible for sin and wickedness. These two evil women in Revelation further enhance that idea. However, we will finally see a beautiful woman, the bride of the Lamb (19:7, 8), clothed in righteousness, who symbolizes the church.

Also, there is the woman in our present text who is the parent of the One who will ultimately rule the nations. She is opposite to Jezebel in every way which refutes the idea that women are somehow responsible for sin on the earth. "Attacked by an evil dragon, she finds protection and refuge provided by God. Her identity has been variously interpreted. Because she bears the Child (capital C), some have seen her as Mary, the mother of Jesus, others as Israel, the collective 'mother' that brought forth the Messiah. The attempts of the dragon to destroy her, along with 'the rest of her offspring' (12:17), may be references to Satan's attempts to destroy Israel and disrupt the messianic line" (*Word in Life Study Bible*). However she is identified, the conflict between this woman and the Dragon is a pictorial of the battle between good and evil.

I. PERSEVERANCE IN PERSECUTION (Revelation 12:1-12)

A. Who Is the Woman? (v. 1)

(Revelation 12:1 is not included in the printed text.)

The woman in this vision is clothed with the sun, the moon is her footstool, and she wears a crown with 12 stars. The only other place in Scripture such symbols are used is in Joseph's dream (Genesis 37:9). Joseph dreamed that the sun, the moon, and 11 stars came and bowed before him. This came to pass when he became the second-in-command ruler of Egypt, and his father and 11 brothers came and bowed down to him. This, then, is a description of the nation of Israel, with Joseph being the 12th star. Paul attributed the human ancestry of Christ to the Jews when he said: "Theirs are the patriarchs, and from them is traced the human ancestry of

Christ, who is God over all, forever praised! Amen" (Romans 9:5, *NIV*). Jesus told the woman at the well of Sychar that "salvation is from the Jews" (John 4:22, *NIV*). Thus, the woman probably represents a picture of restored Israel, or "the Church, if we remember that the Church is the community of God's people in every age," states William Barclay. ("The Revelation of John," *The Daily Bible Study Series*).

Some say the woman represents the church, since the church is seen at the close of Revelation as the bride of Christ. However, the church did not produce the Child. It was the opposite—the Child produced the church.

B. Who Is the Child? (v. 2)

(Revelation 12:2 is not included in the printed text.)

The male child is easily identified as Christ by looking at verse 5. He is the One who will "rule all nations with a rod of iron." This imagery comes from Psalm 2:9, which speaks of God establishing His kingdom on His holy hill of Zion. The "rod of iron" is also referred to in Revelation 2:27, where overcoming believers from the church of Thyatira are promised a position of authority over the nations. The same imagery is repeated in Revelation 19:15.

Ray Stedman says that the rod of iron indicates a millennial scene. Though it is a time of worldwide blessing and prosperity, Christ rules with a strict justice (iron rod), because the curse of sin is still manifest to a certain degree. Stedman also says, "Righteousness reigns in the earth, but it has to be enforced" (*What On Earth's Going to*

Happen?). It is not until the coming of the new heavens and a new earth that there is no longer a need for a rod of iron. At that point sin will have been fully dealt with, and no evil will be able to ever enter the scene again.

C. Who Is the Dragon? (v. 3)

(Revelation 12:3 is not included in the printed text.)

The Dragon is the easiest to identify in this vision. The devil appears as a "great red dragon," with seven heads and 10 horns, and seven crowns on his heads. He is the same as the ancient serpent who deceived Eve, introducing sin into the human race. Portrayed here as a dragon, he is the symbol of satanic worship.

D. Heavenly View of Conflict on Earth (vv. 4-6)

(Revelation 12:4-6 is not included in the printed text.)

To understand this entire chapter, we must realize we are being shown earthly scenes from a heavenly perspective. Stedman says, "When you look at earthly events from heaven's standpoint, time is never a factor; it is not a question of sequence or chronology but simply of occurrence" (*What On Earth's Going to Happen?*) In other words, we are seeing *what* happens, not *when* it happens.

What we view in these verses goes back to the birth of Christ, 2,000 years ago. The great Dragon is watching Israel intently, waiting for the birth of the long-promised Son. He is ready to pounce on the Child at the moment He makes His appearance. Satan knew the Old Testament prophecies of a coming Messiah as well as anyone, but since he is not omniscient, he had to watch just like everyone else.

"The stars of heaven attached to his tail reveal the fact that Satan will take with him in his expulsion from heaven a third of the angels, for the angels are spoken of as 'stars' in the Old Testament (Job 38:7). These 'angels' will be cast with him into the earth. They will not be visible but will secretly sow the seeds of rebellion, and ultimately be cast with Satan into the 'lake of fire' which will be prepared for them (Matthew 25:41)." (Clarence Larkin, *The Book of Revelation*). The Roman Empire was the essence of the Dragon's power during that time. It sought to destroy the Child through Herod. However, God prevented this by sending Joseph and Mary with the baby to Egypt and thereby evading the trap.

Verse 5 says the Child "was caught up unto God, and to his throne." Most expositors see this as a picture of Christ's ascension 30 years later, skipping over His ministry, death, and resurrection. However, when Jesus ascended, He was already beyond the reach of His enemies. Why would He need to escape the wrath of the Dragon? Some see this as a picture of the rapture of the church. The reasoning for this is that all through the New Testament the church is the visible manifestation of Christ on earth. When Saul was blinded on the road to Damascus, Jesus appeared to him and asked, "Saul, Saul, why do you persecute me?" (Acts 9:4, *NIV*). Obviously, it was the church that Paul was persecuting, but Christ used the pronoun *me*.

The *New International Version* of Revelation 12:5 says "her child was snatched up to God and to his throne." Many see the Rapture as being the "Great Snatch." Thus, between this verse and the next verse, the entire church age is covered. When the woman flees to the wilderness, the Child is already gone. In the desert she is taken care of for 1,260 days, indicating that the Rapture has occurred just before the beginning of the Tribulation.

E. War in the Heavens (vv. 7-10)

(Revelation 12:7, 8 is not included in the printed text.)

9. And the great dragon was cast out, that old serpent, called the Devil, and Satan, which deceiveth the whole world: he was cast out into the earth, and his angels were cast out with him.

10. And I heard a loud voice saying in heaven, Now is come salvation, and strength, and the kingdom of our God, and the power of his Christ: for the accuser of our brethren is cast down, which accused them before our God day and night.

The scene suddenly changes from earth to heaven. War has broken out between God's angels and the forces of Satan. Walvoord believes this scene was prophesied in Daniel 12:1: "At that time Michael, the great prince who protects your people, will arise. There will be a time of distress such as has not happened from the beginning of nations until then. But at that time your people—everyone whose name is found written in the book—will be delivered" (*NIV*). In this war Satan and his angels are cast out of heaven, thus confining them to earth. From this we draw the conclusion that Satan will have access to heaven up to the final days. In Job he appeared before God to ask permission to harm Job. In Zechariah he accused the saints before God.

However, at midpoint in the Tribulation, God has had enough of the devil. He sends Michael to force the devil and his angels out of heaven. They are hurled down to earth. In Revelation 9:1 we saw that the great star fell from the sky to the earth.

Verse 10 of our text gives heaven's reaction to the devil being cast out of heaven. This loud voice is apparently the combined voices of the martyrs of Revelation 6 who were given white robes and were seen crying out for vengeance. They now rejoice because their prayers have been answered. "Our brethren" they speak of are apparently the believing Jews who are still on earth, the righteous remnant of Israel. The saints in heaven announce that the time has come for the Lord to reign over the kingdom that was promised to Israel.

F. Overcomers (vv. 11, 12)

(Revelation 12:12 is not included in the printed text.)

11. And they overcame him by the blood of the Lamb, and by the word of their testimony; and they loved not their lives unto the death.

These verses show that believers in any age can overcome the wiles of Satan. Lies, false philosophies, selfish ideals, and sensual temptations face us every day. In addition, Satan still stands in the presence of God hurling accusations against us. We hear those same accusations, but God has provided ways whereby we can overcome, according to verse 11:

1. *The blood of the Lamb.* We simply remind Satan that our sins are covered by the sacrificial blood of Jesus. Even though we are inherently evil, prone to sin, and weak in ourselves, we have a covering. Paul said, "There is now no condemnation for those who are in Christ Jesus, because through Christ Jesus the law of the Spirit of life set me free from the law of sin and death" (Romans 8:1, 2, *NIV*). Stedman says, "There is no way to handle Satan, and avoid the guilt and shame of which he accuses us, without resting upon the work of the Cross, the blood of the Lamb! When Jesus makes you a new creature, Satan can accuse you only of something that is past and gone" (*The Woman and the Serpent*).

2. *The word of their testimony.* Believers are made stronger as they share their freedom in Christ. As we witness, we build strength for ourselves, and bring good news to others.

3. *They loved not their lives unto the death.* Believers are made strong by not permitting anything to replace Christ. Possession, status, or position should never take priority over Christ. As we keep Him our priority, He gives us strength to overcome.

The final verses of chapter 12 (13-17) indicate that the rejoicing in heaven increases the pressure

for those left on earth. Satan is enraged because his time is short. There is only three and one-half years before he will be bound and thrown into a bottomless pit. After being hurled to earth he pursues the woman, but she is miraculously protected. The woman apparently represents those believing Jews who accept Jesus as their Messiah. Unable to touch the woman, Satan then pursues the rest of her offspring.

During the Tribulation how will believers overcome Satan?

II. BLASPHEMY AGAINST GOD (Revelation 13:1-10)

A. The Beast From the Sea (vv. 1-4)

(Revelation 13:1-3 is not included in the printed text.)

4. And they worshipped the dragon which gave power unto the beast: and they worshipped the beast, saying, Who is like unto the beast? who is able to make war with him?

The beast described here corresponds with the fourth beast in Daniel's vision (Daniel 7). Some expositors believe that the sea refers to the Gentile nations. The fourth beast of Daniel's vision was the Roman Empire. The revived Roman Empire will form some sort of coalition of nations representing the same areas that were originally part of Rome. The evil leader of this empire (the Antichrist) will win the admiration of the world. H.A. Ironside expresses this view: "After the church has been caught up to meet the Lord, one man (will arise) who will combine in himself the statesmanship of a Caesar, the military genius of a Napoleon, and the personal attractiveness of a Chesterfield. This man will head a combination of 10 powers, formed, as before mentioned, from the nations that have sprung out of the old Roman Empire" (*Lectures on the Revelation*).

The people of the world will admire the Beast because of his amazing recovery from a deadly wound (v. 3). He apparently actually dies, descends into the Abyss (see 11:7), and returns back to life. Obviously, the world stands in amazement.

B. War With the Saints (vv. 5-10)

(Revelation 13:10 is not included in the printed text.)

5. And there was given unto him a mouth speaking great things and blasphemies; and power was given unto him to continue forty and two months.

6. And he opened his mouth in blasphemy against God, to blaspheme his name, and his tabernacle, and them that dwell in heaven.

7. And it was given unto him to make war with the saints, and to overcome them: and power was given him over all kindreds, and tongues, and nations.

8. And all that dwell upon the earth shall worship him, whose names are not written in the book of life of the Lamb slain from the foundation of the world.

9. If any man have an ear, let him hear.

The empire of the Beast will reflect the past empires symbolized by the leopard, bear, and lion (v. 2; Daniel 7:2-6), but will sur-

pass them all in power because the Dragon (Satan) will empower the Beast (Antichrist) with tremendous authority. This alliance of evil will last for 42 months, the last three and one-half years of the Tribulation. The Beast will fight and conquer the saints, but he will not be able to dominate them spiritually. All the world will accept him, except true believers. Paul warned, "Don't let anyone deceive you in any way, for that day will not come until the rebellion occurs and the man of lawlessness is revealed, the man doomed to destruction. He will oppose and will exalt himself over everything that is called God or is worshiped, so that he sets himself up in God's temple, proclaiming himself to be God" (2 Thessalonians 2:3, 4, *NIV*).

Despite his apparent power, the Antichrist is still a pawn in the hands of Almighty God. "God uses the Antichrist to reveal the depths of the depravity and wickedness of the human race while also purifying the saints and preparing the way for Christ's visible return to earth" (Lotz, *The Vision of His Glory*).

How do we resist the power of Satan in our daily lives?

III. THE MARK OF THE BEAST
(Revelation 13:11-18)

(Revelation 13:13-15 is not included in the printed text.)

11. And I beheld another beast coming up out of the earth; and he had two horns like a lamb, and he spake as a dragon.

12. And he exerciseth all the power of the first beast before

him, and causeth the earth and them which dwell therein to worship the first beast, whose deadly wound was healed.

16. And he causeth all, both small and great, rich and poor, free and bond, to receive a mark in their right hand, or in their foreheads:

17. And that no man might buy or sell, save he that had the mark, or the name of the beast, or the number of his name.

18. Here is wisdom. Let him that hath understanding count the number of the beast: for it is the number of a man; and his number is Six hundred three score and six.

In addition to an infamous political leader (Antichrist), Satan will also exert his influence through a religious leader, the False Prophet (16:13; 19:20; 20:10). He will perform many miracles and signs on behalf of the first beast (the Antichrist). We should be aware that not every miracle or supernatural event is the work of God's hand. Satan was able to duplicate the miracles of Moses. He will be just as deceptive in the future. This beast represents false religions during the Tribulation. Walvoord says, "The identification of the second beast as the head of the apostate church is indicated in many ways in the Book of Revelation."

The first Beast, the Antichrist, came out of the sea. The second one, the False Prophet, comes out of the earth, indicating that he may be Jewish. Some believe that since the first beast is political in character, this religious impostor should be identified as the actual Antichrist. However, most premillennial expositors see the second

beast as a subordinate to the Antichrist. He might best be seen as a "counterfeit of the Holy Spirit. He seems to do good, but the purpose of his miracles is to deceive" (*Life Application Bible*).

John is suddenly given a point of wisdom. Wisdom is the "reverential and worshipful fear of the Lord" (Lotz). It is certainly wise to fear and reverence God alone. Though he may have super-natural power, the Antichrist is still just a man. The number of the Beast is 666. Notice that this is "*a* man's number." However, it is fruitless to search for the Antichrist's identity by assigning numerical symbolism to any political leader, though it has been tried for centuries. Wisdom says to fear God. As believers respond in wisdom, God will reveal the identity of the Antichrist, but not through any mathematical intelligence.

REVIEW QUESTIONS

1. Who is the woman of Revelation 12?

2. What do some believe the sea represents symbolically? Explain the symbolism.

3. How do we differentiate between the wiles of Satan and the temptations of the flesh?

DAILY BIBLE READINGS

M. God's People Oppressed. Exodus 1:8-14
T. God's People Delivered. Exodus 14:15-22
W. Oppressor Defeated. Isaiah 14:12-20
T. Antichrist Unmasked. 2 Thessalonians 2:1-10
F. Deliberate Delay. 2 Peter 3:1-9
S. Spirit of Antichrist. 1 John 4:1-6

God's Judgment Is Right

Study Text: Revelation 14:1 through 16:21

Objective: To grasp the truth that God deals justly with all people and resolve to share the gospel with others.

Time: The Book of Revelation was probably written about A.D. 96.

Place: The Book of Revelation was written on the island of Patmos in the Aegean Sea.

Golden Text: "Who shall not fear thee, O Lord, and glorify thy name? for thou only art holy: for all nations shall come and worship before thee; for thy judgments are made manifest" (Revelation 15:4).

Central Truth: God's righteous character is revealed in His righteous judgment.

Evangelism Emphasis: God gives every person opportunity to prepare for the final judgment.

PRINTED TEXT

Revelation 14:6. And I saw another angel fly in the midst of heaven, having the everlasting gospel to preach unto them that dwell on the earth, and to every nation, and kindred, and tongue, and people,

7. Saying with a loud voice, Fear God, and give glory to him; for the hour of his judgment is come: and worship him that made heaven, and earth, and the sea, and the fountains of waters.

12. Here is the patience of the saints: here are they that keep the commandments of God, and the faith of Jesus.

13. And I heard a voice from heaven saying unto me, Write, Blessed are the dead which die in the Lord from henceforth: Yea, saith the Spirit, that they may rest from their labours; and their works do follow them.

15:4. Who shall not fear thee, O Lord, and glorify thy name? for thou only art holy: for all nations shall come and worship before thee; for thy judgments are made manifest.

5. And after that I looked, and, behold, the temple of the tabernacle of the testimony in heaven was opened:

6. And the seven angels came out of the temple, having the seven plagues, clothed in pure and white linen, and having their breasts girded with golden girdles.

7. And one of the four beasts gave unto the seven angels seven golden vials full of the wrath of God, who liveth for ever and ever.

8. And the temple was filled

with smoke from the glory of God, and from his power; and no man was able to enter into the temple, till the seven plagues of the seven angels were fulfilled.

16:1. And I heard a great voice out of the temple saying to the seven angels, Go your ways, and pour out the vials of the wrath of God upon the earth.

4. And the third angel poured out his vial upon the rivers and fountains of waters; and they became blood.

5. And I heard the angel of the waters say, Thou art righteous, O Lord, which art, and wast, and shalt be, because thou hast judged thus.

6. For they have shed the blood of saints and prophets, and thou hast given them blood to drink; for they are worthy.

7. And I heard another out of the altar say, Even so, Lord God Almighty, true and righteous are thy judgments.

LESSON OUTLINE

LESSON EXPOSITION

INTRODUCTION

Chapters 11-13 of Revelation revealed the awful conditions on earth during the second half of the Tribulation period. The two witnesses are murdered and then are miraculously resurrected; those from Israel and the nations who turn to God are hunted; and the Antichrist and the False Prophet mark the masses with the mark of the Beast.

In chapter 14 we see another parenthetical vision by John. H.A. Ironside says, "This 14th chapter forms a distinct section of the Book. It consists of one vision divided into six parts, and evidently has to do with the closing up of the Great Tribulation and the introduction of the kingdom" (*Lectures on the Revelation*). Charles Caldwell Ryrie sees this chapter as a sort of table of contents for the rest of the book.

The chapter begins by bringing us up to date on the fate of the 144,000. These are the same 144,000 who were sealed in 7:1-8. Through all the evil they faced, what was their fate?

We will actually see the fates of two groups of numbered peoples—the 144,000 Jews who were sealed (14:1-5) and those who accepted the mark of the Beast (vv. 6-20).

Verse 1 begins by showing the 144,000 standing with the Lamb on Mount Zion. Does this mean the mountain in Jerusalem or a spiritual Mount Zion in heaven? Many expositors believe it is the literal Mount Zion, with the scene taking place at the beginning of the millennial reign. Others believe it refers to the heavenly Zion (the heavenly Jerusalem) as mentioned in Hebrews 12:22, 23. In either case the triumphant Jewish believers have endured great persecutions on earth and are now ready to enjoy the eternal blessings of life with God. We are told five things about this group (14:1-5):

1. *They sing a new song.* This is related to the new song that was sung by the 24 elders around the throne in heaven in 5:9. How do these redeemed who are still on earth have such a heavenly privilege to learn this rapturous song? Has God given them special ears that can hear the "raptured church" singing around the throne? We are not given the answer, but it is obvious that this group marches to the "beat of a different drummer"—they hear something that others cannot hear.

2. *They are not defiled with women, for they are virgins.* This does not mean that they are sexual virgins, but that they simply have kept themselves pure before God. Hebrews 13:4 indicates that married couples can still be pure: "Marriage is honourable in all, and the bed undefiled."

3. *They follow the Lamb wherever He goes.* They have faithfully followed the Lord throughout the earth.

4. *These are the firstfruits of the harvest of the Tribulation.* According to John Walvoord, "the term *firstfruits* seems to refer to the beginning of a great harvest. . . . The 144,000 are the godly nucleus of Israel which is the token of the redemption of the nation and the glory of Israel which is to unfold in the kingdom" (*The Revelation of Jesus Christ*).

5. *They are without fault before the throne of God.* They have been changed from *sinners* to *saints* by God's grace. They are cleansed in the blood.

With the beginning of 14:6 the scene suddenly changes. John sees three angels flying through the heavens making profound announcements. We begin our principal study here.

I. THE GOSPEL FOR ALL
   NATIONS (Revelation 14:6-13)

A. The Everlasting Gospel (v. 6)

6. And I saw another angel fly in the midst of heaven, having the everlasting gospel to preach unto them that dwell on the earth, and to every nation, and kindred, and tongue, and people.

The phrase "everlasting gospel" has been controversial to some expositors. John the Baptist preached, "Repent ye: for the kingdom of heaven is at hand" (Matthew 3:2). Then Jesus proclaimed that "this gospel of the kingdom will be preached in the whole world as a testimony to all nations, and then the end will come" (Matthew 24:14, *NIV*). However, during the church age (from the Day of Pentecost to the Rapture), Paul called the message "the gospel of the grace of God" (Acts 20:24). Nevertheless, he also said he preached "the kingdom of God" (v. 25). In another place he said, "But even if we or an angel from heaven should preach a gospel other than the one we preached to you, let him be eternally condemned!" (Galatians 1:8, *NIV*).

Is there any difference in the message? Probably not. Steven Gregg says the everlasting gospel "is the good news, of all ages, that God is sovereign, and man's happiness consists in recognizing His authority. To this blessed fact is added, in the present dispensation, the full truth of the gospel of the grace of God. The gospel of the kingdom is but another aspect of this same news from heaven, emphasizing particularly the Lordship of Christ" (*Revelation—Four Views*).

B. Four Gifts From God (v. 7)

7. Saying with a loud voice, Fear God, and give glory to him; for the hour of his judgment is come: and worship him that made heaven, and earth, and the sea, and the fountains of waters.

Four things are listed here that were made by God—"the heavens, the earth, the sea and the springs of water" (*NIV*). These are all incrementally destroyed by the first four trumpets and first four bowls in chapters 8 and 16. God judges unthankful man by depriving him of the use of resources that were given in love. Romans 1:21 says, "For although they knew God, they neither glorified

him as God nor gave thanks to him, but their thinking became futile and their foolish hearts were darkened" (*NIV*). God has been gracious for many centuries, but finally He deprives man of His wondrous blessings.

C. Fallen Babylon (v. 8)

(Revelation 14:8 is not included in the printed text.)

A second angel announces the fall of Babylon. This is the first time Babylon is mentioned in Revelation. The details of this fall come later in chapters 17 and 18, but here we see a proclamation of something that is as certain to happen as if it had already occurred. This is the same way Isaiah 53 speaks of the death of Christ—as already accomplished, though it would be another seven centuries before actually taking place.

Babylon can be identified in several ways—a literal city, a religious system, a political system, and also as a code name of the Roman Empire. John Walvoord sees Babylon in the first half of the Tribulation as being the apostate church, one which professes to be Christian but is not. In the second half he sees it as an actual city—likely Rome—which will be destroyed at the end of the seven years. Ironside identifies Babylon as a religious system, a false Christianity, one that will be broken and destroyed by God.

D. Fire and Brimstone (vv. 9-12)

(Revelation 14:9-11 is not included in the printed text.)

12. Here is the patience of the saints: here are they that

keep the commandments of God, and the faith of Jesus.

A third angel declares that those who take the mark of the Beast will face eternal judgment. This is one of the most intense passages of Scripture in the Bible. To "drink of the wine of the wrath of God . . . poured out without mixture" (v. 10) indicates the ultimate damnation. In ancient times wine was commonly diluted with water. Here, however, God's wrath is poured out in full strength. "There is no element of grace or hope or compassion blended with the judgment" (William E. Biederwolf, *The Second Coming Bible*). Fire and brimstone describe the worst pain man can experience.

The sin described here matches Christ's description of the unpardonable sin in Matthew 12:31, 32: "And so I tell you, every sin and blasphemy will be forgiven men, but the blasphemy against the Spirit will not be forgiven. Anyone who speaks a word against the Son of Man will be forgiven, but anyone who speaks against the Holy Spirit will not be forgiven, either in this age or in the age to come" (*NIV*). In the verses leading up to this statement by Jesus (22-30), it is clear that crediting the miraculous work of Christ to Beelzebub constitutes this sin. In the same way, accepting the mark of the Beast is equivalent to crediting the evil work of the Antichrist to a holy God. Perhaps in accepting the mark, individuals are asked to express a blasphemous oath. Whatever is required, the true believer will never commit such a heretical act. In fact, verse 12 of our text encourages the

saints to endure patiently and to obey God's commandments.

E. Blessed Are the Dead (v. 13)

13. And I heard a voice from heaven saying unto me, Write, Blessed are the dead which die in the Lord from henceforth: Yea, saith the Spirit, that they may rest from their labours; and their works do follow them.

John is told to write down a promise to those who die in the Lord from that point on, namely those who die as martyrs in the final trying days of the Tribulation. Perhaps this was spoken to allay the fears of those making a righteous stand. The church has already been taken away at this point. Those still on earth might fear the unknown if they are killed. This is the same problem Paul addressed in writing to the Thessalonian Christians (1 Thessalonians 4:13-18). Because Christ had not yet returned and some of the first-generation believers were dying, many feared that since these missed the snatching away of the living saints, these dead would be lost. Paul assured them with these words: "For the Lord himself will come down from heaven, with a loud command, with the voice of the archangel and with the trumpet call of God, and the dead in Christ will rise first" (v. 16, *NIV*).

Why does accepting the mark of the Beast automatically bring eternal doom?

II. PREPARATION FOR FINAL JUDGMENT (Revelation 15:1-8)

A. Seven Angels With Seven Plagues (v. 1)

(Revelation 15:1 is not included in the printed text.)

The general sequence of Revelation continues with 15:1. We have already seen the seven seals and the seven trumpets. Now the final seven last plagues will be revealed. These constitute the most extreme judgments leading to Armageddon. Chapters 4 and 5 showed us a heavenly scene as the Tribulation begins. In chapter 15 we see another celestial scene just before the bowls are poured out in chapter 16.

Notice that there has been an increase in severity from the seals to the trumpets to the bowls. The seals meted out judgment with a destruction ratio of one-fourth; the trumpets increased to one-third; the bowls will cause total devastation. Is there any overlap between the seals, trumpets, and bowls? It is possible to imagine one judgment occurring in a certain region of the earth while another takes place elsewhere. However, because of the difference in severity they should not be viewed as contemporaneous. God's judgments are clear. They increase in intensity as men's hearts grow harder.

B. A Sea of Glass (v. 2)

(Revelation 15:2 is not included in the printed text.)

The very presence of a sea of glass tells us this scene takes place in heaven. This sea was revealed in 4:6 before the opening of the seals. Here, however, there is fire mingled with the sea. There are two possible explanations.

Walvoord says, "Here the sea mingled with fire speaks of divine judgment proceeding from God's holiness" (*The Revelation of Jesus Christ*). Ryrie's view is that the sea "is mingled with fire, perhaps referring to the fiery persecution which these people had suffered under the beast" (*Revelation*).

C. The Song of Moses and of the Lamb (vv. 3, 4)

(Revelation 15:3 is not included in the printed text.)

4. Who shall not fear thee, O Lord, and glorify thy name? for thou only art holy: for all nations shall come and worship before thee; for thy judgments are made manifest.

A triumphant anthem is being sung in heaven by those who were converted and martyred during the Tribulation. The song of Moses was sung by the children of Israel when they crossed the Red Sea (Exodus 15), and again when Deborah led them to victory against the Canaanites (Judges 5). The fact they are singing both the song of Moses and the song of the Lamb indicates that the song of redemption is one continuous song. There is no opposition between the Old and New Testaments. Most expositors see these saints as having been "put to death by the beast, but living in heaven, as disembodied spirits" (Gregg) or "raised from the dead, and raptured during the tribulation period" (Ironside).

D. The Angels With the Seven Last Plagues (vv. 5-8)

5. And after that I looked, and, behold, the temple of the

tabernacle of the testimony in heaven was opened:

6. And the seven angels came out of the temple, having the seven plagues, clothed in pure and white linen, and having their breasts girded with golden girdles.

7. And one of the four beasts gave unto the seven angels seven golden vials full of the wrath of God, who liveth for ever and ever.

8. And the temple was filled with smoke from the glory of God, and from his power; and no man was able to enter into the temple, till the seven plagues of the seven angels were fulfilled.

In 11:15 the seventh trumpet was blown, and in 11:19 the heavenly temple was revealed. Then came the parenthetical visions of chapters 12-14, showing how evil reigns during the second half of the Tribulation. Now we see coming out of the heavenly temple the contents of that trumpet, which turn out to be the seven angels with "seven last plagues." The fact that they come out of the temple indicates that these judgments are "not vindictive but vindicative" (Ryrie). In 5:8 we saw that the four beasts and 24 elders presented bowls of incense representing the prayers of the saints. Here those prayers are being vindicated with bowls of judgment. The bowls will constitute the third woe.

What is symbolized by the fact that the seven angels with the seven bowls come out of the temple?

III. RIGHTEOUS JUDGMENTS
   (Revelation 16:1-7)

(Revelation 16:2, 3 is not included in the printed text.)

1. And I heard a great voice out of the temple saying to the seven angels, Go your ways, and pour out the vials of the wrath of God upon the earth.

4. And the third angel poured out his vial upon the rivers and fountains of waters; and they became blood.

5. And I heard the angel of the waters say, Thou art righteous, O Lord, which art, and wast, and shalt be, because thou hast judged thus.

6. For they have shed the blood of saints and prophets, and thou hast given them blood to drink; for they are worthy.

7. And I heard another out of the altar say, Even so, Lord God Almighty, true and righteous are thy judgments.

A voice out of the temple commands the bowl judgments to begin. Why is there an audible command? There is great precedence for such. In the Creation story of Genesis 1, the phrase "And God said" is repeated over and over. God's speaking out was not necessary for Creation—it was necessary for our understanding. Jesus did the same thing when He called Lazarus to come from the grave: "Father, I thank you that you have heard me. I knew that you always hear me, but I said this for the benefit of the people standing here, that they may believe that you sent me" (John 11:41, 42, *NIV*).

The severity of the judgments have increased in increments. The seals (Revelation 6 and 8) are primarily the result of God's releasing the boundaries of man's evil. The wars, famines, persecution of the saints, and so forth, are the results. The trumpet judgments (chs. 8, 9, 11) are satanic in origin, especially the sixth trumpet where Satan's army of 200 million kills one-third of mankind. The bowl judgments (chs. 15, 16) are direct vindicative judgments of God himself. They come fast, furiously, and decisively.

We see three of these judgments in the verses above. The boils or malignant sores of the first bowl (v. 2) might well be similar to those in Egypt (Exodus 9:9). Hal Lindsey believes they are caused by radioactive pollution. There has also been conjecture that the mark of the Beast could be similar to a tattoo, which after a period of time becomes intensely infected, thus creating a terrible boil. This has a certain logic to it, since only those who have taken the mark are infected.

With the second and third bowls (vv. 3-7), the world's water supply, both salt and fresh, becomes contaminated. Most expositors do not believe the waters turn into literal blood. Ray Stedman suggests this is referring to the phenomenon known as "red tide," where a microorganism multiplies extremely fast, turning the water scarlet and killing all the sea life. Another suggestion is that something destroys all the animal life, and the dead carrion bursts, spewing blood into the waters and turning it red.

However these final plagues take place, they are issued to a wicked world in need of judgment. Walvoord writes, "Even as the saints are worthy of rest and reward, so the wicked are worthy of divine chastening and judgment. The bloodletting during the great tribulation, as saints are slaughtered by the thousands, is without parallel in the history of the human race."

REVIEW QUESTIONS

1. Is there any difference between the "gospel of grace" and the "gospel of the kingdom?" Explain.

2. What modern city is possibly meant when the term *Babylon* is used?

3. Why is accepting the mark of the Beast comparable to committing the unpardonable sin?

4. If the seals destroyed a fourth measure, the trumpets a third measure, then how devastating are the bowl judgments?

5. Why does God use a voice from the temple to declare the beginning of the seven bowl judgments?

GOLDEN TEXT HOMILY

"WHO SHALL NOT FEAR THEE, O LORD, AND GLORIFY THY NAME? FOR THOU ONLY ART HOLY: FOR ALL NATIONS SHALL COME AND WORSHIP BEFORE THEE; FOR THY JUDGMENTS ARE MADE MANIFEST" (Revelation 15:4).

With the advent of televised courtroom proceedings, we have all become legal experts. These programs give us the opportunity to peer into people's lives as we hear their stories unfold before us. Although we may proclaim their sentences from our armchairs, the fact is we still do not know the full story. Our rush to condemn may be unjust.

The Book of Revelation is a reminder of the power and majesty of our God. If we learn nothing else from its record, it would do us all well to learn about its central character—God. God, the ultimate judge of the universe, sits in the courtroom of life. This scene is not a made-for-television event but a chilling reality.

When world history ends, God has the final word. The nations and peoples of the world will gather before Him, awaiting the sound of the final gavel. What will this verdict be? The single most important factor involved is the justice of God. His judgments are always right. His judgments are not influenced by public opinion or filled with loopholes. In the justice hall of God, you and I will stand before Him. Since, unlike many human trials, justice will prevail, all gathered here will receive the correct verdict.

Finally, it should be noted that the quality of legal proceedings depends on the character of the judge. God is holy and righteous, as are His judgments. He gives all people the opportunity to prepare for this moment. Those who have prepared can stand without fear and worry. We can stand before the righteous judge fully clothed in the righteousness of His dear Son.—**Michael S. Stewart, Senior Pastor, First Assembly of God, Raleigh, North Carolina**

SENTENCE SERMONS

GOD'S RIGHTEOUS CHARACTER is revealed in His righteous judgment.

—Selected

GOD GIVES every person opportunity to prepare for the final judgment.

—Selected

THE JUDGMENT of God is the reaping that comes from sowing and is evidence of the love of God, not proof of His wrath.

—Kirby Page

GOD'S JUSTICE AND LOVE are one. Infinite justice must be infinite love.

—Frederick W. Robertson

DAILY BIBLE READINGS

M. Wise Judgment.
1 Kings 3:16-28
T. Plea for Justice. Psalm 43:1-5
W. Christ, the Righteous Judge.
John 5:19-30
T. God Will Judge the World.
Acts 17:22-31
F. God Will Judge Backsliders.
Hebrews 10:26-31
S. Righteousness Rewarded.
2 Timothy 4:1-8

Triumph Over Evil

Study Text: Revelation 17:1 through 20:15

Objective: To realize that Christ, the Living Word, will prevail over evil and submit our lives to His authority.

Time: The Book of Revelation was probably written about A.D. 96.

Place: The Book of Revelation was written on the island of Patmos in the Aegean Sea.

Golden Text: "Alleluia: for the Lord God omnipotent reigneth" (Revelation 19:6).

Central Truth: At His second coming, Jesus Christ will bind and destroy Satan and establish God's eternal kingdom.

Evangelism Emphasis: Christ's triumph over evil enables believers to witness boldly.

PRINTED TEXT

Revelation 19:5. And a voice came out of the throne, saying, Praise our God, all ye his servants, and ye that fear him, both small and great.

6. And I heard as it were the voice of a great multitude, and as the voice of many waters, and as the voice of mighty thunderings, saying, Alleluia: for the Lord God omnipotent reigneth.

7. Let us be glad and rejoice, and give honour to him: for the marriage of the Lamb is come, and his wife hath made herself ready.

9. And he saith unto me, Write, Blessed are they which are called unto the marriage supper of the Lamb. And he saith unto me, These are the true sayings of God.

11. And I saw heaven opened, and behold a white horse; and he that sat upon him was called Faithful and True, and in righteousness he doth judge and make war.

13. And he was clothed with a vesture dipped in blood: and his name is called The Word of God.

15. And out of his mouth goeth a sharp sword, that with it he should smite the nations: and he shall rule them with a rod of iron: and he treadeth the winepress of the fierceness and wrath of Almighty God.

19. And I saw the beast, and the kings of the earth, and their armies, gathered together to make war against him that sat on the horse, and against his army.

20. And the beast was taken, and with him the false prophet that wrought miracles before him, with which he deceived them that had received the mark of the beast, and them that worshipped his image. These both were cast alive into a lake of fire burning with brimstone.

20:1. And I saw an angel come down from heaven, having the key of the bottomless pit and a great chain in his hand.

2. And he laid hold on the dragon, that old serpent, which is the Devil, and Satan, and bound him a thousand years.

7. And when the thousand years are expired, Satan shall be loosed out of his prison,

10. And the devil that deceived them was cast into the lake of fire and brimstone, where the beast and the false prophet are, and shall be tormented day and night for ever and ever.

LESSON OUTLINE

LESSON EXPOSITION

INTRODUCTION

The bowl judgments are devastating and complete. The end of mankind's rebellion has finally come. There are many similarities between the trumpet judgments (8:6—11:19) and the bowl judgments (15:7—16:21), but there are three distinct differences. First, the trumpets cause partial destruction. Second, man still has a chance to repent during the trumpet judgments. There is no such opportunity during the bowls. Finally, some of the trumpet judgments only indirectly affect mankind. They deal more with the elements and nature. During the pouring out of the bowls of wrath, however, man is directly attacked.

Our last lesson ended with the first three bowl judgments:

1. Boils came on all who had taken the mark of the Beast.

2. The seas became like blood, killing all marine life.

3. All the fresh waters of the earth became like blood.

To bring us up to our present text, let us review the other four bowls:

4. *The sun scorches men with fire* (16:8, 9). During the fourth

trumpet the sun, moon, and stars were darkened by one-third each (8:12). Here the opposite takes place. Oppressive, intense heat scorches the earth. Ray Stedman sees this as great nuclear explosions bursting from the sun, creating intense heat on earth. Hal Lindsey sees some sort of full-scale nuclear exchange on earth.

5. *Darkness overtakes the earth* (16:10, 11). The first four bowls had to do with nature. This one apparently has to do with the political power of the Beast. The Beast's kingdom appears to be headed toward anarchy. A darkness, either literal or symbolic, spreads over the land. Also, the sores of the first bowl continue to plague the people. Despite all this, men continue to harden their hearts, blaspheming further against God.

6. *The Euphrates River dries up, clearing the way for the 200-million-man army to move from the east toward Armageddon* (16:12-16). Walvoord sees this as a coalition of the Orient, including Japan, China, India, and other Eastern nations. As part of this bowl, John also sees "three unclean spirits like frogs" moving over the earth (v. 13). Ryrie says, "These frog-like demons are assigned to seduce the leaders of the earth and of the whole world into participating in the battle of that great day of God Almighty." Since the entire world has been under a single government during the Tribulation, how could there be two massive world powers? One suggestion is that the two sets of armies headed toward Armageddon are actually anticipating the second coming of Christ with His forces. The battle could be a coalition of the two earthly armies against the heav-

enly forces. Another possibility is that there is a great rebellion across the earth against the Beast's authority. Thus, the Eastern armies are rising up in insurrection. Walvoord says, "It reflects a conflict among the nations themselves in the latter portion of the Great Tribulation as the world empire so hastily put together begins to deteriorate."

7. *A great earthquake, unparalleled in history, shakes the entire earth* (16:17-21). Lindsey sees this as a full-scale nuclear exchange of the remaining missiles on earth. Stedman also sees this as nuclear warfare proceeding from Armageddon. Absolute destruction takes place around the globe. Ryrie says, "Everything that man has built will crumble before his eyes." Great hailstones of over 100 pounds each then strike the earth. The sad effect of all this is that men refuse to repent, choosing to curse God as they die.

You will notice that our present lesson skips chapters 17 and 18. These largely give a parenthetical vision of the "MYSTERY, BABYLON THE GREAT, THE MOTHER OF HARLOTS" (17:5). In chapter 17, Babylon is generally thought to be a symbol of an apostate world church during the Tribulation years, with headquarters in Rome. Many believe this to be dominated by the Vatican. To throw condemnation on Catholicism is unfair because the apostate church will probably include many groups. "Babylon symbolizes the rebellion of the entire human race throughout all history against God and His people. The roots of Babylon can be traced back to Genesis 11" (Lotz). The word *harlot* insinuates spiritual adultery, indicating all who claim the name of God but are worshiping other gods or idols. The harlot sits on the Beast but later is destroyed by the Beast. This implies that Satan uses a religious system to fool the people, but when the false religion gets in his way, he destroys it. He proclaims himself dictator and sets himself up to be worshiped.

In chapter 18, Babylon seems to refer to a political system centered in a real city (either a rebuilt Babylon or Rome). In her vain boasting, Babylon says of herself, "I sit [as] a queen, and am no widow, and shall see no sorrow" (v. 7). However, her bloodletting of the "prophets and of the saints, and of all who have been killed on the earth" (v. 24, NIV) does not go unnoticed by God, and it is He who comes to destroy her. With a wave of His matchless hand, in just "one hour is she made desolate" (v. 19).

In summary, Revelation 17 gives a picture of Babylon, the great harlot of false religion, being destroyed. This apparently occurs after the midpoint of the Tribulation. Chapter 18 portrays the destruction of the great city Babylon (the political system). This takes place near the end of the Tribulation. Both the religious and political forces of hell have met their doom on earth. This sets up our current lesson, the triumphant church and the marriage of the Lamb.

I. TRIUMPHANT CHURCH
(Revelation 19:1-10)

A. The Roar of Approval (vv. 1, 2)

(Revelation 19:1, 2 is not included in the printed text.)
John hears the sound of giant crowds, crying out in approval over the destruction of the great enemies of God. "Greater and louder even than the expressions of blasphemy on earth are the sounds of victory in heaven!" (Lotz). The apostate church and political system, the great harlot whose false teaching corrupted the population of the earth, have now been judged.

Should we rejoice at the doom of other humans? Frequently, the family of a murder victim will fight for years to get a death sentence assigned to the murderer, only to suddenly have pity on him when the ultimate judgment is given. Such is not the case here. There is no sympathy for the wicked at this point. As God pours out His wrath on earth and its evil inhabitants, the watching universe explodes in approval.

One might ask the question: Do the saints who are in glory see what is occurring on earth today? Very possibly. How, then can they be joyous while viewing the evil on earth—even among their own families? Apparently, a saint's delight in heaven is not determined by what is happening on earth, but rather by the knowledge that God is fully in control and His judgments are righteous. They see the larger scope of God's redemption plan, knowing that restoration is coming.

B. The Cry of "Alleluia" (vv. 3-6)

(Revelation 19:3, 4 is not included in the printed text.)
5. And a voice came out of the throne, saying, Praise our God, all ye his servants, and ye that fear him, both small and great.
6. And I heard as it were the

voice of a great multitude, and as the voice of many waters, and as the voice of mighty thunderings, saying, Alleluia: for the Lord God omnipotent reigneth.

We look again at the heavenly throne John viewed in chapter 4. The 24 elders and four living creatures are consistent in their reverence, falling down and worshiping, just as they did before the unveiling of the judgments in the earlier scene. This speaks to the believer. We should trust God and His integrity; we should trust and worship Him, knowing that His wisdom is perfect and His care for us is complete.

The call for rejoicing of the saints and heavenly hosts over Babylon's downfall was issued in Revelation 18:20. Here we see a response to that exhortation. The word *alleluia* is used four times in the above passage (19:1-4). This word, so universal to Christian worship, is found only here in Scripture.

C. The Marriage of the Lamb
  (vv. 7-10) *after the saints are*
  (Revelation 19:8, 10 is not *gathered* included in the printed text.)

7. Let us be glad and rejoice, and give honour to him: for the marriage of the Lamb is come, and his wife hath made herself ready.

9. And he saith unto me, Write, Blessed are they which are called unto the marriage supper of the Lamb. And he saith unto me, These are the true sayings of God.

The concept that the church is the bride of Christ can be seen clearly in two Pauline passages. In Ephesians 5:25-27, the apostle said, "Husbands, love your wives, just as Christ loved the church . . .

to present her to himself as a radiant church, without stain or wrinkle or any other blemish, but holy and blameless" (*NIV*). In 2 Corinthians 11:2, he also said, "I am jealous for you with a godly jealousy. I promised you to one husband, to Christ, so that I might present you as a pure virgin to him" (*NIV*). "Marriage of the Lamb" is not found anywhere in Scripture other than in the Revelation 19 passage. In Matthew 9:15, Christ says: "How can the guests of the bridegroom mourn while he is with them? The time will come when the bridegroom will be taken from them; then they will fast" (*NIV*). He made a similar reference in Matthew 22:2: "The kingdom of heaven is like a king who prepared a wedding banquet for his son" (*NIV*).

The marriage of the Lamb speaks of an eternal wedlock between Christ and the church. This union has not yet taken place, since the Matthew passages and the text in Revelation see this as a future event. Even though there is a sense that Christ presently abides in the hearts of believers, there is another sense that He is in heaven awaiting us. Perhaps the difference can be compared to the distinction between betrothal and marriage.

There is an unanswered question if we consider the church to be the bride of Christ: What about Israel? The general view is that the Old Testament relationship between God and His special people will be fully restored for eternity. God's marriage to Israel might be pictured in the life of Hosea and his prostitute wife. This restoration takes place when

Israel finally sees Jesus as Messiah during the Tribulation. However, the church has a separate relationship with Christ and is already in heaven at this point. Even though the word *church* is not used, it appears that the bride is the church seen in this vision.

Who is the "bride" of Christ at the marriage of the Lamb?

II. THE CONQUERING CHRIST (Revelation 19:11-21)

A. The Rider of the White Horse (vv. 11-13)

(Revelation 19:12 is not included in the printed text.)

11. And I saw heaven opened, and behold a white horse; and he that sat upon him was called Faithful and True, and in righteousness he doth judge and make war.

13. And he was clothed with a vesture dipped in blood: and his name is called The Word of God.

John sees another vision, as indicated in verse 11, "And I saw heaven opened." There is no mistaking who is riding the white horse in this vision. John sees Christ, accompanied by all the armies of heaven, coming to establish His millennial kingdom. He is identified in many ways:

1. He is called "Faithful and True."

2. His eyes are like "a flame of fire" (v. 12), indicating His wrath against all wickedness and sin.

3. He wears many crowns (v. 12).

4. He has a name no human can express, indicating His divinity. "Knowledge of a name is in antiquity associated with the

power of the god" (*NIV Commentary*).

5. His robe is dipped in blood. Some believe this is the blood of His enemies as He destroys evil mankind. They support this with Isaiah 63:1-6. Others say it is His own blood that was shed on the cross, His blood which washes believers' garments white as snow. Either way, He presents an awesome, terrifying sight in vindicating His anger against sin.

6. His name is called "The Word of God" (v. 13), the same name John used in the beginning of his Gospel. Since this vision reveals two names for Christ, "it may be concluded that the exclusive power of Christ over all creation is now to be shared with his faithful followers (3:21; 5:10; 22:5)" (*NIV Commentary*).

B. Armies Upon White Horses (v. 14)

(Revelation 19:14 is not included in the printed text.)

Some Old and New Testament passages identify the hosts of heaven as being composed of angels (see Psalm 103:21; 148:2; and Luke 2:13). However, these are soldiers riding horses. Their white garments are the same as the Bride's clothing. It is likely that this army includes the saints of all ages, especially the church.

C. The Sharp Sword and Rod of Iron (v. 15)

15. And out of his mouth goeth a sharp sword, that with it he should smite the nations: and he shall rule them with a rod of iron: and he treadeth the winepress of the fierceness and wrath of Almighty God.

Since the sword comes out of His mouth, some writers believe the weapon used by Christ in this battle is His Word. To support this idea they refer to Isaiah 11:4: "He shall smite the earth with the rod of his mouth, and with the breath of his lips he shall slay the wicked." He conquers by the power of His Word, "the instrument of both his judgment and his salvation" (*NIV Commentary*). The "rod of iron" refers back to Psalm 2:9: "You will rule them with an iron scepter; you will dash them to pieces like pottery" (*NIV*). The fact that He will rule with an iron rod indicates to some that everything is not perfect during the Millennium. They believe there will be children born during this time to saints who survived the Tribulation. These children will have the potential for sin. Therefore, strong rule will be necessary. Others see the iron rod as simply a symbol of Christ's absolute authority.

Armageddon is pictured as a winepress where grapes are trodden, scattering the red liquid everywhere. The great assembly of wicked nations will be stomped and trodden upon like grapes in an unmerciful judgment. Their blood will be splattered like the juice from crushed grapes.

D. Destruction of the Beast and His Armies (vv. 16-21)

(Revelation 19:16-18, 21 is not included in the printed text.)

19. And I saw the beast, and the kings of the earth, and their armies, gathered together to make war against him that sat on the horse, and against his army.

20. And the beast was taken, and with him the false prophet that wrought miracles before him, with which he deceived them that had received the mark of the beast, and them that wor-

shipped his image. These both were cast alive into a lake of fire burning with brimstone.

Although the Beast and the wicked kings and nations of the earth try to battle Christ, there is never any chance of their victory. "There is no war at all! The King simply speaks a word, and everyone else drops dead!" (Lotz). The power of the sword in the mouth of Christ defeats every evil alliance.

Pictured here is a gruesome antithesis to the Marriage Supper of the Lamb (19:9). The wicked are slain by the hand of God. Their dead bodies lie lifeless upon the ground for the vultures and birds to eat. The followers of Christ have attended a feast of life in heaven; however, the wicked have themselves become a feast of death on earth at Armageddon.

The Antichrist (the Beast) and his false prophet are thrown directly into the lake of fire. Their followers are cast into hades to await the final judgment (19:20, 21; 20:13), after which they will also be cast into the fiery lake.

What does the sword coming out of Christ's mouth at Armageddon represent?

III. SATAN'S DOOM (Revelation 20:1-3, 7-10)

A. The Binding of the Serpent (vv. 1-3)

(Revelation 20:3 is not included in the printed text.)

1. And I saw an angel come down from heaven, having the key of the bottomless pit and a great chain in his hand.

2. And he laid hold on the dragon, that old serpent, which is the Devil, and Satan, and bound him a thousand years,

The angel described here is possibly Michael, who gained mastery over Satan in chapter 12. Michael is seen in Scripture as the mightiest of God's angels. Satan, the Dragon, is imprisoned for 1,000 years. During this time Christ will rule with perfect justice, grace, peace, and righteousness.

Though Satan is imprisoned and can no longer deceive anyone, it is still possible for sin to exist in individuals. However, it can no longer "be a power forming a fellowship, and thus making a kingdom of sin and Satan" (William E. Biederwolf, *The Second Coming Bible*).

B. Satan Loosed (vv. 7-10)

(Revelation 20:8, 9 is not included in the printed text.)

7. And when the thousand years are expired, Satan shall be loosed out of his prison,

10. And the devil that deceived them was cast into the lake of fire and brimstone, where the beast and the false prophet are, and shall be tormented day and night for ever and ever.

Satan will be released after the Millennium for a little season. There will then be one more rebellion against Christ's reign before the new, eternal creation comes.

The immediate question is, Why would God loose Satan? The answer possibly lies in the fact that at that time He shall rule with a "rod of iron" (2:27; 12:5; 19:15). The earth will be populated during the Millennium with (1) believers who were raptured; (2) believers who died earlier and were resurrected at the Rapture; (3) those who came to faith during the Tribulation, were martyred, and then were resurrected at the return of Christ; and (4) those who somehow managed to survive

the Tribulation and enter the Millennium in their natural bodies. This last group will continue to procreate, and their descendants will still possess sinful, unredeemed natures. By the end of the Millennium this group could make up the majority of the population. Thus, the necessity of a "rod of iron." God will allow Satan to operate to prove the character of these unredeemed descendants. They will have their opportunity to choose between His kingdom and Satan's.

This Satan-led rebellion will culminate in the battle of Gog and Magog (vv. 8, 9). The saints will be camped around Jerusalem. God will fight the battle Himself, sending fire from heaven to devour the armies of Satan. When this is over, the final judgment will come, and all the lost will be resurrected. They will be judged, along with Satan, and cast into the lake of fire for eternity (see vv. 10-15).

REVIEW QUESTIONS

1. Who comprises the army dressed in white, riding white horses at Armageddon?

2. Why are the Beast and the False Prophet thrown directly into the lake of fire at Armageddon?

3. What does Christ's rule with a "rod of iron" possibly tell us about the Millennial Age?

4. Why is Armageddon pictured as a winepress?

5. After the Millennium, who are the people who follow Satan in a rebellion against Christ's reign?

GOLDEN TEXT HOMILY

"ALLELUIA: FOR THE LORD GOD OMNIPOTENT REIGNETH" (Revelation 19:6).

John was rejoicing! The multitudes were rejoicing! This rejoicing was so genuine that it seemed the sea and sky were also joining in the expressions of joy and praise. Neither John nor the multitude were without reasons for sadness. John had been stripped of his civil freedom. He was a banished prisoner on a snake-infested island. Even prior to this, general attempts had been made to deprive him of life itself. The power of Rome was exerting itself to destroy the young church. Yet John and the church were rejoicing.

For believers today the situation has not changed very much. We too live in dark days and experience stormy nights. We see tragedy, corruption, and evil all around us. There is perhaps more hate, fear, despair, and shedding of tears and blood than ever. The world we live in is wicked. But in desperate days we can and should rejoice. We rejoice not because of the evil of the day but in spite of it. For what reason, or reasons, did John and the young church rejoice?

John rejoiced because he believed things were going to get better. He believed in a brighter tomorrow. His belief was not based on the eventual rise of a favored political ideology. He was not rejoicing because a new king was coming with social and economic reforms for the Roman world. He rejoiced because of the coming of the King of kings! The evil world would pass away, and a world of peace and love would come into being. It was easy for John and the young church to believe in the future because they believed in the God who was in charge of the future.

The tense of the word *reigneth* in the Greek New Testament implies a past, present, and continuous action. The song of praise is not merely a celebration of a truth of a bygone time; neither is it simply a matter of the future for which we must wait. "Alleluia: for the Lord God omnipotent reigneth!" Even though it may not seem so, based on circumstances, the Lord who is all-powerful is and always will be the One who rules. Looking at external circumstances, it appears that we have no reason to celebrate. Looking at the truth of the matter, we have every reason to join in the chorus of John.—**R.B. Thomas, D.Litt, Vice President, Church of God Theological Seminary, Cleveland, Tennessee**

SENTENCE SERMONS

AT HIS SECOND COMING, Jesus Christ will bind and destroy Satan and establish God's eternal kingdom.

—Selected

CHRIST'S TRIUMPH over evil enables believers to witness boldly.

—Selected

DAILY BIBLE READINGS

M. The Mighty Warrior.
Isaiah 63:1-6
T. The Lord Executes Judgment.
Ezekiel 38:18-23
W. Gog Defeated. Ezekiel 39:1-10
T. The Son of Man Returns.
Matthew 24:27-31
F. Signs of Christ's Coming.
Luke 21:20-28
S. The Blessed Hope.
Titus 2:11-15

Eternal Inheritance

Study Text: Revelation 21:1 through 22:21

Objective: To examine the believer's eternal inheritance in heaven and rejoice in Christ's provision.

Time: The time of the writing of the Book of Revelation was probably about A.D. 96.

Place: The Book of Revelation was written on the island of Patmos in the Aegean Sea.

Golden Text: "He that overcometh shall inherit all things; and I will be his God, and he shall be my son" (Revelation 21:7).

Central Truth: God has prepared a glorious inheritance for those who trust in His Son.

Evangelism Emphasis: God has prepared a glorious inheritance for those who accept His Son as Savior.

PRINTED TEXT

Revelation 21:1. And I saw a new heaven and a new earth: for the first heaven and the first earth were passed away; and there was no more sea.

2. And I John saw the holy city, new Jerusalem, coming down from God out of heaven, prepared as a bride adorned for her husband.

3. And I heard a great voice out of heaven saying, Behold, the tabernacle of God is with men, and he will dwell with them, and they shall be his people, and God himself shall be with them, and be their God.

4. And God shall wipe away all tears from their eyes; and there shall be no more death, neither sorrow, nor crying, neither shall there be any more pain: for the former things are passed away.

5. And he that sat upon the throne said, Behold, I make all things new. And he said unto me, Write: for these words are true and faithful.

22:1. And he shewed me a pure river of water of life, clear as crystal, proceeding out of the throne of God and of the Lamb.

2. In the midst of the street of it, and on either side of the river, was there the tree of life, which bare twelve manner of fruits, and yielded her fruit every month: and the leaves of the tree were for the healing of the nations.

3. And there shall be no more curse: but the throne of God and of the Lamb shall be in it; and his servants shall serve him:

4. And they shall see his face; and his name shall be in their foreheads.

5. And there shall be no night there; and they need no

candle, neither light of the sun; for the Lord God giveth them light: and they shall reign for ever and ever.

12. And, behold, I come quickly; and my reward is with me, to give every man according as his work shall be.

13. I am Alpha and Omega, the beginning and the end, the first and the last.

14. Blessed are they that do his commandments, that they may have right to the tree of life, and may enter in through the gates into the city.

17. And the Spirit and the bride say, Come. And let him that heareth say, Come. And let him that is athirst come. And whosoever will, let him take the water of life freely.

DICTIONARY

Alpha (AL-fah) and Omega (oh-MAY-guh)—Revelation 22:13—The first and last letters of the Greek alphabet.

LESSON OUTLINE

I. THE HOLY CITY

   A. A New Heaven and a New Earth

   B. The Bride Adorned for Her Husband

   C. The Tabernacle of God

   D. Faithful and True

   E. Alpha and Omega

   F. The Holy City

II. THE GLORIOUS KING

   A. No Need for a Temple

   B. No More Night

III. REWARD AND INVITATION

LESSON EXPOSITION

INTRODUCTION

To introduce this lesson, let us first summarize our last one (chs. 19, 20). At the end of the Tribulation, Christ returns to earth with the saints to fight against the forces of Satan (led by the Beast and False Prophet). Christ triumphs completely, and both the Beast and the False Prophet are cast into the lake of fire. Satan is then bound while Christ rules the earth with an iron rod for a millennium of peace. The saints who rule with Christ during these 1,000 years have all experienced resurrection—the church having done so at the Rapture, while other saints who were martyred during the Tribulation have been resurrected at the Second Coming. There are also a number of saints who somehow survived the Tribulation and enter the Millennium in their natural bodies. They continue to procreate, thus creating a lineage of people who still have the curse of sin in their mortal bodies. This gives eternal credence to the phrase, "Ye must be born again" (John 3:7). These people have the seed of sin but live under the absolute rule of Christ. They become as the "sand on the seashore" (Revelation 20:8, *NIV*) by the end of the 1,000 years.

It is to these unredeemed descendants that Satan is loosed for a short season. Though the seed of sin has been in their hearts, they will never have experienced temptation. They will never have had to exercise their will in choosing right over wrong. They will never have been exposed to anything wrong. "Imagine how vulnerable these descendants will be to Satan's deception! And what will his deception be? Somehow Satan will convince them, 'Living under the lordship of Christ is bad for you! Submitting to the authority of Christ confines your personality and limits your potentiality'" (Anne Graham Lotz). Satan's tactics will be the same as they have always been. God will allow him to tempt the unregenerate in order that they once and for all can make their decisions between living for God and living for self.

The Battle of Gog and Magog settles the issue. Satan is cast into the lake of fire. The unredeemed and wicked of all ages are then resurrected for the final white throne judgment. Both death and hell are destroyed, giving truth to Paul's statement, "The last enemy that shall be destroyed is death" (1 Corinthians 15:26). All whose names are not found in the Book of Life are also thrown into the lake of fire to be forever damned.

With this final lesson on Revelation, we come to the finale of the great drama of human history. However, not only is it a finale but also a new beginning.

In Genesis 1 we saw the creation of the world. With chapter 21 of Revelation we see the creation of a new heaven and earth. In Genesis the devil introduced sin into the world; here we see the devil defeated and destroyed, sin is no longer a factor, and man is once again sinless. In Genesis the earth was subjected to a curse; now the curse is removed. In Genesis mankind was separated from God; now he will live with God forever. In Genesis mankind was barred from the Tree of Life; now he may eat freely of it. In Genesis death entered the world; now death is done away with and man lives forever. In Genesis the languages of earth were confused and different peoples were scattered; now the people of the world come together before Christ, singing His praises forever.

I. THE HOLY CITY (Revelation 21:1-7; 24-26; 22:1-3)

A. A New Heaven and a New Earth (21:1)

1. And I saw a new heaven and a new earth: for the first heaven and the first earth were passed away; and there was no more sea.

The concept of there being a new creation was first intimated by the prophet Isaiah: "For, behold, I create new heavens and a new earth: and the former shall not be remembered, nor come into mind" (Isaiah 65:17). Peter apparently quoted Isaiah when he said, "Nevertheless we, according to his promise, look for new heavens and a new earth, wherein dwelleth righteousness" (2 Peter 3:13). It is obvious that the present earth and heavens are wearing out. Manmade problems of pollution, depletion of natural resources, and radical population growth have debilitated the world we live in. Also, the law of entropy, the second law of thermodynamics, says this present universe is running down, decaying, and losing energy. In contrast, the new heavenly home will be created completely afresh. "Instead of losing energy it will gain it and manifest a unity, stability, symmetry, and beauty that the old heavens and earth never had" (Ray C. Stedman).

Some might be disappointed to read that there will be no more sea. Stedman says that the very reason for the salt seas on this earth was to provide a constant antiseptic to cleanse the planet and make life possible. In the new world to come, there will be no need for cleansing, since there will be no pollutants of any kind. He does, however, feel that there will be large bodies of fresh water for man to enjoy.

B. The Bride Adorned for Her Husband (21:2)

2. And I John saw the holy city, new Jerusalem, coming down from God out of heaven, prepared as a bride adorned for her husband.

The symbolism here suggests a wedding. In 19:7 the announcement of the marriage was made: "For the wedding of the Lamb has come, and his bride has made herself ready" (*NIV*). John's vision here seems to pick up where the earlier one left off, with a bridal procession taking place. However, the earlier passage

occurs before the Millennium, whereas this one is after the 1,000 years. It would appear that the announcement was made before the Millennium, but the final marriage ceremony does not occur until after all trace of potential sin (as well as Satan himself) has been destroyed.

Peter described the new heavens and earth as coming after the destruction of the present cosmos: "That day will bring about the destruction of the heavens by fire, and the elements will melt in the heat. But in keeping with his promise we are looking forward to a new heaven and a new earth, the home of righteousness" (2 Peter 3:12, 13, *NIV*). The question naturally arises as to how God will protect the saints who will have gathered at Jerusalem just prior to the Battle of Gog and Magog. The answer possibly is that God will miraculously move His people to the New Jerusalem as the new earth and heavens are being destroyed. Thus, the New Jerusalem is now the bride, by virtue of the fact that she houses the people who make up the bride.

C. The Tabernacle of God (21:3, 4)

3. And I heard a great voice out of heaven saying, Behold, the tabernacle of God is with men, and he will dwell with them, and they shall be his people, and God himself shall be with them, and be their God.

4. And God shall wipe away all tears from their eyes; and there shall be no more death, neither sorrow, nor crying, neither shall there be any more pain: for the former things are passed away.

The Greek word for *tabernacle* is *skene*, meaning "tent." From this we get the English derivative *scene*, originally indicating the painted tent near a stage where actors changed costumes. The meaning in our present text is that God will tent (live) with men. Since there will be no more sin, God will commune and live directly with men. His presence will no longer be conditional. In Leviticus 26:11, God promised to tabernacle among the Israelites if they remained obedient. This was revoked when the Temple was destroyed in 586 B.C. However, during the Captivity, Ezekiel prophesied a future time of restoration under the new covenant when this privilege would be restored: "My dwelling place will be with them; I will be their God, and they will be my people" (Ezekiel 37:27, *NIV*). Some think this will have been fulfilled during the Millennium, but the most complete fulfillment does not happen until all potential for sin is removed.

There will be no more tears—simply because there will be no reason for tears. Believers will spend eternity in a city where perfect love and peace dwells. They will have a nature confirmed in righteousness. God said in Isaiah, "Behold, I will create new heavens and a new earth. The former things will not be remembered, nor will they come to mind" (65:17, *NIV*). There will be no sad remembrances to bring tears. In fact, the saints apparently will remember nothing of this life at that point.

D. Faithful and True (21:5)

5. And he that sat upon the throne said, Behold, I make all things new. And he said unto me, Write: for these words are true and faithful.

As difficult as the details of the new heavens and new earth might be to comprehend, God's word can always be trusted. John was likely so overwhelmed at what he was seeing that he needed to be assured that the promises were absolutely unfailing.

E. Alpha and Omega (21:6, 7)

(Revelation 21:6, 7 is not included in the printed text.)

The identity of Christ as the beginning and the end of all things is a reiteration of 1:8, 17, 18. The same declaration is made in 22:13. The emphasis is on God's "absolute control over the world as well as His creatorship of everything" (*NIV Study Bible*). The offer of living water is the same that Jesus made to the woman at the well of Sychar (John 4:10), as well as the proclamation He made in the Temple: "If anyone is thirsty, let him come to me and drink" (7:37, *NIV*). To be thirsty a person must need water and at the same time desire it. To such a one Christ promises the free gift of salvation. John realizes that the visions of God's glory among His people, proclaimed as the Word of God, will create a thirst to participate in the reality of this glory. Nothing else is required except to come and drink.

F. The Holy City (21:24-26; 22:1-3)

(Revelation 21:24-26 is not included in the printed text.)

22:1. And he shewed me a

pure river of water of life, clear as crystal, proceeding out of the throne of God and of the Lamb.

2. In the midst of the street of it, and on either side of the river, was there the tree of life, which bare twelve manner of fruits, and yielded her fruit every month: and the leaves of the tree were for the healing of the nations.

3. And there shall be no more curse: but the throne of God and of the Lamb shall be in it; and his servants shall serve him.

These passages are part of a larger segment (21:9-27; 22:1-5) in which an angel carries John away "in the spirit" (21:10) to view the beautiful eternal city. Interestingly, one of these same angels had earlier shown him another city: "Come hither; I will shew unto thee the judgment of the great whore that sitteth upon many waters" (17:1). The harlot city of Babylon was the absolute opposite of what John now sees.

John attempts to give a detailed gaze into the breathtaking sight of the New Jerusalem. His description is limited in much the same way as a primitive jungle native would be today if he were suddenly transported to a large metropolitan city. His descriptions to his friends upon return to the jungle would be totally inadequate. However imperfect John's words may be, he still was inspired by God. Therefore the account can be trusted as true.

From the mention of "nations" (21:24) above, the impression is gained that there will be an organization of the world into nations and rulers. However, there will be no competitiveness or animosity in this true "new world order." Stedman says, "The kings of the earth will bring their glory in, not to compete with the glory of God, but to have it revealed by the light of God. Nothing impure will enter because only the redeemed are admitted."

John sees a glorious picture of fertility, with life radiating everywhere (22:1, 2). Both the "river of water of life" and the "tree of life" are found in Old Testament passages. Psalm 46:4 says, "There is a river whose streams make glad the city of God, the holy place where the Most High dwells" (NIV). The river symbolizes the presence of the Holy Spirit. The Tree of Life was seen in the Genesis account of the Garden of Eden. It is a picture of Jesus himself. "He is the way, the truth and the life, the tree of life. When we obey the Word of God we are eating and feeding on Jesus and drawing life from that nourishment" (Stedman).

The total picture of John's vision of the New Jerusalem is one of the saints' enjoying an eternity of pleasure-filled service to God, an intimate fellowship with Him, and a continual sense of excitement. There will never be any boredom, only constant discovery and anticipation.

Why is the New Jerusalem called the Bride, when earlier the raptured church is seen as the bride of Christ?

II. THE GLORIOUS KING
(Revelation 21:22, 23; 22:4, 5)

A. No Need for a Temple (21:22, 23)

(Revelation 21:22, 23 is not included in the printed text.)

In 2 Chronicles 5 we are given the details of the preparation for the dedication of Solomon's Temple in the 10th century B.C. The Temple was the place God chose to dwell in as a symbol of His being in the midst of His people. Since the people were sinners, His holiness had to be isolated from their sin, thus the very need for the Temple. In the new heavens and new earth, however, there is no sin, since all sinners will have already been judged at the Great White Throne judgment. Also, the new earth will never have been defiled by sin. God will no longer need to be isolated from His people, since they, too, are sinless. His omnipresence will fill the New Jerusalem and the entire new earth. Perhaps the city will provide the inner Holy of Holies, while the entire new earth will be the outer Holy Place where He also will dwell.

Arriving at this perfect place of God's presence is the ultimate hope of every believer. Paul said, "To those who by persistence in doing good seek glory, honor and immortality, he will give eternal life" (Romans 2:7, *NIV*). The Christian already has access to God's presence by faith, as seen in Romans 5:2: "Through whom we have gained access by faith into this grace in which we now stand. And we rejoice in the hope of the glory of God" (*NIV*). Paul recognized, though, that nothing can compare with what is coming: "I consider that our present sufferings are not worth comparing with the glory that will be revealed

in us" (8:18, *NIV*).

B. No More Night (22:4, 5)

4. And they shall see his face; and his name shall be in their foreheads.

5. And there shall be no night there; and they need no candle, neither light of the sun; for the Lord God giveth them light: and they shall reign for ever and ever.

First John 1:5 declares, "God is light; in him there is no darkness at all" (*NIV*). Jesus declared Himself to be the "light of the world" (John 8:12). These verses speak mainly of a spiritual light; nevertheless, physical light is also a manifestation of God's glory. When Solomon's temple was dedicated, the glory of the Lord so filled the place that "when all the Israelites saw the fire coming down and the glory of the Lord above the temple, they knelt on the pavement with their faces to the ground, and they worshiped and gave thanks to the Lord, saying, 'He is good; his love endures forever'" (2 Chronicles 7:3, *NIV*). An illuminated presence also occurred in the Tabernacle (Numbers 16:42). Just how the Shekinah glory will light the entire city of New Jerusalem is impossible for our finite minds to understand, but we can be assured it will be as described.

The seal of God's name (v. 4 of the text) is a promise to the overcomers in the church at Philadelphia (Revelation 3:12). God's seal in the foreheads of the 144,000 is mentioned in 14:1. In 13:16, the False Prophet is seen putting the Antichrist's name on the foreheads of the masses during the Tribulation. This will be a satanic imitation of what God eventually plans to do for all His faithful. Here, we see that bearing the name of the Savior upon the brow is a privilege of all the inhabitants of the New Jerusalem.

Why is there no need for a temple in the New Jerusalem?

III. REWARD AND INVITATION
(Revelation 22:12-17)

(Revelation 22:15, 16 is not included in the printed text.)

12. And, behold, I come quickly; and my reward is with me, to give every man according as his work shall be.

13. I am Alpha and Omega, the beginning and the end, the first and the last.

14. Blessed are they that do his commandments, that they may have right to the tree of life, and may enter in through the gates into the city.

17. And the Spirit and the bride say, Come. And let him that heareth say, Come. And let him that is athirst come. And whosoever will, let him take the water of life freely.

We come finally to the epilogue of John's vision. The speaker is now Jesus himself, and He reiterates themes and promises that have already been given. The words "to give every man according as his work shall be" preaches a powerful message to the saints. At the judgment seat of Christ, rewards will be given for faithfulness and good works. These are certainly not prerequisite for entrance into heaven, for salvation is a free gift. However, the level of rewards of the ages to come is certainly dependent on how the believer spends his time on earth subsequent to salvation. Romans 2:6 says that God "will give to each person according to what he has done" (*NIV*). After just hearing all the wonderful things that are promised in eternity, it would certainly be a shame to enter there with few gifts of works to lay at the Master's feet.

Jesus again speaks of Himself as the beginning and the ending of all things (Revelation 22:13), as well as the root of David and the bright and morning star (v. 16). He had earlier promised Himself in this terminology to the overcomers of the church of Thyatira (2:28). Peter spoke of the morning star rising in the heart of the believer: "And we have the word of the prophets made more certain, and you will do well to pay attention to it, as to a light shining in a dark place, until the day dawns and the morning star rises in your hearts" (2 Peter 1:19, *NIV*).

John had to be mesmerized as the words of Jesus soared. Never was there an orator or preacher who could captivate the listener as the Master himself does now for the apostle's ears. His words swell as four pleading invitations are given to the sinner. First, the Holy Spirit and the Bride give the invitation. Second, everyone who hears this (including John, the one hearing these words) is encouraged to make the plea. Third, the one who is thirsty for righteousness is invited to come. This reiterates one of the Beatitudes: "Blessed are those who hunger and thirst for righteousness, for they will be filled" (Matthew 5:6, *NIV*). Finally, "whosoever will" is implored to come. Thus, we see that the message is for all men. Certainly God does not desire that any be lost. The gifts of eternity are free to all through Jesus' death at Calvary.

REVIEW QUESTIONS

1. What is the Greek meaning for the word *tabernacle*?

2. Explain the symbolism of the "river of water of life" and the "tree of life."

3. The seal of God's name will be on the foreheads of the saints in the New Jerusalem. How did Satan try to imitate this?

4. Why is there no more night or darkness in the New Jerusalem?

5. Who is the final speaker at the end of John's vision? What promises does He reiterate?

SENTENCE SERMONS

GOD has prepared a glorious inheritance for those who trust in His Son.

—Selected

HEAVEN IS NOT a reward for "being a good boy," but is the continuation and expansion of a quality of life which begins when a man's central confidence is transferred from himself to God.

—J.B. Phillips

EVANGELISM APPLICATION

GOD HAS PREPARED A GLORIOUS INHERITANCE FOR THOSE WHO ACCEPT HIS SON AS SAVIOR.

While this lesson gives details of the wonderful life the saints will enjoy for eternity, we cannot help but think of those who will not only miss heaven, but will suffer for endless ages in the lake of fire. What they face is terrifying, to say the least. Look at how other places in Scripture describe the doom of those who are lost:

A place of consciousness—"In hell, where he was in torment, he looked up and saw Abraham far away, with Lazarus by his side. So he called to him, 'Father Abraham, have pity on me and send Lazarus to dip the tip of his finger in water and cool my tongue, because I am in agony in this fire'" (Luke 16:23, 24, *NIV*).

A place of torment and memory of lost opportunities—"For I have five brothers. Let him warn them, so that they will not also come to this place of torment" (Luke 16:28, *NIV*).

Eternal separation from righteous loved ones—"There will be weeping there, and gnashing of teeth, when you see Abraham, Isaac and Jacob and all the prophets in the kingdom of God, but you yourselves thrown out" (Luke 13:28, *NIV*).

No hope of escape—"Then they will go away to eternal punishment, but the righteous to eternal life" (Matthew 25:46, *NIV*).

The temporary pleasures of this life are certainly not worth facing such an eternal damnation.

DAILY BIBLE READINGS

M. A Perfect World. Isaiah 55:9-13
T. New Heaven and New Earth. Isaiah 65:17-25
W. Peace Promised. Isaiah 66:5-13
T. River of Life. Ezekiel 47:1-9
F. A Place in God's Presence. John 14:1-6
S. Looking for Christ's Coming. 2 Peter 3:10-13

Exalt Christ

Study Text: Luke 4:16-19; Philippians 2:5-11; Hebrews 1:5-9; 13:15, 16

Objective: To acknowledge that Jesus Christ is Lord and worship Him.

Golden Text: "God also hath highly exalted him, and given him a name which is above every name" (Philippians 2:9).

Central Truth: Jesus Christ is exalted in the church as we worship and obey Him.

Evangelism Emphasis: As believers exalt Christ, He draws sinners unto Himself.

PRINTED TEXT

Luke 4:16. And he came to Nazareth, where he had been brought up: and, as his custom was, he went into the synagogue on the sabbath day, and stood up for to read.

17. And there was delivered unto him the book of the prophet Esaias. And when he had opened the book, he found the place where it was written,

18. The Spirit of the Lord is upon me, because he hath anointed me to preach the gospel to the poor; he hath sent me to heal the brokenhearted, to preach deliverance to the captives, and recovering of sight to the blind, to set at liberty them that are bruised,

19. To preach the acceptable year of the Lord.

Philippians 2:5. Let this mind be in you, which was also in Christ Jesus:

6. Who, being in the form of God, thought it not robbery to be equal with God:

7. But made himself of no reputation, and took upon him the form of a servant, and was made in the likeness of men:

8. And being found in fashion as a man, he humbled himself, and became obedient unto death, even the death of the cross.

9. Wherefore God also hath highly exalted him, and given him a name which is above every name:

10. That at the name of Jesus every knee should bow, of things in heaven, and things in earth, and things under the earth;

11. And that every tongue should confess that Jesus Christ is Lord, to the glory of God the Father.

Hebrews 1:5. For unto which of the angels said he at any time, Thou art my Son, this day have I begotten thee? And again, I will be to him a Father, and he shall be to me a Son?

6. And again, when he bringeth in the firstbegotten into the world, he saith, And let all the angels of

God worship him.

13:15. By him therefore let us offer the sacrifice of praise to God continually, that is, the fruit of our lips giving thanks to his name.

16. But to do good and to communicate forget not: for with such sacrifices God is well pleased.

DICTIONARY

Nazareth (NAZ-uh-reth)—Luke 4:16—The city in Galilee where Jesus grew up.

synagogue (SIN-uh-gog)—Luke 4:16—A Jewish place of assembly for the reading and exposition of the Holy Scriptures.

Esaias (ee-ZA-yas)—Luke 4:17—The Greek rendering of the word Isaiah (eye-ZAY-uh).

LESSON OUTLINE

I. JESUS IS THE CHRIST

   A. Jesus Honors the Synagogue

   B. The Spirit of the Lord Is Upon Me

   C. The Fulfillment of Scripture

II. CHRIST IS LORD

   A. The Mind of Christ

   B. The Preincarnate Lord

   C. Supreme Condescension— the Incarnation

   D. Jesus Is Lord

III. PRAISE THE LORD

   A. Worthy of Worship

   B. The Sacrifice of Praise

LESSON EXPOSITION

INTRODUCTION

A search of the New Testament reveals that the most often used title for Jesus is *Christ*. Most people today think that this was part of Jesus' name. Actually, His earthly name would have been *Jesus bar-Joseph* (that is, "Jesus, son of Joseph"). The word *Christ* is the English derivative of the Greek word *Christos*, itself being a form of the Hebrew word for *Messiah*. Therefore, by saying "Jesus Christ," one is really saying "Jesus the Messiah." During His earthly ministry, many Jews were appalled to call Jesus by this title. Others used the title, but their conception of the Messiah was incomplete. They were looking only for someone to deliver them from the Romans. When Jesus refused to comply with their notions, they began to question who He really was and refused to consider Him the Messiah.

Interestingly, most people had no problem thinking that Jesus was a prophet. This still holds true today. Many who deny Christ's deity readily admit His role as a prophet. However, a prophet is one whose message absolutely originates with God. If Jesus was a prophet, then His words had to be regarded as truth. But the problem here was that "Jesus as a prophet not only pronounced the Word of God, but declared that He himself was the living and incarnate Word of God. In other words, Jesus not only delivered the Word of God, He was the Word of God" (R.C. Sproul, *Mighty Christ*).

Jesus fulfilled three elements of the Old Testament prophecies concerning the Messiah: He was a prophet (Deuteronomy 18:15); He was a king, because the Messiah would come from the line of King David and would inherit an everlasting kingdom (Isaiah 9:7); He was a priest, because the Messiah was to be a high priest after the order of Melchizedek (Psalm 110:4). The Jews, however, rejected Jesus because they could not see that He filled these roles. They rejected Him as a prophet because He prophesied about Himself. They refused to see Him as a king because their concept was a political-militaristic one. They then refused to see Him as a high priest. A high priest offered sacrifices on behalf of the people. Jesus, however, offered Himself as the sacrifice. He was both the subject and object of the sacrifice. As a whole, the Jews have never yet comprehended this role of Christ.

When Jesus asked Peter to tell Him who he thought He was, Peter's answer was absolutely inspired beyond the knowledge of the fisherman: "'You are the Christ, the Son of the living God.' Jesus replied, 'Blessed are you, Simon son of Jonah, for this was not revealed to you by man, but by my Father in heaven'"

(Matthew 16:16, 17, *NIV*). Peter unwittingly recognized that Jesus was going to fulfill all the requirements of messiahship—prophet, king, and priest.

Jesus acknowledged that Peter had divinely received a word of wisdom. However, just a moment later, Jesus "warned his disciples not to tell anyone that he was the Christ" (Matthew 16:20, *NIV*). Why would He say this? Because Israel was not ready to understand Him, especially His priestly aspect. He would not only be a king and prophet, but He would also be a suffering servant, an ultimate sacrifice for mankind's sins.

Jesus is the Christ. Our lesson this week examines His lordship and encourages us to exalt Him as the Christ, the Son of the living God.

I. JESUS IS THE CHRIST (Luke 4:16-21)

A. Jesus Honors the Synagogue (v. 16)

16. And he came to Nazareth, where he had been brought up: and, as his custom was, he went into the synagogue on the sabbath day, and stood up for to read.

One major significance of this portion of Scripture is often overlooked. Luke's mention of the synagogue and the service Jesus attended there gives us the oldest and most detailed description of what took place in early synagogues. During the Captivity, the Jews in Babylon had no place for communing with God (see Psalm 137 and Daniel 9). They began to meet in local groups for prayer and Scripture reading. After the return from exile, the synagogue became an important part of Jewish life. Even though Zerubbabel rebuilt the Temple, many Jews were scattered, as well as many still living in Persia. The earliest solid evidence dating a synagogue comes from Alexandria, Egypt, about 300 B.C. In Palestine, the oldest known synagogue was at Herod's palace fortress at Masada. This would have been built between 36-30 B.C.

The synagogue became the weekly place of worship for Jews throughout Palestine, as well as for those scattered over the known world. This gave the early church a tremendous precedent for how Christian worship would develop. "Church worship followed the synagogue pattern with Scripture reading, prayer, and a sermon" (*Nelson's Illustrated Bible Dictionary*).

More important here is the fact that Jesus honored the synagogue. "Even though he was the perfect Son of God, and his local synagogue left much to be desired, he attended services every week" (*Life Application Bible*). His example indicates to us the importance of maintaining a "church life." Church attendance, fellowship with other believers, corporate worship, and so forth, are viable parts of solid Christian living. There should be no spiritual hermits. Christians need each other.

B. The Spirit of the Lord Is Upon Me (vv. 17-19)

17. And there was delivered unto him the book of the prophet Esaias. And when he had opened the book, he found the place where it was written,

18. The Spirit of the Lord is upon me, because he hath anointed me to preach the gospel to the poor; he hath sent me to heal the brokenhearted, to preach deliverance to the captives, and recovering of sight to the blind, to set at liberty them that are bruised,

19. To preach the acceptable year of the Lord.

Local synagogues were usually run by one leader with an assistant. Frequently, visiting rabbis were invited to read from the Scriptures and to teach. There is nothing unusual in Christ's being invited to read. His reputation as a teacher had preceded Him, and the local people were anxious to see what kind of person their village had produced.

The passage Jesus chose was Isaiah 61:1, 2. This was a prophecy of the coming Messiah, and it was familiar to virtually every Jew in Palestine. Preconceptions of just what the Messiah would be like were formed, at least to some extent, from these verses. The Jewish populace saw their leader in militaristic terms. They took comfort in thinking that this great leader-to-come would deliver them from their enemies—in this case, the Romans.

The incident in this passage is recorded only by Luke and is fundamental to the writer's development of his account of Christ's life and ministry. Three main themes are seen: (1) Jesus is the bearer of the Spirit. His ministry is marked constantly by the presence of the Holy Spirit, as Isaiah foretold. (2) Jesus is a prophet, fulfilling the mission of proclaiming the gospel, or "good news"

(*NIV*). (3) Jesus is the Messiah. The poor, the brokenhearted, the captives, the blind, and the bruised will all benefit from the special blessing the Messiah brings.

The phrase "acceptable year of the Lord" reminded the people of the Year of Jubilee—every 50th year when debts were forgiven and slaves set free (Leviticus 25:8-17). This indicated a dawning of a new age of salvation and release from bondage. Jesus did not include the last half of Isaiah 61:2: ". . . and the day of vengeance of our God; to comfort all that mourn." This part of the verse excited the people. They looked forward to the Messiah's bringing vengeance on all who had ever harmed Israel. However, this was not the mission of Christ's first coming. He brought the blessings, but not the wrath. That aspect of Isaiah's prophecy will be fulfilled with His second coming.

C. The Fulfillment of Scripture
  (vv. 20, 21)

(Luke 4:20, 21 is not included in the printed text.)

Isaiah made more references to the coming Messiah than any other prophet, yet he was rejected in his own time. Tradition has it that he was sawed in half by the wicked king Manasseh, and was likely the one referred to in the great "Faith Hall of Fame" of Hebrews 11:37, 38. His rejection would be mirrored in the very man he prophesied about.

The congregation in Christ's home synagogue was initially pleased with Him (Luke 4:20-22). His kind manner and wise speech delayed their hostility. Not until

later do the people become angry (v. 28). What happened to stir their animosity? Could it have been Christ's mentioning of the ministry of both Elijah and Elisha to Gentiles instead of to needy Jews (vv. 25-27)? Jesus' words implied that the prophets were sent to the Gentiles by God. The very notion that God might remotely place favor on the Gentiles was enough to enrage the people.

The people appeared favorable toward Jesus until His message countered their ideas about the Messiah, especially as they realized that they would receive no special favors from Him and that He considered Himself above home ties and tradition. The same is true today. Many people accept the notion of an all-loving God, One who accommodates their every need. However, demands of morality, service, standards, and absolutes cross their man-made notions and bring instant rejection.

What did Jesus say or imply that angered His listeners in Nazareth?

II. CHRIST IS LORD
  (Philippians 2:5-11)

A. The Mind of Christ (v. 5)

5. Let this mind be in you, which was also in Christ Jesus.

This entire passage (vv. 5-11) may have been sung by the early church as a hymn. It crystallizes a major message of the gospel into a few words, illustrating Christ's humility and selflessness as the supreme example to follow. Another passage that presents a similar Christological thought is Ephesians 5:25-27, which explains that Christ loves the church as His bride.

A literal rendering of Philippians 2:5 from the Greek might be as follows: "Keep thinking this attitude among you, which was also in Christ Jesus." Obviously, believers cannot duplicate the actions and mind-set of the incarnate Lord, but we can certainly imitate them as our example.

Jesus himself exhorted His followers to imitate Him. In Matthew 20:27, 28, He said, "And whoever wants to be first must be your slave—just as the Son of Man did not come to be served, but to serve, and to give his life as a ransom for many" (*NIV*). Similar appeals can be found in Matthew 11:29; Luke 22:27; John 13:14, 15. After washing the feet of His disciples, Jesus told them, "I have set you an example that you should do as I have done for you" (John 13:15, *NIV*).

B. The Preincarnate Lord (v. 6)

6. Who, being in the form of God, thought it not robbery to be equal with God.

Two aspects of Christ's divine person before He became a man are seen in this verse: (1) He has always existed with God in heaven, and (2) He is equal to God in power, eminence, preexistence, and nature. The exact thoughts were also expressed by John when he wrote, "In the beginning was the Word, and the Word was with God, and the Word was God. He was with God in the beginning" (John 1:1, 2, *NIV*).

The phrase "form of God" elicits interesting thoughts; for example, the idea that the nature of a person remains the same, though the way it is expressed varies. Thus, although Jesus took upon Himself full humanity and lived out a life as a man, He never ceased to have the eternal qualities of God.

C. Supreme Condescension—the Incarnation (vv. 7-10)

7. But made himself of no reputation, and took upon him the form of a servant, and was made in the likeness of men:

8. And being found in fashion as a man, he humbled himself, and became obedient unto death, even the death of the cross.

9. Wherefore God also hath highly exalted him, and given him a name which is above every name:

10. That at the name of Jesus every knee should bow, of things in heaven, and things in earth, and things under the earth.

While Jesus absolutely retained His essence as God when He became a man, He nevertheless made Himself of a lower status in order to live totally as a man so that He would be able to relate completely to mankind. "The *Incarnation* was the act of the preexistent Son of God voluntarily assuming a human body and human nature. Without ceasing to be God, he became a human being, the man called Jesus. He did not give up his deity to become human, but he set aside the right to his glory and power" (*Life Application Bible*). He limited Himself as the rest of mankind is limited with regard to time, place, and physical body. What made His humanity unique was the fact that He was able to live without sin. He showed us as much of the character of God as can be demonstrated within the limitations of humanity.

D. Jesus Is Lord (v. 11)

11. And that every tongue should confess that Jesus Christ is Lord, to the glory of God the Father.

The Greek word for *lord* is *kurios* and has three ascending levels of meaning. On the lowest level it simply means "sir" or "mister." At the next level it refers to the slave-owner relationship. A slave regarded his master as one who owned him. Paul presented himself as a slave in the introductions to some of his letters; for example, "Paul, a servant of Jesus Christ (Romans 1:1) or "Paul, a servant of God" (Titus 1:1). The word for *servant* is the same as the one for *slave*. On the highest level, however, *Lord* refers back to the Old Testament word *Adonai*, which denotes someone who is "sovereign over the kings of the world" (Sproul). When David wrote, "The Lord says to my Lord: 'Sit at my right hand until I make your enemies a footstool for your feet'" (Psalm 110:1, *NIV*), he was saying that God was talking with Someone who was David's *Lord*, or *Adonai*. Our present text reveals that God has given a supreme title to Jesus, one equivalent to that of God himself.

What one distinguishing factor about Jesus' humanity separates Him from all other mankind?

III. PRAISE THE LORD (Hebrews 1:5-9; 13:15, 16)

A. Worthy of Worship (1:5-9)

(Hebrews 1:7-9 is not included in the printed text.)

5. For unto which of the angels said he at any time, Thou art my Son, this day have I begotten thee? And again, I will be to him a Father, and he shall be to me a Son?
6. And again, when he bringeth in the firstbegotten into the world, he saith, And let all the angels of God worship him.

The verses just prior to these in Hebrews express the very same thoughts as our other texts in this lesson (see vv. 2, 3)—the greatness of Christ's position as a member of the Godhead. Jesus is God's spokesman on the earth, and He is God himself. Throughout the Old Testament, God revealed His ways and His will through prophets in dreams, visions, and even face-to-face in the form of a *theophany* (that is, Christ in a preincarnate visitation). With the coming of Christ to earth, God now revealed Himself in person as He spoke through His Son, Jesus.

Jesus is God's firstborn and only Son. In the Jewish family, the firstborn son was given the highest privileges and responsibilities. This passage shows Christ's superiority to all the creation—especially to the angels. Angels are important, but they are only created servants. Christ has always been present with God the Father. The word *firstborn* is symbolic of more than birth order; it can also signify title and position. The term was used to describe Israel in the Old Testament when God instructed Moses, "Then say to Pharaoh, 'This is what the Lord says: Israel is my firstborn son'" (Exodus 4:22, *NIV*; see also Jeremiah 31:9). "Some rabbis used this term to describe God himself: the *firstborn* of the world is the Supreme Being" (*The Quest Study Bible*).

Because He is fully God, Jesus is worthy of all the praise we can give. We thank Him for creating us, for the wondrous blessings we enjoy, the bountifulness of the earth—for everything. In thanking Christ, we are thanking our very Creator.

B. The Sacrifice of Praise
(13:15, 16)

15. By him therefore let us offer the sacrifice of praise to God continually, that is, the fruit of our lips giving thanks to his name.

16. But to do good and to communicate forget not: for with such sacrifices God is well pleased.

To fully understand the concept of "sacrifice of praise," we need to look back to verse 13—

"Therefore let us go forth to Him, outside the camp, bearing His reproach" (*NKJV*). The Jewish-Christian community was now being persecuted as a cult outside of Judaism. Many families and their relatives were being divided, and many believers were now beginning to understand the costs of their commitment to Christ. Most of the Book of Hebrews was written to encourage these Jewish Christians in their faith. The freedom that Christ brings is much greater than the bondage to the

system of Law that they were delivered from. To be "outside the camp" indicates that believers may have to suffer willingly for Christ and be considered unclean, even by those we love. "To follow Jesus, believers must figuratively leave the old tabernacle system of rules and regulations and go outside the camp" (*The Quest Study Bible*). However, no suffering we will endure could exceed that which Jesus underwent.

Because these Christians were shunned by other Jews and excluded from the Temple worship system, they "could consider praise their sacrifice—one they could offer anywhere, anytime" (*Life Application Bible*). The phrase "sacrifice of praise" is a reiteration of the words of Hosea: "Take words with you and return to the Lord. Say to him: 'Forgive all our sins and receive us graciously, that we may offer the fruit of our lips'" (Hosea 14:2, *NIV*).

REVIEW QUESTIONS

1. What does the word *incarnation* mean?
2. In what ways was Jesus subject to human limitations during His earthly ministry?
3. What are the three ascending meanings of the word *Lord*?
4. What does the term "first begotten" mean when it refers to Jesus?
5. What does it mean to offer a "sacrifice of praise"?

GOLDEN TEXT HOMILY

"GOD ALSO HATH HIGHLY EXALTED HIM, AND GIVEN HIM A NAME WHICH IS ABOVE EVERY NAME" (Philippians 2:9).

The above verse is a part of what is believed to be a hymn or poem (Philippians 2:6-11) composed or quoted by the apostle Paul. This magnificent pericope offers the attitude of Jesus as a model to the church at Philippi, a church formed through the sacrificial efforts of the apostle during his second missionary journey. Paul, though writing while incarcerated in Rome, communicated contagious joy while under immense pressure. But, aware that he was a "servant" (Romans 1:1; Philippians 1:1) and "prisoner" (Philemon 1) of Jesus Christ, he pointed his readers not to his own achievement but to Jesus' ultimate self-sacrifice.

As the second person of the Trinity, Jesus voluntarily surrendered at His incarnation the prerogatives of deity while retaining its essence. He experienced childhood, life as a carpenter, and a three-year public mission in proclamation and demonstration of the kingdom of God. During His years of ministry he offered entire obedience to His Father while undergoing ever-increasing hostility from the religious establishment; then He rendered ultimate obedience by dying abjectly on a cross as the price of our redemption from the curse of sin. Here is the most remarkable act of self-sacrifice of history, followed by the most astounding possible result from such an act; for Jesus Christ is now at the "highest place" (Philippians 2:9, *NIV*) and bears a name "above every name," a reference to His ultimate authority over all creation and, particularly, over humankind. He invites us to emulate His example—not in degree of humiliation and exaltation but in voluntary obedience to God, certain to be ultimately followed by our own appropriate exaltation when we reign with Him through eternity.—**Sabord Woods, Ph.D., Professor of English, Lee University, Cleveland, Tennessee**

SENTENCE SERMONS

JESUS CHRIST is exalted in the church as we worship and obey Him.

—Selected

AS BELIEVERS exalt Christ, He draws sinners unto Himself.

—Selected

ANGELS LISTEN for your songs, for your voices rise to the very gates of heaven when you praise the Lord.

—Frances J. Roberts

YOU AWAKEN US to delight in your praise; for you have made us for yourself o' God, and our hearts are restless until they rest in you.

—Saint Augustine

DAILY BIBLE READINGS

M. Exalt His Holiness.
   Psalm 99:1-9
T. Thankful Exaltation.
   Psalm 118:24-29
W. Anointed to Serve.
   Isaiah 61:1-4
T. Exalted at God's Right Hand.
   Acts 2:22-36
F. Glory of God's Grace.
   Ephesians 1:3-14
S. Preeminence of Christ.
   Colossians 1:12-20

Evangelize Sinners

Study Text: Mark 16:14-20; Luke 5:27-32; Ephesians 2:1-7

Objective: To understand that Christ came to save the lost and share the gospel with them.

Golden Text: "Christ Jesus came into the world to save sinners" (1 Timothy 1:15).

Central Truth: Jesus Christ commissioned the church to evangelize the world.

Evangelism Emphasis: Jesus Christ commissioned the church to evangelize the world.

PRINTED TEXT

Luke 5:27. And after these things he went forth, and saw a publican, named Levi, sitting at the receipt of custom: and he said unto him, Follow me.

28. And he left all, rose up, and followed him.

29. And Levi made him a great feast in his own house: and there was a great company of publicans and of others that sat down with them.

30. But their scribes and Pharisees murmured against his disciples, saying, Why do ye eat and drink with publicans and sinners?

31. And Jesus answering said unto them, They that are whole need not a physician; but they that are sick.

32. I came not to call the righteous, but sinners to repentance.

Mark 16:14. Afterward he appeared unto the eleven as they sat at meat, and upbraided them with their unbelief and hardness of heart, because they believed not them which had seen him after he was risen.

15. And he said unto them, Go ye into all the world, and preach the gospel to every creature.

16. He that believeth and is baptized shall be saved; but he that believeth not shall be damned.

17. And these signs shall follow them that believe; In my name shall they cast out devils; they shall speak with new tongues;

18. They shall take up serpents; and if they drink any deadly thing, it shall not hurt them; they shall lay hands on the sick, and they shall recover.

19. So then after the Lord had spoken unto them, he was received up into heaven, and sat on the right hand of God.

20. And they went forth, and preached every where, the Lord working with them, and confirming the word with signs following. Amen.

Ephesians 2:4. But God, who

is rich in mercy, for his great love wherewith he loved us,

5. Even when we were dead in sins, hath quickened us together with Christ, (by grace ye are saved;)

6. And hath raised us up together, and made us sit together in heavenly places in Christ Jesus:

7. That in the ages to come he might shew the exceeding riches of his grace in his kindness toward us through Christ Jesus.

DICTIONARY

Pharisees (FARE-ih-seez)—Luke 5:30—Strict religious followers of Jewish laws, customs, and traditions.

LESSON OUTLINE

I. SEEK THE LOST
   A. The Call of Matthew
   B. Eating With Sinners
   C. Who Needs a Physician?

II. COMMISSIONED TO TELL
   A. Unbelief and Hardness of Heart
   B. The Disciples Commissioned
   C. Signs and Wonders
   D. The Wonder of the Ascension

III. MADE ALIVE IN CHRIST

LESSON EXPOSITION

INTRODUCTION

One great failure of the people of the ancient Jewish nation was their inability to recognize that God had not manifested Himself through them simply for their own benefit. Indeed, Israel was the people through whom God planned to redeem all of mankind—not just that group of descendants of Abraham.

The people of Israel never actually caught sight of their role in the larger scope of creation; likewise, the church has often been guilty of the same flaw. Do we sometimes believe that Christ came only for our particular family, church, denomination, or point of view? Do we have too small a world view of the plan of salvation?

Our lesson deals with the commission of the church to spread the gospel. We deal first with Christ's call of one disciple—Matthew. We will see how God often chooses the most unlikely of people for great roles in the plan of evangelism. We will also see from Matthew's life just what was involved in the invitation "Follow me."

Our second text will deal with the Great Commission. What kind of men were these with whom the Lord was trusting the future of the church? Were they strong, faithful individuals, or were they weak, frightened cowards? How were they transformed into powerful evangelists? What was the message they were given to spread?

Our third text will give us a composite picture of just what Christ did for us by becoming a man and making the ultimate sacrifice for our salvation. The fact that real life has now become available to a race of men who were dead in their trespasses should be enough to excite anyone. Added to this is the promise of a wonderful eternal life to follow this earthly one. We will see that through the redemption plan we are now made fully alive in Christ, raised up to exalted positions in heavenly places with Him, restored to relationship and given access to God himself.

The realization of what has been offered, not only to us but also to all mankind, should give impetus and excitement to spreading the good news—wonderful tidings that all is not lost, that God loves all men, that there is a hope both for this life and a future one to come.

I. SEEK THE LOST (Luke 5:27-32)

A. The Call of Matthew (vv. 27, 28)

27. And after these things he went forth, and saw a publican, named Levi, sitting at the receipt of custom: and he said unto him, Follow me.

28. And he left all, rose up, and followed him.

The calling of Matthew is found in all three synoptic Gospels (see also Matthew 9:9-13 and Mark 2:13-17). Jews commonly had two names; thus he is called Levi by Jesus in this passage. Matthew was a social outcast among the Jews. They saw him as both a sinner and one who mingled with sinners. The name *Matthew* means "gift of God," hardly fitting for his trade. He worked as a tax collector around the city of Capernaum (under the rule of Herod Antipas). "In Jesus' day, land and poll taxes were col-

lected directly by Roman officials, but taxes on transported goods were contracted out to local collectors" (*Nelson's Illustrated Bible Dictionary*). It appears to have been a common practice for these hirelings to squeeze more than was necessary from the people.

The Jews hated tax collectors for more than their corruption, however. The simple fact that they were Jews who worked for Rome placed them in a despised class. They were seen as being on the same level as lepers, murderers, and thieves. It was not even considered wrong to lie to them.

Jesus saw more in this man than human eye could perceive. Matthew's particular talents, traits, and education would prove useful in the years to come. His fluency in both Aramaic and Greek, along with his accuracy in recording events, times, and places, made him perfect to pen the Gospel record to the Jews. The Gospel of Matthew has frequently been described as a "Jew writing to the Jews about a Jew."

Jesus' invitation to follow Him was not just a casual suggestion. Every use of this phrase ("follow me") in the Gospels is an entreaty to leave everything and make a lifetime commitment. In Matthew 4:19-21, Jesus' call caused brothers Peter and Andrew to drop everything: "'Come, follow me,' Jesus said, 'and I will make you fishers of men.' At once they left their nets and followed him" (*NIV*). Jesus apparently made Himself very clear to those He called. He was asking for an absolute commitment: "Whoever serves me must follow me; and where I am, my servant also will be. My Father will honor the one who serves me" (John 12:26, *NIV*). No one was invited to sign on blindly. The costs were well laid out. This can be seen very well in Christ's conversation with the rich young ruler: "When Jesus heard this, he said to him,'You still lack one thing. Sell everything you have and give to the poor, and you will have treasure in heaven. Then come, follow me'" (Luke 18:22, *NIV*). Other passages indicating the same strength of the call to "follow me" can be found in John 1:43; 12:26; and 21:19-22. In this last one, Jesus informed Peter that no other detail in life matters as much as this one thing. Bypassing Peter's question as to John's future, Jesus told the fisherman, "If I want him to remain alive until I return, what is that to you? You must follow me" (John 21:22, *NIV*).

The Evangelical church at the last of the 20th century has often been characterized as a church of "easy believism." Do we make the benefits and joys of the Christian life seem attractive and forget to include the costs of *followership*? Jesus never asked anyone for casual commitment. We should do no less when we encourage men to come to Christ.

B. Eating With Sinners (vv. 29, 30)

29. And Levi made him a great feast in his own house: and there was a great company of publicans and of others that sat down with them.

30. But their scribes and Pharisees murmured against his disciples, saying, Why do ye eat and drink with publicans and sinners?

Matthew did not immediately cut himself off from his old acquaintances and friends. Instead, he went to great effort to introduce them to Jesus. Inviting Jesus to a banquet was the logical method of bringing them into contact with the Master. Perhaps this was a way of saying farewell to his old life. Another possibility is that this dinner occurred long after Matthew's call. If this is true, then Matthew's desire for his friends to meet Jesus was a sustained desire and this is even more substantiated.

Even tax collectors have friends. Jesus once acknowledged this when He said, "If you love those who love you, what reward will you get? Are not even the tax collectors doing that?" (Matthew 5:46, *NIV*). It is obvious that everyone, from the great to the small, has a sphere of influence. There are people that we affect, even when we think we are not witnessing.

The Pharisees so despised the tax collectors that without even thinking they lumped them together with the sinners. The accusers of Jesus in this passage considered a sinner to be anyone who did not agree with every detail of their conscientious scrupulousness. They commonly felt that they held the corner on God's blessing and that all others were condemned.

Evangelical Christians in recent years have been criticized, sometimes rightly so, for "circling the wagons—or, in other words, thinking that everyone else is wrong, that our view of God's plan is without error, and that all others are outside of God's divine will. We must guard ourselves from pharisaical attitudes. Jesus never sacrificed His principles when He mingled with sinners. Paul had strong words to say about this also: "I have written you in my letter not to associate with sexually immoral people—not at all meaning the people of the world who are immoral, or the greedy and swindlers, or idolaters" (1 Corinthians 5:9, 10, *NIV*). Paul went on to say we should only distance ourselves from the one who "calls himself a brother but is sexually immoral or greedy" (v. 11).

Paul also encouraged believers to take opportunities to dine with unbelievers, a means perhaps of reaching them for Christ: "If some unbeliever invites you to a meal and you want to go, eat whatever is put before you without raising questions of conscience" (1 Corinthians 10:27, *NIV*).

C. Who Needs a Physician?
(vv. 31, 32)

31. And Jesus answering said unto them, They that are whole need not a physician; but they that are sick.
32. I came not to call the righteous, but sinners to repentance.

Jesus compares healing physical ailments to healing sinners of their sin. This echoes Isaiah's prophecy about Him (see Isaiah 53:4, 5). Peter also wrote of the Master's dual healing touch: "He himself bore our sins in his body on the tree, so that we might die to sins and live for righteousness; by his wounds you have been healed" (1 Peter 2:24, *NIV*). The sinful need the healing that mercy and forgiveness bring, as much as the sick need a doctor.

The Pharisees completely miscomprehended the purpose of Christ's mission. They had believed that the Messiah would obliterate sinful people and elevate the righteous. Of course they saw themselves in the latter role. They had little use for the One who

received, forgave, and transformed the sinner while dismissing the self-righteous as hypocrites.

Why would Jesus accept Matthew's invitation to a banquet filled with "sinful" people?

II. COMMISSIONED TO TELL
(Mark 16:14-20)

A. Unbelief and Hardness of Heart
(v. 14)

14. Afterward he appeared unto the eleven as they sat at meat, and upbraided them with their unbelief and hardness of heart, because they believed not them which had seen him after he was risen.

The disciples' lack of faith is also elaborated on in John's Gospel (see 20:24-29). Thomas had insisted on seeing Jesus physically before he would believe the Savior had risen from the grave. The doubting disciple was obviously brought to belief when Jesus appeared in the room where they were gathered. Jesus went on to point out that they (the disciples) believed because they had seen Him. He said that even more blessed are those who believe even though they haven't seen Jesus physically.

In the very next verses of Mark's accounting, Jesus presented the disciples with the Great Commission. This might seem odd, given their doubt and unbelief. However, as the Lord told Paul, "My power is made perfect in weakness" (2 Corinthians 12:9, *NIV*). The history of Christianity is one of the Lord's using weak vessels, especially broken ones. No one need think he has to achieve a certain spiritual status before being used of God. The disciples themselves were prime examples of what weakness really is.

B. The Disciples Commissioned (vv. 15, 16)

15. And he said unto them, Go ye into all the world, and preach the gospel to every creature.
16. He that believeth and is baptized shall be saved; but he that believeth not shall be damned.

What is this *gospel* that Jesus commissioned His disciples to spread? It is the "good news" that Christ has paid the penalty for sin. There need be no further alienation of man from God. Notice in verse 16 that belief and baptism are tied together, almost as if they are one act. Belief, an inward act, is to be followed by baptism, an external act of witness to that faith. Salvation includes inwardly believing and externally confessing our belief in Christ.

Baptism is an act of witnessing to the world that a work has taken place in the heart. Thus, the very first thing a believer does upon accepting Christ is to testify in this way to this newfound relationship with Christ.

C. Signs and Wonders (vv. 17, 18)

17. And these signs shall follow them that believe; In my name shall they cast out devils; they shall speak with new tongues;
18. They shall take up serpents; and if they drink any deadly thing, it shall not hurt them; they shall lay hands on the sick, and they shall recover.

Not only the disciples but also all who believe will be used of God with signs and wonders following them. This is the only time in the Gospels that speaking in tongues is mentioned. Obviously this foretells the gift that came at Pentecost. The handling of snakes is never encouraged in Scripture. (Luke 10:19 mentions treading on snakes, but certainly not handling them intentionally.) The intended thrust of the Lord's words here is to communicate that power will be given to all believers to act in the Lord's name.

D. The Wonder of the Ascension (vv. 19, 20)

19. So then after the Lord had spoken unto them, he was received up into heaven, and sat on the right hand of God.
20. And they went forth, and preached every where, the Lord working with them, and confirming the word with signs following. Amen.

The awesome experience of seeing the Lord ascend back to the heavens certainly had a profound effect on the disciples. This, added to the infilling of the Spirit 10 days later, would change a group of common men into some of the greatest witnesses the world would ever see. Verse 20 is unusual in that it seems to summarize the first years of the church. It sounds like a verse from the Book of Acts.

When Jesus ascended back to heaven, the disciples were left with a great void. They no longer had His physical presence with them. Acts 1:11 tells us that it took the miraculous appearance of an angel to shake them from the stupor of their immediate loss. When the Day of Pentecost came soon after, they finally understood how much better it was now that Jesus had gone away. Before, He could be in only one place at a time as a human. Now, with the baptism in the Holy Spirit, the disciples could be led with the ever-constant knowledge of the Lord's full presence.

What is water baptism symbolic of?

III. MADE ALIVE IN CHRIST
(Ephesians 2:1-7)

(Ephesians 2:1-3 is not included in the printed text.)

4. But God, who is rich in mercy, for his great love wherewith he loved us,

5. Even when we were dead in sins, hath quickened us together with Christ, (by grace ye are saved;)

6. And hath raised us up together, and made us sit together in heavenly places in Christ Jesus:

7. That in the ages to come he might shew the exceeding riches of his grace in his kindness toward us through Christ Jesus.

This passage develops the theme of redemption, that is, God's raising of humanity from the despair and hopelessness of sin to a new life of freedom in Christ. When Paul spoke of being dead, he was not referring to physical death or to the final second death (declared at the White Throne judgment in Revelation 20:11-15). He literally meant the present deadness of walking the earth without having any hope or purpose, the condition in which a person's spirit is dead to God, the most important factor in life.

The "prince of the power of the air" (Ephesians 2:2) is certainly identifiable as Satan. This means that his realm, taken literally, is the atmosphere surrounding the earth. The ancients commonly thought the realm of evil to be that area between the earth and the sky. Satan and his demon angels now dominate the spirit world. However, this is only temporary, since Christ defeated him. Jesus is the ultimate sovereign of the entire universe. Only those who choose to follow Satan are under Satan's control.

Power to live life victoriously in Christ and a hope for the future after death are what the good news is all about. These two factors are the primary charges we are given to share in carrying out evangelism. We need not make evangelism complicated. Simply sharing the wonderful life we have been given is the essence of spreading the gospel.

Why is Satan called "the prince of the power of the air"?

REVIEW QUESTIONS

1. What level of commitment did Jesus ask for when He said, "Follow me"?

2. Why did the Pharisees lump tax collectors in the same class with sinners?

3. What kind of vessels does Christ use most efficiently? Explain.

4. Are the works of the flesh to be equated with the works of Satan? How are they different?

5. Give an example of God's grace in your own life.

GOLDEN TEXT HOMILY

"CHRIST JESUS CAME INTO THE WORLD TO SAVE SINNERS" (1 Timothy 1:15).

There is no question that Christ performed miraculous works during His earthly ministry. He opened blind eyes, unstopped deaf ears, cast out demons, cleansed lepers, and raised the dead, to name a few. These were miracles indeed, and they were performed in the will of God.

The reason, however, for Christ's coming to Bethlehem and joining the human race as He did was not to perform miracles. He could have done that without an earthly body. The miracles performed during His incarnation are by no means the first or last of His miracle-working power.

Christ did not come to the world to project an image of being a miracle worker. He came on a salvation mission, as the angel proclaimed to Joseph, "Thou shalt call his name Jesus: for he shall save his people from their sins" (Matthew 1:21). Christ did not leave the ivory palaces of glory and join a world of sin, persecution, and trial, just to gain a title of "miracle worker." He already had that title. Rather, He came "to seek and to save that which was lost" (Luke 19:10).

It is tremendously important that Christ performed healings and other miracles. We shall be eternally grateful. Miracles established in the minds of some people the fact that Christ was truly divine and that He must be the Son of God. But miracles are not why Christ intimately joined the human family. He came to "seek and to save that which was lost."

The love that sent Christ to earth was prompted by lostness, not sickness. For hundreds of years God had seen sickness, but it was the problem of sin that motivated the sending of Jesus Christ. "For God so loved . . . that he gave his only begotten Son, that whosoever believeth in him should not perish, but have everlasting life. For God sent not his

Son into the world to condemn . . . but that the world through him might be saved" (John 3:16, 17).

Christ's primary mission is clearly stated by Paul: "Christ Jesus came into the world to save sinners" (1 Timothy 1:15). Paul stated, not only to Timothy but also to the Galatians, the reason God sent His Son. Christ came to save and cleanse. "God sent forth his Son, made of a woman, made under the law, to redeem them that were under the law, that we might receive the adoption of sons" (Galatians 4:4, 5).—**Joel Harris, M.Div., Pastor, Mobile, Alabama**

SENTENCE SERMONS

JESUS CHRIST commissioned the church to evangelize the world.

—Selected

EVANGELISM is a cross in the heart of God.

—Leighton Ford

THE CHURCH has many tasks, but only one mission—that of winning the lost.

—Arthur Preston

PEOPLE ARE NOT SINNERS because they sin, they sin because they are sinners.

—R.C. Sproul

DAILY BIBLE READINGS

M. A Young Witness.
2 Kings 5:1-4
T. Salvation for Gentiles.
Isaiah 56:1-8
W. An Outcast Is Saved.
John 4:19-26
T. An Unlikely Evangelist.
John 4:27-30, 39
F. Evangelizing a City. Acts 8:4-8
S. Personal Evangelism.
Acts 8:27-38

Equip Believers

Study Text: Acts 13:1-5; Romans 12:3-8; Ephesians 4:11-16

Objective: To recognize the gifts and callings of all believers and find our place of service for the Lord.

Golden Text: "As every man hath received the gift, even so minister the same one to another, as good stewards of the manifold grace of God" (1 Peter 4:10).

Central Truth: The local church should help believers discover, develop, and use their spiritual gifts in service to God.

Evangelism Emphasis: Believers are equipped with spiritual gifts to reach the lost.

PRINTED TEXT

Romans 12:4. For as we have many members in one body, and all members have not the same office:

5. So we, being many, are one body in Christ, and every one members one of another.

6. Having then gifts differing according to the grace that is given to us, whether prophecy, let us prophesy according to the proportion of faith;

7. Or ministry, let us wait on our ministering: or he that teacheth, on teaching;

8. Or he that exhorteth, on exhortation: he that giveth, let him do it with simplicity; he that ruleth, with diligence; he that sheweth mercy, with cheerfulness.

Ephesians 4:11. And he gave some, apostles; and some, prophets; and some, evangelists; and some, pastors and teachers;

12. For the perfecting of the saints, for the work of the ministry, for the edifying of the body of Christ:

13. Till we all come in the unity of the faith, and of the knowledge of the Son of God, unto a perfect man, unto the measure of the stature of the fulness of Christ:

14. That we henceforth be no more children, tossed to and fro, and carried about with every wind of doctrine, by the sleight of men, and cunning craftiness, whereby they lie in wait to deceive;

15. But speaking the truth in love, may grow up into him in all things, which is the head, even Christ:

16. From whom the whole body fitly joined together and compacted by that which every joint supplieth, according to the effectual working in the measure of every part, maketh increase of the body unto the edifying of itself in love.

Acts 13:1. Now there were in the church that was at Antioch

certain prophets and teachers; as Barnabas, and Simeon that was called Niger, and Lucius of Cyrene, and Manaen, which had been brought up with Herod the tetrarch, and Saul.

2. As they ministered to the Lord, and fasted, the Holy Ghost said, Separate me Barnabas and Saul for the work whereunto I have called them.

3. And when they had fasted and prayed, and laid their hands on them, they sent them away.

4. So they, being sent forth by the Holy Ghost, departed unto Seleucia; and from thence they sailed to Cyprus.

DICTIONARY

Lucius (LUH-shi-us) of Cyrene (sy-REE-nee)—Acts 13:1—A Christian from the North African city of Cyrene, who ministered in the church at Antioch.

Manaen (MAN-ah-en)—Acts 13:1—A leader in the church at Antioch and designated as the foster brother of Herod the tetrarch.

LESSON OUTLINE

I RECOGNIZE SPIRITUAL GIFTS

   A. Honest Self-Evaluation

   B. Members of One Body

   C. Different Holy Spirit Giftings

II. EQUIP FOR MINISTRY

   A. Spiritual Equippers

   B. The Ultimate Goal of Ministry

   C. Children No Longer

III. RELEASE INTO MINISTRY

   A. Antioch—A Model for Ministry

   B. Called Out for Special Ministry

LESSON EXPOSITION

INTRODUCTION

Our study unit is on the "Mission of the Church." The mission of the church is to share the good news that Christ is alive, that there is real life to be found in Him, and that there is a reconciliation with God through His Son. We are to go and make disciples of all men, bringing them to a full knowledge of Christ and a relationship with Him.

The mission of the church can be summed up in one word—*ministry*. Ministry is the work of the Lord being done by the people of the Lord. It involves serving others, activating spiritual gifts, utilizing talents and abilities—and most importantly, depending on the Holy Spirit for anointing. Ministry is the responsibility of all church members—not just pastors and professional staff.

Real ministry, however, cannot be carried without mobilizing an army of believers. No army can function if only a few soldiers are doing all the work. A formula has been developing during the late 20th century describing certain aspects of how churches operate.

That formula says that 20 percent of the people give 80 percent of the tithes and offerings. Sadly, it also appears that 20 percent do 80 percent of the work of the church. We must recognize this error and strive to equip all believers for service.

The texts in our lesson show Paul constantly comparing the church to the human physical body. The ultimate goal of the body of believers is to grow more and more like Christ. This process must depend on the inter-relationship of the many organs and parts of the body. It is only when every part is functioning properly that the whole can be viewed as healthy. No one organ or ligament is more important than another. When the smallest muscle aches, the entire body suffers. Although all believers are important and necessary to the total function of the church, there are times when God calls special individuals for specific needs. Our text in point III will deal with how the Holy Spirit sets aside such people. We will see the picture of a model church in its outreach, its concern for others, and its willingness to reach out to all men.

I. RECOGNIZE SPIRITUAL GIFTS (Romans 12:3-8)

A. Honest Self-Evaluation (v. 3)

(Romans 12:3 is not included in the printed text.)

Much has been written in recent years on the subject of a healthy self-image. The great cause of many of society's problems has frequently been diagnosed as having begun with a poor self-image. Even most criminal activity can be traced by psychologists back to unhappy childhoods where individuals were wrongly treated and now have no self-esteem. It would appear, though, that Paul makes a case for the very opposite idea: It is not a lack of self-love that should be guarded against, but rather an overinflated sense of one's own importance.

The real point Paul makes about self-image, however, is not what one thinks of himself, but rather what God thinks of him. "The key to an honest and accurate evaluation is knowing the basis of our self-worth—our new identity in Christ. Apart from him, we aren't worth very much by eternal standards; in him, our worth as a creation of God is infinite" (*Life Application Bible*).

In preparing for carrying out the work of Christ's kingdom, we must put away human standards in terms of how one individual measures against another, and then look to God for His plan. Family heritage, race, gender, and so forth, matter little in His set of criteria. In fact, very often the most qualified person for a job (by human standards) is not the person God chooses, simply because it is easy to depend on talents and natural abilities instead of God himself.

In Romans 12:3, Paul writes that we are to "think soberly, according as God hath dealt to every man the measure of faith." The key word in Paul's advice is *soberly*. Certainly God never expects us to perform in ways He has not equipped us. Generally, our work in the Kingdom will interests. We should make a careful analysis of those things we are capable of doing, surrender those talents to Christ, and then humbly ask for divine help in carrying out any job we are given.

Paul was obviously the most qualified person for the charge he was given in the early church—that of writing the theology of Christianity and of presenting the gospel to the Gentile world. Paul was possibly the most educated man of his day, yet he never boasted in his knowledge and position. Instead, he found that God's grace was what made him who he was: "But by the grace of God I am what I am, and his grace to me was not without effect. No, I worked harder than all of them—yet not I, but the grace of God that was with me" (1 Corinthians 15:10, NIV).

The phrase "to every man that is among you" indicates that every person has some gifting that is useful in the Kingdom. However, all service to Christ must be carried out with humility.

B. Members of One Body (vv. 4, 5)

4. For as we have many members in one body, and all members have not the same office:

5. So we, being many, are one body in Christ, and every one members one of another.

Paul frequently used the illustration of the unity of the human body to describe the church (see 1 Corinthians 12:12). Three distinct truths come from these two verses: (1) the unity of the body; (2) the diversity of the many members of the body; (3) the mutual need of each other.

Every person is essential (using whatever his gifts are) to spreading the Kingdom, and every member needs the others. No one individual is capable of carrying out all the tasks of the church. Thus, even the most menial of jobs should not be viewed as unimportant. There should never be a reason for one seeing his own "ministry" as more vital than that of someone else. Also, all gifts should be dedicated to pure service and not for selfish or personal success.

All members profit from the others' contributions to the whole ministry. Every believer should regularly take stock of how important other Christians are in the scope of both local and far-reaching ministries. Paul encourages an appreciation for one another.

C. Different Holy Spirit Giftings (vv. 6-8)

6. Having then gifts differing according to the grace that is given to us, whether prophecy, let us prophesy according to the proportion of faith;

7. Or ministry, let us wait on our ministering: or he that teacheth, on teaching;

8. Or he that exhorteth, on exhortation: he that giveth, let him do it with simplicity; he that ruleth, with diligence; he that sheweth mercy, with cheerfulness.

Paul does not intend to make an exhaustive list of spiritual giftings, for many such empowerments arise with the varying needs of the church. However, in 1 Corinthians 12:27, 28, a more detailed enumeration is given. In that passage, as well as the present one, Paul refers not so much to natural talents and personality leanings, but rather to specific functional giftings of the Holy Spirit upon individuals for the larger body's use. However, even these direct callings most often take advantage of natural leanings. Prophets are generally required to be strong, bold, and verbally articulate. Exhorters will have a natural love for people. Teachers need to have clear, organized thoughts and the ability to present them. Those who are comforters to the hurting and bereaved should be very caring and compassionate.

Sometimes, however, God does call individuals to areas they might not naturally lean toward. However, He will prepare them for that ministry. For instance, those who never showed compassion for the bereaved will have a change of perspective when they themselves experience a loss. God will use the experiences of life to shape a personality into a useful vessel to fill a ministry need.

We should all be thankful for the variety of gifts and build an appreciation for others. One person's strength will balance another's weakness.

Why aren't all Christians gifted with the same strengths?

II. EQUIP FOR MINISTRY
(Ephesians 4:11-16)

A. Spiritual Equippers (vv. 11, 12)

11. And he gave some, apostles; and some, prophets; and some, evangelists; and some, pastors and teachers;

12. For the perfecting of the saints, for the work of the ministry, for the edifying of the body of Christ.

The list of ministry positions Paul enumerates covers what the modern church would classify as the professional clergy. What is the role of these people? Verse 12 gives the answer. These special individuals have been gifted to equip, or prepare the rest of the body for the work of the Kingdom. This work includes teaching the Word, helping believers overcome their problems and fears that would hinder them, teaching them the skills for reaching out to others with God's love, helping them discover their gifts and how to utilize those gifts. The idea is that everyone in the church ultimately takes part in ministry. These leaders simply show the way for the rest to follow. "Ministry is the calling, privilege, and responsibility of every member of the body of Christ" (*Word in Life Study Bible*).

We should never let the roles of leadership overshadow those of the rest of the assembly. The church should mobilize every person so that it moves as it was intended—one body.

B. The Ultimate Goal of Ministry
(v. 13)

13. Till we all come in the unity of the faith, and of the knowledge of the Son of God, unto a perfect man, unto the measure of the stature of the fulness of Christ.

Fullness in Christ is the goal of all ministry. The "we" here does not mean the entire world, but specifically the body of believers who are in Christ. Paul uses the singular when he says "perfect man," thus indicating that the church as a whole should be one. Individuals within the body of Christ, as well as all believers corporately, should strive to emulate Christ's love, teachings, and example.

With this unity in mind, churches should be very careful about expressing their independence from the rest of Christ's body. We all are part of a larger Kingdom. There should be no mavericks or selfish egoists trying to build individual kingdoms. This only fractures the body.

C. Children No longer (vv. 14-16)

14. That we henceforth be no more children, tossed to and fro, and carried about with every wind of doctrine, by the sleight of men, and cunning craftiness, whereby they lie in wait to deceive;

15. But speaking the truth in love, may grow up into him in all things, which is the head, even Christ:

16. From whom the whole body fitly joined together and compacted by that which every joint supplieth, according to the effectual working in the measure of every part, maketh increase of the body unto the edifying of itself in love.

We are to be children of Christ, but never should we be childish. Paul utilizes a second metaphor by comparing those who do not mature as tossed around like small boats adrift at sea. Such people are "whirled around by every chance gust of fashionable false teaching, which creates dizziness in the mind" (*NIV Study Bible*).

Paul has no use for false teachings. Here, as well as in nearly all his writings, he condemns those who cleverly use false teaching to lead people astray from the larger body of believers.

Should believers be idle when they see others led into false doctrine? Paul insists that deception cannot be left to fester uncorrected. At the same time, every effort should be made to use care and love when attempting to help a brother see the error of his thinking. We should never use the truth as ammunition to wound another believer, no matter how strong his error or how correct we view our own position. Love must be the strong arm of restoration.

What is the secret to restoring believers who have been led into false doctrine?

III. RELEASE INTO MINISTRY (Acts 13:1-5)

A. Antioch—A Model for Ministry (v. 1)

1. Now there were in the church that was at Antioch certain prophets and teachers; as Barnabas, and Simeon that was called Niger, and Lucius of Cyrene, and Manaen, which had been brought up with Herod the tetrarch, and Saul.

Even though Jerusalem was where the church began, Antioch became the first-century center for outreach and ministry. From the moment of the first Gentile conversion (see Acts 10), it was a wrenching process for believers in Jerusalem to accept anyone outside of their Jewish heritage.

There is certainly nothing wrong
with traditions, if they are grounded in truth, but when they super-
sede the real meaning and work of
the gospel, they become a major
hindrance. Jerusalem converts
were positioned at the very heart
of orthodox Judaism, and this
was a difficult barrier to overcome. The church there was slow
in developing a worldview for the
spread of the gospel.

Antioch was a great church
because it had powerful leadership. When Jerusalem believers
had been scattered because of
persecution, a number of them
moved to Antioch and began witnessing with great success. Along
the way some of the Greek Jews
(who were not nearly so narrow-
minded as strict orthodox ones in
Jerusalem) began to witness to
Gentiles. This resulted in great
numbers coming to believe in
Christ. This probably paralleled
Peter's vision and visit with
Cornelius in Joppa (Acts 10).

When the news spread to
Jerusalem, the church leaders
immediately sent Barnabas to
check things out (11:22).
Whether or not they were pleased
with what they had heard is not
known, but likely they were skeptical at best. They did act wisely
by sending Barnabas, for he was
one of the most mature and
respected believers in the
church—"For he was a good man,
full of the Holy Spirit and of faith"
(11:24, *NKJV*).

Upon arrival in Antioch,
Barnabas was quick to recognize
that a true move of God was
under way. He also realized that
this was the perfect time to find
Paul and bring him to work there.

Thus, the leadership that shep-
herded the Antioch outreach was
profound. Also, in response to a
prophecy about famine, the
church there sent provisions to
aid the Jerusalem congregation.
These supplies were carried by
Barnabas and Paul (see 11:28-
30). This helpful attitude and
"social concern" had to have done
much to bridge the prejudicial gap
that still likely remained among
the believers in Jerusalem.

By the time of our present text
the church in Antioch was strong,
not only because of Barnabas and
Paul but because tremendous
other leadership had been developed. Barnabas already had a
reputation for mentoring (because
of his help to Paul, as well as the
fact that he had brought John
Mark back to Antioch with them—
Acts 12:25). Paul's ministry over
the coming years would exemplify
discipleship, especially with
Timothy, Titus, Luke, and Silas.
At Antioch the ministry developed
so strongly that there were three
other prophets and teachers
besides Barnabas and Paul.

B. Called Out for Special Ministry
   (vv. 2-5)

(Acts 13:5 is not included in the
printed text).

**2. As they ministered to the
Lord, and fasted, the Holy
Ghost said, Separate me
Barnabas and Saul for the work
whereunto I have called them.**

**3. And when they had fasted
and prayed, and laid their
hands on them, they sent them
away.**

**4. So they, being sent forth
by the Holy Ghost, departed
unto Seleucia; and from thence**

they sailed to Cyprus.

In the midst of carrying out the daily work of the gospel, the Holy Spirit spoke and instructed that Barnabas and Saul (Paul) be separated for a different outreach. Luke is not explicit as to how the Holy Spirit spoke, but it is obvious that all were in agreement. Interestingly, just what kind of work the two would be separated unto was not immediately told, just that they were to move forth. God never gives us more than we need to know for the present time. As the rest of Acts shows, the plan of missions that these men lived out was at the same time both wonderful and tumultuous. We later see that a great disagreement would arise between the two men. However, even in the midst of personality difference, ultimately the gospel would be spread throughout the Roman Empire.

The church at Antioch gave their blessing to sending the men out. They were not selfish in keeping them to themselves, even though there was plenty for all to do right in the city of Antioch. They probably would not have been so gracious if it were not for the definite move of the Holy Spirit.

Though it is not stated, this would be the beginning of the world outreach to the Gentiles. Even though the two men would go to the synagogues of the cities they visited, soon they would find that their mission was to the world at large. Again, God would reveal His true purposes as they needed to know—and not before.

REVIEW QUESTIONS

1. Is there an exhaustive list of all the giftings of the Holy Spirit?

2. Is there a difference between natural talents and supernatural giftings?

3. How can we guard against being led away into false doctrines?

4. Is there room for maverick individualists in the body of Christ? How should the church deal with those who create dissension?

5. How much does God reveal of His plan for us at one time? Why does He not lay out everything for us to see all at one time?

SENTENCE SERMONS

THE LOCAL CHURCH should help believers discover, develop, and use their spiritual gifts in service to God.
—Selected

BELIEVERS are equipped with spiritual gifts to reach the lost.
—Selected

CHURCHGOERS are like coals in a fire. When they cling together, they keep the flame aglow. When they separate they die out.
—Billy Graham

NO ONE is useless in the world who lightens the burden of it for anyone else.
—Charles Dickens

DAILY BIBLE READINGS

M. Gifts for Skilled Service.
   Exodus 35:30-35
T. Gifted for Administration.
   Numbers 11:16-25
W. Give God the Best.
   Numbers 18:29-32
T. Gifts to Benefit All.
   1 Corinthians 12:1-7
F. Gifts of the Spirit.
   1 Corinthians 12:8-11
S. Gifts for All Believers.
   1 Corinthians 12:12-27

Empowered by the Spirit

Study Text: Acts 1:4-8; 4:31-35; Ephesians 1:3-10

Objective: To understand that the Holy Spirit empowers the church to fulfill its purpose and receive His power for our lives.

Time: The Book of Acts was written between A.D. 61 and 63. The Book of Ephesians was written between A.D. 60 and 61.

Place: The Book of Acts was probably written at Caesarea or Rome. The Book of Ephesians was written from a Roman prison.

Golden Text: "Behold, I send the promise of my Father upon you: but tarry ye in the city of Jerusalem, until ye be endued with power from on high" (Luke 24:49).

Central Truth: The church is empowered by the Holy Spirit to fulfill God's purpose.

Evangelism Emphasis: The Holy Spirit gives believers power to witness.

PRINTED TEXT

Acts 1:4. And, being assembled together with them, commanded them that they should not depart from Jerusalem, but wait for the promise of the Father, which, saith he, ye have heard of me.

5. **For John truly baptized with water; but ye shall be baptized with the Holy Ghost not many days hence.**

6. When they therefore were come together, they asked of him, saying, Lord, wilt thou at this time restore again the kingdom to Israel?

7. **And he said unto them, It is not for you to know the times or the seasons, which the Father hath put in his own power.**

8. But ye shall receive power, after that the Holy Ghost is come upon you: and ye shall be witnesses unto me both in Jerusalem, and in all Judaea, and in Samaria, and unto the uttermost part of the earth.

4:31. And when they had prayed, the place was shaken where they were assembled together; and they were all filled with the Holy Ghost, and they spake the word of God with boldness.

32. And the multitude of them that believed were of one heart and of one soul: neither said any of them that ought of the things which he possessed was his own; but they had all things common.

33. **And with great power gave the apostles witness of the resurrection of the Lord Jesus: and great grace was upon them all.**

34. Neither was there any among them that lacked: for as

many as were possessors of lands or houses sold them, and brought the prices of the things that were sold,

35. And laid them down at the apostles' feet: and distribution was made unto every man according as he had need.

Ephesians 1:3. Blessed be the God and Father of our Lord Jesus Christ, who hath blessed us with all spiritual blessings in heavenly places in Christ:

4. According as he hath chosen us in him before the foundation of the world, that we should be holy and without blame before him in love:

5. Having predestinated us unto the adoption of children by Jesus Christ to himself, according to the good pleasure of his will,

6. To the praise of the glory of his grace, wherein he hath made us accepted in the beloved.

7. In whom we have redemption through his blood, the forgiveness of sins, according to the riches of his grace;

8. Wherein he hath abounded toward us in all wisdom and prudence.

LESSON OUTLINE

I. EMPOWERED FOR EVANGELISM
   A. Waiting for the Blessing
   B. The Baptism With Water Versus the Baptism With the Holy Spirit
   C. Restoring the Kingdom
   D. Ye Shall Be Witnesses

II. EMPOWERED TO ACHIEVE UNITY
   A. A New Filling
   B. Of One Heart and of One Mind

III. ENABLED WITH SPIRITUAL WISDOM
   A. Spiritual Blessings in Heavenly Places
   B. Chosen Before the Foundation of the World
   C. Riches of His Grace

LESSON EXPOSITION

INTRODUCTION

For us as Pentecostals, the coming of the Holy Spirit to birth and empower the church is absolutely essential to our view of Christianity. The "baptism in the Holy Spirit," as experienced by those on the Day of Pentecost (Acts 2), is the distinguishing factor that identifies, and sometimes alienates, us from other Christians.

We believe that the infilling of the Spirit, as evidenced by speaking in tongues and the operation of the gifts of the Spirit, is to be seen as the norm for believers, not just some exceptional manifestation that was available only to the early church. The joy, the enrichment, the glory of praying in the Spirit, the giftings, the receiving of a message to the church in tongues, the interpretation

—these are wonderful components of the Pentecostal experience. However, possibly the greatest reason for the baptism in the Holy Spirit is the subject of this lesson. Jesus himself declared that the power to be witnesses (Acts 1:8) was the reason the disciples were to gather in the Upper Room and wait. The power that came at Pentecost gave purpose, boldness, and wisdom to a group of unlearned and unpolished disciples, transforming them into a body of effective witnessing machines who changed the Roman Empire and the course of history since then.

I. EMPOWERED FOR EVANGELISM (Acts 1:4-8)

A. Waiting for the Blessing (v. 4)

4. And, being assembled together with them, commanded them that they should not depart from Jerusalem, but wait for the promise of the Father, which, saith he, ye have heard of me.

Jesus expressed the importance of the coming of the Holy Spirit by insisting that the disciples do nothing until then. He knew they had to have something more, or they would immediately fail. Had He left them at His ascension with no one to take His place, they would have quickly scattered. This was certainly evidenced by their actions when Jesus was arrested and crucified.

It is interesting to note that when Peter stood and preached his powerful sermon in Acts 2, he was able to quote and expound upon scriptures from the Old Testament, including the prophet Joel and the Psalms. How could he do such? Did a poor fisherman from Galilee have these passages memorized from childhood? Not likely. The 10 days the disciples spent in the Upper Room were given to prayer and pouring over the Scriptures. This time of preparation was necessary before God could use Peter to preach so effectively.

God has an important work for each of us to do today, but He often asks us to wait. As we prepare by studying His Word, praying, and listening for His guidance, we are made ready for the often difficult tasks He sets before us. This waiting time gives us a chance to search our hearts, make sure there is no unconfessed sin, and find illumination from the Scriptures. God never sends His servants out unprepared. We should always view times of waiting as integral to our Christian service.

B. The Baptism With Water Versus the Baptism With the Holy Spirit (v. 5)

5. For John truly baptized with water; but ye shall be baptized with the Holy Ghost not many days hence.

From this verse we know that there is a difference between the two baptisms. Yet, Jesus had earlier told Nicodemus, "I tell you the truth, no one can enter the kingdom of God unless he is born of water and the Spirit" (John 3:5, *NIV*). Was Jesus here distinguishing between physical birth (water) and spiritual birth (Spirit)? Or, was He showing that we are regenerated by the Holy Spirit at salvation, and that this is then demonstrated by water baptism? Could not the water baptism symbolize the cleansing action of the Holy Spirit at the new birth? This seems apparent when Paul writes to Titus: "He saved us, not because of righteous things we had done, but because of his mercy. He saved us through the washing of rebirth and renewal by the Holy Spirit" (Titus 3:5, NIV).

Paul said, "For by one Spirit are we all baptized into one body, whether we be Jews or Gentiles, whether we be bond or free; and have been all made to drink into one Spirit" (1 Corinthians 12:13). John 6:63 says, "It is the Spirit who gives life" (NKJV).

We cannot underestimate the work of the Holy Spirit in our salvation. Any life committed to Christ is a powerful witness. However, it is obvious that the baptism in the Holy Spirit is to be a subsequent empowering to that which the believer has received in salvation.

C. Restoring the Kingdom (vv. 6, 7)

6. When they therefore were come together, they asked of him, saying, Lord, wilt thou at this time restore again the kingdom to Israel?

7. And he said unto them, It is not for you to know the times or the seasons, which the Father hath put in his own power.

"Old habits die hard" is a phrase that aptly describes the disciples at this juncture. The fiery longing of every Israeli was for a political kingdom to be reestablished. When Jesus spoke of the coming Holy Spirit, their dying hopes were suddenly restored. "In Jewish expectations, the restoration of Israel's fortunes would be marked by the revived activity of God's Spirit, which had been withheld since the last of the prophets" (NIV Bible Commentary, Vol. 2). Jesus, however, had something else in mind. His answer to their question was not to deny that there was a future for Israel, but rather to redirect their thinking as to His plans for them. They were to leave to God the matters that were of His concern and to concentrate on their duties.

This might present a "word to the wise" today. Many Christians are so caught up into a "rapture" mentality that they forget the divine commission to "go and make disciples." As much as we would like to understand the events to come, we must keep our feet firmly planted in the work we have to do here on earth.

D. Ye Shall Be Witnesses (v. 8)

8. But ye shall receive power, after that the Holy Ghost is come upon you: and ye shall be witnesses unto me both in Jerusalem, and in all Judaea, and in Samaria, and unto the uttermost part of the earth.

This is one of the most important verses in all of Scripture. Christ's mandate to be witnesses is the theme of the entire Book of Acts. "The Christian church, according to Acts, is a missionary church that responds obediently to Jesus' commission, acts on Jesus' behalf in the extension of his ministry, focuses its proclamation of the kingdom of God in its witness to Jesus, is guided and empowered by the selfsame Spirit that directed and supported Jesus' ministry, and follows a program whose guidelines for outreach have been set by Jesus himself" (*NIV Bible Commentary*, Vol. 2).

We have no record of how the disciples responded to this mandate, for in the very next verse Jesus ascended out of their sight. However, it is very possible that their initial response was not enthusiastic. "All of the places mentioned represented trouble and danger, both real and imagined. Jews—which almost all of Jesus' listeners were—were a small minority in the Roman Empire. . . . They must have wondered: Could He protect them from the inevitable opposition they would encounter? Would they suffer the terrible end that He had?" (*Word in Life Study Bible*, notes on Acts 1:4).

If they did have fears, the disciples at least momentarily forgot them as Jesus suddenly ascended from their sight into heaven. No doubt that moment had to also bring terrible loneliness, just as anyone seeing the departure of a loved one feels an emptiness. It was perhaps to erase those feelings that the two angels appeared immediately to them and gave encouragement (vv. 10, 11).

What did Jesus tell His disciples was the purpose of the Holy Spirit's Coming?

II. EMPOWERED TO ACHIEVE UNITY (Acts 4:31-35)

A. A New Filling (v. 31)

31. And when they had prayed, the place was shaken where they were assembled together; and they were all filled with the Holy Ghost, and they spake the word of God with boldness.

Despite the wonderful things that happened in chapters 2-4, there was also tremendous pressure and stress put on the young church. Just the assimilation of 3,000 new believers on the Day of Pentecost had to have brought monumental problems. The times were wonderful, no doubt. Acts 2:46, 47 says, "Continuing daily with one accord in the temple, and breaking bread from house to house, they ate their food with gladness and simplicity of heart, praising God and having favor with all the people" (*NKJV*). However, anyone who has ever ministered under the anointing of the Spirit knows that there is a tremendous draining effect upon the body. Also, when opposition begins to arise, as it always does, the believer can be further depleted. Very quickly the early church had to face plots against them (4:1-3), as well as threats (vv. 21, 29).

Thus, we come to verse 31 where we see another gathering of the leaders, a new baptism, a renewal of the church. In response to the pressures they were beginning to face, the believers prayed and were given another filling. This presents a strong message to all Pentecostal believers today. We cannot rest in the comfort that we, at some earlier time, received the baptism in the Holy Spirit. There is the constant need for refilling. We should never rest on the laurels of a past spiritual blessing. We face the same draining effect that the early church did. Like them, we should gather in worship and prayer services to seek refueling.

B. Of One Heart and of One Mind (vv. 32-35)

32. And the multitude of them that believed were of one heart and of one soul: neither said any of them that ought of the things which he possessed was his own; but they had all things common.

33. And with great power gave the apostles witness of the resurrection of the Lord Jesus: and great grace was upon them all.

34. Neither was there any among them that lacked: for as many as were possessors of lands or houses sold them, and brought the prices of the things that were sold,

35. And laid them down at the apostles' feet: and distribution was made unto every man according as he had need.

The early church Christians set a high standard in terms of generosity. This giving spirit was obviously a result of the Holy Ghost working in and through them at a special time. It was a season of "great power" and "great grace" (v. 33). There was no pressure for anyone to exhibit such benevolence. Some would say that this was an example of communism. However, there was no intent to set up an economic system, and Scripture never insists on an equal distribution of goods. In addition, the Bible never calls for property ownership to be done away with.

Even as exciting as the times were, they were soon filled with difficulty. Very quickly we see that the giving spirit was not long-sustained nor demonstrated by everyone. The story of Ananias and his wife, Sapphira, in chapter 5 points out again the constant need for refillings of the Holy Spirit.

Have you experienced a renewal, or rebaptism, in the Holy Spirit? Do you seek constant refillings?

III. ENABLED WITH SPIRITUAL WISDOM (Ephesians 1:3-10)

A. Spiritual Blessings in Heavenly Places (v. 3)

3. Blessed be the God and Father of our Lord Jesus Christ, who hath blessed us with all spiritual blessings in heavenly places in Christ.

The phrase "all spiritual blessings" covers a wide territory of wonderful things God has given us: salvation, forgiveness, promise of eternal life, fellowship with Christ through the Holy Spirit while here on earth, the sense of family with other believers, and the empowerment to work for Christ's kingdom—just to name a few. We often think of blessings purely in physical terms (money, possessions, opportunities in life) but so much more has been given to us. Any Christian who has ever ministered under the powerful anointing of the Holy Spirit will testify that there is no wealth on earth to compare to this wonderful blessing.

B. Chosen Before the Foundation of the World (vv. 4-6)

4. According as he hath

chosen us in him before the foundation of the world, that we should be holy and without blame before him in love:

5. Having predestinated us unto the adoption of children by Jesus Christ to himself, according to the good pleasure of his will,

6. To the praise of the glory of his grace, wherein he hath made us accepted in the beloved.

Everything we have is a gift from God. We were spiritually dead, totally unable to respond or resurrect life within ourselves. We died when sin entered the human race, but God graciously provided us new life. "It is not our own awareness that we're sinful people that first turns us to God. Rather, it is God who in his mercy awakens that awareness within us" (*The Quest Study Bible*). Why God would choose to do this is hard to understand, but through Christ's sacrifice we are made holy and blameless. There is no room for pride in us, for it was certainly through no goodness of our own. Before the foundation of the world was laid, God had determined that all who believed on His Son should be saved. Paul used the word *adoption* (v. 5) to show in human terms the immensity of this wonderful provision. In the ancient world slaves were at times adopted by their owners and given full rights as members of the family. In the same sense, we who were enslaved to sin and punishment have been purchased by Christ's sacrifice, and then given the full rights to inherit that which God has.

Some take the term *predesti-*

nated to mean that our salvation is limited totally to God's sovereign choice. By this view, those who would become heirs were picked before time began, and they themselves have no real part in the matter. As Romans 9:16 says, "It does not, therefore, depend on man's desire or effort, but on God's mercy " (*NIV*). In other words, men do not naturally seek God, but rather God's grace frees them to choose salvation (Calvinism). Most of us as Pentecostals take another view (Arminianism), which sees God as having the foreknowledge as to who will accept salvation, but still gives man the freedom to choose for himself. The one thing we must remember is that He is totally fair and just—"The works of his hands are faithful and just; all his precepts are trustworthy" (Psalm 111:7, *NIV*)—and desires that all men be saved (see 1 Timothy 2:4).

C. Riches of His Grace (vv. 7-10)

(Ephesians 1:9, 10 is not included in the printed text.)

7. In whom we have redemption through his blood, the forgiveness of sins, according to the riches of his grace;

8. Wherein he hath abounded toward us in all wisdom and prudence.

In verses 7 and 8, Paul lists some of the blessings that flow from God's grace toward us. Redemption carries the connotation of freedom from slavery or prison. A ransom has been paid for us. The price was the very lifeblood of Christ himself, poured out in his death on the cross.

Forgiveness stems from a verb meaning "to send away," as exemplified by the scapegoat (Leviticus 16:20-22). In the Old Testament, forgiveness was based on the blood of animal sacrifice (17:11). In the New Testament, Jesus' blood was shed for us to become the final and perfect sacrifice.

Grace is God's unmerited favor. It cannot be obtained by our efforts but rather proceeds from His mercy and love.

Wisdom is a gift of knowledge to see things as they really are. This gift is the work of the Holy Spirit in our salvation. It can be better understood if we look at verse 13: "And you also were included in Christ when you heard the word of truth, the gospel of your salvation. Having believed, you were marked in him with a seal, the promised Holy Spirit" (*NIV*). Paul was writing to Gentile Christians to remind them that they were incorporated into the body Christ. Jews were not the only ones who could claim the exclusive rights of God's mercy. Gentiles were to share equally the inheritance, which was sealed with the Holy Spirit.

All three persons of the Trinity are involved in our salvation and subsequent Christian life. The Father has chosen us for His grace (vv. 4-6, 11). Christ the Son offered the sacrifice for sin, Himself paying the penalty and thus extending forgiveness to us (v. 7). The Holy Spirit seals us in Christ, guaranteeing our relationship with God (v. 13). It is the presence of the Spirit that gives us spiritual wisdom. Every believer should recognize the importance of having wisdom to face the difficulties and opportunities of life. The Holy Spirit empowers us to view events and situations from a godly view.

How important is having godly wisdom in the daily walk of a Christian?

REVIEW QUESTIONS

1. Has God placed you in a time of waiting? How are you using this time?

2. What is the difference between water baptism and the baptism in the Holy Spirit?

3. What should we view as the primary role of the baptism in the Holy Spirit in our lives?

4. Describe the generosity of the early church Christians. Should our standards be the same? Explain.

5. Can we take godly wisdom for granted as a continuous blessing, or should we pray and seek for it as a regular part of our daily walk?

GOLDEN TEXT HOMILY

"BEHOLD, I SEND THE PROMISE OF MY FATHER UPON YOU: BUT TARRY YE IN THE CITY OF JERUSALEM, UNTIL YE BE ENDUED WITH POWER FROM ON HIGH" (Luke 24:49).

Notice the divine imperative. In the Greek New Testament, the word *behold* is in the imperative. This always means that the reader or hearer must not ignore that which is about to be revealed. Jesus began this command by calling attention to its importance. We can see why. If the disciples missed this, the kingdom on earth would be over even before it was begun. There would be no Day of Pentecost, no Book of Acts, no Pentecostal church, and no Charismatic Movement. The future of the disciples, the church, and you and me depended on a clear understanding of what Jesus was about to say—not one word must be lost.

Notice the promise of the Father. Joel 2:28-32 and other passages in the Old Testament record God's intention to manifest Himself on behalf of His people in a supernatural, unusual way. Prophets had lived and died, years had passed, and many generations longed for this blessed event. It was coming! The promise would be delivered. It did come, but not in the Temple. It did not come through the priests and the Levites. It did not come to royalty nor the elite. It came to ordinary men and women who heard His word, obeyed His commands, and abandoned all to follow Him.

Notice the connection between the Father, the promise (Holy Spirit), and Jesus. That which was to come is the Holy Spirit. The source of that which was to come is none less than the Father. Jesus said, "I send the promise of my Father upon you." The Trinity converges here to bring a source of energy and power to those who were charged with establishing the kingdom of God on earth. The presence and participation of the triune God in this event signals that this was no small thing that was about to take place. The release of divine energy, promised by the Father, would explode upon the disciples

at the command of Jesus.

Notice the specific instructions given to the disciples. There are many valid reasons why the place should be Jerusalem and why it would be necessary for the disciples to "tarry." Perhaps the most obvious reason was that the Old Testament prophecy might be fulfilled, establishing credibility to the event. The list of reasons could go on and on. What is most significant here is that Jesus gave specific commands. Those commands must be obeyed or nothing happens.

Notice also the power is from on high. It would not come from the Roman Empire; it would not come from the high priest; it would not be the result of "holy wars." It would be "from on high." One of the greatest mistakes God's people now make is to fail to understand this. This is God's kingdom! It is God's work; it is God's plan.—**R.B. Thomas, D.Litt., Vice President for Administration, Church of God Theological Seminary, Cleveland, Tennessee**

DAILY BIBLE READINGS

M. The Spirit in Creation.
   Genesis 1:1-5
T. Empowered to Prophesy.
   2 Samuel 23:1-5
W. Power Over Enemies.
   Isaiah 59:16-21
T. Power to Overcome Temptation.
   Luke 4:1-14
F. Empowered to Witness.
   Acts 4:31-33
S. Empowered as Children of God.
   Romans 8:1-14